Financial Accounting

Understanding and Practice

Second Edition

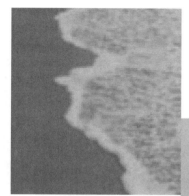

Second Edition

Financial Accounting

Understanding and Practice

Robert Perks

McGraw-Hill Higher Education

London   Boston   Burr Ridge, IL   Dubuque, IA   Madison, WI   New York   San Francisco
St. Louis   Bangkok   Bogotá   Caracas   Kuala Lumpur   Lisbon   Madrid   Mexico City
Milan   Montreal   New Delhi   Santiago   Seoul   Singapore   Sydney   Taipei   Toronto

Financial Accounting: Understanding and Practice, second edition
Robert Perks
ISBN-13 9780077115401
ISBN-10 0-07-711-540-6

Published by McGraw-Hill Education
Shoppenhangers Road
Maidenhead
Berkshire
SL6 2QL
Telephone: 44 (0) 1628 502 500
Fax: 44 (0) 1628 770 224
Website: www.mcgraw-hill.co.uk

British Library Cataloguing in Publication Data
A catalogue record for this book is available from the British Library

Library of Congress Cataloguing in Publication Data
The Library of Congress data for this book has been applied for from the Library of Congress

New Editions Editor: Catriona Watson
Marketing Manager: Vanessa Boddington
Senior Production Editor: Beverley Shields

Text Design by HL Studios, Oxford
Typeset by Fakenham Photosetting Limited
Cover design by Ego Creative
Printed and bound in Great Britain by Cromwell Press, Trowbridge, Wiltshire

First Edition published in 2004 by McGraw-Hill Education

ISBN-13 9780077115401
ISBN-10 0-07-711-540-6

Dedication

To WLL

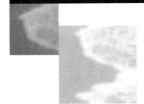

Brief Table of Contents

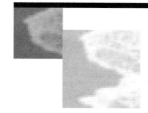

Detailed Table of Contents

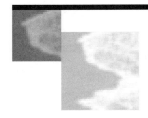

Preface

This book is intended to help readers to understand financial accounting and to see how it can be used in practice, particularly in the interpretation and management of company finances. It should appeal to future managers, rather than to those who want to become accountants. It is intended to be 'user friendly' for those who are put off by conventional presentations of the subject based on arcane rules and procedures. Students from an arts background, for whom figures are sometimes a painful necessity, will probably find that this is as good as it gets with accounting textbooks.

It is an introductory text that is particularly suitable for degree courses in management and business studies, including MBAs and other master's degree programmes. The approach is analytical, critical and evaluative, amply illustrated with real-world examples.

The book goes beyond basic financial accounting, and readers may be interested in its application in relation to the stock market (Chapter 6), financing a company (Chapter 11), investment appraisal (Chapter 12); or in the history and context of financial accounting, and problems in relation to creative accounting (Chapters 3 and 8). In response to requests from users, this new edition provides additional material on bookkeeping and procedural matters (Chapters 14–16) which some modules require; and a new chapter introducing management accounting (Chapter 13). Interpretation of accounts is a problem for many students and a simplified 'ready reference' guide to accounting 'ratios' is now provided in Chapter 4, with more advanced issues dealt with in a separate chapter (Chapter 9). After covering the basics of balance sheets and income statements (Chapters 1 and 2) the book is designed so that any chapter can be studied in almost any order according to the readers' particular interests, or the requirements of a course.

Ample resources are provided to enable readers to understand and apply financial accounting. Self-testing questions (numerical, theoretical and analytical) are included in each chapter, with answers at the end of the book. Assessment questions are provided without answers. Discussion questions and group activities are included to encourage readers to become involved in exploring important questions; and these can be related to current issues in the press by analysing the 'financial accounting in context' illustrations.

All companies produce annual reports and accounts that include a great deal of valuable information if only managers, analysts, financial journalists, economists, bankers and everyone with an interest in business and management would take the time and trouble to understand them. This book is intended to help. Similarly, students who produce projects and dissertations, and politicians and journalists who analyse particular companies and industries, can benefit from a thorough understanding of published financial statements that this book provides. In the main it explains financial accounting as an important resource that has valuable applications; but its approach is also critical, and it encourages readers to think about important issues and to reach their own conclusions.

Guided Tour

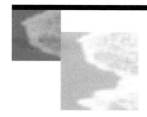

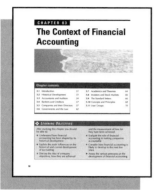

Chapter Contents
A brief list of key chapter contents is highlighted at the start of every chapter.

Learning Objectives
Each chapter opens with a set of learning objectives, summarizing what you should learn from each chapter.

Introduction
Each chapter opens with an introduction, which sets the scene and introduces you to the issues that will be addressed in the chapter.

Illustrations
Each chapter provides a number of examples and balance sheets, which illustrate and summarize important concepts, helping you to apply theory to accounting practice.

Summary
This briefly reviews and reinforces the main topics you will have covered in each chapter to ensure you have acquired a solid understanding of the key topics.

Review of Key Concepts
A brief recap at the end of each chapter is ideal for revising accounting concepts.

Self-testing Questions
These questions encourage you to review and apply the knowledge you have acquired from each chapter and can be undertaken to test your understanding. Answers are provided at the end of the book.

Assessment Questions
This section provides a multitude of questions you may be asked in an exam. They can be used as helpful revision questions or to check your progress as you cover the topics throughout the text.

Group Activities and Discussion Questions
These questions can be used to spark debate in class and can also help readers to think around the topic.

Financial Accounting in Context
Relevant chapters end with a press item that aims to illustrate the main themes of the chapter, allowing you to appreciate how the theory applies in real life.

References and Further Reading
A list of reference from the chapter, plus useful websites, can be used for further research.

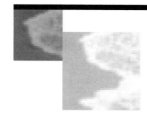

Technology to Enhance Learning and Teaching

*Visit **www.mcgraw-hill.co.uk/textbooks/perks** today*

Online Learning Centre (OLC)

After completing each chapter, log on to the supporting Online Learning Centre website. Take advantage of the study tools offered to reinforce the material you have read in the text, and to develop your knowledge in a fun and effective way.

Resources for students include:
- Learning objectives
- Useful Weblinks

Also available for lecturers:
- Solutions to questions in book
- Additional exam questions
- PowerPoint slides

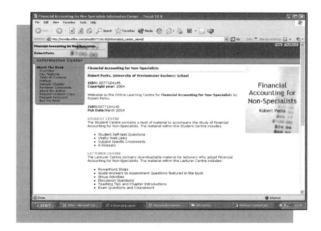

Lecturers: Customize Content for your Courses using the McGraw-Hill Primis Content Centre

Now it's incredibly easy to create a flexible, customized solution for your course, using content from both US and European McGraw-Hill Education textbooks, content from our Professional list including Harvard Business Press titles, as well as a selection of over 9,000 cases from Harvard, Insead and Darden. In addition, we can incorporate your own material and course notes.

For more information, please contact your local rep who will discuss the right delivery options for your custom

publication – including printed readers, e-Books and CDROMs. To see what McGraw-Hill content you can choose from, visit *www.primisonline.com*

Study Skills

Open University Press publishes guides to study, research and exam skills to help undergraduate and postgraduate students through their university studies.

Visit *www.openup.co.uk/ss* to see the full selection of study skills titles, and get a **£2 discount** by entering the promotional code **study** when buying online!

Computing Skills

If you'd like to brush up on your computing skills, we have a range of titles covering MS Office applications such as Word, Excel, PowerPoint, Access and more.

Get a £2 discount off these titles by entering the promotional code **app** when ordering online at *www.mcgraw-hill.co.uk/app*

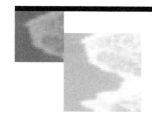

Acknowledgements

Our thanks go to the following reviewers for their comments at various stages in the text's development:

Ian Crawford – University of Bath/University of Reading
Denise Gallagher – University of Leeds
Kathy Grieve – University of Central England
Danny Leiwy – University of Westminster
Dr. Julian Wyn Lloyd Jones – University of Manchester
John Parker – University of Sheffield
Clare Roberts – University of Aberdeen
Trina Small – Dublin City University

Daily Telegraph: Chapter 1, Chapter 4, Chapter 8; *Sunday Telegraph*: Chapter 6, Chapter 7; *Financial Times*: Chapter 3, Chapter 9, Chapter 10 – 2 articles; *Investors Chronicle*: Chapter 5; *Sunday Times*: Chapter 12; *Accountancy Age*: Chapter 11, Chapter 14, Chapter 15; *Accountancy Magazine*: Chapter 2; *Financial Management*: Chapter 13

CHAPTER 01

The Balance Sheet and What it Tells Us

Chapter contents

❖ *Learning Objectives*

After studying this chapter you should be able to:

- ❖ Explain the structure and terminology of straightforward balance sheets
- ❖ Understand how balance sheets can indicate financial weaknesses and strengths
- ❖ Demonstrate how transactions and profits affect balance sheets
- ❖ Discuss the uses and limitations of balance sheets

1.1 Introduction

The term 'balance sheet' is widely used, although most people have never seen one and have little idea of what it shows. This chapter provides a gentle introduction to balance sheets by showing how individuals can prepare their own personal balance sheets, and how similar these are to company balance sheets. It also gives some indication of the usefulness of balance sheets: they can give an indication of what an individual or company is worth (but with severe limitations). They also show what liabilities there are, which can help to predict future bankruptcy.

1.2 An Individual's Balance Sheet

If you want to know how much you are worth as an individual you would probably start by drawing up a list of everything that you own, and then try to put a value on each item. After working for a few years you might own a house, some furniture, a car, some premium bonds and shares that you intend to keep on a long-term basis, and perhaps some short-term investments. You might also have a good stock of food and wine in the kitchen as well as some money in the bank. But you may have debts: a mortgage owed to your bank or building society, an overdraft, money you owe on your credit card, and bills not yet paid for such things as electricity, gas, telephone and council tax.

	£
What I own	
House	300,000
Furniture	4,000
Car	10,000
Premium bonds and shares	6,000
Food and drink	200
Cash and bank	4,800
Total	325,000
What I owe	
Mortgage	222,000
Bills (gas and electricity etc.)	1,000
Credit card	2,000
Total	225,000
What I am worth	100,000

ILLUSTRATION 1.1

It is easy to produce a list of what you own, and a list of what you owe. You can then deduct what you owe from what you own to show your 'net worth'. An example is given in Illustration 1.1.

We can summarize this as:

What I own *minus* what I owe = what I am worth

If you are a full-time student this might be more difficult, or more embarrassing. It may be that the most valuable things that you own are items such as CDs, clothes, books, a stereo and a computer. You may have paid a lot for them, but their value now is questionable – especially if you suddenly needed to sell them. They would cost a lot to replace, and if they were all stolen you would probably claim quite a high value for them if they were insured. But if you try to sell them, their second-hand value would probably be very disappointing: it is likely to be only a small fraction of what you paid for them. Worse still, you may well have a student loan and an overdraft and owe other amounts of money which means that your net worth is zero, or even negative: you owe more than you own. But it is all worth it, you tell yourself, because all the time you are spending money on your education; that is an investment; and what you are really worth is your future earning power. If you go to your bank wanting to borrow money, they will be much more interested in your future earning power than they are in a pile of second-hand clothes and some CDs.

Three main problems arise in trying to establish what any individual or business is worth:

1 What items are we going to list? Are we going to include our 5-year-old computer, our vinyl records, all the food in the kitchen, our educational qualifications and our children? We might think of these as being some of the best things we have, but we would probably exclude them. We need some basis, or principle, for deciding what to include and what to exclude.

2 How do we establish what particular items are worth? We attempt this in several different ways, for example, by looking at what they originally cost, or what the second-hand value is, or what it would cost to replace them.

3 What is our future earning power worth? Whether we look at an individual, or a company, in many cases the money that they can earn in the future is worth a lot more than a collection of bits and pieces that they own. If you want to borrow money, you could tell your bank that you expect to earn at least a million pounds during your working life, and ask to borrow the million pounds now. The bank's response is likely to be short and not very sweet.

You can, of course, make up your own rules, and decide that you are worth £100,000. But if you want to compare your own wealth with someone else's, then you need to agree how the calculation is to be made. Are you going to show your house at the amount you paid for it, or at the market value now? Are you going to show your car at the amount you paid for it, or allow for the fact that it has depreciated since you bought it? If you attempt any comparisons like this you will soon find that you need some agreed rules on what to include, and the basis of valuation to be used. You will need accounting principles.

It is difficult to know what something is really worth until you sell it. I might boast that my house is worth £500,000, but we might agree that it is more objective to show it at cost; and it cost £300,000 a few years ago. The accounting principle would be to list everything that we own, and show everything at the original cost price.

Deciding what principle to adopt for furniture and for a car is more difficult. They have only a limited life, and are likely to depreciate over time as we 'use them up'. We could decide that a car has a 5-year life and write it down by one-fifth each year.

1.3 A Company's Balance Sheet

A company's balance sheet is very much like an individual's balance sheet, except that a standard layout is used, and more impressive terminology is used.

The layout and terminology probably look quite confusing at first and it may be hard to believe that Illustration 1.2 really is the same balance sheet as Illustration 1.1. By using standardized terminology and presentation, accountants say that they are making it easier to compare one company with another. You might think that they are just making it more complicated so that it is 'impenetrable' to non-accountants. But professionals can no longer hide behind their terminology, conventions and so-called 'expertise'. These days many patients question their doctor's recommendations (perhaps by looking things up on the Internet and being instantly more 'expert' than the doctor). Similarly, you are learning to question accountants (and other management 'experts'), and now is the time to make sure that you understand the basic terminology of financial statements.

The terminology used on balance sheets has become more standardized since the widespread application of international accounting standards in 2006. Illustrations 1.2 and 1.3 are both consistent with international standards; the first is in the format illustrated in International Accounting Standard 1 (IAS 1). The second one also complies with the standard, and is also fairly conventional. Unfortunately we have to be able to cope with balance sheets presented in different ways.[1]

In accountant's jargon, what a company owns and what they owe are called *assets* and *liabilities*, and the statement showing assets and liabilities (and *net assets,* or *net worth*, or *equity*, or *capital*) is called a *balance sheet*. The idea is that it 'balances': the total of assets used to be shown on the one side, and the total of liabilities and equity on the other side: the two sides balance. But nowadays it is usual to show the one 'side' at the top, and the other 'side' underneath.

Balance sheet of A Company as at 31 December year 1	
	£
ASSETS	
Non-current assets	
Freehold land and buildings (at cost)	300,000
Furniture (at cost)	4,000
Vehicles (at cost)	10,000
Investments	6,000
	320,000
Current assets	
Inventories	200
Cash and bank	4,800
	5,000
Total assets	325,000
EQUITY AND LIABILITIES	
Share capital and reserves	100,000
Non-current liabilities	
Mortgage	222,000
Current liabilities	
Trade payables	1,000
Short-term borrowings	2,000
	3,000
Total equity and liabilities	325,000

ILLUSTRATION 1.2

---

[1] That is the price of international 'standardization', prior to which there was a standardized UK form of balance sheet which, unfortunately, differed from that of other countries.

A Company
Balance sheet as at 31 December year 1

	£	£
Assets		
Non-current assets		
Freehold land and buildings (at cost)	300,000	
Furniture (at cost)	4,000	
Vehicles (at cost)	10,000	
Total of tangible assets	314,000	
Financial assets (investments)	6,000	320,000
Current assets		
Investories	200	
Cash and bank	4,800	5,000
Total assets		325,000
Current liabilities		
Trade payables	1,000	
Credit card	2,000	3,000
Non-current liabilities		
Mortgage		222,000
Equity		
Share capital and reserves		100,000
Total liabilities and equity		325,000

ILLUSTRATION 1.3

In everyday English we have seen that what I am worth is the total of what I own, minus the total of what I owe. In accountancy terms we would say that the balance sheet value of a company is the total of assets minus liabilities. We could call this 'equity', or net assets, or capital, or net worth. Accountants sometimes talk about 'the balance sheet equation' that has three items (assets, liabilities and equity), which can be arranged in different ways as follows:

(a) assets = liabilities *plus* equity
This shows a total of assets, and then how they were financed: partly with other people's money, and partly by the owners' equity

Or

(b) assets *minus* liabilities = equity
This emphasizes the amount of equity

It is easy enough to establish the 'balance sheet value' of a company, or its 'net asset value', or 'equity', or 'net worth'. In Illustration 1.2 it would be £100,000. It is much more difficult to establish what a company is really worth — because of the same three problems already identified:

1 What items are we going to include on the list?
2 How do we establish what particular items are worth?
3 What is the future earning power of the company as a whole worth?

These problems are addressed more fully later in the book.

1.4 Short- and Long-term Classification

The usual formats for balance sheets make it relatively straightforward to compare one company with another. Both assets and liabilities are classified as being long or short term. Anything that is intended to be around for more than a year is long term. Anything that changes within a year is short term.

Assets

Long-term assets are called 'non-current assets'. They are still often referred to as 'fixed assets' although there is nothing fixed about them: they include cars and aeroplanes just as much as they include land and buildings.

The main categories within the non-current assets section of a balance sheet are:

1 Intangible assets: for example, goodwill, patents, trade marks, licences
2 Property, plant and equipment (tangible fixed assets): for example, land and buildings; plant, machinery and equipment; vehicles; furniture, fixtures and fittings
3 Financial assets or investments: items such as shares in other companies or loans that have been made

We can say that things like vehicles or furniture are *usually* classed as non-current assets, but that is not always the case. If a business intends to use them for a period of years, then they are non-current. But if someone is in business to buy and sell vehicles, or furniture, then any items held short term, awaiting sale, are not fixed assets. Stocks of goods held for sale are labelled as 'inventories' and shown as current assets.

The same arguments apply with investments. Any surplus funds invested in shares, or loaned to someone or another business, might be intended to be long term, and so are 'non-current'. Or they might be intended to be short term, and so are shown as current assets.

Current assets are short term. They include cash and any assets intended to become cash within a year. They include:

1 Inventories (or stocks) of merchandise, production supplies, materials, work in progress and finished goods
2 Trade receivables (or debtors) – money owed to the business by customers and others[2]
3 Investments (those which are not fixed assets)
4 Cash[3]

Current assets are short term, and constantly circulating. They are all cash, or cash equivalents, or things that are intended to become cash within a matter of months. We intend that all our inventories will be sold; even raw materials and components will be incorporated into finished goods that are sold. Investments that are shown as current assets are assumed

---

[2] And even prepayments, and accrued income if you want to be technical!

[3] Cash includes money in the bank, and petty cash in hand. Obviously the two are quite distinct and a bookkeeper needs to account for them separately. But for the sake of simplicity, in interpreting balance sheets, the two can be lumped together.

to be temporary, and so will be sold and converted into cash. The amounts shown for receivables should be received from debtors within a few months.

Liabilities

Liabilities are also categorized as current and non-current (short term and long term).

1 Current liabilities are creditors where the amount is due to be paid within a year. This includes most ordinary trade receivables (creditors for goods and services who have not yet been paid); current taxation payable; and other short-term financial liabilities such as bank overdrafts. Where a company has formally 'proposed' to pay a dividend, but has not yet done so, the 'proposed' dividend is also included in current liabilities.[4]

The balance sheets shown in Illustrations 1.2 and 1.3 clearly show current and non-current asset and liabilities separately from each other.

2 Non-current liabilities include long-term borrowings such as mortgages and debentures.

The distinction between what is short term and what is long term is important in assessing the financial strength or solvency of a business – in assessing whether or not it is likely to go bust!

1.5 Balance Sheets: Financial Strength and Weakness

A balance sheet may suggest that a business is financially strong, although it does not prove it. It can also show signs of weakness – and we ignore these at our peril. Accountants are often criticized when a company gets into financial difficulty because they did not warn in big red letters, 'This company is dodgy. Avoid it like the plague'. But, in most cases, the signs of financial difficulty are there for all to see, long before a much publicized collapse, if only they take the trouble to try to understand the balance sheet.

Companies collapse in one way or another when they cannot pay what they are required to pay: when they are unable to meet their financial liabilities. Many factors may contribute to this situation: poor management, poor marketing, poor planning, trying to do too much with too little money, bad luck, dodgy customers, changes in the world economy and so on. There is usually someone, or something, to blame. But, in the end, either a company can pay its bills, or it cannot. The balance sheet gives a pretty good guide to what bills are due to be paid – and the resources available for paying them.

Although there may be question marks about the reliability of some figures in published accounts, the liabilities[5] figures are among the most reliable. A company needs to have sufficient funds readily available to meet its liabilities when they fall due. A company's 'current liabilities' are shown clearly on the balance sheet. The important question is: does the

---

[4] Although it might be necessary to hunt around in the notes to the accounts to find it.

[5] There are occasions when crooked accountants and directors omit liabilities completely, or hide them as some form of 'off balance sheet finance'. These 'creative accounting' issues are addressed in Chapter 8.

company have enough short-term assets to be able to pay its short-term liabilities as they fall due?

A company's current assets include money in the bank, receivables[6] that are due to become money in the bank within a few months, and inventories, or stocks of goods that the company plans to sell and convert into money in the bank within a matter of months. If a company has a lot more current assets than current liabilities, it should be able to pay its current liabilities when they fall due. If their current assets are two or three times as much as their current liabilities, then they appear to be fairly strong; or in the terminology of accounting, they have a high current ratio.

In Illustrations 1.1 to 1.3, current assets are £5,000, and short-term liabilities are £3,000. The current ratio is 1.67 : 1.[7] This is not particularly high, but it looks as if there is enough cash and near cash available in the short term to be able to pay the short-term liabilities as they fall due.

Although all current assets should become cash within a matter of months, this is more difficult with some items than others. Not all inventories (or stocks of goods) are easily and quickly turned into cash. A half-baked loaf will probably be finished and sold for cash within a matter of hours. A half-built house, in an area where no-one wants to live, could remain unsold for a long time. If most of a company's 'current assets' are actually inventories, their ability to pay creditors quickly may be less than their current ratio suggests. A useful approach to assessing a company's ability to pay their short-term liabilities is to exclude inventories from current assets, and to assess the company's 'liquidity', by comparing their 'liquid assets' with their current liabilities. This is known as the liquidity ratio, or acid test, or quick assets ratio.

Long-term liabilities are also important – a company or individual can go bankrupt because of the weight of long-term creditors. It is difficult to say how much debt is too much – some people, and some companies, seem to manage with huge amounts of debt,[8] whereas others (like Marconi, and a number of airlines recently) collapse. An individual who has lots of money can afford to borrow lots of money. Similarly, a company with a large amount of equity, or shareholders' funds (the company's 'own' money) can afford to borrow more money than a company with very little equity. In Illustrations 1.1–1.3 the amount of equity is £100,000, so it would seem reasonable to borrow another £100,000. If a business is financed half by borrowing, and half from its own shareholders' funds, then the borrowing is high, but probably not excessive. But in these illustrations, the borrowing is much more than the equity. If we add together all the long-term funds (shareholders' funds, plus long-term creditors = £322,000), then we can see that the assets of the business are mainly[9] financed by borrowing. In accounting terminology such a company is 'high geared', which usually means high risk.

---

[6] Receivables are debtors; these are customers who have not yet paid for the goods and services with which they have been supplied.

[7] £5,000 ÷ £3,000 = 1.67.

[8] At the end of 2005 ICI had long-term liabilities totalling £5,600 million; total equity amounted to only £486 million. This is most unusual!

[9] £222,000 of £322,000 is almost 69 per cent.

But high gearing, or high amounts of long-term debt, does not particularly matter if the individual or company has a substantial amount of income with which to pay the interest, and to repay the creditors (or borrow more!) when repayment is due. Individuals who have to pay mortgage interest of £20,000 a year should have no problems if their annual income is £100,000 a year or more. Someone who has to pay £20,000 a year mortgage interest from an annual income of £25,000 is likely to have real problems! It is worth comparing the amount of interest that has to be paid each year, with the income available to pay that interest. If the interest is covered, say, 5 times by the income, then it is probably all right. But if the interest is covered only 1.25 times by the available income, then there are likely to be problems.

In assessing the financial strength of a company, or how likely it is to go bankrupt, it is worth calculating the current ratio, the liquidity ratio, the capital gearing ratio and the interest times cover.

1.6 Depreciation and Balance Sheet 'Values'

Before looking at the published balance sheet of a real company, it is useful to know that all assets are not simply shown at cost. Some non-current assets, particularly land and buildings, are revalued from time to time. Most property,[10] plant and equipment ('tangible non-current assets') are depreciated each year.

If you buy a car for £10,000, you might decide that you will keep it for 4 years, and expect that at the end of the 4 years you will be able to sell it for £2,000. This is a plan, or an accounting policy. After one year you can show the car as being £8,000; after 2 years it would be £6,000 and so on. This does not mean that the car is 'worth' £8,000 after one year. What we need to do is to show three things:

1 The car cost £10,000
2 After 1 year the cumulative depreciation is £2,000 (after 2 years it would be £4,000; after 3 years it would be £6,000)
3 After 1 year the net book[11] value of the car would be £8,000 (after 2 years it would be £6,000; after 3 years it would be £4,000).

It is important that *all three* of these can be found on the balance sheet, or in notes to the balance sheet: the cost of an asset, the cumulative depreciation and the net book value. As the above example shows, the net book value is not an attempt to show what the asset is really worth now. We decided to write off the initial cost of the car, down to an estimated trade in value when we have finished with it, and to charge the same amount of depreciation each year[12] for 4 years. A published balance sheet does not, of course, show individual assets; totals for groups of similar assets are shown.

In Illustrations 1.1–1.3 depreciation has been ignored to simplify it. The car is shown at

---

[10] Yes, even property.

[11] The amount shown in the 'books' of the company, or its balance sheet value.

[12] Depreciation does not have to be on a 'straight line' or 'equal annual instalments' basis. Businesses can choose to charge more depreciation in the early years by using a 'diminishing balance' basis.

£10,000. If we decided that a depreciation charge, or expense, of £2,000 is appropriate, there would be *two effects* on the balance sheet: (i) the car (assets) would be reduced by £2,000; and (ii) the equity would be reduced by £2,000. The basic balance sheet equation, shown below, would still balance.

$$\text{Assets} - \text{liabilities} = \text{equity}$$

Illustration 1.4 shows how the balance sheet changes as a result of charging expenses, earning income and making a profit.

1.7 Balance Sheets and Profit

A successful individual or business is likely to show an increase in capital or equity or net worth each year.

Expenses, such as depreciation, decrease assets and decrease equity. Most expenses reduce the asset of cash when they are paid.[13] If they have not yet been paid, then there is an increase in liabilities – shown as payables (which has the same effect as a reduction in assets). Whether they are paid out in cash or not, the effect of all expenses is to reduce equity.

Revenues, mainly from sales, increase assets and increase equity. If they come in the form of cash, then the asset of cash is increased. If the customers have not yet paid, then the increase in assets shows up as an increase in receivables.[14] Whether they are received in the form of cash or not, the effect of all revenues is to increase equity.

In a successful business revenues should be greater than expenses. This means that profit is earned; the net effect is to increase equity. Profit is added to equity.

If we take the balance sheet at the end of one year, and compare it with the balance sheet at the end of the next year, we can get a fairly good idea of the amount of profit that was made in the period between the two dates. All we do is compare the figure for equity (or net assets, or shareholders' funds) on the most recent balance sheet with the equivalent figure a year ago. This is shown in Illustration 1.4. The profit has shown up in additional stocks, debtors and cash: they have increased by £29,000. But fixed assets have gone down by £2,800 (depreciation), and there are additional liabilities of £1,200; the total effect of these is an increase in net assets of £25,000. That £25,000 should be added to equity: until the question mark has been replaced by £25,000 of 'retained earnings', the balance sheet will not balance.

Without more evidence we cannot always be sure that the increase in net assets is the profit for the year, for three main reasons:

1 It could be that the amount of equity has increased because shareholders have put more money into the business; there has been a new issue of shares. Any extra coming in from the issue of shares does not count as profit, and so should be deducted from

---

[13] Depreciation is an expense that reduces the fixed asset; it does not reduce the cash – it is not paid.

[14] Or debtors.

Balance sheet of A. Reader Company Limited as at 31 December

	Year 1 £	£	Year 2 £	£
Non-current assets				
Tangible assets				
Freehold land and buildings (at cost)	300,000		300,000	
Furniture (at cost less depreciation)	4,000		3,200	
Vehicles (at cost less depreciation)	10,000		8,000	
	314,000		311,200	
Investments	6,000	320,000	6,000	317,200
Current assets				
Inventories	200		9,000	
Trade receivables	–		20,000	
Cash and bank	4,800		5,000	
		5,000		34,000
Total assets		325,000		351,200
Current liabilities				
Trade payables		3,000		4,200
Non-current liabilities				
Mortgage		222,000		222,000
Total liabilities		225,000		226,200
Equity				
Capital and reserves		100,000		100,000
Retained earnings for year 2				?
		325,000		351,200

ILLUSTRATION 1.4

the increase in equity shown on the balance sheet to arrive at the profit figure for the year.

2 All the profits that have been made do not necessarily stay within the business. Most companies pay out dividends. They can make a substantial profit, and pay most of it out as dividends. Dividends do not reduce profits, but they do mean that the whole of the profit for the year does not increase equity. If we are to calculate the amount of profit for the year using the balance sheet, dividends must be added to the amount of retained profit for the year to arrive at the total profit for the year.

3 Sometimes the amount shown for equity has increased because the company has revalued its assets. An increase in the value of assets does not count as profit. In Illustration 1.4 if the company had wanted to revalue their land and buildings from £300,000 to £350,000 there would be two effects: the amount for the asset would increase by £50,000; and the amount of equity would have increased by £50,000. This has not happened in Illustration 1.4.

If there has been an increase in the amount shown for equity from one year to the next, this is an indication of profit; but adjustments may need to be made for the three items listed above to arrive at the correct profit figure for the year.

A balance sheet is not the most convenient way of calculating profit, but it can be done! Profit for the year is the increase in equity during the year, minus any additional shares that have been issued, plus any dividends that have been declared, minus any amounts resulting from the revaluation of assets.

Some may argue that even an increase in asset values should count as profit. But the traditional accountant would not be impressed with such an 'all inclusive' view of profit.

1.8 A Company's Published Balance Sheet

A recent published balance sheet of Ted Baker plc for the year ended 28 January 2006 (slightly simplified) is shown in Illustration 1.5. It is presented in a form that became normal practice in 2006, following IAS 1. It provides useful indications in relation to several aspects of a company, especially when comparing one year with another.

1 *Size and growth*[15] The book value of Ted Baker increased from £36.8m in January 2005 to £42.2m in January 2006, an increase of 11.5 per cent. There has been an increase both in current assets and in non-current assets.

2 *How the business is financed* The balance sheet equation, assets *equals* liabilities *plus* equity, shows that a business finances its assets partly with other people's money (liabilities), and partly with the owners' money (equity). Ted Baker's increase in assets has been financed mainly by an increase in equity. The increase in equity was as a result of generating profits; no additional shares were issued.

The increase in current assets (£5.7m) was financed partly by an increase in current liabilities (£2.8m).

3 *Profits* Comparing balance sheets of two different dates does not show the amount of profit made in the intervening period, unless a few adjustments are made, as explained above. It does not show what dividends were paid; but even after deducting the dividends we can see a substantial increase in Ted Baker's retained profits (£5.2m).

4 *Solvency* Balance sheets show the amount of liabilities, and give some indication whether or not these are excessive. This can be done in two stages as follows.

Current Liabilities

Are these excessive in relation to current assets? The amounts are as follows:

	2006	2005
	£000	£000
Current assets	46,775	41,090
Current liabilities	24,740	21,929

Current liabilities are amounts that have to be paid out in the short term. Current assets include cash and items that should become cash within a year. As Ted Baker has a lot more

[15] In assessing size and growth it is useful also to look at sales revenue, profits and market capitalization. On Monday 19 June 2006 the market capitalization of Ted Baker was shown in the *Financial Times* as £209m.

	28 January 2006 £'000	**29 January 2005** £'000
Non-current assets		
Intangible assets	501	506
Property, plant and equipment	18,667	17,346
Other assets	1,719	567
	20,887	18,419
Current assets		
Inventories	23,475	22,725
Trade and other receivables	11,764	8,762
Cash and similar assets	11,536	9,603
	46,775	41,090
Current liabilities		
Trade and other payables	17,507	15,806
Borrowings and similar items	689	–
Current tax payable	6,544	6,123
	24,740	21,929
Non-current liabilities		
Borrowings	750	750
Total liabilities	25,490	22,679
Net assets	42,172	36,830
Equity		
Share capital	2,149	2,149
Share premium	6,983	6,983
Retained earnings	33,040	27,698
	42,172	36,830

ILLUSTRATION 1.5 Ted Baker plc

current assets than current liabilities, there should be no problem in paying those liabilities as they fall due. This is often expressed as the *current ratio,* which is the ratio of current assets to current liabilities, which is:

1.9 : 1   1.9 : 1

The ratio is lower than the 2 : 1 that some textbooks recommend, but it is in line with most retailers where current ratios tend to be lower than average.

With some current assets such as inventories, it could take many months before they are turned into cash. Liquidity can be assessed by taking only 'quick assets' and comparing them with current liabilities. This is the 'acid test'. If stocks are excluded from current assets, the *liquidity ratio* is calculated as follows:

	2006	2005
	£000	£000
Current assets excluding inventories	23,300	18,365
Current liabilities	24,740	21,929
Liquidity ratio	0.9 : 1	0.8 : 1

The liquidity ratio is less than 1 : 1 which, at first sight, looks rather weak: there are not enough liquid assets to pay current liabilities at the moment. But this is the normal position with retailers, and is not likely to be a problem in this case.

Non-current Liabilities

Ted Baker's balance sheet shows that borrowings (or '*debt*') are the only long-term liability, and the amount is fairly low. The total equity ('E' or shareholders' funds) amounted to over £42 million in 2006, but there was only £0.75 million of long-term borrowings ('D' or debt). This can be expressed as a *gearing ratio* for each year by asking the question: what proportion of long-term finance was borrowed (as opposed to being part of shareholders' funds)? This can be expressed as: what D as a proportion of D + E?

	2006	2005
	£000	£000
D Long-term borrowings	750	750
E Equity	42,172	36,830
D + E Total long-term finance	42,922	37,580
D as a percentage of D + E	1.7%	2.0%

The gearing is less than 2 per cent which is low; this means that the company has little dependence on long-term borrowings, and so the company is financially strong. Many companies have gearing ratios of 20 per cent or 30 per cent without problems. A company might be regarded as being highly geared, and so more risky, if the ratio is around 50 per cent.

In assessing if there is too much borrowing it is important to see how much interest the company has to pay, and if their operating profits are high enough that the interest is amply covered by the earnings available to pay it.

The published annual reports of companies show a lot more detail than the simplified balance sheets included in this chapter, and it can look frighteningly complex. A great deal of additional information is shown in notes to the accounts. In studying balance sheets it is important to have a few clear questions in mind; to concentrate on the larger figures; and not to become lost in detail that is hard to understand.

1.9 Role and Limitations of Balance Sheets

Balance sheets can be useful in a number of ways.

1 We saw that the balance sheet, or a statement of assets and liabilities, can be useful in showing what a person or business is worth. But there are problems in establishing agreed rules as to exactly which assets (and perhaps even which liabilities) should be

included, and in determining the basis upon which they should be valued. There is also the problem that the value of a business as a whole is likely to be different from the value of all of its assets (less liabilities) added together. The real value of a business (or an individual) might depend more on the income that it can generate (as a whole entity) in the future than upon whatever amounts might be shown for individual assets and liabilities.

2 We also saw that, in listing the various liabilities that have to be paid, short and long term, we can get an idea of the financial strength of a business. If its liabilities are too high, and it cannot pay them, it is likely to get into serious financial difficulties, and perhaps go out of business. Balance sheets can give a good indication of whether liabilities are too high, or whether the business is reasonably strong. The balance sheet is the basis for assessing the financial position of a company.

3 We can also measure profit using the balance sheet. There are easier ways of measuring profit, but it is useful to calculate it in two different ways so that one checks the other. The balance sheet approach to measuring profit is one of the two main approaches, and one that may increase in importance.

4 Balance sheets play an important role in 'stewardship'. Shareholders put their money into a company; directors and managers are the 'stewards' of that money; and shareholders want to know what has happened to their money. The balance sheet shows what money has been put in by the shareholders, and what retained profits have been added to it; this amount is shown as equity (or shareholders' funds). Examination of the balance sheet, the assets and liabilities, shows what that money is now financing or, if you like, what has happened to it.

5 In order to produce a balance sheet it is necessary to produce a listing of all the company's assets and liabilities. This can be useful in keeping track of various assets, and ensuring that all are being put to good use and are earning their keep. When a company gets into financial difficulties it sometimes seems that they manage to find assets that they had previously forgotten about, or done nothing with. There may be investments that are not much use; sports and social facilities that are hardly used; debtors who have been neglected and have got away with not paying for too long (perhaps because of a half-forgotten dispute); a workshop developing a new product that made little progress; machinery, or components and raw materials that were specially bought for a new product that was quietly abandoned; too many premises or branches; an expensive head office in the centre of London; a training centre, kitchens, computer workshops and maintenance facilities that should have been sold or re-deployed when these activities were outsourced.

   Many companies do not even know what assets they own, or how many laptop computers have 'walked' out of the door, and they do not even have an up-to-date fixed assets register. The process of producing listings of assets in order to compile a balance sheet can be a useful housekeeping exercise.

6 In addition to providing a basis for assessing the financial *position* of a company, the balance sheet also provides a basis for assessing the financial *performance* of a company. The shareholders of a company are likely to be concerned about perform-

ance in terms of profitability. They are not concerned merely with the amount of profit the company makes; they are concerned with how much profit the company makes in relation to the amount of capital employed. A profit of £1 million may look good for a company with capital employed of £5 million; it would look pathetic in relation to capital employed of £100 million. It is the balance sheet that shows the amount of capital employed. The ratio of profit to capital employed is a key ratio in assessing and improving a company's financial performance.

7   Financial accounting is a whole system, and the balance sheet is an essential part of it in checking, balancing and controlling other parts of the system. If a company's balance sheet does not balance, there is definitely something wrong! Accountants are only (or nearly!) human, and inevitably some mistakes are made with figures. The financial accounting system is designed to show up errors, and to find where they occurred. An accounting system can also show up fraud and theft. When a balance sheet does balance, we cannot be sure that there is no fraud or error. If it does not balance, we can be sure that something is wrong; and if we do make a mistake, it will probably show up during the accounting processes before producing a balance sheet.[16]

But we should not expect too much from balance sheets. They were never properly designed to achieve anything very useful. When double-entry bookkeeping first became widely used, the balance sheet was just a matter of bookkeeping convenience. It was not even necessary to produce one every year. Until the eighteenth century a balance sheet was often not produced until the ledger was full; then a balance sheet was a summary of the assets and liabilities that were transferred to the new ledger. Any remaining old balances, mostly revenues and expenses, were written off. The balances shown on the balance sheet are items that are continuing, but they tend to be shown at the cost price when they are first entered in the business's books.

By the end of the eighteenth century the production of balance sheets on an annual basis became normal. During the nineteenth century it became a requirement for companies to publish annual balance sheets; and during the twentieth century legislation became increasingly specific about what should be shown on a balance sheet. Towards the end of the twentieth century accounting standards laid down more detailed requirements, and since 2006 companies have been following International Accounting Standards in the same way as many other countries.

The main limitations of balance sheets have already been referred to:

1   What items are we going to include?

2   How do we establish the value of particular items?

3   The value of a company as a whole is likely to be very different from the total net value of the individual assets and liabilities.

Sometimes it is very difficult to decide whether or not an item should appear on the balance sheet. If a company running a number of hotels buys an additional hotel, that is clearly an extra fixed asset that would be shown on the balance sheet, and the

---

[16] Mistakes usually show up in the trial balance – if it does not balance!

amount shown would be the amount paid for it. If such a company pays for routine cleaning of a hotel, there is no additional asset, and the amount paid should not appear on the balance sheet as an additional asset. A payment for cleaning will reduce assets (cash) and also reduce equity. Routine redecoration, like cleaning, is an expense that does not appear on the balance sheet. Improvements, such as installing double glazing, an extension, or additional bathrooms, are 'capital expenditure': the amounts are added to fixed assets on the balance sheet. Sometimes the boundary between 'capital expenditure' (which appears on the balance sheet, and does not reduce equity) and 'revenue expenditure' (which does not appear on the balance sheet, and does reduce equity) is not clear and there may be scope for creative accounting.

Where there is a lack of clear principles to determine what should be included on a balance sheet, and the basis or valuation that is to be used for the various items, the value of balance sheets is restricted. A series of official 'Financial Reporting Standards', now on an international basis, has been produced to deal with this problem, and the development of financial accounting has steadily encouraged users to expect more from balance sheets. It would be difficult for them to satisfy all the different expectations that interested parties might have. But we cannot even begin to assess a company's financial position and performance without a good understanding of balance sheets.

1.10 Financial Accounting and Management Accounting

Financial accounting is mainly concerned with producing financial statements for shareholders, creditors and others who are outside the organization concerned. The main financial statements are the balance sheet, the income statement and the cash flow statement. In published accounts these are supported by substantial additional information, notes and explanations. The Companies Acts, and official accounting standards, regulate the information that is published. Within the company a sophisticated bookkeeping system is required to record all the transactions that form the basis of these financial statements. Bookkeeping systems are explained in Chapter 14. In large-scale businesses managers do not rely very much on published financial accounting information; they have access to much more detailed and relevant management accounting information.

Management accounting is concerned with producing information for managers who are concerned with planning, decision-making and control. Management accounting information is not usually published, and it is designed to meet the needs of the managers of the organization concerned; it does not have to comply with official regulations. The subject of management accounting is introduced in Chapter 13 where it is clearly distinguished from financial accounting.

Summary

A balance sheet shows the liabilities of a company, and can provide useful information about a company's financial position. Solvency ratios can give an indication of whether a company is likely to become insolvent. Assets are not usually shown at their current value, and care is needed in using balance sheets as an indication of the value of a company. A business as a whole, as a going concern, is usually worth much more than the total of its net assets.

Review of key points

- A balance sheet shows what a company owns (assets) and what it owes (liabilities).
- By deducting liabilities from assets we arrive at the figure for 'equity', or 'capital', or 'net assets'.
- Assets and liabilities are classified as being long or short term. UK balance sheets usually begin with non-current assets, followed by current assets. The second part of the balance sheet shows how the assets were financed: by liabilities (current and non-current) and by equity.
- A successful business is usually worth more than the balance sheet figure for its net assets.
- Balance sheets show how a company is financed and may indicate if a company has excessive liabilities.
- Comparing this year's balance sheet with last year's can provide a basis for calculating profit
- The main financial accounting statements are published; management accounting information is different, and is internal to the organization.

Self-testing questions

1 Which of the following are shown on a balance sheet?
   Assets; expenses; liabilities; sales; share capital; profit for the year
2 What is the difference between a non-current asset and a current asset?
3 Give examples of non-current (or 'fixed') assets. In what circumstances would some of the items you have listed be current assets?
4 Arrange the three main balance sheet items (assets, liabilities, equity) as an equation.
5 A balance sheet appears to show what a business is worth. What are the main problems with this statement?

Self-testing questions (continued)

6 You are given the following simplified balance sheet of the Sandin Castle Company:

	£	£
Non-current assets		50,000
Current assets		
Inventories (at cost)	24,000	
Receivables	12,000	
Cash	9,000	
		45,000
Total assets		95,000
Current liabilities		
Payables		22,000
Equity		
Share capital	50,000	
Retained earnings	23,000	
		73,000
		95,000

a Calculate the current ratio.

b Calculate the liquidity ratio.

c After preparing the balance sheet, the company sells inventories, which had cost £4,000, for £8,000, which it immediately receives in cash. Show how the balance sheet would appear after this transaction.

d How does the above transaction affect the current ratio and the liquidity ratio?

7 You are given the following simplified balance sheets of the Windysand Company as at 31 December:

Simplified[17] balance sheet of the Windysand Company as at 31 December

	Year 1	Year 2
	£	£
Non-current assets	320,000	350,000
Current assets	5,000	45,000
Total assets	325,000	395,000
Equity	100,000	183,000
Non-current liabilities	222,000	202,000
Current liabilities	3,000	10,000
	325,000	395,000

a How much profit does it at first seem that the company made during year 2?

b How would your answer to (a) be affected if you found out that the company had paid £10,000 in dividends; that additional shares with a value of £20,000 had been issued; and that fixed assets had been revalued upwards by £30,000?

---

[17] The order of items on this balance sheet follows the illustration given in IAS 1; it differs from the order given in Ted Baker's balance sheet. We have to be prepared for balance sheets that show items in a different order.

Self-testing questions (continued)

8 You are given the following simplified balance sheets of two very similar companies; Domer Castle Company and Warmer Castle Company, as at 31 December year 1.

	Domer Castle Ltd £	Warmer Castle Ltd £
Non-current assets		
Tangible assets		
Freehold premises (at cost)	300,000	100,000
Furniture (at cost less depreciation)	4,000	80,000
Vehicles (at cost less depreciation)	10,000	90,000
	314,000	270,000
Investments	–	44,000
	314,000	314,000
Current assets		
Inventories	8,000	19,000
Receivables	12,000	10,000
Cash	14,000	5,000
	34,000	34,000
Total assets	348,000	348,000
Equity		
Share capital	100,000	100,000
Retained earnings	131,000	31,000
	231,000	131,000
Non-current liabilities		
10% Debentures	100,000	200,000
Current liabilities		
Trade payables	17,000	17,000
Total equity and liabilities	348,000	348,000

During year 1 the operating profit (earnings before interest and taxation) of the Domer Castle Company amounted to £31,000. The operating profit of the Warmer Castle Company amounted to £32,000.

Which of the two companies appears to be financially weakest, and why? You should calculate the current ratio, the liquidity ratio, the capital gearing ratio and the number of times interest is covered by operating profit.

9 You are given the following simplified balance sheet of the Stonefolk Company as at 31 March year 4.

	£
Non-current assets	158,000
Current assets	
Inventories (at cost)	110,000
Receivables	120,000
Cash	20,000
	250,000
Total assets	408,000
Equity	
Share capital	250,000
Retained earnings	38,000
	288,000
Current liabilities	
Trade payables	120,000
Total equity and liabilities	408,000

a The following transactions took place in April year 4. Show how each would affect the balance sheet. (Each transaction must affect two or more figures, and the balance sheet must continue to balance.)

i A building, which had cost £80,000, was sold for £100,000, which was immediately received in cash.

ii Inventories, which had cost £30,000, were sold to Mr Spliff for £80,000. Mr Spliff agreed to pay for the goods by the end of May year 4.

iii The company paid £40,000 of the amount that it owed to creditors, which are shown on the balance sheet as 'payables'.

b Show how the balance sheet would appear after these transactions have been recorded.

1 What are the main functions of a balance sheet?

2 You are given the following simplified balance sheet of the Hackin Company as at 30 June year 9.

Assessment questions (continued)

	£
Non-current assets	250,000
Current assets	
Inventories (at cost)	60,000
Receivables	40,000
Cash	120,000
	220,000
Total assets	470,000
Current liabilities	
Payables	100,000
Equity	
Share capital	250,000
Retained earnings	120,000
	370,000
Total equity and liabilities	470,000

a Calculate the company's current ratio and liquidity ratio.

b The following transactions take place during July year 9:

   i New plant and equipment are bought for £80,000, and payment is made in cash.

   ii Additional inventories of goods are bought for £15,000; it is agreed that they will be paid for in August.

   Prepare a revised balance sheet after these transactions have been recorded.

c How do these transactions affect the current ratio and the liquidity ratio?

3 You are given the following simplified balance sheets of the Fourpine Company as at 31 December.

	Year 1	Year 2
	£	£
Non-current assets	520,000	450,000
Current assets	45,000	55,000
Total assets	565,000	505,000
Equity		
Share capital	300,000	310,000
Retained earnings	35,000	60,000
	335,000	370,000
Non-current liabilities	200,000	100,000
Current liabilities	30,000	35,000
Total equity and liabilities	565,000	505,000

a How much profit does it at first seem that the company made during year 2?

b How would your answer to (a) be affected if you found out that the company had paid £25,000 in dividends?

4 You are given the following simplified balance sheets of the Port Andrew Company and the Port Edward Company as at 31 December year 1.

Assessment questions (continued)

	Port Andrew Ltd	Port Edward Ltd
	£	£
Non-current assets		
Tangible assets		
Freehold premises (at cost)	100,000	200,000
Plant (at cost less depreciation)	200,000	100,000
Vehicles (at cost less depreciation)	100,000	100,000
	400,000	400,000
Investments	200,000	30,000
	600,000	430,000
Current assets		
Inventories	70,000	40,000
Receivables	50,000	90,000
Cash	10,000	60,000
	130,000	190,000
Total assets	730,000	620,000
Equity		
Share capital	300,000	300,000
Retained earnings	60,000	140,000
	360,000	440,000
Non-current liabilities		
10% Debentures	300,000	100,000
Current liabilities		
Trade payables	70,000	80,000
Total equity and liabilities	730,000	620,000

During year 1 the operating profit of the Port Andrew Company amounted to £61,000. The operating profit of the Port Edward Company amounted to £40,000.

Which of the two companies appears to be the financially weaker, and why? You should calculate the current ratio, the liquidity ratio, the capital gearing ratio and the interest times cover.

5 You are given the following simplified balance sheet of the Whiting Company as at 31 August year 6:

	£	£
Non-current assets		350,000
Current assets		
Inventories (at cost)	90,000	
Trade receivables	80,000	
Cash	30,000	200,000
Total assets		550,000
Current liabilities		
Trade payables		130,000
Equity		
Share capital	380,000	
Retained earnings	40,000	420,000
		550,000

Assessment questions (continued)

a The following transactions took place in September year 6. Show how each would affect the balance sheet. (Each transaction must affect two figures, and the balance sheet must continue to balance.)

  i A new machine costing £10,000 was purchased and paid for in cash.

  ii Inventories which had cost £50,000 were sold to Mrs Fish for £90,000 and paid for immediately in cash.

  iii £30,000 was received from debtors, which were shown as 'receivables' on the balance sheet.

b Show how the balance sheet would appear after these transactions have been recorded.

Group activities and discussion questions

1 Each individual in the group should attempt to answer the question 'How much am I worth?' There is no need to disclose actual figures or personal information. The objective is to determine – and for members of the group to agree – the way in which the question would be answered. What principles or rules would you use?

2 Each member of the group should choose two listed companies, and obtain their published balance sheet (from the companies' websites; or by using the *Financial Times* Annual Reports Service). Try to assess how financially strong each company is (or is it likely to collapse?). The group should rank each of the companies that members have examined from the strongest financially, to the weakest. The group should discuss, and try to agree, criteria to form the basis for this assessment.

3 Is it possible to calculate the value of a company? If not, why not? If so, how?

4 Which of the following should be included as assets on a company's balance sheet: money which is owed to the company; the cost of an advertising campaign; machinery that is over 20 years old but which is still used occasionally; key employees who have a high market value; money paid as 'commission' to a government minister in Wayawayaland that has helped to secure a lucrative contract; brand names; money receivable under a contract that was signed yesterday and that will be earned next year; machinery that the company does not own, but for which they have signed a 5-year lease.

Financial accounting in context

Eurotunnel secures 'Chapter 11' protection

By Tom Stevenson

Daily Telegraph, 3 August 2006

Discuss and comment on the following extract from the press with particular reference to how balance sheets can help to predict the bankruptcy of a company.

Source: Reproduced with permission by the *Daily Telegraph*.

EUROTUNNEL has won up to 18 months protection from its creditors after a French court appointed an administrator to help put together a rescue plan for the heavily indebted Channel Tunnel operator.

The 'safeguard procedure', which is similar to Chapter 11 protection in the US, follows 15 months of failed negotiations over the restructuring of a £6.2bn debt mountain, which has brought Eurotunnel to the brink of bankruptcy.

The protection will allow Eurostar trains, and the freight and vehicle-carrying shuttle trains that use the tunnel between Britain and France, to keep running while a deal is thrashed out.

Chairman Jacques Gounon has warned that Eurotunnel could collapse as early as next January unless two sets of warring creditors can agree on the terms of a debt-for-equity swap by September.

He said yesterday: "I am convinced that we now have the conditions necessary to achieve a financial restructuring for Eurotunnel within the time allowed."

Eurotunnel is due to begin repaying debt in January. If agreement is not reached in time, senior creditors – principally the banks that funded the construction of the tunnel 20 years ago – have the right to take control of the tunnel.

A spokesman for the senior creditors said: "We continue to work to try and achieve a consensual deal based on economic reality."

A proposal that would see senior bank creditors take up to 87pc of the company in exchange for writing off some of Eurotunnel's outstanding borrowings was blocked last month by a group of bondholders representing £1.9bn of lower ranking debt.

The deal, proposed by Mr Gounon with backing from Goldman Sachs and Australia's Macquarie, left open a slim chance of shareholders retaining control. They could do this if Eurotunnel were able to generate enough cash to buy back part of a new £1.2bn bond before its conversion into shares in three to five years' time.

Even if the bond was to convert in full, shareholders would be left with 13pc of the company under the Gounon plan. Eurotunnel has around 800,000 shareholders, mainly in France. Bondholders, led by Deutsche Bank have been pushing for a share of the proposed bond. They also believe that the 13pc minimum stake earmarked for existing shareholders is too generous. A spokesman for the bondholders said they would "actively co-operate in order to reach a balanced and satisfactory solution for all parties involved, and for Eurotunnels' future".

The French court delayed a decision on the protection order last week in order to give more time for agreement between the various groups of creditors.

Eurotunnel said it believed there had been "a convergence of views amongst the principal creditors who consider that [the Gounon] proposal constitutes the basis for pursuing negotiations that will lead to a reconciliation of their positions".

Eurotunnel, an engineering and operational success, has been a financial disaster ever since construction costs doubled to £10bn, the tunnel opened a year late in 1994 and traffic forecasts proved too optimistic after ferry operators responded to the new cross-Channel threat by launching a price war.

References and further reading

International Accounting Standard 1 *Presentation of Financial Statements*. (December 2003, amended March 2004). IASB.

Pendlebury, M. and R. Groves (2003) *Company Accounts: Analysis, Interpretation and Understanding* (6th edition). Thomson Learning.

Wood, F. and A. Sangster (2005) *Business Accounting* vol. 1 (10th edition). FT Prentice Hall.

www.frc.org.uk (gives details of the Financial Reporting Council and arrangements for accounting standards in the British Isles)

www.iasb.org.uk (gives details of international accounting standards)

www.tedbaker.co.uk (select: share info; click for full financial information; select financial reports or other information as required)

CHAPTER 02

The Income Statement (Profit and Loss Account)

Chapter contents

❖ LEARNING OBJECTIVES

After studying this chapter you should be able to:

❖ Explain the structure and terminology of straightforward income statements

❖ Understand that there are different reasons for measuring profit, and different views of what profit is

❖ Describe the main categories of expenses

❖ Assess some possibilities for 'creative accounting' in measuring profit

❖ Discuss the role and limitations of income statements

The term 'profit and loss account' has been widely used for many years, but following international accounting standards the term 'income statement' is increasingly used instead.

2.1 Introduction

In Chapter 1 we saw that the amount of profit a company makes during a year can be calculated by comparing the balance sheet at the beginning of the year with the balance sheet at the end of the year. Some additional information may be needed, and it is not the easiest way of calculating profit. Income statements (or profit and loss accounts) provide more straightforward presentations of profit figures. But even a brief examination of the published income statement of a company shows a complex assortment of different profit figures, and it can be difficult to know where to start.

At first sight the notion of profit seems very straightforward. If you buy something for £6 and sell it for £10, you have made £4 profit. But accountants would say that this is 'gross profit', which is the first of the profit figures shown on an income statement. We need to deduct expenses before we arrive at operating profit. There are more deductions, and profit is shown both before and after tax.

To begin with, we need to be clear about (a) terminology, and (b) the usual formats for presenting the information. Most people are clear that they want to know the profit figures, but they are much less clear about exactly what profit means, and what the profit figures are to be used for. If we are clear about the function(s) of profit figures, we can then see what principles for measuring profit are appropriate.

2.2 Terminology and Format

Income statements show profit for the year[1] and the term 'income statement' has now generally replaced the term 'profit and loss account'.

An income statement shows the calculation on the basis that expenses are deducted from revenues.

$$\text{Revenues } \textit{minus} \text{ expenses} = \text{profit}$$

'Revenues', 'turnover' and 'sales' are much the same thing, and are shown on an income statement along with any 'other income'.[2] The words 'expenses' and 'costs' mean much the same thing, but payments (of cash) are quite different. It sometimes seems as if accounting terminology is designed to be confusing!

One thing we need to be very clear about is that the word 'receipts' is nothing to do with income or profit; it means receipts of cash. Similarly, the word 'payments' is nothing to do with expenses or profit measurement; it means payments of cash. The differences between receipts and payments of cash, and profit are essential to an understanding of financial accounts. They are dealt with in Chapters 7 and 16.

The usual format of an income statement calculates profit in four main stages, as shown in Illustration 2.1.

---

[1] An income statement can be for a year, a month or any period you like. A balance sheet is never for a period – it is always 'as at' a given date.

[2] It is easier to think of 'income' as being revenues for the period, before expenses are deducted; but, unfortunately, some accountants use the word 'income' to mean profit. Accounting terminology can be very confusing!

Income statement of Simple Company Ltd for the year ended 31 December year 3

	£000
Revenue	100
Cost of sales	60
Gross profit	**40**
Distribution costs	(12)
Administration expenses	(9)
Operating profit**	**19**
Financing costs	(3)
Profit before taxation	**16**
Tax on profit for year	(4)
Profit after taxation for the year**	**12**

Statement of changes in equity of Simple Company Ltd for the year ended 31 December year 3

Balance at 31 December year 2	500
Add Profit for the year	12
Deduct Dividends for the year	(5)
Balance as at 31 December year 3	507

ILLUSTRATION 2.1

First, there is 'gross profit', which is the difference between the sales figure and *the cost of the goods that have been sold*.[3] This phrase, more simply expressed as *cost of sales*, is very important in profit measurement.

Second, there is 'operating profit', which is arrived at after deducting the main categories of expenses, which are distribution costs and administrative expenses. Operating profit is an important figure: it shows how much profit has been made from the normal operations of the business before deducting any interest payable.

Third, there is 'profit before taxation', which is arrived at after bringing in interest receivable and interest payable – usually shown as 'finance costs'.

Fourth, there is 'profit after taxation', which obviously comes after deducting the company's tax charge for the year, and is the net amount that has been earned for the shareholders.

Each of the above four versions of profit may be useful in assessing different aspects of a company's performance. The fourth figure shows profit available after taxation that is the basis for determining the amount of dividend to be paid to shareholders.

The dividend[4] for the year is shown on a separate 'Statement of changes in equity for the year'. As we saw in Chapter 1 we can compare the balance sheet at the beginning of the year with the balance sheet at the end of the year to show the amount by which 'equity' has changed: it is increased by the amount of profit earned during the year; it is reduced by the amount of dividends to be paid for the year; and it may be changed by other items such as

---

[3] It excludes the cost of goods that have not been sold (closing stock or inventory), which is carried forward to be treated as an expense in the following period.

[4] The dividend for the year is the amount paid to shareholders; it is usually part of the profit (after tax) for the year. The remaining profits are 'retained' within the business.

a revaluation of assets. The 'Statement of changes in equity for the year' shows these items and anything else that has changed the amount of equity during the year.

Although company income statements can be almost infinitely complex, it is also possible to have versions that look relatively simple, as shown in Illustration 2.1. Each of the different profit figures has its uses, but the two marked with asterisks are perhaps the most important in assessing the overall performance of a company. It is useful to compare the profit figures for the current year with those of previous years to see what improvement (if any) there has been. It is also useful to compare the profit figures with the amount of resources invested in the company to see if a reasonable return has been achieved.

The income statement emphasizes what profit has been earned for the shareholders. The final figures on a published income statement show the 'earnings per share' (EPS). This is the total amount of profit after tax that the company has earned during the year, divided by the number of shares that the company has. This figure is widely used as a measure of a company's success. Not all of the EPS is paid out to shareholders as dividends: the total earnings for the year can be compared with the dividends for the year on the statement of changes in equity. In Illustration 2.1 the Simple Company Ltd made profits of £12,000 during the year; £5,000 of this was paid to shareholders as dividends; the remaining £7,000 was retained in the business.

An income statement might show a substantial increase in profits, but this does not necessarily mean that the shareholders are going to be better off. If profits have increased by 50 per cent, but the number of shares has doubled, then the EPS will be reduced. EPS is sometimes seen as being the most important figure in assessing company performance. Shareholders expect to see it increase year after year, and some companies even aim for 'double-digit' growth in EPS – they want it to increase by at least 10 per cent each year. Not many companies manage to achieve this for more than a very few years.

2.3 Reasons for Measuring Profit

There are many good reasons for measuring profit. It is a symbol of success for companies and their managers. A company that shows steadily increasing profits is likely to go from strength to strength. A company that shows losses, or falling profits, is likely to find itself in difficulties.

More specifically, the main reasons for measuring profit, or functions that profit measurement may serve, are as follows:

1 It is a measure of *performance*. Shareholders want to know how well the directors and managers of a company are doing, running the company for its owners (the shareholders).

2 It is a guide to dividend policy. A company chooses how much profit is paid out as dividends. Occasionally, a company pays out more dividends than it earns in profits, but it cannot do that for very long. A company must earn profits if it is to continue paying

dividends. There is a Companies Act requirement that dividends should be paid only when there are sufficient accumulated realized, retained earnings to justify them.

3 Directors and managers may have a direct interest in such performance for their own reasons: they are often shareholders themselves, and they may have some sort of performance-related pay, which means that they get extra salaries or bonuses[5] if profits achieve specified levels.

4 It is a measure of the *efficiency* of a company. Efficiency is about the relationship between inputs and outputs. To maximize efficiency is to minimize the cost per unit of output; or to maximize the outputs per £ of cost. For a company the inputs are shown as costs; outputs are shown as sales; the difference between sales and costs is shown as profit. Maximizing profits, therefore, maximizes efficiency.

5 It is a measure of the *effectiveness* of a company. Effectiveness is about the relationship between outputs and objectives. An effective organization (or individual) is one that achieves what it is intending to do. If we assume that companies intend to maximize profits, then maximizing profits maximizes effectiveness.

6 It is a guide to the financial strength of a company. A company that is profitable is more likely to survive, and be able to pay its liabilities when they fall due, than one which is loss-making.

7 It is a basis for taxation. The government lays down various rules for taxation purposes (e.g., what rate of depreciation or 'writing-down allowance' should be used), which means that the profit figure shown in a company's published accounts may be quite different from the figure used in calculating the amount of corporation tax payable.

8 It is relevant in pricing decisions. In most circumstances prices are determined more by what the market will bear, and the company has to find ways of keeping costs below the market price (and/or ways of pushing up what the market will bear). In some circumstances (e.g., in public utilities that were previously publicly owned) there are official restrictions on price increases that are related to profits.

9 Employees have an interest in profits. They may believe that a profitable company is the best guarantee of long-term employment. They may also believe that good profits present an opportunity for pressing for increases in wages and salaries.

10 Profits are sometimes seen as being the key to a successful economy and a successful country. Companies that are most profitable find it easier to raise capital, at lowest cost; and so resources in the country flow into the most profitable companies, which are also the most efficient and effective. Companies that are least profitable find it hardest to raise capital, have to pay more for it, and so the least efficient and effective companies tend to decline.

Some of the above may be questionable, or political, and you are, of course, free to take very different views. You may believe that profit is a measure of the success of the strong in

---

[5] Or they may have share options. Or they may be 'fat cats' who get good bonuses even when the company does badly. Or their bonuses may depend on the share price achieving a particular level. Or they may have share options that are valuable only when the share price achieves particular levels. As directors are supposed to be accountable to shareholders, it is worth considering the effectiveness of accountability arrangements; these are discussed later.

exploiting the weak; that big business makes too much profit; that more should go to the workers; that profit fails to measure social costs; and all of the above ignores issues such as health and safety, child labour, damage to the environment and non-sustainable development. You can, if you wish, take the view that profits are a 'bad thing'. It is probably a 'good thing' if this book encourages you to think about these issues!

It is, however, worth being explicit about the general assumptions that seem to lie behind the measuring and reporting of profit. Many different people and groups in society are likely to be in favour of companies making good and increasing profits for many different reasons. In some circumstances governments may try to restrict the amount of profit that monopolies (or near monopolies) are allowed to make. But increasing profits are generally favoured by shareholders, managers (and the Treasury who are usually happy to rake in more in taxation), and the company's bankers and professional advisers (whose fees seem to keep going up), the financial press, many employees and anyone else who can jump on the gravy train. There is enormous pressure on managers to perform, and to produce profits. And if they cannot, they are liable to be replaced by others, sometimes by managers who can produce profits out of thin air,[6] like magicians. There are always some who can make use of creative accounting techniques for their own advantage. But, like magicians, such managers do not want to be watched too closely, and the more successful ones move on rapidly to other companies to display their tricks and illusions.

Given that profit figures are likely to be used for many different purposes, it is not surprising that there are different approaches to profit measurement. The principles of profit measurement could be based mainly on comparing balance sheet values from one period to the next. They can also be based on the income statement, and how revenues and income are defined and measured.

2.4 What is Included as Revenues (or Income)

The income statement begins with the figure for revenue, which could also be called sales or turnover. It includes all the sales that have been made during the period, not just of goods, but, depending on what kind of business it is, also of services, and it can include other items such as rents receivable. The turnover figure is shown net of such things as value added tax.

It includes all sales that have been made during a period, even if the money for those sales is not received until a later period. This principle is important. It means that a rapidly expanding business might be making very good sales each month, and good profits, but the amount owed by debtors will increase each month, and the cash that comes into the business lags behind the profits that are being earned. This could mean that a rapidly expanding and profitable business has much less money than the sales figures suggest.

It is also important because it is sometimes not clear exactly when a sale has been made. It could be that a sale is initially agreed by telephone; a few days later an order is received; then a few weeks later the goods are completed ready for despatch; then, a few days later, the goods are received by the purchaser; then the seller sends out the invoice. Payment for

---

[6] Such 'creative accounting' is examined in Chapter 8.

the goods is probably not made for another month or two. There is a need for a clear accounting principle that determines the exact point, or the critical event, at which a sale is recognized. In practice, an accounting system usually recognizes a sale when the invoice is sent out. But it is easy to see that temptations can arise to recognize sales at an earlier date. When sales are below target, perhaps in the last month of the year, and managers see their bonuses disappearing, or even their jobs, it is not difficult to create a few extra sales by bringing some forward, or sending invoices out early; they can be reversed the following month. It is a bit like a shop assistant borrowing from the till, with the intention of paying back before the final reckoning comes: you can get away with it for a while, but eventually it will catch up on you. You can bring forward your revenues one year, but you cannot bring them forward more and more each year.

Other items of income are included in published income statements such as profits on sales of fixed assets, investment income, interest receivable, various 'exceptional items' and any share of profits from associated companies.

2.5 What is Included as Expenses

There are more problems with defining and measuring expenses, and no shortage of accounting standards or principles attempting to deal with them. Expenses are recognized in accordance with the *accruals concept,* which means that it is not the amount of cash paid out during a period that is counted; it is the amount incurred in earning the revenue that is recognized during the period. This is also about *matching*: after recognizing the turnover for a period, we match against it those expenses that have been incurred in earning that turnover. This is particularly important with cost of sales and with depreciation.

Cost of Sales

The first expense on the income statement is cost of sales, or cost of goods sold. This means that if you buy 100 items, but sell only 70 of them, only the 70 count in the cost of sales. The other 30 are 'closing inventory' (stocks remaining at the end of the period), and are carried forward to be treated as an expense in the following period (see Illustration 2.2).

As the calculation of gross profit (or any other profit) is dependent on the closing inventory figure, the way in which this is determined is important. If, in Illustration 2.2, Raj had made a mistake, and his closing inventory figure was really £3,000, then his cost of sales would be only £8,000, and the gross profit would be £7,000.

If his real closing inventory figure was only £1,500, then his gross profit would be only £5,500. If a higher closing inventory figure is shown, then the profit figure will be higher, and the assets[7] and equity figures on the balance sheet will be higher. If a lower closing inventory figure is shown, then the profit figure will be lower, and the assets and equity figures on the balance sheet will be lower. This has important consequences: if Raj overstated his closing inventory figure by £1 million, his income statement and balance sheet

---

[7] Closing inventory is shown as an asset on the balance sheet.

At the beginning of March, Raj's shop had inventories of goods amounting to £1,000. During March he bought goods for resale costing £10,000.[8] His sales figure for March was £15,000.

Raj, therefore, had £11,000 worth of goods available for sale. But that is not the cost of sales figure. Some of the goods he had available for sale were not sold, and we cannot calculate the cost of sales or the gross profit until we know the closing inventory figure.

His stock of unsold goods at the end of March was £2,000.

The cost of the goods which he sold can now be calculated as follows:

Opening stock	£1,000
Purchases	£10,000
Cost of goods available for sale	£11,000
Deduct Closing inventory	£2,000
Cost of goods sold (or cost of sales)	£9,000

The cost of sales figure is then compared with the sales figure, and the difference, £6,000, is the gross profit.

Sales	£15,000
Cost of sales	£ 9,000
Gross profit	£ 6,000

ILLUSTRATION 2.2

would look better by £1 million. Clearly, we need some clear rules and principles for determining closing stock figures. The general rule is that stocks of goods are shown at cost price.[9]

In a retailing business it is relatively easy to establish the cost price of goods. In a manufacturing business it is more difficult because we need to establish the cost of manufacturing the goods, which involves some difficult decisions in allocating overheads.

The cost of sales figure includes only the costs of buying, or producing goods and services. It includes an appropriate share of production overheads, including the costs of running the factory or other production facilities (including rent, lighting, heating, depreciation and maintenance of machinery, and factory supervision costs). Cost of sales does not include the general administration costs of the business, or the selling and distribution costs.

Gross Profit Ratio

In examining the income statement of a business, analysts usually calculate the gross profit ratio. This expresses gross profit as a percentage of sales as follows:

$$\frac{£6,000}{£15,000} = 40\%$$

Mark-up

The cost of the goods that Raj sold was £9,000. He marked them up by £6,000 and sold them for £15,000. The mark-up can be expressed as a percentage as follows:

---

[8] That is what he bought during March. He probably did not pay for them until April. But actual payments of cash, and receipts of cash, are quite distinct from revenues and expenses, that are used in profit measurement.

[9] Or, more precisely, closing inventories are shown at the lower of cost and net realizable value.

$$\frac{£6,000}{£9,000} = 66\tfrac{2}{3}\%$$

It is important not to confuse percentage mark-ups with gross profit percentages, and it is worth playing with a few calculations to become familiar with them. A 25 per cent mark-up becomes a 20 per cent gross profit ratio (e.g. buy for £80, sell for £100). A 33⅓ per cent gross profit ratio comes from a 50 per cent mark-up (e.g. buy for £100, sell for £150).

Depreciation

Figures for depreciation are less obvious on a published income statement; they are usually included under several headings with the detail hidden away in the notes to the accounts. When a business buys a non-current asset (a fixed asset) such as a piece of machinery, it is not immediately treated as an expense. The asset is shown on the balance sheet; the business decides how long the useful life of the asset is expected to be; and the figure is written down, or depreciated, each year. Depreciation is an expense in calculating profit that sounds straightforward enough. But it causes problems to students of accounting because:

1 They often think that expenses are paid out in cash; but depreciation is not paid out in cash. The fixed asset has already been bought, and the cash has already flowed out. Depreciation is a bookkeeping entry, not a flow of cash. Profit is always calculated *after* charging depreciation. If we want to know what cash flow a business is generating, then we have to add depreciation back on to profit. Some people say that a business's cash flow is its profit plus depreciation, which is roughly right. Some even see depreciation as being an inflow of cash, but that is completely wrong: depreciation is something that, in calculating profit, we treat as if it is paid out as cash (but it is not) so we add it back to profit to indicate the cash that has been generated during the period.

2 They see depreciation as part of a process of valuing assets, which it is not. The objective is to write down the cost of a fixed asset, year by year, as the useful life of the fixed asset is being used up. Usually[10] this results in asset figures being shown on the balance sheet that are closer to current values, but that is incidental. The main point is to charge, as an expense in calculating profit, the amount of the fixed asset that has been used up.

3 They think that a provision for depreciation is a pool of money that can be used to replace fixed assets when they come to the end of their lives. But there is no money in a provision (or in 'reserves'). If you want to know what money (or cash and bank) there is in a business you have to look in current assets. The provision for depreciation is a bookkeeping entry, not an allocation of cash. It reduces profits, and as companies usually relate dividend decisions to the level of profits, the fact that depreciation is charged may limit the amount of dividends paid out – a way of achieving 'capital maintenance'.

Even for sophisticated users of accounts, there are problems with depreciation. Different companies have different depreciation policies, and we never really know how long a

---

[10] But not always. Companies are expected to depreciate buildings as their effective lives are 'used up', even if they are increasing in value.

fixed asset will last, or how long we will keep it, or how much it will be sold for when we have finished with it. We might buy a car for £10,000, and *plan* to keep it for 4 years, and then to sell it for £2,000. But that might change; we might keep it much longer, or sell it much earlier; and the amount we sell it for might be much more, or less, than we planned.

The easiest approach to depreciation is to use the 'straight line' method. If we buy a car for £10,000, and plan to sell it for £2,000 after 4 years, then the total amount to be depreciated is £8,000, which works out at £2,000 a year for 4 years.

Slightly more complicated, but still reasonably popular, is the 'diminishing balance' method.[11] If we charged 33 per cent[12] per annum on this basis, the figures would be as follows:

Initial cost of car	£10,000
Year 1 depreciation 33% of £10,000	£3,300
Balance at end of year 1	6,700
Year 2 depreciation 33% of £6,700	£2,211
Balance at end of year 2	4,489
Year 3 depreciation 33% of £4,489	£1,481
Balance at end of year 3	3,008
Year 4 depreciation 33% of £ 3,008	993
Balance at end of year 4	2,015

This method of depreciation results in higher depreciation in the early years, and lower depreciation in the later years. Occasionally, depreciation is calculated in more obscure ways. A vehicle could be depreciated in relation to the number of miles it does each year.

If a company suddenly changed its policy and planned to keep its vehicles (or ships, or aeroplanes, or machinery) for twice as long as they had previously planned, that could halve their depreciation charges, and produce a very significant increase in profits. Such a change in policy, and its financial effects, would have to be disclosed in a note to the financial statements. But there is inevitably some scope for individual judgement or manipulation as there is no certainty in the future lives, or residual values, of fixed assets.

Depreciation figures and policies should be disclosed fully in the notes to the financial statements, but they do not usually appear on the face of a published income statement. The three main categories of expense (cost of sales, distribution costs and administration expenses) may all include some depreciation as there may be fixed assets involved in producing the goods and services, in selling and distributing them, and in the administration of the business.

Impairment of Goodwill

When one company buys another business, the amount of money they pay is partly for the net assets of the business, and partly for their 'goodwill', a term that covers a multitude of attributes of a business that enable it to earn profits. If a company buys a business with excellent prospects, they may pay a lot for 'goodwill', and the amount must be shown on the balance sheet as a non-current asset; and, as with other fixed assets, it is likely to be

---

[11] Also known as the reducing balance method.

[12] Thirty-three per cent. Not 33⅓ per cent – that would give a different answer.

'used up' over a number of years. Traditionally, accountants would 'amortize' goodwill in much the same way as they depreciated other fixed assets. But it is difficult to know how long the goodwill will last, and so it is difficult to decide whether it should be written off over 5 years, or 20 years, or some other period. What happens now is that there is an 'impairment test' each year: the company assesses the amount by which the goodwill has been impaired, or used up, during the year. An impairment charge is then made, which is, in effect, depreciation or amortization of goodwill.

Goodwill and its amortization are controversial areas in accounting. The traditional view was that if goodwill is an asset, its value is dubious and it should be written off as soon as possible. A more current view is that, provided the business is well run, goodwill should last indefinitely, and there is no need to amortize it each year – especially as this can lead to massive reductions in reported profits. The official requirement is that goodwill should be subject to an annual impairment test, and then written down accordingly. A business may decide that it has been impaired very little during the year or not at all. Some subjectivity is inevitable, and the door is wide open for creative accounting. Companies are not allowed to *increase* the amount they show for goodwill. Regardless of the requirements of financial reporting standards, many companies and investment analysts choose to emphasize profit figures that have not been charged with amortization of goodwill.

Classification and Disclosure of Expenses

A business can produce an income statement showing as much detail as they wish – with separate figures for wages and salaries, repairs and maintenance, cleaning, rent and rates, lighting and heating, insurance, telephones, stationery, postage, newspapers, directors' fees, auditors' fees, lawyers' fees and many other things. But the published accounts of companies are in standardized formats, such as the one shown in Illustration 2.1, which group most expenses under the general headings 'cost of sales', 'distribution costs' and 'administrative expenses'. The income statements included in the published annual reports and accounts of companies probably look more complicated, but the basics are the same as shown in Illustration 2.1.

If you plough through the notes to the accounts, and the directors' report, you will find lots more detail of expenses, including wages and salaries, directors' remuneration, costs of hiring plant and machinery, auditors' remuneration, depreciation and amortization, charitable and political donations. Other items disclosed include exceptional items such as profits or losses on disposals, the results of discontinued operations, and of new acquisitions, and an analysis of results classified as different segments.

As long as an expense is clearly recognized as such, which heading it is included under is less important. The chief executive may spend part of his time dealing with production issues (arguably part of the cost of sales), part dealing with distribution issues and part dealing with administration. But there is no need to bother with allocating the costs of employing him to these different headings, and it is acceptable to treat the whole cost as being administrative expenses. Gross profit ratios[13] may be important, but it is sometimes difficult to be clear about just which expenses have been included in cost of sales.

---

[13] Gross profit expressed as a percentage of sales revenue.

2.6 A Company's Published Income Statement

The income statement for Ted Baker plc is shown in Illustration 2.3. It is called a 'group income statement' because it includes the results of subsidiary companies that the Ted Baker Company owns.

Group income statement of Ted Baker Company for the 52 weeks ended 28 January 2006

	Note	52 weeks ended 28 January 2006 £'000	52 weeks ended 29 January 2005 £'000
Revenue	2	117,832	105,753
Cost of sales		(48,979)	(43,357)
Gross profit		68,853	62,396
Distribution costs		(39,007)	(34,417)
Administrative expenses		(15,339)	(15,089)
Other operating income		3,827	3,515
Operating profit		18,334	16,405
Finance income	4	129	68
Finance expenses	4	(109)	(221)
Profit before tax	3	18,354	16,252
Income tax expense		(5,435)	(4,884)
Profit for the period		12,919	11,368
Attributable to			
Equity shareholders of the parent company		12,931	11,347
Minority interests		(12)	21
Profit for the period		12,919	11,368
Earnings per share			
Basic	5	30.6p	26.8p
Diluted	5	29.7p	26.2p

Group statement of changes in equity of Ted Baker Company (simplified extract) for the 52 weeks ended 28 January 2006

	£'000
Balance at 29 January 2005	36,830
Add Profit for the period	12,919
Deduct Dividends	(4,775)
Other items	(2,802)
Balance at 28 January 2006	42,172

ILLUSTRATION 2.3

The main feature to note, from the shareholders' point of view, is that the 'profit for the period' has increased from about £11.4 million to nearly £13 million. This is a good increase (13.6 per cent), and the company is expanding fairly rapidly. Sales revenue has increased by 11.4 per cent (from £105.8 million to £117.8 million). The balance sheet (shown as Illustration 1.5, p. 13) shows that equity has increased from about £36.9 million to about £42.2 million (an increase of 14.5 per cent). Shareholders would be happy to see a good increase in sales and profits; but they may be less happy to see that so much more of their money (the increase in equity) was needed to achieve those results.

The main categories of expenses shown are:

- Cost of sales
- Distribution costs
- Administrative expenses
- Finance expenses

Finance expenses relate to interest payable by the company. Ted Baker's borrowings are very low, and so there is little interest to pay; in the most recent year they received more interest than they paid (finance income is greater than finance expense). In Chapter 1 we saw that some companies are very dependent on borrowings; interest costs can be high in relation to profits; and such companies may be at risk if they are unable to pay their liabilities as they fall due. Ted Baker is very low geared and with no real risk in relation to borrowings.

We can see that total profits have increased, and that most of the various categories of expenses have increased. This is not surprising as the business has expanded: total revenues have increased. It is worth examining whether or not expenses have increased faster than revenues; whether expenses seem to be carefully controlled, or whether they are rocketing upwards even faster than turnover. The main expenses are expressed as a percentage of sales, including cost of sales. It is more usual to express gross profit as a percentage of sales; both are shown as follows:

	2006	2005
Cost of sales/revenue	48,979/117,832	43,357/105,753
	41.6%	41.0%
Gross profit/revenue	68,853/117,832	62,396/105,753
	58.4%	59%
Distribution costs/revenue	39,007/117,832	34,417/105,753
	33.1%	32.5%
Administrative expenses/revenue	15,339/117,832	15,089/105,753
	13.0%	14.3%

The gross profit ratio seems fairly high. It would be interesting to compare it with other clothing retailers.

Other operating expenses seem to be under control. Distribution costs have increased as a percentage of sales, but administrative expenses are lower. From the notes to the accounts other information about expenses, and some explanation of the increases, can be found.

2.7 Income Statement Detailed Items

Examining the published income statement of a company usually reveals more complexities than have been outlined so far.

Company or Group

Most large companies that are listed on the stock market own a number of subsidiary companies. It is most useful to look at the group results that include all the results of the subsidiary companies

Minority Interest

A company often owns only, say, 90 per cent of a subsidiary company, but the income statement includes 100 per cent of the results of all the subsidiaries. At the end of the income statement, after profit for the period has been calculated, an item for 'minority interest' is shown. This is the part of the group's profit that belongs to shareholders outside the group (e.g. 10 per cent of the shareholders of a subsidiary company). The amount of profit remaining (after deducting the minority interest) belongs to the shareholders of the parent company.

Associates and Joint Ventures

A company (e.g. H) may invest in other companies (e.g. A or J), but own only between, say, 20 per cent and 50 per cent of A or J's shares. H is likely to have significant influence over A or J. But H does not include 100 per cent of A or J's profits in its income statement. Instead, H includes, say, 20 per cent to 50 per cent, according to the proportion owned.

Dividends Receivable

A company (e.g. H) may have only a small shareholding in another company (e.g. I) as an investment. If H has no significant influence over I, then I is not part of the group, and the group's income statement does not include a share of I's profits. Instead, the group income statement includes dividends (not profits) from such companies.

Acquisitions, Discontinued Operations and Continuing Operations

Large companies often sell off parts of the business, and buy new businesses. If you want to assess the future performance of a business, it is not much use doing so on the basis of information that includes parts of the business that have been closed down or disposed of. If you want to assess the past performance of a business, it is not much use comparing last year's figures with this year's figures if there has been a major acquisition; in that case we would expect to see a significant increase in this year's figures. To make meaningful comparisons we need to separate the figures for new acquisitions from continuing operations, and we need to separate the figure for operations that have been discontinued or disposed of.

Income statements provide the information under the three headings (acquisitions, discontinued operations, continuing operations) for sales and for operating profit.

Segmental Reporting

Many large companies combine together a number of different businesses, perhaps with very different products, or with very different geographical areas. International Accounting Standard (IAS) 14 requires companies to disclose their revenues, profits and capital employed for each major geographical and business segment. This can be very useful if you are trying to forecast a company's future performance and you believe that one area of business is going to perform better than another in the future. It can also be useful in assessing whether the management of one company has been as successful as others in dealing with areas of growth, and areas of decline.

Exceptional Items

A company's results are sometimes affected by 'one-off' exceptional items such as a profit on selling part of the business or some assets; inventories being written down; some write-offs to reflect the impairment of fixed assets; or the costs of redundancies and reorganization. These are usually shown as a separate item on the income statement, with more detail shown in the notes. The profit for the year and the basic EPS are shown after deducting (or crediting) all exceptional items. However, companies sometimes show a second EPS figure that may exclude any bad news that they have managed to label as 'exceptional items'.

2.8 Subjective Measurement and Creativity Problems

Creative accounting is an important subject in its own right, but even an introductory look at income statements reveals several areas where subjective judgements are required, and where there may be scope for creative accounting.

Capital Expenditure and Revenue Expenditure

Capital expenditure adds to the amount for fixed assets that are shown on the balance sheet as 'property, plant and equipment', under the heading 'non-current assets'. The balance sheet shows the amount of assets that the company owns at the year end. In an expanding company this usually increases each year because the company buys additional fixed assets during the year. 'Capital expenditure' is the term used for buying additional fixed assets; its effect on profit figures is delayed, and spread over a number of years as depreciation. The net effect of capital expenditure and depreciation is shown on the balance sheet, and more detail is shown in the notes to the accounts. Revenue expenditure appears on the income statement, not the balance sheet, and is an immediate charge against profit. Buying a new car, premises or machinery is capital expenditure. Maintaining them, and the costs of using them, are revenue expenditure.

The important distinction between capital expenditure and revenue expenditure is usually clear, but there are some grey areas and sometimes there may be a temptation to 'capitalise'[14] expenditure that is more like revenue expenditure and should be treated as an expense immediately. If a company can make most of its 'repairs and maintenance' expenditure look more like improvements and additions to fixed assets, they can avoid charging them as expenses on the income statement, boost profits and show higher asset figures on the balance sheet.

There are areas, such as research and development, where companies can capitalize large amounts of development expenditure in this way. It is also possible, when constructing a fixed asset (perhaps building a new hotel) to treat the cost of interest during the period of construction as part of the capital expenditure rather than revenue expenditure.

---

[14] Treat it as adding to fixed assets.

Depreciation

There is inevitably scope for differences of view on the lives of fixed assets, likely values at the end of their lives and in choosing what method of depreciation to use.

Valuation of Inventories

The value of inventories at the end of the year affects profits: if closing stocks are overstated, then profits and assets are overstated. Although the general rule is that stocks are shown at cost price (or net realizable value if it is lower), there may be some room for manoeuvre, especially when the company has itself manufactured the unsold items. There are important rules to determine which costs should be included in the cost of production, and which costs should be treated as expenses immediately. There is also a grey area in assessing 'net realizable value'. If an item has cost £100 to make or buy, it should continue to be included in the accounts at that price, until it seems that it can only be sold for a lower figure. It is possible for a company to be too optimistic in assessing net realizable values or to be too pessimistic; either approach can lead to unrealistic profit figures.

Timing

The rules on when sales should be recognized are not very clear and there is sometimes scope for bringing forward the recognition of sales, and so boosting the sales figure for the year.

2.9 Role and Limitations of Income Statements

The main role of the income statement is to set out the profit that a business has made during the period, and its component parts. The old term 'profit and loss account' may still be preferred because it shows the profits and losses from the various activities undertaken by the company. There are many good reasons for measuring profit, as set out in Section 2.3.

The income statement also has a role in indicating how and where profits might be increased. Comparing this year's results with last year's is a useful monitoring exercise. Most businesses expect their sales figure to increase each year, with an increase in cost of sales and an increase in gross profit. But they also hope to at least maintain their operating margins: that gross profit as a proportion of sales will be maintained or increased. The same kind of analysis should be applied to the main categories of expenses. As sales increase, expenses might also be expected to increase. But management should be monitoring the various expenses as a proportion of sales, and trying to ensure that expenses, as a percentage of sales, do not increase. Sometimes, as a matter of policy, a business might decide to increase particular items of expense (e.g. spending more on marketing). But, more generally, a business should expect some economies of scale as it expands, and monitor the results to see if each category of expense really is declining as a proportion of sales.

The information shown in the income statement can be useful in comparing this year's results with last year's as part of the financial control.[15] It can also be useful comparing one company's results with another. Of course, a large supermarket chain makes more profits than a small one; but detailed analysis of the income statement, looking at the various expenses as a proportion of sales, can show where one company is doing better than another, and where there is room for improvement.

In comparing companies with each other, we need to look carefully for explanations of difference in performance. One company might lease all its premises and equipment while another owns them. One might have very old fixed assets, and so have very low depreciation charges, while another has much newer fixed assets. One company might be financed wholly by shareholders' funds, and so have no interest charges, while another is largely financed by borrowing (i.e. it has high gearing) and so have high 'finance expenses' (interest charges). There might also be different accounting policies, and where there is scope for 'creative accounting', it may be difficult to make meaningful comparisons between one company and another. Among the functions of IASs are to aid comparisons between different companies, and different countries, and to minimize the scope for manipulation and creative accounting.

It is also important to realize that profits are not the same as cash flow. A company might do very well in selling equipment and civil engineering products to what the Americans call 'rogue states'; but there could be massive delays in receiving the money from these sales, which rather takes the shine off the performance. Income statements should be interpreted together with cash flow statements. Indeed, the main published financial accounting statements should be taken as a whole. Making profits is not enough. Profits need to be sufficient, when compared with the amount of money invested in the business, to justify that investment. Companies need to make a good return on capital employed (ROCE), and assessing the performance of a company requires the use of figures both from the income statement and from the balance sheet.

Summary

An income statement (previously known as a profit and loss account) shows the profit for a period, typically a year. Profit is based on the difference between revenue (or sales or turnover), and the costs incurred in earning those sales. Profit figures are useful in many different ways, and care is needed in interpreting the information. Profit is calculated after charging cost of sales (which requires a value to be put on closing inventories) and depreciation; these are examples of expenses where there is an element of subjectivity.

IASs permit a variety of different ways of presenting balance sheets and income statements, provided the same information is disclosed (sometimes on the face of statements; sometimes in the notes to the accounts). Illustration 2.1 will probably prove to be the most popular way of presenting income statements in the UK. But, with additional items, many look much more complex.

---

[15] The exercise is often carried out comparing budgeted (or planned) income statements with the actual results achieved.

Review of key points

- The income statement (or profit and loss account) shows the profit for a period by deducting from sales (and any other revenues) the costs incurred in earning those revenues.
- It is useful to measure profit as an indication of a company's performance and as a basis for dividend decisions.
- Profit figures are also useful to a range of different groups in society.
- There is some subjectivity in profit measurement; for example, in depreciation and in valuing closing inventories.
- Profit figures are most useful when they are used in making comparisons.
- Profit is different from cash flow.

Self-testing questions

1 What are the main differences between a balance sheet and an income statement?

2 What is an expense? How does an expense differ from an asset? Can an asset become an expense?

3 How are inventories valued? Why does it matter? Would it be a good idea to show inventories at selling price?

4 Why is depreciation charged?

5 What is the difference between capital expenditure and revenue expenditure?

6 Which of the profit figures shown in a simplified income statement (Illustration 2.1) are shareholders likely to be most interested in, and why?

7 The Kingsdun Company buys a delivery van for £25,000 and a boring machine for £25,000. They decide that the delivery van should be depreciated at 25 per cent per annum on a diminishing balance basis, and that the boring machine should be depreciated at 10 per cent per annum on a straight line basis. Calculate the depreciation charge for each of the first four years of the assets' lives, and the net book value of each at the end of year 4.

8 The Dargate Retailing Company sells a range of different products, some with modest gross profit margins, and some with much higher gross profit margins. For example, they buy Fargs for £100 each, apply a 25 per cent mark-up, and sell them for £125 each; the gross profit on Fargs is, therefore, 20 per cent (£25 gross profit is 20 per cent of the selling price). Employees often confuse percentage mark-ups with percentage gross profit. To avoid confusion you are asked to produce a definitive list showing the cost, mark-up percentage, selling price and

gross profit percentage of each product by completing the gaps in the table that follows:

Product	Cost price £	Mark-up %	Selling price £	Gross profit %
Fargs	100	25	125	20
Gargs	100	10		9.09
Hargs	50		100	
Jargs	40		80	
Kargs	80			33⅓
Largs		20	60	16⅔
Margs		30	40	
Nargs			50	10
Pargs	75			25

9 Banterbury Company Ltd

Income statement of the Banterbury Company Ltd for the year ended 31 December

	Year 3 £000	Year 4 £000
Revenue	100	120
Cost of sales	(60)	(73)
Gross profit	40	47
Distribution costs	(12)	(14)
Administration expenses	(9)	(12)
Operating profit	19	21
Finance expenses	(3)	(3)
Profit before taxation	16	18
Taxation	(4)	(3)
Profit for the year	12	15

Statement of changes in equity of Banterbury Company Ltd for the year ended 31 December

	£000	£000
Balance at beginning of year	93	100
Profit for the year	12	15
Dividends paid	(5)	(6)
Balance at end of year	100	109

The chairman of the company boasts that sales, profits and dividends are at record levels and that the amount of shareholders' funds in the business has increased to £109,000 at the end of year 4.

Critically assess the performance of the company.

Assessment questions

1 The Broadstores Company:

Income statement of Broadstores Company for the year ended 31 December

	Year 7	Year 8
	£000	£000
Revenue	200	220
Cost of sales	(120)	(131)
Gross profit	80	89
Distribution costs	(22)	(24)
Administration expenses	(40)	(41)
Operating profit	18	24
Finance expenses	(10)	(18)
Profit before taxation	8	6
Tax on profit for year	(3)	(2)
Profit after tax for the year	5	4

Statement of changes in equity of Broadstores Company for the year ended 31 December

	£000	£000
Balance at beginning of year	50	51
Profit for the year	5	4
Dividends paid	(4)	0
Balance at end of year	51	55

The chairman of the company states that the management of the company have performed well in a very difficult economic climate, and that increased profits have been retained within the business to finance profitable expansion.

A shareholder at the annual general meeting of the company claims that the reduction in profits and the absence of dividends prove that the management of the company is a disaster.

Assess the evidence for each point of view.

2 The Billygate Company operates with a 40 per cent mark-up on the goods that they buy. What is their gross profit ratio?

The Sillygate Company operates with a 40 per cent gross profit margin. What percentage mark-up do they use?

3 Roger, a graduate of the University of South East England, has been running a business called 'SuperSoftService' since he completed his IT degree six years ago. He sells software and prides himself on providing fast delivery using his sports car, and he has an extensive stock of software, catering for the latest developments as well as meeting demand for software for old operating systems – he still can still supply most things for Windows 95 and makes the occasional sale of old software.

About half of his sales are on a cash basis, and about half are on credit. He sells on credit only to friends, graduates and people he knows, and has no experience of bad debts.

Assessment questions (continued)

The business is very profitable, and is almost entirely financed by borrowing from his father. But his father is concerned that Roger keeps borrowing more and more money to keep the business afloat.

His summarized financial statements are shown as follows:

Income statement of SuperSoftService for the year ended 31 December year 6

Revenue		£100,000
Cost of goods sold		
Opening inventories	60,000	
Purchases	40,000	
	100,000	
Less Closing inventories	(80,000)	20,000
Gross profit		80,000
Administration and distribution expenses		(50,000)
Net profit		30,000
Drawings for personal expenditure		(29,000)
Retained profit for year		1,000

Balance sheet of SuperSoft Service as at 31 December year 6

Non-current assets		
Car at cost 1 January year 1		18,000
Less Provision for depreciation		(9,000)
		9,000
Current assets		
Inventories at cost	80,000	
Receivables	80,000	
	160,000	160,000
Total assets		169,000
Current liabilities		
Payables	3,000	
Overdraft	3,000	6,000
Loan from father		150,000
Equity		
Roger's capital	6,000	
Roger's retained earnings	7,000	13,000
		169,000

a Comment on the financial position and performance of the business.

b How 'real' are the profits?

Group activities and discussion questions

1 Profit figures are wanted by so many different groups of people for so many different purposes that it is not possible to define and measure profits in such a way as to meet all of those different needs. Discuss.

Group activities and discussion questions (continued)

2 Attempt a definition of 'profit'. You can use other books. Can all members of the group agree on the definition? Is the definition clear and robust enough to provide a basis for measuring profits in all businesses? You could have a formal debate with two people arguing in favour of a particular definition of profit, and two could argue against that definition. Or two could argue that it is possible to produce a workable definition, and two could argue that it is not.

3 Last year a company's balance sheet showed freehold land and buildings at cost, the amount being £4 million. This year the properties have been revalued at £7 million. Is the company £3 million better off? Have they made £3 million profit?

4 Why do companies aim to earn profits? Should all organizations attempt to earn profits? If you think that some organizations should not attempt to earn profits, on what basis would you decide which should earn profits, and which should not?

5 Do companies have too much freedom to determine the methods and rates of depreciation that they use for their published accounts? Where governments specify methods and rates of depreciation to be used to calculate profits for taxation purposes, should companies be required to use those same rates in their published accounts?

6 You are a shareholder in a listed company and are told that last year the company's net profit after tax increased from £100 million to £130 million, and that the management of the company are therefore performing extremely well.

   a What additional information would you want in order to assess the effectiveness of management? (Produce a list, and don't look at (b) until you have done that!)

   b Obtain the published annual report and accounts of a listed company. How much of what you wanted to know does it tell you?

7 Examine Ted Baker's results since 2006. Has the expansion of the company been successful in leading to a big enough increase in profits?

8 Compare the gross profit ratios of a number of different retailers. Are the differences very substantial? How do you explain or justify such differences?

Financial accounting in context

The Top 10 for turnover

Accountancy Magazine 2006

Discuss and comment on the following extract from the press with particular reference to the importance of turnover and profit figures in assessing the effectiveness of an organization.

Source: Reproduced with permission by *Accountancy Magazine*; originial source Deloitte.

Manchester United (3)
The club came third in 2005 but topped the league for turnover (£159m) and profitability (£33m). Man U was only second to Chelsea in its wages bill of £77m. Auditor: PwC.

Chelsea (1)
Despite a turnover of nearly £149m the club still turned in an operating loss of £16.7m, putting it firmly at the bottom of the table in 2005. This didn't stop the team winning the double though, as the Blues topped the league and lifted the League Cup in the same season. Auditor: KPMG.

Liverpool (5)
Fifth in the league but the second most profitable club after Man U (£25m); it scored a turnover of £122m. Europe provided a spectacular finish to the season when it came back from 3-0 down to win on penalties. Auditor: PKF.

Arsenal (2)
The north London club narrowly missed out to its west London rivals. But at least off the pitch the Gunners can boast operating profits of £20m on a turnover of £115m. Auditor: Deloitte.

Newcastle United (14)
The club had the second largest average gate (51,844) and fifth largest turnover (£87m). Auditor: KPMG.

Tottenham Hotspur (9)
Mid-table on the pitch, but Spurs was the fifth most profitable at £12.8m, and £53m turnover. Auditor: Deloitte.

Manchester City (8)
The club remained in profit at £3.5m with a turnover of £61m and scored the third highest average gate of 45,192. Auditor: KPMG.

Everton (4)
Finished the season one place higher than its Merseyside rivals but with only half the turnover of £60m and a credible £10m profit. Auditor: Deloitte.

Bolton Wanderers (6)
Scored the same number of points as Liverpool but with the Reebok stadium only holding 28,000, the Trotters' turnover of £53m only produced a profit of £6.8m. Auditor: Deloitte.

Middlesbrough (7)
Finished the season in its highest ever position in the Premiership and turned in a healthy profit of £17m on a turnover of £52m, to boot. Beating Man City meant the Boro went on to Europe the following season. Auditor: PwC.

League position in brackets.

Source: Deloitte

References and further reading

International Accounting Standard 1 *Presentation of Financial Statements*. (December 2003, amended March 2004). IASB.

Pendlebury, M. and R. Groves (2003) *Company Accounts: Analysis, Interpretation and Understanding* (6th edition). Thomson Learning.

Wood, F. and A. Sangster (2005) *Business Accounting* vol. 1 (10th edition). Prentice Hall.

www.frc.org.uk (gives details of the Financial Reporting Council and arrangements for accounting standards in the British Isles)

www.iasb.org.uk (gives details of international accounting standards)

www.tedbaker.co.uk (select: share info; click for full financial information; select financial reports or other information as required)

CHAPTER 03

The Context of Financial Accounting

❖ LEARNING OBJECTIVES

After studying this chapter you should be able to:

- ❖ Understand how financial accounting has been shaped by its historical development

- ❖ Explain the main influences on the historical and current development of accounting

- ❖ Discuss the idea of company objectives, how they are achieved and the measurement of how far they have been achieved

- ❖ Evaluate the role of financial accounting in making companies accountable

- ❖ Consider how financial accounting is likely to develop in the next few years

- ❖ Assess the various pressures on the development of financial accounting

3.1 Introduction

It is easy to criticize financial accounting for failing to do whatever it is that you think it is supposed to be doing. There seem to be endless financial scandals, companies (unexpectedly?) getting into financial difficulties and cases where companies' financial statements are incredible or incomprehensible; and there are always accountants involved. It is a similar story with traffic jams, crime and football hooliganism: the police always seem to be around. But it is not the police who are to blame for all that goes wrong in society. It is their job to get involved and to try to sort things out. Similarly, accountants are not to blame for all company financial scandals; but they are usually involved in trying to sort them out.

But what is it that financial accounting is supposed to achieve? Why do things so often seem to go wrong? Whatever definitions of its 'objectives' are produced, financial accounting is usually found wanting. In part this is due to unrealistic expectations. Financial accounting cannot predict all financial scandals and corporate collapses;[1] it cannot prevent rogue directors from bending rules or being outright crooks; and it cannot show the 'true value' of a company, because that depends on future performance which no one knows.[2] We have come to expect a lot from financial accounting, and, if we are to understand it as it operates today, we need to examine its origins: how it came about. We also need to understand which interest groups in society influence accounting and how their power is exercised. Accounting emerged and developed over hundreds of years in response to the needs of business and the pressures of various interest groups.

3.2 Historical Development

Financial accounting as it exists today was not designed by anyone, or any group of people, to meet any specific objectives. It has evolved over hundreds of years, mainly to meet the needs of various businesses. We cannot understand accounting as it exists by reading the official pronouncements of the Accounting Standards Board (ASB) and then deciding what 'improvements' are needed for it to meet a particular set of objectives today. It is important to understand that accounting has evolved in response to the needs and objectives of a range of different interest groups, and will probably continue to do so.

Financial accounting has developed from double-entry bookkeeping that was first described by Luca Pacioli, a Franciscan monk/friar, in Italy in 1494. He did not invent the system – nobody did. It emerged naturally from the practices of international traders, particularly in medieval Italy, who needed to keep records of their cash, sales, expenses, debtors, creditors and so on. They kept accounts of their various ventures, such as voyages or consignments of spices. The priority was record-keeping; the idea of annual financial reports came much later.

Business in medieval Italy was international and relatively complex. There were voyages around Europe and to the East. There were partnerships, many of which were short term for a particular voyage or venture. Much of the business was done on credit. It was essential to

---

[1] Although it can and does provide lots of evidence that can help to predict such events.

[2] No one; not even the so-called 'experts'.

keep records not just of cash, but of debtors, creditors and other assets and liabilities. The results of a particular venture also needed to be worked out: what revenues it generated, what expenses were incurred and, when it came to an end, who owed how much and to whom. Almost everything that double-entry bookkeeping required was recorded anyway. It became a matter of convenience to complete the double entry. Every transaction was recorded twice: once as a debit, and once as a credit. The total of debits could then be compared with the total of credits to see if it balanced, and to find errors.

The British did not take kindly to the new Italian system of double-entry bookkeeping, and the old English systems ('charge and discharge') and single-entry bookkeeping continued declining for several hundred years. But the 'Italian system' spread steadily from Italy; Pacioli's book was translated into English and Dutch early in the eighteenth century; it became a standard system throughout the business world. Its main functions were to record transactions and to keep a record of who owed what and to whom. Accuracy was its most important attribute.

Bookkeeping was, of course, originally done in books or ledgers; and books eventually become full. When the book was full, it was necessary to transfer to a new book all the balances which still mattered. Everything that was to go into the new book would be summarized on a 'balance sheet'. Old balances that were finished with were written off to a 'profit and loss account', which showed all the profits and losses on the various activities undertaken. At first, balance sheets and profit and loss accounts were produced only when necessary: when the book was full. By the end of the eighteenth century, it had become normal to produce these statements annually, and managers and others were starting to see accounting as being more than mere record-keeping; it could provide useful statements.

Following the industrial revolution, the nineteenth century saw the next major development of financial accounting with the establishment of companies. The cost of financing major industrial enterprises and railways required more capital than individuals and their partners could provide. It was necessary to find a larger number of investors, and partnership was not the best way of attracting investors. All partners are liable for the debts of the business, and a partner could lose everything if the business went wrong. Individuals who had modest sums to invest, and who knew little about the business or the people running it, would want to be sure that their potential liability (the maximum amount that they could lose) was limited to the amount that they had invested.

The vehicle for more substantial investment became the limited liability company. Investors' potential liability was limited to the amount that they had invested in the company, and they could be relatively passive investors. But they needed to be able to trust the company's directors to take proper care of their money: directors had 'stewardship' responsibilities for shareholders' funds. This had several important consequences:

1 Company shareholders had annual general meetings, and the annual report and accounts became the major vehicle by which directors were accountable to shareholders. Management and directors became separated from ownership (with large companies), and there was a need for directors to be accountable to shareholders.

2 Shareholders wanted to see what had happened to the money that they had invested, and the balance sheet was the easiest way of showing this. On one side the capital that shareholders had invested was shown; on the other side the assets were shown in which it had been invested – perhaps a railway line from London to Warmington-on-

Sea. In a successful company the assets side would steadily increase, and the increase in net assets was reflected on the other side of the balance sheet as 'reserves', which became part of shareholders' funds.

3 The establishment of companies with 'limited liability' made the position of creditors less secure. When creditors are owed money by an unincorporated business (a sole trader or partnership) with unlimited liability, if the business does not pay them what is due, they can, when all else fails, recover the amounts from the personal assets of the proprietors. With small businesses, banks are often keen to secure any loans on the private property (particularly houses) of the proprietors. With companies there is no recourse to the private assets of the directors or shareholders. Limited liability may be seen as a privilege that government legislation has established, and creditors have to accept if they want to do business with companies. In return for that privilege, companies' financial information is opened up to the public: annual reports and accounts are deposited at Companies House for all to see.

4 Shareholders also wanted the company to do well and to pay an annual dividend. Directors could easily find the money to pay a dividend to shareholders – perhaps by borrowing,[3] or issuing more share capital. But dividends should come out of profits, not from share capital, and this is a basic principle of accounting. By today's standards it would be a fairly unsophisticated fraud to pretend that a company is making profits, and to pay dividends simply by raising more share capital. As long as new shareholders can be conned into investing in a company that appears to be doing well, the company could keep going. But companies are not allowed to pay dividends out of capital, and the principle of 'capital maintenance' is central to modern accountancy.

5 If capital is to be 'maintained' before any dividends can be paid, that is not a problem for a railway company. Most of their capital was invested in the railway line; the railway line had to be maintained; and a railway line can be assumed to last for ever – if it is properly maintained. But some fixed assets have only a limited life, and a company cannot be said to have made a profit unless provision is made for depreciation of fixed assets. Thus, it became necessary to charge depreciation as an expense, and to separate capital expenditure (which adds to fixed assets) from revenue expenditure (which reduces profits) in order to determine profits; this is to help to assure investors that dividends were paid out of profits, not out of capital.

6 Another important consequence of the development of companies is that financial accounting practices came to be based on new company laws, and company laws came to reflect accounting practice: they were intended to reflect the better accounting practices of the day, not the worst! From time to time various financial and accounting scandals arise, and governments need to be seen to respond to these in various ways, such as setting up committees of inquiry and developing proposals for more rigorous company laws and more effective implementation and enforcement.

7 Following the development of companies, and increases in their accounting requirements[4] there was lots more work for 'accountants' to do, and professional accountancy

---

[3] Many still do.

[4] There were also increases in the amount of work for accountants in liquidations and bankruptcies.

bodies were established to add to the credibility of accountants, and to represent their interests. Although governments took responsibility for revising company law, the professional accountancy bodies increasingly came to be seen as the 'experts', and in many ways governments left regulation of accountancy to the professional bodies.

In the second half of the nineteenth century governments had a *laissez-faire* attitude to businesses and accountancy: let them get on with it in their own way. By about 1900 governments started to (and continue to) take a more active role in the development of accountancy. But changes in accounting practice are not the result of any single dominant person or force. They result from the interplay of a range of interested parties, including accountants and auditors; bankers and creditors; companies and their directors; governments and the law; academics and theorists; investors and stock markets; and the standard setters.

3.3 Accountants and Auditors

The status of a profession seems to depend partly on its antiquity, and in this respect accountants are way behind doctors, priests and lawyers. The first professional accountancy body in the world was established in Scotland (1854) with England and Wales, Canada, Australia, the USA, Ireland, New Zealand and the Netherlands following by 1895. The early development of professional accountancy bodies in these countries is associated with a distinctive development of accountancy, which differs from most of continental Europe. Sweden was the first of the other European countries to develop an accountancy profession; Germany and France came much later.

Another peculiar feature of the UK accountancy profession is that it has far more members[5] (per head of the population) than any other country. In the 1980s predictions were made that, if present tendencies continued, by the middle of the twenty-first century every man, woman and child in the UK would be an accountant! There are a number of possible explanations for the UK having so many accountants. UK accountants are not just auditors. We include as 'accountants' members of professional accountancy bodies who are engaged in a wide range of different financial and management positions. Professional accountancy qualifications are also highly regarded. As criticisms of some educational standards has increased, the respect for tough professional examinations has been further strengthened.

Sixty years ago accountants were not a particularly impressive bunch and were relatively poorly educated. Equipped with just a few GCE 'O' levels they would pay to become articled to a chartered accountant, and study for their modest examinations by correspondence course. But other managers were even less impressive, typically having no professional training, limited numerical ability, and little knowledge or understanding of finance. Accountants of reasonable ability soon gained promotions and senior management positions. In the last 30 years or so the calibre of accountants has increased substantially. The large professional firms require a very high standard in the trainees they recruit. Personality

---

[5] Members of professional accountancy bodies. Anyone can call themselves an accountant; but you have to be a member of one of the professional bodies to be a 'chartered accountant'.

is important, and most recruits have good 'A' levels, and a good degree from a good university. Those who also manage to pass the tough professional accountancy examinations and get into senior positions with major professional firms are generally people of formidable ability.

Professional accountancy firms have become important and powerful organizations, not least because of their size, ability and economic resources. Power also lies in the professional accountancy bodies themselves[6] – various organizations where accountants have effective representation (such as the ASB and the International Accounting Standards Board (IASB)). The large professional accountancy firms are powerful – and on a worldwide basis. Illustration 3.1 shows that there are only three or four major players (and they do the audits of the vast majority of listed companies in the UK). Their resources and skills are enormous and their ways of seeing and operating in the worlds of business, accounting and finance tend to predominate.

The power, prestige and status of professional accountants should not be underestimated. Governments and regulatory bodies that try to 'interfere' in the sphere of professional accountants are likely to find themselves up against very tough opponents who can run rings around them and argue them into a corner. It may be that professional accountants act mainly in the interest of the public – to ensure true and fair financial reporting, the proper operation of capital markets, and so the efficient allocation of resources in society – but, sometimes, it may be that the self-interest of accountants predominates.

Firm	Number of UK offices	Fee income 2005–6 £m	% Increase on previous year	Audit/ accounting fees	Consultancy fees £m
PricewaterhouseCoopers	30	1,780	12.6	861	405
Deloitte & Touche	18	1,550	14.4	485	375
KPMG	22	1,281	20.2	357	225
Ernst & Young	21	945	14.5	476	–
Grant Thornton	32	284	11.1	92	–
BDO Stoy Hayward	15	275	20.6	89	–
Baker Tilly	30	184	6.4	91	–
Smith Williamson Ltd	10	137	7.4	23	–
PKF	22	117	2.7	49	22
Tenon Group plc	30	100	10.5	61	–
RSM Robson Rhodes	9	95	10.4	35	14
Moore Stephens	28	90	8.7	34	11

ILLUSTRATION 3.1

Source: *Accountancy*, July 2006. No figures for consultancy were shown for several large firms. The PwC consultancy figure includes corporate recovery and corporate finance; the Robson Rhodes figure is what they describe as 'risk advisory services'; the Deloitte & Touche figure is partly estimated.

---

[6] The Institute of Chartered Accountants in England and Wales (ICAEW); the Institute of Chartered Accountants of Scotland (ICAS); the Institute of Chartered Accountants in Ireland (ICAI); the Chartered Association of Certified Accountants (ACCA); the Chartered Institute of Management Accountants (CIMA); and the Chartered Institute of Public Finance and Accountancy (CIPFA).

In spite of the strength and prestige of many large firms of auditors and their professional bodies, there are also many examples of disappointment with auditors. Every time a company gets into financial difficulties or there is a fraud or a scandal, the auditors seem to come in for criticism. Many have unrealistic expectations of what auditors could or should do. Some of these 'expectations' are listed in Illustration 3.2, together with comments indicating what would be a more realistic expectation.

Expectation	More realistic
1 The financial statements are prepared by the auditors; the auditors agree with everything in them and are responsible for them	The directors are responsible for preparing the financial statements. Auditors agree only that they represent one of perhaps several possible 'true and fair' views
2 The financial statements are correct and accurate; a different auditor would produce the same financial statements from the same basic information	The auditors do not prepare the financial statements, and as there are many areas requiring judgement, different accountants would probably come to different conclusions (e.g. on rates of depreciation, or the appropriate provision for bad debts). The decisions belong to the directors
3 The financial statements show what a company is worth; assets have been properly valued	Most assets are shown at some variation of historic cost. Even if they were shown at some sort of current value, the value of the business as a whole would almost certainly be very different from the value of the separable assets less liabilities
4 The auditors have checked and ascertained that no significant fraud or irregularities have taken place	The auditors are on the look-out for fraud, but they are not responsible for finding it all. And even if they find some, provided it is not too enormous, they will still say that the financial statements show a true and fair view
5 The business is a going concern, and is not likely to collapse or fail in the foreseeable future	The auditors check to see if there are any doubts about the business being a going concern, and report accordingly. But there can be no guarantee that it will not collapse in the near future
6 The management of the company are reputable, competent, efficient and effective	Auditors are usually happy to take fees from even the most hopeless managers, and are not likely to disclose any incompetence!
7 The audit report draws attention to any doubts about the company's finances	If there are doubts about the company's immediate financial survival, the auditors should comment
8 Auditors are independent and cannot be got rid of by directors	In theory auditors have great security and independence. But directors can easily put an audit out to tender, and replace existing auditors
9 Auditors are controlled and disciplined by a professional body that clearly specifies what is required of them	This is a reasonable expectation
10 Auditors are more concerned with their duty to the public and their reputation than with maximizing their own remuneration	This is more a matter of opinion!

Some of these issues are explored more fully in Chapter 8.

ILLUSTRATION 3.2

3.4 Bankers and Creditors

Although financial statements are said to have many different 'users', including employees, customers and competitors, the two most important groups are shareholders and creditors.

It is usual to make a distinction between short-term creditors (trade creditors who supply goods and services; overdrafts), and long-term creditors (loans and debentures). Both have a similar interest: will they get their money back when they are supposed to?

Ideally, what creditors want to see is a business with lots of valuable assets, very few liabilities, and one that generates lots of 'free cash flow'[7] with which to make necessary repayments. In Illustration 3.3, the Dodge Company has lots more assets and lots more equity than the Wadge Company, but it also has lots more liabilities. The Wadge Company looks safer from the point of view of creditors. We can express liabilities as a percentage of net assets. In the Dodge Company 65 per cent of net assets are financed by liabilities; in the Wadge Company only 30 per cent of net assets are financed by liabilities. It may seem unlikely, but if the companies get into financial difficulties, and the assets are difficult to sell (or if they have been overvalued), there might not be enough funds in the Dodge Company to pay all the creditors. If the net assets could realize only 60 per cent of their book value (£1,200,000), the creditors could not be paid in full, and there would be nothing left for the shareholders. In the Wadge Company, if net assets realized only 60 per cent of their book value (£540,000), the creditors could be paid in full, and there would be a decent amount left over for the shareholders.

This leads to an interesting question: how reliable are asset values as shown on the balance sheet? When a business gets into difficulty, any forced sale of assets is likely to result in low prices. Creditors want to know that the assets are really worth *at least as much* as the balance sheet shows. That is their security. They have an interest in *prudent* asset values. This is true of all

	Dodge Company	Wadge Company
	£000	£000
Net assets	2,000	900
Liabilities	1,300	270
Equity	700	630

ILLUSTRATION 3.3

creditors, and banks are important in this respect. Conservatism or prudence was for long a fundamental concept of financial accounting, particularly in much of Europe where banks have been more important sources of finance for businesses than stock markets. In the UK and similar countries, conservatism has now been de-emphasized. The basis of accounting is moving away from giving priority to the information needs of creditors; the equity investors' view is becoming dominant.

3.5 Companies and their Directors

Accountancy has evolved mainly to meet the needs of businesses; companies have become the dominant form of business organization; accountancy has, therefore,

---

[7] 'Free cash flow' is explained in Chapter 7.

developed mainly to meet the needs of companies. We could say that financial accounting exists mainly to meet the needs of companies, or shareholders, or company directors. We could say that it exists primarily to serve the needs of companies. Unfortunately, the words 'company', 'shareholders' and 'directors' are sometimes used as if they mean the same thing. Each should be considered separately.

Objectives of Companies

If accountancy is to serve the needs of companies, we need to be clear what the objectives of companies are – if companies can have objectives. A company is an organization of different individuals, each with their own particular aims, interests, powers and priorities. The directors are the most powerful, but employees, shareholders and others also affect what a company does. Companies succeed in operating cohesively by maintaining the myth that they all have an interest in achieving objectives such as those considered in the following list.

1 Survival: avoiding going bankrupt, or into liquidation, or being taken over by a 'predator'. Financial accounts can show if a company appears to have excessive liabilities and if it is generating sufficient cash flows to meet its obligations.

2 Maximizing profits: it is often assumed that this is the primary objective of companies. But the *amount* of profit a company makes is much less important than their return on capital employed (ROCE) or their *profitability*. If a company increases its profits from £10 million to £12 million, the increase in profits of £2 million might at first seem impressive. But if, at the same time, the company's capital employed has increased from £100 million to £140 million, the ROCE has fallen.[8] It is easy to make lots of profits if there is lots of capital employed to play around with.

3 Maximizing profitability or ROCE is a better objective in terms of improving performance. If profits increase from £10 million to £12 million, and at the same time capital employed is reduced from £100 million to £90 million, that is a much better result.[9] The test of good management is whether they can increase profits by a bigger proportion than any increase in capital employed.

4 Growth often seems to be the objective of companies. Many act as if increases in sales will, in due course, be followed by increases in profits. But some companies succeed in increasing turnover at too high a cost. In reading chairman's statements, it is worth looking to see if they are too keen on pursuing growth – at the expense of the 'bottom line' (profit). It is also worth looking to see if increases in sales are matched by increases in profits. With new ventures it often takes a while for profits to build up; but it is not hard to find examples of companies where profits never seem to catch up.

5 Dominating an industry. Some companies take pride in being the biggest operator in a particular industry. Tesco dominates the supermarket industry; Asda rivals with Sainsbury, and Morrisons struggle to stay in the same league. If a company can become the dominant force in a particular industry, it is in a more powerful position to make profits; it also appeals to the vanity of chairpersons and directors.

---

[8] From 10 per cent to 8.6 per cent.

[9] £12 million as a percentage of £90 million is 13 per cent.

6 Meeting the needs of customers. Few companies claim to be interested only in making as much profit as possible (even if they are!), and claim to be doing all sorts of good for society, employees, customers, the environment, disabled people and anything else that puts them in a good light. We may each have our own opinions regarding the ways in which companies present themselves. It seems likely that, to be successful and to continue in business, companies do have to meet the needs of customers. If they are to continue to do this, they also need to survive financially.

7 'Satisficing' or balancing the needs of different interest groups around the company. A company cannot fully meet everyone's objectives. Customers might want better products at a cheaper price. Employees might want higher wages and salaries for working fewer hours. Suppliers might want to charge higher prices and be paid more quickly. Shareholders might want as much dividend income as possible. And the directors might want increases in their fees and fringe benefits. A company cannot give everyone what they want. They have to find some sort of balance that 'satisfices' all the different demands.

8 Maximizing shareholders' wealth. This is often assumed to be the objective of financial management. Shareholders' wealth comes from two (related) sources: dividends, and the share price.

Maximizing Shareholders' Wealth

At first sight the idea of maximizing shareholders' wealth seems fairly straightforward. If a company maximizes profitability, then it is in a position to maximize dividends payable to shareholders, and it is a reasonable expectation that the share price would be maximized. But, unfortunately, life is not so simple. We can never be sure exactly what determines share prices, but companies appear to act as if they can influence share price in ways other than maximizing profitability.

1 Listed companies tend to have shareholder relations departments, which may be seen as companies' 'spin doctors'. Careful presentation can make a company's record and prospects look better than the statements that a boring accountant would produce. Companies that tell a good story are likely to have more highly rated shares than those that have a good story to tell, but which give insufficient attention to the telling, the presentation and to 'spinning'. Sometimes when companies believe that their shares are underrated they launch a 'charm offensive': making presentations to institutional shareholders in the hope of improving the performance of their shares.

2 Much rests on the reputation of management: management must appear to be in control, to know what they are doing, to have sensible plans, and to be able to implement them and achieve the results that investors have been led to expect. A company that announces that it expects profits to increase by 5 per cent in the coming year, and then, 12 months later, finds that they have increased by 30 per cent does not look very credible. An unexpectedly good year could easily be followed by an unexpectedly bad year – and the share price is likely to suffer.

  If management announce a reorganization programme that will lead to a 2 per cent reduction in profits in the coming year, followed by a 6 per cent increase the following year, then 'double-digit' growth thereafter, the share price is not likely to suffer – as long as they maintain credibility and deliver what they have said.

3 In real life profits do not always increase in line with management expectations, and there is a temptation to indulge in some form of 'creative accounting'[10] to give the impression that they do. The idea of 'income smoothing', if it can be pursued with credibility, is likely to benefit the share price. Investors seem to like to see a pattern of steadily increasing profits every year. If management can succeed in hiding away some of the profits in the good years (the idea of 'secret reserves' used to be popular), they can boost profits in the lean years and maintain the image of steadily increasing profits.

4 Jumping on bandwagons may also be seen as a good way of maximizing shareholder wealth – at least in the short term. In the 1990s, when share prices were booming (a 'bull' market), companies had to be seen to be involved in e-business if they were not going to lose out. Some companies sought reclassification from boring, underrated sectors into more highly rated sectors. A glance at the *Financial Times*[11] indicates which sectors are most highly rated at a given time. The price/earnings ratio (P/E ratio) shows how expensive shares are in relation to profits. Sectors with high P/E ratios in mid-2006 were electronics and electrical equipment, mobile telecommunications, and oil equipment and services. Less fashionable, with lower P/E ratios, were mining, real estate, and software and computer services.

5 Much emphasis is given to maximizing earnings per share (EPS), and, obviously, increasing profitability helps a lot with this. But if a company is struggling to make good profits, arithmetically there is a simple solution to increase EPS: reduce the number of shares. Companies can buy their own shares on the stock market and cancel them. Reducing share capital is also a way of increasing ROCE. A company needs to have the money to be able to buy a significant number of shares. Sometimes this seems to be the best use of surplus funds – more effective (in maximizing shareholders' wealth) than increasing dividends.

6 One way of finding the money for the company to buy its own shares is to borrow; or to have a sale and leaseback arrangement on its properties. Such arrangements are fairly common practice among large retailers.

7 Companies also use dividend policy to try to influence share price. If a company has a record of steadily increasing dividends, not marred by short-term fluctuations, it is likely to be beneficial to their share price.

8 Careful use of gearing is also often seen as having an effect on share price. Modest use of borrowing, when profits are steadily increasing, can 'gear up' the return earned for ordinary shareholders. But excessive borrowing can make a company look too risky, and have an adverse effect on share price.

The extent to which companies can influence the price of their shares on the stock market is debatable, and perhaps limited by the 'efficient market hypothesis', which suggests that markets are efficient, and share prices are fair, in the sense that they already reflect all infor-

---

[10] Creative accounting is explored in Chapter 8.

[11] FTSE Actuaries Share Index – included on the same page as share prices.

mation that is available. This may suggest that there is little point in companies trying to rearrange and re-present their affairs in the hope of increasing their share price. But this theory does not seem to stop them from trying.

Whatever we think that companies are doing, or attempting, financial accounting can help them to achieve their objectives. It also indicates to shareholders and other interested parties how successful or otherwise the company has been in achieving many of those objectives. Most shareholders may care more about the share price than they do about the financial accounts. Financial accounts do not explain fully what happens to share prices, but they are an essential part of the story.

Accountability

The directors of companies are supposed to be accountable to the shareholders who own the company, and they are required to give an annual account of their activities. They are free to embellish these accounts with whatever additional information they wish, which they often do to show themselves in a more favourable light. In some ways they are like politicians seeking re-election, and a company's annual report and accounts may be seen as being their election address. But politicians somehow manage to avoid most of the really difficult areas of their performance, and to include only the most favourable aspects of their performance (with some loss of credibility as a result). It is harder for directors to avoid the difficult questions because there are very specific disclosure requirements; the share price is there for all to see; and the arrangements for the accountability of directors are more thorough than they are for politicians.

Companies Acts lay down the information that a company has to disclose each year in its annual report and accounts, and these requirements are generally effective. In addition, 'accounting standards' specify additional disclosures, although these are not always meticulously followed. The information that is disclosed also has to be audited – directors cannot just make it up, as politicians sometimes seem to! It is also made public: the annual reports have to be filed at Companies House for all to see; and they are very easy to see using the Companies House website.[12]

But if shareholders do not like what they read, their options are limited. How many shareholders really read the annual report and accounts is not clear, but they usually know about their company's performance, especially the share price. If the company is doing badly, the annual report and accounts usually provide plenty of information to demonstrate why this is the case, and perhaps even to show how the directors are to blame.[13] But it is the directors who have produced the annual report and who are responsible for the contents. They have usually made sure that, in addition to the information that is required by law, there is also plenty of information intended to demonstrate what a good job they have done, and to justify their re-election.

It is not easy to get rid of directors. Contested elections are almost unknown; directors are usually re-elected unopposed. Directors usually have some shares themselves; many shareholders sign proxies to allow directors to vote on their behalf; and financial institu-

---

[12] For a small fee. Most large companies have their own websites on which annual reports can be accessed free of charge.

[13] It is difficult to find examples of directors taking the blame for poor results; they usually take the credit for good results, but the blame for poor results usually lies elsewhere!

tions, who have enormous potential voting power, tend either to support directors or avoid being involved at all. Although directors are supposed to be the 'agents' of shareholders, this relationship has its problems and costs, and it sometimes seems as if directors are running companies mainly for their own benefit. It is often a problem for shareholders to assert their theoretical power over the activities of directors, and significant institutional shareholders are likely to be more effective than individual ones. When institutions do take an active role in changing the management of a company, it usually spells trouble for the existing chairperson and chief executive! But sometimes company directors (Unilever in 2003) complain that institutional investors are too inactive.

The *Financial Times* (6 August 2003) reported that:

> 66 Unilever has turned the corporate governance debate on its head by asking
> 10 of its major shareholders to account for their failure to register their votes
> at the last annual general meeting. 99

The Anglo-Dutch group's unorthodox questioning of its own shareholders will add to the pressure on institutional investors to be more active custodians of their clients' money. The current (mid-2006) government proposals for company law reform specifically seek to enhance shareholder engagement, partly with a view to developing a long-term investment culture.

This was immediately after Unilever had reported disappointing half-year results. Their 'path to growth' plan, concentrating on their strongest brands, had resulted in a fall in sales, profits and share price. This would seem to be a good time to be glad that institutional shareholders are keeping quiet. But perhaps attack is the best form of defence!

Shareholders have little chance of carrying a resolution against the wishes of the directors at an annual general meeting, and even if they do, directors can just ignore it. If shareholders find that the performance of their company is unsatisfactory there is not usually much they can do other than bail out and sell their shares. The trouble is that when it becomes clear that a company is doing badly, the share price has already fallen; if many shareholders sell when the price is falling, it is likely to fall further and they can lose out badly. Eventually share prices fall until someone thinks that they are good value and starts buying them. Directors are not usually keen on seeing 'their' company being bought up, on the cheap, by operators who may have very different ideas about the future of the company – or about the future of the existing directors! Existing directors usually do their best to maintain the share price, partly for their own survival, and partly because they probably have lots of shares in the company themselves, and perhaps they also have favourable options to acquire more shares.

The growth and development of companies, and the need for directors to be accountable to their shareholders, continues to be one of the major influences on the development of financial accounting.

3.6 Governments and the Law

Governments have long been involved in the regulation of companies. Prior to the 1844 Joint Stock Companies Act there were very few companies, and most of them were incorporated by a special Act of Parliament. The important change introduced in 1844 was that companies could be incorporated simply through registration. The Act also brought in the requirement to maintain books of account; and to produce a full and fair balance sheet, which had to be audited, presented to annual general meetings and filed with the Registrar of Companies. Little was laid down about the content of the balance sheet, and almost anyone could be an auditor. The 1856 Act introduced model articles of association for companies, which were more thorough and prescriptive than the requirements of the 1844 Act, but the adoption of them was voluntary. Indeed, the attitude of governments until the end of the nineteenth century was very much *laissez-faire*: leave companies to carry on their businesses as they saw fit. The relationship between directors and shareholders was a matter for them, not for governments.

The pattern in the twentieth century was rather different. There was a major Companies Act roughly every 20 years; each Act strengthened the accounting and auditing requirements; and some of the requirements of each Act were responses to abuses and scandals where previous Acts had proved inadequate. Governments no longer accepted that the accountability of directors to shareholders and others was a private matter for them to agree among themselves; governments became increasingly involved in the specification of accounting and auditing requirements. But a lot of the detailed implementation was left to accountants, auditors and their professional bodies who operated within the framework of the Companies Acts.

The 1900 Companies Act required an annual audit for registered companies; and the 1908 Companies Act required the publication and audit of balance sheets. These reversed the *laissez-faire* approach since 1856.

The 1929 Act brought in important new requirements, including the publication of a profit and loss account. But little detail on the content was specified – disclosure of turnover came much later.

The 1948 Companies Act established the basis for a whole generation of accountants. It established the main disclosure requirements. Consolidated accounts (for groups of companies) were required. Auditors had to have specified qualifications. And the audit report had to state if the published financial statements showed *a true and fair view*, which has become a key phrase in financial accounting.

The 1967 Act continued the trend with additional disclosure requirements, including turnover. Additional disclosures were also specified for the directors' report (such as exports, charitable and political donations, and the market value of investments).

The 1981 Companies Act clarified rules for determining distributable profits, specified additional disclosure requirements (including cost of sales) and implemented the European Economic Community's (EEC's) 4th Directive, specifying formats, principles and valuation rules. It also ensured that *a true and fair view* became the overriding consideration.

The 1985 Companies Act was a major consolidating piece of legislation. It also did little to reverse previous trends of constantly strengthening accounting and auditing requirements: small and medium-sized companies were allowed to disclose less information.

The 1989 Companies Act implemented the EC's 7th and 8th Directives (group accounts; qualifications for auditors), and allowed companies the option of distributing only summary statements to shareholders.

At times governments seem only to have flirted with the idea that they should be involved with determining financial accounting requirements, but, increasingly often, they have been forced by events to become actively involved. Since 1981 major changes have been very much influenced by Europe, with a more prescriptive approach to measurement and disclosure. There has also been a tendency to concentrate on increasing the accounting requirements for larger companies while allowing some exemptions for smaller companies.

The Labour Government (since 1997) has continued discussing the possibility of new companies legislation, and is heavily involved in negotiations with the accountancy profession. Any legislative changes are likely to come as a result of agreement. In 2006 their proposals included introducing statements of directors' duties making it clear that they are supposed to develop the company for the benefit of the shareholders (rather than for themselves, perhaps), and simplifying administration, particularly for smaller companies, with new model articles of association; and a proposal to 'update company financial and narrative reports'.

In the meantime, the role of self-regulation continues and the development and promulgation of international financial standards has been taken over by the IASB; these define accounting terminology and specify methods of measurement, and information to be disclosed. Within the European Union (EU) the consolidated accounts of listed companies are now required to comply with International Financial Reporting Standards (IFRSs), and the Committee of European Securities Regulators (CESR) (established by the European Commission) are advising on the implementation of these standards, and developing a role in relation to enforcement.

3.7 Academics and Theorists

Financial accounting has mostly been a practical subject rather than a theoretical one, but it does have some respectable academic roots. In Scottish universities it tended to develop in law faculties, and the subject may have been seen differently from England. Perhaps the practice of accountancy was primarily the application of legal concepts. In English universities the subject has developed more within an economics framework, with a London School of Economics' view rapidly spreading and predominating since the late 1940s.

The *ad hoc* nature of financial accounting served well enough until financial statements came to be seen as hopelessly unrealistic as a result of the ravages of high inflation in the 1970s. One theoretical solution to the problems was found in the work of Sweeney (1936) who advocated general price level adjusted financial statements. This became the accountancy profession's favoured solution in the ill-fated 'provisional' Statement of Standard Accounting Practice (SSAP) 7. Replacement cost accounting was a more radical solution, and modified versions of this (current cost accounting (CCA)) came to be favoured. This used 'deprival value' in measuring assets and profits, and it became the basis of the accountancy profession's (equally ill-fated!) SSAP 16. But the approach is still favoured by many economists, and still permeates the thinking of accounting standard setters. The idea is to move financial accounting away from being a system that merely records transactions and summarizes them: balance sheets (and profit measurement) are to be based on attempts to value assets.

The idea that assets should be shown at some sort of current value, or 'fair value', rather than historic cost (HC), emerged over a long period. Fixed assets have long been shown at cost less depreciation. Inventories are shown at the lower of cost and net realizable value. Receivables are shown after deducting a provision for bad debts. All the early moves away from pure HC were in the direction of conservatism or prudence. Although investments on balance sheets are still generally shown at some sort of 'book value', the current market value is also shown. But, increasingly, there are revaluations of land and buildings to show current (higher) values. Gradually, prudence is going out of the window.

Accountants have long sought some sort of 'conceptual framework': a statement of principles that could be seen as underlying all financial accounting. The idea is presented as if accounting is a subject something like economics or mathematics. If we had a basic set of principles, then all accounting standards and rules could be built upon the implementation of these principles. Where a detailed standard has not yet been produced, then the principles would serve as guidance in the absence of a standard. Such principles could also reduce the need for offering detailed guidance on every new problem and issue that arises: accountants and auditors would just have to follow the principles. The Accounting Standards Board could present itself as having an orderly approach to the steady application of principles. In recent years it has been criticized for taking what is seen as a 'fire-fighting' approach: rushing in to deal with problems and crises as they arise, and for neglecting many issues if they do not seem to be urgent. The existence of principles would also reduce the effectiveness of 'political' lobbying in the accounting standard setting process. There is wide consultation in the process of developing accounting standards and it is clear that the standard setters are under pressure to allow accounting treatments that favour the interests of powerful lobby groups.

The idea of having answers to fundamental questions is also appealing: what is the definition of profit, and how is it measured? What is an asset, and how do we measure its value? The credibility of accounting statements, and the accountancy profession, would be enhanced if people believed that accounting was all based on a sound theoretical framework. Such a framework would also enhance the respectability of accounting as an academic subject.

There have been many attempts to develop such a framework. In the 1940s and 1950s the American Institute of Certified Public Accountants (AICPA) produced a series of Accounting Research Bulletins, and this work was consolidated by the Financial Accounting Standards Board (FASB) in the 1970s and 1980s. In the UK the 1975 *Corporate Report* was a remarkable and liberal framework that was respected for many years.

The early parts of developing a conceptual framework are not very difficult. There is usually agreement on the objectives of financial reporting by businesses, and on the desirable characteristics of financial information. Financial reporting is intended to provide information about the company's financial performance and position that is useful to users (mainly investors) for assessing management's stewardship of the company, and for making economic decisions. The information should be relevant, reliable, comparable and understandable; other characteristics that contribute to this are that the information should be neutral, accurate, complete, prudent and consistent.

The ASB's SSAP 2 specified four fundamental accounting concepts: going concern, accruals, consistency and prudence. Although a whole generation of accountants was brought up on this idea, it did not provide a very satisfactory basis for the development of accountancy. The four seemed to conflict with each other, but prudence was supposed to prevail. The ASB's *Statement of Principles* has de-emphasized these four concepts and now the debate is more about *reliability* versus *relevance* in accounting information, and deciding which should prevail.

In the 1970s it seemed that effort was put into producing long lists of desirable characteristics (or accounting concepts, or doctrines, principles), and long lists of 'users'. The UK's *Corporate Report* (1975) listed just about everyone as a user of a company's accounts, including competitors, journalists, and all *potential* shareholders and potential employees.

The next stage in developing conceptual frameworks was quite easy too: it is assumed that what all these users want is a balance sheet, an income statement, and probably a cash flow statement and a few other bits and pieces. It is rather more difficult to define exactly what should be included in these statements. But the stumbling block was (and probably still is) determining on what basis these should be measured. While academic theorists favoured some sort of current cost accounting, traditional accountants preferred HC and have usually managed to block the compulsory replacement of HC accounting by some form of current cost accounting.

The ASB published its *Statement of Principles* in December 1999, and that is deemed to be the basis of financial reporting standards. It is a formidable document that should effectively discourage non-accountants from questioning the adequacy of the theoretical basis of financial accounting. It is significant in examining the ways in which profits and assets are defined and measured. These issues are explored in Chapters 5 and 11. The IASB and the American Financial Accounting Standards Board (AFASB) are now working together to develop a joint conceptual framework, probably based on the idea of 'fair value'; there are still deep-seated differences and there is little sign of a world-wide conceptual framework at present.

3.8 Investors and Stock Markets

Those countries that were first to develop professional accountancy bodies also tend to be the ones where stock markets are most important. The countries with the largest number of listed companies are the USA, the UK, Japan, Canada and Australia. Although France and Germany are much larger countries, they have only about half the number of listed companies as Canada, and less than a third of the number in the UK. The message seems to be that accounting has developed in this group of countries very much based on the supposed needs of shareholders, under the eye of stock markets, and with the aid of professional accountants.

At times the organized stock exchanges have been influential in pressing for more and better disclosure of financial information for investors. Their influence is less obvious today, but their importance may be seen in their support of the work of the accounting standards setting bodies, and in the push for international financial reporting standards.

3.9 The Standard Setters

Long ago when accountants were not sure how to account for particular items, they had nothing to rely on but a few well-worn accountancy textbooks. The early ones seemed to be modelled on Pacioli's 1494 work, but better books like the well-known 'Spicer and Pegler' acquired authority, and, in due course, the ICAEW produced its 'N' series: Recommendations on Accounting Principles (1942–69).

A major change came at the end of the 1960s with a series of well-publicized accounting scandals, including the GEC–AEI takeover, and Pergamon Press. In October 1967, when AEI was defending itself from a takeover by GEC, they produced a profits forecast for the year 1967. As 9 months of the year had already passed, they should have had a pretty good idea of what the results for the year would be. But GEC's takeover succeeded, and AEI's 'actual' profits for 1967 were published. Instead of being a substantial profit, it turned out to be a substantial loss. It was announced that the differences were due partly to matters of fact, and partly to matters of judgement. The public could be forgiven for thinking that there were no accounting principles at all. It seemed that different accountants, using the same basic data, could come up with entirely different profit figures; and losses could be turned into profits, just by using different 'principles'. Robert Maxwell proved to be very successful at this. A Department of Trade report on a Pergamon Press takeover included some amazing examples of how accounting practices could be selected to produce the required result. It was as miraculous as turning water into wine; accounting had moved a long way since it did no more than record transactions and then summarize them as balance sheets and profit and loss accounts; and accountancy has never looked back.

The professional accountancy bodies set up the AS's Steering Committee at the end of 1969, which was intended to narrow the areas of difference and variety in accounting practice by promulgating a series of 'accounting standards' or SSAPs. Twenty-five SSAPs were produced. They started off as Exposure Drafts (EDs) for consultation, and, when agreed by the main professional accountancy bodies, they became authoritative statements. They did much to clarify definitions and alternatives, and to improve disclosure practice. But too often they allowed more than one treatment, and there was no effective enforcement mechanism. By the 1980s they were losing credibility as 'creative accounting' became well known.

A new accounting standards regime was established in 1990. The Accounting Standards Board produces Financial Reporting Exposure Drafts (FREDs), which, after consultation, become Financial Reporting Standards (FRSs). By 2003, 19 FRSs had been produced, and 30 or so FREDs. The Accounting Standards Board worked under the supervision of the Financial Reporting Council, alongside the Financial Reporting Review Panel (FRRP). Overall, the new arrangements worked better than the old Accounting Standards Committee. The FRSs (together with the SSAPs that they adopted) had more legal backing, and auditors are required to state if they have been followed; attempts are being made to reduce the number of permitted alternative treatments; and the FRRP gradually developed an enforcement role. Where questionable accounting treatments were referred to the FRRP they insisted on the accounting statements being revised. The role of standard setting in the UK is now based on international arrangements.

The IAS Committee has been superseded by the IASB, and in the EU the IFRSs were applied to listed companies in 2005. The IASB is working with the USA's FASB for greater harmonization of accounting standards. There is still a substantial gulf between US requirements on the one hand, and continental European accounting traditions on the other. But there is an enormous force behind current proposals for internationalization, and it seems likely that the idea of countries having their own accounting standards will soon be a thing of the past. This will probably be only a minor problem for countries like the UK, which was always closely linked with the IASB; and IFRSs seem to follow the UK and US practice of prioritizing the needs of shareholders. It is likely to be more of a problem in some European countries with different accounting traditions. IFRSs will, no doubt, be applied to listed companies; but significant changes to accounting traditions in the bulk of smaller businesses will take longer to be effective.

3.10 Concepts and Principles

Financial accounting was said to be based on four fundamental accounting concepts between 1970 and 1999. These were as follows:

1 *Going concern*: assumes that the business will continue in operational existence for the foreseeable future; that there is no intention to liquidate the business or to curtail it significantly. This was used to justify showing assets at cost (adjusted for such things as depreciation), rather than attempting to show them at the amount for which they could be sold at the balance sheet date.

2 *Accruals*: revenues and costs are recognized as they are earned or incurred, not as money is received or paid; they are matched with one another and dealt with in the income statement of the period to which they relate. Profit measurement is based on accruals and matching, not on receipts and payments of cash. This is used to justify a whole range of accounting adjustments including accruals and prepayments; capitalization of fixed assets and annual depreciation charges; and carrying forward the cost of unsold inventories to be treated as an expense when they are sold.

3 *Consistency*: there is consistency of accounting treatment of like items within each accounting period, and from one period to the next. This means, for example, that it is not acceptable to depreciate some vehicles but not others; or to change depreciation policies from one year to the next (unless full details are disclosed).

4 *Prudence*: revenues and profits are not anticipated, but are recognized only when realized as cash (or other assets, the ultimate cash realization of which can be assessed with reasonable certainty[14]); provision is made for all known liabilities (expenses and losses) whether the amount of these is known with certainty or is a best estimate. This conservatism is intended to ensure that profits, assets and income are not overstated; and that expenses and liabilities are not understated. The assumption is that the financial position of a business should be *at least* as good as the financial statements show.

A fifth concept, 'separate valuation', is usually added because it was specifically referred to in the 1985 Companies Act along with the other four. It requires that the amount for each item included in the financial statements should be determined separately. One item should not be offset against another; and (e.g.) a fleet of vehicles should not be valued as a whole: the amount for each vehicle should be determined separately, and then added together.

Over the years a whole range of other concepts, doctrines, principles, postulates, statements of the obvious and pieces of nonsense have been added. The entity concept means only that financial statements are produced for a business entity that is separate from the owners or managers. The materiality concept suggests that minor items will not affect 'a true and fair view', so that, for example, there is no need to capitalize and depreciate a pencil

---

[14] It is acceptable to recognize sales before the money has been received from customers, provided it is reasonably certain how much cash will be received.

sharpener although it might last for several years. The HC concept suggests that items are shown in accounts at their original cost (adjusted for such things as depreciation), not at a current market value (although market values are given for some assets). Duality indicates that every transaction must have two aspects so that it can be recorded twice in a double-entry system, as a debit and as a credit. Disclosure suggests that all information should be disclosed, which is likely to be relevant to the needs of users. Verifiability suggests that items should be included only where there is verifiable evidence (such as documents) of their existence. Objectivity and neutrality suggest that those responsible for producing financial statements are not biased in favour of a particular point of view. Money measurement indicates that items in financial statements are given monetary values. Substance over form suggests that financial statements should show the economic reality of an item rather than its legal form. Odd writers have suggested that financial accounting is based on other conventions such as the arithmetic convention, which seems to be a statement of the obvious; and the assumption that the value of the pound is constant, which is nonsense.

Even the old Accounting Standards Committee recognized contradictions within their own four fundamental concepts, and argued that the prudence concept should prevail over the accruals concept. Other 'concepts' indicated above do not form any coherent framework or basis for accounting.

More recently the ASB's *Statement of Principles for Financial Reporting* (December 1999) refers to objectives and constraints rather than concepts. In producing financial accounting statements, the most appropriate accounting polices are those that meet four objectives:

1 *Relevance* to the needs of users in predicting the future or confirming the present or past.

2 *Reliability*, which means that accounting information represents faithfully the substance of the underlying transactions; is neutral (there is no deliberate or systematic bias); is free from material error; is complete within the bounds of materiality; and, where conditions are uncertain, judgements and estimates have been made with a degree of caution.

3 *Comparability*, which means that the financial statements of one entity can usefully be compared with those of another; this requires a combination of disclosure and consistency.

4 *Understandability* suggests that users should be able to understand financial statements (provided they have a reasonable knowledge of business, economics and accounting; and a willingness to study the information diligently).

The idea of prudence has been downgraded from being a fundamental accounting concept to being only part of reliability, and applying only in conditions of uncertainty; it relates only to a degree of caution being used in making judgements and estimates. The idea of general prudence has gone; it has been dismissed as being likely to result in systematic bias in financial statements. Similarly, consistency has been downgraded to being part of comparability. The accruals concept continues to be central to financial accounting. With regard to the going concern concept, companies are now required to disclose information where there may be uncertainties about its continuance as a going concern.

The idea of understandability may be just wishful thinking. The published financial statements of companies are now generally more complex and more difficult to understand than ever before.

3.11 User Groups

Published financial statements are supposed to meet the information needs of a variety of different 'users'. The main groups of users, and their information needs, are summarized below.

1 Shareholders, including potential shareholders, who are considering buying or selling shares in the company. They are interested in such things as the value of the company, the profits, dividends and cash flows that it has generated in recent periods, and what its performance is likely to be in future periods; and in its financial position and survival prospects.

2 Creditors and suppliers including potential creditors. They are interested in the company's cash flows and ability to meet their liabilities in general and to pay their creditors on time.

3 Lenders both short term (e.g. banks in relation to overdrafts) and long term (e.g. debenture holders and those considering lending) have similar information needs to other creditors. They want to know about their company's ability to repay the loans, their current financial position and their future prospects. They are interested in financial position (balance sheets), performance (income statements) and cash generation (cash flow statements).

4 Employees and potential employees want to know about the future prospects of their companies, whether they will survive and prosper and be able to pay wages and salaries and provide expanding career prospects in the future. They are also interested in companies' pension schemes, and whether they are viable or in deficit. When going for an interview with a company, applicants are well advised to find out all they can about their potential employer, including type of business, and their proposed developments.

5 Customers may be interested in the financial position and prospects of a company, although this is a bit unlikely in relation to most consumer goods. If a government or large company is considering entering into a substantial or long-term contract, they will want to know if proposed contractors are reputable, and in a strong enough financial position to meet the commitments that are being considered.

6 Government and public sector bodies are interested in companies (and not just as potential customers). They are interested in gathering information about businesses in relation to a whole range of public policy concerns, including employment levels and policies, research and development, investment and growth, their impact on the balance of payments, pricing and inflation, mergers, takeovers and competition policy, and environmental and public health. Wherever politicians see a public policy impact, or evidence of voters' concerns, they are likely to want to know what companies are doing, and to consider gathering more information, and implementing additional regulations.

7 HM Revenue and Customs are responsible for collecting corporation tax, income tax, value added tax, and customs and excise duties, which they do on the basis of specific forms and information requirements. But as part of their general checking and control procedures, they are likely to be interested in the published accounts of companies, and investigating any apparent discrepancies.

8 Managers and directors are likely to be interested in the annual financial statements of their companies and even more interested in monthly statements. But financial accounting information is primarily designed for people outside the business. Managers should have access to specially produced internal management accounting information on a regular basis. But there are many small companies that produce little management accounting information other than monthly income statements, balance sheets and cash flow statements, which are relied on by managers and directors.

9 Financial analysts and advisers come in all shapes and sizes, and have many different information needs. Some may be advising the company concerned on raising additional finance or on a potential takeover bid. More generally, there are investment analysts who carry out fundamental analysis of the financial information about a company and produce recommendations to those considering buying or selling shares in the company. They are interested in the financial position and performance, and still more interested in its future prospects, in attempting a valuation of a company based on the future cash flows that it will generate, and in assessing whether or not the current share price represents good value in relation to future prospects.

10 Competitors usually like to compare their own results with those of their rivals, perhaps to gloat where they are doing better, and to learn what they can to improve their own performance. They are interested in how much their competitors are expanding, their profit margins and in how the different segments of the business are performing.

11 The public, special interest groups and students between them are likely to seek an almost infinitely wide range of information about a company, much of which can be found in annual reports and accounts. There are environmental lobby groups, animal welfare groups, local people interested in possible building expansion, trade unions acting on behalf of employees, people concerned with health, safety and accidents, and many others. The Internet is usually the first port of call for students undertaking projects; but they should not overlook the company's annual report and accounts, which is the company's official information intended mainly for shareholders, and includes much more than students usually expect.

The information needs of some of these groups should not be taken too seriously because they are in a position to get most of what they want to meet their specific needs directly from the company. These groups include governments, HM Revenue and Customs, and managers and directors. Lenders such as bankers are usually given much more information than is included in published financial statements, including forecast information, monthly breakdowns and cash budgets. Similarly financial advisers are likely to be given most available information if they are acting for the company concerned (but not if they are acting for competitors!).

In some cases the information that particular groups want is so detailed and specific that it would be impractical to include it in a general purpose annual report. Expansion plans at a supermarket site, safety records at a particular factory and employment prospects at a particular location may all be matters of interest locally, but it would be impractical to expand annual reports to include all the detail that some groups might want in respect of a particular location. Annual reports are necessarily 'general purpose'. Many of the supposed information needs of the various groups are a matter for legitimate public concern, but perhaps it should be governments who act on behalf of the public and obtain appropriate information; it is unrealistic to expect everything to be included in a company's annual report and accounts.

A major problem with the information needs of the various groups is that most want to know what is going to happen in the future. Shareholders, creditors, lenders and employees all want to know what the company's future prospects are. Will they be able to meet their liabilities? Will shares be a good investment? Will the company thrive and provide good career prospects? These are all legitimate questions, but financial statements deal almost entirely with what has already happened. Many users are concerned to assess the value of published, historic financial information by assessing the extent to which it provides an effective basis for future forecasts, and there are increasing pressures for companies to publish additional forecast information. Many see the role of financial statements as being to provide a basis for predicting future cash flows.[15]

As it is not possible for a company to publish exactly the information that everyone wants, the emphasis is on balance sheets, income statements and cash flow statements, which are primarily designed for the benefit of shareholders and creditors.

The general presumption now[16] is that focusing on the interests that investors have in the financial performance and position of a company will, in effect, also be focusing on the common interest that all users have. The income statement, balance sheet and cash flow statement are assumed to meet most information requirements of users of financial statements, which is not much more than a truism: those are the statements that are available; those are the statements that they use, so those must be the statements that they want to use.

Summary

Financial accounting is based on a myth (perhaps many myths): it exists primarily to provide financial information for investors and creditors. But what investors really want to know about is the future. What will future profits, dividends and share prices be? Will creditors all be paid on time or will the company get into financial difficulties? But we cannot know the future, and any estimate of value, or even (last year's) profit, rests on assumptions about the future. Perhaps there is a natural human need to have faith that someone can help us to predict what will happen in the future. If prophets and religion are declining, it may be that the need for faith in accountant's profits and other figures is increasing. But if accountants are now expected to fill this human need for guidance about the future,[17] there are bound to be problems with credibility. We have the Accounting Standards Board, and even the International Accounting Standards Board, to help us to have faith in complex financial reports. Published financial statements can provide valuable information. But we should be realistic about what we can expect from a system that has traditionally done little more than record and summarize transactions.

---

[15] Cash flows are, of course, different from profits. These differences are explored in Chapter 7.

[16] In line with the ASB's *Statement of Principles*, December 1999.

[17] We cannot measure profit without making assumptions about the future of assets. For example, we need a figure for closing inventories and what their net realizable value is likely to be; we need to estimate how long fixed assets will last and how much depreciation is appropriate.

Review of key points

- Financial accounting has evolved in response to the needs of businesses; it was never designed as a whole.
- Its development has been effectively influenced by accountants and auditors; bankers and creditors; companies and their directors; governments and the law; the standard setters; academics and theorists; and investors and stock markets.
- The accountability of directors to shareholders is central to financial accounting.
- The ASB has produced the *Statement of Principles* upon which financial reporting standards should be based and attempts are being made to produce a comparable statement that is internationally agreed.
- Financial accounting statements meet some of the information needs of a wide range of different users, but the needs of investors predominate.

Self-testing questions

1 Who are the main users of financial accounting, and what are their information needs?
2 To what extent and in what ways is the financial accounting information that creditors want different from that which shareholders want?
3 Who determines what is to be included in company annual reports and accounts?
4 Why does there seem to be a lot of criticism of auditors?
5 What have been the main influences on the development of financial accounting in the UK?

Assessment questions

1 Compare the idea and practice of the 'accountability' of governments with that of companies.
2 In what ways, and to what extent, can financial accounting indicate the extent to which companies have achieved their objectives?
3 For what reasons might financial accounting for listed companies differ from financial accounting for unlisted companies?
4 Explain the meaning of 'relevance' and 'reliability' and discuss the importance of each in financial reporting.
5 In what ways is it helpful to understand the historical development of financial accounting?

Group activities and discussion questions

1 Making use of your knowledge of other subject areas (perhaps the armed forces; the church; the UK constitution; the transport system; universities; football), discuss the view that we cannot understand how something operates today without knowing about its historical development.

2 The chapter referred to the interests of a number of different groups in society. With the legal and medical professions we can say that there is also a 'public interest' (in justice; in health). Is there a 'public interest' in accountancy?

3 As a group, make a list of about 10–15 professions. You may wish to discuss what you mean by a 'profession'. As individuals, rank each of the professions with the best at the top of the list; be aware of what criteria you are using to rank the different professions. As a group, try to agree which criteria you want to use to rank professions. Is accountancy the best profession? If not, why not?

4 Select two or three businesses that you know something about (perhaps Manchester United, your own university, the University of Buckingham, Scottish Power, EMI, Severn Trent Water, BP). To whom should they be accountable, and for what, and how? To what extent would you expect accountants to be able to implement accountability in a form that you would like to see?

5 (For groups of students from different countries.) How has the historical development of accountancy in your country/countries differed from the UK? Discuss the relative importance of the government, bankers, stock markets and the accountancy profession in that development. What are the main problems to be overcome in implementing International Accounting Standards in all countries?

Financial accounting in context

Show of hands packs punch in boardroom

By Sundeep Tucker

Financial Times, 26 January 2006

Discuss and comment on the following item taken from the press. What does it indicate about the effectiveness of arrangements to make directors accountable to shareholders?

Source: Reproduced with permission by the *Financial Times*.

YESTERDAY'S confirmation that the government has ruled out new legal curbs on "rewards for failure" marks a symbolic victory for shareholder activists. Tellingly, the Department of Trade and Industry has decided against legislation because it believes investor activism is having the desired effect.

As little as five years ago investors had little control over the worst boardroom excesses, and winced as directors walked away with millions of pounds having presided over a deteriorating share price. Shareholders were not helped by the lack of disclosure on directors' contracts in annual reports.

That all changed in 2003 when the Labour government – sensitive to accusations that it was being too soft on "fat cat" pay – opted not to legislate but to hand investors greater powers to control boardroom pay.

Directors were told to publish their pay packages and, crucially, shareholders were given the right to vote on executive deals at company annual meetings.

It was not long before investors flexed their muscles. In May 2003 they voted down plans that would have allowed Jean-Paul Garnier, chief executive of GlaxoSmithKline, to pocket a "platinum parachute" payment of £22m if he left the company.

Peter Montagnon, Association of British Insurers' head of investment affairs, described the GSK vote as a "watershed". "Companies are now aware that they can lose a vote and, as a result, there is more dialogue surrounding pay issues."

However, there have been some high-profile exceptions, largely with pay plans that were arranged before investors got to approve them.

There was fury last year when it emerged that TV boss Michael Green in October 2003 had been awarded £15m in cash and shares, largely because Carlton merged with Granada, and similar anger in the summer when Sir Peter Davis, chairman of J Sainsbury, walked away from the ailing grocer with a £2.6m bonus.

Such rows are now increasingly unlikely. Companies are so worried about losing a vote they are flocking to have pay plans approved by shareholder Groups, in advance of the annual meeting. Last year the ABI received delegations from 209 companies, more than double that of three years ago, and, ironically, is now complaining about the levels of consultation.

Geoff Lindsey, an adviser to the National Association of Pension Funds, said: "In general, the banging of heads over corporate governance has gone. Confrontation between shareholders and companies is in no one's best interests."

Susannah Haan of the CBI employers' organisation said: "Shareholder activism is the best way to police directors' pay. Legislation would have generated unnecessary legal complexity and uncertainty. Investors are the most credible judges of performance, not the law courts."

However, investors have pledged to remain vigilant over the structure of directors' pay, which they believe is an important driver of the company's performance. And not everybody believes that the days of boardroom excess are over.

Brendan Barber, Trades Union Congress general secretary, said: "Top directors still award themselves pay rises many times those given to staff and continue to give themselves VIP pensions when many employees are seeing their schemes close."

Even some pay advisers are sympathetic to that view. Cliff Weight, a director of Independent Remuneration Solutions, has published research showing that despite greater investor focus on pay, remuneration for leading chief executives had risen by 170 per cent over the past five years to £2m. He said: "The new regulations have reduced the payments for failure but not the rewards for average performance. Reward for success [has] gone up as it is now more closely linked to performance and that's a good thing."

BOARDROOM PAY ROWS

Sir Peter Davis, J Sainsbury
July 2004
The board of J Sainsbury escaped defeat thanks to the backing of the Sainsbury family against the fury of shareholders over proposals to pay the maximum bonus to Sir Peter Davis, the chairman, who left amid poor sales and profit warnings.

Michael Green, Carlton
October 2003
Michael Green received £1.8m compensation for loss of office, in addition to £13.2m in share awards triggered by the merger of Carlton and Granada. Shareholders later moved to tighten the rules on 'windfall' payments triggered by changes of control.

Jean-Paul Garnier, GSK
May 2003
Investors threw out plans to pay chief executive Jean-Paul Garnier a 'platinum parachute' of £22m should he lose his job.

Jonathan Bloomer, Prudential
May 2002
The chief executive's pay package, including a potential bonus of £4.6m, was withdrawn after opposition by shareholders.

References and further reading

Accounting Standards Board (1999) *Statement of Principles for Financial Reporting*. ASB.

Accounting Standards Steering Committee (1975) *The Corporate Report*. ASSC.

Lewis, R., D. Pendrill and D. S. Simon (2003) *Advanced Financial Accounting* (7th edition). FT Prentice Hall.

Perks, R.W. (1993) *Accounting and Society*. Chapman and Hall.

Spicer, E. and E. Pegler (1908) *Book-keeping and Accounts* (1st edition). 16th edition by W.W. Bigg, H.A.R.J. Wilson and A.E. Langton (1964) HFL Publishers Ltd.

Sweeney, H.W. (1936) *Stabilized Accounting*. Harper and Row.

www.iasb.co.uk (deals with international accounting standards)

www.icaew.co.uk (site of the Institute of Chartered Accountants in England and Wales; the other professional accountancy bodies also have websites)

www.fasb.org (deals with US accounting standards)

www.frc.org.uk (deals with UK accounting standards)

CHAPTER 04

Ratios and Interpretation: a Straightforward Introduction

Chapter contents

❖ LEARNING OBJECTIVES

After studying this chapter you should be able to:

❖ Calculate and interpret four solvency ratios from a company's published financial statements

❖ Calculate and interpret four overall profitability ratios; three dealing with the profitability of sales; and five dealing with the utilization of assets

❖ Calculate and interpret four stock market ratios

❖ Understand the role of working capital management and apply relevant ratios

❖ Appreciate the importance of financial structure and apply relevant ratios

❖ Understand the limitations of ratio analysis and the importance of suitable bases for comparison

4.1 Introduction

This chapter shows how financial accounting provides information that can be useful in assessing the financial strength of a company, and in analysing and improving its performance in terms of profitability in a straightforward way. Complexities, and more advanced aspects of interpretation, are dealt with in Chapter 9.

This chapter also introduces the use of financial accounting information in interpreting the performance of a company's shares on the stock market. These issues are dealt with more fully in Chapter 6.

Interpretation of accounts is not about memorizing a number of ratios and then calculating them. It is about examining a set of accounts, with some clear questions in mind, and then carefully arranging the evidence to answer those questions.

Presentation of 'Ratios'

Accounting 'ratios' are presented in a number of conventional ways, most of which are percentages or some other measures, rather than 'ratios' in the strict sense of the word.

1   *Ratios* Current ratios and liquidity ratios are presented as ratios, in the form 2 : 1

2   *Percentages* Many so-called ratios are really expressed as percentages. A dividend yield might be 3.5 per cent. Return on capital employed (ROCE) might be 12 per cent. The 'gross profit ratio' is also expressed as a percentage (e.g. 25 per cent)

3   *Number of times* Dividend cover is expressed as a number of times, for example 2.2 times. Interest cover and asset turnover ratios are also expressed as, for example, 6 times, 1.9 times. A 'price/earnings ratio' (e.g. 16) is the share price divided by earnings per share: it is the number of times earnings per share would be multiplied by to arrive at the share price.

4   *Number of days (or weeks)* A debtors 'ratio' is often shown as being, for example, 36 days.[1] Similarly, the stock turnover ratio is often expressed as a number of days. A 'creditors ratio' is often shown as being the average payment period for creditors.

5   *Sum of money* Earnings per share are expressed as a sum of money (e.g. 10p)

There are three main groups of questions in interpreting financial statements and a number of related ones.

1   *Financial strength/solvency* Is the business likely to survive? Can it pay its liabilities as they fall due? Is it financially strong? Is there too much debt?

2   *Profitability* Is the business sufficiently profitable? Is it making the best use of the resources available to it? How can profitability be increased?

3   *Stock market* How are the company's shares performing on the stock market? Are they likely to be a good investment?

The chapter demonstrates how ratios can be used to tackle each of these questions in relation to Druisdale plc for year 5. Readers are invited to calculate and interpret the equivalent ratios for year 6. (The answers are provided at the end of the book, pp. 492–4.)

---

[1] Alternatively, it could also be expressed as sales divided by debtors, giving perhaps 10 times per annum.

Other related questions include different aspects of profitability, working capital management, financial structure and cash flows. This chapter introduces most of these issues. Cash flows are dealt with in Chapter 7. Stock market ratios are dealt with more fully in Chapter 6. More advanced interpretation of financial statements and some complexities are dealt with in Chapter 9 .

The final part of the chapter provides an overview of ratio analysis, followed by a 'ratios ready reference' section.

4.2 Financial Strength/Solvency

A balance sheet shows what a company owns (assets) and what it owes (liabilities). Unless the company is a complete disaster, it should have more assets than liabilities, and the excess of assets over liabilities is called 'equity'. If someone owns a house worth £200,000, and has a mortgage of £120,000, their 'equity' in that house is £80,000.

A company can collapse in many different ways: bankruptcy, liquidation, receivership, winding up, reorganization and takeover. Many different reasons are put forward to explain what went wrong, including bad management and bad luck. But, in the end, a company collapses if it is unable to pay its liabilities as they fall due. Balance sheets show liabilities clearly, and it is worth trying to assess if those liabilities are excessive – if the company owes so much that it is likely to get into financial difficulties.

The balance sheet clearly separates short-term assets and liabilities from long-term assets and liabilities, and the assessment can be done in two stages: short term, and long term.

Short Term

The key question is: can a company meet its short-term liabilities as they fall due? Current liabilities are clearly shown on balance sheets. If a company has current liabilities of £1 million, and they have £2 million in the bank, then there should not be a problem. There are companies with so much money in the bank that they do not know what to do with it, but that is not the norm. Even if a company does not have lots of money in the bank, it is worth looking at their current assets as a whole. Current assets include cash, and things like stocks and debtors that should become cash within a matter of months. If a company has lots more current assets than current liabilities, then they look reasonably strong.

If we look at the Druisdale plc's balance sheet at the end of year 5 (Illustration 4.1), we can see that current liabilities amount to £60m. If all their current assets are turned into cash there should not be a problem: current assets amount to £120m. Current assets are twice as much as current liabilities – a ratio of 2 : 1. This relationship between current assets and current liabilities is called the current ratio.

In some businesses stocks are not easily converted into cash. In looking at what money is immediately available with which to pay current liabilities we should, perhaps, exclude stocks. Some inventories, such as stocks of food in a supermarket, should be sold and converted into cash within a few weeks. Other inventories may take a long time to be converted into cash; for example raw materials and components that have not yet been incorporated

Balance sheet of Druisdale plc as at 31 December

	Year 5 £m	Year 6 £m
Assets		
Non-current assets		
Property, plant and equipment	180	200
Current assets		
Inventories	60	60
Trade receivables	40	50
Cash	20	10
	120	120
Total assets	300	320
Equity and liabilities		
Equity		
Share capital	100	100
Retained earnings	80	100
Total equity	180	200
Non-current liabilities		
Long-term borrowings	60	40
Current liabilities		
Trade payables	60	80
Total liabilities	120	120
Total equity and liabilities	300	320

Income statement of Druisdale plc for the year ended 31 December

	Year 5 £m	Year 6 £m
Revenue	300	350
Cost of sales	(200)	(230)
Gross profit	100	120
Distribution costs	(15)	(20)
Administrative expenses	(25)	(31)
Operating profit	60	69
Finance costs	(5)	(4)
Profit before tax	55	65
Income tax expense	(15)	(15)
Profit for the period	40	50

Statement of changes in equity of Druisdale plc for the year ended 31 December

Balance at beginning of year	165	180
Profit for the period	40	50
Dividends	(25)	(30)
Balance at end of year	180	200

Additional information
Druisdale plc's share capital consists of 100m ordinary shares with a nominal value of £1 each. Assume that the share price on 31 December year 5 was £5.60, and on 31 December year 6 it was £7.50.

ILLUSTRATION 4.1

into saleable products, or partly built houses – perhaps where demand is currently slack. In Druisdale plc there is £20m of cash, and £40m of trade receivables that should become cash within a month or so. In other words 'liquid assets' of £60m (excluding stocks) are just enough to meet current liabilities of £60m as they become due. This is a liquidity ratio of 1 : 1.

On year 6 balance sheet there are not enough liquid assets (£60m) to meet current liabilities (£80m). The liquidity ratio has gone down to 0.75 : 1. Their liquidity position has deteriorated, and problems could arise.

Long Term

A company is likely to find itself in financial difficulties if it has too much debt, whether it is short term or long term. One way of assessing if debt is too high is to compare it with equity. If someone has a mortgage (debt) of £120,000 it is probably not serious if the house is worth £200,000 – there is £80,000 of the owner's equity. It is still less of a problem if the house is worth £500,000: the owner's equity would amount to £380,000. The more equity there is in relation to the total value of the house, the less risky the borrowing is. The more borrowing there is in relation to the total value of the house, the more risky the borrowing is.

It is also necessary to look at an individual's, or a company's, ability to service the loan. If interest of 8 per cent per annum is payable on a loan of £120,000, the cost of the loan is £9,600[2] per annum. If an individual or company earns only £10,000 a year, they are going to have problems paying the interest. If they earn £30,000 a year we can say that the interest is 'covered' just over three times, which might be satisfactory. It would be much more comfortable if the income available to pay the interest was £96,000 a year: we could say that the interest is covered 10 times.

Balance sheets show the relationship between equity and long-term borrowings. At the end of year 5 Druisdale plc's equity amounted to £180m; their long-term borrowings were £60m. We could say that as long as equity is a lot more than borrowings, the position is satisfactory. Or we could present a 'gearing ratio' that relates 'debt' (long-term borrowings) to equity. The total amount of long-term funding available to Druisdale is (180 + 60 =) £240m. Of this total, £60m is borrowed: the gearing ratio is therefore 25 per cent.[3]

Druisdale should have little difficulty in servicing their loan. The income statement for year 5 shows 'finance costs' of £5m. The profit available to provide that interest amounted to £60m. We could arrive at this figure simply by taking profit before tax, and adding back the interest. Or we could use the 'operating profit' figure (which is the same), which is gross profit minus operating costs for distribution and administration (100 − 15 − 25 =) £60m. Interest is covered 12 times,[4] which should be very safe.

---

[2] 8% × £120,000 = £9,600.

[3] 60 ÷ 240 × 100 = 25%.

[4] 60 ÷ 5 = 12.

An Overall View

The approach so far has been to calculate four widely used 'ratios' for year 5, which are as follows.

    1 *Current ratio* (or working capital ratio)   2 : 1

    2 *Liquidity ratio* (or quick assets ratio, or acid test)   1 : 1

    3 *Capital gearing ratio*   25%

    4 *Interest times cover*   12 times

A current ratio of 2 : 1 is conventionally regarded as being fairly safe. If it falls below about 1.7 : 1 it may look rather risky.

    A liquidity ratio of 1 : 1 is satisfactory: there are just enough liquid assets to pay current liabilities. If it falls below about 0.7 : 1, it may look rather risky.

    A gearing ratio of 25 per cent is fairly average. Anything much above 50 per cent reliance on borrowing begins to look a little risky.

    Interest times cover of 12 times looks fairly safe. Cover of much less than 5 begins to look risky.

The above comments need to be interpreted with care, and what is satisfactory depends on the type of business. Retailers often have low current and liquidity ratios. Companies with very reliable income such as property companies often have very high gearing (with loans secured on property and the rental income receivable from it). It is also useful to look at trends rather than at just a single year.

Activity 4.1

Complete the following table for Druisdale plc by inserting the figures for year 6, and commenting on the changes that have taken place.[5]

Ratio	Year 5		Year 6		Comment
1 Current ratio	120 : 60	2 : 1			
2 Liquidity ratio	60 : 60	1 : 1			
3 Gearing ratio	60/240	25%			
4 Interest cover	60/5	12 times			

    This conventional approach separates short-term liabilities from long-term liabilities. It may also be important to look at the total of all liabilities in forming an assessment of a company's financial strength and survival prospects.

    In assessing the financial strength of a company there are many other factors to take into consideration; indications of many of these can be found in the financial accounting statements. The balance sheet alone will not tell us all we want to know. We also have to look

---

[5] A completed table is provided at the end of the book (see p. 492).

at the income statement in order to calculate interest cover. Profit is by no means a guarantee of survival, but creditors of a profitable company are likely to be much more secure than creditors of a loss-making company. A company that is making profits is much more likely to survive than one that is making losses.

Creditors are interested in whether or not they are likely to be paid on time. A calculation of the average time it takes to pay creditors is provided in ratio 16 (see p. 88 – creditors ratio).

In terms of survival, it may be that cash flow matters more than profit, or any of the above ratios. As long as a company is generating lots of cash it can pay its liabilities and survive. The calculation and interpretation of these ratios and the evaluation of solvency are considered more fully in Chapters 7 and 9.

4.3 Profitability

Profitability is examined here in three sections:

- Overall profitability
- Profitability of sales
- Utilization of assets

Overall Profitability

An income statement shows how much profit a company has made for the shareholders in a given period. Druisdale plc's profit for year 5 was £40m, after finance costs and taxation (but before deducting dividends, which are shown on a separate statement). Shareholders may reasonably ask: was that enough? Should the company be more profitable?

Druisdale's balance sheet shows the total equity as being £180m at the end of year 5. If the shareholders' funds had been put into a deposit account at a bank, they might have been paid about 4 per cent per annum interest, with virtually no risk. Shareholders would expect a company to earn a much better return than that[6] in view of the risk inherent in investing in companies. A return of 4 per cent per annum on £180m would produce £7.2m profit a year. As Druisdale earned £40m in year 5, the shareholders may be satisfied. The return earned for them is as follows:

5 *Return on shareholders' funds*

$$\frac{\text{Profit for the year}}{\text{Equity at year end}} \times \frac{100}{1} \qquad \frac{£40}{£180} \times \frac{100}{1} = 22.2\%$$

We might consider that any return on capital employed (ROCE) of more than about 10 per cent is satisfactory; anything over 20 per cent is good.

The ROCE is often regarded as the being most important, or key, or primary ratio, particularly in measuring profitability. Where there is a good, and increasing ROCE, we can

---

[6] Even if much of the profit or income earned is retained in the business and not paid out to shareholders as dividends.

conclude that the management of the company are using its resources effectively. It is important to consider the *total* of shareholders' funds (£180m), not just the share capital (£100m).

The above calculations are from the shareholders' point of view. The ratio measures the return on *shareholders'* capital employed, or the return on equity.[7] In assessing management, however, we should consider all the funds for which they are responsible more generally, and look at the return on *total long-term capital*. The balance sheet at the end of year 5 shows that in addition to shareholders' funds of £180m, the company had long-term borrowings of £60m. Profit is earned for the shareholders; interest is the return to lenders. If we are going to calculate a return on total long-term capital, we must include interest, in addition to profit, as being part of the return. In year 5 the profit was £40m, and the finance cost (presumably interest) was £5m. Rather than just adding the two together it is easier to consider the return before taxation; sometimes the figure is described as earnings before interest and taxation (EBIT), or as operating profit.

6 *Return on total long-term capital employed*

Profit £40m, plus tax expense £15m, plus finance cost £5m = £60m
Or gross profit of £100m, minus £15m distribution costs, minus £25m administrative expenses = £60m
Total capital employed is equity (£180m), plus long-term borrowings (£60m) = £240m
Operating profit

$$\frac{\text{Operating profit or EBIT}}{\text{Equity} + \text{long-term borrowings}} \times \frac{100}{1} \qquad \frac{£60m}{£240m} \times \frac{100}{1} = 25\%$$

As is the case with most ratios, this figure is most useful when making comparisons with previous periods (or other companies). It is important to ensure that all ratios are calculated in the same way when making comparisons, but it is particularly relevant with ROCE as there are several different ways of doing it.

Directors and shareholders often want to see an increase in the ROCE and there are two[8] ways of achieving this.

- Increasing the return, or profit, in relation to the amount of capital employed. This can be done by reducing costs, and/or increasing sales. The important thing is to increase the difference between costs and sales; in other words to increase profit as a percentage of sales. This is assessed in ratio 7, and considered in more detail using ratios 9–11 on page 86
- Reducing the amount of capital employed (in relation to the amount of sales); or increasing the amount of sales (in relation to the amount of capital employed). This means making more intensive use of assets, or capital employed; or increasing 'asset turnover'. This is assessed in ratio 8, and considered in more detail using ratios 12–16 on pages 87–8

---

[7] When there are preference shares the return on equity (ordinary shareholders' funds) will be different from the return on total shareholders' funds (ordinary shareholders' funds plus preference shares).

[8] Perhaps *only* two.

7 *Operating profit[9] as a percentage of sales*

In year 5 Druisdale's operating profit as a percentage of sales was

$$\frac{\text{Operating profit}}{\text{Sales}} \times \frac{100}{1} \qquad \frac{\text{£60m}}{\text{£300m}} = 20\%$$

8 *Asset turnover*

In year 5 Druisdale's asset turnover may be measured by relating the sales figure to net operating assets.[10]

Fixed assets plus current assets minus current liabilities (£180m + £120m − £60m) = £240m

Or, equity plus long-term borrowings (£180m + £60m) = £240m

The £240m may be shown as FA + CA − CL

Sales revenue £300m

$$\text{Asset turnover} = \frac{\text{Sales}}{\text{Fa + CA − CL}} \qquad \frac{\text{£300m}}{\text{£240m}} = 1.25 \text{ times}$$

The last three ratios considered can be related together as follows:

6 Return on total long-term capital employed   25%

7 Operating profit as a percentage of sales   20%

   25 ÷ 20 = 1.25

8 Asset turnover   1.25 times

Activity 4.2

Complete the following table for Druisdale plc by inserting the figures for year 6, and commenting on the changes that have taken place.[11] Check the relationship between ratios 6, 7 and 8.

Ratio	Year 5		Year 6		Comment
5 Return on shareholders' capital employed	40/180	22.2%			
6 Return on total long-term capital employed	60/240	25%			
7 Operating profit as a percentage of sales	60/300	20%			
8 Asset turnover	300/240	1.25 times			

---

[9] Profit before deducting finance charges.

[10] Net operating assets may be defined as total assets (current plus non current) minus current liabililties. This should be equal to equity plus non-current liabilities.

[11] A completed table is provided at the end of the book (see p. 492).

When these four ratios have been calculated for each of the two years, it will be clear whether profitability has increased, and why.

In order to increase its profitability it is necessary to consider (a) the profitability of sales (and analyse costs), and (b) the utilization of capital employed, or asset turnover (and analyse 'activity ratios').

Profitability of Sales

Any costs can be expressed as a percentage of sales. The first cost on an income statement is cost of sales, but it is more usual to express gross profit as a percentage of sales. If cost of sales is two-thirds of sales, then gross profit is one-third of sales. The figures for Druisdale plc for year 5 are as follows:

9 *Gross profit ratio*

$$\frac{\text{Gross profit}}{\text{Sales}} \times \frac{100}{1} \qquad \frac{£100\text{m}}{£300\text{m}} \times \frac{100}{1} = 33\tfrac{1}{3}\%$$

It may be more useful to express the cost of raw materials or labour as a percentage of sales. But the most readily available costs from published accounts are distribution costs and administrative expenses. The ratios for Druisdale plc for year 5 are shown below.

10 *Distribution costs as a percentage of sales*

$$\frac{\text{Distribution costs}}{\text{Sales}} \times \frac{100}{1} \qquad \frac{£15\text{m}}{£300\text{m}} \times \frac{100}{1} = 5\%$$

11 *Administrative expenses as a percentage of sales*

$$\frac{\text{Administrative expenses}}{\text{Sales}} \times \frac{100}{1} \qquad \frac{£25\text{m}}{£300\text{m}} \times \frac{100}{1} = 8\tfrac{1}{3}\%$$

Whether or not these ratios are satisfactory depends on the business; the figures mean little, except by comparison.

Activity 4.3

Complete the following table for Druisdale plc by inserting the figures for year 6, and commenting on the changes that have taken place.[12]

Ratio	Year 5		Year 6		Comment
9 Gross profit ratio	100/300	33⅓%			
10 Distribution costs as a % of sales	15/300	5%			
11 Administrative expenses as a % of sales	25/300	8⅓%			

---

[12] A completed table is provided at the end of the book (see p. 492).

Utilization of Assets

Where there is a problem with the asset turnover ratio (number 8 above), there is a need to improve the utilization of assets. The first step is to see whether the problem lies with non-current assets or with current assets.[13] This can be done by comparing one year with the next, as demonstrated in Activity 4.4 below.

12 *Sales/fixed assets*

$$\frac{\text{Sales}}{\text{Non-current assets}} \qquad \frac{300\text{m}}{180\text{m}} = 1.67 \text{ times}$$

If it is established that there is a problem with fixed assets (there are too many fixed assets in relation to the amount of sales), further analysis can be done by comparing different categories of fixed assets with sales.

13 *Sales/current assets*

$$\frac{\text{Sales}}{\text{Current assets}} \qquad \frac{300\text{m}}{120\text{m}} = 2.5 \text{ times}$$

If it is established that there is a problem with current assets (there are too many current assets in relation to the amount of sales), further analysis can be done by comparing different items of current assets, and current liabilities, with sales. The most widely used ratios are in relation to stocks, debtors and creditors. These may be measured in terms of the number of times the item is 'turned over' in a year (e.g. a stock turnover ratio). However, it is preferable to express each of stocks, debtors and creditors as a number of days.

14 *Stock turnover ratio*

The stock or inventory figure taken from the balance sheet is shown at cost price (not selling price), and so must be compared with the cost of sales figure (not the sales revenue figure). The inventories are divided by cost of sales to give a proportion of a year (365 days):

$$\frac{\text{Inventories}}{\text{Cost of sales}} \times 365 \qquad \frac{60\text{m}}{200\text{m}} \times 365 = 109.5 \text{ days}$$

This figure seems rather high, but it does depend on the type of business. A supermarket would probably have only a few weeks' stocks on hand at any one time.

15 *Debtors ratio*

The trade debtors or trade receivables figure taken from the balance sheet is shown at selling price (that is the amount that the customer owes, not the cost price), and so must be compared with the sales revenue figure (not the cost of sales figure). Again, it is expressed as a proportion of a year:

$$\frac{\text{Debtors}}{\text{Sales revenue}} \times 365 \qquad \frac{40\text{m}}{300\text{m}} \times 365 = 48.7 \text{ days}$$

---

[13] The problem might also lie with current liabilities. Increasing current liabilities can increase profitability (it reduces the amount of capital employed), but it might make solvency ratios look weaker.

If all sales are on credit, and customers are expected to settle their accounts by the end of the month following the month in which the sale takes place, 49 days is reasonable.

If some or all sales are on a cash basis (as is the case with most retailers), a much lower average figure would be expected. If possible, credit sales should be separated from cash sales, and the debtors figure should be compared only with the credit sales figure.

16 *Creditors ratio*

The trade creditors, or trade payables figure taken from the balance sheet is shown at cost price (that is the amount owed to suppliers), and so must be compared with the cost of sales figure in the same way as with the stock turnover ratio above:

$$\frac{\text{Payables}}{\text{Cost of sales}} \times 365 \qquad \frac{60m}{200m} \times 365 = 109.5 \text{ days}$$

On the balance sheet of Druisdale plc, it happens that the amount for inventories is the same as the amount for payables, and so the two payment periods are the same.

We do not necessarily know what is included in payables. Ideally, we should compare like with like, and payables for raw material purchases would be compared with amount of raw material purchases. As always, we have to use the best information available, and even relatively crude measures can provide valuable information, such as: is the company taking longer to pay their creditors than they did a year ago?

Activity 4.4

Complete the following table for Druisdale by inserting the figures for year 6, and comment on the changes that have taken place.[14]

Ratio	Year 5		Year 6	Comment
12 Sales/fixed assets	300/180	1.67 times		
13 Sales/current assets	300/120	2.5 times		
14 Stock turnover ratio	60 ÷ 200 × 365	109.5 days		
15 Debtors ratio	40 ÷ 300 × 365	48.7 days		
16 Creditors ratio	60 ÷ 200 × 365	109.5 days		

4.4 Stock Market Ratios

Investors can compare the share price of a company with information from that company's financial statements to assess how expensive the share is in relation to the last known level of earnings (income), dividends and underlying asset values.

---

[14] A completed table is provided at the end of the book (see p. 493).

17 *Price/earnings ratio*

'Earnings per share' is a widely used measure and is calculated by dividing the profit for the period by the number of shares that the company has. This shows how much profit was earned for each share. The amount of profit that Druisdale plc earned for its shareholders in year 5, after deducting all expenses and taxation, was £40m. The company had share capital of £100m, all in £1 shares.

$$\text{Earnings per share} = \frac{\text{Profit for the year}}{\text{Number of shares}} \quad \frac{£40m}{100m} = 40p \text{ per share}$$

Investors in that company might think that earnings per share will continue at 40p for the foreseeable future, and be willing to pay five or ten times as much as that for each share; that would result in the share price being £2 or £4. If shareholders are optimistic that future earnings will increase substantially, they might be willing to pay more than ten times as much as the earnings per share figure. At the end of year 5 investors were paying £5.60 for each share, so they must have been reasonably optimistic.

$$\text{P/E ratio} = \frac{\text{Share price}}{\text{Earnings per share}} \quad \frac{£5.60}{40p} = 14$$

A P/E ratio of 14 means that the amount investors are willing to pay for shares is 14 times the last known earnings per share figure. That is not particularly high. If shareholders are very optimistic about the future of a company, they would be prepared to pay much more for the shares, and P/E ratios of 20 or 30 are not unusual. A high P/E ratio suggests that investors are optimistic about the future prospects of the company.

18 *Dividend yield*

Investors are interested not only in the amount of profit that has been earned for them, but also in how much dividend is being paid. Companies usually pay out only a part of their profits as dividends. Druisdale plc paid out dividends of £25 million in year 5 (as shown on the statement of changes in equity). This amounts to 25p per share (there are 100 million shares).

$$\text{Dividend per share} = \frac{\text{Total dividends}}{\text{Number of shares}} \quad \frac{£25m}{100m} = 25p \text{ per share}$$

This may seem like only a modest return for shareholders. They have to pay £5.60, and at that time the last known dividend per share was 25p. The dividend yield is calculated by expressing the dividend per share as a percentage of the share price.

$$\text{Dividend yield} = \frac{\text{Dividend per share}}{\text{Share price}} \times \frac{100}{1} \quad \frac{£0.25}{£5.60} = 4.5\%$$

Investors hope for higher dividends in the future and pay a lot more for shares where substantial growth is expected. If Druisdale's share price doubled (to £11.20), the dividend yield would halve (to about 2.25%).

19 *Dividend cover*

Some companies pay out a higher proportion of their profits than others. If a company pays out only a quarter of its profits as dividends they are more likely to be able maintain dividend levels in the future than a company that pays out most or all of its profits as dividends. Investors may want to know to what extent their dividends are 'covered' by earnings.[15]

Dividend cover[16] can be measured on a 'per share' basis, or in total for the company.

$$\frac{\text{Earning per share}}{\text{Dividend per share}} \quad \text{or} \quad \frac{\text{Total profit for the period}}{\text{Total dividends}}$$

$$\frac{40p}{25p} \quad \text{or} \quad \frac{£40m}{£25m}$$

$$\text{Dividend cover} = 1.6 \text{ times}$$

Companies typically pay out about half of their profits as dividends; on average dividend cover is around 2 (i.e. dividends are covered twice by profits).

20 *Net assets per share* (or balance sheet value per share)

Investors may be interested in the asset value underlying the share price. The balance sheet of Druisdale at the end of year 5 shows net assets as being £180m. This may be calculated in two different ways, each giving the same answer:

  i Non-current assets, plus current assets, minus non-current liabilities, minus current liabilities. £180m + £120m − £60m − £60m = £180m

  ii Total equity = £180m. Obviously it is easier to do it this way, but it is worth making the point that (i) above, which is usually called 'net assets', is equal to total equity

The amount net assets per share is calculated as:

$$\frac{\text{Net assets}}{\text{Number of shares}} \quad \frac{£180m}{100m} = £1.80$$

The value of the shares on the stock market at the time, at £5.60, was much higher. This is usually the case with a successful company: it is worth significantly more than the balance sheet indicates.

Activity 4.5

Complete the following table for Druisdale plc by inserting the figures for year 6, and commenting on the changes that have taken place.[17]

---

[15] Just as debenture holders may want to know to what extent their interest is 'covered' by operating profits, which are available to pay that interest (ratio 4).

[16] Here it is assumes that there are no preference shares.

[17] A completed table is provided at the end of the book (see pp. 492–4).

Ratio	Year 5		Year 6		Comment
17 Price/earnings ratio	£5.60 ÷ 40p	14			
18 Dividend yield	25p ÷ £5.60 × 100	4.5%			
19 Dividend cover	40/25	1.6 times			
20 Net assets per share	£180/100	£1.80			

4.5 Working Capital Management

Working capital management is concerned with balancing two contradictory pressures:

- The need to ensure that there are sufficient funds to pay liabilities as they fall due. Having large sums of money in the bank, and plenty of money due from debtors (plus additional money tied up in stocks) should reassure creditors. If creditors are paid rapidly, the figure for creditors is minimized, and that contributes to maximizing the amount of working capital. The larger the amount of working capital, the more creditors are reassured about the company's solvency.

- The need to ensure the profitable use of capital employed. Having large sums of money tied up in current assets undermines profitability (by increasing capital employed). Similarly, minimizing the amount of creditors undermines profitability (also by increasing capital employed). The smaller the amount of working capital, the greater the profitability is likely to be.

The first of these is about maximizing solvency, and the usual ratios for assessing this are dealt with above.

  1 Current ratio: are there enough current assets to cover current liabilities?

  2 Liquidity ratio: are there enough liquid assets to cover current liabilities?

  16 Creditors ratio: how long does it take to pay creditors? Are we paying them too slowly?

The second is about maximizing profitability, particularly in the utilization of assets (ratio 8, asset turnover). More specifically the main ratios are:

13 Sales/current assets: are current assets excessive in relation to turnover?

14 Stock turnover ratio: are stocks excessive in relation to turnover?[18]

15 Debtors ratio: are debtors taking too long to pay?

16 Creditors ratio: are we paying creditors too quickly to maximize profitability?

Working capital management is considered more fully in Chapter 11.

---

[18] More specifically: stocks in relation to cost of sales.

4.6 Financial Structure/Gearing

The way in which a business is financed is often called *financial structure*. It is particularly concerned with the balance between equity (shareholders' funds) and debt (long-term borrowing). This is also called capital gearing, and is introduced above as ratio number:

> 3 Capital gearing ratio: is there too much borrowing in relation to the amount of equity?

From the point of view of creditors, the lower the gearing (the lower the amount of borrowing), the greater is their security. Low gearing may be seen as an aspect of solvency or financial strength. High gearing suggests high risk.

But high gearing can be advantageous in maximizing profitability. A company may be able to borrow money at modest interest rates, perhaps 6 per cent per annum; they may then be able to invest that money in the business to earn a return[19] of more than, say, 10 per cent. In that situation, maximizing borrowings will maximize profits. But this can be a risky strategy and companies usually seek to avoid excessive borrowings.

Capital gearing is considered more fully in Chapters 9 and 11.

4.7 Limitations and Comparisons

A systematic use of ratios can provide valuable insights into a company's financial position and performance. It is better to have some clear questions in mind than to simply read through the financial statements as presented by the company. Annual reports often emphasize the favourable aspects of a company's performance, and some systematic investigation is required to arrive at a more balanced view. Financial statements provide substantial and increasing amounts of detail, but they can still leave important questions unanswered. A detailed ratio analysis is likely to indicate areas for further investigation at least as much as it produces full and final answers.

Bases for Comparison

The figures and ratios from an analysis of financial statements are meaningful only by comparison with something. The easiest thing, in all companies' accounts, is to compare this year's results with last year's; they are presented side by side for that very purpose. We can immediately see whether a company's financial position and performance are improving or deteriorating, as a whole, and in detail, using many different figures and approaches.

The following comparisons may be used:

1 With previous years for the same company. Published financial statements always show one previous year, but a comparison over a number of years is more valuable

2 With other (similar) companies

3 With other divisions or branches within the same company

---

[19] Ratio 6. Return on total long-term capital employed. The return is measured before deducting the cost of interest.

4 With stock market or sector averages

5 With conventional wisdom, for example about acceptable levels of gearing, or 'safe' current and liquidity ratios

6 With market levels; a return on shareholders' funds may be compared with the general level of interest rates

7 With policy: a company may have a policy of requiring debtors to pay within 45 days

8 With budgeted or planned results. This can indicate the success of management in implementing their plans and achieving the intended results

Limitations of Ratio Analysis

The main limitations of ratio analysis are as follows:

1 What basis for comparison should be used? To know that a company's stock turnover ratio is 64 days does not mean much, except by comparison. Is it better or worse than last year? Or than planned? Or than a similar company? Stock turnover of more than a few weeks would be unacceptable for a fresh food business, but might be quite good in a gift shop.

2 Comparisons may be limited where companies have different accounting policies. Some companies may capitalize software or development expenditure, where others write them off immediately. There may be differences on approaches to depreciation of fixed assets or amortization of goodwill. Some companies' accounting policies are more prudent than others, and some may indulge in 'creative accounting'.

3 Comparisons may be limited where companies have different financing policies. Some companies rely more on overdrafts and short-term borrowing; others rely more on long-term borrowing; others have little or no borrowing. Some companies own most of their fixed assets; others lease them on finance leases (which show up in the financial statements); others lease them on operating leases (which do not show up in the financial statements). Some companies spend substantially on fixed assets every year, others have major expenditure only every 3, or 5, or 10 years. Some companies sell on a cash only basis; others sell partly or mainly on credit. Ratio analysis shows up many of these differences, but care is needed in interpretation, for example where a company changes its policy in a particular year (e.g. reducing short-term debt by issuing shares or debentures).

4 Comparisons may be limited where companies have different policies to achieve growth. Where internal growth is pursued, there may be substantial investments in fixed assets in a particular year that do not earn their keep at first. Where external growth is pursued, substantial amounts may be paid for goodwill in acquiring other companies, with a subsequent charge for impairment; and there may be substantial one-off benefits from rationalization (e.g. closing down operations in some locations where there is duplication).

5 Comparisons may be limited where companies have different operating policies. Some companies do most of their manufacturing in the UK (and so have substantial amounts of fixed assets); others subcontract their manufacturing, perhaps to overseas companies, and so have less money tied up in fixed assets. Some companies produce only for specific orders, or in batches, while others have mass production of standard items: this is likely to affect profit margins and stock levels.

6 Comparisons may be limited where companies have different accounting dates, especially in seasonal businesses. Retailers with a year end a few weeks before Christmas are likely to have substantial stocks and creditors shown on their balance sheets, and perhaps some short-term liquidity problems. The balance sheet of a retailer a few weeks after Christmas is likely to show lower stock levels, and more liquid resources.

7 Results may be influenced substantially in particular years by 'exceptional items', such as losses incurred in closing down a production facility, or profits made in selling particular fixed assets (especially land and buildings).

8 Balance sheets show the position only on a given date. They are not necessarily typical for the whole year. Some companies indulge in 'window dressing' to try to make the position look better at the year end when the financial statements are published.

9 Balance sheets are usually based on historic cost, and the amounts shown for assets are not necessarily their current values. Some fixed assets are revalued from time to time, and in comparing results with different companies, we cannot always be sure that we are comparing like with like. The amount shown for 'equity' on a balance sheet does not usually reflect the current value of the assets; nor does it indicate the market value of the equity (the 'market capitalization') on the stock market.

10 Most of the information included in financial statements is for the business as a whole and so most ratios are an average for the business. Some parts of it are likely to be performing much better than others. Companies produce some 'disaggregated' or 'segmental' information about different parts of the business, but this is rather limited.

11 Financial statements do not normally show the effects of inflation. A company's sales and profits may increase every year, but a 3 per cent increase is not an indication of success if the inflation rate was 4 per cent.

12 Financial statements and their analysis are based on information relating to the past; much of it is inevitably out of date. And the past is not necessarily a guide to the future.

13 Ratio analysis is usually limited to the information that companies are required to show in their published annual reports. There is likely to be a great deal of other information, financial and non-financial, that would be important in evaluating the financial position and performance of a company.

4.8 Ratios Ready Reference

The ratios below are illustrated taking the figures from the financial statements of Garwick Ltd for year 7. Activity 4.6 lists these ratios and invites readers to calculate the equivalent ratios for year 8, and to comment on them. A solution is provided at the end of the book (see p. 494).

Balance sheet of Garwick Ltd as at 31 December

	Year 7 £000	Year 8 £000
Assets		
Non-current assets		
Property, plant and equipment	50	60
Current assets		
Inventories	10	13
Trade receivables	14	16
Cash	18	1
	42	30
Total assets	92	90
Equity and liabilities		
Equity		
Share capital	20	20
Retained earnings	15	20
Total equity	35	40
Non-current liabilities		
Long-term borrowings	40	30
Current liabilities		
Trade payables	17	20
Total liabilities	57	50
Total equity and liabilities	92	90

Income statement of Garwick Ltd for the year ended 31 December

	Year 7 £000	Year 8 £000
Revenue	101	110
Cost of sales	(70)	(74)
Gross profit	31	36
Distribution costs	(7)	(7)
Administrative expenses	(5)	(6)
Operating profit	19	23
Finance costs	(4)	(3)
Profit before tax	15	20
Income tax expense	(4)	(5)
Profit for the period	11	15

Statement of changes in equity of Garwick Ltd for the year ended 31 December

Balance at beginning of year	32	35
Profit for the period	11	15
Dividends	(8)	(10)
Balance at end of year	35	40

Additional information

Garwick Ltd's share capital consists of 100,000 ordinary shares with a nominal value of 20p each. Although the company is too small to be listed on a stock market, for the purpose of this question assume that the share price on 31 December year 7 was £1.87, and on 31 December year 8 it was £2.85.

Four Financial Strength/Solvency Ratios

1 Current ratio (or working capital ratio)

$$
\begin{array}{ccc}
\text{Current assets} & : & \text{Current liabilities} \\
£42,000 & : & £17,000 \\
2.47 & : & 1
\end{array}
$$

2 Liquidity ratio (or quick assets ratio, or acid test)

$$
\begin{array}{ccc}
\text{Current assets excluding inventories} & : & \text{Current liabilities} \\
£32,000 & : & £17,000 \\
1.88 & : & 1
\end{array}
$$

3 Capital gearing ratio (financial gearing, or leverage)

$$
\frac{\text{Long-term borrowings}}{\text{Equity plus long-term borrowings}} \times \frac{100}{1}
$$

$$
\frac{£40,000}{£75,000} \times \frac{100}{1} = 53.3\%
$$

4 Interest times cover

$$
\frac{\text{Profit before deducting interest}}{\text{Interest}} \qquad \frac{£19,000}{£4,000} = 4.75 \text{ times}
$$

Four Overall Profitability Ratios

5 Return on shareholders' funds

$$
\frac{\text{Profit for the period}}{\text{Total equity}} \times \frac{100}{1} \qquad \frac{£11,000}{£35,000} \times \frac{100}{1} = 31.4\%
$$

6 Return on total long-term capital employed

$$
\frac{\text{Operating profit}[20]}{\text{Total equity plus long-term borrowings}} \times \frac{100}{1} \qquad \frac{£19,000}{£75,000} = 25.3\%
$$

7 Operating profit as a percentage of sales (or profit/sales ratio)

$$
\frac{\text{Operating profit}}{\text{Sales}} \times \frac{100}{1} \qquad \frac{£19,000}{£101,000} = 18.8\%
$$

8 Asset turnover

$$
\frac{\text{Sales}}{\text{Operating assets}[21]} \qquad \frac{£101,000}{£75,000} = 1.35 \text{ times}
$$

---

[20] Profit before deducting tax and interest, or EBIT, or gross profit minus operating expenses.

[21] Fixed assets plus current assets minus current liabilities. This is the same as equity plus non-current liabilities.

Three Profitability of Sales Ratios

9 Gross profit ratio

$$\frac{\text{Gross profit}}{\text{Sales}} \times \frac{100}{1} \qquad \frac{£31,000}{£101,000} \times \frac{100}{1} = 30.7\%$$

10 Distribution costs as a percentage of sales

$$\frac{\text{Distribution costs}}{\text{Sales}} \times \frac{100}{1} \qquad \frac{£7,000}{£101,000} \times \frac{100}{1} = 6.9\%$$

11 Administrative expenses as a percentage of sales

$$\frac{\text{Administrative expenses}}{\text{Sales}} \times \frac{100}{1} \qquad \frac{£5,000}{£101,000} \times \frac{100}{1} = 5\%$$

Five Utilization of Assets Ratios

12 Sales/fixed assets

$$\frac{\text{Sales}}{\text{Fixed assets}} \qquad \frac{£101,000}{£50,000} = 2.02 \text{ times}$$

13 Sales/current assets

$$\frac{\text{Sales}}{\text{Current assets}} \qquad \frac{£101,000}{£42,000} = 2.4 \text{ times}$$

14 Stock turnover ratio

$$\frac{\text{Inventories}}{\text{Cost of sales}} \times 365 \qquad \frac{£10,000}{£70,000} \times 365 = 52.1 \text{ days}$$

15 Debtors ratio

$$\frac{\text{Receivables}}{\text{Sales}} \times 365 \qquad \frac{£14,000}{£101,000} \times 365 = 50.6 \text{ days}$$

16 Creditors ratio

$$\frac{\text{Payables}}{\text{Cost of sales}} \times 365 \qquad \frac{£17,000}{£70,000} \times 365 = 88.6 \text{ days}$$

Four Stock Market Ratios

17 Price/earnings ratio (P/E ratio)

$$\frac{\text{Share price}}{\text{Earnings per share}} \qquad \frac{\pounds 1.87}{11\text{p}} \qquad \text{P/E} = 17$$

18 Dividend yield

$$\frac{\text{Dividend}}{\text{Share price}} \times \frac{100}{1} \qquad \frac{8\text{p}}{\pounds 1.87} \times \frac{100}{1} = 4.3\%$$

19 Dividend cover

$$\frac{\text{Earnings per share}}{\text{Dividend per share}} \quad \text{or} \quad \frac{\text{Profit for the period}}{\text{Dividends for the period}}$$

$$\frac{11}{8} \quad \text{or} \quad \frac{\pounds 11,000}{\pounds 8,000} = 1.4 \text{ times}$$

20 Net assets per share (balance sheet value per share)

$$\frac{\text{Total equity}}{\text{Number of shares}} \qquad \frac{\pounds 35,000}{100,000} = \pounds 0.35 \text{ per share}$$

Activity 4.6

Calculate the ratios for Garwick Ltd for year 8 and comment on them.

Ratio	Year 7	Year 8		Comments
1 Current ratio	2.47 : 1			
2 Liquidity ratio	1.88 : 1			
3 Capital gearing ratio	53.3%			
4 Interest times cover	4.75 times			
5 Return on shareholders' funds	31.4%			
6 Return on total long-term capital employed	25.3%			
7 Operating profit as a % of sales	18.8%			
8 Asset turnover	1.35 times			
9 Gross profit ratio	30.7%			
10 Distribution costs as a % of sales	6.9%			
11 Administrative expenses as a % of sales	5%			
12 Sales/fixed assets	2.02 times			

Ratio	Year 7	Year 8		Comments
13 Sales/current assets	2.4 times			
14 Stock turnover ratio	52.1days			
15 Debtors ratio	50.6 days			
16 Creditors ratio	88.6 days			
17 Price/earnings ratio	17			
18 Dividend yield	4.3%			
19 Dividend cover	1.4 times			
20 Net assets per share	£0.35			

Summary

There are a number of conventional ratios that can be calculated from balance sheets and income statements that give a good indication of a company's solvency and profitability. Care is needed in selecting and interpreting the most appropriate figures, and the exercise is more useful if comparisons are made over a number of years. Companies need to be solvent to survive. But profitability is also important, and is best indicated using figures for ROCE. Careful analysis of gross profit, operating profit and various costs as a percentage of sales can indicate where improvements may be made. But utilization of assets is also an essential part of profitability: there should not be excessive assets in relation to the amount of sales generated. Ratio analysis also provides useful insights into the management of working capital and financial structure. Accounting ratios often raise as many questions as they answer, but are a valuable tool of analysis, particularly in making comparisons, provided their limitations are recognized.

There is no limit to the number of ratios that can be calculated. This chapter has concentrated on a few key questions, and a total of 20 widely used ratios that help to answer those questions.

Review of key points

- The current ratio, liquidity ratio, capital gearing ratio and interest times cover can be used to assess a company's solvency, but care is needed in calculating and interpreting them.
- There are two main ways of calculating ROCE; each can be used to assess a company's profitability and how it might be improved.
- One side of ROCE can be used to assess all costs as a proportion of sales.

Review of key points (continued)

■ The second side of ROCE can be used to assess the utilization of each group of assets by relating them to sales.

■ Stock market ratios can be used to assess how expensive shares are in relation to the most recent levels of earnings, dividends and net asset values.

■ The chapter is based around 20 widely used ratios and provides opportunities to practise calculating and interpreting them.

■ Accounting ratios are most useful when used in making comparisons, but care is needed in comparing different types of business and in realizing the limitations of the figures.

■ Published financial statements often contain a lot of detail that is hard to understand; it is important to be clear about key questions, to select the most appropriate figures and to focus on those.

Self-testing questions

1 Describe how to calculate:

   a Current ratio

   b Liquidity ratio

   c Capital gearing ratio

   d Interest times cover

2 Why are inventories excluded from current assets when calculating a liquidity ratio?

3 How is the return on ordinary shareholders' capital employed calculated?

4 If debentures are included as part of capital employed, what figure is used for 'return'? How and why does it differ from the 'return' figure used for calculating return on ordinary shareholders' capital employed?

5 If a company's gross profit ratio has increased, what does that tell us about the volume of sales and selling prices?

6 You are given the following balance sheet information about the Nikkigra Company.

   You are required to comment on the financial position and performance of the company, making use of appropriate ratios.

Self-testing questions (continued)

Balance sheet of Nikkigra as at 31 December

	Year 1 £000	Year 2 £000
Assets		
Non-current assets		
Property, plant and equipment	1,000	900
Current assets		
Inventories	1,200	1,000
Trade receivables	600	500
Cash	68	600
	1,868	2,100
Total assets	2,868	3,000
Equity and liabilities		
Equity		
Ordinary 50p shares	1,000	1,000
Retained earnings	434	500
Total equity	1,434	1,500
Non-current liabilities		
10% Debentures	1,000	900
Current liabilities		
Trade payables	294	451
Taxation	60	65
Proposed dividends	80	84
	434	600
Total liabilities	1,434	1,500
Total equity and liabilities	2,868	3,000

Income statement of Nikkigra for the year ended 31 December

	Year 1 £000	Year 2 £000
Revenue	3,600	3,780
Cost of sales	3,225	3,396
Gross profit	375	384
Distribution costs	(50)	(48)
Administrative expenses	(30)	(31)
Operating profit	295	305
Finance costs: interest	(100)	(90)
Profit before tax	195	215
Income tax expense	(60)	(65)
Profit for the period	135	150

Statement of changes in equity of Nikkigra for the year ended 31 December

	Year 1	Year 2
Balance at beginning of year	1,379	1,434
Profit for the period	135	150
Dividends	(80)	(84)
Balance at end of year	1,434	1,500

Assessment questions

1 Why would you expect retailers to have lower current ratios than manufacturers?

2 What information (in addition to the current ratio, liquidity ratio, capital gearing ratio and interest times cover) would you want to assess a company's solvency?

3 Accounting ratios are said to be most useful when making comparisons. If you had a set of ratios for a company, what comparisons would you make?

4 What are the main limitations of accounting ratios?

5 How could a company increase its profitability when sales are falling (assuming that they are unable to increase sales)?

6 You are given the following balance sheet information about the Jackdan Company. You are required to comment on the financial position and performance of the company, making use of appropriate ratios.

Balance sheet of Jackdan Ltd as at 31 December

	Year 1 £000	Year 2 £000
Assets		
Non-current assets		
Property, plant and equipment	300	330
Current assets		
Inventories	70	90
Trade receivables	50	70
Cash	30	40
	150	200
Total assets	450	530
Equity and liabilities		
Equity		
Ordinary 50p shares	200	200
Retained earnings	50	60
Total equity	250	260
Non-current liabilities		
8% Debentures	100	150
Current liabilities		
Trade payables	38	45
Taxation	32	40
Proposed dividends	30	35
	100	120
Total liabilities	200	270
Total equity and liabilities	450	530

Assessment questions (continued)

Income statement of Jackdan Ltd for the year ended 31 December

	Year 1 £000	Year 2 £000
Revenue	492	550
Cost of sales	(369)	(410)
Gross profit	123	140
Distribution costs	(12)	(12)
Administrative expenses	(10)	(9)
Operating profit	101	119
Finance costs: interest	(8)	(12)
Profit before tax	93	107
Income tax expense	(32)	(40)
Profit for the period	61	67

Statement of changes in equity of Jackdan Ltd for the year ended 31 December

Balance at beginning of year	239	250
Profit for the period	61	67
Dividends	(50)	(57)
Balance at end of year	250	260

Group activities and discussion questions

1 Which is more important: increasing ROCE, or increasing earnings per share, and why? Can a company increase its earnings per share year after year, although its ROCE is steadily falling?

2 In what circumstances can a substantial improvement in a company's position result in a reduction in their ROCE?

3 In what circumstances can a steady increase in a company's ROCE be a symptom of a company being in decline?

4 Most companies' profitability is lower than it should be because they have too much money tied up in assets. They should aim to have a zero level of assets. This would lead to a ROCE of infinity. Discuss the practicability of these suggestions.

5 Most efforts to reduce the amount of funds tied up in assets are wasted because one type of asset is turned into another: inventories and surplus buildings become receivables and cash. The total capital employed, and the total profitability is unaffected. Discuss the validity of these statements.

6 The Executive Service Company has high levels of stock, and fine premises; their sales/net assets ratio is 1 : 1. The QuickValue Service Company has low levels of stock, and backstreet premises; their sales/net assets ratio is 2 : 1. Does that mean that the QuickValue Service Company is more profitable?

Making use of this example, discuss the idea that the use of ratios shows the effects of companies choosing to do business in different ways; ratios do not indicate how businesses should be run.

Financial accounting in context

Here comes a bankruptcy boom

By Iain Dey

Daily Telegraph, 30 July 2006

Discuss and comment on the following item taken from the press with particular reference to assessing when gearing levels are too high.

Source: Reproduced with permission by the *Daily Telegraph*.

'WE THINK OF ourselves as the eraser on Wall Street's pencil," says Wilbur Ross, the investor more commonly known as the King of Bankruptcy. "And we are expecting to see plenty of opportunities over the next couple of years."

Ross has made a career out of buying companies at death's door. Last week, he sold his boutique investment firm, WL Ross, to Amvescap, the fund management group, in a £200m deal.

At 68, one could be forgiven for assuming that Ross was planning to retire. In fact, he has committed to staying on for at least five years; he struck the deal with Amvescap partly to give WL Ross access to the additional financial muscle he believes it will need to get involved in bigger and more complicated rescue deals.

As far as Ross is concerned, corporate insolvencies will inevitably start to rise within the next few months. Debt levels are too high, margins too slim and valuations unrealistic. And he is not alone in believing that some of the big deals completed in recent years will turn sour.

In the UK, the major lending banks have been tightening the terms of their loans and adding staff to their "work-out teams" – the bankers who sort out problematic corporate debts. Law and accountancy firms have been recruiting heavily for their restructuring teams in anticipation of problems ahead. Investment banks have been doing likewise at the same time as beefing up their distressed debt trading desks.

And there are an increasing number of finance houses raising recovery funds similar to those run by Ross – Alchemy Partners and HSBC are both marketing recovery funds to investors.

Nonetheless, the appetite for debt seems insatiable. Last week the biggest-ever bid tabled by a private equity company was launched when Kohlberg Kravis Roberts agreed a deal worth more than $30bn (£16bn) to buy HCA, the American healthcare firm. What is more, Blackstone, another heavyweight private equity player, is attempting to trump the deal.

"We are at a very interesting inflection point," explains Ross. "In 2006 to date, default rates of high-yield bonds are at historic lows globally, down around the 1 per cent level. But looking at some of the transactions being done, it seems clear to me there will be a very high propensity for those to go into work-out.

"A few weeks ago we submitted a bid for a company to bring it out of bankruptcy. Then a bank – a regular commercial bank – came along with a competing proposal toward which they were willing to lend more dollars than we were willing to pay for the whole company. That totally staggered me. It was a sizeable company, a $700m transaction. Either we're totally nuts or they are. Time will tell."

The high levels of debt being taken on by companies in private equity deals are the main concern behind fears that a collapse could be coming. Even though economic conditions are benign and interest rates, although on the rise, remain low, the extraordinary levels of gearing in corporate buyouts have left little room for operating targets to be missed. Any operational shortcoming could push companies into breach of debt covenants and spark financing difficulties.

In 2002 the average European buyout deal was priced at nine times earnings, according to research for *The Sunday Telegraph* based on Mergermarket data. Last year, that figure crept up to 11.2 times earnings, and in the first six months of this year it nudged up to 12.5. The amount of debt being taken on to support those buyout deals is rising even faster. In 2001 the total amount of debt in the average buyout deal was roughly 3.8 times the earnings of the company being acquired. This figure now stands at 7.8.

"The significance of [such] statistics is quite simple to see," explains Ross. "When you put that kind of value on something, then you leverage it to a high degree, what you've done is reduce the margin of error available to management. We believe that while default rates have been low in 2006, as we move out into 2007 they will have doubled and tripled and eventually, maybe into the latter part of 2007 and 2008, they will be running above the historic average."

Alan Hudson, a corporate restructuring partner at Ernst & Young, also anticipates problems. "With businesses as geared as they are, there's not going to be a lot of leeway. If they start to underperform, they will hit problems very quickly and soon find themselves sitting round the table with their stakeholders."

Official government insolvency statistics due to be published at the end of this week are expected to show a jump of about 25 per cent in the total number of companies going into administration or liquidation in the UK.

Some of the mid-market retailers that have been taken private in recent years are among those expected to encounter difficulties over the next few months, according to insolvency experts. There have already been signs of trouble in the sector; for example, Hamsard, the fashion retailer behind the QS and Be-Wise fashion chains, went into administration in March and was subsequently rescued.

A clutch of private equity-backed retailers, such as Focus, the DIY chain, Maplin Electronics and Ethel Austin, all had to renegotiate the terms of their debt last year.

Further clues on the health of the corporate credit environment should emerge later this week as each of the UK's Big Five banks reveals its half-year results. Broadly speaking, the City believes the banks will indicate that credit quality remains fairly good. But there will be some signs of weakness emerging. Lloyds TSB has warned that impairment charges in its wholesale banking division will be sharply higher than last year, although that is from a low base.

But the big banks are not the guide to credit quality they once were. Turnaround experts say it is increasingly rare to find themselves dealing with the banks that wrote a company's debt by the time it is in trouble. Increasingly, the banks are selling off their bad loans in the secondary debt market, where a proliferation of hedge funds and investment bank trading desks are active, creating a huge pool of liquidity.

Bonds are highly sought after, thanks to the need for steady cash flows being demanded by pension funds and charities, which have been increasing their exposure to bonds over the past two to three years. Even junk bonds are popular. According to research by Close Brothers, only 1 per cent of the high-yield bonds issued in 2001 were rated CCC, or junk, at the time of their issue. In 2005 that figure was closer to 30 per cent.

"Right now it is pretty difficult for any mid to large-sized company to go bust," says Andrew Merrett, a director of the European Special Situations group at Close Brothers. "People out there want to restructure the balance sheet and put in operational turnaround guys. There's a great supply of new money in the marketplace to refinance them."

He adds: "You could have an increase in restructuring activity without having a massive downturn in the economy, and that's mainly because of what's been going on in the debt market. You've got much greater complexity in deal structures, and the availability of money has led to a deterioration in the credit quality of some of the issuers. Those factors combined will inevitably unwind in the next couple of years."

Although there is lots of money available to refinance companies, this in turn is making the structure of those deals more complicated and hence more difficult to unravel.

Similarly, as private equity deals have increased in size, so has their complexity. With all those elements of the debt tradeable, it can often be difficult for companies to know who their creditors are, let alone who would be owed what in any restructuring proposal.

Hedge funds are changing the shape of insolvencies, as they are all areas of the financial markets. Many restructuring experts believe their appetite for risk is helping to keep afloat companies that would previously have been closed down. Others argue that the liquidity in the debt markets is such that the parties negotiating a rescue package for a troubled company will change so often during the course of the negotiations that it is impossible ever to reach an agreement.

"The participation of hedge funds in distressed debt is not guaranteed long-term," says Ross. "Right now a lot of hedge funds are coming into it because they can borrow at a cheaper rate than they are lending. But what's going to happen when these debts start to default?"

References and further reading

Lewis, R., D. Pendrill and D. Simon (2003) *Advanced Financial Accounting* (7th edition). FT Prentice Hall.

McKenzie, W. (2003) *Financial Times Guide to Using and Interpreting Company Accounts* (3rd edition). FT Prentice Hall.

Pendlebury, M. and R. Groves (2003) *Company Accounts: Analysis, Interpretation and Understanding* (6th edition). Thomson Learning.

Sugden A., P. Gee and G. Holmes (2004) *Interpreting Company Reports and Accounts*. FT Prentice Hall.

www.cifc.co.uk (select: benchmarking and interfirm comparison; a standardized basis for using ratios to compare different firms)

Profits: Definitions, Role and Measurement

❖ LEARNING OBJECTIVES

After studying this chapter you should be able to:

❖ Explain the main functions of profit measurement

❖ Appreciate that there are different ways of defining and measuring profit

❖ Relate profit measurement to economic theory

❖ Understand how the balance sheet approach to profit measurement can differ from the income statement approach

❖ Identify different elements of profit in published accounts and appreciate their relevance in predicting profits

❖ Understand the limitations of historic cost (HC) accounts in a period of rising prices

❖ Evaluate proposed changes including current purchasing power (CPP) and current cost accounting (CCA)

5.1 Introduction

Nearly everyone seems to believe that profit is important, even if they are not sure why. But they do not seem to know what 'profit' means, or how to define it, or how to measure it. This chapter explores these issues. The first section explains why profit figures are important: there are several good and different reasons for measuring it and reporting it. The second part of the chapter examines in more detail two main ways of measuring profit: the income statement approach; and the balance sheet approach. In practice, at present, the two different approaches produce the same figure. But profit figures often do not provide the information that people want or expect from them. Any attempt to provide 'better' or more useful profit figures ought to be based on some clear theoretical basis if we are to have credible profit figures that are comparable from one organization to another.

5.2 Functions of Profit Measurement

The widespread belief that profit is important is based on the idea that profit figures tell us something useful. Profit figures may be useful in many different ways.

As a Guide to Dividend Decisions

The more profit a company makes, the more it can pay out as dividends. The idea of capital maintenance is important: dividends are paid out of profits, not out of shareholders' capital. Profits must be calculated after making provision for depreciation so that, as the useful life of assets declines, the amount of shareholders' funds invested in assets does not. Charging depreciation ensures that an equivalent amount stays within the business, whether in the form of cash or other net assets, and is not paid out as dividends.

When companies decide how much of their profits to pay out as dividends they consider other factors, not just the current year's profit. In some years, even if profits are very low, they may maintain, or even increase dividends. But they cannot do this indefinitely. In the long run, profits are the main guide to dividend decisions. The 1985 Companies Act limits the amount a company can distribute as dividends to the total of accumulated, realized profits, less accumulated losses.

Measuring the amount of profit available for distribution as dividends may also be seen as measuring how much can be consumed during a period without reducing the amount of capital at the beginning of the year, that is without 'living off capital'.

To Indicate Cash Generated

Many people talk about making money as if it is the same as making profits. The differences between cash flow and profit are central to financial accounting, and are illustrated in the examples at the end of this book (see pp. 441–7), and explained in Chapter 7. To some extent we could argue that it is mainly a matter of timing: in the end, all profits should eventually show up as cash. Profits may be tied up in inventories and receivables, but, in due course, the stocks are sold, and the debtors pay up. But profits may also be tied up in additional fixed assets and used up in other ways (such as paying off long-term debt or

The Quirkar Company was established on 1 January year 1 with £10,000 capital. The business bought and sold second-hand cars. All profits generated were either paid out as dividends, or used to increase the stocks of cars. At the end of year 3 the company's balance sheet was as follows:

	£
Stocks of cars	100,000
Share capital	10,000
Retained earnings	90,000
	100,000

ILLUSTRATION 5.1

reducing the company's own share capital). Although we can say that profits do generate cash, there is no reason to expect profits will still be around as cash at any given time.

The Companies Act requirement that dividends should be paid only out of *realized* profits goes along with the idea that profits turn up as cash, and are 'available'. Profits are realized when a sale is made. Unrealized profits, such as those that result from revaluing buildings and other fixed assets, are not available for distribution as dividends – until the assets are sold, and the profits are realized.

Even the idea of profits being 'available' for distribution as dividends implies that profits are a pool of cash that can be used either to pay out as dividends, or to spend on more fixed assets, or whatever the company chooses to do with them. It is one of the hardest things for non-accountants to understand: reserves or retained earnings are not cash. The fact that reserves are not usually available as cash is shown in Illustration 5.1.

The company has made £90,000 profit,[1] but none of it is 'available' to pay out dividends because, as the profit and cash flow was generated, it was all paid out, and more cars were bought. Legally, £90,000 is 'available' to pay out as dividends; but in cash terms there is nothing available – only cars.

Although the idea of using profit figures to indicate the amount of cash that a company has generated may have some popular appeal, it must be rejected as misleading, impracticable and simply wrong. It is more useful to examine cash flow statements to see what has happened to the profits that have been generated.

To Indicate How (Un)successful the Management of the Company is

Companies are expected to make profits. Shareholders elect directors to run the company for them. If the directors manage the company successfully they will make lots of profit for the shareholders. If they do not make decent profits, then they are failing and should be got rid of. This might be a bit simplistic, but it is essentially what companies are about.

A more sophisticated version would be that the aim of the financial management of companies is to maximize shareholder wealth; shareholder wealth is made up of dividends and the value of the shares; maximizing profits is likely to maximize dividends and share

---

[1] It probably made much more, some of which was paid out as dividends; the £90,000 is retained earnings, after paying out dividends.

price. It is easy to make lots of profits if the company has lots of capital employed; profits as a proportion of capital employed are, therefore, most important.

It might be possible to think up circumstances where directors succeed in maximizing shareholders' wealth without making much profit. This was happening during the dotcom bubble as share prices went up to unsustainable levels. But it is difficult to maximize share-holders' wealth for very long without making profits. In most circumstances, directors have to deliver good and increasing profits if they are to be seen as performing well. We should not be surprised to find that directors sometimes try to manipulate profit figures to make their performance look better. Some naïve economists seem to believe that there are such things as 'correct' profit figures, and if we have proper accounting and auditing standards, directors would not be able to indulge in such creative accounting. But, as will become increasingly clear, there are no 'correct' profit figures; there are many difficult areas in profit measurement; and profit figures in practice are, at least in part, the result of negotiation rather than 'economic reality' (whatever that is!).

As a Basis for Taxation

Governments expect companies to pay corporation tax on their profits and so have an interest in the way in which profits are measured. In the UK, HM Revenue and Customs lays down rules for profit measurement for taxation purposes, and these rules are different from those used for financial reporting. This sometimes surprises people from some other countries where companies had to follow the rules laid down by taxation authorities for financial reporting purposes. It does not surprise those who just assume that there is something dis-honest about it: some profits are hidden from the tax authorities. But there is nothing dishonest about it; there are two distinct regimes for profit measurement, and two sets of rules.

Current trends for the harmonization of accounting standards on an international basis are likely to end the system in those countries where government taxation rules have to be followed for financial reporting purposes. But, one day, the argument could be turned on its head. At present the International Accounting Standards Board (IASB) seems to be making a good job of producing International Financial Reporting Standards, but the history of these things is not encouraging. The day may come when the accounting standard setters lose credibility and there is a call for the rules for profit measurement to be laid down by governments and tax authorities.

To Guide Investors in Deciding to Buy or Sell a Company's Shares

The main users of financial accounts are supposed to be investors, particularly (a) those who are thinking of buying shares in the company; and (b) those who already have shares in the company and are considering selling them, or deciding whether to retain the ones they already have. These investors want to know about future performance and hope that the profits of the last few years will provide the appropriate guidance. The priority is therefore to find profit figures that have predictive value. One way of forecasting future profits is to analyse previous years' profits into various elements, some of which are likely to continue along with known trends, some of which are one-off, some of which are coming to an end. In recent years official disclosure requirements have specified increasingly detailed analysis of the various different elements of profit, as shown in Section 5.3.

To Guide Creditors

Creditors may be more interested in the balance sheet, to calculate current ratios, liquidity ratios and gearing ratios. But, in assessing a company's ability to pay amounts due to creditors, it is not just the assets available at the balance sheet date that matter; it is also the company's ability to generate assets, particularly in the form of profits. If a company is making losses, the security that creditors see in assets can soon disappear as the assets are diminished by losses.

We could say that investors and creditors are mainly interested in the future cash flows that the company will generate, and that principles for profit measurement should be selected to provide the best basis for prediction. Perhaps the companies themselves should provide more predictions.

Profit figures are used as a survival indicator. A company that makes profits is more likely to survive than one that makes losses. Various sophisticated versions of 'Z scores' have been developed to predict corporate failure that incorporate measures of working capital, debt and equity; but the biggest single element is usually some measure of profitability.

To Indicate Economic Efficiency

Efficiency is concerned with the relationship between inputs and outputs. An organization that maximizes the ratio of outputs to inputs is maximizing efficiency. There are, of course, difficulties in defining the inputs and outputs that should be counted, and how to measure them. In a company, the simplest approach is to say that the main output is sales or revenues; and the main input is costs. The difference between sales and costs is profit. Maximizing profit, therefore, maximizes efficiency. Efficiency can be increased by (a) increasing sales; (b) reducing costs; (c) increasing sales and costs, but increasing sales by more than the increase in costs; (d) reducing sales and costs, but reducing costs more than the reduction in sales. This is all very simplistic, and the overall approach could ignore many inefficiencies. It also ignores costs to society, and costs to employees and other interested parties. This idea does, however, underlie much of our thinking: a profitable company is efficient; an unprofitable company is inefficient. In organizations that are not primarily intended to make profits, it is more difficult to assess efficiency.

A profitable company is also assumed to be an effective company. Effectiveness is concerned with the relationship between outputs and objectives. An effective organization is one that achieves its objectives. If we assume that profitability is a primary objective of companies, then it is also a measure of effectiveness.

Profits are also assumed to be concerned with efficiency in the economy as a whole, particularly the allocation of resources in the economy. The most profitable companies will attract investment and resources most easily; companies that are not profitable will have difficulty in finding funds for investment. Investment in the economy, therefore, goes to the most profitable, and so the most efficient, organizations.

This idea is also rather simplistic; but in attempting to understand what goes on in the economy, and how it is justified, these arguments about efficiency and effectiveness should not be ignored.

To Indicate Anything You Like

Profit figures seem to be quoted in many different contexts to indicate a wide variety of different matters of concern to individuals, groups or society. Employees and their representatives are likely to look at profits as an indicator of how much companies can afford to pay out in wage increases, or as an argument against closures and redundancies. Socialists may see profits as an indicator of how much companies exploit others. Profits are also relevant in any government-imposed price controls, for example with privatized utility companies. Such companies are usually allowed to make a reasonable return on capital, but are not expected to use their monopoly or near monopoly positions to make excessive profits.

Different profits figures seem to be required for different purpose. It is reasonable to expect financial statements to identify different versions of profit to meet the needs of the various different users of financial statements.

5.3 Different Elements of Profit

It might be appealing to have a single profit figure that tells us everything that we want to know about a business, but businesses make profits in different ways, and from different sources, some of which might be expected to continue, and some of which are more exceptional, or are derived from parts of the business that have since been disposed of. Financial reporting standards require the reporting of different elements, including those that arise from different segments of the business; discontinued operations; exceptional items; and income from investments.

Segments

It is sometimes surprising to find that a company operates a number of very different business segments. Marks and Spencer sell pensions; British Gas sells electricity; GUS (primarily a retailer) owns a credit rating agency, which it may de-merge. There are different geographical segments (such as the UK, Europe and Asia) and different business segments (such as men and women's clothes; or retail and wholesale).

International Accounting Standard (IAS) 14 requires companies to disclose information about the assets, liabilities, revenues, expenses and 'result' (operating profit) for each segment. Disclosure of information about the different segments of a business is usually shown in a note to the accounts. Illustration 5.2 shows part of Ted Baker's segmental disclosures. The company also provides equivalent information for geographical segments, though there are only two (the UK and Other).

When making forecasts of the performance of a company, it is useful to identify separate segments where different growth rates and economic and competitive conditions may be identified. Detailed examination of Ted Baker's results might, for example, show that sales of menswear are growing faster than sales of womenswear; that retail sales are growing slightly faster than wholesale sales, but wholesale sales are much more profitable.

2) Segment information

The revenue and profit before taxation are attributable to the Group's principal activities, the design and contracted manufacture of high quality fashion clothing and related accessories for wholesale and retail customers.

a) Analysis of revenue by brand

	52 weeks ended 28 January 2006	52 weeks ended 29 January 2005
	£'000	£'000
Menswear	66,403	57,137
Womenswear	45,920	41,492
Other	5,509	7,124
	117,832	105,753

b) Primary reporting format – divisional segments

52 weeks ended 28 January 2006	Retail	Wholesale	Total
	£'000	£'000	£'000
Revenue	80,055	37,777	117,832
Cost of sales	(27,136)	(21,843)	(48,979)
Gross Profit	52,919	15,934	68,853
Operating costs	(44,081)	(10,265)	(54,346)
Operating contribution	8,838	5,669	14,507
Other operating income			3,827
Operating profit			18,334
Net finance income			20
Profit before taxation			**18,354**
Total assets	47,816	19,846	67,662
Total liabilities	(17,308)	(8,182)	(25,490)
	30,508	11,664	42,172
Capital expenditure	4,692	403	5,095
Depreciation	3,518	302	3,820

52 weeks ended 29 January 2005	Retail	Wholesale	Total
	£'000	£'000	£'000
Revenue	71,669	34,084	105,753
Cost of sales	(23,795)	(19,562)	(43,357)
Gross Profit	47,874	14,522	62,396
Operating costs	(39,977)	(9,529)	(49,506)
Operating contribution	7,897	4,993	12,890
Other operating income			3,515
Operating profit			16,405
Net finance expenses			(153)
Profit before taxation			**16,252**
Total assets	43,274	16,235	59,509
Total liabilities	(15,376)	(7,303)	(22,679)
	27,898	8,932	36,830
Capital expenditure	6,996	503	7,499
Depreciation	3,220	231	3,451

ILLUSTRATION 5.2 Ted Baker plc 2006 annual report (extract)

Discontinued Operations

It is not unusual for companies to change the range of products and services that they offer; to sell off substantial parts of their business; and to buy new businesses. With some companies, it sometimes seems that it is a story of constant change: underperforming parts of the business are disposed of; new parts are acquired and developed. If investors are trying to predict future profits, figures for the year that has just ended may be very misleading. It is not much use basing profit predictions on figures that include products that the company no longer provides. Care is also needed with predictions based on newly acquired lines of business; they may grow more quickly than existing lines of business; and last year's profit figures may include only a month or two of the new line of business.

In Illustration 5.3 the Oke Company has one line of business that is discontinued; one line of business that is continuing; and one newly acquired line of business. Without the detailed analysis, the picture is one of a modest decline (1 per cent) in sales, and a slightly larger decline (4 per cent) in operating profit. A potential investor might reasonably assume that the pattern will continue. By looking at the different segments we can see that if Bokes are discontinued, and excluded from the results, sales of Cokes have increased by 2 per cent and operating profit on them has increased by 4.6 per cent. With the addition of the new product, Dokes, it no longer seems to be a declining business.

There are different ways of dealing with a decline in sales and profits. Where it is decided to introduce new products or divisions, and withdraw from poorly performing ones, segmental reporting can show the effectiveness of these actions.

Income statements are required to show separately the revenues, expenses and pre-tax profit of discontinued operations.

Exceptional Items

Some elements of the previous year's profit (or loss) need to be regarded separately in making predictions of future profits. There are often exceptional, extraordinary or one-off items that are not likely to be repeated. Examples might include profits or losses resulting

---

The Oke Company makes Bokes and Cokes. Bokes are not very profitable and the company ceased producing them in the autumn of year 8. On 1 December year 8 they bought a Doke manufacturing business, and they believe that the demand for Dokes will increase rapidly. Their results for the years ending 31 December years 7 and 8 may be summarized as follows:

	Year 7	Year 8
Sales (of Bokes, Cokes and Dokes)	£1,000,000	990,000
Operating profit	£ 100,000	96,000
Sales of Bokes	500,000	440,000
Sales of Cokes	500,000	510,000
Sales of Dokes	–	40,000
Operating profit Bokes	35,000	20,000
Cokes	65,000	68,000
Dokes	–	8,000

ILLUSTRATION 5.3

from the disposal of a major part of the business; costs of a significant reorganization; the results of war and terrorism; uninsured losses; damages payable or receivable as a result of a legal case; the effects of epidemics; losses or gains resulting from changes in exchange rates. The list could go on for ever. Some chairman's reports seem to put forward an endless variety of 'exceptional' causes of poor results: the Central line was not working; a flu epidemic; a health or safety scare; the sales manager broke her leg while skiing; the lorry broke down; Mary had a headache; the cat had kittens.

Some of these 'exceptional' items are, of course, very genuine, and it is helpful for investors to be able to identify them and to quantify the financial effects of them. Companies have enormous discretion over what they disclose as 'exceptional'. In the end, the final earnings per share (EPS) figure must take into account all these so-called exceptional items, whether they are favourable or unfavourable. They should not be hidden. Companies are free to disclose more than one version of their EPS. Their basic EPS figure should follow all the accounting rules to make sure it is after charging (and crediting) just about everything. Many companies also disclose an alternative measure of EPS. It is always worth looking at the justification for such an alternative. Sometimes it seems that companies are saying that (their version of) EPS increased from 10p to 12p because of good management. But if we take into account the loss on disposal of their premises in Amblebridge, the costs of a reorganization, depreciation of premises and amortization of goodwill (as the accounting rules say we should), their EPS actually fell to 4p. Analysts seem unclear and inconsistent in how they treat alternative measures of EPS. Sometimes sophisticated analysis is built up on the basis of very dubious earnings figures.

Following the adoption of International Accounting Standards, the term 'exceptional' is disappearing from financial statements, but there are still plenty of such specially identified items disclosed. In 2005 and 2006 Morrison Supermarkets showed two versions of their results including, and excluding, the costs of integration and conversion of Safeway stores. Ottakar's showed two exceptional items in 2005 amounting to £5.5 million; these were for asset impairment, and for 'corporate activity' (costs relating to a proposed merger). Tesco showed profit arising on property-related items (£77 million) and a loss of £10 million from discontinuing an operation (selling their Taiwan operation to Carrefour partly in exchange for Carrefour's Czech and Slovakian operations).

Investment Income, Subsidiaries, Associates, Joint Ventures

Large companies usually have investments in other companies and the shareholders of an investing company are provided with information on the performance of these investments in three main categories:

1 *Subsidiary companies*   Where the investing company has a controlling interest in other companies, all the revenues, expenses, assets and liabilities are included in the consolidated (or group) income statement and balance sheet. If a proportion of the subsidiary company belongs to outside shareholders, this 'minority interest' is also shown.

2 *Associates and joint ventures*   Sometimes the investing company has 'significant influence' over companies in which it has invested, but not enough influence to control those companies. Typically, this would be a shareholding of between 20 per cent and

50 per cent. With these investments the group accounts include the group's share of the profits (or losses) of the associates and joint ventures. The group balance sheet shows the investment as an asset that increases as the companies make and retain profits (but the investment is reduced if they make losses).

3 *Simple investments*   Where the investing company has shares in another company, but exercises no control or significant influence, the position is simpler. The investing company takes credit for dividends receivable (not profits or losses; they have no influence over these); and on the balance sheet the investment is usually shown at cost, with a note of its current market value.

The financial performance of each of these categories of investment can be noted. A return on capital employed (ROCE) can be calculated for each category, and trends can be monitored.

Accounting disclosure requirements in recent years have required increasingly detailed disclosure of the items that make up profit for the year. Users of financial statements are able to select particular figures and, in effect, define profits in their own way. There can be no single measure of profit that suits all purposes and the standard setters have developed the idea that profit figures are made up of many very different elements, and discouraged the idea of a single figure that suits all purposes. But, somehow, journalists, analysts and others seem to be attached to the idea of a single, correct figure that tells us all we want to know. Over the years, income statements have steadily provided more detail, and more analysis. But they always finish with the EPS figure – a single figure that is presented as if it encapsulates everything.

5.4 Two Approaches to Profit Measurement

There are two basic approaches to profit measurement. One is based on the income statement; the second is the balance sheet approach.

In the first approach, the *income statement* takes priority. The emphasis would be on reporting revenues, and carefully determining the costs that should be matched against those revenues in order to determine the amount of profit. The balance sheet would then be a statement of left-over balances with no pretence that they represent the current *value* of assets.

When we measure depreciation, the emphasis is on profit measurement: we allocate the cost of the asset over its estimated useful life. There is no pretence that the balance left over after a few years' depreciation represents the current value of the asset.

Profit may be defined as sales and any other revenues earned during a period, minus the costs incurred in earning those sales and revenues. This seems straightforward enough. Sales are not very hard to identify, and most costs are obvious. Both are shown on a profit and loss account or income statement. It starts off with showing the sales figure, then the cost of goods sold is deducted to give a gross profit figure; then various other expenses are deducted to give net profit figures (before tax, then after tax).

Determining exactly which costs should be 'matched' against the revenues of a period is, in most cases, done with little difficulty, although it does mean dealing with asset values, or 'unexpired costs'.

If a company buys goods for £100, and sells half of them for £120, they have made £70 profit. The cost of goods was £100, but half of the costs are 'unexpired' or unsold: those stocks are still there to be shown as assets on the balance sheet. The gross profit requires the 'cost of goods sold' to be deducted from sales.

Accountants have traditionally been prudent in valuing closing inventories. They may be difficult to sell, and they may eventually have to be sold for less than the cost price of £50. Accountants should be prudent. The figure for closing stock needs to be assessed carefully and it may not be acceptable simply to show it at cost price. Christmas trees sell well in December, but not in January. A hit record may be almost impossible to sell a few months after it has peaked. It is not prudent enough to show stocks always at cost. When the net realizable value of the stocks is less than the cost price, the closing stock must be written down. In the above example, if the net realizable value of the closing stock, which had cost £50, was only £35, then the cost of goods sold[2] would be £65, and the gross profit would be £55. If the closing stock value falls by £15, then profit falls by £15.

There are also problems in the treatment of fixed assets, and calculating depreciation based on estimates of how long the asset's useful life will be, and what its scrap value will be at the end of its life. There may also be problems with debtors (and estimating provisions for bad debts) and other assets or unexpired costs.[3]

Most revenues and expenses can be established with reasonable certainty and accuracy, but there are inevitably some difficult or subjective areas in profit measurement.

In the second approach the *balance sheet* could take priority. The emphasis would be on correct definition and valuation of assets and liabilities. Any increase in a company's net asset value would be the profit figure.[4] This is an 'all inclusive' version of profit. The emphasis of financial accounting would change from being mainly the recording and summarizing of transactions (at cost price) to being mainly concerned with the valuation of assets. The income statement would be downgraded, but would provide some detailed breakdown of the elements that have made up the overall gain.

Profit would be calculated as the increase in net assets during a period (after deducting any additional share capital sub-scribed, and adding back any dividends paid), as shown in Illustration 5.4.

Conventional accounting uses both approaches at the same time with a statement of changes in equity to reconcile the income statement with the balance sheet. At present,

Net assets at 31 December year 4	£45 million
Net assets at 1 January year 4	£35 million
Increase during year	£10 million
Minus Additional proceeds of share issue	(£5 million)
Plus Dividends paid	£7 million
Profit for year	£12 million

ILLUSTRATION 5.4

---

[2] Cost of goods sold, or cost of sales, is opening inventory (zero), plus purchases (£100), minus closing inventory (£35) = £65.

[3] Sometimes the benefit from paying for something (such as advertising or development expenditure) may extend over several periods and it is necessary to determine how much of it is to be treated as an expense in the current period, and how much should be carried forward as an unexpired cost, or asset, to future periods.

[4] Except that any additional share capital has to be deducted, and any dividends have to be added back.

some accounting figures are an uneasy compromise between income measurement and asset measurement.

Unfortunately, it is not possible to measure profits without having to decide on the amount to be shown for some assets. To measure cost of goods sold an amount for closing stock has to be shown. The requirement to charge depreciation also means that some value for fixed assets has to appear on the balance sheet.

Similarly, in an income statement credit is taken for all sales, even if payment has not yet been received for them. The amounts that debtors owe from sales are shown on the balance sheet as receivables. But it is likely that a proportion of debtors will not pay up, and a provision for bad debts is made, and this, in effect, becomes a revaluation of debtors.

Even if we decide that the income statement is most important, we cannot avoid having to determine some asset values for the balance sheet.

Cash Flow Statements

It is important to be clear that the definition and measurement of profit is very different from cash flow. Many people talk about making money and making profits as if they are the same thing. However, we saw in Chapter 2 that profit is not cash flow. This is explained and illustrated in Chapters 7 and 16, and clarified in some of the exercises.

If a business buys some goods for £6, and sells them for £10, it has made £4 gross profit, even if not a penny has changed hands. It is normal business practice to buy goods on credit, and to sell goods on credit. The payment for the goods follows about a month later. But the profit has still been made before any cash has flowed.

If a business buys some goods and pays £6 cash for them, and then sells half of them for £10, which it receives in cash, they have generated a net cash flow of £4. But the gross profit is £7. Gross profit is the difference between sales (£10) and the cost of the goods that have been sold (£3).

A business can generate profits, but if the profits are tied up in inventories and receivables, it can take some time before they materialize as cash. In some circumstances it might be only a matter of time before profits turn up as cash. But a company that is continuing to expand, and to invest in more assets, may find itself short of cash year after year. Profits are used as a guide to dividend decisions. But even if a company makes good profits that appear to justify good dividends, they do not necessarily have enough cash to pay dividends. Cash flow statements indicate what has happened to the cash that profits are supposed to generate, and neatly reconcile profit figures to available cash balances.

5.5 Economic Theory and Profit

Profits cannot be measured without requiring some assets to be valued. The move towards emphasizing asset values and the balance sheet in profit measurement is also influenced by economic theory.

We saw in Chapter 3 that profit and loss accounts (and income statements) originally emerged more as a convenience of bookkeeping than as any serious attempt to measure profit. But with the development of companies, the idea of 'capital maintenance' became essential. This involved no very complex theory. The main change was that fixed assets had to be depreciated: no dividends could be paid except out of profits; and there was no annual profit unless annual provision for depreciation had been made. With high inflation in the 1970s, depreciation provisions had proved to be insufficient, and various *ad hoc* solutions to this problem had been around for 30 years or more. But the great and the good of the accountancy profession sought something more sophisticated: a theoretical basis was required for profit measurement.

The Hicks (1946, p. 172) definition of profit or income can be applied to the dividend decision. He stated that 'The purpose of income calculations in practical affairs is to give people an indication of the amount which they can consume without impoverishing themselves'. The idea of companies 'impoverishing themselves' may seem a little obtuse, and the quotation has been adapted to mean that profit is the amount that a company can pay out as dividends without making itself less 'well off' at the end of the year than it was at the beginning. The emphasis is on how well off a business is – the net worth of its net assets – not how much income it has earned. The idea is that income measurement is based on periodic valuation of assets.

The Hicks definition is derived from ideas expressed by Fisher (1919, p. 38) who stated that:

> Income is derived from capital goods, but the value of the income is not derived from the value of the capital goods. On the contrary, the value of the capital is derived from the value of the income. Not until we know how much income an item will probably bring us can we set any valuation on that capital at all. It is true that the wheat crop depends on the land which yields it. But the value of the crop does not depend on the land. On the contrary, the value of the land depends on its crop.

In a sense this is no more than a statement of the obvious. The value of an asset depends on what you can get out of it. If we want to establish the value of something, we need to estimate the future cash flows that it will produce, and then 'discount'[5] those cash flows to arrive at a net present value. This approach to the valuation of assets (net present value; sometimes called *economic value* or *value in use*) is increasingly important in financial accounting. It is based on *future estimates*, not on recording past transactions.

As we have seen with inventories, receivables and depreciation of fixed assets, it is not possible to measure profits without some estimates of the future benefits that assets will generate. Any measure of profit is, to some extent, dependent on assumptions about the future.

The distinction between the two approaches to profit measurement is not as stark as it might at first appear. The income statement approach depends on asset values. The balance sheet approach necessitates an analysis of the total change in 'well-offness' that an income statement provides. Both approaches have theoretical and practical problems. Chapter 10 deals with problems in the definition and measurement of assets, liabilities, revenues and expenses. In any attempt to decide which approach is 'better', it may be a question of emphasis. The need for accuracy, reliability and verifiability might lead to a preference for

---

[5] To allow for the loss of interest during the periods that we have to wait for the cash flows. Obviously the value *now* of a cash flow receivable in 5 years' time is less than the same cash flow receivable today.

the income statement approach: if revenues and expenses can be reliably measured, reliance on asset valuation can be minimized. The need for a theoretically robust definition of profit (based on measurement of 'well-offness' – with all its subjectivity) might lead to a preference for a balance sheet approach to profit measurement.

5.6 Adjusting Financial Statements for Rising Prices

Financial accounting has always been based on the recording of transactions; transactions are recorded on the basis of costs; and balance sheets and income statements are traditionally based on these 'historic cost' (HC) figures, not current values. But prices change, the value of assets changes, and it has long been recognized that cost figures need to be modified in particular ways. Creditors feel safer if they know assets are worth *at least as much* as the balance sheet shows, and prefer a prudent approach to asset valuation. Fixed assets are depreciated; inventories are shown at the *lower* of cost and net realizable value; and it is recognized that all debtors may not pay up and so a provision for bad debts is created, which reduces the receivables figure accordingly. Companies can continue to show any investments they own at cost or 'book value'; but they also have to show the current market value at the balance sheet date. It would, therefore, be wrong to suggest that we ever had a 'pure' HC system. It has been modified in various ways to reflect changes in prices and values, and to make financial statements more prudent or conservative. As the level of inflation steadily rose after the 1960s, the usefulness of financial statements was increasingly affected, and various *ad hoc* ways of dealing with it were adopted. But there were also pressures to develop different systems of accounting, moving away from HC. Since the peak of the inflation accounting debate, inflation in the UK has fallen from over 20 per cent per annum to less than 4 per cent, and the problem is now seen as theoretical rather than urgent.

The Problem

Price increases affect the usefulness of traditional HC financial accounts in a number of important ways.

1 *The cost of sales is understated*   If a company buys oil at £60 a barrel, and sells it at £65 a barrel, it seems to have made £5 a barrel profit. But if prices are rising, by the time they come to replace the oil that they have sold, it may cost them £64 a barrel to buy. Most of their so-called 'profit' will be used up merely to continue operating at the same level as they were before; they are only £1 a barrel better off; in real terms they have made only £1 a barrel profit.

   The same argument is true with all companies where prices are rising and they need to replace the goods they have sold. It is most obvious with a trading company or a retailer. Part of their 'profits' are needed simply to replace what they have sold because the replacement cost has increased. If they paid out all their profits as dividends, they would no longer be able to afford to finance[6] the same level of operations. They would not have maintained capital in real terms.

---

[6] Unless they had another source of finance, such as borrowing.

Another way of looking at this is to say that there are two kinds of gain. In the oil trading above they made a *holding gain* of £4 a barrel and an *operating gain* of £1 a barrel. We could say that the £1 a barrel operating gain is profit that could be paid out as dividends without reducing the operating capacity of the business. But the holding gain of £4 a barrel is needed to continue to finance existing inventory levels.

2 *Depreciation is understated*   Depreciation is an expense that reduces profits by the amount of fixed assets that is deemed to have been consumed during a period. It is usually based on the original cost of the fixed assets. When the asset comes to the end of its life, the cost of buying a new one is likely to be much higher than the amount of depreciation that has been charged. Depreciation is understated, and profits are overstated.

If all profits are paid out as dividends, a company would not be able to afford[7] to replace the fixed assets at the end of their lives, and they would not have maintained capital in real terms.

3 *Receivables*   The amount of receivables increases in line with prices. An additional charge can be made against profits to allow for the extra cost of financing receivables.[8]

4 *Overstated profits*   The effect of rising prices on HC accounts is that profits are overstated because they do not allow for the extra cost (due to price rises) of replacing assets. If dividends are based on profits, then dividends are likely to be excessive. If corporation tax payments are based on profits, then corporation tax payments are likely to be excessive. The effect of these, together with the additional cost of replacing assets at higher prices, means that companies are likely to suffer liquidity problems. If companies distribute all their profits as dividends, they will probably need to borrow quite a lot of money if they are to carry on financing the same level of activities.

5 *Asset values understated*   If assets are shown on the balance sheet at cost (or some modified version of cost), as prices rise, so the amounts shown for assets become increasingly unrealistic. Attempts to use the balance sheet to indicate what a company is worth are, to say the least, difficult. Creditors may be reassured by low asset values if they can be sure that assets are worth *at least as much* as the balance sheet shows. But company directors might like to see higher asset valuations in order to support additional borrowing.

6 *Return on capital employed is overstated*   If profits are overstated, and asset values are understated, both factors will lead to a company's ROCE being overstated, as shown in Illustration 5.5.

We can generalize from this during a period of rising prices. A company may be showing a reasonable ROCE, but if profits and assets are restated, the ROCE will be significantly lower. It depends on the rate of inflation, and the circumstances of particular companies, but Illustration 5.5 could be typical: a company's 'real' ROCE might only be about half of what the conventional published accounts show.

---

[7] Again, they could borrow.

[8] This is done using a net receivables figure (receivables minus payables, or debtors minus creditors).

Last year the Luxgud Company had a return on capital employed of 12 per cent, calculated as follows:

	£000
Fixed assets plus current assets less current liabilities	100
Shareholders' funds plus long-term liabilities	100
Earnings before interest and taxation	12

The company's auditors, RiceSlaughterhouse, estimated that profits were overstated by £4,000 because of the effects of rising prices, and that asset values were understated by £33,333.

The return on capital employed, after adjusting for rising prices, was $\frac{8}{133} \times \frac{100}{1} = 6\%$

ILLUSTRATION 5.5

7 There are other practical and theoretical problems with HC accounts. The idea of adding together items expressed in different units of currency is, to say the least, dubious. Not many would find the following extract from a balance sheet acceptable:

Fixed assets	Land and buildings	€10 million
	Plant and machinery	$5 million
	Vehicles	£2 million
	Total	17 million

It is usually acceptable to add together all items expressed in pounds, even if the items were acquired at very different dates, and the value of the pound was very different at those dates. If the land and buildings had been bought 20 years ago, and the plant and machinery 10 years ago, we would happily add the two together if they were both expressed in pounds. But the value of a US dollar or a euro is closer to the value of a pound than the value of a pound 20 years ago. One solution to this problem would be to express everything in an inflation-adjusted unit of currency: this came to be called pounds of current purchasing power (as at the balance sheet date). The CPP approach to accounting is explained in Section 5.7.

8 Conventional HC accounts also fail to show the gain that a business can make by borrowing lots of money. If a business borrows money, it usually has to pay interest, and that is properly shown in the financial accounts. But if they borrow £1 million to invest in tangible, non-monetary assets (such as land, buildings, machinery, inventories), these assets are likely to go up in line with inflation. The assets will increase to, say, £1.1 million, while the amount of the loan stays the same. There is a gain to the company of £100,000.

Many assets can be expected to increase roughly in line with inflation. But money sitting in the bank does not. If a company has no borrowings, but has a spare £1 million in the bank, it will earn interest, and that will be properly shown in the financial accounts. What will not be shown is the fact that, after inflation of say 10 per cent, they will not be able to afford to buy the same amount of assets that they could one year ago. They still have their £1 million, but what they could have bought for £1 million a year ago will now cost £1.1 million. In real terms they have lost £100,000.

Conventional HC accounts do not reflect the gain that is made by holding more monetary liabilities than assets, or the loss that is made by holding more monetary assets than liabilities.

Most of the time companies can live with the effects of inflation on their financial statements, especially when inflation levels are modest. They may also like to see their profits and ROCE exaggerated if it makes their performance look better. Companies like to boast that each year they have made record sales, and record profits. But they are not so keen on paying excessive taxation, or having serious liquidity problems. When inflation levels are very high, the effects on conventional financial statements can be serious.

Some Solutions

Accountants have long been aware that the effect of changing prices is to limit the usefulness of conventional financial statements and the Institute of Chartered Accountants in England and Wales (ICAEW) has given advice on the subject since as far back as 1949. They recognized that the usefulness of conventional profit figures was severely limited by the effects of rising prices, and recommended caution in interpreting the figures, and that companies should not pay out all their profits as dividends.

During the 1950s and 1960s various *ad hoc* ways of dealing with the problem were used. Some helped to produce more realistic balance sheet figures. Some helped to produce more realistic profit figures. The use of current values on balance sheets increased, and a requirement was introduced to show the market value of investments in addition to the book value.

Fixed assets could also be revalued, although there was little agreement on how this should be done. Many companies were happy to show more healthy-looking balance sheets, with higher asset values, and so higher equity figures. But if fixed assets are revalued upwards, the depreciation charge should be increased accordingly; and this reduces profit figures. Companies were less inclined to implement higher depreciation charges.

LIFO[9] was another partial[10] solution. During a period of rising prices, if the cost of sales figure is based on the most recent purchases it will be higher;[11] profits will be lower, and closer to being based on current costs. But the use of LIFO means that the items left in stock (and shown on the balance sheet) are at old, low, irrelevant prices.

By the early 1970s a more thorough-going solution was required. Inflation was extraordinarily high; and the credibility of the accountancy profession was extraordinarily low. A number of different suggestions have been made, including a pure replacement cost accounting system, and systems based on using net realizable values. But, as is so often the case, the solution to the problem depends on the way in which the problem is defined. It came to be seen as a problem of capital maintenance. Profit for the year is seen as being the maximum amount that a company can pay out as a dividend without being less 'well off' at the end of the year than it was at the beginning. Maintaining 'well-offness' means

---

[9] Last in first out: a method of pricing stocks that is widely used in the USA but not acceptable for taxation purposes in the UK.

[10] Perhaps all solutions are 'partial' in one way or another.

[11] Higher than using FIFO: first in first out.

maintaining capital. The debate has been dominated by different versions of capital maintenance, such as the following:

1 *Money capital or financial capital*   If a company starts the year with net assets of £100, and ends the year with £120,[12] it has made £20 profit. Inflation is ignored. This is traditional HC accounting.

2 *General purchasing power*   If a company starts the year with net assets of £100, and ends the year with £120, but there has been 12 per cent inflation during the year, distributable profits are only £8. To maintain the original capital, in terms of general purchasing power, it must go up in line with inflation to £112 before there are any distributable profits. This is CPP accounting.

3 *Operating capability*   A company might start the year with £100 invested in operating assets. By the end of the year the balance sheet shows a total of £120 (HC). But the cost of financing the same level of operating capability might have increased to £108. In current cost terms their profit is £12. This is based on the specific price rises that affect the company, not the general level of inflation. This is CCA.

As inflation faded, and interest in adjusting accounts to reflect changing prices faded with it, the Accounting Standards Committee came up with a compromise solution that combined CPP with CCA in their 1988 document *Accounting for the Effects of Changing Prices: A Handbook.*

5.7 Inflation: Current Purchasing Power

The accountancy profession's first set of proposals to deal with the problems was to require, in addition to conventional historical cost accounts, a set of inflation-adjusted accounts using CPP accounting. The accountancy profession's provisional Statement of Standard Accounting Practice (SSAP) 7 on CPP used the Retail Price Index to adjust accounts.

In principle it is very simple. All items[13] in the financial statements are multiplied up by the rate of inflation since the item first arose to express them in pounds of CPP as at the balance sheet date.

The effects on the income statement are shown in Illustration 5.6. We can assume that most transactions (sales, purchases, expenses) take place on average in the middle of the year. We convert them to year-end prices by multiplying them by the year-end index, and divide by the mid-year index; most items are simply multiplied up to year-end prices by the rate of inflation since mid-year. Depreciation has a much bigger uplift because fixed assets were bought some years ago. Opening inventory (an expense) has a bigger uplift than most items, because it was bought at least 6 months before mid-year. Closing stock (a deduction from expenses) has the smallest uplift because it was bought not long before the year end.

---

[12] Assuming there was no additional capital subscribed or dividends paid out.

[13] No change is required to monetary items (such as cash, receivables, liabilities) as they are already expressed in pounds of CPP at the balance sheet date.

The Retail Price Index was at 100 on 1 January year 1. By 31 December year 1 it had risen to 120.

Summarized income statement for the year ended 31 December year 1

	£HC 000	Conversion	£CPP 000
Sales		<u>1,500</u>	<u>120</u> 110		<u>1,636.36</u>
Opening stock	100		<u>120</u> 98	122.45	
Purchases	1,100		<u>120</u> 110	1,200.00	
	1,200			1,322.45	
Deduct					
Closing stock	(110)		<u>120</u> 118	(111.86)	
Cost of goods sold		(1,090)		(1,210.59)	
Gross profit[14]		410		425.77	
General expenses		(200)	<u>120</u> 110	(218.18)	
Depreciation		(200)	<u>120</u> 80	(300.00)	
Net profit		10		(92.41)	

Opening stock was bought before the beginning of the year, so we need to estimate when it was bought, and what the index was then. In this instance we assume that the index was 98 when it was bought.

Closing stock was bought before the end of the year; we estimate that the price index was 118 when it was bought.

Fixed assets were bought some years ago; in this instance we assume that the price index was 80 when they were bought. Depreciation is multiplied up in line with the amount of inflation since the assets were bought.

ILLUSTRATION 5.6

The effect of applying CPP in Illustration 5.6 is to convert a HC profit of £10,000 into a loss of £92,410. CPP accounting also requires the calculation of a gain or loss on holding monetary items. If a company has net monetary assets (e.g. lots of cash in the bank), its purchasing power declines during the year, and a loss on holding net monetary assets is shown. If a company has net monetary liabilities (e.g. they have borrowed lots of money) there is a gain because the assets in which the borrowings have been invested are assumed to go up in line with inflation, but the amount of the borrowing stays the same.

The distinction between monetary and non-monetary items is also important on the balance sheet. Non-monetary items (mainly fixed assets and inventories) are multiplied up in line with inflation. With monetary items (such as cash, bank, receivables, debentures) there is no change. Perhaps the most important figure is share capital. It is multiplied up in line with inflation: this is intended to maintain capital in terms of general purchasing power.

---

[14] In this instance the adjustments increase sales by more than the cost of sales, and so a higher gross profit figure is shown. It will often be the case that the adjustments increase the cost of sales more than the sales, resulting in a lower CPP gross profit.

Profits are regarded as being available for distribution as dividends only if the total amount of shareholders' funds has increased more than in line with inflation.

A CPP balance sheet does not show the 'real' value of tangible assets: it shows HC (less any depreciation), multiplied by the rate of inflation since the assets were purchased. The market value at the balance sheet date might be higher or lower than the £CPP figure (but 'prudence' suggests that if CPP values are significantly in excess of current value, they should be written down).

CPP has many advantages. It is relatively easy to implement because it does not mean that we need to change all existing financial statements and systems. It introduces a supplementary statement expressed in pounds of CPP. It is a fairly credible and effective system. It deals with the main problems that arise from the effects of inflation on financial statements. Indeed, it is the only real 'inflation accounting' system. It appealed to accountants because they could just about understand it, while at the same time it baffled most non-accountants. Moreover, it does not introduce any additional subjective judgement. The HC figures are taken as given, and multiplied up for inflation. This also means that the figures can be as easily verified by auditors as HC accounts.

CPP is a system that should 'maintain capital' in a very particular sense. Profits are not regarded as distributable unless equity has been maintained in real terms. The main drawback is that it does not reflect the specific price changes that affect particular businesses. The Retail Price Index is based on the price of bread and butter, steak and kidney pies, rents and council tax, shoes and socks, and all the things that make up the cost of living for a household. This is not very relevant to an oil company when the price of oil has just doubled, or halved. On average, CPP might produce relevant figures for average companies. But the figures are of questionable value to particular companies dealing with particular price changes.

In practice, the main problem with CPP accounting was that the government(s) at the time were not happy with it. They were afraid of the idea of general indexing. They were trying to control prices and incomes, and did not want either to go up automatically in line with inflation. That might be a recipe for still worse inflation. And they certainly did not want to see government borrowing indexed so that they had to repay inflation-adjusted amounts.

5.8 Maintaining Operating Capability: CCA

Just before SSAP 7 was issued the government appointed the Sandilands Committee on Inflation Accounting to consider whether, and how, company accounts should be adjusted to allow for price changes. The Committee was asked to look at the profession's CPP proposals and other possible accounting methods. They were requested to take into account the financial requirements of investors, creditors, employees and the public; the efficient allocation of resources through the capital market; and management decision-making and the efficiency of companies. In addition they were required to consider some of the economic concerns of the government, including the need to restrain inflation, and the taxation of company profits and capital gains.

The Sandilands Report was published in 1975 and recommended against CPP. Instead CCA should be adopted. Current cost accounts should be the main published accounts, not supplementary statements. Assets should be shown at *value to the business,* which in most (but not all) cases would be the written-down replacement cost. The profit for the year would be *operating profit,* which would be calculated by charging against sales the 'value to the business' of the assets consumed in generating that revenue. Holding gains and losses would be shown separately from operating profit. The Report was clear and well written; its recommendations seemed realistic; they were based on a system of replacement cost accounting that had been used by the Dutch electrical company Philips for many years. The Report was widely welcomed. Perhaps Sandilands' neatest move was to pass it to the accountancy profession to produce the detailed recommendations on how the system should be implemented.

The Accounting Standards Committee (ASC) established the Morpeth Committee to work on the detailed implementation of CCA, and their recommendations were published in October 1976 as Exposure Draft (ED) 18. At first this, too, was widely welcomed: at last there was a solution to the problems of price changes and financial statements! But that was before people read the detailed recommendations. Most accountants found it far too complicated, and they did not want to move away from HC accounting. It was like asking a vicar to give up the Bible, or a toddler to give up its security blanket: it may be full of holes, but it had served them well for a long time, and how could they cope in a world without that which they know best?

A large proportion of the ICAEW's members were against the proposals. An extraordinary general meeting was called; a vote against the proposals was carried; and the accountancy profession was left with egg on its face. The only answer was for the ASC to set up another committee. This time it was under William Hyde, and it produced the 'Hyde Guidelines' as an interim measure. These recommended retaining HC accounts as the main accounts; large companies should, in addition, publish a supplementary statement that made a number of current cost adjustments to arrive at current cost profit. These guidelines became the basis of SSAP 16 that was issued in 1980.

The basic principle is that current cost operating profit should be calculated after allowing for the effect of price changes on funds needed to continue the business and maintain its operating capability. It is the specific price changes that affect the business that matter, not the general level of inflation. When prices increase, a business needs the funds to finance more assets. Even if the business is not expanding, or increasing its operating capability, the cost of replacing the existing level of assets increases. They need to replace inventories as they are sold; they need to replace fixed assets as they are used up; and they probably need to finance a higher level of receivables.[15]

Current cost adjustments are made to HC profit to allow for the extra funds needed to finance the higher amount of assets that is due to price increases. A company cannot afford to distribute all its HC profits as dividends; they need to retain some of those so-called profits to finance the additional cost of replacing assets.

There are four adjustments to HC profit, and the first three are very similar. We can assume that most items on an income statement (sales, purchases, most expenses) take place, on average, in the middle of the year. The current cost of most of these items is, there-

---

[15] Net receivables, that is receivables minus payables.

fore, matched against current revenues, and so no adjustment is required. The three exceptions where adjustment is required are:

1 *Cost of sales adjustment* Opening inventory is increased to mid-year prices, which increases the amount charged against profit. Closing inventory is reduced to mid-year prices, which reduces the credit to profit. The effect of both of these is to reduce HC profit.

2 *Depreciation adjustment* The depreciation charge is increased in line with the change in the price of the fixed assets concerned since the date that they were acquired.

3 *Monetary working capital adjustment* It is easier to think of this in terms of amounts for (net) receivables. As prices increase, so the amount of receivables increases; and the business needs to finance that higher level of receivables. Receivables are treated in the same way as inventories and fixed assets: all need more finance because of price increases; an appropriate charge is made against profit to allow for the maintenance of operating capability, and to ensure that the necessary part of profits are retained in the business and not paid out as dividends.

If receivables are wholly financed by payables, there is no need for such an adjustment. We can assume that as prices increase, payables go up in line with receivables, and there is no need for a monetary working capital adjustment to allow for the financing of additional receivables.

If a company has more payables than receivables, the creditors are not only financing the debtors but also financing other assets. The effect of inflation would be to increase the amount of payables, and reduce the amount of funding the company needs to finance other assets. A monetary working capital adjustment would then be a *credit* that offsets the effect of the cost of sales adjustment.

The total effect of the first three adjustments is a reduction in HC profit to allow for the increased cost of financing assets. The assumption so far is that it is shareholders' funds (or retained profits) that have to do all the financing. But many companies are partly financed by borrowing. If a company is financed two-thirds by shareholders' funds and one-third by borrowing, we can assume that this will continue to be the case. Any increase in assets will be financed partly by shareholders' funds (two-thirds), and partly by borrowing (one-third). The effect of the first three adjustments is to charge shareholders' funds with *all* the financing of the additional assets. A fourth adjustment allows for the fact that part of the financing is likely to be from borrowing.

4 *Gearing adjustment* The proportion of the business financed by monetary items is calculated. If only two-thirds of the business is financed by shareholders' funds, then only two-thirds of the first three adjustments remain as a charge against profit. One-third is credited back in arriving at current cost operating profit; this is the gearing adjustment.

The use of liabilities to finance assets usually involves an interest cost; the benefit of the gearing adjustment is shown after the cost of borrowing (interest), as shown in Illustration 5.7. The amount available for distribution as dividends is shown after charging interest and taxation, and after crediting the gearing adjustment.

Income statement of the Currant Quest Company for the year ended 31 December year 3

		£000	£000
HC profit before interest and taxation			100
Deduct			
	Cost of sales adjustment	(20)	
	Monetary working capital adjustment	(15)	
	Depreciation adjustment	(25)	
			(60)
Current cost operating profit			40
Deduct			
	Interest payable	(12)	
	Taxation	(23)	
		(35)	
Add	Gearing adjustment	20	(15)
Current cost profit attributable to shareholders			25
Deduct	Proposed dividends		(30)

ILLUSTRATION 5.7

The Currant Quest Company paid a dividend of £30,000 which seemed to be well covered by HC profits after interest and tax. HC accounts showed £65,000[16] as being available for dividends. The dividend was covered 2.16 times. But after making the current cost adjustments, we can see that too much dividend was being paid. The company was failing to maintain their operating capability.

A current cost income statement is based on mid-year prices. A current cost balance sheet is based on year-end prices or, to be more exact, it is based on value to the business at the year end. The main differences between a HC balance sheet and a current cost balance sheet are in relation to fixed assets, inventories and the current cost reserve.

The first step in calculating current cost[17] of fixed asset and inventories is to establish their replacement cost. What would it cost to buy an equivalent asset at the balance sheet date? This could be established very specifically by looking at suppliers' price lists. With fixed assets, allowance must be made for depreciation: obviously it costs more to buy a new asset than the amount that would be shown on the balance sheet for an old one. The nearest equivalent asset must be established, and an allowance made for (say) 3 years' depreciation if the asset is (say) 3 years old. An easier way to get at an appropriate replacement cost is to apply a price index, but it must be a specific price index dealing with that type of asset, not a general price index such as the Retail Price Index.

CCA is not the same as replacement cost accounting. In most circumstances the use of replacement cost is appropriate. But sometimes the replacement cost is too high; the business would not want to replace an asset.

---

[16] £100,000 minus interest (£12,000) and taxation (£23,000).

[17] Or value to the business or deprival value.

> The Stainleigh Company bought a machine 4 years ago for £10,000. Its book value is now £6,000. An equivalent new asset would cost £20,000 today; the written-down value would be £12,000. But the company does not use the asset very often, and it would not be worth buying a replacement. The existing machine could be sold for £4,000, but the company prefers to keep it as it still generates some revenues. The company estimates that, over its remaining life, the economic value[18] of the machine to the business is £5,000.
>
> The company will not sell the machine for £4,000 because it is worth £5,000 to them. They would not replace it: the cost (even the written-down replacement cost) is more than the machine is worth to the business. The value to the business of the machine is £5,000; that is the amount at which it would be shown on a current cost balance sheet.
>
> **ILLUSTRATION 5.8**

When the replacement cost of an asset is more than the asset is worth to the business, the 'value to the business' is not the replacement cost; it is the 'recoverable amount'. With the Stainleigh Company (see Illustration 5.8), its economic value (continuing to use it) was more than its net realizable value. The value to the business is, therefore, its economic value. Sometimes it is not worth continuing to use an asset: its economic value is less than it could be sold for;[19] in this situation the value to the business is the net realizable value.

We could think of an asset as being worth what we can get out of it. This might be what we can sell it for (net realizable value), or how much we can make out of it by using it (economic value). The 'recoverable amount' for an asset is the higher of net realizable value and economic value. If the replacement cost is so high that we would not replace the asset, then the value to the business is the recoverable amount.

After making all the above alterations to HC accounts, the resulting balance sheet will not balance. The easiest thing is to put in 'reserves' as the balancing figure – but that is cheating! It is useful to separate out what has happened to the HC balance sheet:

1 Retained profits for the year have been reduced by the current cost adjustments

2 Asset values have been increased to a current cost basis

The current cost balance sheet will show two categories of reserves: retained profits (on a current cost basis), and a current cost reserve that includes unrealized surpluses on revaluation of assets.[20]

CCA has a number of advantages compared with HC accounting. It deals with most of the problems with HC accounting that were identified in the first part of Section 5.6. It provides a more defensible measure of profit and indicates the amount that could be distributed as dividends while still maintaining the operating capability of capital. But full and detailed implementation is complex, expensive and time-consuming. It is also very dependent on subjective judgement about valuations, and is, therefore, open to manipulation. It also puts auditors in a difficult position: most HC figures are a matter of fact that

---

[18] The net present value of the future cash flows it will generate.

[19] As is normally the case with assets such as inventories that the business intends to sell.

[20] Offset by the current cost adjustments to the income statement.

can easily be verified. But companies can easily defend a wide range of different figures for the value of assets; this can make it difficult for auditors to verify the figures with any real certainty.

5.9 From Compromise to Fair Value and All Inclusive

After the debate between CPP accounting and CCA, the accountancy profession produced a compromise, *real terms accounting*. But as levels of inflation fell to very low levels, interest in adjusting financial statements for price changes faded away. The emphasis in financial accounting is now moving towards fair value accounting, and developing an all-inclusive income statement that is intended to report comprehensive income.

A Compromise

The ASC's 1988 *Handbook* suggested a voluntary, compromise proposal combining CPP and CCA. It seemed like the accounting profession's last attempt to deal with the problem before interest in it faded away.

The proposals involve using current cost balance sheets (based on the idea of value to the business), and calculating profit by comparing the net assets at the beginning of the year with the net assets at the end of the year.[21] As the intention is to maintain capital in 'real terms' (allowing for inflation), the opening balance is multiplied by the amount of inflation during the year. If the net assets figure at the end of the year is more than the opening balance (after adjusting for inflation), then a profit in real terms has been made. This profit will include realized operating gains; it will also include unrealized gains from revaluing assets. The system may be seen as implying that such gains are regarded as being distributable as dividends; but normal accounting rules (and company law) do not regard unrealized gains as being distributable. They are, however, an indicator of the performance of a company.

In many cases the amount by which shareholders' funds have to be uplifted to allow for inflation will more than offset the amount of unrealized holding gains. In Illustration 5.9, unrealized gains on fixed assets and stocks amount to £80,000. But as there was 20 per cent inflation during the year, shareholders' funds needed to increase by £200,000. There was therefore no real holding gain. The HC profit was reduced from £150,000 to £30,000 because of a real holding loss.

The balance sheet shows that total shareholders' funds have increased by £230. But £200 of this was needed just to keep up with inflation. The total real gain was only £30.

In some instances there will be a real holding gain (when the current cost of fixed assets and stocks increased by more than the rate of inflation), which is added to the HC profit. Whether such unrealized holding gains should be regarded as being part of profit for the year is debatable. But clear identification of the various elements that make up any increase in 'well-offness' during the year should provide more useful information to the careful user of financial statements.

---

[21] After adding back any dividends and deducting any additional share capital.

Balance sheet extract as at 1 January

	£000
Net assets at current cost	1,000
Share capital	500
HC reserves	400
Unrealized holding gains (on fixed assets and stocks)	100
	1,000

Balance sheet extract as at 31 December

	£000
Net assets at current cost	1,230
Share capital	500
HC reserves	550
Unrealized holding gains (on fixed assets and stocks) (100 + 80)	180
	1,230

Income statement extract for the year ended 31 December

Historic cost profit after taxation		150
Add Unrealized holding gains (on fixed assets and inventories during year)	80	
Deduct Inflation adjustment to shareholders' funds	(200)	
Real holding loss		(120)
Total real gain		30

ILLUSTRATION 5.9

Fair Value Accounting

Extensive discussion is taking place within the IASB, and the ICAEW, with new publications at frequent intervals, and it is not yet official policy. But it seems clear that the preference is moving towards 'fair value' as a basis for asset values; the adoption of this will, in turn, affect the measurement of profit. There is not yet an agreed or rigorous definition of fair value, but it is based on a current market value rather than HC. There have already been a number of significant moves away from HC as a basis for financial statements; it remains to be seen how far this will go.

All Inclusive

The IASB has proposed amendments to the income statement that would extend it to include a whole range of items that are not included in 'profit for the year'. These include exchange differences on translating foreign operations; cash flow hedges; gains on property revaluation; gains or losses on defined benefit pension plans; and other items that add up to a total of recognized income and expense for the year. The inclusion of property revaluations is likely to be the most controversial.

Summary

There are many different reasons for measuring the amount of profit that a company has made during the year; and there are at least as many different profit figures. The idea that one single figure can tell us most of what we want to know about a company is unrealistic. It is as unrealistic as pretending that we can measure the performance of an individual in a single figure (such as IQ or GCE 'A' level points). As individuals we are each a combination of strengths and weaknesses, and our performance varies from time to time. Companies are similar to individuals in this respect. A single 'correct' EPS figure, the final figure on the income statement, a neat summary of company performance, is an appealing idea, but oversimplistic. It is easy to criticize financial accounting for failing to provide just what we want. But if we took the trouble to be very clear and specific about what we want to know about a company's performance, we will find that there is a wealth of information in published financial statements that gives as good an indication of what we want to know as it is realistic to expect.

Review of key points

- Profit figures are useful as a guide to dividend decisions, the success of management, as a basis for taxation, to guide investors and creditors, to indicate economic efficiency and to provide information to other users of accounts.
- Different elements of profit such as segments, exceptional items and investments can be monitored.
- The income statement approach to profit measurement emphasizes revenues generated and the costs incurred in generating them.
- The balance sheet approach emphasizes asset valuation.
- Financial statements based on HC have serious limitations; if they were adjusted for price increases they would show lower profits.
- HC accounts can be adjusted using CPP or CCA.
- It is unrealistic to rely on a single profit figure; different figures may be useful for different purposes.

Self-testing questions

1 What are the main reasons that profit is measured?

2 Explain how profit can be calculated using balance sheets. How does this approach differ from profit measurement using income statements?

3 There are likely to be different rates of growth in the profits of the various activities that a company undertakes (and different levels of risk). What detail is given in published financial statements of the performance of the different activities of a company?

4 Explain why it is not possible to measure profit without making predictions about the value of assets in the future.

5 What are the main differences between CPP and CCA?

6 (*Do not attempt this question unless you are good at basic statements – and can manage Chapters 14–16 to this book. You could look at the answer: it illustrates some important points.*) Mary runs a small business buying and selling Bibles. All transactions are on a cash basis. She started last year with 100 Bibles, which had cost her £10 each. During the year she bought 1,000 Bibles for £11,000; and she sold 1,000 Bibles for £15,000. At the end of the year she had 100 Bibles in stock, which had cost her £1,200. She decided to give all her profits to charity.

Required:

a The balance sheet at the beginning of the year

b The income statement for the year

c The balance sheet at the end of the year before giving profits to charity

d How much could the business afford to give to charity?

e How would the results have been different if she had used LIFO?

7 Jackie received £30,000 compensation for unfair dismissal and plans to set up in business running a taxi. The vehicle will cost £30,000 and will have a trade-in value of £3,000 after 9 years. Taxi fares, all received in cash, will amount to £40,000 per annum. Expenses (petrol, road tax, insurance, repairs), all paid in cash, will amount to £20,000 per annum. Jackie plans to take all the profits out of the business, as cash, each year.

Required:

a The balance sheet at the beginning of the business

b The income statement for a typical year

c How much will Jackie draw out of the business each year?

d The balance sheet at the end of 9 years

e What does this tell us about capital maintenance?

Assessment questions

1 Are profits usually overstated when HC accounting is used? Explain.

2 Using Illustration 5.3, produce a prediction of profits for year 9.

3 Using the segmental report for Ted Baker (Illustration 5.2), what additional ratios can you calculate? How useful are these?

4 On 1 January year 5, Smele Ltd was set up with 250,000 fully paid 50p shares. On the same day the company bought a freehold property for £100,000, and purchased 12,000 items of stock for £24,000.

On 31 December year 5, two-thirds of the inventory that had been bought on 1 January 1995 was sold for £40,000; 2,000 units of identical stock were purchased for £5,000; and the total expenses for the year of £12,000 were paid.

There were no other transactions during the year. All items were settled in cash on the date of the transaction.

The company uses FIFO. Freehold property is depreciated on a straight line basis over 50 years. The relevant index for property prices is:

1 January   120

31 December   150

Required:

a Prepare an income statement for Smele Ltd for the year ended 31 December year 5, and a balance sheet on that date, using replacement cost accounting.

b Explain how and why the results differ from using HC accounting.

5 The Floatus Car Company has a car showroom and is in business to sell sports cars. They decide to use CCA. In their window they have, as an advertising gimmick, a 1936 Rolls-Royce, and they are unsure what amount should be shown for it on their balance sheet. It originally cost them £10,000, 5 years ago. It has no engine in it, and it would cost about £8,000 to make it saleable; with an engine it could be sold for about £25,000. If it needed to be replaced it would be extremely difficult to find exactly the same model; it could probably be obtained from a specialist collector for £150,000. As an advertisement they reckon it is worth £10,000 a year for the next 5 years after which it would have a net realizable value of £20,000.

Since they bought the car the Retail Price Index has increased by 100 per cent; the average price of second-hand cars has increased by 80 per cent. The company's cost of capital is 12 per cent per annum.

Outline the principles for asset valuation using CCA, and attempt to apply them to Floatus's Rolls-Royce.

6 The following is a summary of the balance sheet of the Flaxey Company for the last 2 years:

Assessment questions (continued)

	Year 6	Year 7
	£000	£000
Fixed assets at cost	500	500
Provision for depreciation	(300)	(350)
	200	150
Inventories	100	140
Receivables minus payables	50	80
	350	370
Debentures	100	100
Share capital and retained earnings	250	270
	350	370

The price index of equivalent fixed assets has increased from 80 to 240 since the fixed assets were bought. The price index applicable to inventories, receivables and payables increased by two points a month from 84 at the end of October year 5 to 112 at the end of December year 7.

You are required to calculate the following, making and stating appropriate assumptions:

a Cost of sales adjustment

b Depreciation adjustment

c Monetary working capital adjustment

d Gearing adjustment

Group activities and discussion questions

1 a Profit is an essential indicator of company performance. Accounting standards setters are steadily improving its reliability and we will soon have reliable, consistent and comparable company profit figures on an international basis.

b The meaning of 'profit' changes as often as accounting standards change and companies find new ways of bending the rules for profit measurement. Undue importance is attached to a figure that is no more reliable than predictions by astrologers, weather forecasters and experts who tell us what will happen to house prices.

Present a case in favour of each of the above views. A group could be divided into two parts; one to present a case in favour of each. Or there could be a third subgroup that assesses the cases presented by each of the other two subgroups.

2 Inflation makes a company's performance look better, and this is to everyone's advantage. Discuss this statement. You should consider the point of view of (i) directors, (ii) shareholders, (iii) creditors, (iv) employees, (v) the government and

Group activities and discussion questions (continued)

(vi) the public. The discussion could take the form of a formal debate. Alternatively, role play could be used with each member of the group representing the interests of one group of users of financial statements.

3 Why has inflation accounting (and CCA and all its variants) generally fallen into disuse? What would be likely to revive it?

4 Profitability is a good measure of efficiency and effectiveness in companies. It is very difficult to measure efficiency and effectiveness in 'not-for-profit' organizations. Governments do not want to be responsible for organizations that make losses and are criticized for being inefficient and ineffective. Governments are increasingly privatizing organizations so that their activities can be seen to be efficient and effective.

Explain and assess the above argument.

Financial accounting in context
Unfavourable impressions
By Mr Bearbull

Investors Chronicle, 16 June 2006

Discuss and comment on the following item taken from the press and what it reveals about the difficulties of defining, measuring and interpreting profit figures.

Source: Reproduced with permission by the *Investors Chronicle*.

OKAY, SAY I WANT TO IMPRESS SOMEONE – A new girl friend, a potential employer, whomever. So I use my credit cards to buy a Paul Smith suit and hire an Aston Martin for the day – things I can barely afford. But, even if I'm confident that, somehow, I'm going to get a payback from this spending, is it a sensible thing to do? The reasoned answer would have to be: "No way. You've either got it or you haven't, and no amount of posing will change that."

However, what is self-evidently sensible conduct for people can become blurred when applied to companies. Take software supplier iSOFT, whose best-known activity is selling a key package in the £6bn scheme to install joined-up computing throughout the NHS. Like all of us, iSOFT has people it wants to influence – institutional investors, potential customers, etc. So clearly, it's easier to do that if it turns up with the corporate equivalent of a fine suit and a fast car – fat profits. And iSOFT's profits have apparently been fat, rising from £7m in 2000–01 to £70m in 2004–05.

It made these from selling licences for customers to use its software and providing installation and maintenance. But exactly how much revenue should be attached to selling licences, which are lump sums

recognized immediately, and how much to on-going contrasts, is fuzzy. ISOFT decided to attach a significant proportion to its licence fees, which was jolly helpful for its profits. It's likely, too, that its customers were happy to pay that way because iSOFT arranged it so that they didn't actually pay immediately. Instead, they gave iSOFT letters of credit, which were turned into cash for iSOFT via loans that the company itself guaranteed. At the end of April, iSOFT was guaranteeing £85m-worth of such IOUs. In addition, it had received £65m-worth of payments via financing arrangements that it did not guarantee – material amounts for a business whose turnover in 2005–06 was around £200m.

However, all good things come to an end. Modernising the NHS's computer systems is now looking like a nightmare for iSOFT. Back in January, it acknowledged that its NHS-modernisation revenues for 2005–06 would be £30m rather than the £85m expected. Now it seems iSOFT has yet to earn a penny from the NHS programme – or that much is implied by a change in its accounting policy for revenue recognition. Under the new policy, £165m-worth of licence revenue has evaporated. ISOFT's bosses say, 'don't worry, those revenues have just been deferred –

possibly £100m will be recognised this year and next, with the balance in the following two years'. However, maximum scepticism would be the correct investor response, especially as some revenue relates to licences that were sold four years ago.

There may be worse to come, too, because restating profits means that iSOFT is now in breach of its banking covenants, so the terms of the off-balance-sheet debt that funds licence sales may have to be renegotiated. That could mean a higher cost of debt. It might even mean a rescue fund-raising, which could leave little for existing shareholders.

Despite all this, I still wonder if there is value in iSOFT's shares – now down to 58p, which gives the group a stock market value of £133m. The chief reason is that, when all is said and done, iSOFT still has annual maintenance revenues of about £90m from its installed base of software. That should generate about £19m of taxed profits each year and prompts the question: what's that worth as an annuity? Even if I assumed that there was absolutely no other value within iSOFT, the group's current market value demands that a £19m annuity yields 14 per cent. That seems a bit risk-averse – especially as iSOFT had possibly £70m of surplus cash at the end of October.

However, there remains an issue of management credibility. It helps that chief executive Tim Whiston has fallen on his sword, acknowledging that "my continued role with the company may represent a source of negative speculation". Shareholders should not want new chairman John Weston, former boss of BAE Systems, to be the stand-in chief executive for long. Better that he is a heavy-weight non-executive chairman, working with a credible chief executive who can talk frankly to shareholders, rather than with the flannel that has characterized iSOFT's corporate communications.

Instinct tells me there is worse news to come from iSOFT but, paradoxically, that may have a cathartic effect and push its shares higher. So the brave decision may be to buy a small stake and wait to see what happens when the company announces its 2005–06 results on 11 July. Granted, the wish to act is heightened by the fact that the stock-market shake-out has pushed two holdings in the Bearbull Speculative Portfolio through their stop-loss levels. I sold the fund's holding in electronic components maker MTL at 415p for an 88 per cent profit, and its shares in IT services supplier Dimension Data for 42p and a 17 per cent loss.

Whatever I do, though, I mustn't be influenced by the desire to impress. If the iSOFT affair has any moral, it is that this rarely works in the long run.

References and further reading

Fisher, I. (1919) *Elementary Principles of Economics*. Macmillan.

Hicks, J.R. (1946) *Value and Capital* (2nd edition). Oxford University Press.

International GAAP (2005 or latest edition). LexisNexis (Ernst & Young).

Lee, T. (1996) Income and Value Measurement: Theory and Practice (3rd edition). Thomson Learning.

Lewis, R. and D. Pendrill (2003) Advanced Financial Accounting (7th edition). FT Prentice Hall.

www.fasb.org (US accounting standards)

www.frc.org.uk (UK accounting standards)

www.iasb.co.uk (international accounting standards)

CHAPTER 06

How the Stock Market Assesses Company Performance

❖ LEARNING OBJECTIVES

After studying this chapter you should be able to:

❖ Discuss various factors that influence share prices

❖ Understand the main information shown by the *Financial Times London Share Service*

❖ Calculate and interpret P/E ratios, dividend yield and dividend cover

❖ Explain why cash flows may influence share prices

❖ Understand the relationship between share prices and balance sheet values

❖ Critically assess the possible influence of a variety of other factors on share prices

6.1 Introduction

The performance of companies' shares on the stock market is part of our everyday news agenda, but it is difficult to be sure about what really influences share prices, and why it is important. Share prices are determined by supply and demand for a company's shares; this in turn is influenced by a number of factors, and the information revealed in financial accounts is perhaps the most important. It is easy to see which companies are doing well, but by the time this is obvious, their shares are usually already quite expensive. Similarly, by the time a company's performance is obviously poor, the share price has already fallen. Unfortunately, this chapter cannot teach you how to 'beat the market', but it does a lot to explain what happens.

6.2 Investing in Shares

When we talk about investing in shares, we usually mean buying shares that are listed on the London Stock Exchange (LSE), or other leading international stock markets. There are many thousands of private companies in the UK, most of them very small, typically with only about two shareholders; their shares are not available on any stock market. There are also many public companies, some quite large, which are also not listed on stock markets. You may be invited by friends or family to buy shares in an unlisted company; you may set up your own company; and you may inherit some shares. But unless the company is a listed one, buying and selling the shares is usually difficult because there is no ready market.

The shares in listed companies are bought and sold frequently, sometimes every few minutes or seconds, on the stock market, and it is easy to buy and sell them. If you want to buy or sell shares in listed companies, you need to have a stockbroker; or you could ask your bank to act for you; or you could register with a stockbroker who arranges for you to deal directly on the Internet. In the bull[1] market of the 1990s many private individuals became 'day traders', buying and selling shares on the same day, and making more profit than they could earn by working for a living. It is not difficult to make profits when share prices are rising.

Companies do not buy and sell shares themselves. If you go to Marks & Spencer or Boots and ask to buy some shares, you will be referred elsewhere. Shares are, in effect, bought and sold by investors (companies, institutions and individuals) via an established stock market. The price or current value of the shares is not calculated, or determined, by the company or individual. It constantly changes as a result of supply and demand for a particular company's shares. If demand for a share is very high, the price will be marked up; this will encourage some investors to sell their shares so that others can buy. When the price goes up too high, demand for the company's shares will slacken, and an equilibrium is reached. If a company's shares are not in demand, the price will fall until some investors decide that the shares have become good value.

Sometimes there are exaggerated short-term effects on share prices. If there is a rumour that there will soon be a takeover bid for a particular company, demand for those shares

---

[1] A bull market is when share prices are rising; a bear market when share prices are falling market.

might increase rapidly until the situation is resolved. When a company has some bad news, or there is bad news from comparable companies, there might be a sudden, exaggerated decrease in the share price, which may prove to be only temporary.

6.3 What Influences Share Prices?

Many different factors influence share prices. Some have nothing directly to do with the company itself but are more to do with general sentiments about investing and the economy. Such factors include expectations about interest rates, growth or recession in the economy, and exchange rates. To some extent stock markets in different countries move in line with each other, and it often seems that the UK stock market follows the USA.

The most widely used measure of share price performance is the FTSE 100 ('Footsie'). This is the *Financial Times* index[2] of the share prices of the 100 largest companies, based on their market capitalization. The FTSE 250 covers the next 250 largest companies and the FTSE All Share is the index for all listed companies. The constituent companies of the index change slightly on a regular basis as the value of their shares change. During the 1990s there were substantial increases in share prices and the index reached an all-time high on the last trading day of the century. During the first three years of this century there were substantial falls in share prices generally. The market rose steadily in the period 2003–2006 with the Footsie reaching a peak of about 6,100 in 2006. Currently, it is not clear if this bull market is now coming to an end.

The FTSE 100 is widely used, and some 'tracker' investment funds simply buy shares in the companies that make up the index; the performance of these funds is often better than funds where the managers use their own expertise to select the best investments. Inclusion, or non-inclusion in the index can affect a company's share price. It may be partly a matter of prestige and status. It is also a result of increased demand for shares that are going into the index; the managers of tracker funds have to buy them. And when companies are about to be removed from the index (because of a relative fall in their market capitalization), the share price is hit by the need for tracker funds to sell those shares.

A company's share price is also influenced by what is happening to other companies in the same sector. When one retailer reports relatively poor results, the share prices of many retailers may suffer too because it is anticipated that their results will also be poor. It also seems that sectors go in and out of favour.

Other factors influencing a company's share price are more directly to do with the company itself. Fundamentals of solvency and profitability are important, and so is growth. The (perceived) quality of management can also affect share prices. When a company has been through a bad time, chief executives often lose credibility and their jobs. When new chief executives are appointed they, and the company's share price, often enjoy a honeymoon period while the market awaits the delivery of improved results. Share prices are also influenced by the reputation of the company, by actual or rumoured takeover bids and by all sorts of rumours, speculation, scandal and gossip.

---

[2] The index is calculated by taking the average share prices of the 100 largest companies on the LSE. The index is 'weighted' so that the largest companies have most influence on the index.

As we do not know what will happen to share prices in the future, there is inevitably some risk in investing in shares. Some risk is because of what happens to the market generally: this is known as systematic risk. Other risk is because of what happens with particular companies: this is known as unsystematic risk, and it is possible to have a balanced portfolio of shares in different companies that eliminates this unsystematic risk.

There may be individuals who really understand how the various factors operate and affect share prices. If such individuals exist, they are likely to keep their advice to themselves, and to act on it, and to become extremely rich. When you read advice from investment analysts, bankers and other 'professionals' you may be tempted to believe them. But you might also wonder why they are giving you this advice or selling it to you so cheaply. Why do they not simply take their own advice and make more money that way? There are a number of possible explanations for this:

1 Investment analysts are fair-minded individuals, solely interested in pursuing the truth, with no interest in making money for themselves, and with more interest in helping others to make money.

2 They do not really know. Like journalists, they are just writing for a living and putting out any credible stories for which they get paid.

3 For some reason they want you to follow their advice and buy and sell shares when they suggest that you should.

There are infamous tales of financial journalists who offered share tips to readers. They would choose a company with a credible story about its future prospects; then they would buy themselves a few thousand shares at the current price, say £1 each. Then they would recommend readers of the *Daily Whatsit* to buy the shares at £1 each. Once such a recommendation is published (unless it is total rubbish) the share price is likely to go up immediately – even prior to publication. By the time the poor readers of the *Daily Whatsit* get their shares, the price has gone up to, say, £1.10, and they are likely to stay at this increased level for at least a few days. The journalists then sell their shares at, say, £1.10, having made a nice little profit. They can then boast to readers that the share price increased as they predicted it would. Financial journalists may be influential enough to cause temporary price increases, but readers receive the advice too late to act on it. Some might argue that the market is too 'efficient' for individuals to influence share prices. But if we are talking about a major investment bank, or the chief executive of the company concerned, what they say, and what is reported in the financial press, may have a significant effect on share prices.

At any one time there are likely to be hundreds or thousands of theories around about which shares are going to do particularly well in the future. Some of those theories will prove to be correct, while most will be quietly forgotten.

Most investors want to buy shares when they are cheap, and sell them when they are expensive. If you think that the true value of a particular share is £2, and you can buy it for £1.80, then it seems 'cheap', and you might buy some. If, soon after buying them, you still think that they are worth £2 each, but the market price has risen to £2.20, it seems 'dear' and you would make a decent profit by selling. The problem is determining what a share is really worth.

Unfortunately, there is no 'true value' with which the market price of shares can be compared. It does not mean much to say that a share with a market value of £2.50 is cheaper than a share with a market value of £3. We can, however, say that a share price is expensive or cheap in relation to key information such as the amount of earnings, or dividends, or net assets per share.

6.4 Accounting Information and Share Prices

Investors and investment analysts make their investment decisions and recommendations using financial accounting information, and whatever other relevant and/or credible information they are able to find. Share prices reflect the information that is available to investors, and financial accounting information is central to this. Share prices may be influenced by any information that a company discloses, but the most important figures are probably:

1 The profits earned by a company
2 The dividends paid out by the company
3 The net asset (or balance sheet) value of the company
4 The cash flows generated by the company

Each of these can be related to the most recent share price that gives an indication of whether a share is 'expensive' or 'cheap' in relation to that information. Investors are guided by the most recent figures for each of these; predictions are also sometimes available, which is what investors really need; but predictions have varying degrees of credibility, and should be compared with the actual results when they become available.

Profits

From the shareholder's point of view, the most relevant profit is the amount that was earned for them in the most recent financial year. It is the figure after all expenses, including interest and any exceptional items, have been deducted, and after charging taxation for the year. It usually has a straightforward label such as 'profit for the year', and that is the amount that has been earned for the shareholders during the year. Some of it is paid out as dividends; the rest remains in the business and becomes part of the retained earnings shown on the balance sheet.

If there are preference shareholders, then part of the profit earned for the year belongs to them; preference dividends have to be deducted from profits for the year to arrive at the amount earned for ordinary shareholders.

There is a relationship between the value of a company, and the amount of profits that the company earns. If a company earns £1 million a year, the company might be worth, say, £10 million or £15 million. The relationship is called the 'price[3]/earnings ratio', which, in this example, would be 10 or 15. It can be calculated by relating the company's *total*

---

[3] The 'price' is the price of one share: in this example it is worth 10 or 15 times the amount of profits earned per share.

earnings for the year to the *total* market value for all of its shares.[4] Alternatively, it can be calculated by relating the earnings *per share* to the market price *per share*.

Dividends

Some shareholders are more interested in the dividends that a company actually pays out than in how much profit the company makes. If a shareholder needs the income, profits are all very well, but it is the cash dividend that the shareholder actually receives that helps to pay the bills.

Companies usually declare dividends in pence per share, perhaps 4p per share. This means that the shareholders receive a 4p dividend for each share that they own. The amount varies from year to year, and companies usually try to increase it a little each year.

A company usually pays a dividend twice a year: an 'interim' dividend and a 'final' dividend. The shareholders are most interested in the total amount for the year.

Dividend Yield

There is a relationship between the value of a company's shares and the amount of dividend paid. If a company pays a dividend of 4p per share and each share is worth, say, £1, then the 'dividend yield' is 4 per cent. If the share price increased to £2, the dividend yield would fall to 2 per cent. The dividend yield is usually calculated by showing the most recent annual dividend per share (interim plus final) as a percentage of the current share price. The same dividend yield figure would be produced if the company's total dividends for the year are expressed as a percentage of the company's market capitalization.

Dividend Times Cover

There is also an important relationship between the amount of profits a company earns and the amount that they choose to pay out as a dividend. If a company pays out a lot less than half of its profits as dividends, then the dividend looks reasonably secure: the dividend is well covered by profits. If a company pays out nearly all its profits as dividends, then the dividend looks less secure. Analysts divide the profit by the dividend and say, for example, that the dividend is covered 1.6 times by profits. If a company earned £100 million profits, and paid out £62.5 million as dividends, then the dividend is covered 1.6[5] times by profits.

'*Dividend cover*'[6] can be calculated using earnings and dividend figures for the company as a whole or on a per share basis.

Net Asset (or Balance Sheet) Value

A company's balance sheet clearly shows the amount for equity or shareholders' funds, which is the same as the amount for 'net assets'. But the total value of the company's shares on the stock market is likely to be very different from what the balance sheet shows. Share prices result from the interplay of supply and demand for shares, rather than from recording financial transactions within the business. If a company's prospects are seen to be very

---

[4] The total market value of all the shares is called the *market capitalization*.

[5] £62.5m × 1.6 = £100m.

[6] Dividend cover should not be confused with interest cover.

Company	Closing price on previous day (pence)	Change in price (pence) since previous day	52-week high	52-week low	Yield %	P/E	Volume '000s
Morrison	199	+ .25	218	158	1.9	–	3422
Sainsbury	325 xd	+ 1.75	360	270	2.5	54.1	3904
Tesco	331 xd	– 0.5	351	292	2.6	16.5	4197
GUS	921	+ 6	£11.36	£7.87	3.4	16.1	5848

ILLUSTRATION 6.1

good, there is a strong demand for the shares, and the share price tends to increase. Generally, with a successful company, the market price of the shares is much higher than the net asset value per share (based on balance sheet values).

Cash Flows

Many analysts do not rely on profit information alone, but also analyse the company's cash flow statement, and are likely to have more confidence in a company that has healthy cash flows.

6.5 The *Financial Times*

The *Financial Times* shows key figures and ratios in respect of each listed company on the London[7] Stock Exchange on a daily basis. On Tuesdays to Saturdays the P/E ratio and the dividend yield are shown for each company together with various other information (see Illustration 6.1).

On the day that the figures in Illustration 6.1 were published[8] the average yield for the FTSE 100 companies was 3.39 per cent and the average P/E ratio was 12.91.

In Illustration 6.1 we can see that Tesco and GUS have very similar P/E ratios that are rather higher than the stock market average. Morrisons does not have a P/E ratio because the company had no earnings; they made a loss. Sainsbury's P/E ratio was extraordinarily high because it is based on the previous year's low earnings, and a rapid recovery is expected.

The content of the columns is as follows:

1 Name of company, usually abbreviated

2 Various notes (not included in Illustration 6.1). The most useful is the ♣ symbol which indicates that the *Financial Times* will supply a copy of the company's annual report and accounts if you telephone 020 8391 6000. If the ♣ symbol is not shown, the

---

[7] Comparable information is shown on preceding pages for many other shares and markets in the world.

[8] The two FT extracts are from Monday 19 June and Tuesday 20 June 2006.

annual report and accounts can be obtained by contacting the company directly or on the company's website

3 Share price at close of business on the previous day (closing mid price[9])

4 Amount by which the share price changed during the previous day

5 The highest the share price has been during the previous 52 weeks

6 The lowest the share price has been during the previous 52 weeks

7 Yield: the latest known dividend per share expressed as a percentage of the share price

8 P/E: expresses the relationship between the share price and the latest known profit, or earnings, per share.

9 Volume: the number of shares traded on the previous day in thousands

On Mondays, as there was no previous day's trading, the *Financial Times* provides different information as follows, and as shown in Illustration 6.2.

1 Name of company as above

2 Various notes (not included in Illustration 6.1) as above

3 Price at the close of business on the previous Friday

4 The percentage change in the share price during the previous week

5 The amount of the last known annual dividend expressed in pence per share

6 The dividend cover: earnings per share (EPS) divided by dividend per share

7 Market capitalization: the share price multiplied by the number of shares that the company has in issue

8 The date when the share became 'ex-dividend'. The most recent dividend was payable to whoever owned the shares on the day before the 'xd' date. If the dividend is 4p per share, we might expect the share price to fall by about 4p on the 'xd' date, because whoever owns the share on that date will not receive the 4p dividend, and will probably have to wait 6 months before another dividend is due

9 City line. This is a four-digit telephone number that gives live, up-to-the-second share prices, if you dial 0906 003, or 0906 843, followed by the four-digit number. Normal trading hours are 8.00 a.m. to 4.30 p.m.

On the date that these figures were published the average dividend times cover was 2.29.

In Illustration 6.2 we can see that GUS shares had the biggest increase during the week. GUS also paid the largest dividend of the four companies, but this piece of information by itself does not mean much as the price of their shares is much higher than the other companies. What matters is the dividend yield: the dividend as a percentage of the share price. On this measure GUS still looks good, partly because the shares are not too dear (e.g. in relation to the previous year's earnings).

The dividend cover indicates how safe the dividend is. Tesco and Marks & Spencer's dividend cover look reasonably safe: they were paying out less than half of their profits as dividends (i.e. dividends were covered more than twice by profits). Sainsbury paid out more

---

[9] There is always a 'spread' between the buying price and selling price: the mid-point is shown.

Company	Closing price on Friday	% Change during last week	Dividend in pence per share	Dividend cover	Market capitalization £m	Date when share last became ex-dividend	City line telephone
Morrison	199.25	− 0.5	3.7	–	5,329	26.4	3422
Sainsbury♣	323 xd	+ 1.9	8	0.8	5,529	24.5	3904
Tesco♣	332 xd	− 0.6	8.63	2.3	24,925	3.5	4197
Marks & Sp	573 xd	+ 4.2	14	2.3	9,561	31.5	3292
GUS	921	+ 0.9	31.5	–	8,117	4.1	2740

ILLUSTRATION 6.2

dividend than they earned in profit, perhaps anticipating an increase in profits in the following year.

The market capitalization is a measure of the size of a company. It is the current share price multiplied by the number of shares in issue. Using this measure we can see that Morrison and Sainsbury are companies of similar size; GUS and Marks & Spencer are much larger; and Tesco is way ahead. Other measures of the size of a company include turnover, net asset (balance sheet) value, profits and number of employees.

When a company declares a dividend it is payable to all who own the shares on a particular date. Anyone buying the shares after that date will not receive the company's most recent proposed dividend. If the dividend is, say, 20p per share, we can expect the share price to drop by 20p on the day that it becomes ex-dividend. It is important to know the date that a share becomes ex-dividend (and the amount of the dividend), if we are to make sense of share price movements.

The City line telephone number is a service provided by the *Financial Times*. For up-to-the-second share prices anyone can call 0906 843 followed by the four-digit code provided for each company.

For information about net asset values and cash flows it is necessary to look at the annual report and accounts; alternatively information produced by investment analysts and in the financial press can be examined.

6.6 Price/Earnings (P/E) Ratios

Calculating the P/E Ratio

The 'P/E' ratio is perhaps the most widely used stock market indicator. It shows clearly the relationship between the last known EPS figure and the most recent share price. Illustration 6.3 shows how the P/E ratio can be calculated on a per share basis (g) or for the company as a whole (e).

What the P/E Ratio Can Tell Us

In the example in Illustration 6.3, Cronky plc has a P/E ratio of 10. If we pay £2.00 for a

	Cronky plc	Voddy plc
a Number of ordinary shares	1,000,000	1,000,000
b Current share price	£2.00	£3.20
c Market capitalization (a × b)	£2,000,000	£3,200,000
d Total profits after taxation attributable to ordinary shareholders	£200,000	£160,000
e P/E ratio (c ÷ d)	10	20
f EPS (d ÷ a)	£0.20	£0.16
g P/E ratio (b ÷ f)	10	20

ILLUSTRATION 6.3

share, and the company earns 20p per share each year, the share will have paid for itself[10] in 10 years. That seems rather a long time for an investment to pay for itself. But the position with Voddy plc is even worse: it would take 20 years. These figures are not unusual. At the time of writing, the average P/E ratio on the London Stock Market was about 13. This could mean that most shares are hopelessly overpriced. It is more likely to mean that investors expect EPS to increase significantly in the coming years. The share price looks high in relation to the previous year's earnings, but (hopefully) not in relation to future earnings.

If share prices seem high it is because demand for them is high; and if demand is high it is usually because investors are optimistic about the future prospects of the company. Investors in Voddy plc do not assume that the EPS will remain at 16p for the next 20 years: they expect or demand *growth* in EPS.

If earnings grow at a constant rate of 10 per cent per annum, they will double in less than 8 years. If they grow at 15 per cent per annum, they will double in just less than 5 years. Not many companies manage to maintain such rates of growth in earnings, but they may be needed to justify high share prices, that is, to justify high P/E ratios. We can assume that, generally, a high P/E ratio means that investors are expecting high rates of growth, although they may, of course, be disappointed. In the late 1990s many share prices were very high, with high P/E ratios, particularly technology, media and telecommunications, together with computing, and anything vaguely connected with the dotcom bubble. But most companies failed to deliver the rapid growth in earnings that was needed to justify the high P/E ratios, and many high share prices crashed. In the 1990s many investors jumped on the bandwagon of high P/E ratios, only to be disappointed. In 2003 more modest P/E ratios and more realistic expectations of growth were the order of the day and several years of steadily increasing share prices followed. There were signs of this peaking in late 2006.

We can get a feel for P/E ratios by looking at the back page of the *Financial Times*. It gives the average for the London Stock Market as a whole, the average for the top 100 companies (the FTSE 100) and the average for about 35 different sectors. At the time of writing, the average P/E ratio for the FTSE 100 was 12.91. Sectors with high P/Es included mobile telecommunications, oil equipment and services, and electronic and electrical equipment. Sectors with low P/Es included mining and food producers.

---

[10] In terms of profit that the company earns, not in terms of dividends that the company pays out.

Sudndip plc has 10 million ordinary shares in issue. Their total profits after tax, earnings per share (EPS) are shown below. The share price and P/E ratio shortly after the results were published are also shown.

	Year 1	Year 2	Year 3	Year 4	Year 5
Net profit after tax	£1m	£1.1m	£1.25m	£1.45m	£50,000
EPS	£0.10	£0.11	£0.125	£0.145	£0.005
Share price	£1.20	£1.43	£1.87½	£2.61	
P/E ratio	12	13	15	18	

ILLUSTRATION 6.4

We can generalize that high P/E ratios are associated with expectations of high rates of growth. If the average P/E is 13, then any company with a P/E of much more than about 18 is expected to deliver high rates of growth if investors are not to be disappointed. A company with a P/E of less than about 9 is not expected to produce so much growth in EPS.

Most companies have a P/E of between about 9 and 25. But care is needed in interpreting these, especially if the P/E is unusually high or low. Sometimes P/E ratios are abnormally high – so high as to be meaningless. In Illustration 6.4 Sudndip plc had four very successful years. Profit increased each year by more than 10 per cent, and at an increasing rate. This raised expectations, and the P/E ratio went up from 12 to 18 during the period. Then, in year 5, earnings collapsed; EPS are minute. We could be fairly sure that the share price would collapse too. Maybe it would go down to £1 or even to 80p. But with a tiny EPS figure, even at 80p the P/E ratio would still be 160, which is so far out of the normal range as to be misleading. It still means that the share price is very high in relation to the latest EPS, but the explanation is more to do with exceptionally low earnings than it is to do with a high share price.

The drop in earnings shown in Illustration 6.4 is rather extreme, but it is often the case that a high P/E ratio signifies that the previous year's earnings were unusually low, and better results are expected soon. Many hotel companies suffered a loss of business in 2003 (partly due to the SARS epidemic and the Iraq war), but their P/E ratios stayed fairly high: the shares were expensive in relation to the previous year's earnings, but not in relation to anticipated earnings. In 2006 Morrisons and Ottakars made substantial losses; their share prices remained at reasonable levels, but as there were no earnings, there was no P/E ratio.

Although International Financial Reporting Standards (FRSs) lay down clear rules on how EPS should be calculated, it is not always clear which EPS figures have been used in calculating the P/E ratio, particularly in the financial press. Unusual P/E ratios are often the result of unusual earnings figures, such as exceptional profits, or losses on the sale of a subsidiary, or charges for the impairment of goodwill. Companies often produce two different EPS figures, choosing to exclude particular items for one of them. In the financial press use is sometimes made of P/E ratios based on future forecast earnings that may be referred to as prospective or forward P/E ratios.

6.7 Dividend Yield

Calculating the Dividend Yield

The dividend yield is another widely used stock market indicator. It shows clearly the relationship between the last known amount of annual dividend and the most recent share price. It can be calculated on a 'per share' basis, by dividing the most recent annual dividend by the most recent share price.[11] Alternatively, it can be calculated for the company as a whole, by dividing the company's total dividends payable for the most recent year[12] by its 'market capitalization' (the most recent share price multiplied by the number of shares that the company has in issue).[13]

The calculation, for two companies, is shown in Illustration 6.5.

In this example, Cronky has a significantly higher dividend yield than Voddy, but care is needed in interpreting this. It does not mean that Cronky's dividends are higher than Voddy's; both companies are paying the same dividend per share, that is, 10p. Cronky's higher dividend yield means that it has a lower share price than Voddy. A high dividend yield means that the share price is low (in relation to dividends); a low dividend yield means that the share price is high in relation to dividends.

What the Dividend Yield Can Tell Us

In the 1990s, little attention was given to low dividend yields. The average dividend yield on shares was only around 2 per cent at a time when it was possible to get 5 per cent or more from a bank or building society deposit account. Dividend yields looked very low, partly because share prices were very high. Although interest rates can vary, there is no 'growth' in the amount of interest paid on deposit accounts. But the hope and expectation is that dividends will increase, year after year, and in the majority of companies they still do. If someone invests £100 in shares, and the only dividend they get is £2, that is a yield of 2 per cent but it looks miserable. But the following year it might be £2.15, then £2.35

		Cronky plc	Voddy plc
a	Number of ordinary shares	1,000,000	1,000,000
b	Current share price	£2.00	£3.20
c	Market capitalization (a × b)	£2,000,000	£3,200,000
d	Total ordinary dividends	£100,000	£100,000
e	Dividend yield (d ÷ c × 100)	5%	3.1%
f	Dividend per share (d ÷ a)	£0.10	£0.10
g	Dividend yield (f ÷ b × 100)	5%	3.1%

ILLUSTRATION 6.5

[11] And multiplying by 100 to express it as a percentage.

[12] After deducting any preference dividends.

[13] And multiplying by 100 to express it as a percentage.

the next year, then £2.55; and, after a number of years (hopefully before the investor retires!), the dividend might look very respectable in relation to the original £100 invested, with every prospect that it will continue to increase, at least in line with inflation. With a successful investment, the share price also increases, which means that the dividend yield still looks low: it is the *amount* of dividend that the investor hopes to see increasing each year, not the dividend yield.

It is 'normal' for the average yield on shares to be lower than interest rates on deposit accounts, because investors expect there to be growth in dividends on ordinary shares. But interest rates on deposit accounts fell in the first few years of this century; share prices were also falling, and dividend yields steadily increased. Shares on average were yielding nearly 4 per cent in 2002–3 and it was possible to invest in shares that yielded more than bank deposit account rates. The average yield is now about 3.3 per cent, and interest rates are, more normally, higher than this.

Low dividend yields are mainly the result of high share prices, and low dividend yields go hand in hand with high P/E ratios. Shares that are expected to deliver rapid and sustained growth have high prices, and, therefore, high P/E ratios, and, therefore, low dividend yields. But many of the growth portfolios of the 1990s did not deliver, and share prices collapsed as the twentieth century ended. In the early years of this century investors' faith in growth stocks[14] steadily evaporated, and there has been more focus on shares that represent real value: low P/E ratios and higher dividend yields. The return of a bull market (rising prices, 2003–6) was due partly to improved company performance, and there has (so far) been no return to the very high P/E ratios of the late 1990s.

It might be a rational strategy for investors to choose companies with high dividend yields, provided they can be sure that the dividends will continue to be high. We do not know what future dividends will be. For a time in 2002–3 Abbey National had a high dividend yield (10 per cent), but there was no guarantee that this level of dividend would continue. The dividend yield looked high in relation to the previous year's dividend, partly because the share price had collapsed,[15] and it was rumoured that the following year's dividend would be reduced. The company was finally taken over by the Santander Bank.

At present, interest rates are still relatively low: it is difficult to get more than about 4.5 per cent from a deposit account. Although the average yield on shares is only 3.4 per cent, there are plenty of shares with yields higher than 4 per cent, which look reasonably sound, and have prospects of steadily increasing dividends. But yields of more than about 6 per cent may be suspicious: the share price is low in part because investors think that there may be problems with future dividends. Many individual and institutional investors are attracted to 'good value' shares with a reasonable dividend yield. It is possible to get some guidance on how sound such an investment might be by looking at the company's record over a number of years (profits and dividends), and by looking at their cash flow statements.

---

[14] Stocks or shares – much the same thing.

[15] The P/E ratio was down to 4.6, one of the lowest on the stock market. Investors were really pessimistic about the company's growth prospects.

6.8 Dividend Cover

The easiest and most widely used indicator of how likely it is that a company's dividend will be maintained and increased is 'dividend cover'. This is the relationship between profits and dividends. If a company pays out only a small proportion of its profits as dividends, then the dividend looks reasonably secure: even if profits fall in the following year, there should still be more than enough to pay the same level of dividend.

Dividend cover is calculated by dividing earnings per share by dividend per share. It can also be calculated by dividing the total profits attributable to ordinary shareholders by the total amount of ordinary dividends payable for the year.

The calculations for Cronky plc and Voddy plc are shown in Illustration 6.6.

		Cronky plc	Voddy plc
a	Total profits after taxation attributable to ordinary shareholders	£200,000	£160,000
b	Total ordinary dividends	£100,000	£100,000
c	Dividend cover (a ÷ b)	2 times	1.6 times
d	Earnings per share	£0.20	£0.16
e	Dividend per share	£0.10	£0.10
f	Dividend cover (d ÷ e)	2 times	1.6 times

ILLUSTRATION 6.6

On this basis, Cronky's dividend looks more secure than Voddy's. We must expect profits to fluctuate from time to time. Cronky can afford a bigger percentage reduction in profits before the dividend looks threatened than can Voddy. If each company suffered a 40 per cent reduction in profits, the EPS would be:

	Cronky plc	Voddy plc
Earnings per share	£0.12	£0.096

If each company continued with a 10p per share dividend, the dividend cover would be:

Dividend cover	1.2 times	0.96 times

Although it is acceptable for a company to pay out more in dividends than it earns in profits from time to time, perhaps when there is an unusually bad year, clearly this cannot continue for very long. A dividend that is not well covered by profits looks insecure. The average company on the stock market had a dividend cover that increased from about 1.7 times to 2.3 times in 2006. Many companies try to maintain the amount of dividend that they pay, even in years when profits are not good; their dividend cover then looks weaker.

6.9 Net Asset (or Balance Sheet) Value

It is easy to calculate the net asset value of a company, or the value of its equity, from the balance sheet. It is simply the total figure for equity, including share capital and all retained earnings and reserves. The amount for preference shares (if there are any) should be deducted because we are usually assessing only the value of the ordinary shareholders' funds.

This amount can be compared with the company's 'market capitalization' – the total value of all the company's shares, using the most recent share price. The comparison can be made using these total figures for the company as a whole. Alternatively, it can be made on a per share basis, comparing the net asset value per share with the share price.

In most cases the market value of a company is much higher than the net asset value shown on the balance sheet. This is for two main reasons:

1 Balance sheet values may be understated, often being based on historic cost (HC) rather than current values; and some assets are not shown on the balance sheet – human assets, skills and any 'internally generated'[16] goodwill.

2 Share prices are determined by supply and demand for the shares, and the balance sheet usually has a minor influence on demand for shares. The major influence is expectations of future profits and dividends, and expectations that the share price will rise in the future.

Some traditional manufacturing companies may have huge amounts of assets, and their market capitalization may not be very much more than their net asset value. Many modern companies have relatively small amounts of tangible assets, and their value lies in their skills, expertise, reputation, brands and other intangibles not shown on the balance sheet. Such companies might easily be worth 5 or 10 times their net asset values, especially at the height of a bubble!

The *Financial Times* does not regularly publish net asset values – which might be taken as an indication that they are not seen as being particularly important. They can easily be calculated from a company's balance sheet, and usually feature in reports by investment analysts, and are published by journals such as the *Investors Chronicle*. Some examples are shown below.

Company	Share price (pence)	Net asset value per share	Intangibles included in net asset value
Halfords (Car and cycle accessories)	297	89	113
Fuller Smith & Turner (Pubs and brewery; travel and leisure)	1,112	1,221	192
Northumbrian Water (Water utilities)	243	58	15
Lonrho Africa (Mining, mini-conglomerate)	26	13	–

In a successful company it is normal for the market price of the share to be higher than the net asset value per share. In many companies a large part of the net assets consists of 'intangible assets' (mainly the amounts paid for goodwill when another company is taken over).

---

[16] When a company buys another business, any amount paid for 'goodwill' has to be shown. But when a company generates its own goodwill, this is not shown on a balance sheet.

If such intangible assets are excluded, then the tangible asset of a company may be very low indeed compared with the share price.

In a minority of cases the net asset value of a company falls below its market capitalization. If the difference is substantial, this might invite an asset-stripping takeover bid: it may be possible to buy up the company at a bargain price, and then sell off all the separate parts of it at a profit. Investment analysts often assess the market value – not just the balance sheet value – of the separate parts of a business, and when this falls below the market capitalization, there are danger signs for management: another management team may be able to take over and do a better job for the shareholders.

In some cases, such as property companies, the market capitalization is usually significantly less than the market value of the underlying assets. In part this may be because the balance sheet shows properties at fairly full current valuations, and it may be difficult to sell the properties at those prices. It may also be because it is difficult to generate much growth in profits: rental income is relatively stable, and safe, but does not produce 'double-digit' growth in profits.

6.10 Cash Flow

Cash flow may be a better indicator of a company's performance than profit. A company that generates substantial profits on paper, but cannot back them up with cash flows, raises serious questions. A company that makes profits year after year, but has to keep raising more money (by borrowing or making rights issues) may be unpopular with investors. Cash flow statements explain how and why a company's cash flow differs from its profit, as explained in Chapter 7.

The first question is: does the company generate cash from its normal operations? If it does not, there is a need to establish why not.

The second question is to do with expansion. Is the company investing in more fixed assets and buying other businesses? This is clearly shown on the cash flow statement. Such expansion may require additional borrowing or the issue of more shares. Amounts invested in expansion can be compared with the amounts raised as additional share capital and borrowings. It is a danger sign if the company is raising lots more capital, without any evident increase in profitable investment. It is more healthy if a company is investing in additional capacity and this is partly financed from operating cash flows, and not totally dependent on raising additional funds.

Cash flow statements show three categories of cash flows:

1 *Cash generated from operating activities*   Investors expect to see a positive figure here, even after financing any increases in working capital

2 *Cash flow from investing activities*   Investors expect to see a negative figure here, with the company investing in additional fixed assets and perhaps buying up other businesses

3 *Cash flow from investing activities*   Investors want to know about the company's financing, including what dividends have been paid, how any expansion has been financed, and whether the company has been increasing or reducing borrowings.

Some analysts emphasize profit plus depreciation and amortization as being the key figure. The cash flow from operations figure is perhaps the most useful and readily available. Others look for 'free cash flow' that can be deduced from somewhere in the middle of the cash flow statement, by estimating how much of the amounts paid for additional fixed assets is essential, and how much is for expansion.

6.11 Other Indicators/Predictors of Performance

There is no shortage of investment analysts, experts and charlatans giving advice on how to pick winners when investing on the stock market. Most accountants are more cautious, but not all! It is difficult to be clear about who is an expert, who is a charlatan and who is advising investing in particular shares for reasons of self-interest. Even the 'experts' do not seem to be able to get it right, and are often carried along with the fashionable conventional wisdoms of the day. In the late 1990s it was not difficult to spot that shares in telecommunications companies were overpriced, but many still jumped on the bandwagon until the bubble burst, and share prices collapsed. The effects were serious for a few years until share prices started to rise again.

All financial accounting information can be analysed with a view to guiding investment decisions. Many different ratios can be calculated, and an examination of trends over a number of years can be revealing.

The relationship between a company's turnover figure and its market capitalization is one of many ratios that might be worth following. The idea is that if a company's market capitalization is higher than its turnover, the shares are overpriced. If a company's turnover is very much higher than its market capitalization, the shares are good value. The theory is that if a company has a high level of sales (in relation to share price), profits will follow. The hardest thing is to achieve a high level of turnover. If the present management cannot make good profits from a high level of sales, a future management will. This may be no more than a hypothesis. It would probably turn out to be a good basis for investment in some companies, in some years, but not for other companies in other years. This is probably true for most decision rules that are supposed to form the basis for investment decisions.

During the period of enthusiasm for shares in telecommunications companies, emphasis was given to measures such as earnings before interest, taxation, depreciation and amortization.[17] A decision rule emerged that a company should be worth about three times this figure; but ideas like this soon faded.

The more fully past data are analysed, the more models can be developed that appear to predict future share prices. It is not difficult to find past data which, if analysed in a particular way, would have predicted share prices. But we cannot assume that such relationships will hold good in the future. In choosing between different accounting policies, accountants often favour those policies that seem to have most predictive value; but we can know only those that would have had most predictive value in the past. Markets are constantly changing. Companies and activities that did well in the 1990s may be a disaster

---

[17] Known as EBITDA.

between 2000 and 2003, then recover brilliantly in the next few years. Past performance is no guide to the future.

The same arguments apply with technical analysis: it is difficult to believe that graphs of share prices over time show patterns that enable us to predict future share prices.

Although financial accounting cannot give us all the answers that we might like, the information that it provides is central in making investment decisions, and in monitoring how successful those decisions turn out to be.

6.12 A Further Illustration

The main stock market ratios are shown in Illustration 6.7. The figures suggest a typical, average company, and may be used to make comparisons with other companies and to see how the ratios have been calculated. The P/E ratio, the dividend cover and the dividend yield may all be calculated using figures for the company as a whole, or on a per share basis.

The figures for Stoutmouth plc are in many ways typical of a listed company. At the time of writing, the average P/E ratio of the 100 largest companies quoted on the LSE was 13; the average dividend yield was 3.4 per cent; and the average times cover for dividends was 2.3. The market capitalization of each of the companies in the largest 100 is between £2 billion and £120 billion. But the market capitalization of most listed companies is nearer to that of Stoutmouth plc.

	Stoutmouth plc
Share capital (25p shares)	£ 5,000,000
Retained earnings	£31,000,000
	£36,000,000
Net profit after tax for year	£6,400,000
Dividends for year	£4,000,000
Number of shares	20,000,000
Market price of shares	£5.44
Market capitalization	£108,800,000
EPS	£0.32
Dividend per share	£0.20
P/E ratio	17
Dividend times cover	1.6 times
Dividend yield	3.7%
Net assets per share	£1.80

ILLUSTRATION 6.7

Summary

One of the main objectives of financial management is to maximize shareholders' wealth. Dividends, which are dependent on profits, contribute to this. But the main element of shareholders' wealth is the value of their shares. Directors and chief executives are usually well motivated to maintain and increase their company's share price: they own shares themselves; they may have options to buy shares at predetermined prices; and their remuneration may include substantial incentives related to share price performance. If they fail, and the share price languishes, they risk the wrath of shareholders, and leave themselves open to a hostile takeover bid with a new management team replacing them.

Accounting measures of solvency and profitability are central to the performance of share prices. If a company is seen as having excessive debt, the share price will suffer. Profitability is essential to maintaining and increasing share prices, although more attention seems to be paid to earnings per share than to return on capital employed (ROCE). Growth, and expectations of future growth in sales, profits and dividends make a major contribution to increases in share prices. Sometimes it seems that expectations of share price increases are the main cause of share price increases. Share prices are influenced by expectations, rumours and many other factors that are difficult to define and measure, particularly in the short term. In the long run, sound finances and growth in EPS are likely to be the main contributors to increasing share prices.

Review of key points

- Many different factors influence share prices.
- A company's P/E ratio, dividend yield and dividend cover are widely used measures of share price performance.
- Growth and expectations of growth of sales and profits help to boost share prices.
- Many influences on share prices are difficult to quantify.
- Company directors and shareholders have an interest in maintaining and increasing share prices.
- Claims to be able to predict share prices should be treated with caution.
- Financial accounting information helps to explain changes in share prices.

Self-testing questions

1 Explain the meaning, calculation and significance of each of the following:

   a P/E ratio

   b Dividend yield

   c Dividend times cover

2 Is a company's balance sheet value (net asset value) likely to be higher or lower than its market value? Explain.

3 If a company currently has a dividend yield of 10 per cent, does that mean that someone investing £100 today will receive £10 dividend in the coming year? Explain.

4 You are given the following information about two companies. You are required to fill in the missing items for Beermouth plc.

	Alemouth plc	Beermouth plc
Share capital (20p shares)	£1,600,000	£ 2,000,000
Retained earnings	£3,200,000	£18,000,000
	£4,800,000	£20,000,000
Net profit after tax for year	£3,520,000	£1,200,000
Dividends for year	£3,200,000	£800,000
Number of shares	8,000,000	10,000,000
Market price of shares	£4.40	£1.80
Market capitalization	£35,200,000	£18,000,000
EPS	£0.44	£0.12
Dividend per share	£0.40	£0.08
P/E ratio	10	–
Dividend times cover	1.1 times	–
Dividend yield	9.09%	–
Net assets per share	£0.60	–

5 Comment on the dividend yield of Alemouth plc.

6 Comment on the relationship between the net assets per share of Beermouth plc and its share price (or on the relationship of the total of shareholders' funds to the market capitalization).

Assessment questions

1 What is the level of the FTSE 100 today? What is the average P/E ratio of the top 100 companies? What is their dividend yield and dividend cover?

You are given the following information about the FTSE 100:

	Index	P/E	Dividend yield	Dividend cover
16 September 2003	4299	17.6	3.3%	1.72
19 June 2006	5597	12.8	3.4%	2.3

What do you think are the main causes of the changes

a between September 2003 and June 2006;

b since June 2006?

2 You are given the following information about two companies, partly extracted from their most recent balance sheet and income statement, and partly taken from the financial press. You are required to fill in the missing items for Drinkmouth plc.

	Cidermouth plc	Drinkmouth plc
Share capital (20p shares)	£ 4,000,000	£1,200,000
Retained earnings	£14,000,000	£2,400,000
	£18,000,000	£3,600.000
Net profit after tax for year	£3,400,000	£1,800,000
Dividends for year	£2,000,000	£ 900,000
Number of shares	20,000,000	6,000,000
Market price of shares	£3.40	–
Market capitalization	£68,000,000	£45,000,000
EPS	£0.17	£0.30
Dividend per share	£0.10	–
P/E ratio	20	25
Dividend times cover	1.7 times	–
Dividend yield	2.9%	2.0%
Net assets per share	£0.90	–

3 You are given the following information about Swin Gin plc:

	Year 1	Year 2	Year 3	Year 4	Year 5*	Year 6	Year 7
EPS	£0.50	£0.55	£0.62	£0.01	£1.20	£0.83	£0.90
Share price	£6.00	£7.70	£9.92	£6.00	£7.20	£12.45	£15.30

(after publication of results for year)

* In year 5 the company sold their head office building in London making a profit that amounted to 45p per share.

You are required to calculate the P/E ratio for each year, and comment on how the market appears to have reacted to changes in EPS.

4 Assess the usefulness of P/E ratios and suggest how they might be misleading.

5 Select a recent takeover bid (e.g. the 2006 bids for Ottakars and for British Airports Authority). Assess the various factors that determined the price that was eventually agreed for the company which was taken over.

Group activities and discussion questions

1 Look at the shares listing in the *Financial Times*. What is an average P/E ratio? Select some companies with high P/E ratios. Do they seem to have anything in common? How useful are the P/E ratios given for different sectors in the 'FTSE Actuaries Share Indices'? Select some companies with low P/E ratios. Do they seem to have anything in common?

2 Look at the shares listing in the *Financial Times*. What is an average dividend yield? Select some companies with high dividend yields. Do they seem to have anything in common? How useful are the dividend yields given for different sectors in the 'FTSE Actuaries Share Indices'? Select some companies with low dividend yields. Do they seem to have anything in common?

3 Each member of the group selects one or two companies in which they believe the shares are likely to increase in price during a selected period. A long period may be preferable, but in a 12-week module the selection could be made in week 4; the shares monitored for 6 weeks; and the 'final' results assessed in week 10.

Each member of the group is required to give a justification for selecting a particular share in week 4. Then, in week 10, each member should present an explanation of what has happened to their company's share price.

There would be a competitive element (who would have made most money?). There should also be an assessment of the quality of the presentations; this assessment could be done partly or wholly by the students themselves.

4 Each group forms one or more hypotheses about how to select companies where the increase in share prices is expected to be higher than the average for the FTSE 100 companies. Examples might include (with variations) such things as:

i companies with a dividend yield of between 4 per cent and 5 per cent where the cover is not less than 2

ii companies where sales have increased by more than 20 per cent per annum (over a given number of years), but profits have not (yet) increased

iii companies where profits have increased by more than 10 per cent since last year, but the share price is lower

This exercise might be more fun if it is done live. But it is difficult to complete it during the 12-week period of a typical module. It is easier to do it historically. The decision rules are selected first, then they are applied to a sample of companies.

Some competition between different groups can produce interesting results. The results produced by the winners might need careful scrutiny.

5 Each group chooses three different sectors (e.g. pharmaceuticals and biotech; construction and building materials; transport and retailers). The key stock market indicators are found for each sector and compared with the average for the FTSE. These are shown in the *Financial Times* as 'FTSE Actuaries Share Indices'. Suggest factors that make each sector different from the FTSE average.

Financial accounting in context

M&S shares looking sharp

Sunday Telegraph, 2 July 2006

Discuss and comment on the following item taken from the press. How valuable are financial journalists' views about investing in particular companies' shares likely to be?

Source: Reproduced with permission by the *Sunday Telegraph*.

TWO YEARS into Marks & Spencer's turnaround under Stuart Rose, the chief executive, we think that it is time to buy shares in the retailer.

M&S (587p) has enjoyed a steady recovery over the past year and is now trading at a hefty premium to the 400p a share that Sir Philip Green, the retail entrepreneur, wanted to pay for the chain in 2004.

The shares languished below the 400p level until last autumn – leading some to question whether Rose could turn the company around – but their rise since then has proven doubters wrong as M&S has surged ahead. By early May this year, M&S's shares had almost doubled over the previous eight months to 634.5p.

The shares have fallen back recently on profit-taking (including by two large M&S holders – Baugur of Iceland and Brandes of the US) and a falling stock market. They are now down 8 per cent on May's eight-year high and we think it is a good time to pick up stock.

The strong share price performance has reflected success on the shop floor. Like-for-like sales at M&S over the first four months of this calendar year rose by 6.8 per cent, and a trading update next week to coincide with a shareholder meeting should contain even better news.

So what have Rose and his team done? Seymour Pierce, the broker, points out that Rose has "totally revolutionised" the retailer's supply chain, has increased margins through better procurement and reducing money-off sales, has cut overheads, and is spending £500m a year refitting stores. M&S has also cut its entry prices, allowing shoppers to buy its clothes at prices normally only offered by downmarket rivals.

On the fashion side, M&S has sharpened up its act and is getting its message across via well-received adverts featuring models such as Twiggy and Erin O'Connor.

Seymour Pierce has a price target of 630p and Lehman Brothers has one of 640p. Buy.

References and further reading

Berger, D. and J. Carlisle (2002) *The Motley Fool UK Investment Guide*. Boxtree.

Brealey, R., S. Myers and F. Allen (2005) *Corporate Finance*. McGraw-Hill.

Brett, M. (2003) *How to Read the Financial Pages*. Random House Business Books.

Lumby, S. and C. Jones (2003) *Corporate Finance: Theory and Practice*. Thomson Learning.

McKenzie, W. (2003) *Financial Times Guide to Using and Interpreting Company Accounts*. FT Prentice Hall.

Rees, B. (forthcoming) *Financial Analysis* (3rd edition). FT Prentice Hall.

Financial Times (daily newspaper)
Investors Chronicle (weekly magazine)
www.ft.com
www.londonstockexchange.com

CHAPTER 07

Cash Flow and Profit

❖ *LEARNING OBJECTIVES*

After studying this chapter you should be able to:

❖ Understand the differences between cash flow and profit

❖ Explain the accruals concept

❖ Understand and interpret cash flow statements

❖ Explain the difference between a cash flow statement and a cash budget

❖ Understand how incomplete records differ from accruals-based accounting

❖ Appreciate the importance of having both accruals- and cash flow-based financial information

❖ Prepare and interpret a cash budget

7.1 Introduction

It is tempting to say that the performance of a company should be judged by the amount of cash that it generates. A successful company generates lots of cash. An unsuccessful company runs out of cash. The accountant's job would be very easy: there is no need to do more than record all receipts and payments, and to report on a regular basis which is higher. The analyst's job would be easy: the company that generates most cash is most successful. There would be no problems of credibility, or subjectivity, or manipulation of asset values and exaggeration of profits. Everything could be easily checked by looking at the company's bank statement.

But generating lots of cash is not necessarily a sign of success. Few of us would be impressed by a company that massively increased its cash balances simply by selling off assets and borrowing lots of money. A company that succeeds in generating large amounts of cash is not necessarily a successful company.

Similarly, a successful company might pay out far more cash than it receives. A profitable company might be paying out substantial sums of cash to buy assets that are going to increase future profit; the company is performing well even though it is using up lots of cash.

In many companies, profit and cash[1] flow go hand in hand and tell a similar story. But they can also tell very different stories, and the distinction between cash flow and profit is vital to an understanding of financial accounting, and to the survival of many businesses.

Many people go into business in order to 'make money', even though they are not very clear what 'making money' means. Does it mean making profit, or do they mean generating cash? And what is the difference?

The differences between cash flow and profit are not easily understood and are dealt with as follows:

1 The *accruals concept* is the theoretical basis of the distinction between cash flow and profit. It is dealt with in this chapter.

2 *Cash flow statements* are illustrated and interpreted in this chapter. A cash flow statement provides a reconciliation between the amount of profit generated during a period, and the amount by which cash balances have increased or decreased during the period. The detailed preparation of cash flow statements is dealt with in Chapter 16.

3 *Incomplete records* are often kept by small businesses. They do not have a full set of double-entry accounts, but a summary of receipts and payments of cash can be constructed from bank statements. The process of converting receipts and payments into an income statement and the production of a balance sheet illustrate how cash flow differs from profit. This is explained and demonstrated in Chapter 16.

4 A *cash budget* is a plan of future receipts and payments of cash, typically prepared for the coming year. It shows the cash received and the payments made each month, and the balance remaining (or overdraft) expected at the end of each month. It can be compared with a budgeted income statement to see how profit differs from cash flow.

---

[1] The word 'cash' is used to include both petty cash (coins and notes) and money in the bank.

A cash budget is sometimes loosely referred to as if it is a 'cash flow statement', but it is important to distinguish between the two. A cash budget is a forecast or plan of *future* receipts and payments. A cash flow statement is prepared in a standardized format for publication to reconcile profit and changes in cash balances; it is based on what has happened in the *past*.[2]

7.2 The Accruals Concept

Balance sheets and income statements are based on the *accruals concept,* which means that profit is the difference between the revenues earned during a period (regardless of when the money is received), and the costs incurred in earning those revenues (regardless of when cash is paid out).

The accruals concept has long been regarded as a *fundamental accounting concept.*[3] It requires that revenues and costs are accrued, and matched with one another so far as their relationship can be established or justifiably assumed. They are dealt with in the income statement of the period to which they relate, which is often not in the period when cash is received or paid.

The profit figure for a particular period is, therefore, likely to be very different from the amount of cash generated in that period. A naïve, non-accountant might think that:

Profit   =   receipts of cash   less   payments of cash

But they would be seriously mistaken.

Financial accounting is based on the accruals concept which means that for a particular period:

Profit   =   revenues earned   less   costs incurred in earning those revenues

The words are important. Receipts and payments apply to cash. Revenues or income and costs or expenses apply to profit calculation.

The accruals concept is applied throughout financial accounting. Gross profit is the difference between sales and the cost of goods sold. In calculating profit, it is the amount of sales revenue earned during a period that matters, not when the money is received. The cost of goods sold uses the purchases figure, which is the total amount purchased during the period, regardless of when they are paid for. The cost of goods sold figure also adjusts for inventories. The expense 'cost of sales' is based on the cost of the goods that were actually sold during the period. Unsold inventories from one year become a cost for the following year as they are included in cost of sales as opening inventory. Closing stocks of unsold stocks of goods at the end of one period are the opening stocks of unsold goods at the beginning of the next year.

---

[2] It is also possible to produce a *forecast* cash flow statement in the standardized format; this would look different from a cash budget, but the two should easily be reconciled.

[3] Statement of Standard Accounting Practice (SSAP) 2 specified four fundamental accounting concepts: going concern; accruals; consistency; and prudence (or conservatism).

Any payment made to buy fixed assets that is made this year (or which it is agreed will be paid in another year) is not an expense for this year. The cost is spread out over the life of the fixed asset and is charged as depreciation each year. The timing of cash paid out for buying fixed assets is very different from the timing of the depreciation expense which is charged in calculating profit.

It is important to be clear that:

1 Not all payments of cash are expenses; some payments are not a charge against profits

2 Not all receipts of cash are revenues; some receipts do not add to profits

3 Not all expenses are payments of cash; some expenses are charged against profits although no payment of cash is required in the year that the expense is charged

4 Not all revenues are receipts of cash; some revenues are added to profits although there is no receipt of cash in the year that credit is taken for the revenue

There are examples of each of the above four differences. But, in interpreting financial statements, it is important to look for the big differences. Substantial inflows of cash are likely to come from borrowings, issuing share capital and selling off assets;[4] none of these count as revenues for the purpose of calculating profit. Substantial outflows of cash are usually for buying fixed assets, but such payments are not charges against profit for the year. The biggest expense, which is not paid in cash, is depreciation and that can easily cause confusion!

Some of the examples of differences are relatively minor timing differences. But they are all important in explaining the difference between cash flow and profit. And, in some circumstances, 'minor' items can become very significant.

1 *Payments of cash that are not expenses*: purchase of fixed assets; investing in other companies; repaying loans; payments to buy stocks of goods that are not sold until the next period; payments to creditors for expenses incurred in the previous period.

2 *Receipts of cash that are not revenues*: sale of fixed assets; borrowing money; proceeds from issuing shares; receipts from debtors this period in respect of sales for the previous period.

3 *Expenses that are not payments*: depreciation and amortization;[5] expenses incurred this period but which are not paid for until the next period; creating a provision; increase in a provision for bad debts; discount allowed to customers for settling their accounts promptly.

4 *Revenues that are not receipts*: sales that are made during this period, but the money is not received until the next period; discount allowed by suppliers for settling accounts promptly; reduction in a provision.

There are also examples where the cash receipt is very different from the revenue figure. When a fixed asset is sold, all the cash received is credited to the cash account. But in cal-

---

[4] Any profit on selling a fixed asset counts towards income for the year; the full amount of the sale proceeds does not.

[5] Amortization is really the same as depreciation, but the word is usually applied to leasehold property and to intangible fixed assets such as goodwill. 'Impairment' of goodwill or other assets is comparable.

The Floughin Company has a small assembly plant at Jurbeigh that originally cost £30,000; cumulative depreciation is £6,000. The government decided to develop an international airport nearby, and the company was able to sell their plant for £40,000.

The receipt of cash is £40,000. The net book value of the plant is (£30,000 − £6,000 =) £24,000. Only the profit of £16,000 is credited towards profit for the year.

ILLUSTRATION 7.1

culating profit, only the difference between book value and the sale proceeds is credited to profit, as shown in Illustration 7.1.

It is sometimes argued that cash flow would be a better basis for accounting than the accruals concept because it is more objective. But total cash flows (including receipts from borrowing and payments to acquire fixed assets) mean little unless there is some classification of the receipts and payments. The need for classification would remove the supposed objectivity. Almost all accountants agree that profit measurement[6] and the use of the accruals concept are essential.

7.3 Cash Flow Statements

A *cash flow statement* provides a reconciliation between the amount of profit generated during a period, and the amount by which cash balances have increased or decreased during that period. The idea is that profits generate cash, but cash tends to flow away. The statement shows where it has gone.

It starts off by showing how much operating profit was generated during the period; then it shows what happened to the profits. Some of it may be tied up in additional stocks and debtors; some may have gone in paying interest and taxation; some may have gone in buying more fixed assets or repaying loans. The final figure shows how much cash is left; that final figure at the end of a cash flow statement is the same as the cash balance shown on the balance sheet at the year end.

Most of the information required to prepare a cash flow statement can be found by comparing two balance sheets. In Illustration 7.2 we can see that Ebbing plc made a profit in year 2.[7] But, as the illustration shows, a company may be making, and retaining, decent profits, but because of the need to finance more fixed assets and higher levels of stocks and debtors, they end the year with less cash than they started with. In Illustration 7.2 Ebbing plc started year 2 with £160,000 in the bank; they retained profits during the year of £15,000, but they ended the year with only £35,000 in the bank. By comparing the two balance sheets it is easy to see where the money went: £100,000 extra was tied up in fixed assets; there were additional stocks of £40,000; and there was an additional £30,000 tied up in

---

[6] The reasons why profit is measured are explored in Chapter 5.

[7] Retained earnings increased from £120,000 to £135,000. Profits retained in year 2 amounted to £15,000; that figure is after deducting dividends and taxation. Pre-tax profits would be much greater.

Balance sheet of Ebbing plc as at 31 December

	Year 1	Year 2
Assets	£000	£000
Non-current assets	200	300
Current assets		
Inventories	80	120
Trade receivables	60	90
Cash	160	35
Total assets	500	545
Equity and liabilities		
Equity		
Share capital	240	240
Retained earnings	120	135
Non-current liabilities		
Long-term borrowings	50	50
Current liabilities		
Trade payables	90	120
	500	545

A simplified reconciliation might appear as follows:

		£	£
Increase in	Non-current assets	100,000	
	Inventories	40,000	
	Payables	30,000	
		170,000	
How was this financed?			
Retained profit for the year (135,000 – 120,000)			15,000
Reduction in cash balances (160,000 – 35,000			125,000
Increase in current liabilities (120,000 – 90,000)			30,000
			170,000

ILLUSTRATION 7.2

debtors. How were these additional assets financed? The money came partly from retained profits, partly by reducing cash balances and partly by owing more to trade creditors.

The above reconciliation is rather simplified, and the cash flow statements published by companies are in a standardized format so that businesses can readily be compared with each other. They start by identifying cash flows from operations, which are as follows.

Operating Activities

1 Net profit before deducting taxation and interest
2 Depreciation
3 Increase in working capital
4 Interest paid
5 Taxation paid

1 *Net profit* is normally positive and is an inflow of cash. Where the business makes a loss, this outflow of cash is shown in brackets.

Any increase in retained profits can be established by comparing the balance sheet at the end of the period with the balance sheet at the beginning of the period. The figure required for a cash flow statement is net profit before deducting taxation and interest, which is found from the income statement (or profit and loss account).

2 *Depreciation* is shown as an inflow of cash. Profit is shown as if all expenses are outflows of cash. But depreciation is an expense that is not paid; there is no outflow of cash for depreciation. It is, therefore, necessary for depreciation to be added back to profit. It is an oversimplification to say that cash flow consists of profit plus depreciation, but it is useful to remember this as being the first part of a cash flow statement.

3 Any *increase in working capital* is an outflow of cash or a negative cash flow, and so it is shown in brackets. This usually means that profits have been used to finance higher levels of inventories and payables. Any reduction in working capital is shown as a cash inflow.

The main components of working capital are inventories, receivables and payables (stocks, debtors and creditors) and these can be shown individually instead of using a single figure for working capital.

Any increase in inventories and receivables is shown as an outflow of cash; any decrease in inventories and receivables is shown as an inflow of cash.

Any increase in payables is shown as an inflow of cash; any decrease in payables is shown as an outflow of cash.

This is explained as follows:

i *Debtors or receivables*   Not all the revenue from sales (which is included in the profit figure) is immediately a cash inflow. Where the amount of debtors has increased, this is treated as an outflow of cash (to reduce the inflow included in profit arising from sales). Where the amount of debtors has gone down during a period, more money has been received from them, and the reduction is treated as an inflow of cash.

ii *Creditors or payables*   Not all the expenses that have been recorded in arriving at the profit figure have in fact been paid. Where the amount of creditors has increased, this is treated as an inflow of cash (to reduce the outflow included in profit in respect of purchases and expenses). Where the amount of creditors has decreased during the period, this is treated as an outflow of cash (because more has been paid out than has been charged as an expense in calculating profit).

iii *Stocks or inventories*   In calculating profit, only the cost of goods that have been sold is treated as an expense. The cost of goods that have not yet been sold (closing stocks) is not yet an expense, but those goods still have to be paid for. Any increase in stocks is, therefore, treated as an outflow of cash. Any reduction in stocks is treated as an inflow of cash.

4 *Interest paid* is an outflow of cash, and is shown in brackets. Any interest receivable is an inflow of cash. In some cases the interest receivable is greater than the interest payable, and so the net figure is an inflow of cash.

5 *Taxation paid* is an outflow of cash, and is shown in brackets. Sometimes there is a cash inflow where there has been a tax rebate, perhaps after the company has been making losses.

The first part of a cash flow statement, dealing with cash flows from *operating activities*, is often the most complex. The second and third parts of the cash flow statement deal with *investing activities* (buying and selling fixed assets and investments) and *financing activities* (raising additional finance by issuing additional shares or debentures, or perhaps reducing share capital and borrowings). The reconciliation of cash flow and profit for Ebbing plc is shown in the form of a cash flow statement in Illustration 7.3. Some additional information[8] has been included to make it more realistic.

Cash flow statement of Ebbing plc for the year ended 31 December year 2

		£	
Operating activities			
Net profit, before taxation and interest		48,500	
Depreciation		16,000	
		64,500	
Increase in working capital			
Inventories	(40,000)		
Receivables	(30,000)		
Payables	30,000	(40,000)	
Interest paid		(4,000)	
Taxation paid		(13,500)	
		7,000	(A) Total inflow from operating activities
Investing activities			
Purchase of fixed assets[9]		(116,000)	(B) Investing outflow
Financing activities			
Dividend paid		(16,000)	(C) Financing outflow
Decrease in cash		(125,000)	Net outflow A – B – C
Cash at beginning of year 2		160,000	
Cash at end of year 2		35,000	
		(125,000)	

ILLUSTRATION 7.3

---

[8] Additional information. Depreciation £16,000; interest paid £4,000; taxation paid £13,500; dividends paid £16,000. The increase in retained profits for year 2 is still £15,000, but profit before taxation is (£15,000 + £13,500 taxation + £4,000 interest + £16,000 dividends =) £48,500.

[9] Fixed assets at the end of year 1 were £200,000. In year 2 the amount deducted for depreciation was £16,000. This would have reduced the amount to £184,000. But at the end of year 2 the amount shown for fixed assets was £300,000; expenditure on additional fixed assets must, therefore, have been £116,000.

International Accounting Standard (IAS) 7 specifies that cash flow statements should report inflows and outflows of cash under three headings as follows:

1 *Operating activities*   This should include all the receipts and payments resulting from sales and costs based on the profit figure. Not all of the profit figure shows up as cash because of changes in current assets and current liabilities, as was illustrated with Ebbing plc in Illustrations 7.2 and 7.3.

Depreciation has to be shown separately. It is treated as an expense in calculating profit as if cash has been paid out. But, unlike other expenses, no cash is paid out for depreciation. To arrive at a cash flow figure it is, therefore, necessary to add depreciation (and amortization) to the net profit figure. Interest and taxation paid are also usually included as operating activities.

Ebbing plc made a decent enough profit which, when added to depreciation, produced a cash flow of £64,500. But after financing the increase in working capital, and paying interest and taxation, there was only £7,000 left, which was not enough to pay for additional fixed assets and to pay the dividend.

2 *Investing activities*   This includes all payments for additional fixed assets and expenditure on buying investments in other businesses. Cash inflows include receipts from disposals of fixed assets.

Ebbing plc spent £116,000 on additional fixed assets. Fortunately, they had sufficient money to pay for them because they started the year with £160,000 in the bank.

3 *Financing activities*   The main cash flows here are from issuing or redeeming shares and long-term loans.

Dividends paid are also usually included as a financing activity. Cash outflows include redemption of loans and a company may buy back some of its own shares.

Ebbing plc did not raise any additional loan or share capital during the period as they had enough cash to meet their needs.

The cash flows arising from operating activities is perhaps the most important figure, and it should be positive, even after paying interest and taxes. This is the case with both Ebbing plc (Illustration 7.3) and Reet Aylor plc (Illustration 7.4). In year 3 Reet Aylor plc generated £4.1m from operating activities. But this was not enough to finance the £9.3m they spent on property and equipment. They raised a sum of money from selling off equipment (£0.4m); but the net payment for investing activities was £8.9m. In most businesses this would lead to the need to raise additional funds through long-term loans or issuing shares. But Reet Aylor plc started the year with £7m of cash in the bank, which was more than enough to finance the shortfall and to pay the dividend for the year. The company decided to pay back some of its borrowings, and ended the year with a £1m overdraft.

The financing activities in year 4 were rather different. The cash generated from operating activities was higher at £5.5m, but this was still not enough to finance the £6.3m of additional fixed assets in year 4. The shortfall was financed by a substantial share issue that raised £3.3m. The additional funds raised were also used to pay off the £1m overdraft.

In a reasonably successful company, the cash generated by operating activities should be enough to finance the dividend and some increase in fixed assets. Where there is a

Cash flow statement of Reet Aylor plc for the year ended 31 December

	Year 3 £000	Year 4 £000
Cash flows from operating activities		
Profit before financing costs	7,900	8,200
Depreciation	5,700	6,100
	13,600	14,300
Increase in trade receivables	(2,000)	(1,700)
Increase in inventories	(4,100)	(3,800)
Increase in trade payables	200	300
Cash from operations	7,700	9,100
Interest paid	(1,100)	(900)
Income taxes paid	(2,500)	(2,700)
Net cash from operating activities	4,100	5,500
Cash flows from investing activities		
Proceeds from disposal of equipment	400	300
Purchase of property and equipment	(9,300)	(6,600)
Net cash from investing activities	(8,900)	(6,300)
Cash flows from financing activities		
Proceeds of issue of shares	200	3,300
Repayment of borrowings	(2,100)	–
Dividends paid	(1,300)	(1,400)
Net cash used in financing activities	(3,200)	1,900
Net (decrease)/increase in cash	(8,000)	1,100
Opening cash	7,000	(1,000)
Closing cash	(1,000)	100

ILLUSTRATION 7.4

substantial increase in fixed assets, it is usually necessary for some financing activities to raise additional long-term funds.

In Reet Aylor plc the increase in dividend was very small considering the substantial increase in share capital. If the additional shares were issued towards the end of year 4, a substantial increase in the amount of dividends paid might be expected in year 5.

7.4 Interpreting Cash Flow Statements

Free Cash Flow

The term 'free cash flow' is widely used by financial journalists. The idea is that profit plus depreciation generate additional cash flows; some of this has to be used to finance increases in working capital and to pay interest and taxation. What then remains is 'free cash flow': companies are free to use it how they wish: to pay dividends; to invest in fixed assets or other businesses; and to repay borrowings or share capital.

It is perhaps easier to regard free cash flow as being the net amount of cash arising from operating activities. For example, in Reet Aylor plc (Illustration 7.4) the amount was £4.1m in year 3. Unfortunately, there is no clear definition of what is meant by 'free cash flow'. Most companies do not identify such a figure. Some companies who show it use a variety of different definitions. Although companies are generally 'free' to decide whether or not to pay dividends, care is needed in interpreting cash flow statements: some companies show a 'free cash flow' figure *after* deducting dividends.

The treatment of fixed assets is also a problem. Businesses regularly need to replace some of their fixed assets as they come to the end of their lives; cash flow is not 'free' if it has to be used for essential replacements. But some fixed assets are purchased as part of an expansion plan, and companies are free to decide whether or not to go ahead with such expansions. It would be sensible to say that 'free' cash flow is arrived at after payments for essential replacements of fixed assets, but before funding any expansion. Unfortunately, the distinction between essential replacements and fixed assets for expansion is hard to determine. Sometimes an arbitrary compromise is used, such as deciding that one-third of expenditure on fixed assets is for essential replacement; free cash flow is arrived at after deducting such a proportion of expenditure on fixed assets.

Cash Flow Ratios

Conventional ratio analysis can be adapted to use cash flow figures rather than profit figures. It is important that, in such analyses, a clear definition of cash flow is used consistently. The most straightforward figure to use is the net cash flow generated from operations in the first part of a published cash flow statement. It is seen as being a key indicator of a business's ability to generate cash flows from its operations to pay dividends, repay debt and finance investments in fixed assets to maintain and increase its operating capability (without having to raise additional long-term share or loan capital).

Unfortunately, IAS 7 does not have a firm definition of what is to be included in net cash flow generated from operations with regard to interest and dividends. Interest paid is probably best included under operating activities, but the standard also allows it to be included under financing activities.

Interest and dividends received are probably best included under operating activities, but the standard also allows them to be included under investing activities (as they are the product of investments that have been made). Dividends paid are probably best included under financing activities, but the standard also allows them to be included under operating activities.

The following cash flow ratios are useful provided the definition used for cash flow is clear and consistently applied. The term is sometimes used to mean simply profit plus depreciation. It would be better to use the total figure for operating activities taken from the cash flow statement.

Interest and Dividend Cover

These figures can be calculated to indicate the extent to which interest and dividend payments are covered by cash flows generated. The figures for Reet Aylor plc are as follows:

	Year 3	Year 4
Net cash from operating activities[10]	£4.1m	£5.5m
Dividends paid	£1.3m	£1.4m
Dividend times cover	3.15 times	3.93 times

The dividend cover has increased because although the dividend payment has increased a little, the operating cash flow has increased by a bigger proportion.

	Year 3	Year 4
Net cash from operating activities[11]	£4.1 million	£5.5 million
Interest	£1.1 million	£0.9 million
Cash flow available to cover interest	£5.2 million	£6.4 million
Interest times cover	4.73 times	7.11 times

The cover has increased because the amount of interest payable has reduced (because some borrowings have been repaid) and operating cash flow has increased.

Cash Return on Capital Employed (ROCE)

This figure can be calculated to indicate the extent to which the business generates cash (as opposed to profit) for the shareholders.

$$\frac{\text{Net cash from operating activities}}{\text{Equity}} \times 100$$

Cash Flow per Share

This figure can be calculated in the same way as earnings per share (EPS), but using cash flow from operating activities instead of profit. The cash flow figure is divided by the number of shares in issue. Comparing cash flow per share with EPS is much the same as comparing total cash flow with total earnings.

Published Cash Flow Statements

Published cash flow statements can be quite daunting and include many details and complexities that are hard to understand, even after wading through pages of complicated notes. Generally, figures shown in brackets are outflows of cash, and figures not shown in brackets are inflows of cash. But the proliferation of subtotals and negative figures (outflows) can be confusing, and sometimes the use of brackets is not consistent. It can be helpful to begin by summarizing the main figures, and then asking a number of key questions. The following are likely to be helpful in respect of Reet Aylor plc.

	Year 3	Year 4
	£000	£000
Cash from operating activities	4,100	5,500
Cash (used in) investing activities	(8,900)	(6,300)
Cash (used in)/from financing activities	(3,200)	1,900
(Decrease)/increase in cash	(8,000)	1,100

---

[10] This figure is taken before deducting dividends; it is all available to cover dividends.

[11] This figure is provided *after* interest has been deducted; the interest is, therefore, added back to establish the amount available to cover interest.

Suggested questions in interpreting cash flow statements:

1 Was there a positive cash flow from operating activities? If so, how was it used? If not, why not?

2 Has working capital increased, and how was it financed? Has there been a reduction in working capital, and what is the significance of this reduction?

3 Have there been significant investing activities? Is there a substantial increase in fixed assets? Have there been substantial investments in other businesses? How were these financed?

4 Has there been a reduction in investments in fixed assets and other businesses? How much money was raised, and how was this used?

5 Has the business been raising substantial long-term financing? Why do these funds seem to be needed? Have they been invested in long-term assets? Were they needed to finance shortfalls in cash flows from operating activities? Were they needed to pay off overdrafts?

6 Are the cash flows from financing activities negative (i.e. has there been a reduction in long-term funding)? What does this suggest? Is the business contracting? Or are cash flows from operating activities sufficient to finance expansion?

7 Has one form of long-term capital been used to redeem another (perhaps issuing shares to repay debentures)? Why might this have been done?

8 Was the amount of dividend covered by cash flows from operating activities? Does the dividend appear to be justified by available cash flows?

9 Did the cash balance increase or decrease during the year? Why – what were the main contributors to this?

A cash flow statement provides useful information in relation to questions such as these, but it may not provide full answers. It is important (as always with interpretation of financial statements) to compare this year's figures with the previous year and to identify trends. It is also usually necessary to examine the balance sheet and income statement for further explanation. All three statements should be considered together.

A Published Cash Flow Statement

Interpretation

A quick overview of Ottakar's 2006 financial statements (Illustration 7.5) shows that they generated £23m from operating activities and used almost £8m of that in investing activities, buying additional plant and equipment. Over £4m was used in financing activities, mainly repaying borrowings and paying dividends. That left almost £11m to increase the amount of cash that they held. As they started the year with *negative* cash of over £10.5m, they ended the year with positive cash of just less than £0.4m.

Their 2005 financial statements show that they generated £3.9m from operating activities, but managed to spend almost £9m on investing activities, buying additional plant and equipment. They also used up over £3m in financing activities (repaying borrowings and paying dividends). The result was that they ended up with £8.2m less cash than they started the year with: their overdraft increased from £2.4m to £10.6m.

Cash flow statement of Ottaker's plc

Statement of cash flows[12] for 52 weeks to	28 January 2006 £000	29 January 2005 £000
Cash flows from operating activities		
(Loss) Profit for year before tax	(4,551)	6,866
Depreciation	6,165	5,609
Financial expense	1,373	1,113
Impairment of property and equipment	3,398	–
Loss on disposal of property and equipment and other items	368	62
	6,753	13,650
Increase in receivables	(456)	(2,023)
Decrease/(increase) in inventories	3,031	(4,106)
Increase in payables	16,395	23
Cash generated from operations	25,723	7,544
Interest paid	(1,375)	(1,134)
Taxes paid	(1,250)	(2,543)
Net cash generated from operating activities	23,098	3,867
Cash flows from investing activities		
Proceeds of disposal of property and equipment	1	426
Purchase of property and equipment	(7,986)	(9,387)
Net cash used in investing activities	(7,985)	(8,961)
Cash flows from financing activities		
Proceeds from issue and sale of shares	321	229
Repayment of borrowings	(3,000)	(2,000)
Repayment under finance leases	(90)	(82)
Dividends paid	(1,410)	(1,262)
Net cash used in financing activities	(4,179)	(3,115)
Net increase/(decrease) in cash and cash equivalents	(10,934)	(8,209)
Opening cash and equivalents	(10,562)	(2,353)
Closing cash and equivalents	372	(10,562)

ILLUSTRATION 7.5

A closer examination shows that the performance for 2006 was worse than that for 2005. The biggest item in the cash generated from operations resulted from increase in short-term liabilities: they had £16.4m more because they owed £16.4m more. Profit plus depreciation should be the main generator of operating cash flows. The 2005 figure was (£6.9m + £5.6m =) £12.5m. For 2006 it was only £1.6m (£4.6m loss; £6.2m depreciation).

A loss of £4.6m looks bad, but part of it (£3.4m) was due to 'impairment of property and equipment', which is rather like depreciation, and could be added to the £1.6m to give £5m for profit plus depreciation (compared with £12.5m in the previous year). That still looks bad, as does the huge increase in payables (current liabilities). It is interesting to note that

---

[12] Summarized and simplified.

while in previous years inventories had increased, there was a substantial reduction (£3m) in 2006, although turnover was still increasing, which helped to increase cash generated from operating activity. This may have been due partly to bringing in cash by selling off stocks; there may also have been an element of writing inventories down to net realizable value, a process comparable with depreciation.

In spite of their 'losses' Ottakar's continued to invest substantially (almost £8m), in additional property and equipment in 2006, and to pay off borrowings (£3m). It is unusual that this was, in effect, financed by increasing short-term creditors.

7.5 Cash Budgets

Most of us have some sort of cash budget in mind for our own personal receipts and payments. We like to know that, each month, there is enough coming in to meet the payments that we plan to make. Or we may plan it the other way around: we will spend no more than the cash that will be available to us. Failure to plan properly typically leads either to unexpected overdrafts and credit card borrowing – with crippling rates of interest; or we simply run out of money before the end of the month and cannot afford to eat or drink until our next salary comes in.

It is a similar story for companies. They need to plan their monthly[13] receipts and payments for at least the next year. It may be that a company is very profitable and expanding rapidly, but they may not be producing enough cash to meet their monthly commitments. Some companies make substantial profits, but end the year with less cash than they started. Other companies may not be particularly profitable, but they generate lots of cash. Comparing a company's budgeted income statement with their cash budget for the coming year shows how their monthly cash flows differ from their monthly profits or losses, and why. The budgeted income statement gives a good indication of the viability of the business. The cash budget shows whether they are likely to have cash surpluses (which they may wish to invest), or whether there is going to be insufficient cash to get by. If a cash shortage problem is identified in advance, ways around the problem can be planned before it becomes a crisis. This can be seen by examining Illustration 7.6, the Holly Day Company.

A cash budget shows all the (planned or expected future) receipts and payments of an organization, typically on a monthly basis for the next year.

The receipts figure includes all cash that comes in directly from cash sales. It also includes receipts from debtors; they usually come in a month or two after the sales are made, so the figure is different from that shown on a profit and loss account. In Illustration 7.6 it was assumed that all sales were on credit. There may be other receipts such as money that comes in from dividends, interest, rent, commission and royalties. The cash budget will show the money as a receipt in the month when the money is expected. An income statement shows it in the month in which it is earned (or it 'accrues') regardless of when the cash is received.

---

[13] Or weekly or even daily.

The Holly Day Company
Question

The Holly Day Company manufactures seasonal goods for holidaymakers, and supplies them to retailers in many seaside resorts. There has been little change in their seasonal sales patterns in recent years. Sales start off at £15,000 a month in January, and increase by £15,000 a month until they peak at £120,000 a month in August; they fall to £90,000 a month in September; £30,000 a month in October, and then to £15,000 a month in November and December. Customers pay for the goods, on average, two months after the sales are made.

The materials are bought and used in the month before sales take place; they are treated as an expense in the month that the finished goods to which they relate are sold; and they are paid for one month after purchase (i.e. in the month that the sale takes place). The cost of materials for making the goods amounts to one-third of the selling price.

There is a basic labour force costing £4,000 a month in October–January each year. This increases to £6,000 a month in February, and £8,000 a month in March. The labour costs in the busy time of the year are £16,000 a month, from April to September inclusive.

The only other expense is depreciation, which amounts to £3,000 a month. One of the machines is getting towards the end of its life and will be replaced by a new one, costing £60,000, which will be paid for in June. Depreciation on the new machine will be charged at 20 per cent per annum on a straight line basis. The old machine will be sold for £15,000 (which is its net book value) at the end of the year (in December).

Taxation of £50,000 is payable in March, and dividends of £55,000 will be paid in May.

Required:
a Prepare the income statement for the coming year, showing sales, expenses and profit for each month, and in total.
b Prepare the cash budget for the coming year, showing receipts and payments for each month; the net cash surplus or deficit for the month; and the bank balance at the end of each month. Assume that the business starts the year with £50,000 in the bank.
c Explain why the company has generated more profit than cash during the year.
d From examining the cash budget, what changes in plan would you suggest to minimize the need for an overdraft?

Answer
b Cash budget of the Holly Day Company

	Jan £000	Feb £000	Mar £000	Apr £000	May £000	Jun £000	Jul £000	Aug £000	Sep £000	Oct £000	Nov £000	Dec £000	Total £000
Receipts													
From debtors	15	15	15	30	45	60	75	90	105	120	90	30	690
Sale of machine	—	—	—	—	—	—	—	—	—	—	—	15	15
	15	15	15	30	45	60	75	90	105	120	90	45	705
Payments													
Materials	5	10	15	20	25	30	35	40	30	10	5	5	230
Wages	4	6	8	16	16	16	16	16	16	4	4	4	126
Fixed assets						60							60
Taxation			50										50
Dividends	—	—	—	—	55	—	—	—	—	—	—	—	55
	9	16	73	36	96	106	51	56	46	14	9	9	521
Net receipts or (deficit)	6	(1)	(58)	(6)	(51)	(46)	24	34	59	106	81	36	184
Opening balance	50	56	55	(3)	(9)	(60)	(106)	(82)	(48)	11	117	198	
Closing balance	56	55	(3)	(9)	(60)	(106)	(82)	(48)	11	117	198	234	234

ILLUSTRATION 7.6

a Budgeted income statement

	Jan £000	Feb £000	Mar £000	Apr £000	May £000	Jun £000	Jul £000	Aug £000	Sep £000	Oct £000	Nov £000	Dec £000	Total £000
Receipts													
Sales	15	30	45	60	75	90	105	120	90	30	15	15	690
Expenses													
Materials	5	10	15	20	25	30	35	40	30	10	5	5	230
Wages	4	6	8	16	16	16	16	16	16	4	4	4	126
Depreciation	3	3	3	3	3	4	4	4	4	4	4	4	43
	12	19	26	39	44	50	55	60	50	18	13	13	399
Profit	3	11	29	21	31	40	50	60	40	12	2	2	291

ILLUSTRATION 7.6 continued

Some receipts do not appear on an income statement. These include receipts from issuing shares or debentures; borrowing money; and sales of fixed assets.[14]

The payments figure includes all the money that it is expected will be paid out. Payments for purchases are usually made a month or so after the purchases are made (and recorded for profit and loss account purposes). The cash budget also shows payments for expenses that will also appear on the profit and loss account. With most expenses the payment is made after the expense is incurred. Some expenses (such as rent, and perhaps advertising) are paid in advance. Again, in the cash budget, it is the period in which the payment is actually made that matters. In the income statement it is when the expense is incurred that matters.

The cash budget also shows when tax and dividends are to be paid. These items also appear on the profit and loss account, but, again, the timing might be different. A company typically shows its tax charge on the income statement of one year, but the cash is actually paid in the following year. Similarly a company typically decides on their final[15] dividend in one year and the cash is paid out in the following year.

Some payments do not appear at all on an income statement. Cash has to be paid out to acquire non-current assets (fixed assets), and there may be payments to buy investments such as shares in other businesses, and to repay loans.

A cash budget shows the change in the cash balance each month. There is an opening balance at the beginning of the month. Total receipts and total payments are calculated to give a figure for net receipts (or payments) for the month. Net receipts are added to the balance at the beginning of the month to show the closing balance for the month. That then becomes the opening balance for the next month.

Figures can, of course, be the other way around. If the budget shows an overdraft at the beginning of the month, net receipts for the month will reduce the overdraft.

---

[14] The profit arising on the sale of a fixed asset is included in the income statement. That is the difference between the net book value of the asset and its sale proceeds.

[15] Companies typically pay an interim dividend part way through the year, and a final dividend after the end of the year.

The budget should also show the total increase or decrease in cash expected during the year. This will be different from the budgeted profit figure, and it is useful to compare the two to see how and why the profit figure for the year differs from the cash flow figure. This is illustrated in this chapter with the Holly Day Company (Illustration 7.6) and with Rachel's business (Self-testing question 6).

Summary

In many businesses, generating profits and generating cash flows go hand in hand. Good profits are likely to result in healthy cash flows, but the two are unlikely to be identical. In many circumstances the profit (or loss) for the year can be very different from the increase (or decrease) in cash. The differences between the two show up well on a cash flow statement. Having cash available to meet liabilities as they fall due is essential for business survival, and healthy businesses should generate healthy cash flows. Businesses also need to generate profits if they are to survive and be healthy. If a business makes a profit, its wealth increases. That increase in wealth is used in many different ways (such as paying dividends and investing in more assets); it is unlikely to be matched by an exactly equal increase in cash.

We could debate whether cash flow or profit is more important to the survival and success of businesses. That would be a bit like debating whether eating or drinking is more important to the survival and success of people. Both are essential.

Review of key points

- Profit is not the same as cash flow. The accruals concept may be seen as being the theoretical justification and explanation of the difference.
- A cash flow statement provides a reconciliation between operating profit for the year and the net increase or decrease in cash during the year.
- A company's operating profit may be used to finance higher levels of stocks and debtors; to pay interest and taxation; and to buy additional fixed assets.
- A detailed cash flow statement shows other differences between cash flow and profit in a standardized format.
- A cash flow statement should be interpreted alongside the related balance sheets and income statements, and can reveal important aspects of a company's performance.
- A cash budget shows planned receipts and payments of cash, typically on a monthly basis for the next year.
- The budgeted net receipts of cash are likely to be very different from the budgeted profit figure.

Review of key points (continued)

- Some differences between cash flow and profit are relatively minor, relating to the timing of receipts and payments compared with the timing of recognition of revenues and expenses.
- Depreciation is an important expense in calculating profit; there is no equivalent payment in cash terms.
- Some of the biggest receipts and payments (such as issue of shares; purchase of fixed assets; and paying back loans) have no direct effect on profit.
- The availability of cash to meet liabilities as they fall due is essential to business survival. Making profits is essential if the business is to become 'better off'.

Self-testing questions

1 What is meant by the 'accruals concept'? Why is it important in financial accounting?

2 In what circumstances is a very profitable business likely to find that it has serious cash shortages?

3 Is it possible for a company to make losses year after year, but still increase its cash balances? Explain.

4 What is meant by 'free cash flow'? Estimate the amounts of free cash flow for:

   a Ebbing plc for year 2 (Illustration 7.3)

   b Reet Aylor for years 3 and 4 (Illustration 7.4)

   Comment briefly on each.

5 You are given the cash flow statements for the last two years for Deek Lining plc, which are shown overleaf.

Self-testing questions (continued)

Cash flow statement of Deek Lining plc for the year ended 31 December

	Year 3 £000	Year 4 £000
Cash flows from operating activities		
Profit before financing costs	3,400	(1,200)
Depreciation	2,600	2,800
	6,000	1,600
(Increase)/Decrease in trade receivables	(600)	300
(Increase)/Decrease in inventories	(400)	200
(Decrease)/Increase in trade payables	(100)	100
Cash from operations	4,900	2,200
Interest paid	(200)	(150)
Income taxes paid	(1,300)	(100)
Net cash from operating activities	3,400	1,950
Cash flows from investing activities		
Proceeds from disposal of equipment	100	1,100
Purchase of property and equipment	(3,700)	(150)
Net cash from investing activities	(3,600)	950
Cash flows from financing activities		
Proceeds of issue of shares	–	–
Increase/(Decrease) in borrowings	200	(1,000)
Dividends paid	(600)	(700)
Net cash raised from (used in) financing activities	(400)	(1,700)
Net (decrease)/increase in cash	(600)	1,200
Opening cash	700	(100)
Closing cash	100	1,100

An extract from the chairman's statement reads as follows:

Year 4 was another successful year, producing a positive cash flow which enabled us to pay off a substantial amount of borrowings, to invest in new fixed assets, and to increase the dividend for ordinary shareholders.

Critically appraise this statement.

6 Rachel owns a specialist boring-digging machine that she hires out, together with an operator/driver, to builders and farmers. A few years ago her accountant worked out that she should charge £500 a day and that should give her a comfortable living. In the last year demand has fallen, particularly in the winter months when the weather restricts the use of the machine, and in the summer months when many people are on holiday. In the coming year (year 3) she estimates that she will have 10 days' work a month in January and February; 20 days' work a month in March, April, May and June. Then it will fall to 12 days a month in July and August. In September, October and November she expects 20 days' work a month, and only 5 days in December.

At the end of year 2 her debtors figure was £5,000, of which she expects to receive half in January and half in February.

On average, customers pay 2 months after the work is done.

Self-testing questions (continued)

Operating expenses, including fuel and labour, amount to £100 per day. Expenses are paid in the month that they are incurred.

Her fixed overheads, including depreciation, are £3,000 per month. The machine originally cost £140,000 and is expected to have a 5-year life, with a residual value of £20,000. She uses straight line depreciation.

At the end of last year she had only £1,000 in her business bank account.

Rachel would like to take £45,000 a year out of the business to cover her personal living expenses. But she does not want to have an overdraft, and she does not want to be living off capital.

Required:

a Prepare the income statement for the coming year, showing sales, expenses and profit for each month, and in total.

b Prepare the cash budget for the coming year, showing receipts and payments for each month; the net cash surplus or deficit for the month; and the bank balance at the end of each month.

c Explain why the company has generated more cash than profit during the year.

d How much do you think that she can afford to take out of the business as drawings (or dividends if it is a company) during the year? Give your reasons.

Assessment questions

1 Explain the effect of the accruals concept on the treatment of inventories, fixed assets, receivables and payables.

2 Shareholders are mainly interested in a company's ability to pay dividends. If a company increases the amount of cash it has available during the year, it is able to pay more dividends. A company should, therefore, aim to maximize the amount of cash it has available. Explain the flaws in these statements.

3 You are given the cash flow statements shown overleaf for Ink Reasing plc.

Required:

a Write a report explaining what the above cash flow statements reveal.

b The company's bankers stated that in view of the £1m increase in the company's overdraft, and the additional borrowings of £2.2m, the increase in the amount of dividends paid is not justified. Do you agree? Explain.

Assessment questions (continued)

Cash flow statement of Ink Reasing plc for the year ended 31 December

	Year 1 £000	Year 2 £000
Cash flows from operating activities		
Profit before financing costs	1,800	2,500
Depreciation	1,500	1,900
	3,300	4,400
Increase in trade receivables	(800)	(1,200)
Increase in inventories	(600)	(1,300)
Increase in trade payables	100	200
Cash from operations	2,000	2,100
Interest paid	(600)	(600)
Income taxes paid	(400)	(600)
Net cash from operating activities	1,000	900
Cash flows from investing activities		
Proceeds from disposal of equipment	–	100
Purchase of property and equipment	(2,100)	(4,000)
Net cash from investing activities	(2,100)	(3,900)
Cash flows from financing activities		
Proceeds of issue of shares	2,000	–
(Repayment of) increase in borrowings	(600)	2,200
Dividends paid	(400)	(500)
Net cash (used in) raised from financing activities	1,000	1,700
Net (decrease)/increase in cash	(100)	(1,300)
Opening cash	400	300
Closing cash	300	(1,000)

4 Judas has developed a plan for a rapidly expanding business selling and installing software for individuals using computers at home. He will operate on a 100 per cent mark-up (50 per cent gross profit ratio) on the software that he sells, and will employ a team of highly paid technicians/sales staff. He has piloted his business model on a number of customers, and he knows that they are particularly afraid of computer viruses; he will provide a guarantee of 12 months free of viruses. But, somehow, after a year or so he knows that there will always be a return of viruses and most of his customers will request his services again. During the next 12 months he aims to build up his customer base, and make a small profit.

He has discussed his business plan with his accountant, and the following seems to be soundly based.

i Sales in January will be £220,000 and will then increase by £20,000 per month. Customers pay 2 months after the sale is made.

ii Suppliers are paid 1 month after purchases are made. Stocks amounting to £100,000 will be bought in the first month and maintained at that level. Purchases will be made each month that are sufficient to supply sales for that month.

Assessment questions (continued)

iii Wages and expenses will be £100,000 a month for the first 4 months of the year; then they will increase to £150,000 a month for the following 3 months; then they will be £200,000 a month for the next 5 months. They are paid during the month that they are incurred.

iv At the beginning of the year he will spend £840,000 on fixed assets. All fixed assets are depreciated over 10 years. Depreciation is charged on a monthly basis. In June additional fixed assets of £360,000 will be bought.

His accountant advises him that although the business should make a modest profit, there will be substantial cash outflows to begin with. She prepared a monthly budgeted profit and loss account, and a monthly cash budget. But Judas had £1m available to finance the business and reckoned that there would be no problem. He refused to pay her fees and so she did not show him the monthly budgets.

You are required to:

1 Prepare a monthly profit and loss account for the first year of the business showing the profit or loss each month, and for the year in total.

2 Prepare a cash budget for the year showing the receipts and payments for each month, and the cash surplus or deficit each month.

3 Explain and comment on the results.

Group activities and discussion questions

1 Study a number of published cash flow statements. In what ways (if any) are they more useful than relying on just a balance sheet and an income statement?

2 Discuss the idea of 'free cash flow'. To what extent are companies 'free' to refrain from investing in fixed (non-current) assets?

3 Would you rather see a summary of receipts and payments of cash during the year than see a conventional cash flow statement? What are the advantages and disadvantages of each?

4 Cash flow statements are usually in respect of the previous year; cash budgets are usually in respect of the coming year. What would be the advantages of showing a budgeted cash flow statement for the coming year?

5 Do you prepare a cash budget for yourself for the coming year? What is the case for and against bothering to do this? Is it *essential* for a company to prepare a cash budget? Is it *essential* for you?

6 Shareholders are interested in whether their company has increased its equity (using accruals-based accounting), and what dividends are justified. They are not interested in the management of cash; that is a matter for the directors. Discuss.

7 Does it matter if a company's cash flow from operations is negative? Explain.

Financial accounting in context

We have made 130 times our money and are still playing

By James Hall

Sunday Telegraph, 23 October 2005

Discuss and comment on the following extract from the press with particular reference to the distinction between making

profits and generating cash.

Source: Reproduced with permission by the *Sunday Telegraph*.

PHILIP GREEN, the retailing entrepreneur who owns the Arcadia and Bhs chains, claims that he will not be celebrating this weekend.

"I'm sleeping this weekend. I'm exhausted," he says from the back of his Gulfstream G550 jet en route to Monaco, where he lives.

But Green has ample reason to raise a glass or two. Last week he paid himself a £1.2bn dividend from Arcadia, the TopShop to Dorothy Perkins retailer that he bought for £850m in 2002. The figure is the largest ever personal dividend paid in UK corporate history. Green is well known for his sumptuous lifestyle, but last week's payout took his personal resources to new levels.

Green and his family own 92 per cent of Arcadia, with the remaining 8 per cent owned by HBOS, the bank. The bumper payout is all the more staggering given that at the time of the 2002 deal only £10m of pure equity was invested in Arcadia – £9.2m from Green and £800,000 from HBOS.

Green's £1.2bn dividend represents a return on his initial investment of 130 times. "We have made 130 times our money and we are still playing," he says gleefully. HBOS received a dividend of more than £100m for its 8 per cent share, taking the total payout to £1.3bn.

As noteworthy as the jaw-dropping size of the dividend is the fact that it is not being financed from the company's coffers. The cash will come from a seven-and-a-half year loan from a banking syndicate [led] by HBOS. Green has geared up the business in order to finance the dividend.

News of the dividend left Green's retail rivals impressed, partly because it was announced with a strong set of full-year

profits – a rarity in the current harsh retail environment. Arcadia's operating profit rose by 10 per cent to £326.1m over the year to 27 August. Sales rose 6.8 per cent to £1.77bn, with like-for-like sales rising 1.3 per cent. The gross margin increased too.

"He's done well, hasn't he?" says Phil Wrigley, the chief executive of New Look, the fashion retailer, with just a touch of understatement. "Absolute credit to him. He has quite rightly claimed some of the bragging rights. What a story. The debt [for the dividend] looks perfectly serviceable."

So how has Green done it? Two years before he bought Arcadia the company was on the critical list. And over the year to August 2002 – when Arcadia had made a recovery under Stuart Rose, its then chief executive and now head of Marks & Spencer – the retail group made a pre-tax profit of £106m. How has Green managed to grow profits so strongly and make so much money out of a retail deal?

There are three reasons. The first centres around the way that the Arcadia deal was structured. The second is about how Arcadia was run before Green bought it. And the third is the importance that Green – a lifelong, hands-on retailer – places on the importance of generating cash when running a store chain.

To finance the £850m deal for Arcadia, Green borrowed £775m from HBOS. In addition, he put in the £10m of equity (along with HBOS). The rest came from two subordinated loans totalling £65m.

Through cutting fat from Arcadia and increasing sales and margins, Green was able to pay back £500m of the debt and increase operating profits by 95.8 per cent, to £227.9m, within a year of buying Arcadia.

More importantly, cash flow surged. Green took a sprawling PLC with substantial central costs and a rigid structure and all but eliminated the head office – and he gave Arcadia's seven store chains their autonomy.

He increased the amount of goods that Arcadia sourced from cheaper suppliers in the Far East and Central Europe. And he bought smaller amounts of stock, reducing stockholding costs, but increased the frequency of purchases. Result: fewer markdowns to shift unwanted stock.

This better buying – and Green's ability to instill a cost-conscious culture throughout a company – meant that sales and margins rose. "It is about being focused on every area of the business whether we are buying pencil sharpeners or hotel rooms or flights or telephones or tyres for cars. We try to do the best we can in every case. I don't call it cost-cutting. I just call it doing your job," he says.

Analysts say that Arcadia's position as a private company has helped him, since he has not suffered from the pressure felt by many listed companies to drive up turnover even when that turnover is unprofitable.

Anyway, by last October – when Green announced Arcadia's second set of full-year results – he had paid off all the debt that he had borrowed from HBOS four years ahead of schedule.

With Green making so much cash out of Arcadia, he has been accused of buying it "on the cheap". David Dummings, a fund manager at Standard Life Investments, which held 9 per cent of Arcadia before Green bought it, famously said that he felt short-changed after Green revealed Arcadia's maiden results under his ownership.

But that's not what most shareholders felt when they sold out. After Rose joined Arcadia in November 2000 its shares were at 51p having been as low as 38p a few months previously. Earlier that year the company had been close to breaching its banking covenants.

Just a year later its performance had improved and Baugur, the Icelandic retailer with a 20 per cent stake in Arcadia, tried to buy the company at between 280p and 300p per share, valuing it at under £600m. However, talks were eventually called off in February 2002 when the Arcadia board, which had been keen to recommend the bid, concluded that Baugur was unable to raise the funds.

Green bought Arcadia in the autumn of 2002 for 412p a share, or £850m (the deal was actually for 408p a share plus a 4p special dividend). He had moved upwards from an initial indicative offer of 365p. The final offer was a 36 per cent premium to the share price before news of his bid broke.

Although analysts now value Arcadia at £2bn – a substantial increase on the £850m he paid – Green angrily dismisses talk that his bid was "low ball".

"You have got to look at where Arcadia came from. The fact is that Stuart tried to exit at the beginning of 2002, but couldn't because Baugur couldn't raise the money. So on the basis that the board were prepared to recommend 280p to 300p, how the f****** hell can 412p be low ball eight months later?", he asks.

Green doubts that he will have any problems in paying back the new debt of £1.35bn that he has taken on. As well as the loan to finance the dividend, Green has taken out £260m worth of long-term mortgages on Arcadia's stores (a clever move as it means that the company still owns its properties and has resisted the move to sell them and lease them back).

"This is not aggressive leveraged finance. This is traditional financing. Risk is a definition," he says, explaining that the debt is only equal to three times Arcadia's EBITDA.

"If you can find me a retailer that I can buy for three times EBITDA I will turn my plane around and arrive with my chequebook," he says.

Observers agree that Green will not be stretched. "Philip is probably the best judge of business risk there is. He is measured and considered," says Richard Hyman, the chairman of Verdict, the research company.

On this basis Philip Green, dividend king, can sleep easy this weekend.

References and further reading

Elliott, B. and J. Elliott (2005) *Financial Accounting and Reporting.* FT Prentice Hall.

International Accounting Standard 1 *Presentation of Financial Statements.* (December 2003, amended March 2004). IASB.

International Accounting Standard 7 *Cash Flow Statements.* (December 1992, amended March 2004). IASB.

International Accounting Standards Board *Framework for the Preparation and Presentation of Financial Statements* (1989, amended 2001). IASB.

Lewis, R., D. Pendrill and D. Simon (2003) *Advanced Financial Accounting* (7th edition). FT Prentice Hall.

www.frc.org.uk (UK accounting standards)

www.iasb.co.uk (international accounting standards)

Creative Accounting

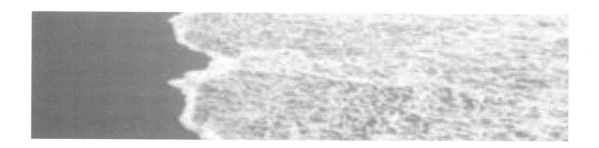

❖ LEARNING OBJECTIVES

After studying this chapter you should be able to:

❖ Explain what is meant by *creative accounting* and understand that the term is sometimes applied to very different practices

❖ Explain why creative accounting practices have developed

❖ Give examples of a number of creative accounting practices

❖ Describe how existing accountancy arrangements are intended to restrict creative accounting

❖ Evaluate a variety of different approaches to deal with creative accounting

8.1 Introduction

This chapter examines what is meant by 'creative accounting', explains a number of different practices that have been described as creative accounting, and then assesses a variety of different ways in which the problem might be tackled.

8.2 What is Creative Accounting?

The term 'creative accounting' is used in relation to a variety of different accounting practices. At one extreme it is used to describe fraudulent and criminal activities. At the other extreme it might be viewed more benignly: as being no more than producing an honest presentation that emphasizes the favourable aspects of a company's performance. There is a natural desire for companies to put a positive spin on their financial position and performance.

It is unlikely that a company's annual report will say:

> The company has three divisions. Division A is the largest and is a complete disaster; losses continue to mount. Division B is going downhill and is now running at a loss. Division C is small, but it did make a tiny profit.

They are more likely to say:

> Division C has expanded rapidly and sales and profits are at record levels. Division B is coping well with difficult world economic conditions. Division A has made good progress in meeting its targets and is expected to show further progress in the coming year.

Investors and other users of annual reports and accounts can look at the published, audited figures to establish the relationship between management claims, and the 'real' financial performance and position. One of the functions of annual reports is to enable those who use them to assess the competence of the company's management. They can do this by comparing their fine words with the financial results that their companies produce.

The Development of Creative Accounting

There have, no doubt, always been examples of directors, accountants and auditors who bend or breach the rules to show company performance in a more flattering light. Such abuses have been tackled by Companies Acts and by the accounting and auditing professions. As attention has been drawn to particular abuses, so action has been taken to try to stop them. The regulatory framework of accounting has steadily become more strict and detailed. But even 60 years ago there were relatively few accounting rules; they were very flexible; and enforcement was not strong.

In the late 1960s there were some serious and high-profile accounting scandals from which it seemed that companies could choose almost any accounting principles they liked. What was a profit to one accountant would be a loss to another, and confidence in the accountancy profession was at a low ebb.

The accountancy profession set up the Accounting Standards Committee (ASC) which, in the 1970s and 1980s, produced a series of Statements of Standard Accounting Practice (SSAPs), which were intended to raise standards of financial reporting, and to reduce the areas of difference and variety in accounting practice. They had some success in improving financial reporting, but it was in the 1980s that the term 'creative accounting' came to be widely used, even in the popular press.

Popular books on creative accounting by Griffiths (1986), followed by Jameson (1988), argued that companies had a wide choice of accounting principles, policies and practices, and could justify almost any profit figures that they wished. The reputation of the ASC suffered, and, following the recommendations of the Dearing Committee (1988) the accounting standards setting arrangements were revamped, and the Accounting Standards Board (ASB) was established.

The situation improved in the 1990s, but the scandals did not go away. In a new version of his book, Griffiths (1995) argued that some order had been brought to the chaos of the regulatory framework of accounting, and that the ASB had made tremendous progress in restoring the integrity and credibility of accounting standards. The more flagrant abuses had been banned, but an extensive range of techniques was still available that could be used to massage the figures. The Financial Reporting and Review Panel (FRRP) was demonstrating that it could be effective in enforcing the application of accounting standards. But, he argued, 'creative accounting still flourishes ... there is still tremendous scope for manipulation'. He concluded that his basic 1986 premise still held: companies were still fiddling their profits.

Other books popularized the idea that creative accounting was (and probably still is) widespread. Smith and Hannah (1991) highlighted a number of creative accounting practices. They produced a list of major companies, and put a number of 'blobs' against them: one blob for each of the questionable practices that the company adopted. Some companies came out with a clean bill of health, but serious questions were raised about the credibility of the financial statements of others. More recent versions by Smith show that the problems have not gone away. Other books in the 1990s (e.g. McBarnet and Whelan, 1999; Pijper, 1993) continued to highlight the problems of creative accounting in the UK.

But, in 2001–2, the limelight was taken by US companies, with a number of major accounting scandals that overshadowed what came to be seen as relatively minor problems in the UK.

In November 2001 Enron, one of the world's largest energy groups, admitted that between 1997 and 2000 various 'special purpose entities' should have been included in the group's accounts, which would have substantially reduced profits. In December 2001 they filed for bankruptcy. Arthur Andersen, Enron's auditors, admitted shredding or deleting thousands of relevant documents and were found guilty of obstructing the course of justice. Arthur Andersen, one of the world's largest accountancy firms, collapsed and their business was split up and taken over by rival firms. Enron had paid Andersen $25m in audit fees for 2001 and another $27m for other non-audit services.

The next major scandal was WorldCom where the founder and chief executive, Bernie Ebbers, and the chief financial officer, Scott Sullivan, resigned after admitting that the US's Securities and Exchange Commission (SEC) was investigating the company's accounting practices. There were claims of frauds amounting to $3.8 billion in the company.

Soon it seemed that newspapers were making comments on almost every company's annual report suggesting problems of creative accounting: Xerox, Vivendi, Computacenter, Elan – the list went on and on. Many of the accounting policies that were criticized at the peak of the controversy had previously hardly been a matter for comment. Suddenly the climate changed and they were presented as scandals or abuses. The main scandals seemed to be in the USA, and action was taken with stricter requirements under the Sarbanes–Oxley Act. By 2006 there was a period of relative stability. Former Enron chief executives Kenneth Lay and Jeffrey Skilling were found guilty of the biggest fraud in corporate history after their energy giant collapsed into bankruptcy. Others became more cautious. But creative accounting had not disappeared. There are still problem areas in accounting standards, for example with revenue recognition; there are still differences between international and US standards; and there are signs that 'mutual recognition' of differing standards is emerging rather than general agreement between different standard setting regimes.

The Effects

The main and obvious intention and effect of creative accounting is to boost reported profits (or to reduce reported losses). When a company gets into financial difficulties, and a different team of accountants starts examining what has been going on, it sometimes comes to light that the company has been exaggerating profits in one way or another. A different team of accountants reinterprets the accounting data and comes up with very different profit (or loss) figures.

Exaggerated profits can have a number of effects. The share price is likely to be favourably affected as long as the profits have credibility. When the credibility goes, the share price collapses.

An increasing proportion of the remuneration of chairpersons and chief executives (often the majority, and sometimes in millions of pounds) is performance-related pay. It is usually linked to the company's profits and its share price. It is only to be expected that chief executives will do what they can to maximize profits and share price. That is what the shareholders put them there to do.

Sometimes creative accounting is more concerned with 'income smoothing' than with maximizing profits in a particular year. In a year when the company's performance is very good, there is a temptation to understate profits, and to keep something back to supplement profits in leaner years. Investors are probably more impressed by a company that manages to increase its profits every year than by one that seems to swing from profits to losses. This is, of course, against all accounting rules, but it is likely that, at the margin, judgements in some companies are exercised in a more prudent way when the profits are very good, and in a less prudent way when profits have fallen.

Creative accounting is not only about reported profits. It can be used to manipulate key ratios that are used by analysts, and to produce more healthy looking balance sheets. If a company wants to demonstrate that they have a high return on capital employed (ROCE) they will want to maximize profits; but they will not want to see high figures for capital employed. Such companies may avoid increasing asset values, and find ways of reducing asset values that do not hit profits too hard, particularly in relatively lean years.

Other companies may have a need to borrow, and will want to emphasize the asset backing for such borrowings. Existing borrowings often come with covenants to protect the position of existing lenders. Such covenants may require the company not to exceed specified gearing ratios and other defined ratios. In these circumstances companies might seek to maximize assets and equity. If land and buildings are revalued (upwards), that automatically increases the figure for equity and may then make it easier for the company to borrow more money.

The use of creative accounting may be attractive to a new management team that has just taken over a company. The new team are likely to be under pressure to prove that they are more successful than their predecessors. The use of 'provisions' may be a tempting way of doing this, as outlined in the section on page 196.

Judgement Becoming Creative

There is inevitably a need for judgement in many areas of accounting. There are no single, correct, objective figures, even in traditional, straightforward accounting, which operated successfully for many years, long before sophisticated creative accounting techniques were developed.

Depreciation is an area where there is a need for judgement. We can rarely be sure how long a fixed asset will be used, or what its residual value will be. If an airline changes its depreciation policy so that aircraft are depreciated over 25 years rather than 15 years, it will make a massive difference to profits. It should be reviewed every year, but it would not be amazing if, when profits are looking a little low, the company decides that fixed assets will be kept for longer than was previously the case.

We cannot be sure what the net realizable value of inventories of unsold goods will be.[1] When a company is doing well they probably have time to check that all stocks really are being written down to net realizable value. It would not be amazing, if, when profits are looking a little low, there are other priorities than estimating the latest net realizable value figures and ensuring that everything has been written down accordingly.

Perhaps provisions for bad debts are more prudent in some years than others. Similarly, in a year of low profits, there may be no harm if a few repairs and renewals get classified as capital expenditure. And it is only natural to delay doing repairs when times are hard. It can all start off fairly harmlessly and almost unconsciously: where there is a margin for error or judgement we understate profits a little in the good years, so that when the bad years come we can review our accounting policies to release something held back by our previous caution.

Gradually, there can be more pressure to increase profits, and accounting policies seem to be twisted in one direction only. At first this might all be legitimate, and within the rules. But it can go to dubious, illegal and criminal extremes.

A company might operate a number of hotels, and be reasonably successful for many years. Then occupancy levels drop, perhaps because of the international situation. Keeping the hotels in a good state of repair, and maintaining their appearance is a major expense that hits profits. At first the company might decide to try to maintain profits by deferring all but essential repairs. Carpets are not replaced until they are threadbare and dangerous; rooms are not redecorated until the paper is peeling off the walls, and the smart

---

[1] Inventories should be shown at the lower of cost and net realizable value. It is, of course, necessary to know what the net realizable value is if it is to be compared with cost.

white paintwork has either turned to a gentle shade of puce or gone mouldy, and the furniture is starting to fall apart. After a few years it is not repairs that are needed, but a total refurbishment. Fortunately, refurbishment can be classified as capital expenditure, and does not hit profits. A new policy emerges: the expense for repairs virtually disappears; all hotels are refurbished every 4 or 5 years.

If there are still no profits from running the hotels, more extreme accounting policies are needed. Suppose that the company owns a hotel that originally cost £8m, but now needs £2m spending on it for refurbishment. It has a market value of £10m. The company sells the hotel to a friendly building company for £10m. The building company does the refurbishment, and sells the hotel back to the hotel company for £13m. The building company is happy with the contract: they have made £1m profit. The hotel company is happy with the arrangement: what might have been an expense for repairs, over the years, of £2m has become a profit (on sale of the hotel) of £2m; and their balance sheet looks better. Instead of having a tatty old hotel shown as £8m, they have a newly refurbished one shown at £13m; and they had to borrow only £3m to achieve this.

It could get worse and more dubious, and illegal. Maybe the hotel is not really worth £10m. But there may be ways of finding a building company willing to enter into a contract to buy it for £10m, if there is a guaranteed profit of £1m. Perhaps there is more profit to be made from specialized arrangements to buy and sell hotels than there is from actually running hotels.

Other strange contracts can be created. A hotel might find that it expects spare room capacity worth £1m at quiet times of the year. They might be glad to sell that spare capacity to a Package Holiday Company for £500,000, giving the hotel company £500,000 of revenues that they would not otherwise have had. The Package Holiday Company might then find that it has more capacity than it needs, and sell on half of what it has bought to a Conference Company for £600,000 (making £100,000 profit for doing almost nothing). Then the Conference Company sells part of what it has bought, and the Conference Company buys some surplus capacity on an airline's routes from London to one of the places where it has hotel capacity; the airline has bought that spare capacity from another airline, and they had bought it from a hotel who had bought it from another airline, or perhaps it was the original airline, or hotel, or conference company. OK, I am making this up about hotels and airlines (I think), but it did happen with telecommunications companies, making profits by selling spare capacity to each other.

Creative accounting can start with cautious use of judgement that varies a little from year to year depending on the circumstances. It can end with serious fraud and criminal activity, and with the company going into liquidation with lots of people losing their livelihood, their pensions and their savings. But some people probably manage to get out in time, after making a lot of money. Creative accounting can be a mechanism for redistributing wealth from the poor, weak and vulnerable to those who are strong, clever and ruthless. Financial accounting has an important role to play in trying to prevent and disclose such activities.

How Bad are the Various Techniques?

Where there are suggestions or accusations that creative accounting has been used, we could ask, on a scale of 1 to 10, how bad is it? Number 1 would be almost nothing wrong at all; number 10 would be the worst possible. The following is not intended to be authoritative or definitive, but it does give an idea of the range of different activities that some might classify as being 'creative accounting'.

1 There is nothing questionable about the financial statements, but information has been presented to emphasize the more favourable aspects of financial position and performance, and to de-emphasize the least favourable.

2 The emphasis on the favourable aspects is so strong as to suggest more of a propaganda exercise than a balanced report.

3 All financial statements are properly drawn up, but somehow the rules seem to flatter the company's performance whereas a different selection of accounting policies and measurements would be less flattering.

4 All financial statements have been properly drawn up in accordance with the requirements of company law and accounting standards. Where the official accounting requirements allow choice or flexibility, the company selects those options that tend to flatter the financial statements.

5 There are departures from accounting standards, but these have been properly disclosed and explained, and the financial effects have been quantified.

6 There is just a suspicion that there are departures from accounting standards that have not been disclosed. Some of the figures seem to be a bit questionable.

7 Rules and definitions have been pushed to the limit, and perhaps a little beyond. Judgements have been exercised to come up with treatments that the auditors have been persuaded to accept, but on the face of it, other accountants would find such treatments unacceptable.

8 Transactions and arrangements seem to have been deliberately designed to take advantage of, or to avoid, particular rules or accounting treatments.

9 Clear breaches of accounting standards without proper disclosure of departures or reasons for them.

10 Criminal activity, fraud and deception.

8.3 Some Problem Areas

One of the difficulties of describing the problem areas and neatest tricks of creative accounting is that by the time they come to be described in books such as this, they have become so well known that the accounting standard setters have brought in measures to stop them.

There have always been the areas of judgement such as the amounts to be charged for depreciation, the amount to be shown for closing stock, provisions for bad debts, and with the difficult, grey area between capital expenditure and revenue expenditure. Other areas, such as the following, are worth careful examination.

Exceptional and Extraordinary Items

In the 1970s one of the most controversial areas was extraordinary items and exceptional items, such as profits on sales of fixed assets or losses on reorganizations and disposals.

Sometimes companies would treat profits from such one-off transactions as an 'exceptional' item, which means that they were separately disclosed, and counted as part of earnings per share (EPS). But losses might be classified as 'extraordinary items'; these were shown 'below the line' – they were ignored in calculating EPS. This was all allowed by the old SSAP 6, although companies were expected to justify the treatment that they had adopted.

This problem was effectively tackled by Financial Reporting Standard (FRS) 3. Extraordinary items were virtually abolished. In the unlikely event that a company could defend something as being extraordinary, it still had to be counted in calculating EPS. FRS 3 also required specific disclosure of profits or losses on the sale or termination of an operation; costs of fundamental reorganizations; and profits or losses on the disposal of fixed assets. All these have to be counted in calculating EPS.

But companies are still free to calculate two different EPS figures: one according to the official rules, and one dealing as they think appropriate with unusual (and not so unusual) items. They can give whatever interpretation and spin they wish to the EPS figure that they have chosen for themselves. Some companies prefer to ignore non-routine bits of bad news (such as losses on a sale or reorganization of a business), or even fairly routine items (such as losses resulting from currency fluctuations, or impairment of goodwill). Unsophisticated investment analysts may even agree with the company's interpretation, and decide that the company's performance is better than is suggested by the figures resulting from strict adherence to the measurement rules in accounting standards.

Provisions

Strange things can happen when one company is taken over by another company. The 'victim' company may have been pottering along quite nicely with modest profits. Then along comes a new management, and what looked like last year's profits suddenly become substantial losses. The new management say that inventories and fixed assets are mostly obsolete and write them down to much lower values. There will have to be reorganizations and redundancies, and a provision must be made against the most recent profit figure to allow for this. Some of their customers look in poor shape and might not pay up, so a large provision for bad debts is created. Any intangible assets that the 'victim' has paid for are likely to be virtually worthless, and so are written down to very low values or written off completely. Last year's expected profits are suddenly converted into a substantial loss, and it is all blamed on the previous management.

The new management, perhaps they are company doctors,[2] are able to transform the company's performance. The dreadful losses that they inherited are suddenly turned into substantial profits the next year.

For some managements there may be a temptation to throw all sorts of dubious expenses and write-offs into a 'big bath' or massive provision. All the bad news can be got rid of in one year; future years can then only be better. FRS 12 *Provisions, Contingent Liabilities and Contingent Assets* is intended to curtail such (ab)use of provisions. A provision is defined as a *liability* of uncertain timing or amount. It is not just an *intention* to do something, and it is certainly not somewhere to credit good profits in one year so that they can be taken out

---

[2] Perhaps even witch doctors who can create a massive improvement in a company's performance, as if by magic.

> The draft income statement of Slowco for the year ended 31 December year 5 showed a profit of £2m for the year. The company was taken over by Fastgro on 31 January year 6. Fastgro reviewed the accounting policies of Slowco, wrote down a number of assets, and created a provision for reorganization. As a result the draft profit of Slowco for year 5 became a loss of £1m.
>
> Slowco had inventories of raw materials, components, work in progres and finished goods that were originally shown at cost of £800,000. Fastgro wrote these inventories down to £200,000, which they considered to be the net realizable value.
>
> In year 6 Fastgro managed to sell all the inventories concerned for £500,000.
>
> Inventories that had originally cost £800,000 had been sold for £500,000; Fastgro showed this as a profit of £300,000 in year 6. The loss of £600,000 in year 5 (when the stocks were written down) was blamed on the previous management.
>
> Twelve months later the new management were able to announce that Slowco had made record profits in year 6. Not many people examined the underlying performance.

ILLUSTRATION 8.1

again[3] in a subsequent year. A provision should be recognized only where there is an *obligation* to make a payment. This might be a legal obligation, but a 'constructive obligation' is also an acceptable basis for a provision (see Illustration 8.1). This may be based on past practices or published policies that lead to a valid expectation that a payment will be made; this is rather more subjective and may allow some scope for creative accounting.

There is also a problem in that we continue to use provisions for depreciation, and provisions for bad debts, although these are clearly not liabilities.

The Accounting Standards Board (ASB) has produced stricter definitions of provisions than the Companies Act 1985, and requires additional disclosure. But they also positively encourage the regular review of asset valuations, and the possibility of these being used to push profits down in one year and up in another year can never be eliminated entirely.

Goodwill

Goodwill arises in financial statements when one company buys another company, and pays more for it than its net asset value as shown on the balance sheet. This is normal practice. If a company has a net asset value of, say, £10m, it is very unlikely that the owners of that company would be willing to sell it for £10m, especially if the company has had a good profit record for a number of years. Assets are often undervalued on balance sheets, and when one company takes over another, the assets should be revalued to 'fair value'. A company might have net assets with a balance sheet value of £10m, and a 'fair value' of, say, £12m. But if the company is successful and profitable, anyone wanting to take it over should expect to pay more than £12m. Perhaps they pay £15m.

If we buy a business with net assets of £12m, and we pay £15m for that business, there should be no problem recording the payment of £15m, or the net assets of £12m that have been bought. But £3m has been paid for goodwill. Is this to be recorded as an expense or as an asset? Treating it as an expense would hit profits too hard. Showing it as an asset might be open to question: does the business really own something worth £3m?

---

[3] The bookkeeping would be debit provision account, credit income statement.

The old ASC preferred a treatment that avoided this stark choice. Goodwill was deducted from retained earnings on the balance sheet. It did not have to be written off as an expense on the income statement; and it did not need to be shown on the balance sheet as a rather questionable asset. But if a company had reserves of only, say, £1m, it was difficult to deduct £3m from retained earnings without making the balance sheet look very weak indeed. With many 'modern' businesses, the main asset is often goodwill, and it is now not unusual when buying a business to pay more for goodwill than the retained profits available against which it could be written off.

By the 1990s standard practice was that purchased goodwill should be shown as an intangible fixed asset on the balance sheet, and it should be amortized as an expense over its useful economic life. The life could be 5 years, or 10 years, or almost any period. Companies could argue that the useful economic life would be more than 20 years, or indefinite, provided they carried out annual impairment reviews. Now there is no requirement for systematic amortization: an annual impairment review has to take place instead. The rules appear to be fairly strict, but there is still some room for creativity in deciding the extent to which goodwill has been impaired in a given year.

Reducing Choices

In a number of areas, standard setters are attempting to reduce the choices available to management by establishing criteria for deciding between alternatives; the criteria appear to be fairly clear.

There has long been a problem with expenditure on research and development, and whether it should be written off as an expense when it is incurred, or whether it could be carried forward as an asset on the balance sheet. The old SSAP 13 laid down that research expenditure should be written off when it is incurred, and that is still the case. But development expenditure *could* be carried forward as an asset on the balance sheet *provided* it met certain criteria: companies could choose. Now IAS 38 lays down that development expenditure *should* be recognized as an internally generated intangible asset (and carried forward on the balance sheet, not immediately written off through the income statement) if, and only if, certain things can be demonstrated (such as that the project is technically feasible; that when completed it can be used or sold; how it will generate economic benefits; the availability of sufficient resources to complete it; and the ability to measure reliably the resources required to complete it). If these criteria are all met, then it should be recognized as an asset; there appears to be no choice. However, a company can choose whether (a) to put in sufficient effort and resources to demonstrate what is required; or (b) simply to write it off as an expense (as many pharmaceutical companies do).

Currently, there are also areas where choices still remain. When a company constructs its own fixed assets (perhaps building a hotel), most of the costs are capitalized and become part of the cost of the fixed assets. A company is likely to borrow money while building, and to incur interest costs. Most traditional accountants might say that interest costs should be written off in the period in which they are incurred. But some would choose to capitalize them, and treat interest as being part of the cost of the fixed asset. IAS 23 specifies that writing off interest as an expense is the benchmark (or normal) treatment; but it is an allowed alternative treatment to include attributable interest payable as part of the cost of a fixed asset on the balance sheet.

It is not always clear exactly when a sale takes place, and when the revenues from sales should be recognized. For bookkeeping convenience, a sale may be recognized in an accounting system when the invoice is sent to the customer. But sometimes companies who are not doing very well are tempted to bring forward the date on which sales are recognized; this will have the effect of increasing the sales in the current period.[4] They might, for example, choose to recognize the revenue when an order for goods or services is first received, and this is allowed. The problem of 'revenue recognition' is explored more fully on pages 260–2. Currently, the issue is still 'work in progress' for the standard setters. Meanwhile, some companies are choosing to recognize revenues as soon as a contract is signed, even though it might be years before a service is delivered and the cash flows appear.

The standard setters are steadily trying to reduce the number of areas where there are still choices, and where no guidance exists. But there are also likely to be some clever accountants working to find new ways of creating choices as fast as the standards setters curtail the old ones.

Fuzzy Rules

The accounting standards setters have tried to move away from allowing companies a free choice between alternative treatments. They have done this by specifying the circumstances in which each should apply. Unfortunately, such specifications and rules tend to become fuzzy at the edges as some companies interpret them creatively.

The fuzzy rules, and the choice between the 'acquisition' and the 'merger' methods of producing consolidated accounts, all but disappeared when strict criteria were specified for the use of the merger method. Now, with International Financial Reporting Standard (IFRS) 3, there is no choice: the merger method is prohibited.

There are other areas where the standards setters have tried to establish clear rules, including provisions; deferred tax; definition of associates; recognition of profits on uncompleted long-term contracts; the basis on which production overheads are included in inventory valuations; and defining exactly which leases should be shown on the balance sheet. The rules appear to be clear; there appears to be no choice. But there is always some fuzziness in rules in marginal cases. And it is always possible that companies structure financial transactions in a particular way so as to be able to use the accounting treatment that shows their results in the best light.

Detecting Creative Accounting

Sometimes accountants are creative in producing profit figures that are not supported by the company's underlying performance. Perhaps people who work for the company know that it is going downhill; perhaps there are terrible delays in paying creditors. But still healthy-looking profit figures are produced.

One way of detecting questionable accounting is to compare the amount of tax a company is paying with their reported profit figures. If a company is paying virtually no corporation tax, they must be telling HM Revenue and Customs that they are making virtually no profits. But if at the same time they are declaring substantial profits in their annual

---

[4] If sales are brought forward to be included in this year, the sales figure for the following year is reduced.

reports, it is worth further investigation. It may be that the company has invested heavily in fixed assets, and so has generous writing-down allowances for corporation tax purposes, or it may be more suspicious.

A cash flow statement can also give indications of what is 'really' going on if profit figures seem questionable. It is easier to generate fictitious profit figures than to produce fictitious cash. Sooner or later a company is going to need more cash to keep going. A genuinely profitable company generates cash; and a healthy company can usually raise cash without much difficulty, typically by borrowing. But if a company keeps needing to borrow more, it may raise questions, and their balance sheet will start to look very weak if burdened by too much debt. The company may try to borrow in ways that do not appear on the balance sheet.

Off Balance Sheet Finance

When a company wants more fixed assets they may (a) borrow the money and buy the fixed assets; or (b) lease the fixed assets.

In the first instance there is clearly an asset and a liability; both appear on the balance sheet. In the second instance, the financial effects are very similar: the company has the use of the asset just as if they own it; and they have to make repayments, just as if they had borrowed the money. Leasing was seen as a way of, in effect, borrowing money, but keeping the borrowings off the balance sheets. Creditors would not know the extent of the company's commitments to make payments under leasing agreements, and might be misled into lending more money.

SSAP 21 and IAS 17 put a stop to this. Some leases are defined as 'finance leases' and treated just as if the company owned the fixed asset that they had leased: both the asset and the liability to pay for it had to be shown on the balance sheet. One way of raising money 'off balance sheet' had been ended, but companies sought other methods. The temptation to raise additional financing through dubious off balance sheet arrangements was a key feature of the major accounting scandal with Enron in 2002, and its subsequent collapse.

Increasingly sophisticated, even devious, forms of off balance sheet finance were developed, and the need to report the 'economic substance' of an arrangement rather than its legal form became accepted. Now, the requirements of IAS 32 and IAS 39 are detailed and complex. Whatever the legal technicalities might be, if a company has incurred a financial commitment, it must be shown as such. In the USA the rules appear to be stricter, but the more strict and clear the rules are, the easier it is to create financial arrangements that just fall within the letter of the rules, but are a breach of the spirit of them. The UK approach errs on the side of principle rather than strict rules, and the idea of 'economic reality' takes priority over 'legal form'. It may be, however, that the international standards will be increasingly 'rules-based' in line with US standards.

Share Options

If a company wants to minimize the amount of salaries that count as an expense, employees can be paid in share options instead of money. This became fairly common practice at the height of the dotcom boom (see Illustration 8.2).

> Dorothy accepted a job with the e.vilwich company, selling potions on the Internet. The job carried no salary or commission, but she was given the option of buying 100,000 shares in the company for £1 each. When she joined the company the market price of the shares was only 50p. But before she left the company the market price had gone up to £11.
>
> Dorothy bought her 100,000 shares for £100,000, and then immediately sold them for £1,100,000. She had received no salary; she had cost the company nothing; and she had become a millionairess.

ILLUSTRATION 8.2

Conclusion

Accounting standard setters are steadily becoming more strict; they are reducing and eliminating choices; and more effective enforcement mechanisms are being implemented. But it seems unlikely that the problems of creative accounting will ever be completely solved. Perhaps it is unrealistic to expect (m)any problems to be completely solved. The present trend is for a steady increase in the length and complexity of accounting standards. But as the rules get fuller and more detailed, so some practitioners find increasingly complex ways around them. This in turn leads to the need for even more detailed standards to close loopholes that have been found. When these become pressing, FRSs are frequently revised, and additional guidance is given. Finding ways around the additional guidance becomes more complex, and so it goes on. If present trends continue, by the time the average reader of this book reaches the present age of the writer, there will be more accounting and auditing standards, rules, principles and guidance than anyone could read in a lifetime. In July 2006 the International Accounting Standards Board (IASB) recognized the problem of too many standards being produced, 'constant tinkering' with them and the need for preparers and users to catch up; they promised that companies will not have to implement any new requirements that are now being developed before January 2009.

In spite of the efforts of the accountancy profession and the standards setters, many would argue that creative accounting is still alive and well. A wide range of choices in the way that companies can measure and report their financial performance still remains. Perhaps we need different approaches to tackling the problems; and we may need to look at the problem in different ways.

8.4 How to Curtail Creative Accounting

Many different suggestions have been made for dealing with the problem of creative accounting. One group of suggestions builds on what is already happening. Work should continue on improving accounting standards, rules and principles; enforcement mechanisms should be improved. Problems with auditing arrangements should be sorted out. Offenders should be punished.

More radical proposals might take a right-wing approach (leave it all to the market), a left-wing approach (let the state take it over), or examine the problem from a different perspective.

Moderate Evolutionary Changes

Many assume that there is little wrong with the existing systems for accounting, auditing and the production and implementation of accounting standards. They acknowledge that there is a need for continuing reform and improvement. They also recognize that there are sometimes individual wrongdoers who either gently bend or sidestep the rules, or who are guilty of flagrant breaches of the rules. It is necessary to take action against such individuals. But the approach seems to assume that, generally speaking, the framework for accounting and auditing is proceeding in the right direction, and any serious threat to existing vested interests is inappropriate. The main suggestions within this approach are outlined below.

1 *The production of clearer accounting standards that reduce or eliminate choices*
There are still some accounting standards that specifically allow a choice of accounting treatments. The accounting standards setters are continuing to work towards producing more clear-cut accounting standards. But there is the danger that companies may invent new, alternative treatments faster than the standards manage to reduce existing variations. The accounting standard setting bodies have steadily become more powerful, and more resistant to special pleading to produce compromise solutions that meet the needs of different interest groups. But it is likely to be some years before the permitting of different treatments is phased out.

2 *The 'benchmark' argument* This recognizes that there will never be 100 per cent agreement or standardization, and that as long as companies have the power to do so, some will continue to push variations in accounting treatment that make their own position look better. Standards should lay down a single recommended treatment that is a 'benchmark' against which all other treatments are measured. Where a company adopts a different treatment, the financial effects of doing this should be quantified and disclosed. This means that users of accounts should not be misled: reported figures can always be converted back to the preferred benchmark treatment.

3 *Stronger legal backing for accounting standards* The position of the old ASC was weakened by the lack of legal backing for the enforcement of accounting standards, but the position has since improved. The 1989 Companies Act gives legal recognition to official accounting standards, but falls short of requiring companies to adopt them. Directors have to state whether accounts have been prepared in compliance with these standards, and declare any departures from them; but such departures are allowed, and there is still the overriding requirement for accounts to show what the directors consider to be 'a true and fair view'. Legal opinion suggests that accounting standards have, in effect, become a source of law, and it is difficult for companies to argue against the idea that following accounting standards is the most effective way of showing a true and fair view. But they can, and sometimes they do, and creative accounting still flourishes. The present accounting standards regime continues to work largely by consent, which means that standards have sometimes avoided difficult, clear-cut and controversial requirements. Firmer legal backing for standards has proved to be necessary, and this has reduced the tendency to compromise with difficult issues.

4 *Relying on international standards* In some respects International Financial Reporting Standards (IFRSs) are more prescriptive than UK ones. International standards have

become generally accepted since the European Union (EU) requirement that listed companies should adhere to international standards from 2005.

If the problems of creative accounting can be tackled effectively by improving accounting standards on an international basis, major steps forward have been taken in the last few years. Differences between European and UK financial reporting are now largely resolved. The approach in the USA differs significantly from Europe, but attempts are being made at convergence of accounting standards. In general this is likely to lead to better standards. The need for compromises might still leave options open, and some areas of creative accounting might not be tackled effectively. But the strength of the movement towards clear and effective IFRSs is now irreversible.

5 *More effective monitoring and enforcement* The Financial Reporting and Review Panel (FRRP), which operates under the auspices of the Financial Reporting Council (FRC), continues to investigate non-compliance with the requirements of the Companies Acts and accounting standards, both in response to complaints received, and by sampling companies on its own initiative. It does have legal teeth but, so far, all instances of suggested non-compliance have been resolved voluntarily. There have been significant improvements in enforcement in the last few years, but regulatory and enforcement bodies are still underfunded compared with the equivalent bodies in the USA. Enforcement mechanisms in the EU (including the Committee of European Securities Regulators (CESR)) are still at an early stage of development and we are largely dependent on company directors and auditors.

6 *Principles rather than rules* The fashionable defence of accounting in the UK, in the light of the US accounting scandals following Enron, is that UK accounting is based on principles rather than rules: difficulties arose in the USA because their approach depends on rules rather than principles. The argument is that simply following the rules can lead to creative presentations that do not represent 'economic reality'. The 'superior' UK approach depends on 'substance', or 'economic reality' being more important than the rules or 'legal form'; and that the professional judgement of accountants and auditors about what is a true and fair view is more important than following the rules.

This is a curious argument in a number of respects. Some of the worst US problems seem to be due to people *not* following the rules. The fact that there were more serious accounting scandals in the USA than in the UK may be more a matter of chance than it is due to perceived differences in the emphasis on rules rather than principles. The idea that UK accounting is based on principles may be hard to defend: most accounting standards were produced before the ASB produced its *Statement of Principles* (1999); and our principles are not always very clear, and they seem to change almost as regularly as accounting standards change. As the ASB might have said: if you don't like our principles, we have others.

7 *Current cost accounting (CCA)* Those who advocate CCA may hope that clear principles about asset valuation might reduce the amount of freedom to indulge in creative accounting. But moving away from historic cost (HC), which is based on objective, verifiable transactions, is more likely to increase the scope for creativity than reduce it.

8 *Cash flow accounting* If accounting was based simply on receipts and payments of cash, as opposed to the accruals basis for measuring profit, most scope for creative accounting would be eliminated. There would, of course, be a need to classify cash flows: the total figures alone would tell us little. We would probably want to separate payments for acquiring fixed assets from payments for normal operating expenses. Such classifications would be to some extent a matter for judgement, and the supposed objectivity of receipts-and-payments based accountancy would immediately disappear. More seriously, it would be, in effect, abolishing accounting as we know it: there would be no profit figure, and there would be nothing to show on the balance sheet apart from cash.

The term 'cash flow accounting' is sometimes used to mean something quite different. Some people advocate the production of balance sheets that use valuations based on the net present value of the future cash flows that an item is expected to generate. The amount of profit for a period would be based on the increase in the net asset value of the business between the two balance sheet dates. Given the amount of subjectivity involved in estimating future cash flows, this seems more like another way of encouraging creative accounting than it does a way of curbing it.

Improving Auditing Arrangements

Auditors are often seen as one of the main safeguards against creative accounting. Directors might favour a variety of weird and wonderful ways of calculating profit that serve to flatter their own management performance; auditors are expected to play a role in curbing such creative accounting. But if auditors are to be effective in this, they must be clearly independent of directors. If the auditors are in the directors' pocket, with directors determining their appointment and remuneration, they are in a weak position if they need to stand up to directors. Areas where there are suggestions to increase the independence of auditors include the following.

1 *Rotating senior audit partners more often* It is sometimes argued that auditors can become too close to directors and too easily influenced by them. The Institute of Chartered Accountants in England and Wales (ICAEW) has responded to recent criticisms by reducing the maximum period that a partner can be responsible for a particular audit from 7 years to 5 years.

2 *Audit fees being set by an independent body* The idea that an auditor can be independent from directors, while at the same time negotiating their fees with the directors, strains credibility. In view of this, their fees are, in theory, decided by shareholders, but in practice it is the directors who decide. The moderate response to this problem is that auditors' fees should be approved by non-executive directors as part of a company's audit committee. A more extreme response would be that directors should not be involved at all: fees should be set by a completely independent body.

3 *Auditors being appointed by an independent body* The arguments are much the same as with audit fees. The idea that auditors can be independent from directors while at the same time negotiating to be reappointed as auditors is questionable. In theory, the appointment is made by shareholders; but in practice it is the directors who decide. It could be a matter for the audit committee, which should be independent from the executive directors.

4 *Prohibiting non-audit work*   Criticism of auditors' lack of independence because they are always looking for remunerative consultancy work is widespread. The European tradition is that auditors are restricted to auditing duties, and the USA has moved strongly in this direction since the WorldCom and Enron scandals. Following criticisms of auditing arrangements, many of the large international accountancy firms sold off their consultancy businesses in the first years of this century. But much of their consultancy business has since been rebuilt, and they continue to offer a wide range of services to their audit clients. It seems only natural that when they are carrying out an audit they are able to make recommendations to improve a client's accounting and computing systems, and also to offer taxation advice. This can be very remunerative for the auditors.

It is now a requirement that a company's annual report shows not only the audit fee for the year, but also any other fees payable to their auditors for other services. Very often the fees paid for additional services are greater than the audit fee. Sometimes auditors have been accused of 'low-balling': deliberately quoting low audit fees in order to get other, more remunerative work from their audit clients. It is difficult to believe that auditors are really independent of directors when they seem to be on the look-out for additional lucrative work from those directors.

There are also criticisms when the individual accountants who audit a particular company subsequently leave their appointment with the auditing firm, and take up employment as a senior accountant with a former audit client. The idea of independent auditors seems to be compromised if we know that some of the auditors may be keen to impress the management of companies that they are auditing in the hope of a lucrative job offer.

The professional accountancy bodies have made progress in shoring up the reputation of auditors in relation to the problems of independence, and audit committees play an important part in this. But the professional accountancy bodies may be seen as acting primarily on behalf of their members, rather than on behalf of investors or the general public. Auditors are supposed to be there to act on behalf of shareholders, but sometimes seem to be more interested in supporting the directors, and protecting their own remuneration.

Punishing Offenders

It is sometimes convenient to blame individuals for problems that arise from creative accounting, and in some cases this is clearly appropriate. Individuals may be guilty of fraud, or deception, or breaches of relevant legislation, or criminal offences. Often it is the accounting and auditing systems that should be given credit for exposing such offences. But sometimes there are serious questions about the adequacy of systems where they have for long periods failed to detect problems.

Some might argue that, where accounting scandals have arisen because of wrongdoing by individuals, this is not a creative accounting issue. It is a matter for the criminal and civil law enforcement authorities.

But the line between wrongdoing and 'innocent' creative accounting is not always clear. The existence of creative accounting is due partly to weaknesses in the regulatory framework of accounting, and partly to the existence of a minority of individuals who are prepared to bend and break the rules in pursuit of their own advantage. In the USA the political response to the accounting scandals of 2002 sometimes seemed to be concerned more with blaming particular individuals than with challenging the vested interests of the accounting and auditing establishment. Although it is appropriate to take legal action against those who have clearly broken the law and abused their positions of trust, it is unrealistic to expect all accountants, auditors, regulators, chief executives, managers, executive directors and non-executive directors to behave like saints. Some need clearer and stronger rules to restrict the excesses of their bad behaviour. Others need clearer and stronger rules to support their attempts at good behaviour. Those who are trying to ensure that creative accounting is minimized, and that auditing and accounting requirements are properly implemented, can be severely hampered if close examination of accounting and auditing standards reveals that there are loopholes; if the rules that they are trying to enforce are not really clear; and there is still scope for those who are tempted by creative accounting practices.

Proposals for improving corporate governance and companies' auditing and accounting practices often rely heavily on the supposed role of non-executive directors. Even if there are enough competent people to carry out the functions expected of them, and there are more saints than sinners among them, it is difficult for anyone to be better than the system within which they operate. Punishing a few wrongdoers does not solve the problems of the system within which they operate.

Having powerful legislation, and the clear prospect of imprisonment for wrongdoers, can effectively change attitudes, as we have seen with the Sarbanes–Oxley Act (2002) in the USA, which followed some serious financial scandals. Under that Act the responsibility for financial statements is clearly put on the shoulders of company chief executive officers and chief financial officers. Each is required to certify financial information personally. Auditing firms are required to register with and report regularly to an Oversight Board. An audit committee becomes a requirement of listed companies and is to be responsible for the appointment, remuneration and oversight of the company's independent auditor who reports directly to the audit committee. The audit committee is required to deal with any disagreements between the auditors and management on accounting policies, and to be involved in analysing any deficiencies in internal controls, and any fraud.

The Act prohibits accounting firms from offering many non-audit services to audit clients, although the SEC may grant exemptions. Other non-audit services, such as taxation, may be provided only if approved in advance by the company's audit committee, and such approvals must be publicly disclosed.

In many ways the Sarbanes–Oxley approach is in line with the UK approach, although it is perhaps more heavy-handed. The controls are a step or two away from direct government control, and rely heavily on audit committees. Companies (on both sides of the Atlantic) are very keen to ensure that they have appropriate compliance arrangements in place – if only to keep their chief officers out of prison. The major accounting and auditing firms have been only too keen to provide appropriate advice and support to ensure compliance, and to charge for their services. Increased regulation and control tends be financially rewarding to the accountancy profession.

Radical Proposals

Right Wing

We could argue that the whole regulatory approach to accounting is a waste of time and money; it serves only to build up the bureaucratic empires of the regulators; it will always be unsatisfactory, and will always lead to demands for more resources for the regulators. Accounting and auditing are matters for agreement between the shareholders and the directors.

A right-wing perspective could take a *laissez-faire* approach, or it could rely on freedom of access to information.

1 *Laissez-faire*   The market-based argument is that there is no need for legislation or public involvement in the ways in which companies do their accounting, or in the existence, role or operations of auditing firms. Companies have a vested interest in supplying credible information to capital markets, and auditing firms have a financial interest in maintaining their reputations. Companies that supply duff information will be punished in the capital markets; share prices will collapse; the companies will be taken over at bargain basement prices; and the directors will lose their jobs when their more credible competitors take over. Similarly, auditing firms that give their names to incredible accounting treatments will soon lose credibility, and be of no use to their clients. Eventually they will end up like Arthur Andersen – the major international accounting firm that collapsed with the Enron scandal. The market takes care of everything. There is no need for public involvement.

   This argument is out of favour at present. As long as there are financial scandals, governments want to be seen to play a role in dealing with the problems. The UK approach tends to be gentle and consultative and the accountancy profession can usually talk governments around to their way of thinking. Following Enron, WorldCom and other scandals, the USA adopted very strong measures with the Sarbanes–Oxley Act .

2 *Freedom of access to information*   Financial statements provide summaries of transactions and of what can be a huge amount of financial data. In the early days of companies, when there were fewer shareholders and fewer financial transactions, it was practicable to open up the books of account to individuals[5] who could see all transactions for themselves. If someone chose to present 'creative' accounts of what had happened, it would be difficult to pull the wool over the eyes of shareholders who could inspect everything for themselves. Such an approach became impractical as the number of shareholders and the number of financial transactions increased enormously. Shareholders became dependent on the version of events that was created for them by accountants, directors and auditors. But computerization may have changed all that. When we read that schoolboys with computers in their bedrooms can penetrate the secrets of Pentagon defence systems, and fraudsters or pranksters can penetrate the security of banking systems – perhaps just for fun – we can no longer pretend that company accounting systems are inviolate. The public need no longer be dependent on accountants as intermediaries to present company financial stories in ways that suit company directors.

---

[5] Something similar happens with local authorities today.

Such open access to information is potentially revolutionary, and could be associated with a dramatic shift of power in society. There could be no secrets in relation to creative accounting. But, unfortunately, very few people seem to be interested in the details of company transactions.

Accounting and auditing arrangements are no longer a matter just for directors and shareholders. When companies are listed on stock markets, the listing agreement requires appropriate arrangements to be in place. A stock exchange does not want its reputation undermined by companies that have chosen to opt out of accounting regulations. The most substantial shareholders are institutional investors, such as pension funds. They are unlikely to invest in companies that lack normal accountability mechanisms.

Left Wing

Many assume that that there is a legitimate public interest in the numbers that purport to represent the profits, assets and liabilities of companies. This is because they are relevant in the allocation of resources in the economy, the amount of taxation paid by companies, or because of the importance attached to 'the system' and avoiding financial scandals. The left-wing view would be that it is better to rely on a public sector body to act in the public interest, rather than relying on the accounting profession, a variety of power groups and vested interests. When, as happens from time to time, there are accounting scandals, and financial reporting seems to be collapsing, there are increasing demands for more direct government/public control.

1 *HM Revenue and Customs rules OK!* Many Europeans are surprised to find that, in the UK, profits for financial reporting purposes do not simply follow the rules laid down by the government for taxation (and other) purposes, and that this is deemed to be quite legitimate. The idea that companies can choose to depreciate ships or aircraft over 10 or 20 or 30 years – or almost any period they like – seems quite fantastic. Perhaps it is central to the Anglo-American notion of 'freedom', which includes freedom to be creative with accounting.

   If we want to argue for clearer, more effective and enforceable accounting rules to curb creative accounting, we can argue that this should come from the government, and it can build on what HM Revenue and Customs already does. To someone from eastern Europe this would seem only natural. But the argument is rarely advanced in Anglo-American accounting cultures. It is argued that governments lack the necessary expertise in accounting, and that they would be too slow to respond to changing business and accounting circumstances and practices.

   But if governments lack accounting expertise, they can easily buy it, as companies do. And if governments are slow to respond to changing circumstances, they may be no worse than the accounting profession. The Chancellor of the Exchequer is usually criticized for producing too many changes in the taxation system too quickly, not for slowness to respond.

2 *A state auditing board* It may be too extreme to suggest nationalizing the whole of the auditing profession. However, if auditing is seen as not operating in the public interest, but is instead operating for the benefit of vested interest groups, this must remain the ultimate solution. A state auditing board, as advocated by Lyall and Perks (1976), could

do much to shift the balance of power without full nationalization. If there is a public interest in auditors being independent from directors (which is supposed to be the case), it is hard to defend a system where, in effect, the directors:

- Decide which firm of auditors should be appointed, and how long they should serve
- Decide what level of remuneration to pay to auditors
- Allocate substantial contracts to auditors for non-audit work

A public or state auditing board could be responsible for appointing auditors to particular companies, determining the level of fees and the period of appointment, and deciding to whom non-audit work should be allocated.

Such a board would also have a vested interest in establishing and implementing clear-cut accounting rules that could be expected to minimize creative accounting.

Accountancy and Power

Anyone who believes that there is such a thing as 'correct' accountancy is likely to favour existing accountancy arrangements whereby accounting standard setters struggle with the problem of how particular items should be measured and reported. They then produce the best solution, and accountants and auditors have to ensure that these are properly applied.

But many accounting numbers and accounting standards are the result of negotiation, rather than being based on any underlying truth, principle or economic reality. Accounting standard setters have changed their conclusions and recommendations on issues such as the amortization of goodwill, providing for deferred taxation and capitalization of development expenditure. A negotiated settlement is reached, but it may be changed a few years later. No new 'truth' is discovered. In negotiations the strongest usually get their way, and the way in which accountancy is applied is as a result of bargaining among powerful interest groups. Any serious attempt to change the way in which accountancy is applied in practice would involve a change in the balance of power between the different vested interest groups in society that influence accounting.

Summary

Many accounting and financial scandals arise because of illegal (sometimes criminal) activity by company directors and others. It is often normal accounting and auditing routines and reports that uncover the problems.

Creative accounting also arises where the rules are not clear and so technically there is no wrongdoing. There will continue to be problems with creative accounting as long as directors have substantial control over the ways in which financial reports are presented. The problems of creative accounting can only be curbed, not cured; and the process may be slow, especially if reliance is placed on moderate, evolutionary changes. The UK is unlikely to implement radical right-wing or left-wing proposals, and will proceed by international consensus.

There may be potential for restricting creative accounting by requiring companies to use HM Revenue and Customs' taxation rules for measuring profit, as is (or was) the case in some European countries. But, somehow, the US–UK approach usually seems to win in any contest with European approaches. It may be unrealistic to expect a thorough, authoritative set of measurement rules to be developed and enforced that will close all the creative accounting loopholes. Substantial improvement can come from fuller and more clear-cut disclosure requirements. The most effective curbs would come from the most significant shifts of power over the presentation of accounting information.

The most likely outcome is that we will continue with gentle reforms, become increasingly international, and largely preserve the status quo. More effective changes come as statutory requirements for additional specific disclosures are increased; and from restricting the powers of directors over auditing and accounting. Those who have the power to do so, create knowledge, accounting principles and determine accounting practice. If creative accounting flourishes, it is because it is in the interest of those who have the power to allow it. Perhaps it can be effectively restricted only if there is a radical shift away from the existing power structures of the accountancy profession, standard setters, directors and auditors.

Review of key points

- The term 'creative accounting' is applied to a wide range of accounting practices.
- The exercise of judgement is inevitable in some areas of accounting, and it may be tempting to exercise it in a creative way, and to extend this to other areas.
- Some companies use questionable accounting practices to boost profits, to improve key ratios, to boost equity on the balance sheet and to smooth out profits and losses from year to year.
- Problem areas have included exceptional and extraordinary items, provisions, goodwill, and off balance sheet finance.
- Accounting standards setters have reduced the scope for creative accounting, but there are some 'fuzzy' rules, and some areas of choice remain.
- Moderate evolutionary changes are steadily reducing the scope for creative accounting.
- Creative accounting is still a problem and more radical solutions may be considered.

Self-testing questions

1 In what areas of accountancy has there always been a need for subjective judgement and scope for creative accounting?

2 Give examples of techniques that have been used in 'creative accounting'.

3 Is creative accounting illegal?

4 In what ways can accounting standards be improved to restrict creative accounting?

5 In what ways have auditors been criticized for lack of independence?

6 The Platto Company produced the following draft income statements in early January year 9, shortly before being taken over by the Uppit Company in February year 9.

	Draft income statement for year ended 31 December year 8 £000	Budgeted income statement for year ended 31 December year 9 £000
Sales revenue	800	790
Opening inventory	80	90
Purchases	650	636
	730	726
Closing inventory	(90)	(88)
Cost of sales	640	638
Gross profit	160	152
Depreciation	(40)	(38)
Operating expenses	(90)	(92)
Profit	30	22

In February year 9 the Uppit Company revised the draft accounts of the Platto Company for year 8 as follows:

a Closing inventories were written down to net realizable value, estimated at £50,000.

b Fixed assets in Chipping Sodbury were written down to an estimated fair value that led to an impairment charge of £55,000. The net book value of the assets was reduced from £120,000 to £65,000.

During year 9 the actual results of the Platto Company were much the same as had been budgeted, except that:

c Sales were reduced by £32,000 because inventories left from year 8, which were originally expected to be sold for £112,000, were, in fact, sold for £80,000.

d The fixed assets in Chipping Sodbury were sold for £90,000; as a result the total depreciation charge for year 9 was reduced from a budgeted level of £38,000 to an actual level of £26,000. The total of other operating expenses was unaffected.

You are required to:

i Show the summarized income statement for the Platto Company for year 8, as modified by the Uppit Company.

ii Show the summarized income statement for the Platto Company for year 9.

iii Explain and comment.

Assessment questions

1 In what ways are the problems of creative accounting being tackled at present?

2 What more radical solutions do you think should be considered?

3 In what areas is it particularly difficult to restrict creative accounting?

4 Examine the case for more government involvement in the setting and enforcing of accounting standards, and in the regulation of auditors.

5 What is likely to happen to a company that overstates its profits year after year?

Group activities and discussion questions

1 Obtain the annual reports of about four companies, two being major, well-known companies, and two being much smaller. Compare the reports in terms of the public relations material and 'spin' that they put on the results. Can the reports be ranked on a scale indicating the extent of 'spin'? Do some reports contain little or nothing more than the minimum required? Why do some companies provide a lot more information, comment and explanation than is strictly required?

2 Try to find a company whose accounting practices have been criticized. (Look for critical comments in the *Financial Times, Accountancy* or *Accountancy Age* after the company has published its annual report and accounts.) Obtain a copy of the annual report and accounts (telephone the company or look on their website if it is not one supplied by the Financial Times Annual Reports service on 020 8391 6000; www.ftannualreports.com). Do you think that the company has been unduly 'creative'?

3 A company has a duty to maximize reported profits. If it uses creative accounting techniques to do so, it does not matter, as long as those profits have credibility. Discuss.

4 Examine a number of company accounts in detail. Express the taxation charge as a percentage of the profit before taxation, and compare the companies. Examine the cash flow statements of the companies. Do these comparisons reveal anything that causes you to question reported profit figures?

5 Produce a list of recent accounting standards, and select a few for detailed examination. Read the stated objectives in the standards, and try also to read between the lines. Can you suggest what 'creative accounting' techniques (if any) they are designed to address?

6 Should the rules for profit measurement be laid down by governments?

Financial accounting in context

Auditors toast lucrative new rules

By Cosima Marriner

Daily Telegraph, 28 June 2006

Discuss and comment on the following item taken from the press. In whose interests do improved accounting standards operate?

Source: Reproduced with permission by the *Daily Telegraph*.

ACCOUNTANTS are benefiting from a increased regulatory burden imposed on companies, with income at Britain's top 60 firms rising £1bn to £7.7bn last year.

The boom in audit work boosted fees by 14pc in 2005, according to Accountancy magazine's annual league table. In 2004, growth was reported at 5pc.

PricewaterhouseCoopers remains the biggest earner, with income of £1.8bn, up 13pc. It also has the most staff (14,000) and partners (755).

But it was the third-ranked KPMG which enjoyed the biggest increase in fee income of the top five firms. 2005 was KPMG's most successful year in the UK on record, with income up 20pc to £1.3bn.

The strong growth in accountancy income is a turnaround from just three years ago, when the top 60 firms were reporting flat fee income. Accountancy editor Chris Quick attributed the rise to the increased workload created by the US Sarbanes-Oxley Act and the International Financial Reporting Standards (IFRS) in Europe.

"Partners of accountancy firms will be toasting a mixed bag for their success," Mr Quick said. "Messrs Sarbanes and Oxley for their lucrative legislation, Brussels bureaucrats for introducing IFRS, and of course former Enron chiefs Jeffrey Skilling and Ken Lay for starting the crisis that led to such a regulatory backlash."

The growth in firm income is trickling down to partners, whose earnings were up 13 pc in 2005. Average fees per partner [have] now reached £839,000. The decline in partner numbers has also been halted, with the total number of partners in the top 60 up to 4,914 from 4,847. In another sign that confidence is returning to the sector, merger activity increased, though mainly at the smaller end of the industry.

But the accountancy profession expects fee rises to level off this year as companies get used to the new regulations. "The question for the big firms is how they maintain their fee income levels going forward now that Sarbox (Sarbanes-Oxley) and IFRS changes are starting to bed down inside companies," Mr Quick said.

Women remain under-represented at a senior level in UK accountancy. This month, Deloitte appointed the first female to its executive board when it made Sharon Fraser managing partner for talent of the UK business. Accountancy magazine found just over 10pc of the 4,914 partners in the top 60 firms were female, an increase of only 0.25pc. Of the Big Four, Ernst & Young has the highest average, with 17pc of its partners female.

The figures are published in the July issue of Accountancy magazine, out later this week.

TOP FIVE FIRMS

2006 League table of fee income earned by UK accountants

1 PricewaterhouseCoopers: £1.8bn (+13pc)
2 Deloitte & Touche: £1.6bn (+14pc)
3 KPMG: £1.3bn (+20pc)
4 Ernst & Young: £945m (+14.5pc)
5 Grant Thornton: £284m (+11pc)

References and further reading

Accountancy (monthly journal of the Institute of Chartered Accountants in England and Wales).

Accounting Standards Board (1999) *Statement of Principles.* ASB.

Dearing Committee (1988) *The Making of Accounting Standards.* ICAEW.

Gilbert Welytok, J. (2006) *Sarbanes–Oxley for Dummies.* Hungry Minds Inc., USA.

Griffiths, I. (1986) *Creative Accounting: How to Make Your Profits What You Want Them to Be.* Sidgwick and Jackson.

Griffiths, I. (1995) *New Creative Accounting.* Macmillan.

Jameson, M. (1988) *A Practical Guide to Creative Accounting.* Kogan Page.

Lyall, D. and R. Perks (1976) Create a State Auditing Board? *Accountancy,* June.

McBarnet, D. and C. Whelan (1999) *Creative Accounting and the Cross Eyed Javelin Thrower.* Wiley.

Mulford, C.W. and E.E. Comiskey (2002) *The Financial Numbers Game: Detecting Creative Accounting Practices.* Wiley.

Pijper, T. (1993) *Creative Accounting: The Effectiveness of Financial Reporting in the UK.* Macmillan.

Schilit, H. (2002) *Financial Shenanigans: How to Detect Gimmicks and Fraud in Financial Reporting.* McGraw-Hill.

Smith, T. and R. Hannah (1991) *Accounting for Growth.* UBS Phillips and Drew.

www.fasb.org

www.frc.org.uk

www.iasb.org.uk

CHAPTER 09

Advanced Interpretation
of Financial Statements

❖ *LEARNING* *OBJECTIVES*

After studying this chapter you should
be able to:

❖ Identify key information in
published financial statements
required to assess companies'
solvency

❖ Explain how financial accounting
information can be used to calculate
Z scores, and predict financial
distress and understand the main
elements included in Z scores

❖ Analyse the performance of
companies using most of the

detailed information included in
published financial statements

❖ Describe segmental reporting and
make use of the information
disclosed to assess the performance
of different segments

❖ Analyse the performance of
investments made by companies

❖ Make use of financial information
disclosed by companies in addition
to that included in balance sheets,
income statements and cash flow
statements

9.1 Introduction

In Chapter 4 we saw how 20 widely used 'ratios' can be used to assess three key aspects of a company:

1 Its solvency and ability to meet its liabilities as they fall due

2 Its profitability and how this can be increased

3 How its shares are rated on the stock market

It is not too difficult to calculate these ratios when the information is provided by a textbook in a convenient format. It is more difficult to find and use appropriate information from a complex looking annual report and accounts.

This chapter begins by providing extracts from the 2006 published financial statements of Wm Morrison Supermarkets plc. The 20 ratios are calculated for 2006 (p. 221), together with guidance on selecting the appropriate figures, and some interpretation. Students are invited to calculate the equivalent 20 ratios for 2005 and to provide more detailed interpretation The answers are provided at the back of the book (see p. 463).

Sections 9.3 and 9.4 of the chapter provide more detailed guidance on assessing solvency and profitability. More detailed consideration of a company's performance on the stock market is provided in Chapter 6. The final part of this chapter (Section 9.5) examines other information available from annual reports and accounts.

9.2 Calculating Ratios from Published Accounts

The information provided in respect of Wm Morrison Supermarkets plc is pages 38 and 39 of their 2006 annual report and financial statement and Note 22 from page 52 (see Illustration 9.1). The information in respect of ratios 17–19 for 2006 is derived from the *Financial Times* as shown in Chapter 6 (Section 6.5, pp. 145–7). The share price in 2005 is assumed to be 199p.

The 20 ratios introduced in Chapter 4 are shown in Illustration 9.2 (p. 221) for 2006, followed by an explanation of the figures that have been used. You are invited to calculate the equivalent ratios for 2005; this is Self-testing question 1, and an answer is provided at the end of the book (see p. 463).

1 The current ratio is the ratio of current assets to current liabilities. It is expected to be low with a retailer because there are few receivables or debtors.

2 The liquidity ratio is the ratio of current assets excluding inventories to current liabilities. This is even lower with retailers, because there are substantial inventories or stocks.

3 The gearing ratio relates debt (or borrowings) to equity. In this instance both long- and short-term borrowings have been included. It is acceptable to use only long-term borrowings; or to use the total figure for non-current liabilities, provided the interpretation is clear and the same basis is used in making comparisons. In this instance total borrowings have been expressed as a percentage of the total of equity plus total borrowings. It is also acceptable to use borrowings as a percentage of equity.

Wm Morrison Supermarkets plc

Consolidated balance sheet
29 January 2006

	Note	2006 £m	2005 £m
Assets			
Non-current assets			
Goodwill and other intangibles	8	–	103.2
Property, plant and equipment	9	6,143.9	5,708.1
Lease prepayments	10	217.8	230.5
Investment property	11	225.3	218.5
Investment in Joint Venture	12	–	78.4
Financial assets	19	36.4	37.0
		6,623.4	6,375.7
Current assets			
Stocks	14	399.4	424.6
Debtors	15	157.4	224.2
Cash and cash equivalents	16	135.3	93.5
		692.1	742.3
Non-current assets classified as held for sale	13	128.6	582.5
		820.7	1,324.8
Liabilities			
Current liabilities			
Creditors	17	(1,471.2)	(1,437.2)
Other financial liabilities	18	(296.6)	(274.7)
Current tax liabilities		(39.0)	(0.5)
		(1,806.6)	(1,712.4)
Non-current liabilities			
Other financial liabilities	18	(1,022.7)	(1,016.7)
Deferred tax liabilities	21	(422.6)	(501.6)
Pension liabilities	28	(416.2)	(408.1)
Provisions	20	(127.2)	(55.8)
		(1,988.7)	(1,982.2)
Net assets		3,648.6	4,005.9
Shareholders' equity			
Called up share capital	22	267.3	265.8
Share premium	22	36.9	20.1
Merger reserve	24	2,578.3	2,578.3
Retained earnings	24	766.1	1,141.7
Total equity		3,648.6	4,005.9

The financial statements on pages 34 to 66 were approved by the Board of Directors on 22 March 2006 and were signed on its behalf by:

Robert Stott
Chief Executive

Richard Pennycook
Group Finance Director

ILLUSTRATION 9.1

Wm Morrison Supermarkets plc

Consolidated balance sheet

52 weeks ended 29 January 2006

	Note	2006 Before Safeway integration & conversion costs £m	2006 Safeway integration & conversion costs £m	2006 Total £m	2005 Before Safeway integration & conversion costs £m	2005 Safeway integration & conversion costs £m	2005 Total £m
Turnover	1	12,114.8	–	12,114.8	12,103.7	–	12,103.7
Other operating income		18.5	–	18.5	18.3	–	18.3
Raw materials and consumables		(9,155.5)	–	(9,155.5)	(9,110.3)	–	(9,110.3)
Gross profit		**2,977.8**	**–**	**2,977.8**	3,011.7	–	3,011.7
Staff costs	2	(1,630.8)	(86.1)	(1,716.9)	(1,536.9)	(31.4)	(1,568.3)
Depreciation	3	(256.9)	–	(256.9)	(259.2)	–	(259.2)
Impairment and other asset write offs	4	–	(124.2)	(124.2)	–	(40.0)	(40.0)
Profit/(loss) on sale of property, plant and equipment		7.5	(16.7)	(9.2)	14.5	(14.9)	(0.4)
Other operating expenses	4	(986.1)	(147.4)	(1,133.5)	(834.7)	(52.9)	(887.6)
Operating profit/(loss)		**111.5**	**(374.4)**	**(262.9)**	395.4	(139.2)	256.2
Finance costs	5	(73.2)	–	(73.2)	(86.5)	–	(86.5)
Finance income	5	21.0	–	21.0	21.1	–	21.1
Share of post tax profits from BP joint venture	12	2.2	–	2.2	2.2	–	2.2
Profit/(loss) before taxation	3	**61.5**	**(374.4)**	**(312.9)**	332.2	(139.2)	193.0
Taxation	6	(15.6)	78.2	62.6	(112.4)	24.4	(88.0)
Profit/(loss) for the period		**45.9**	**(296.2)**	**(250.3)**	219.8	(114.8)	105.0
Earnings/(loss) per share (pence)	7						
– Basic		1.73		(9.46)	8.66		4.14
– Diluted		1.73		(9.46)	8.62		4.12
Ordinary dividends (pence per share)							
Interim – paid				0.625			0.625
Final – proposed				3.075			–
– paid				–			3.075

Consolidated statement of recognised income and expense (SORIE)

52 weeks ended 29 January 2006

	Note	2006 £m	2005 £m
(Loss)/profit for the financial period		(250.3)	105.0
Actuarial loss arising in the pension scheme (net of taxation)	28	(28.2)	(56.5)
Total recognized income and expense for the financial period		**(278.5)**	48.5
Prior year impact on retained earnings of first time adoption of IAS 39		3.4	–
Attributable to equity shareholders		**(275.1)**	48.5

ILLUSTRATION 9.1 continued

Note to the financial statements
52 weeks ended 29 January 2006

21 Deferred tax continued
The deferred income tax credited/(charged) to equity during the period is as follows:

	2006 £m	2005 £m
Actuarial gains/losses – taken through the SORIE	**13.3**	23.0
Share options	**(3.3)**	–

22 Called up share capital

	Number of shares millions	Share capital £m	Share premium £m	Total £m
At 30 January 2005	2,658	265.8	20.1	285.9
Share options exercised	15	1.5	16.8	18.3
At 29 January 2006	**2,673**	**267.3**	**36.9**	**304.2**
At 1 February 2004	1,574	157.4	15.9	173.3
Share options exercised	2	0.2	3.6	3.8
Acquisition of subsidiary (note 27 (b))	1,079	107.9	–	107.9
Shares issued	3	0.3	0.6	0.9
At 30 January 2005	**2,658**	**265.8**	**20.1**	**285.9**

The total authorised number of ordinary shares is 4,000m shares (2005: 4,000m shares) with a par value of 10p per share (2005: 10p per share).

Potential issues of ordinary shares
Certain eligible employees hold options to subscribe for shares in the Company at prices ranging from 77.5p to 239.3p under the share option schemes approved by shareholders. Options on 15m shares were exercised in 2006. The number of shares subject to options, the periods in which they were granted and the periods in which they may be exercised are given in note 23.

23 Share-based payments
(a) Share-based payments
The Group operates a number of share-based payments schemes; the Executive share option scheme, the Sharesave scheme, the Safeway Customer Care Performance Share Ownership Plan ("CCPSOP") and a Long Term Incentive Plan ("LTIP"). In line with IFRS 2 *Share-based payment*, the Group has fair valued all grants of equity instruments and shadow equity instruments after 7 November 2002 which were unvested as of 1 January 2005.

The total charge for the period relating to employee share-based payment plans was £4.0m (2005: £2.6m), of which £0.7m (2005: £0.4m) related to equity-settled share-based payment transactions. After deferred tax, the total charge was £2.3m (2005: £1.5m).

Executive share option scheme

In May 1995 the Group adopted the 1995 Senior Executive Share Option Scheme which is available to Directors and other senior employees. The scheme offers options at the market price two weeks prior to the date of the grant which are normally exercisable between three and ten years from the date of grant. The maximum exercise value of the ordinary shares subject to options held by an individual must not exceed the greater of four times earnings and £100,000. The exercise of options under the scheme is subject to performance criteria broadly requiring an increase in Group operating profits of at least 20% between the year prior to the date of the grant and its third or any succeeding anniversary. The scheme is equity settled.

ILLUSTRATION 9.1 continued

Those options which have been granted after 7 November 2002 have been fair valued using the Binomial stochastic option pricing model. The fair value per option granted and the assumptions are as follows:

Grant date	12/11/2004	02/04/2003
Share price at grant date	£2.33	£1.81
Fair value of options granted	£1,427,070	£1,886,816
Exercise price	£2.22	£1.75
Dividend yield	1.43%	1.49%
Annual risk free interest rate	4.61%	4.12%
Expected volatility*	29.4%	29.4%

*The volatility measured at the standard deviation of expected share price returns is based on statistical analysis of weekly share prices over the last six years.

ILLUSTRATION 9.1 continued

4 Interest cover is calculated by taking the profit available for paying interest (or operating profit; this is gross profit *minus* all operating expenses, but before deducting finance costs) and dividing it by the amount of interest paid (shown as finance costs). As there was an operating loss in 2006, the interest is not covered. (Alternatively it could be calculated as a negative figure.)

5 The profit for the period (after tax) is expressed as a percentage of the total amount for equity. As there was no profit in 2006, the return is shown as zero. (It could be calculated as a negative figure.)

6 Operating profit (before deducting interest and taxation) is expressed as a percentage of total capital employed, using the figure from number 3 above. It is important to use comparable figures. The operating profit is shown before including the profits from the BP joint venture; in 2006 the amount shown for the investment in the joint venture was zero; no adjustment is required. In 2005 the investment in the joint venture is shown as £78.4m; this amount should be deducted from the total amount of capital employed so that neither figure includes the results of the joint venture. (Alternatively, the operating profit could be increased to include the profit from the joint venture.)

As finance costs (interest) relate to both current and non-current borrowings, the total of all such borrowings has been included in 'long-term' capital employed; this treatment is consistent but not strictly correct. The alternative is to estimate how much of the finance costs relates to short-term borrowings, and treat these as an operating expense; the result would be a lower operating profit that would be expressed as a percentage of long-term capital employed (equity plus 'other financial liabilities' shown under non-current liabilities, but excluding current financial liabilities).

7 Operating profit is expressed as a percentage of sales revenue (turnover).

8 Sales (turnover) is divided by operating assets; this includes all operating assets regardless of what long-term financing was used. It is usually taken as the total of all assets (current and non-current) *minus* current liabilities. It is equal to equity plus non-current liabilities.

Ratio	2006		2005
1 Current ratio		820.7 : 1,806.6	0.45 : 1
2 Liquidity ratio		421.2 : 1,806.6	0.23 : 1
3 Capital gearing ratio	$\dfrac{296.6}{\dfrac{1,022.7}{1,319.3}}$		
	$\dfrac{3,648.6}{\dfrac{1,319.3}{4,967.9}}$	$\dfrac{1,319.3}{4,967.9}$	26.6%
4 Interest times cover		(262.9) ÷ (73.2)	Not covered
5 Return on shareholders' funds		$\dfrac{(250.3)}{3,648.6} \times 100$	Negative
6 Return on total long-term capital employed		$\dfrac{(262.9)}{4,967.9} \times 100$	Negative
7 Operating profit as a % of sales		$\dfrac{(262.9)}{12,114.8} \times 100$	Loss
8 Asset turnover	$\dfrac{6,623.4}{\dfrac{820.7}{\dfrac{(1,806.6)}{5,637.5}}}$	$\dfrac{12,114.8}{5,637.5}$	2.15 times
9 Gross profit ratio		$\dfrac{2,977.8}{12,114.8} \times 100$	24.6%
10 Staff costs as a % of sales		$\dfrac{1,716.9}{12,114.8} \times 100$	14.2%
11 Other operating costs as a % of sales	$\dfrac{256.9}{\dfrac{124.2}{\dfrac{9.2}{\dfrac{1,133.5}{1,523.8}}}}$	$\dfrac{1,523.8}{12,114.8} \times 100$	12.6%
12 Sales/fixed assets		12,114.8 ÷ 6,623.4	1.83 times
13 Sales/current assets		12,114.8 ÷ 820.7	14.76 times
14 Stock turnover ratio		$\dfrac{399.4}{9,155.5} \times 365$	15.9 days
15 Debtors ratio		$\dfrac{157.4}{12,114.8} \times 365$	4.7 days
16 Creditors ratio		$\dfrac{1,471.2}{9,155.5} \times 365$	58.7 days
17 Price/earnings ratio		199 ÷ (9.46)	Negative
18 Dividend yield		$\dfrac{0.037}{1.99} \times 100$	1.9%
19 Dividend cover		Loss	Negative
20 Net assets per share		3,648.6 ÷ 2,673m	£1.36

ILLUSTRATION 9.2 Financial ratios for Wm Morrison Supermarkets plc

9 Gross profit is expressed as a percentage of sales revenue (turnover).

10 and 11 Most companies disclose two categories of operating expenses: distribution costs and administrative expenses. In most cases these are expressed as a percentage of sales revenue (turnover). In interpreting financial statements we have to make the best use we can of the information available. In this instance staff costs have been separately identified and used in ratio 10. Other operating expenses have then been grouped together for ratio 11. Other variations are possible.

12 Sales revenue (turnover) is divided by the total for non-current assets to show the number of times that fixed assets were 'turned over' during the year.

13 Sales revenue (turnover) is divided by the total for current assets to show the number of times that current assets were 'turned over' during the year. This is then analysed in more detail in ratios 14 and 15 (and 16).

14 Cost of sales is used here, not sales, because the stocks figure is shown at cost price (not selling price). Inventories (stocks) are divided by cost of sales (which is sales *minus* gross profit); this is then multiplied by 365 to show how many days stocks are held.

15 The sales figure is used here (not cost of sales) because receivables (debtors) are shown at selling price. Trade receivables (debtors) are divided by sales (turnover) and then multiplied by 365 to express the amount of receivables in days, which indicates how long debtors take to pay. The figure is usually relatively low with a retailer because most customers pay cash and there are not many debtors.

16 Cost of sales is used here, not sales, because the amounts owing to creditors are at cost price. Trade payables (creditors) are divided by cost of sales, and then multiplied by 365 to indicate the number of days taken to pay creditors.

17 This is calculated as the share price (current, perhaps taken from the *Financial Times*) divided by the amount of earnings per share (EPS). As Morrisons made a loss in 2006 there is no meaningful P/E ratio.

18 The most recent annual dividend usually comprises an interim dividend that has already been paid, and a proposed final dividend for the year (which has not yet been approved at the balance sheet date, and which most companies show tucked away in a note to the accounts). Morrisons conveniently show these figures on the face of the income statement. The dividend is expressed as a percentage of the current share price.

19 EPS is divided by last year's dividend per share. Earnings were negative in 2006 and so there was no cover for the dividends.

20 The amount shown for total equity is divided by the number of shares, which is shown in note 22. Although the company did badly in 2006, the share price is still higher than the net assets per share.

9.3 Solvency and Predicting Financial Distress

The words 'financial distress' are widely used to cover a variety of different situations in which a company may find itself when it is unable to meet its liabilities as they fall due. Liquidation, receivership, bankruptcy, and voluntary or compulsory winding up are all variations on a theme. Companies can negotiate arrangements with their bankers and other creditors. A few years ago Marconi plc had to give their creditors almost all the company's share capital in exchange for the debts it owed them. The result was that previous shareholders were left with only a tiny proportion of the company: almost all their investment had disappeared. Something similar is happening to Eurotunnel at present. In other situations a company may be the unwilling victim of a takeover bid; an agreed bid or merger may be sought; or parts of the business may be sold off to a variety of different companies, venture capitalists, and other investors and institutions.

If debt is excessive, the result is usually that the creditors' interest in the company is as well protected as circumstances allow, but some sort of capital reorganization and restructuring results in the ordinary shareholders, the owners of the business, losing out. If the shareholders have financed the bulk of the business, and creditors have financed only a small proportion, then the creditors are relatively well protected: the greater the shareholders' equity in relation to debt, the greater is the financial security, at least for the creditors. We saw in Chapters 1 and 4 that this relationship between debt and equity is a key indicator in assessing a company's financial strength and solvency.

In the end, a company gets into financial difficulties for one reason only: they are unable to pay their debts. All sorts of factors can lead to this situation: bad management, poor products, a weak economy, problems with exchange rates, government policies, poor industrial relations, changes in demand for products and services. There is usually no shortage of explanations for poor performance, and it can be difficult to identify these various factors until it is too late. It is easy to see when a company is getting into a lot of debt by using conventional ratio analysis. It is difficult to be sure when debt is excessive, and what is acceptable does vary from business to business, and from time to time. But it is not difficult to observe a trend of increasing debt. It is worth examining the figures over a period of several years to see if debt is continuing to increase.

When introducing the idea of assessing the solvency of a company, it is convenient to separate short-term liabilities from long-term liabilities: that is the way in which a balance sheet is presented. But it is the overall level of debt that matters. It is not difficult for companies to reduce their short-term liabilities by long-term borrowing if their current ratio is starting to look too low. Similarly, it is not difficult to replace some long-term debt with current liabilities if the amount of gearing is looking too high. It makes more sense to look at the overall level of debt.

A straightforward calculation of capital gearing can be supplemented by a variety of calculations relating *all* liabilities to the amount of equity or shareholders' funds. There are different ways of doing this. For example, there might be some debate about whether deferred taxation and some provisions should be included with liabilities. The important thing is to be consistent from year to year and from company to company in making comparisons. If the amount of liabilities as a percentage of equity is steadily increasing over a number of years, it is a cause for concern, and other information should be examined, as indicated below.

A high level of debt is not necessarily a cause for concern, especially if the company is well placed to meet all interest payments as they fall due. The repayment of the loan itself (the principal) is usually done by borrowing more money; it is worth keeping an eye on the creditworthiness of the company generally to see if this is likely to be problematic. Credit ratings are published for most major companies. If a company's rating weakens, it usually means that they will have to pay higher interest rates.

Interest is payable on borrowings (but not on all liabilities). The total amount of interest payable by a company is shown as finance costs on their income statement, but it does not distinguish between interest on short-term borrowing and interest on long-term borrowing. It is worth calculating the average amount of borrowings a company has during the year; this can be estimated by taking the figure at the beginning of the year, adding it to the figure at the end of the year, and dividing by two. The total amount of interest paid during the year can then be expressed as a percentage of the average amount of borrowings. The rate can then be compared with interest rates payable in the market generally. If the company seems to be paying an interest rate that it too high, it may be that they are suffering from a poor credit rating; or it may mean that their actual level of borrowings during the year was higher than the balance sheets suggest. Such 'window dressing' at the year end is not unusual.

Profits

If the company has very healthy profits there should be no problem in paying interest, and avoiding financial difficulties. Earnings before interest and taxation for the year can be divided by the amount of interest payable; this gives the number of times interest is covered by earnings available to pay that interest. A company with an interest cover of 10 or more is obviously much safer in this respect than one where the cover is only 2 or 3 times.

It is worth trying to assess how 'healthy' the profits are by looking at the type of industry the company is in, and their record over a number of years. If they are in a cyclical industry that seems to have very good years followed by very bad years, or in a declining industry, a cover of 3 or 4 times may be a serious sign of weakness. If they are in an industry with very stable earnings (such as a property company or a utility company), interest cover of 3 times may be quite satisfactory.

Assets

Solvency is often assessed by relating the amount of liabilities to the amount of equity or shareholders' funds. The amount of equity is determined by the amount of net assets owned by the company. It is worth looking at the kind of assets that a company owns, and how they have been valued. If a company's borrowings are starting to look high in relation to equity, they may be able to revalue some assets; an increase in assets will increase the amount of equity; as a result the relationship between liabilities and equity immediately looks healthier.

Some assets represent very good security for creditors. Cash is obviously most readily available to pay them, and there are often other investments that are easily turned into cash, and the balance sheet should show their current value. Debtors should become cash within a matter of months. Inventories are less liquid, but in most businesses they should be sold and producing cash within a year. Fixed assets provide varying degrees of security to creditors. Freehold property is usually the asset that creditors prefer, and loans are often secured on such property. Properties held on short leases are more of a mixed bag: some may be very valuable; some may be very hard to dispose of (such as an unprofitable shop in a declining area): the company might be committed to continuing to pay rentals on properties that only produce losses. Plant and machinery and other tangible fixed assets offer reasonable security where there is a ready market for them. Traditionally all assets should be prudently valued, but users of accounts may need to make their own estimates of how prudent the values are.

Goodwill is an asset that might be very difficult to dispose of; it is not really a 'separable' asset – it can be sold only as part of the business as a going concern. If the amount shown for goodwill is overstated, then the amount shown for equity is overstated, and the relationship between liabilities and equity may be misleading. Goodwill may be properly shown in accordance with all accounting standards and rules, but that does not mean that it has any value to creditors if the company gets into financial difficulties. It is not unusual for a company's main asset to be goodwill. In many companies, if goodwill was excluded from assets, there would be a negative net asset value; this would mean negative equity, and that assets provide little or no security for creditors.

Cash Flows

A company that generates healthy cash flows is less likely to get into financial difficulties than one that does not. As explained in Chapter 7, profits and positive cash flows do not always go together. Sometimes companies are successful in generating profits, but they never seem to show up as cash; the company continues to expand and pour money into additional assets. This may look good, but it does not pay the creditors. There are also sometimes suspicions about creative accounting: the company appears to be making profits, but somehow these are not backed up by cash being generated.

Lenders are interested in a company's business plans, particularly their cash budgets, and how soon a company is likely to be able to repay their debts. Published financial statements often include comments about this aspect of a company's financial situation, but cash budgets are not usually published.

Differences between cash flow and profit are explored in Chapter 7, and the use of published cash flow statements in explaining the differences between a company's cash flow and their profit is explained.

Z Scores

It is possible to find out which factors have been most closely associated with companies that find themselves in financial distress. A list of companies that have 'failed' in one way or another is produced. The financial data for those companies are compiled for a number of years, including amounts of profit, equity, working capital, cash flows and so on. The data are then manipulated until a way of selecting and arranging them is found that best predicts impending failure. Altman (1983) found that the key data were:

- Working capital
- Total gross assets
- Retained profits
- Earnings before interest and tax
- Market value of equity
- Book value of debt
- Sales

By arranging these as five ratios, and giving a weighting to each, he calculated a Z score, which gave the best prediction of corporate failure.

Ratio	Weighting
1 Working capital ÷ total gross assets	× 1.2
2 Retained profits ÷ total gross assets	× 1.4
3 Earnings before interest and tax ÷ total gross assets	× 3.3
4 Market value of equity ÷ book value of debt	× 0.6
5 Sales ÷ total gross assets	× 1.0

Altman did not claim to be stating the causes of failure; it was a statistical calculation which, in his sample, gave the best results. Companies with a Z score of more than 2.99, using the above calculation, did not fail; companies with a Z score of less than 1.81 did fail. The outcome of companies with a score of between 1.81 and 2.99 was less predictable, but overall the prediction was accurate in 96 per cent of cases.

His model suggests that the following are important in predicting failure:

1 The amount of working capital (in relation to total assets)

2 The amount of retained profits (in relation to total assets)

3 Some measure of return on capital employed (ROCE)

4 Some measure of gearing, and the market value of equity

5 Some measure of utilization of assets (or turnover of assets).

This calculation of a Z score in Illustration 9.3 suggests that Morrisons are below the 'safe' level of 2.99, but well above the 'unsafe' level of 1.2. It may be that the book value of debt has been overstated because all liabilities have been included. It must be remembered that most retailers have very low or negative levels of working capital (number 1); Morrisons' Z score is also adversely affected because they made a loss in 2006 (number 3). The score is buoyed up by the high market value of equity in relation to debt (number 4), and by the high level of sales in relation to total assets (number 5).

Altman's sample was based on manufacturing companies in the USA more than 40 years ago. But similar work has been done by Taffler (1983) and Taffler and Tisshaw (1977) more recently in the UK. Taffler found that the key ratios included:

	Weighting
1 Profit before taxation ÷ current liabilities	53%
2 Current assets ÷ total liabilities	13%
3 Current liabilities ÷ total assets	18%
4 (Immediate assets − current liabilities) ÷ operating costs excluding depreciation	16%

Taffler did not publish full details on the calculations but it is clear that the key information, manipulated in different ways, could give very good indications of corporate failure in a different environment.

The message is clear: published financial statements, if interpreted with skill and care, can give very good indications of a company's solvency, or how safe it is from financial collapse. Important information is available from financial statements, the most important

	Ratio	£m		Weighting	
1	WC/TGA	(986.1) ÷ 7,444.1 = (0.1325)		× 1.2	(0.1590)
2	RP/TGA	766.1 ÷ 7,444.1 = 0.1029		× 1.4	0.1441
3	EBIT/TGA	(262.9) ÷ 7,444.1 = (0.0353)		× 3.3	(0.1165)
4	MV equity/BV of debt	5,329.2 ÷ 3,795.5 = 1.4041		× 0.6	0.8425
5	Sales/TGA	12,114.8 ÷ 7,444.1 = 1.6274		× 1.0	1.6274

Workings				
	Current assets	820.7	Z score	2.3385
	Current liabilities	(1,806.8)		
	Working capital	(986.1)		
	Non-current assets	6,623.4		
	Current assets	820.7		
	Total gross asset	7,444.1		
	Current liabilities	1,806.8		
	Non-current liabilities	1,988.7		
		3,795.5		

ILLUSTRATION 9.3 Z score for Wm Morrison Supermarkets plc 2006

being profits, assets, liabilities, cash flows and Z scores. But other information is also important, including trends, quality of management, competition, and what is happening in the markets in which the company is operating.

9.4 Performance

At an introductory level, most interpretation of accounts concentrates on the performance of a company as a whole. Profitability is measured using ROCE, and this is analysed into its various components showing (a) costs and profits in relation to turnover;[1] and (b) utilization of assets,[2] relating sales or cost of sales to different categories of assets in varying degrees of detail. Cash flows are also analysed for the company as a whole.

There are good reasons for wanting to analyse the performance of different parts of the business. If investors and analysts are interested in forecasting the future sales, profits and cash flows of a company, they are likely to assume different growth rates, different rates of profitability, and varying amounts of risk for different types of business – even if they are unable to do it exactly. At the end of the twentieth century it was assumed that there were great growth prospects in areas like telecommunications, pharmaceuticals and leisure. But investors were disappointed in the short run.

Investors are also concerned with assessing the competence of management. Many companies are becoming increasingly diversified, making money in one area where

---

[1] Chapter 4, ratios 7, 9, 10, 11.

[2] Chapter 4, ratios 8, 12, 13, 14, 15, (16).

they have expertise and success, then investing it in other areas that need careful monitoring.

In many cases diversification is very successful. GUS made money in retailing, and now has a very successful credit rating business in Experian. As one area declined (home shopping), so another expanded, and it is an area that has very modest levels of capital employed. UK water companies operate in a tightly regulated market, and have diversified with varying degrees of success into other areas where they are more free to make more profits. The US GEC has expanded successfully from being an electrical manufacturer into almost any kind of business that makes money, from vehicle hire to life assurance and perhaps even financing the underwear you are wearing at the moment.[3] Meanwhile the UK GEC, which was cautiously and successfully built up by Arnold Weinstock over many years to make just about everything electrical – and a huge pile of cash – divested and diversified disastrously, and was destroyed almost as fast as an airline(r) can crash. They sold off boring electrical manufacturing too cheaply, and borrowed excessively, in order to buy more exciting, overpriced telecommunications manufacturers just as the market was collapsing. Their share price fell from over £12 to less than £0.02!

Unfortunately, there are many other examples of unsuccessful diversification. Marks & Spencer expanded abroad, but their results suffered and they began selling off their overseas operations. Now it seems that they are planning to expand abroad again. If they do this by franchising, rather than investing in significant additional assets, their ROCE is likely to increase. Detailed examination of annual reports enables us to calculate the profitability of each segment of the business. Abbey National was a very successful retail bank, and had all the expertise necessary; they then diversified into wholesale banking, where their expertise was limited, and ended up having to write off many hundreds of millions of pounds, and were finally taken over by Bank of Santander. Boots are a successful pharmacy and retailer of a limited range of products; but their venture into Halfords was not successful; their other diversifications are questionable; and their strategy is now based on the merger with Alliance Unichem.

Many successes and failures of diversification are made public. We do not know how many attempts at diversification have failed and been quietly brushed under the carpet. Fortunately there are official disclosure requirements that enable us to find out about different *segments* of a business, about *continuing and discontinued* operations, and about the results of investments in *associates* and *joint ventures*.

Reporting Financial Performance

The idea that the financial performance of a company can be distilled into a single figure is appealing, and the EPS figure is the most suitable for this purpose. If EPS increases each year, that must be a good thing. If it falls, that must be a bad thing.

But a single measure of performance is likely to cover a multitude of sins. Investors who are trying to forecast future EPS figures need to consider whether or not this year's EPS figure has taken into account the following:

---

[3] GE Finance provides credit cards for the Burton Group, including Top Shop.

1 The results of parts of the business that have since been discontinued

2 The results of new acquisitions that have yet to come fully on stream

3 Any exceptional items such as large, one-off profits on the sale of fixed assets or investments

4 Exceptional write-offs of goodwill or other assets

5 Exceptional provisions for future reorganizations and redundancies

6 Impairment of goodwill

7 Depreciation

8 Interest

9 Unrealized profits on revaluation of assets

10 Exchange rate gains or losses on translating the financial statements of overseas subsidiaries

The requirements of international standards are clear on this: the EPS figure takes into account the first eight items, but not numbers 9 and 10. Items such as 9 and 10 have the effect of changing the total amount of equity shown on the balance sheet, but they are not reported in the income statement. They are separately disclosed on a statement of total recognized gains and losses for the year.

Companies and investors may be unhappy about including all of items 1–8 in the EPS figure. What is the use of a EPS figure that includes all sorts of odd items that are unlikely to occur again?

One solution adopted by many companies is to produce two EPS figures: one fully in accordance with accounting standards, which takes into account items 1–8 above. They also produce a second EPS figure, which excludes some of these items. This may be done to give what they consider to be a more true and fair view, or to provide a better basis for predicting future earnings. Sometimes it looks as though they try to exclude items that would show lower earnings figures.

The solution adopted by the accounting standard setters is to require a lot of information to be disclosed so that users of accounts can produce their own earnings figure that meets their particular needs. All[4] the items listed above in 1–8 have to be disclosed separately unless they are too small to be of any significance.

Companies are required to disclose both turnover and operating profit separately for continuing operations and for discontinued items. Some also separately disclose the results of new acquisitions.

Segments

A careful examination of the annual report and accounts of most large companies reveals information about the different segments of the business that enables us to assess the performance of the different parts. In Chapter 5 we saw that Ted Baker made 'segmental' disclosures for menswear and womenswear, and for wholesale and retail. Morrisons make

---

[4] The requirement for separate disclosure of the results of acquisitions have quietly been dropped with the adoption of IASs.

no segmental disclosures as they operate exclusively in the UK, and 'The Directors consider that there is only one business segment being grocery and related retailing and vertically integrated manufacturing'.[5] The BOC group disclose revenues and operating profits for five different business segments (Process Gas Solutions; Industrial and Special Products; BOC Edwards; Afrox hospitals; and Gist), and for five geographical segments (Europe; Americas; Africa; Asia; and South Pacific). Associated British Foods disclose revenue and operating profit for five business segments (Grocery; Primary food; Agriculture; Ingredients; and

TATE & LYLE
CONSOLIDATED INCOME STATEMENT

	Notes	Year to 31 March 2006 £m	2005 £m
Sales	5	**3 720**	3 339
Operating profit	6	**75**	229
Interest income	10	**45**	34
Finance expense	10	**(78)**	(58)
Profit before tax		**42**	205
Income tax expense	11	**(69)**	(55)
(Loss)/profit for the year		**(27)**	150
(Loss)/profit for the year attributable to:			
Equity holders of the Company		**(30)**	146
Minority interests		**3**	4
		(27)	150
		pence	pence
(Loss)/earnings per share attributable to the equity holders of the Company	12		
Basic		**(6.3)**	31.0
Diluted		**(6.3)**	30.6
Dividends per share	13		
Interim paid		**5.9**	5.7
Final proposed		**14.1**	13.7
		20.0	19.4

All activities relate to continuing operations.

Analysis of profit before tax		£m	£m
Profit before tax		**42**	205
Add back:			
Exceptional items	8	**248**	45
Amortisation of acquired intangible assets	14	**5**	4
Profit before tax, exceptional items and amortisation of acquired intangible assets		**295**	254

The notes on pages 71 to 123 form part of these Group financial statements.

ILLUSTRATION 9.4

---

[5] Annual report and financial statements 2006, Wm Morrison Supermarkets plc.

Retail), and for four geographical segments (UK; Rest of Europe; The Americas; Australia, Asia and Rest of world).

The consolidated income statement for Tate & Lyle for the year to 31 March 2006 is shown in Illustration 9.4. Readers of the previous edition of this book will note how much briefer this is than the 2003 equivalent statement (shown as Illustration 5.3 on p. 115 of the previous edition). In the first part of the statement (prior to EPS) 23 lines of data and 3 columns have been reduced to 10 lines in a single column. Much of the information previously shown on a complex profit and loss account is now included in notes to the simplified income statement.

Tate & Lyle in 2006 show both the interim and final proposed dividend per share on the face of the income statement, which makes it easy to compare the amount of dividends with the amount of earnings. As final dividends are not now recognized as a liability until after they have been approved by shareholders, which is after the financial statements are published, it is often difficult to find the current year's dividends (including proposed dividends) in the accounts. The amount shown for dividends in a cash flow statement is the amount actually paid during the year, which is different from the amount proposed for the year.

Tate & Lyle provide segmental information for four different geographical segments, but their main segmental disclosures are for five different business segments (Food and industrial ingredients, Americas; Food and industrial ingredients, Europe; Sucralose; Sugars Americas and Asia; Sugars Europe). This information is summarized in Illustration 9.5.

This segmental information enables us to produce much more detailed analysis of the company's performance indicating, for example, the growth in each of the areas identified, as shown in Illustration 9.6.

The percentage increases (Illustration 9.6) should be interpreted with care. The percentage increase in sales of Sucralose was very substantial (23.5 per cent), but the amounts were relatively small, and the increase in sales of Sugars Europe were more substantial. Percentage changes in operating profits look massive where there is a move from a profit to a loss (or vice versa), and the percentages above 100 per cent can be misleading. The very substantial increase in the net operating assets of Sucralose suggest that it is seen as good future potential.

	Food Americas	Food Europe	Sucralose	Sugars Americas	Sugars Europe	Total
Year to 31 March 2006 £m						
Sales	1 127	719	142	273	1 459	3 720
Operating profit	138	(217)	64	28	62	75
Net operating assets	674	428	172	125	450	1 849
Year to 31 March 2005 £m						
Sales	1 037	761	115	237	1 189	3 339
Operating profit	41	40	42	36	70	229
Net operating assets	492	564	66	80	296	1 498

ILLUSTRATION 9.5

	Food Americas	Food Europe	Sucralose	Sugars Americas	Sugars Europe	Total
Year to 31 March 2006 % increases						
Sales	8.7%	(5.5%)	23.5%	15.2%	22.7%	11.4%
Operating profit	236.6%	(100%+)	52.4%	(22.2)	(11.4%)	(100%+)
Net operating assets	37.0%	(24.1%)	161%	56.3%	52.0%	23.4%

ILLUSTRATION 9.6

The use of conventional accounting ratios provides more useful information. These are shown as Illustration 9.7 for the year 2005 and are the equivalent of ratios 6, 7 and 8 in Chapter 4. Readers are invited to calculate equivalent figures for 2006, and to comment on them. The answers are provided at the end of the book (Self-testing question 4, p. 464).

In 2005 the ROCE was reasonably good (15.3 per cent), and each product made a positive contribution to this profitability, with Sucralose being the most profitable in relation to capital employed. The overall operating profit/sales ratio was 6.9 per cent, with each product making a positive contribution; Sucralose had the highest profit/sales ratio, and Food Americas had the lowest. Utilization of assets overall was 2.2 times with Sugars Europe producing most sales in relation to capital employed; Food Europe the least. We might conclude that the company should concentrate on expanding their production and sales of Sucralose, and that ways must be found of making Food Europe more profitable.

These three ratios are the key ones in interpreting profitability and for showing which products are the most profitable. But they tell us more when we compare one year with another to see where profitability has increased and where it has declined. You are invited to calculate the figures for 2006 and to comment on them.

It is worth analysing the performance of the different segments of a company in this way, and comparing this with the comments made by the chairman or directors about the progress and prospects of different parts of the company.

	Food Americas	Food Europe	Sucralose	Sugars Americas	Sugars Europe	Total
Year to 31 March 2006						
Operating profit/net operating assets						
Operating profit/sales						
Sales/net operating assets						
Year to 31 March 2005						
Operating profit/net operating assets	8.3%	7.1%	63.6%	45%	23.6%	15.3%
Operating profit/sales	3.9%	5.3%	36.5%	15.2%	5.9%	6.9%
Sales/net operating assets	2.11 times	1.35 times	1.74 times	2.96 times	4.02 times	2.23 times

ILLUSTRATION 9.7

Investments

It is possible to assess how successful management has been in making investments in other companies and other securities by comparing the dividends and interest receivable from those securities with the amount of shareholders' funds tied up in them. Investments are usually shown on balance sheets at cost, but some indication of current value should also be given. The income statements show dividends and interest receivable.

In most cases such 'normal' investments are relatively small. Companies are likely to make major investments either:

a by taking a controlling interest in another company, which then becomes a *subsidiary*; its results are then 'consolidated' with those of the company which makes the investment, and included in group accounts; or

b by taking a significant shareholding in other companies, which then become *joint ventures* or *associates*.

With these major investments what matters is the profits or losses made by the company in which the investment has been made; dividends receivable are of much less significance. This is because profits are an indication of performance; dividends are a matter of choice, and increasing dividends are sometimes paid when performance is deteriorating.

Subsidiary Companies

Most large listed companies are in fact groups of companies: a listed company typically holds 50–100 per cent of a number of subsidiary companies. It is possible to get separate information about each of the separate companies in the group but for most purposes this is not really necessary. They produce 'group accounts' that include figures for all the subsidiary companies. These figures are included in the holding company's figures: separate figures for each subsidiary are not provided in group accounts.

Group balance sheets include all the assets and liabilities controlled by the group, even where the holding company owns only, say, 75 per cent of the subsidiary; the net assets of the subsidiary that are owned by the 25 per cent of the shareholders outside the group are shown, next to shareholders' funds, as 'minority interest'.

The first parts of a group income statement includes 100 per cent of the results of all subsidiary companies. Each item from turnover down to profit after taxation includes the figures for the subsidiary companies. But then it is recognized that part of the profit after taxation belongs to subsidiary company shareholders who are outside the group. Their 'minority interest' in the profits is then deducted to arrive at the profit attributable to group shareholders. Profit for the period, after deducting minority interest, is the key figure in interpreting financial statements. It is compared with dividends for the year to calculate dividend cover; it is the figure used to calculate earnings per share; and it is the profit figure for calculating return on equity (or return on shareholders' capital employed). The figure shown on an income statement for minority interest may be compared with the balance sheet figure for minority interest to assess the profitability of those subsidiary companies that are not wholly owned.

Joint Ventures and Associate Companies

Joint ventures and associates (as with subsidiaries) are special categories of investments in other companies where we are less concerned about any dividends receivable than we are about the profits and losses earned by those companies.

A joint venture as a contractual arrangement whereby two or more parties undertake an economic activity that is subject to joint control. Two or more companies might decide to set up a new operation jointly to share the expenses and benefits.

An associate is an enterprise in which the investor has significant influence but which is neither a subsidiary nor a joint venture. If the investor has 20 per cent or more of the voting power, then 'significant influence' is assumed.[6] One company may buy a substantial shareholding in another company; that company remains separate and independent from the investing company, but the investing company exercises significant influence over it.

There are technical differences between the way accounting is done for joint ventures and the way it is done for associates. Rather more information may be disclosed for joint ventures than for associates. With joint ventures the amounts of assets and liabilities are shown separately; with associates they are combined. With joint ventures the amount of turnover is disclosed; with associates this is not required.

The investing company's share of the profit or loss of joint ventures and associates is clearly disclosed. The amount of the investing company's share of the net assets of the associates and joint ventures is also easily identified. This includes any amounts paid for goodwill. It is based on the original cost of the investment, including any amounts paid for goodwill; each year the amount will be reduced to reflect any impairment of goodwill, and increased to bring into account retained profits for the year (or reduced by any losses).

The fact that there is a figure for capital employed and a figure for profit means that it is possible to compare the ROCE in associates and joint ventures with the ROCE for the company as a whole.

The information[7] to assess the success of joint ventures and associates is found in the group (or 'consolidated') financial statements. Different companies present the information in different ways, and there is some variation in the amount of detail disclosed. It is usually the operating profit figure that is shown for joint ventures and associates, which is calculated after depreciation charges and impairment of goodwill (which may not be separately identified), but before deducting interest, any exceptional items and taxation (which are usually separately identified). Care must be taken to ensure that calculations of ROCE are made on as comparable a basis as is possible, given limited information.

It is possible to calculate ROCE using the operating profit figure (comparable with EBIT), which is taken before deducting interest. Normally, this would be expressed as a percentage of total long-term capital employed, which includes borrowings. But as the borrowings of joint ventures and associates are not usually separately shown, the

---

[6] Unless it can be proved otherwise, for example if another investor has more than 50 per cent of the voting power, and there is no evidence of significant influence being exercised by the 20 per cent investor.

[7] In each case it is the investing company's proportion (e.g. 25 per cent) which is shown, not the total figures for the joint venture or associate company as a whole (unlike with subsidiary companies where the total is shown at first, and then a 'minority interest' figure is deducted later).

figure for capital employed would include only shareholders' funds. In calculating ROCE it is, therefore, preferable to take the results of joint ventures and associate companies, and then deduct interest and taxation (if this information is available) and express the result as a percentage of the shareholders' funds invested in those associates and joint ventures.

There is no requirement to disclose the sales revenue of associated companies, although some companies with investments in associates do so. Companies are expected to publish the names of significant associates, and the proportion that they own; by obtaining the financial statements of the associate company separately, it is possible to obtain the sales figure and further additional information.

Where the sales figure is available, the performance of associates can be measured using the same three ratios used in assessing segmental performance.

9.5 Other Information from Annual Reports

Users of financial statements may be concerned with other aspects of a company's activities, not just their solvency and profitability. They may be seeking more detailed explanation of what is revealed by the balance sheet, the income statement and the cash flow statement, and they may be looking for information about future prospects and performance. Companies may choose to disclose all sorts of things in their annual reports, and there is often a chairman's statement full of fine-sounding information in the style of advertising and public relations. But there is also quite a lot of useful additional information that is required by law, and which is presented by companies in a fairly standard way.

Directors' Report

Companies are required to produce a directors' report that contains a great deal of fairly standardized formal information, including the following:

- *Principal activities* of the company, and any changes
- *Business review* of the activities during the year and of the position at the year end
- *Future developments*
- *Research and development activities*
- *Post balance sheet events*: any important changes since the balance sheet date
- *Value of land and buildings*: significant differences between balance sheet values and market value of land and buildings
- *Statement about employee involvement*: policies on providing information to employees, consulting them, any schemes for employees' shares, and increasing understanding of shared ideas about factors affecting the company's success (in companies with over 250 employees)
- *Number of disabled employees* and employment policies regarding disabled employees (in companies with over 250 employees)

- *Donations* to charities and to political parties are each disclosed separately
- *Purchase of own shares*: number of shares purchased, amount paid, and reasons for doing it
- *Information about directors:* their names and the number of shares held by each at the beginning and end of the year
- *Creditor payment:* the company's policy should be disclosed, and a calculation of the average number of days taken to pay creditors

Substantial information is also provided about *directors' remuneration* and how it is determined, and about *corporate governance* and how the directors run the company. There is an *auditor's report* that usually looks fairly complicated, but uses standard wording and says very little; and a statement of *directors' responsibilities* that makes it clear that the financial statements are the responsibility of the directors, not the auditors.

The financial statements include an *income statement*, a *balance sheet*, a statement of *changes in equity* and a *cash flow statement*. With large listed companies there are usually parent company versions of these statements together with a consolidated version (which includes all the subsidiary companies). These are followed by substantial *notes to the financial statements* that include some vital information although they appear forbiddingly complex: it sometimes seems that the company is more interested in obfuscation than in clarification. There is usually also a *five-year summary* of results although these vary considerably: it may not be for five years, and the companies may disclose very little, or a great deal of, information for previous years in a standardized format. Serious analysts may want to analyse previous years' financial statements for themselves, or to follow up particular items in them; most large listed companies now have good websites from which it is possible to download previous years' annual reports and financial statements.

Operating and Financial Review

The UK Accounting Standards Board (ASB) has, since 1993, recommended that an *operating and financial review* should be published by companies. It is only a recommendation, and it is rather less specific than a directors' report. The ASB (unsurprisingly) recommend that it should be fair (balanced and objective), showing both favourable and unfavourable aspects; focused on significant items; and be designed to be helpful to users who want to understand the financial circumstances of the business.

The operating section of the review should discuss the results for the year, indicating what factors are likely to be most influential in the future, and how the business is investing to meet future needs.

The financial review should deal with financing, borrowing and gearing; cash flow and current liquidity; and any restrictions on transferring funds from overseas.

The information specified for the directors' report is all required by law and is fairly specific. The operating review is only a recommendation, and is set out in general terms only, leaving it to directors to decide exactly what should be shown and how.

Smaller Companies

Disclosure requirements are significantly reduced for small- and medium-sized companies. It is not difficult to get the annual report and accounts for any company (if necessary via Companies House); but the amount of information disclosed for smaller companies is very disappointing compared with that for a public company that is listed on the stock exchange.

Social and Environmental Reporting

Most financial accounting requirements are based on providing information for actual and potential shareholders and creditors. It is sometimes argued that companies have much wider responsibilities, and should be accountable to many other groups in society, and to society as a whole. This book is intended to help readers to understand financial accounting as it is, not to argue a political case for or against particular disclosures to various groups in society. The ASB's *Statement of Principles* considers a number of different users of accounts: investors, lenders, suppliers and trade creditors, employees, customers, governments and their agencies, and the public. But they come to the conclusion 'that financial statements that focus on the interest that investors have in the reporting entity's financial performance and financial position will, in effect, also be focusing on the common interest that all users have in the entity's financial performance and financial position'. This comes close to saying that all users are interested in balance sheets and income statements, and so the production of these will meet the common interest of all users of accounts. The possibility that other users of accounts might want different information is brushed aside.

But from the information required in directors' reports, we can see that there are concerns to make companies accountable more widely in some senses. There are concerns about employees: their numbers, their remuneration and policies for consultation and involvement. There are similar concerns about disabled employees. Although the overwhelming concern is with investors, there are also concerns about trade creditors, and whether or not companies are taking too long to pay them. The requirement to disclose political and charitable donations may be seen as a concern with companies' social involvement more generally. But the amount of disclosures intended primarily for employees, customers, environmentalists, idealists and so on is very small indeed.

There is an argument that a requirement to disclose information can change the ways in which companies behave. Much of the case for corporate social reporting rests on this idea. It does appear that the requirement to disclose how long companies take to pay their creditors is associated with improvements in this aspect of companies' behaviour. Even the requirement to disclose fees to auditors for non-audit work is at last having some effect, but some large companies still pay consultancy fees to their auditors in excess of the amount of the audit fee, apparently compromising their independence.

Many companies voluntarily provide substantial additional information on various aspects of their performance including their practices regarding social and environmental issues; some even produce separate environmental and social reports. Scottish Power produces a substantial (30 page) Environmental and Social Impact Summary Report with, in addition, seven separate Performance Reports covering governance, environment, health and safety, customer, workplace, community and procurement.

Summary

It is not very difficult to learn to calculate a dozen or so standard accounting ratios based on the simplified versions of company accounts that are usually presented in textbooks and examinations. But when examining the complexities of real companies' financial statements it is easy to be overwhelmed. Relatively straightforward real company financial statements were introduced early in the book. More complicated financial statements should be seen as a challenge and as an opportunity: a challenge to answer the same basic questions about solvency and profitability that have already been introduced, and an opportunity to make use of more detailed information that is available to produce a fuller analysis.

Substantial and detailed information is available to assess the solvency of a company; its performance and how its profitability might be improved; and the performance of its shares on the stock market. The amount of information disclosed is generally increasing, partly in response to official requirements, and partly because companies want to be seen to be socially and environmentally responsible.

Review of key points

- More sophisticated assessments can be made of a company's solvency than the main ratios shown in Chapters 1 and 4.
- Companies disclose key information that enables us to analyse the performance of the different business and geographical segments in which the business operates.
- Companies also disclose important information that enables us to assess the performance of investments that they have made in different other companies.
- The directors' report and operating and financial review provide additional information that can help us to assess companies' performance.
- Most information that is disclosed is in relation to companies' financial performance, financial position and cash flows; some information is provided on other aspects of companies' activities.

Self-testing questions

1 Calculate the 20 ratios for Wm Morrison Supermarkets for 2005 to complete the table in Illustration 9.1. Assume the share price for 2005 was £1.77.

2 What accounting information is most useful in assessing a company's solvency?

3 What key information is disclosed to assess the profitability of the various segments of a company?

Self-testing questions (continued)

4 Calculate the appropriate ratios for Tate & Lyle for 2006 to complete the table in
   Illustration 9.7, and comment on the figures produced.

5 You are given the following information about Gobbiediggan International plc.

Segment	UK		Africa		South America	
	Year 1	Year 2	Year 1	Year 2	Year 1	Year 2
	£000	£000	£000	£000	£000	£000
Sales	800	860	300	270	100	180
Operating profit	80	78	40	44	20	21
Operating assets	900	760	200	175	40	60

Making use of appropriate ratios, comment on the performance of each of the
geographical segments.

   One of the directors of the company considers that the UK market should be
abandoned because profits are declining. A second director considers that the
Africa market should be abandoned because sales are declining. A third director
considers that the South America market should be abandoned because it keeps
needing additional investment. Critically assess each of these views.

Assessment questions

1 Select one or two companies' annual report and accounts and assess the financial
   position and performance of their various segments and investments in as much
   detail as the information permits.

2 If a company analyses the ROCE of every division, branch, investment or segment
   that it operates, and closes down all of those with a below average ROCE, then the
   average ROCE for the company as a whole is bound to increase. Assess this
   approach to managing a large business.

3 You are given the following segmental information about the Willaston Company.

Segment	Men's things		Women's things		Children's things	
	Year 1	Year 2	Year 1	Year 2	Year 1	Year 2
	£000	£000	£000	£000	£000	£000
Sales	400	405	800	820	60	130
Operating profit	80	95	90	92	(20)	(4)
Operating assets	200	180	250	260	10	11

Making use of appropriate ratios, comment on the performance of each of the
segments.

Assessment questions (continued)

4 You are given the following information about the Goodwynne Company:

	Year 2	Year 3
	£000	£000
Sales	1,000	1,100
Operating profit	100	115
Operating assets	700	800

Making use of appropriate ratios, assess the view that the company should concentrate on reducing its operating assets.

Group activities and discussion questions

1 What information would you like to see disclosed in company annual reports and accounts in addition to that which is at present required? Examine the annual report of a few companies that provide a lot more information than the minimum required. To what extent does that information provide you with what you want?

2 It is possible to calculate an almost infinite number of ratios from a company's annual report. What ratios other than the 20 emphasized in this chapter do you think would be useful? Why?

3 Think of a number of companies, or types of company, that have gone bankrupt or have found themselves in serious financial difficulties recently (perhaps airlines, telecommunications companies, Polaroid, Eurotunnel). What do you think led to their financial difficulties? Try to identify some comparable companies, and examine their annual report and accounts. Is there evidence of impending financial difficulties?

4 It is unrealistic to assess the performance of a company on the basis of one figure, such as EPS. To what extent do the complexities in producing this figure undermine its usefulness?

5 Companies that generate cash surpluses can afford to diversify, but they should return the money to the shareholders, and it is for shareholders to decide the extent to which they wish to diversify their investments. Companies that cannot afford to diversify often borrow money that they cannot afford and make their shareholders' investments more risky; it is for shareholders to decide whether or not they want more risk. Critically assess these statements.

6 Z scores are only the beginning. Sophisticated statistical models that produce accurate predictions of share prices are becoming available. Discuss the practicability, limitations and implications of these statements.

Financial accounting in context

Strong support for operating reviews

By Barney Jopson

Financial Times, 26 June 2006

Discuss and comment on the following extract from the press with reference to what additional disclosures you think should be required from companies.

Source : Reproduced with permission by the *Financial Times*.

More than three-quarters of investors and analysts want companies to publish full operating and financial reviews in spite of the government's last-minute decision to drop the requirement, research has found.

The results of a survey for IR Magazine contrast with advice that led ministers to scrap mandatory OFRs in November. The decision caused an outcry among governance experts, unions and green lobby groups.

Of fund managers and analysts, 78 per cent thought companies should publish a full OFR, providing narrative on their performance and prospects to supplement the data in annual reports.

"A full review would be best because without it, it is difficult to tell what is going on in the company," said one fund manager questioned in the survey of 250 City professionals, due to be published on Thursday.

Gordon Brown received different messages in briefings that led to the decision that he announced after apparently scant consultation with cabinet colleagues.

The chancellor was told in Treasury documents that Hermes, asset manager of the BT pension scheme, felt the OFR was "colossally over-engineered." The London Stock Exchange was said to be concerned that investors would not use the information.

A Mori poll quoted to the chancellor in October found 41 per cent of fund managers supported the compulsory OFR. The Treasury documents were released following legal action brought against Mr Brown by Friends of the Earth, the environmental lobby group.

The dropping of OFRs was presented as a deregulatory move that would benefit listed companies. Some businesses, represented by the CBI employers' body, had said the cost of complying with the regulation would outweigh the benefits.

But the end of mandatory OFRs marked the start of a policy-making saga punctuated by government U-turns. The result was that mandatory OFRs would be replaced by a looser European Union requirement to produce an annual business review.

Ministers last month stood by the chancellor's original decision, but they acceded to demands to give directors "safe harbour" protection against litigation over the content of business reviews.

Companies can still choose to produce an OFR. A survey last month by Radley Yeldar, a communications consultancy, suggested most companies had gone beyond the basics of the review but fallen short of the original OFR requirements.

Only 7 per cent of 55 companies assessed in the FTSE 100 produced detailed, forward-looking information. Three-quarters failed to make a reasonable attempt at explaining the markets in which they operated and 90 per cent did not define the key indicators they used to measure their performance.

References and further reading

Altman, E.I. (1983) *Corporate Financial Distress*. Wiley.

Gray, R. and J. Bebbington (2001) *Accounting for the Environment*. Paul Chapman.

Lewis, R., D. Pendrill and D. Simon (2003) *Advanced Financial Accounting* (7th edition). FT Prentice Hall.

McKenzie, W (2003) *Financial Times Guide to Using and Interpreting Company Accounts* (3rd edition). FT Prentice Hall.

Pendlebury, M. and R. Groves (2003) *Company Accounts: Analysis, Interpretation and Understanding* (6th edition). Thomson Learning.

Rees, B. (2006) *Financial Analysis* (3rd edition). FT Prentice Hall.

Reid, W. and D.R. Myddelton (2005) *The Meaning of Company Accounts* (8th edition). Gower Publishing.

Sugden A., P. Gee and G. Holmes (2004) *Interpreting Company Reports and Accounts*. FT Prentice Hall.

Taffler, R.J. (1983) 'The assessment of company solvency and performance using a statistical model – a comparative UK-based study'. *Accounting and Business Research*, Autumn.

Taffler, R.J. and H. Tisshaw (1977) 'Going, going, gone – four factors which predict'. *Accountancy*, March.

www.cifc.co.uk (select: benchmarking and interfirm comparison; a standardized basis for using ratios to compare different firms)

www.experian.com (a credit rating agency)

www.investorschronicle.co.uk/public/home.html (a variety of information about companies, interpretation and performance)

www.morrisons.co.uk (click investor information, financial statements and trading updates, for annual reports)

www.tateandlyle.com (click investor relations, select an area, annual report)

CHAPTER 10

Assets, Liabilities, Revenues and Expenses

❖ LEARNING OBJECTIVES

After studying this chapter you should be able to:

- ❖ Define assets, liabilities, revenues and expenses

- ❖ Explain a number of reasons for measuring and disclosing assets

- ❖ Outline the historical development of approaches to asset valuation

- ❖ Assess a number of different bases for asset valuation

- ❖ Describe and understand the main categories of assets and liabilities shown on balance sheets

- ❖ Discuss and analyse various types of provision

- ❖ Understand all the main items shown on balance sheets

- ❖ Understand and describe the main items shown as revenues, income and expenses in financial statements

- ❖ Appreciate the problems in defining when revenues are recognized

- ❖ Explain items that are included in an income statement but which do not look much like revenues or expenses

- ❖ Know which expenses can be found in a company's annual report

- ❖ Understand that some items increase or reduce equity but are not revenues or expenses, and appear on a statement of changes in equity, not on an income statement

10.1 Introduction

Assets and liabilities were introduced in Chapter 1 (the balance sheet), and revenues and expenses in Chapter 2 (the income statement). Their importance in relation to profit measurement was explored in Chapter 5 where it was explained that profits can be measured either in relation to an increase in net assets, or as being the difference between revenues and expenses. It is important to understand what is included under each of these headings, and how the items are measured, in order to understand and interpret financial statements and throughout financial accounting. This chapter provides further explanation of these four key elements and an opportunity to consider how they are defined, measured and presented in financial statements.

10.2 Assets

Definition

It is easier to think of an asset as being anything that a business (or individual) owns that is worth something. Tangible assets include land and buildings; plant and machinery; furniture, fittings and equipment; vehicles; inventories of goods; receivables; and money in the bank. Financial assets include all kinds of investments. Intangible assets include such things as goodwill, patents, brand names and copyright.

The International Accounting Standards Board's (IASB's) *Framework for the Preparation and Presentation of Financial Statements* (1989) defines an asset as 'a resource controlled by the enterprise as a result of past events and from which future economic benefits are expected to flow to the enterprise'. The Accounting Standards Board's (ASB's) *Statement of Principles for Financial Reporting* (1999) defines assets as 'rights or other access to future economic benefits controlled by an entity as a result of past transactions or events'. Both definitions emphasize control rather than ownership. It is the control of the right to economic benefits that matters, not the ownership of a 'thing'.

A piece of machinery is obviously an asset if a business owns it and it is of some value (i.e. it will bring economic benefits to the business). Surprisingly, it is also an asset if the business hires it using a finance lease (usually a long-term lease). It is control that matters, and the right to receive the economic benefits. It has always been accepted that a long lease on a building (perhaps 99 years) is an asset. There is more controversy around the idea that something like machinery that is held on a shorter lease should also be treated as an asset (and that future amounts that the company is committed to paying under the terms of the lease should be treated as a liability) on the balance sheet. The 'economic reality' or 'substance' of holding an asset under a finance lease is regarded as being much the same as owning it.

The principle that it is control that matters, rather than ownership, is also seen on group balance sheets. If Company A owns 60 per cent of the shares of Company B, then Company B is a subsidiary of Company A, and Company A controls it. When consolidated accounts are prepared for the group controlled by Company A, the group balance sheet includes 100 per cent of the assets of Company B, although only 60 per cent are owned.[1]

---

[1] The 40 per cent that is not owned is included in 'minority interest' on the balance sheet, and shown alongside equity.

Goodwill is also an asset. If a business has such things as a good reputation, a trained workforce, established customers, and provides high quality goods or services, these are all likely to bring economic benefits. We have seen that the market value of a business as a whole, if it is successful, is likely to be much higher than the total of the values of all its separate assets. If a successful company has net assets of £10 million, and someone buys it, they are likely to have to pay much more than £10 million for it for all sorts of reasons (i.e. all the things that make it a successful business as opposed to a collection of dead assets). If someone paid £22 million for the business, they would have paid £12 million for goodwill. The goodwill is a right to future economic benefits that are controlled by the entity as a result of the transaction. It may be referred to as purchased goodwill, and is recognized as an asset on the balance sheet. Goodwill is not usually a 'separable' asset: it cannot be sold separately from the business. It is an intangible asset that is an integral part of the business.

Of course, a business is creating goodwill all the time. Efforts put into advertising, public relations, market research, the development of products and information systems, recruiting and training staff, all contribute to the goodwill of the company. But such 'internally generated' goodwill is not recognized as an asset. It only counts as an asset if it has been bought as part of a transaction in buying another business.

When a business creates tangible fixed assets, these are included on the balance sheet as assets (unlike internally generated goodwill). A business can choose to buy such things as buildings, machinery and information systems, or they can build or make their own. Capital expenditure creates or adds to fixed assets. Revenue expenditure is a charge against profits (and so it reduces equity). One of the problems of defining fixed assets is distinguishing between capital and revenue expenditure. Building an extension is capital expenditure; repairing a building is revenue expenditure. But there is a grey area between the two. If rotting, draughty, wooden window frames are replaced by modern, plastic double-glazed windows, it is partly an improvement (capital expenditure; adding to the value of a building), and partly ordinary maintenance (revenue expenditure).

Another problem in deciding exactly what an asset is arises with research and development costs. In the good old/bad old days before (the original) Rolls-Royce collapsed, a company could spend a lot of money on research and development, in developing a new aero engine for example, and there were no rules on whether this should be regarded as normal revenue expenditure, or whether the expenditure could be regarded as creating an additional asset to be shown on the balance sheet. Eventually accounting standards were produced (International Accounting Standard (IAS) 38 and Statement of Standard Accounting Practice (SSAP) 13) that said that all research expenditure was revenue expenditure; but development expenditure, if it met specified conditions, could be treated as capital expenditure; or it could be treated as revenue expenditure; the company can decide. Perhaps there can be no watertight definition of an asset. It is possible only to provide guidelines.

There are particularly difficult areas in defining and measuring assets such as goodwill, research and development, human assets, and leased assets. Annual reports often include statements from the chairman saying something like 'our employees are our most valuable asset', but they are not included on the balance sheet. Assets that 'count' can be something that is not tangible; something that is not separable; and something that the company does not even own. It must be something of value, and something that the company has bought or created. Traditionally goodwill was always seen as being a rather questionable asset; bankers and other creditors are not interested in assets that cannot be separately sold, and so do not provide security for them. If we are to have a satisfactory basis for determining what is to be counted as an asset, and what should be included on the balance sheet, we need to consider the purposes of defining and measuring assets.

Reasons for Showing and Valuing Assets

For many years the idea of 'valuing' assets was largely irrelevant in financial accounting. Assets were simply recorded and shown at cost.

When double-entry bookkeeping first evolved, the idea of listing assets and liabilities was of little importance. What mattered was to record transactions, and to know who owed what and to whom. The accuracy of the recording system was (and still is!) important, and producing a listing of debit and credit balances that had not been written off was a useful check in the double-entry bookkeeping system. For many years no one pretended that such listings of balances in the form of a balance sheet were of any particular use unless such a listing was needed, because the old ledger was full, and the balances needed to be transferred into a new ledger.

Major changes came with the development of companies in the middle of the nineteenth century. Industrialization led to many businesses needing much more machinery and other assets, which in turn meant that they needed more money to finance their activities. Potential investors were attracted to the idea of investing in companies where their liability for potential losses was limited to the amount of capital they had invested. A company would have many different shareholders who could not manage the investment themselves: they elected directors to look after it for them. The idea was (and should still be) that directors manage companies on behalf of the shareholders who own the company, and the directors are accountable to the shareholders who want to know what has happened to their money; a balance sheet shows the assets in which it is tied up. The origins of modern accountancy are in the requirement for companies to provide accounts of their activities to shareholders.

Today, shareholders want steady growth in company profits, year after year, and to see this reflected with the value of their shares steadily increasing. In the nineteenth century they were more concerned to see that the directors had not run away with their money. If the company is successful the net assets and the amount of equity should increase each year, unless the company opts to pay out all profits as dividends. The important thing was to maintain the amount of the original capital invested; any dividends must be paid out of profits, and there could be no profit unless the amount of capital originally invested had been maintained. As fixed assets became worn out and used up, a depreciation charge had to be made, and there were no profits available to be paid out as dividends unless the capital (now invested in assets) had been maintained.

Asset values are important in determining how much a company can pay out as dividends. Unless a company has maintained the value of its shareholders' funds (by ensuring that the amount of net assets in which they are invested is not less than the shareholders had invested in the company), then it cannot pay dividends. Dividends must come out of profits that the company has earned, not out of the capital that the shareholders invested in the company.

Companies may still want or need more long-term funding as they expand and invest in more fixed (and current) assets. They may borrow money by issuing debentures, or by persuading others such as banks to lend money to them. Balance sheets can provide reassurance to actual and potential creditors, by showing what asset backing there is, and creditors have an interest in seeing that balance sheets are prudently prepared: that the company's assets are worth *at least* as much as the balance sheet states. If a building is shown at cost, £1 million, but, after a number of years, it is really worth £2 million, then the creditors are happy: their security has increased. Where businesses are particularly dependent on banks to finance their activities, such a prudent approach is welcomed by the banks.

At least until the middle of the twentieth century, most of the reasons for valuing assets pointed towards conservative or prudent valuations. The assumption was that assets are worth at least as much as the balance sheet showed. Prudence was seen as being a fundamental accounting concept.

The effects of rising prices, particularly in the 1970s, led to pressures to move away from historic cost (HC). This was partly to do with the asset values shown on the balance sheet and partly to do with profit measurement. The effects of rising prices meant that the HC of assets was seen as being too low in relation to current values. It also undermined the idea of 'capital maintenance' in profit measurement: maintaining the historic amount of capital was no longer enough to keep the business going when assets needed to be replaced at higher prices.

There were other pressures to revalue assets upwards. In many companies the current market value of assets was much higher than the balance sheet indicated, and asset stripping became an art form. If a company was not doing particularly well it was sometimes possible to buy a whole company for less than the total value of all its separate assets. A company might have a net asset value – according to its balance sheet – of, say, £10 million. If they were making only £1 million a year, it might be possible to buy the whole company for, say, something between £12 million and £15 million. But if someone managed to estimate the current value of all the various parts of the business, and it came to £20 million, they were well placed to make a killing. If it is possible to buy a company for less than £15 million and sell the various parts of it for £20 million, many would see this as being good business.

The best defence against such takeovers is to have a good profits record, and a high share price, so that it would cost a lot more than the net asset value to buy the company. Revaluing assets on the balance sheet to give more realistic, up-to-date figures is no guarantee against unwelcome takeover bids. But the values are there for all to see, and it is less likely that someone will succeed in buying up a company for less than its net asset value. But, even when assets are shown at current values, if a company is doing badly, the value of the company as a whole can still be less than the value of its separate assets.

The desire or need for companies to borrow increasing amounts of money encourages them to adopt current values for assets, particularly property. Lenders are concerned that a company's borrowings should not be excessive in relation to the company's own money, or equity. Low asset values result in low figures for equity, which in turn can restrict the amount of money that a company can borrow. Property companies generally revalue their properties every year; with other companies there is little consistency – some revalue frequently, while others revalue infrequently or not at all.

Although most practitioners seem to be happy enough to continue with a wide variety of different asset valuation bases, the ASB's *Statement of Principles for Financial Reporting* (1999) should offer some sort of theoretical justification for what happens and suggest some consistency. But it accepts HC with all its many modifications, and also moves towards ideas of fair value. Readers of financial statements will realize that there is still a hotchpotch of valuation bases. Companies do disclose what basis they have used for each category of asset, but it is necessary to study the notes to the accounts and assess the information about asset values carefully.

The reasons for showing assets on the balance sheet have changed over the years. Originally 'stewardship' was the main reason for showing assets on a balance sheet. The directors of a company act as 'stewards' for the money invested by shareholders who want to know where their money is. Until the last few decades of the twentieth century, prudence was the order of the day. Creditors wanted reassurance that companies had adequate assets to meet their liabilities. When companies wanted to increase their borrowings, it became important for companies to show higher asset figures. Asset valuation is also necessary for profit measurement. Today, increasing importance is given to 'fair values' for assets, based on market values. We should be wary of the idea that a fair value can be established for each asset, and that the total of these values would be equal to the value of a business – even if that is what some economists think that a balance sheet should show, and what investors really want to know. The value of a business and its assets depends on the future, and the idea that financial statements can tell us about the future should be treated with caution.

A Variety of Asset Values

There are many different ways of valuing assets, and the number of possible combinations of asset valuations on a single balance sheet is almost infinite.

The main approaches are:

1 *HC* This is objective, verifiable, and the true market value at the time of the transaction. It appears increasingly irrelevant as time goes by.

2 *HC less depreciation* This allows for the fact that fixed assets wear out, or are partly used up each year. There are many different ways of estimating depreciation.

3 *Net realizable value* This means the amount for which the asset could be sold, after deducting any necessary costs of getting it into a condition and location that enable it to be sold. Net realizable value could be estimated in two different ways, giving two different answers: on the basis of an asset being sold in the normal course of business, or in the event of a forced sale.

4 *Economic value,* **or** *net present value* **or** *value in use* This is based on the future cash flows that an asset is expected to generate, discounted at an appropriate discount rate. This is easy to apply where there are long-term debtors, and the dates on which they will pay are known; similarly, with investments in gilts and debentures where amounts and dates of interest receivable are known, and the redemption date is fixed. It is much more difficult to estimate with most other assets.

5 *Replacement cost* This can be based on list prices for equivalent assets, or it can be

estimated using appropriate price indices and applying them to HC. Where technology is changing rapidly, a company would not replace an existing asset with an identical one. Instead they may try to identify an equivalent alternative asset, perhaps equivalent in productive capacity or operating capability.

6 *Face value* Notes and coins are usually shown at face value. Receivables and some investments may also be shown at face value.

7 *Face value less a provision* Receivables are usually shown at face value minus a provision for bad debts.

8 *Market price* The market price for an asset is likely to be very different depending on whether you are buying or selling, as anyone selling or buying a second-hand car knows. Market price, when we are buying, is replacement cost; market price when we are selling is net realizable value. The difference could be quite extreme, for example with a railway line. If it is uneconomic and closed down, the net realizable value of a narrow strip of land in a rural area could be very small, or even negative if it was accompanied by obligations to maintain fences, ditches, bridges and rights of way. But the replacement cost, or the cost of building a new railway line, for example Crossrail between Paddington and Liverpool Street, is likely to be many millions of pounds.

Market price is most easily used in relation to listed investments such as shares, debentures and government gilt-edged securities.

9 *Directors' estimate of market value* With investments that are not listed, the easiest alternative to HC is to have an estimate of market value made by the directors. Inventories are sometimes valued on this basis, perhaps where there are unsatisfactory records.

10 *Valuer's report* Land and buildings, especially investment properties, are sometimes revalued regularly on the basis of valuers' reports produced by specialist valuers, who provide a report, for a fee; this can be verified by the company's auditors. Valuers are, of course, like auditors: they are independent professional experts, and their opinions are objective and neutral, and not influenced by what the company's directors want or by their need to earn fees.[2]

11 *Insurance values* Assets are insured on the basis of the valuation that insurance companies put on them. As insurance premiums are usually based on the asset value, they are likely to be overstated rather than understated. If a company is desperate, and can think of nothing better, they might use insurance values as the basis for valuing some assets.

12 *HC adjusted for inflation* The basis of inflation accounting (current purchasing power (CPP)) is to adjust all non-monetary items in the financial statements by the amount of inflation since the transaction was recorded. This gives very unrealistic asset values where price changes for specific types of assets are very different from the average change in retail prices recorded by the Retail Price Index.

13 *Fair value* This is a market value: the amount for which an asset could be exchanged between knowledgeable, willing parties, in an arm's-length transaction. The idea is of

---

[2] And you will probably believe in Father Christmas too, it is in your interest to (appear to) do so.

increasing importance in the development of both international and US financial reporting standards, but there is no agreed definition, and it is not clear how to apply the idea of fair value where there is no ready market for a particular asset.

14 *Deprival value* or *value to the business* This is the basis used in CCA. It is usually the same as replacement cost, but where replacement cost is too high (so that it would not be worth replacing the asset), then deprival value is either net realizable value or economic value, whichever is the higher.

Most balance sheets incorporate a variety of different approaches to asset valuation, and it is very unlikely that there will be general agreement on a single approach that is applicable to all assets.

Even if we could produce reliable asset values, perhaps based on the net present value of future cash flows, we should be wary of the idea that a total of such asset values has much meaning or much use. It does not show what the assets could be sold for, and it does not show what the business is worth as a whole. Most successful businesses should be worth a lot more than the amount shown for its separate assets on the balance sheet. This is because, in a successful business, there is 'internally generated' goodwill that has not been recorded. If the accounting standards setters are moving towards a world when even internally generated goodwill is shown on a balance sheet, based on estimates of its net present value, then perhaps the total of the net asset value of a company will be equal to its market capitalization on the stock market. We will then have moved to a world where accountancy, based as it is on recording transactions, is superseded by predictions, fictions, economic theory and fantasy.

Categories of Assets

A balance sheet usually starts by listing assets under two headings: non-current assets, and current assets.

Non-current assets include the following that should be separately identified:

1 Property, plant and equipment. This heading includes most of the usual tangible fixed assets such as most land and buildings; plant, machinery and equipment; furniture, fixtures and fittings; vehicles

2 Investment property

3 Intangible assets, including goodwill

4 Financial assets, including most long-term investments

5 Investments in associates

Current assets include the following that should be separately identified:

1 Inventories, including stocks of raw materials and components, work in progress and finished goods

2 Trade and other receivables

3 Cash and cash equivalents

Summary

If there was one, simple, clear reason for wanting to know the amount that should be shown for assets on company balance sheets, it might be easy to specify exactly what should be included, to define what we mean by an asset, and to decide the basis on which assets should be valued. But there are many different reasons for wanting to know the amount of assets, which in turn means that there are different ways of defining exactly what should be included as an asset, and ways of valuing or measuring assets.

The debate on asset valuation sometimes seems to proceed as if there is a 'correct' answer, as if accountants have been at fault for years for failing to show 'true' values. But we never really know the value of an asset until it is sold and the price is agreed; HC was a 'true' value when it was first recorded. We can produce asset valuations that are more up to date, and accept some loss of reliability, but we must remember that even if we are able to value all assets on an acceptable and consistent current basis, the total of the values is of limited meaning. We need to deduct liabilities to arrive at a net asset value. But the resulting figure tells us neither what the individual separable assets could be sold for, nor what the value of the business as a whole is. The value of a business depends on investors' expectation of the future cash flows that the business will generate.

10.3 Liabilities

Definition

A liability may be thought of as being something that a business or individual has to pay or repay. Normal current liabilities are trade receivables (creditors), overdrafts, and any amounts due to HM Revenue and Customs (taxation). Non-current liabilities include debentures and other long-term loans. It is not usually difficult to list the amounts that an individual or company owes, but some problem areas are considered below.

The IASB's definition of a liability is 'a present obligation of the enterprise arising from past events, the settlement of which is expected to result in an outflow from the enterprise of resources embodying economic benefits'. It is worth noting the phrase 'present obligation ... from past events' because it excludes some prudent but vague 'provisions' that companies used to make even though there was no 'present obligation' at the balance sheet date, and the events that might require a payment to be made lay in the future. Such vague provisions are no longer permitted. All provisions must be liabilities within the above definition.

IAS 1 lists five categories of liability to be shown on a balance sheet. These may be current or non-current:

1 Trade and other payables

2 Provisions

3 Other financial liabilities (mainly borrowings)

4 Liabilities for current tax

5 Deferred tax liabilities

Companies typically disclose separately any liabilities for pensions.

Liabilities should not be thought of as being 'negative assets' – an idea that has largely disappeared. Some assets are reduced by deducting provisions (for bad debts or for depreciation), but they should not be reduced below zero.

Current Liabilities

Current liabilities were previously known as 'creditors: amounts falling due within one year'. Most of the figures are fairly straightforward.

Company balance sheets invariably show trade payables (creditors) for the usual purchases and expenses that they have bought or incurred during the year just ended, but which have not yet been paid for. The term 'accruals' is just an extension of this. At the year end estimates have to be made of all expenses that have been incurred during the year although no bookkeeping entries have yet been made for them. At the balance sheet date there will always be some expenses such as electricity and gas, and perhaps interest, which have to be 'accrued'.

In addition, most companies are likely to have current liabilities for taxation. Proposed dividends are no longer regarded as a liability until after they have been approved at the annual general meeting (after the balance sheet date), and so these should no longer appear as current liabilities. Companies often also have overdrafts and other short-term borrowings from banks and other institutions that are shown as current liabilities.

Longer-term liabilities that eventually are paid (and not all are, as explained below) become current liabilities during the last 12 months before they are paid. Most of the items that are shown as long-term liabilities eventually become current liabilities as the date for payment approaches.

Non-current Liabilities

The most substantial long-term liability is usually in the form of debentures or other borrowing where the amount is due to be repaid more than a year after the balance sheet date. There are also various provisions for liabilities and charges, which are described below.

When a company acquires fixed assets under a finance lease, the interest accrues annually, and is shown as an expense in the profit and loss account; if it is unpaid at the year end, it is shown as a current liability. The main part of the liability – the capital element or the principal – is identified as a finance lease liability, and included under financial liabilities, alongside borrowings; often it is detailed in a note to the balance sheet.

Provisions

Provisions are created as a result of a charge against profits. If a provision of £100,000 is created, the profits are reduced by £100,000. If the provision is increased in the following year by £50,000, the charge against profits is £50,000, and the total provision shown on the balance sheet is £150,000. In a later year, when the provision is reduced, profits are increased by the amount of the reduction. Provisions have been used in 'creative accounting',[3] particularly in 'income smoothing': to reduce the profits in booming years, and to boost them in lean years.

---

[3] See Chapter 8.

The Companies Act 1985 defines provisions as 'amounts retained as reasonably necessary to cover any liability of loss which is either likely or certain to be incurred'. This gives companies a fair amount of freedom in deciding how much use to make of provisions. They are typically labelled as being for reorganizations, redundancies, disposals, legal liabilities, decommissioning costs, and future losses and costs of various sorts.

UK and international FRSs have created a stricter definition: a provision is a liability of uncertain timing or amount. It is, therefore, a liability, and there must be an obligation to transfer economic benefits. It is supposed to be much like any other liability; the difference is the uncertainty of the timing or amount. Provisions have sometimes been established where there is no real obligation to transfer economic benefits, and even today Financial Reporting Standard (FRS) 12, allows provisions where there is no legal obligation, but only a 'constructive' obligation.

According to FRS 12, provisions should be recognized only where there is a (constructive or legal) obligation to transfer economic benefits as at the balance sheet date; it is probable that the transfer will be required; and that a reliable estimate can be made of the amount of the obligation. It is difficult to eliminate an element of subjectivity in deciding whether to create provisions, and the amounts to be shown.

The accounting standards setters are in a difficult position. If they allow too much freedom in creating, increasing and reducing provisions, they leave the door open to creative accounting. But if they are too strict in not allowing provisions, there would often be cases where companies knew of some likely bad news, and kept quiet about it. A prudent set of financial statements would disclose all potential liabilities including 'contingent liabilities'.

Warranties

Companies may make specific provisions for the cost of guarantees or warranties and other after-sales service that they are expected to provide. This may appear on a balance sheet as a provision, or it may not be separately disclosed. Sometimes companies deduct appropriate provisions from the figure for sales; sometimes it is included in a more general provision.

Contingent Liabilities

Contingent liabilities can arise as a result of legal action. Maybe the company will have to pay out a lot of money as a result of losing a case; but the result has not yet been determined. A contingent liability is a possible obligation whose existence will be confirmed only by the occurrence of an uncertain future event, or it can be where a transfer of economic benefits is not probable, or the amount cannot yet be measured reliably. Contingent liabilities should not be shown on a balance sheet. They should be disclosed as a note to the accounts (unless they are only a remote possibility).

In assessing the solvency or creditworthiness of a company, it is worth looking not only at the actual liabilities shown on the balance sheet, but also at the contingent liabilities; there may a risk of substantial payments having to be made.

Deferred Taxation

Deferred taxation arises because the rules for calculating profit for inclusion in annual reports and accounts are different from the rules for taxation purposes. Depreciation allowances for taxation purposes ('writing down allowances') are typically quite high in the early years of a fixed asset's life; these high allowances reduce taxable profits, which means that the amount of corporation tax payable is much reduced in the first years after substantial acquisitions of fixed assets. Profits for tax purposes are much lower than the profits reported in the annual accounts, which would make the tax charge look peculiarly low, and might mislead shareholders by exaggerating the after-tax profits available for dividends.

A few years later this reverses. As the fixed assets get towards the end of their lives (and if there have been few additional purchases of fixed assets) the position reverses: allowances for tax purposes are smaller; the amount of tax payable is larger; and this might mislead shareholders by showing low after-tax profit being available for dividends.

Deferred taxation is a bit like a taxation equalization account. In the early years after acquisitions of fixed assets, the tax actually payable is low, but a higher charge against profits is made; this extra 'deferred taxation' is not yet payable, but is shown as if it is a liability. After a few years it may reverse: the tax actually payable is higher, but only a modest 'equalized' charge is made against profits; the extra is charged against the balance for deferred taxation that was built up for that purpose in the early years of the fixed asset's life.

In many cases the amount shown as a long-term liability for deferred taxation will never actually be paid. If a company continues to invest in additional fixed assets, it is likely that the writing down allowances on the new fixed assets will have the effect of building up the credit balance on the deferred taxation account faster than it is used up by the smaller writing down allowances on the older fixed assets. The old Accounting Standards Committee (ASC) experimented with a 'partial provision' for deferred taxation, based on the idea that provisions should be made only for amounts that it was reasonably probable would become payable. But this was rather subjective and not consistent with international practice.

FRS 19 required full provision for deferred taxation for all timing differences. The effect can be to build up a substantial provision on the balance sheet that might never actually become a liability. This makes interpretation of financial statements, and the calculation of accounting ratios, rather difficult. Some people simply ignore it: they exclude it from capital employed, and from liabilities, but this can lead to inconsistent ratios that never properly add up or reconcile.

Deferred taxation is normally shown as a non-current liability, identified separately from other liabilities. As in so many areas of interpretation of financial statements, there may be no definitive 'right' answer. The important thing is to treat it in a consistent way in comparing one company with another, and comparing one year with another.

Deferred Income and Deferred Credits

Most items of revenues and income are credited to the income statement and contribute towards profit immediately. Sometimes, revenues are received in advance of the company providing the goods or services, and these should not (yet) be credited to the income statement. They may be shown as liabilities for deferred income, or as deferred credits.

When a company receives a government grant towards the cost of acquiring fixed assets, this should not be credited to the income statement immediately. The income should be spread over the life of the asset. This can be done by showing it as a deferred credit on the balance sheet; each year part of this is credited to the income statement in line with depreciation. (An alternative is to deduct it from the cost of the asset: this has the same effect on profit, by reducing depreciation charges.)

Pension Funds

Companies with pension funds have usually built up assets to meet the need to pay future pensions. Each year companies and their employees put money into a fund, and the money is invested in shares, debentures, government bonds, property and, occasionally, in less conventional assets such as works of art. As the company expands, so there are more employees; more money is put into the fund; and the investments increase in value; and, with a bit of luck, the income from the investments is more than enough to pay the pensions as they fall due.

There used to be cases where companies took a 'pensions holiday', and made no contribution to the pension fund because its value was more than enough to meet all expected liabilities. Such 'holidays' helped to boost companies' profits.

In some cases there are no serious problems with pension funds. The scheme may be one where the amount that has to be contributed each year is defined, but there is no definition of the amount of pensions that has to be paid. If the pension fund turns out to be very valuable, pensions may be generous. If the fund turns out to be rather poor, then pensions are rather poor.

Most employees prefer a 'defined benefit' or 'final salary' scheme where the amount of pension they will receive depends on the level of salary they are earning before retiring. If they have been in the pension scheme for, say, 30 years, their pension may be 30 sixtieths, or 30 eightieths of their final salary. Each year when companies prepare their annual accounts they have to estimate what their future liability for pensions will be, and disclose any shortfalls.

Where the number of employees in a company is declining, the level of contributions to the pension scheme is also declining. More seriously, pension funds have typically depended heavily on investments in equities, and the value of these declined substantially between the beginning of the year 2000 and the middle of 2003. This, together with the fact that people are living longer, has resulted in many pension schemes being in deficit; in some cases the deficits are enormous. This information has to be disclosed in the annual reports of companies.

Discounting

If the amount of a liability is not due to be paid for some years it may be appropriate to 'discount'[4] it. That means applying a discount factor (or interest rate) to it to allow for the number of years. If a company owes £10 million that is due to be paid four years in the

---

[4] Discounting is explained in Chapter 12.

future, and an appropriate discount rate is 10 per cent, the amount would be shown at its 'present value', which is (£10 million × 0.683 =) £6.83 million.

The definition and measurement of liabilities is generally less problematic than with assets. Accounting standards have made it clear that everything on the balance sheet must be assets, liabilities or equity. This should eliminate vague provisions that are not really liabilities at all. Provisions for depreciation and for bad debts are still deducted from the amounts shown for the assets, but these are unlike provisions specifically shown on balance sheets.

10.4 Revenues and Income

The terms 'revenue' and 'income' are sometimes used to mean much the same thing. An income statement usually begins by showing revenue, which is income from sales, also known as turnover. The figure is based on the amount *earned* during the period, not the amount of cash received (in accordance with the accruals concept); there is usually some delay in receiving money from debtors.

An income statement usually then identifies various other items of income that might include other operating income (perhaps rents receivable), finance income (interest receivable), profits on disposal of fixed assets, and share of profits from joint ventures or associates.

One approach to the definition of income is to say that it includes anything that adds to the value of the business, or increases the amount of equity (excluding, of course, any increase in equity that is the result of issuing more shares). Most of this is recognized in the USA's definition of revenue[5] that defines revenues as 'inflows or other enhancements of assets of an entity or settlements of its liabilities (or a combination of both) from delivering or producing goods, rendering services, or other activities that constitute the entity's ongoing major central operations'.

The IASB's framework provides a more inclusive definition of income as being 'increases in economic benefits during the accounting period in the form of inflows or enhancements of assets, or decreases of liabilities, that result in increases in equity, other than those relating to contributions from equity participants'.

The US definition of revenue excludes income from anything other than the business's major central operations. The IASB's definition of income includes almost anything that increases equity, which could include revaluations of assets. It is clear that sales are revenues that should be included on an income statement. It is not clear what other income should be included.

There is room for debate on the extent to which reductions in the value of assets should be recognized in the income statement. When such reductions are recognized, the profit for that period is reduced. The HC convention of accounting might seem to permit continuing to show assets at cost, even if their value has declined. But HC has always been moderated by 'prudence'. Inventories are shown at the lower of cost and net realizable value; provisions are made for bad debts; and fixed assets are depreciated. Where there has been an

---

[5] SFAC 6 para 78.

additional reduction in the value of assets or 'impairment', most accountants would probably say that this should be recognized as an expense in the income statement for the year, perhaps separately disclosed as an 'exceptional item'. But, generally, companies can choose whether to show assets at cost or at current value.

There is less room for debate on unrealized gains on holding assets, at least in the eyes of a traditional, prudent accountant. The ASB talks about 'the re-measurement of assets and liabilities', which really means 'revaluation', and this may result in a decrease or an increase in the value. The idea that it may be necessary from time to time to 'write down' assets is certainly normal accounting practice, and such write-downs are an expense. They certainly reduce the earnings per share (EPS) figure. But revaluing (or 're-measuring') assets upwards is a different matter. If assets increase in value then that is, on paper, a 'gain' to the owners (the shareholders), but it is certainly not a 'realized' profit until the asset is sold. The Companies Act permits the payment of dividends from profits that have been realized, not from unrealized profits. It is inappropriate to include unrealized gains on an income statement if one of the main functions of that statement is to provide a basis for dividend decisions.

A separate *statement of changes in equity for the year* is included in published financial statements. This shows gains and losses that it is not appropriate to include on the income statement and which are not recognized as being part of profit for the year. The main examples of such gains or losses are on revaluing fixed assets, and, because of differences in exchange rates, on translating the financial statements of overseas investments into the home currency. The statement is necessary to reconcile profit for the year with the amount by which total retained profits on the balance sheet have increased or decreased during the year.

In theory it may be only the total of gains less losses that matters. But for those who want a full and detailed analysis of a company's performance, it is important that all the various elements are separately disclosed.

There is room for disagreement on whether or not profits on sales of fixed assets are 'revenues'. They are clearly 'gains', and they are gains that have been 'realized': a sale has taken place, some payment is receivable, and the amount realized is usually very clear. They should be disclosed as separate items on an income statement, and they should be included in the EPS figure. The reason for separate disclosure is to enable users of accounts to separate out any exceptional gains if they wish to do so, perhaps to provide a better basis for predicting future years.

The ASB's emphasis on gains and losses rather than revenues and expenses suggests a preference for an 'all inclusive' measure of profit, based on the balance sheet, rather than refining income statements. But they are not suggesting that there should be a single figure for profit, in which 're-measurement' gains and losses are hidden. The emphasis in recent developments is on increasingly detailed disclosures of the various items that make up the overall gain or loss during a period. One way of presenting this information is shown in Illustration 10.1. This is based on an example provided in the IASB's 2006 proposed amendment to IAS 1 *Presentation of Financial Statements*. It indicates the move towards a more 'all inclusive' view of profit, partly prompted by the move towards the US Financial Accounting Standards Board's (FASB's) approach. A distinction is made between 'profit for the year', and 'total recognized income and expense for the year'. The detail of

Statement of recognized income and expense of XYZ Group for the year ended 31 December 20XX

	£
Revenue	390,000
Cost of sales	(245,000)
Gross profit	145,000
Other income	20,667
Distribution costs	(9,000)
Administrative expenses	(20,000)
Other expenses	(2,100)
Finance costs	(8,000)
Share of profit of associates	35,100
Profit before tax	161,667
Income tax expense	(40,417)
Profit for year from continuing operations	121,250
Loss for year from discontinued operations	–
Profit for year	121,250
Other recognized income and expense	
Exchange differences on translating foreign operations	5,334
Available-for-sale financial assets	(24,000)
Cash flow hedges	(667)
Gains on property revaluation	933
Actuarial gains (losses) on defined benefit plans	(667)
Share of other recognized income and expense of associates	400
Income tax related to components of other recognized income and expense	4,667
Other recognized income and expense for the year, net of tax	(14,000)
Total recognized income and expense for the year	107,250

ILLUSTRATION 10.1

the distinction between the two is provided. It is worth noting that there is no longer a requirement to separately identify a figure for operating profit (which is usually profit before deducting finance costs).

Companies' income statements are credited with various income from investments such as interest receivable, dividends receivable and a proportion of the profits from investments in associated companies and joint ventures. These are clearly 'gains', but whether or not they should be called 'revenues' is a matter that can be debated. Many of these items can, of course, be negative. A company may pay more interest than it receives, and interest payable is clearly an expense. If a company has invested in an associate company, and the associate makes a loss, then the profit and loss account of the company that made the investment must include their share of that loss; the loss would look very much like an expense, but somehow the word 'loss' seems more appropriate.

Additional revenues can come from such things as rents receivable, and from patents, licences, copyrights, all of which are disclosed in varying degrees of detail in published financial statements. The main difficulty in interpreting these published figures is to realize that:

1 Not all items of revenue are separately identified and published. Modest amounts of rents receivable would not be shown separately.

2 Revenues are accounted for on an accruals basis. This means that credit is taken for them as they are earned, not as and when the money for them is received.

Some items are credited to the income statement as if they are revenues, although they may seem more like accounting adjustments than revenue. Examples include discount received, exceptional items and reversals of provisions.

Discount Received

Companies that buy goods on credit, and pay for them reasonably promptly, often 'receive' a discount for so doing. If a company owes £200, and the discount receivable is 2.5 per cent, they pay only £195. This is recorded as an expense of £200 (typically as part of cost of sales), and 'revenue' of £5 is recorded. This is a sensible way of recording it if the intention is to measure the relationship between sales and cost of goods sold (the gross profit ratio) without it being distorted by an item that is more to do with financing decisions than to do with the cost of the goods that are being sold. It is not usually separately identified in published accounts.

Exceptional Items

Exceptional items can be gains or losses, or a company may have both. Some have to be disclosed; companies decide to disclose some others. Most companies buy fixed assets fairly frequently, and dispose of old ones. When a fixed asset is sold, it is unlikely that it will be sold for exactly its book value; the actual sale proceeds usually lead to a profit or loss on disposal being recognized. Gains on sales of fixed assets are shown on the income statement as exceptional items as part of revenues or income.

Reversal of a Provision

Exceptional items can also be reductions in provisions. A substantial provision for reorganization may no longer be required, and so part or all is credited back to the income statement. This is not revenue: it is a reversal of a previous over-provision for expenses.

Given the traditional accounting emphasis on prudence, it is not surprising that it sometimes turns out that expenses were over-provided, or assets had been written down excessively. The reversal of excessive prudence is a credit to the income statement. But it looks more like an accounting adjustment than an item of revenue.

Illustration 10.2 shows the effect of an exceptional write-off of inventories which is subsequently reversed.

Companies routinely make provisions for bad debts. Experience might suggest that normally a proportion of debtors will not pay up, and the company might show a provision for bad debts of, say, 5 per cent of debtors. On the balance sheet, if the company has

A publishing company has 5,000 rather boring history of art books in stock. They originally cost £4 per unit to produce, and were intended to sell for £20 per unit. But after a year they were remaindered, and the company was able to realize only £2 per unit when selling them. The books were, therefore, written down to the net realizable value of £2 per unit.

The company added a new cover to the book that featured some erotic art and cost £1 per book. There was also a revival of interest in history of art. The books began to sell at £8 per unit.

As stocks should be shown at the lower of cost and net realizable value, the books were then written up to (£4 original cost + £1 for the cover =) £5 per unit. This was a credit to the income statement.

ILLUSTRATION 10.2

receivables of £100,000, the net figure, £95,000, is shown. In most years the provision is likely to increase, and that increase is treated as an expense. Sometimes a company decides to reduce the provision, perhaps because of more reliable customers, better credit control procedures, or because they have been too prudent in the past. Such reductions are credited to the income statement as if they are income. But there is usually no separate disclosure of modest changes in provisions for bad debts.

Substantial or 'exceptional' changes in provisions should be separately disclosed.

Revenue Recognition

One of the main problems with revenues is determining the date on which they should be recognized. There is considerable variation in practice, and little official guidance. It is probably easier to say that revenues are recognized when the customer is invoiced: the act of raising the invoice introduces the transaction into the bookkeeping system. But when should the invoice be raised?

A sale may go through various stages such as those shown below, and there is the possibility of recognizing it as a sale at any of these stages.

27 February	Customer telephones with order for special-purpose machine to be manufactured
1 March	Raw materials and components are ordered so that the machine can be manufactured
2 March	Written confirmation of order received from customer
10 March	Manufacture of machine is completed
11 March	Machine is despatched to customer
12 March	Customer receives the machine
13 March	Written confirmation arrives showing that customer has received the goods
14 March	Invoice is sent to customer
16 April	Customer receives free after-sales service for machine
18 April	Cheque received from customer in full payment
24 April	Cheque is cleared by bank

There is a case for recognizing revenue at almost any of these points in the process. It is tempting to say that the exact date does not really matter: the sale took place in March. But it would matter if the company's year end happened to be 28 February, or 10 March, or 31

March, or any of the dates between 7 February and 24 April. Is it going to count as a sale in the year just ending or not?

In most cases it probably does not really matter at what stage the revenue is recognized, provided there is consistent practice from one year to the next. But it can be a fertile ground for creative accounting practices. Most listed companies are under pressure to increase profits year after year. If, as the year is coming to an end, it is clear that sales and profits are lower than planned, various ways may be found to boost sales in the last month of the year. Sales staff, who may be incentivized by special bonuses to increase sales just before the year end, could encourage customers to buy extra goods and increase their stocks by offering special discounts, or offering goods on a sale or return basis. Orders could be received just before the year end, and recognized as sales, only to be cancelled a week or two later.

Accounting staff may find ways of speeding up their procedures, especially if it means recognizing the sales at an earlier stage, and so increasing sales in the current year. In the above listing of stages the invoice was sent to the customer on 14 March. This could be brought forward to 11 March when the goods are despatched, or perhaps to 2 March when the written order is received; or perhaps to 27 February when the order is received by telephone. The effect of bringing forward the date in one year is to increase the sales (and profits) for that year. It is even possible to bring the date forward a little each year for several years, although this could not continue indefinitely. There have been some well-publicized cases of companies bringing forward revenues and profits by changing the date on which sales are recognized.

Unfortunately, there is no clear rule as to when sales should be recognized, nor any standard practice. There is little problem with most retailers: a sale is recognized when the cash is received, or when the customer's PIN is accepted for a credit card payment. Apart from straightforward retailers, there is wide variation from one type of industry to another.

In some industries, such as gold or diamond mining, revenues are sometimes recognized as soon as the materials are obtained. There is an immediate and ready market for the products, and it is getting the gold or diamonds out of the mine that is the most critical event. The sale easily follows. But the practice of recognizing revenues when the materials are obtained is unusual. In some industries, for example where there are long-term building contracts, revenues are recognized during the production process. If a company has a contract for a major civil engineering project (e.g. to build a new road, railway, tunnel or pipeline) that will take several years, there are usually established procedures to take credit for revenues and profits on a regular basis as parts of the job are completed, and probably in line with progress payments receivable. It should, of course, be done on a prudent basis; but it is generally accepted that it is more realistic to recognize the revenues in stages – and to show realized profits that can justify dividends – than to wait until the contract is finally completed.

If the business already has the goods in stock (or perhaps if it is very easy to obtain them immediately), it may be justifiable to recognize the revenue immediately that the order is received. But this is not normal practice.

It is more usual to recognize the revenue when the goods are delivered to the customer. But even here there may be some flexibility on whether it is the date of despatch, the date of delivery or the date on which confirmation of delivery is received. Although delivery may be seen as the 'normal' event that justifies revenue recognition, there may be good reasons for not recognizing 100 per cent of the revenue. Some or all of the goods may be returned by the customers as being unsatisfactory, or not exactly what they thought they had ordered; the customer may not pay for them, or may not pay the full amount; and there may be future liabilities under warranty.

When goods are sold on a 'sale or return' basis – with the option to return the goods within, say, one month – it might be prudent not to recognize the revenue until that period has expired. But if a company's experience suggests that such returns are unusual they would probably justify recognizing the sale when the goods are delivered or first accepted by the customer.

In some types of business the 'accretion' approach to recognizing revenues is normal. Where a business has rents receivable, it is appropriate to recognize the rental income as it accrues, on a daily basis. With the production of crops, timber or livestock, it is common practice to recognize revenues as they grow and mature. The balance sheets show stocks at valuation (costs[6] of growing crops and animals may be difficult to measure or irrelevant), which has the effect of recognizing the revenue before anything is sold.

Problems of revenue recognition also arise with the provision of services. A solicitor, or an architect, or an accountant, whose clients know that the charge is £x per hour, could justify recognizing the revenue as soon as some work is done. It is more usual to recognize it when an invoice is sent to the client. It might be more prudent, especially in some types of professional practice, to wait until the client has actually paid. When a professional practice is going to be sold, or when the practitioners' personal remuneration depends on revenues generated, there may be a temptation to bring forward the recognition of revenues as much as possible.

There are continuing difficulties in agreeing official guidance on how and when revenues should be recognized. The general rule is likely to be that revenue should be recognized at the point of sale, but other possibilities will remain. Official requirements are likely to be that revenue should not be recognized until the risks in the operating cycle have been substantially eliminated; this is a move away from strict adherence to the idea that revenue should be 'realized' before it is recognized. There seems to be increasing acceptance of the idea of recognizing some revenues during the course of production, although this should be the exception rather than the rule.

10.5 Expenses

Businesses have a good deal of freedom in the amount of detail that they disclose about expenses, and the way in which they are presented either on the face of the income statement, or in the notes to the accounts. There is, however, a lot of information that companies are *required* to disclose.

The usual format in the UK for presenting expenses on the income statement shows the following:

1 Cost of sales; this is deducted from sales revenue to show gross profit

---

[6] Costs such as the provision of sun and rain to make things grow.

2 Distribution costs

3 Administrative expenses

Distribution costs and administrative expenses are sometimes shown together as 'operating costs'. Sometimes an additional heading 'other operating expenses' is included. These expenses are usually deducted from gross profit to show 'operating profit' (or EBIT: earnings before interest and taxation), although there is no requirement to show this

4 Finance costs; this includes interest payable. There is often also an item for 'finance income' (interest receivable)

It may be convenient to include all expenses as just four items on an income statement, but more detailed information has to be shown in the notes to the accounts including, for example, depreciation of tangible non-current assets and impairment of goodwill. The detail may be tucked away in the notes. Almost all 'expenses' are included in the income statement, perhaps in the name of prudence, rather than being deducted directly from retained earnings.[7] A few items, such as losses on translation of overseas currencies, hedges and revaluations are now shown on the statement of changes in equity that links the balance sheet with the income statement.

Expenses were defined by the FASB as 'outflows or other using up of assets or incurrences of liabilities (or a combination of both) from delivering or producing goods, rendering services, or carrying out other activities that constitute the entity's ongoing major or central operations'.

The IASB's definition of expenses is broader: 'decreases in economic benefits during the accounting period in the form of outflows or depletions of assets or incurrences of liabilities that result in decreases in equity, other than those relating to distributions to equity participants'. It seems that any reduction in asset values, or anything that reduces equity (apart, of course, from the paying out of dividends), counts as an expense. The convention has been that increases in asset valuations (e.g. land and buildings) add to equity (now via the statement of changes in equity), but do not go through the income statement, and do not affect EPS. Reductions in valuation (now typically shown as charges for impairment) are included in the income statement, and do affect EPS. The idea of prudence lives on, although it is under threat.

Expenses are usually seen as being the costs incurred in earning the revenues that are recognized during that period. This is the basis of the accruals concept: costs are matched against the revenues earned.

As with revenues there are a number of problem areas:

1 Not all items of expense are separately identified and published. There is usually no separate disclosure of most expenses such as lighting and heating, postage, stationery and telephones, rates, insurance, repairs and maintenance. But, as shown below, a surprising amount of detail about expenses is available for those who bother to hunt around in the notes to the accounts and the directors' report.

2 Expenses are accounted for on an accruals basis. This means that they are charged as

---

[7] Which used to happen with so-called 'extraordinary items'. These have now disappeared.

they are incurred, not as and when the money for them is paid. The major differences between payments and expenses are that:

a Purchases are not charged as an expense: it is the cost of the goods that are sold that is the expense

b Depreciation is an expense; the amount incurred to buy fixed assets is not (yet) an expense.

3 Some items are shown in the income statement as if they are expenses, although they may seem more like accounting adjustments than revenue. Examples include losses on sale of fixed assets, discount allowed and increases in provisions.

The income statement shows separately any debits or charges (that are, in effect, expenses) for interest payable, and for losses incurred by companies where investments have been made in associates or joint ventures. Other kinds of investment may result in losses, but companies do not necessarily show these on the income statement (as expenses). With relatively modest investments (usually less than about 20 per cent of the shares of another company) credit is taken for dividends receivable, not for a proportion of the profits earned. If the company in which such an investment is made makes losses, there is no requirement for investors to charge a proportion of those losses in their profit and loss accounts.

Companies that own properties, shares in other companies and other forms of investment usually show them on the balance sheet at the price they originally paid for them, at least in the early years. They are also required to show the market value of those investments, or if they differ significantly from the value shown on the balance sheet. If the market value goes down, there is no requirement to show this immediately. But, if the reduction in value looks as though it is long-lasting, the company will probably write down the asset. This is rather like depreciation. It reduces the amount shown for the asset on the balance sheet, and the amount of the reduction is shown as an expense or a loss on the balance sheet. It is usually separately disclosed as an 'exceptional item'.

The following additional information about expenses should be available in notes to the accounts:

1 Segmental information, including the operating expenses of the different business segments in which the company operates.

2 Directors' remuneration, in total, and giving details of gains made from exercising share options, amounts receivable under incentive schemes and company contributions to pension schemes.

3 Depreciation: on the face of the income statement, depreciation is not shown as a separate expense; it is included in cost of sales, distribution costs and administration expenses, as appropriate. Depreciation of machinery that is used to make the goods that the business sells is included in cost of sales; depreciation of vehicles that are used to distribute the company's products is included in distribution costs; and depreciation of office furniture and equipment is included in administration expenses. But there is no requirement to disclose the amount of depreciation included under each of these headings. The year's depreciation charge for each category of fixed asset (e.g. property, plant and equipment) is separately shown.

4 Impairment of goodwill is separately shown.

5 The aggregate amount of expenditure on research and development should be disclosed. Where development costs have been capitalized (and treated as an intangible asset) they must be amortized, and the amount of amortization is disclosed.

6 Auditors' remuneration is disclosed, showing separately the amount paid for audit work, and the amount for non-audit work.

7 Staff costs are disclosed, showing separately: wages and salaries; social security costs; and other pension costs. In addition, the average number of people employed is shown for the UK and other areas. This enables average levels of remuneration to be calculated.

Depreciation of Tangible Fixed Assets

It is tempting to think of depreciation as being the reduction in value of a fixed asset over time. The reduction may be due to the asset becoming worn out, or used up, or obsolete. But depreciation is not an attempt at valuing an asset. It is usually seen as being an allocation of the cost of the fixed asset, so that it is treated as an expense over a number of years.

IAS 15 defines depreciation as being the systematic allocation of the depreciable amount of an asset over its useful life. FRS 12 is rather more forthcoming: depreciation is the measure of the economic benefits of tangible fixed assets that have been consumed during the period. It is usually based on the original cost of the asset, as shown in Illustration 10.3. But if the asset is revalued, then depreciation is based on the revalued amount. It may seem strange that an asset can be revalued upwards; the amount shown for the asset is then reduced through depreciation. It may seem to be two contradictory processes going on at the same time.

Fixed assets normally have a limited life, and so they must be written off over the length of that life. Some assets, such as freehold land, are assumed to last for ever, and so depreciation is not required. It is sometimes argued that as buildings often increase in value, it seems pointless to depreciate them. If the buildings are held as investments, and not for use, this argument is accepted: special accounting rules apply to investment properties.[8] If the buildings are used as fixed assets, then the principle that they have a limited life must apply. Companies can argue that the life of a building may be 100 years or more, and that as they keep it in good condition, then the depreciation is negligible. They, therefore, choose not to make a charge for depreciation because the amount involved is so small. But, if they choose

---

The Adle Company buys a new machine for £256,000, and intends to use it for 5 years, after which it is expected to have a trade-in value of £36,000.

The company decides to use straight line depreciation. The amount of depreciation charged as an expense each year for 5 years is, therefore, £44,000.[9]

ILLUSTRATION 10.3

---

[8] IAS 40 allows (but does not require) gains or losses on investment properties to be recognized in the income statement; depreciation is not required.

[9] Depreciable amount is (£256,000 − £36,000 =) £220,000 ÷ 5 = £44,000.

The Adle Company buys a new machine for £256,000, and decides to use the reducing balance method of depreciation, charging 25 per cent per annum. The amount of depreciation charged as an expense each year is as follows:

	Depreciation charge for year	Remaining balance
Cost of machine £256,000		
Year 1	£64,000	£192,000
Year 2	£48,000	£144,000
Year 3	£36,000	£108,000
Year 4	£27,000	£81,000
Year 5	£20,250	£60,750

ILLUSTRATION 10.4

not to charge depreciation, they are required to carry out an annual impairment review. For companies that own a lot of properties (e.g. retailers with shops or breweries with pubs) this is a small price to pay if the alternative is to have to reduce profits with a substantial depreciation charge.

In Illustration 10.3 'straight line' was used: the company charged the same amount of depreciation each year. IAS 16 requires that the depreciation charge should reflect the pattern of consumption of the benefits that the asset brings over its useful life. If a fixed asset is 'used up' more in its early years than its later years, a depreciation method can be chosen that reflects this. The 'reducing balance'[10] method is widely used; its calculation is shown in Illustration 10.4.

As can be seen from Illustration 10.4, the reducing balance method charges much more for depreciation in the early years; much less in the later years; and it would take for ever to get down to zero.

Companies have a wide measure of freedom in determining what method of depreciation to use. All sorts of weird and wonderful methods of depreciation can be devised but, in practice, most companies use the straight line or the diminishing balance method.

There is inevitably an element of subjectivity in deciding the period over which a fixed asset is to be depreciated, the method of depreciation and what value, if any, the asset will have when it comes to the end of its economic life. Whatever assumptions are originally made when the asset is first acquired, what subsequently happens is likely to be different: the asset may have a shorter or longer life; depreciation may be revised; the asset may be revalued; and when it is finally disposed of the sale proceeds are usually different from the book value. These changes to the original assumptions may be regarded as 'exceptional items', but there is nothing exceptional about normal depreciation, and it should always be regarded as an expense and charged as such in the calculation of EPS.

---

[10] Or 'diminishing balance'.

Impairment of Goodwill

Most large listed companies are really groups of companies with a number of subsidiaries. When a subsidiary company is first acquired it is usually the case that the price paid to acquire the business is higher than the balance sheet value of the net assets acquired. If the balance sheet of a successful company shows a net asset value of £10 million, the owners of the company are unlikely to be willing to sell it for as little as £10 million. They will expect an extra payment for the goodwill of the company. Perhaps the agreed price will be £22 million, of which £12 million is paid for goodwill. Goodwill is an intangible fixed asset, and, like other fixed assets, it should be written off as it is used up.

The treatment of goodwill has varied over time, and the amounts involved have tended to increase. It used to be regarded as being very questionable, and was typically written off immediately by deducting it from retained earnings; it did not pass through the income statement. That was a problem when the amount of goodwill was greater than the amount of retained earnings! In the last few decades of the twentieth century the usual policy was to recognize goodwill as a fixed asset, but to amortize it systematically, as an expense, via the income statement, over its expected useful life (which could be 10 years or 20 or more years).

Now, IAS 36 requires that there should be an annual impairment review of goodwill, although it is recognized that goodwill does not generate cash flows separately from the assets with which it is associated. The impairment review is of a cash-generating unit, and any impairment is recognized as an expense in the income statement. This, of course, leaves open the possibility that a company will decide that there has been no impairment and so no charge is required.

Deferred Expenditure

Not all expenditure is charged as an expense in the income statement for the year in which it was incurred. Capital expenditure – buying or adding to fixed assets – is not an expense in calculating profit; it is the annual depreciation that is an expense. As we have seen, there are sometimes problems in drawing an exact line between capital expenditure and expenses that are to be charged in the current year. Problem areas include repairs to buildings that are more like improvements, or improvements to buildings that also include an element of repair.

Sometimes expenditure incurred in one year is 'deferred' and charged as an expense in future years; we have seen that this sometimes happens with development expenditure. Sometimes other expenditure may be deferred. The cost of advertising that is expected to benefit future periods may be deferred, even if this does not seem very prudent. There can be conflicts between the accounting concepts of prudence (write it off immediately) and accruals (match it against the revenues it is expected to generate). In any such conflicts today, the decision should be based on whether or not an asset exists: if, at the balance sheet date, the expenditure represents an asset, then it should be carried forward to future periods. If there is no asset, it should be written off.

The prudent accountant might argue that this approach leaves a door wide open: many expenses (e.g. advertising, publicity, staff recruitment, training, the provision of medical, counselling and welfare services to staff, investor relations departments) add to the goodwill of a company. There could be a case for deferring all such expenditure that would significantly boost most companies' profits. But the costs of such internally generated goodwill should be treated as an expense.

Capitalization of Interest

There is no doubt that creating a new fixed asset is capital expenditure, even if the company creates their own new fixed assets. When it takes a long time to construct an asset, substantial borrowing costs are often incurred during the construction process. If a company bought such an asset from a builder, the price paid would have to cover the interest costs incurred by the builder. But if the company constructs the asset itself, it may regard the interest cost as being part of the cost of the building (a fixed asset) rather than an expense. The idea of capitalizing interest may be controversial, but it is permitted in circumstances specified by IAS 23, provided appropriate disclosures are made.

Share options

Some companies have chosen to give part or all of their employees' remuneration in the form of options to buy shares rather than in cash. This became particularly common in the dotcom boom, where companies were not generating much cash, and so wanted to minimize the payments that they made. Their share prices were going up and up, and employees found the idea of being paid in share options very attractive. When the company's shares were trading at £2 each, they might be given the option to buy 100,000 shares at £2.50 each. That seemed like giving them nothing; and no expense was recorded. But when the company's share price increased to, say, £4.50 each, the employee could make £200,000 (= 100,000 × [£4.50 − £2.50]), apparently at no cost to the company.

But such an arrangement does have a cost to the original shareholders: suddenly they own a smaller proportion of the company. In 2003 Microsoft set the trend by treating the issue of stock options as an expense. The accounting standard setters are attempting to find a way of recording such an 'expense' that will command general acceptance.

Summary

It is easy to criticize variations in practice and uncertainties in definitions and rules produced by accounting standards setters. It is much more difficult to come up with clear-cut and consistent definitions, and measurement bases, which are both reliable, and relevant to the needs of those who use accounts. Increasingly, sophisticated accounting standards have led to a situation where a wealth of information about companies is published, and – with care and some reservations – the information is available to meet a wide range of users' needs. Net asset value is an important figure, but it needs to be interpreted with care. EPS is often seen as being more important, and it is the result of what is included in the income statement as revenues and expenses. But perhaps too much emphasis has been given to finding principles and rules for determining a single, correct figure that is expected to summarize a company's performance. The detailed items that make up revenues and expenses, and the assumptions that underlie them are more important.

Increasingly, detailed information is available based on standards that are generally accepted internationally. Accountants may need to know all the requirements in detail. But there is no permanent agreement on how assets, liabilities, revenues and expenses should be defined, measured and disclosed. Requirements change as often as fashions. It is worth considering what we are really trying to achieve with financial reporting, and which objectives International Financial Reporting Standards are likely to meet. A PwC survey in 2006[11] reported that 85 per cent of finance executives in FTSE 350 companies felt that IFRSs had made their accounts more difficult to explain, and 40 per cent said they were unhelpful to the board. But an earlier survey of fund managers found that 66 per cent of fund managers thought IFRSs had improved financial reporting; and 59 per cent welcomed the introduction of fair value accounting.

Review of key points

- Assets include all the things that a company owns, but the official definition includes all rights or other access to future economic benefits that are controlled by the company.
- The emphasis in asset valuation has changed over the years from more 'prudent' approaches to more 'relevant' approaches.
- There was never a 'pure' HC system for reporting assets.
- Measuring and reporting assets has a useful role in assessing solvency, measuring profits and providing other important information to those who use companies' financial statements.
- Liabilities are obligations to transfer economic benefits resulting from past transactions or events.
- Provisions are included in the liabilities section of the balance sheet, but there are often provisions that do not seem much like liabilities.
- Definition and measurement of liabilities is generally more straightforward than it is with assets, but there are some problems.
- An income statement includes revenues and expenses; they are recognized on an accruals basis.
- Revenues arise from a number of different sources, and there are problems in defining when revenues should be recognized.
- Expenses appear in summary form on an income statement; more detail is available in the notes.
- Income statements include some accounting adjustments that do not look much like revenues and expenses.

---

[11] Reported in *Accountancy Age*, 27 July 2006.

Self-testing questions

1 Define assets and liabilities.
2 What purposes are served by measuring and reporting a company's assets?
3 List at least 12 different methods of asset valuation and explain the basis of each.
4 Why do we not have 'pure' HC accounting?
5 List the main categories of asset and give examples of each.
6 List the main categories of liability and give examples of each.
7 Are provisions different from other liabilities? Explain.
8 Explain how increases in equity differ from revenues.
9 Explain how decreases equity differ from expenses.
10 How does the accruals concept affect what is recognized as expenses?
11 What are the main categories of expense shown on the face of an income statement, and what is included in each category?
12 What are 'exceptional items'?
13 How could companies avoid charging depreciation on land and buildings? How could they avoid writing off goodwill?

Assessment questions

1 Is an asset simply something that a company owns?
2 Discuss the role of 'prudence' in accounting.
3 Produce a list of different approaches to asset measurement or valuation. Give each a mark out of ten for (a) relevance and (b) reliability, and provide a brief justification for each of the marks given. You might choose to do this in respect of typical assets for which that approach could be used. Alternatively, you could select two or three particular assets, and give a score for the relevance and reliability of each approach to asset management in respect of those particular assets.
4 Discuss the view that it is a reasonable generalization to say that liabilities are more easily defined and measured than assets.
5 What income is recognized in financial accounts other than sales revenue?
6 Give examples of losses that do not seem like expenses.
7 Why is depreciation of fixed assets not normally disclosed as a separate expense in the income statement?
8 What is the importance of 'exceptional items'?
9 At what point should revenues be recognized?

Group activities and discussion questions

1 Depreciation of fixed assets reduces earnings per share; appreciation does not increase earnings per share. How is this practice justified?

2 What additional detail about expenses would you like to see published in company financial statements?

3 Revenue recognition should not be a problem. A sale should be recognized when the goods or services have been delivered or provided to the customer, and when a legal contract for the sale exists. Discuss these statements, and explain why revenue recognition is a problem area in accountancy.

4 Definition and measurement of revenues and expenses are no more reliable than the definition and measurement of assets and liabilities. Discuss.

5 In the light of question 4, is it therefore essential that profit is measured in two different ways (balance sheet and income statement) and that the two are made to agree?

6 Assess the case for including key employees on the balance sheet (presumably as assets).

7 The balance sheet is said to show assets less liabilities as being equal to equity. Is it oversimplistic to assume that all items that should be included on balance sheets may legitimately be included under one of these three headings?

8 Have a competition to describe the asset that it is most difficult to put a value on. Each member of the group should describe one such asset, and explain why a meaningful valuation is (almost) impossible. Other members of the group should suggest ways in which the asset could realistically be valued.

   The assets chosen must be ones that the group agree exist, and are of a type that is likely to be owned or controlled by a business. The group would probably not agree to trying to value ghosts, Uranus, a marriage or someone's soul.

   Does the group agree that it is possible to put a meaningful value on all items that could legitimately be described as a business asset?

9 Should a Tobacco Company include on its balance sheet a liability for damage done to its customers' health by smoking? When and how would such a liability be recognized?

Financial accounting in context

Golden Wonder's £50m pension poser

By Maggie Urry

Financial Times, 19 January 2006

Discuss and comment on the following extracts from the press, with reference to the implications of pension deficits.

Source: Reproduced with permission by the *Financial Times*.

THE PENSION FUND DEFICIT at Golden Wonder, the snack company that went into administration last week, amounts to £50m on the conservative "buy-out" basis.

That figure, produced by Integra, which administers the pension scheme, is what it would cost to pay an insurance company to take over the fund's liabilities

Kroll, the administrator to Golden Wonder, has not revealed how much the company's creditors are owed.

But it is unlikely that the sale of the business could generate sufficient cash to repay creditors and cover the pension deficit.

Yesterday, the Pension Protection Fund received formal notification that Golden Wonder had become insolvent and the pension scheme had insufficient funds to match the level of benefits that the fund would provide.

There now follows a one-month validation period, which is expected to lead to an assessment period likely to take a year.

This will determine if the PPF, a statutory fund, will assume responsibility for Golden Wonder's scheme.

Meanwhile, the scheme's 530 pensioners will continue to be paid in full.

The remaining 1,200 active and deferred members of the scheme will receive 90 per cent of their pensions, up to an annual maximum of £25,000, if the PPF took over the scheme.

Paul Wilson, of Integra, who is secretary to the trustees, said the deficit at the end of 2004 was £19m on an FRS 17 accounting basis and using an actuarial valuation carried out in April 2004.

In 2004, the company lost £10.8m on sales of £87.8m.

Kroll last week sold the Pringles Mini business to Tayto, the Northern Irish group. It also said it had 60 expressions of interest for the rest of Golden Wonder.

Financial accounting in context

BA's pension deficit stands at £2bn

By Norma Cohen

Financial Times, 19 January 2006

BRITISH AIRWAYS' pension deficit, as measured by its actuaries, has roughly doubled to about £2bn since the last valuation in March 2003. If the company were to close its scheme and wind it up, it would crystallise a debt of £3bn to £4bn, compared with BA's market capitalisation yesterday of £33.6bn.

The dire situation was spelled out to representatives of the company's unions yesterday and signalled months of tense negotiations on pay and pensions.

BA has told its workers that it would be seeking changes to the way they accrue pension benefits. The scheme was closed to new members in 2003 but existing members are continuing to earn benefits that are considered more generous than those in many other final salary schemes.

The news comes as several other companies try to curb their pension liabilities. In December, Rentokil Initial became the first FTSE 100 company to close its final salary scheme to existing workers. Co-op Group has announced that workers will accrue benefits based on salaries earned over an entire career rather than at retirement.

Balpa, the pilots' union, has threatened industrial action if BA tries to close the final salary scheme to existing workers.

BA representatives at the meeting yesterday ruled out closing the scheme completely, noting that to do so would crystallise the liability, union representatives said.

Pilots' pensions are expensive for BA relative to those for other staff. According to the valuation report for the New Airways Pension Scheme – its main scheme for active members – and assuming that BA had no deficit at all, the company would have had to contribute 3.8 times the sum contributed by pilots themselves against 2.5 times that contributed by the bulk of its workforce.

BA has said it is contributing £5 for every £1 in worker contributions. However, that figure includes contributions aimed at filling the existing deficit.

BA yesterday declined to comment on the meeting, saying that the talks are confidential. However, a spokesman said BA had sought to inform the union representatives about the exact financial position. "We did outline to them some of the challenges facing the company and the scale of the deficit."

Separately, union representatives said BA had declined to present any proposals on changes to early retirement benefits or severance terms in spite of a request in December to include these items in a discussion of pensions.

References and further reading

Accounting Standards Board (1999) *Statement of Principles for Financial Reporting.* ASB.

Elliott, B. and J. Elliott (2005) *Financial Accounting and Reporting.* FT Prentice Hall.

International Accounting Standard 1 *Presentation of Financial Statements* (December, 2003, amended March 2004). IASB.

International Accounting Standard 37 *Provisions, Contingent Liabilities and Contingent Assets.* (1998, amended March 2004). IASB.

International Accounting Standard 38 *Intangible Assets.* (March 2004). IASB.

International Accounting Standards Board *Framework for the Presentation of Financial Statements.* (1989, amended 2001). IASB.

Lewis, R., D. Pendrill and D. Simon (2003) *Advanced Financial Accounting* (7th edition). FT Prentice Hall.

www.frc.org.uk (UK accounting standards)

www.iasb.co.uk (international accounting standards)

Financing a Business

❖ LEARNING OBJECTIVES

After studying this chapter you should be able to:

❖ Describe the main sources of finance used by companies

❖ Appreciate the differences between the various sources, and evaluate the appropriateness of each in different circumstances

❖ Understand the advantages and disadvantages of high gearing

❖ Evaluate different dividend policies

❖ Understand how published accounts indicate companies' financing needs and policies

❖ Define working capital and explain its importance in relation to solvency, overtrading and profitability

❖ Explain how to manage debtors and calculate the financial implications of different policies for managing debtors

❖ Discuss stock control and apply the economic order quantity (EOQ) model

❖ Explain how to plan, control and manage cash, and how to manage and avoid cash crises

❖ Understand the role of control and management of creditors

❖ Take an overall view of the financing of businesses, combining a number of different approaches

11.1 Introduction

Businesses own a variety of different assets, and balance sheets show how these have been financed. There are non-current assets (e.g. land and buildings, plant and machinery, furniture and fittings), and current assets (such as inventories, receivables and cash). These have been financed from three main sources:

1 The money or capital that was put into the business by its owners. In a company this is the share capital which is part of 'equity' or shareholders' funds

2 Borrowing: a company may borrow money on a long-term basis (e.g. by issuing debentures), and on a short-term basis (e.g. as a bank overdraft);

3 Retained earnings: a successful company makes profits, some of which are paid out to shareholders as dividends; what is left is retained in the business, financing an increase in net assets.

When starting a business the owners usually put in a large amount of their own money ('equity') and/or to borrow substantial sums. If the business is to expand, they will need to make profits, retaining some within the business. There are, however, other ways of financing the setting up of a business and its subsequent growth. Although businesses tend to own the premises that they occupy and the vehicles and equipment that they use, they may choose to lease them instead. Although many businesses finance inventories of goods, many find that, by buying on credit, they do not need to provide the finance themselves. Similarly, many businesses finance 'receivables' themselves, whereas others manage to get their customers to pay cash (so that there are few, if any, debtors), or even to require them to pay in advance. It can be very expensive to finance a manufacturing facility (factory premises, plant and machinery; inventories of raw materials, components, work in progress and finished goods); an alternative is to subcontract (or 'outsource') the manufacturing,

---

The three main sources of finance are shown in the following simplified company balance sheet:

	£
Non-current assets	
Property, plant and equipment	2,600
Current assets	
Inventories, receivables and cash	1,200
Total assets	3,800
Equity	
Share capital	1,000
Retained earnings	1,000
	2,000
Non-current liabilities	
Debentures	1,000
Current liabilities	
Payables	800
Total equity and liabilities	3,800

ILLUSTRATION 11.1

perhaps to a country where these things cost less, leaving the subcontractor to provide the finance.

The three main sources of finance to a business (share capital, borrowing and retained earnings as shown in Illustration 11.1) are examined in the next three sections of this chapter. But it is always worth considering other ways of financing. Careful control of working capital can substantially reduce financing requirements, and ways of doing this are examined in Section 11.5. Finally, 'other sources of finance' are considered, including other ways of doing business that reduce the need for external finance. In most situations a combination of different ways of financing the business is used.

In this instance the three long-term sources of finance are each £1,000, making a total of £3,000. There is also short-term funding (current liabilities or creditors) of £800. The £800 has financed most of the current assets; perhaps their stocks of goods have been financed by the company's creditors. The £3,000 has financed all the long-term assets, leaving £400 for working capital.

11.2 Share Capital

Share capital is perhaps the most important source of finance for companies, and it is mostly 'ordinary' share capital. There are other types of share, including a variety of preference shares.

Ordinary Shares

When a company is established it issues a number of ordinary shares. With a small, new company, they may be issued only to a few family members. The shareholders are the owners of the company. They also bear most of the risk. If the company gets into financial difficulties, all the creditors have to be repaid before anything is returned to the shareholders. Shareholders can lose everything that they put into a company, but their liability is limited to that amount. There can be no call on the shareholders' personal assets to pay any amounts due to creditors; that is the nature of limited liability.

A company may start off as a small, private limited company, with a restricted number of shares. If it grows and wants more shareholders it becomes a public limited company. Very large plcs may become listed on a stock market, for example the London Stock Exchange (LSE), to raise additional finance from many more shareholders, with an Initial Public Offering (IPO) of shares.

The initial nominal (or par) value of the shares may be £1 each (or 50p, or 10p, or any amount). In a successful expanding company the market value of shares is likely to increase. New shareholders will not be invited to buy shares at an old, low price. New shares are normally issued at a premium, as shown in Illustration 11.2, where additional £1 shares are issued for £2.50; the premium is £1.50 per share.

There is no requirement for a company to pay dividends on ordinary shares. In a very small company, where there are only two or three shareholders, they may easily agree what dividends, if any, are to be paid. In large, listed companies the directors normally propose a dividend for approval by shareholders at the annual general meeting. There is usually an interim dividend paid part way through the year, and a final dividend after the year end.

Big Company agrees to pay £2,500,000 to take over Little Company. Big Company's shares are highly regarded by investors, and their market value is £2.50. The £2,500,000 is paid not in cash, but by the issue of one million £1 shares.

The effect of this transaction is that Big Company's balance sheet will show £1,000,000 of additional share capital, and £1,500,000 of share premium. The total, £2,500,000, was issued in exchange for assets (Little Company).

Shares may be issued in exchange for cash or any assets.

ILLUSTRATION 11.2 Share premium

Companies sometimes decide not to pay a dividend, perhaps because they have been making losses, or have some other financial problem. In 2006 British Ariways again did not pay a dividend, for the fifth year in a row, although they had returned to profitability after a difficult period in which many airlines had found themselves in severe financial difficulties. Similarly, Ryanair and many other companies do not pay dividends.

The fact that there is no requirement to pay a dividend may make ordinary shares seem to be an attractive, cost-free source of finance. But many shareholders, especially institutional shareholders (such as pension funds), expect and rely on a steady (and increasing) stream of income from dividends. The shareholders are the owners of the company, and directors who regularly disappoint shareholders are likely to find themselves out of a job. Most companies pay regular and increasing dividends.

Growing companies might not seek a full listing on the stock exchange to begin with. They may first invite a financial institution or venture capitalist to buy some shares. Companies such as 3i invest in growing companies that are not yet large enough for a stock market listing. The formalities, administrative burden and costs of a full stock market listing may be too much for companies of modest size and they are likely to seek a listing on the Alternative Investment Market (AIM). AIM is regulated by the LSE but has less demanding rules, and a listing is less costly than being on the LSE's Official List.

Companies often increase their share capital a little each year, especially when there is some sort of incentive scheme for directors and other staff that provides them with shares. But any significant increase in funding through the issue of shares is a major event for a company, and does not happen very often. Similarly, a company may, from time to time, buy back some of its own shares and so reduce share capital. Companies do not keep a supply of shares for investors to buy and sell: investors buy and sell shares from each other, usually via a stock exchange. Investors cannot go to Marks & Spencer and buy a few shares along with their new underwear and microwave dinner! They have to go via a stockbroker, and there are lots of easy and flexible ways of buying and selling shares via a range of banks and other financial institutions, and on the Internet.

The Right Company has one million ordinary shares with a nominal value of 50p each, and a market value of £2.00 each. The company decides to make a rights issue, offering existing shareholders one share for every five that they already hold, at a price of £1.50 per share.

Shareholders might choose to exercise their rights (by buying the additional shares), or to sell them.

After the rights issue, the theoretical value of the company will be:

Existing one million shares at £2.00 each	£2,000,000
Cash raised from rights issue 200,000 at £1.50	300,000
	£2,300,000
Number of shares after issue	1,200,000

Theoretical share price after rights issue

$$\frac{£2,300,000}{1,200,000} = £1.92$$

ILLUSTRATION 11.3

Rights Issue

When a company wants to raise substantial additional funds by issuing shares, they often make a *rights issue* to existing shareholders. This usually means that they offer new shares at a price lower than the current market price (see Illustration 11.3).

A *rights issue* is the normal way in which established companies raise additional funds, and it is intended to be attractive to existing shareholders. If the current market price of a company's shares is £2, the right to buy more shares at £1.50 each sounds attractive. After the rights issue the total value of the company will, in theory, be worth the amount it was worth before the rights issue, plus the amount of money raised from the rights issue. In practice, if investors believe that the additional funds will be invested sufficiently profitably, the total value of the company will increase by more than the amount of cash raised.

If shareholders take up all the rights to which they are entitled, they will continue to own the same proportion of the company. The right to buy shares cheaply may look attractive, but the record of rights issues is mixed. Sometimes it seems that companies make rights issues because they are in financial difficulties. Sometimes it is a sign of success, and additional funds are needed for expansion.

Bonus Issue

A bonus issue (or a scrip issue) is quite different: it raises no additional funds, and so should not really be included in a chapter on sources of finance!

Many shareholders like receiving bonus shares, although they really receive nothing. Most people would probably rather have two pieces of cake than one. But if the second piece of cake is created just by cutting the original piece of cake in half, there is no gain. In effect that is what a bonus issue does. A one-for-one bonus issue means that everyone has twice as many shares, but nothing has changed; each still owns the same proportion of the same total. In Illustration 11.4 there was a 'two-for-one' bonus issue. For example, anyone who held 200 shares would be given an additional 400 shares, giving them a total of 600 shares. The total number of shares the company had, therefore, increased from 2 million to 6 million; share capital was increased by £4 million; retained earnings were reduced by £4 million. But the assets (and liabilities) of the company are unchanged.

Scriptease plc

	Before bonus issue £000	After bonus issue £000
Non-current assets	5,300	5,300
Current assets		
Inventories and receivables	3,000	3,000
Cash	500	500
Total assets	8,800	8,800
Trade payables	300	300
Equity		
Share capital (£1 shares)	2,000	6,000
Retained earnings	6,500	2,500
	8,800	8,800

ILLUSTRATION 11.4

In practice, a bonus issue is more likely to be one new share for every three, or four, or five shares already held. Shareholders may think that they will still receive the same amount of dividend per share, and so they will be better off. Bonus issues are often associated with good performance and optimism, which could lead to an increase in demand for the shares, and so an increase in share price and in the total value of the company.

One of the justifications for bonus issues is that it is often said that share prices higher than about £8 or £10 become less 'marketable': shareholders would rather buy five shares at £2 each than one share for £10. But there are plenty of successful companies where the share price is £10 or £20 or more.

Preference Shares

Preference shareholders take less risk, and can expect less reward than ordinary shareholders. Preference shares have a fixed rate of dividend, perhaps 7 per cent. This means that for each £1 preference share, investors receive a 7p dividend each year. Sometimes a company might decide not to pay the preference dividend (perhaps when profits are low), but if no preference dividend is paid, then no ordinary dividend can be paid either. The preference shareholders have preference over ordinary shareholders with payment of dividends.

Preference shares are usually *cumulative*, which means that if the preference dividend is not paid in some years, all arrears of preference dividends must be paid before any ordinary dividends can be paid. But preference shares are not very popular for a number of reasons. Ordinary shareholders always have the prospect that the company might do really well, and there could be a substantial increase in profits, dividends and share price: they might make loads of money! Preference shareholders are more secure, but their level of dividend is fixed, whether the company does well or badly.

Preference shares can be made more attractive if they are *participating* and/or if they are *convertible*. Participating preference shares can participate in higher levels of dividend when the company does well, and ordinary dividends rise above some predetermined level.

The Fastgro company issues £1 ordinary shares at a premium of 50p per share. On the same date it issues 6 per cent convertible £1 preference shares giving the shareholders the right to convert three preference shares into one ordinary share at any date they choose.

In the early years, preference shareholders are unlikely to give up three preference shares, worth about £3, for one ordinary share, worth £1.50. But if the company is successful the market price of the ordinary shares might increase steadily to, say, £10 per share. An investor with 900,000 preference shares, worth about £900,000, could then convert them to 300,000 ordinary shares worth £3m; this would give a profit of over £2m!

ILLUSTRATION 11.5

Convertible preference shares can be more attractive: they can be converted to ordinary shares, at a predetermined rate (see Illustration 11.5).

The prospect of a substantial capital gain if the company is successful can make convertible preference shares seem very attractive to investors; they get a decent dividend in the short term, with reasonable security. But the dividend is likely to be very expensive to the company, mainly because dividends (unlike interest) are not allowable as an expense to be charged against taxation. If we assume a corporation tax rate of 30 per cent, then a company needs to earn a £10 profit to pay a £7 dividend. It is cheaper for the company to borrow money: a company earning a £10 profit could pay £7 in interest and still have £3 (pre-tax) profit left for shareholders.

Interpretation of Balance Sheets

When interpreting balance sheets, for most purposes the total figure for 'equity' is used. Equity (or ordinary shareholders' funds) includes all shareholders' funds (share capital, share premium and all reserves/retained profits) except preference share capital. This figure is used in calculating gearing, and in calculating the net assets per share. It is also used in calculating the profitability of ordinary shareholders' funds: net profit after tax (and after deducting any preference share dividends) is expressed as a percentage of equity. It is usually a mistake (often made by students) to use the share capital figure instead of including all of shareholders' funds.

The nominal value of shares is of little or no importance except perhaps in calculating the number of shares that make up share capital. Calculations of earnings per share (EPS), dividend per share and net assets per share are based on the number of ordinary shares.

11.3 Borrowing

Some very prudent individuals and businesses may think that it is dangerous to borrow: the business may not be able to meet the interest and repayments, and there is always the risk of insolvency if the business gets into difficulties. Those who want to minimize risk probably want to minimize borrowing. But if they are so risk averse, they should probably not go into business, and will probably never make much money.

It is safer and easier to put your money in a bank, and earn a steady, low rate of interest, with little or no risk. But people invest in businesses because they think that it is worth the

Two companies in the same industry each have a return on capital employed of 10%, and they are each able to borrow money at an interest rate of 7%.

Prudent plc borrows an extra £1m

Cost of additional borrowings: £1m at 7%	£70,000 per annum
Additional earnings: £1m at 10%	£100,000 per annum
Net additional earnings	£30,000 per annum

Profitable plc borrows an extra £100m

Cost of additional borrowings £100m at 7%	£7,000,000 per annum
Additional earnings: £100 billion at 10%	£10,000,000 per annum
Net additional earnings	£3,000,000 per annum

ILLUSTRATION 11.6

risk in order to earn more money. If banks are paying, say, 5 per cent interest, investors hope to earn more than that by investing in companies. Perhaps they expect a return on capital employed (ROCE) of 10 per cent or more. A business could argue that if the cost of borrowing is less than the return on capital employed that they can earn, then the more they borrow, the more profit they will make. If you can borrow money at 7 per cent per annum, and invest it to earn 10 per cent per annum, then the more money you borrow, the more profit you will make, as shown in Illustration 11.6.

Borrowing can increase the return to shareholders, as is demonstrated in Illustration 11.7. Borrowing can also be relatively cheap, and is a cheaper source of finance than issuing ordinary shares because the interest is allowable as an expense for tax purposes; and

Low-geared company			Capital structure:	Equity	£100m
				10% debentures	£ 10m
					£110m
	Year 1	Year 2			
	£m	£m			
EBIT	10	12	+20%		
Interest	1	1			
Pre-tax profit	9	11			
Tax (say) 30%	2.7	3.3			
Profit after tax	6.3	7.7	+22.2%		
High-geared company			Capital structure:	Equity	£ 50m
				10% debentures	£ 60m
					£110m
EBIT	10	12	+20%		
Interest	6	6			
Pre-tax profit	4	6			
Tax (say) 30%	1.2	1.8			
Profit after tax	2.8	4.2	+50%		

ILLUSTRATION 11.7

because shareholders expect a higher return as they are taking more risk than lenders. But what they expect and what they get can be very different.

In both cases EBIT (earnings before interest and taxation) increased by 20 per cent between years 1 and 2, but the effect of gearing was a larger increase in the profit after tax earned for the ordinary shareholders. In the low-geared company, the return earned for ordinary shareholders increased by 22.2 per cent. In the high-geared company, it increased by 50 per cent.

There are other good reasons for borrowing rather than issuing more shares. In a family-controlled company, the existing shareholders and directors might not want to risk issuing more shares if it would result in new and different people becoming shareholders and controlling the company. In spite of what some textbooks say, directors do not always make rational economic decisions: many like to keep their positions of power and influence, even if (by not issuing more shares) they restrict the growth and profitability of the company. The costs involved in issuing shares also tend to be higher than the costs in obtaining loans.

Another advantage of borrowing is that it comes in many forms, and can be very flexible. It may be short or long term. The most flexible way of borrowing is through an overdraft. Interest rates are negotiable, and are usually a number of percentage points above base rate. Individuals with unauthorized overdrafts may find that they are charged with ridiculously high interest rates, perhaps even 10 or 15 points above base rate. A company ought to be able to negotiate an overdraft interest rate just a little above base rate. Some businesses are seasonal and need to borrow at particular times of the year. A business such as a seaside hotel is likely to be flush with cash in October, after the holiday season, but by March they need short-term borrowings until the money starts coming in for the next holiday season.

Many businesses have plenty of money in the middle of the month, but need to borrow at the end of the month, when wages and salaries are paid. Overdrafts are most appropriate for such short-term financing because interest is payable only for the actual days that the overdraft facility is used. There is no point in having a fixed loan throughout the year, and paying interest throughout the year, if the money is needed only for a few days each month, or for a few months each year.

Although overdrafts are supposed to be a short-term source of finance, many individuals and companies seem to have significant (and increasing!) overdrafts that go on for years. Banks are interested in converting overdrafts into fixed loans for a few years, if they can earn more interest by so doing. Businesses need to work out carefully how much it is appropriate to borrow with fixed-term loans and fixed interest rates, and how much it is appropriate to use overdraft facilities for.

Debentures are a form of long-term borrowing (typically 5–10 years), usually with a fixed rate of interest, which can be listed on a stock market. Investors can, therefore, sell them when they wish, and the company can choose to buy them back on the market, if they have nothing better to do with their money. Debentures are usually 'secured' on some assets of the company; perhaps on land and buildings; on perhaps a floating charge on most of the assets of the company. The effect is a bit like taking out a mortgage: if the company does not meet its payments as they fall due, the debenture holders can eventually get their money back by selling off the company's assets.

Debentures are sometimes 'convertible' into ordinary shares; this can make them very attractive to investors if it is expected that the company's shares will do very well in the future. Investors in a new or expanding business may be attracted by the security of a debenture with a reasonable interest rate to begin with, together with the possibility of conversion to ordinary shares (and increases in the share price and increasing dividends) once the venture has proved to be successful.

The main attraction of borrowing is the idea that the more you borrow, the more profit you can make. It may be an attractive idea, but there are a number of problems with ever increasing borrowings:

1 Borrowing may be no problem as long as the company can be sure of always having earnings above the required level of interest payments. But businesses tend to have good years and bad years; the economy tends to run in cycles; some industries are particularly cyclical; and some industries run into bad patches, with bad luck and/or bad management. If in some years the company does not earn enough to make the necessary interest payments, lenders may repossess vital assets and force the business to curtail its activities or close down.

2 The more you get into debt, the more difficult it is to borrow more money. There is probably always someone or some bank that will lend to you, but as you get more into debt, the higher the interest rates become to compensate the lender for additional risk.

3 Lenders usually look for some sort of security. It is easy to borrow money secured on land and buildings. Lenders may be happy to take some sort of 'floating charge' on whatever other assets the company has. But when all assets have already been used as security, it is increasingly difficult to borrow more money.

4 Those who have already lent money to the company often lay down conditions to restrict the ability of the company to borrow more. These 'restrictive covenants' may specify that a company's total borrowing must not exceed some (small, e.g. 1 or 1.5) multiple of the amount of equity.

5 Companies that are heavily in debt may get a reputation as being 'high risk', and other businesses may be reluctant to do business with them. Sometimes investors steer clear because the risk is too great.

A good, old-fashioned view might be that a company should keep increasing its borrowing, as long as it can get away with it. Theory suggests that eventually lenders will see that the company has borrowed too much (gearing is too high), and they will start to charge higher interest rates. As borrowing increases, interest rates increase until eventually the cost of borrowing is higher than the return that the company can generate from the borrowings. High levels of borrowing are also associated with high risk, and this can affect the share price, especially if it starts to look as if the company is so heavily in debt that it might be forced into liquidation. There is, thus, in this traditional view, an optimal level of borrowing (although it is difficult to establish what this level is).

A different perspective was offered by Modigliani and Miller (1958) suggesting that the level of gearing has no effect on share price. Even if the amount of borrowing changes, it is still the same business, with the same earnings stream and the same business risk.

Modigliani and Miller's presentation is sophisticated, but it depends on a number of unrealistic assumptions, and it is often misinterpreted. Their emphasis is on the value of the company, which depends on the investments that they have, and the cash flows that they will generate; how the company is financed is a secondary issue. More recent work, recognizing the impact of taxation (interest is an allowable expense for taxation, and so the cost of borrowing is likely to be lower than the cost of equity), together with lower interest rates, and the actual behaviour of companies, suggests that there may be some optimal level of gearing; but this is hard to find, and views about acceptable levels of gearing change from time to time.

In practice, many companies seem to borrow as much as they can get away with. Some companies constantly need additional funds because of expansion and development. But some companies (like some individuals!) do not seem to be able to live within their means, and borrow until they go bust.

In Illustration 11.1 (see p. 276), the company had total long-term funds of £3,000 of which £1,000 was borrowed. In other words, one-third of their long-term funding was borrowed, or their gearing ratio was 33⅓ per cent. There is, of course, no 'correct' or 'best' level of borrowing, nor is there a single correct way of measuring gearing.[1] Companies that are able to borrow extensively are likely to have a steady, secure income stream so that they can be confident about being able to pay the necessary interest every year. They are also likely to have lots of good quality assets (particularly land and buildings) to offer as security to lenders. Companies in very cyclical industries should avoid high gearing, but many do not, and they get into financial difficulties. The airline industry is noticeably susceptible to epidemics of war, terrorism and disease; many airlines are highly geared; and many found themselves in serious financial difficulties in 2002–3.

When the telecommunications industry was expanding and share prices were booming at the end of the twentieth century, many companies got away with very high levels of borrowing – for a while. Then the business climate turned against them, and many share prices collapsed. British Telecommunications (BT) plc had a debt mountain of £30 billion, which did not look too bad in relation to the market value of their equity when share prices were high. But in comparison with the balance sheet value of equity it looked terrible. And when telecommunications share prices took a nosedive, the amount of debt looked unsustainable in relation to the market value of equity. BT has taken decisive action, and has substantially reduced debt.

As interest rates have remained low in recent years, higher levels of gearing have become acceptable. Sometimes one company buys another company and finances the purchase almost entirely by borrowing; this is called a 'leveraged buyout'.[2]

---

[1] If Borrowing is represented as D; and Equity is represented as E; gearing can be measured by taking D as a percentage of D + E; or as a percentage of E. D is sometimes taken to include overdrafts; sometimes it refers only to long-term borrowing.

[2] The purchase of another business can, instead, be financed by issuing additional ordinary shares.

11.4 Retained Earnings

A successful company makes profits that materialize in the form of additional cash or other net assets. The company may choose to pay out all its profits as dividends, in which case profits will not be a source of funds. Most companies choose to pay out a proportion (perhaps around 40 per cent) of their profits as dividends; the rest are retained and used to finance the business. Obviously, the more profit a company makes, the greater is the potential for using retained profits as a source of finance. Raising finance through retained profits depends on how profitable the business is. It also depends on the company's dividend policy.

Dividend Policy

In deciding how much dividend to pay, or what proportion of profits are to be paid out as dividends, companies need to consider some important matters. Dividend policy usually requires striking a balance between (a) paying out *all* profits as dividends, and (b) paying *no* dividends at all.

Pay Out All Profits as Dividends

There is a case for paying out all profits as dividends: profits belong to the shareholders, not the directors. The directors might see retained profits as being too easy a source of finance, and not bother to ensure that they are reinvested in the company properly and profitably. As profits are earned, they may simply disappear into higher levels of stocks and debtors, or even cars and 'conference centres' for the comfort of directors.

Many companies find themselves with surplus funds that they invest in disastrous diversification (ad)ventures or waste on more or less (un)successful takeover bids and mergers. Abbey National lost millions of pounds attempting to move from its secure base in retail banking into areas of wholesale banking where they had no experience. Marks & Spencer lost millions of pounds in spreading its operations overseas, and then withdrawing. Marconi wasted millions of pounds investing in overpriced telecommunications companies just before they collapsed. Some companies have a history of merging with others, and then demerging, or selling off the bits they no longer want (e.g. Kingfisher, Hays). The evidence so far suggests that a takeover is more likely to destroy shareholder value than create it.

There are, of course, plenty of exceptions: well-managed companies that succeed in reinvesting retained profits year after year and that have a good record in increasing profits and dividends; some even succeed in increasing their ROCE, and, with a bit of luck, the company's share price. There are also many companies where the directors know that they are unable to do this. Arnold Weinstock of GEC sat on mountains of cash rather than risk wasting it on ill-advised investments. Other companies, knowing that there are limited opportunities for successful investment of surplus funds, simply return them to shareholders as special dividends, or they use the money to buy their own shares on the market and cancel them.[3]

---

[3] This is a way of increasing earnings per share (EPS) even if total earnings do not increase, the number of shares decreases, and so the EPS increases.

The EPS and the dividend per share of the Cycle Company for the last few years are shown below (in pence).

Year	1	2	3	4	5	6	7
EPS	100	134	60	116	180	10	191
Dividend	50	53	56	59	63	64	70
Cover	2	2.5	1.1	2.0	2.9	0.2	2.7

ILLUSTRATION 11.8

Many companies, or their directors, cannot be trusted to invest retained profits successfully. But there are good reasons for not expecting companies to pay out all their profits as dividends.

1 Rising prices, or inflation, usually mean that companies need to retain some of their profits, not for expansion, but merely to maintain the existing level of operations. More funds are required to finance receivables (as selling prices increase); to finance inventories (as replacement costs increase), and to replace fixed assets as the cost of these increases. Inflation in the UK in recent years has been very low, and the cost of replacing many items (e.g. computers and electronic equipment) has actually fallen. But few businesses can afford to finance even their existing level of operations without retaining some profits.

2 Investors, particularly financial institutions, generally want to see dividends increasing steadily each year, preferably by rather more than the rate of inflation. Illustration 11.8 shows how company profits can fluctuate, but attempts are made to keep dividends steady.

3 Many companies boast that they have succeeded in increasing dividends every year since anyone can remember. Compared with dividend expectations, profits are less predictable, less controllable, more cyclical and more affected by one-off 'exceptional' items. Companies usually prefer to increase dividends only modestly in the very good years so that there is more scope for maintaining or increasing dividends in the lean years.

Pay Out No Dividends

There is a case for paying no dividends at all, even in successful companies. When a company is making serious losses, or when they have massive borrowings, scrapping the dividend for a year or two makes good sense. Companies at an early stage of their development need all the money that they can get hold of and so are not inclined to pay dividends. In the great dotcom and TMT[4] bubble of the late 1990s, many companies did not pay dividends. A quick look at the *Financial Times* today will show which companies are not paying dividends; usually there are plenty of mining companies and pharmaceuticals and biotechnology companies that have not yet found their pot of gold or wonder drug, and are burning up cash in their efforts; there is unlikely to be a dividend until a worthwhile discovery has been developed.

---

[4] Technology, media and telecommunications.

	FTSE 100	Compass	Royal Bank of Scotland	United Utilities	Pearson	BP	BT
Dividend cover	2.3	1.3	2.3	0.5	2.7	1.5	1.5
Proportion of profits distributed	43%	77%	43%	200%	37%	67%	67%

ILLUSTRATION 11.9
Source: Financial Times, 12 June 2006.

If a company can invest the shareholders' money and earn a better rate of return than the shareholders can themselves, then there is a case for the company to keep the money, and not pay dividends. If the money stays within the company, the value of their shares should increase. If shareholders need some income, they can sell a few shares, and (they hope!) the value of their shares will increase because of all the retained profits being re-invested. If they sell a few shares, they may have to pay capital gains tax, but for many shareholders the taxation of capital gains is lower than the taxation on income from dividends. Paying no dividends at all may suit some companies and some shareholders – sometimes.

Dividend Policy in Practice

Most companies do not opt for the extremes of no dividends, or 100 per cent distribution. Usually a proportion of profits is distributed. Listed companies typically pay out rather less than half their profits as dividends. Recent figures for the FTSE 100 index and a number of companies are shown in Illustration 11.9.

Company profits tend to fluctuate from year to year, not least because of 'exceptional' items such as profits or losses arising from the sale of fixed assets, or closing down part of the business. As shown in Illustration 11.8, it makes more sense to try to maintain a record of steady and increasing dividends, rather than to pay out the same proportion of profits each year. Some companies pay an extra 'special' dividend in a particularly good year, but most try to keep an upward trend, even when profits fall. And many seem to increase their dividends more than the underlying profits justify; this results in the dividend cover declining over a number of years, and the dividend begins to look less safe.

In making dividend decisions, companies need to consider what 'signal' any change in dividends gives to investors. A sudden reduction in dividends suggests that directors are not confident about future years. Companies also need to consider what cash is available to pay dividends and their plans for expansion, investment and borrowing.

11.5 Management of Working Capital

The planning and management of working capital is an important part of the financing of a business. High levels of inventories and receivables tie up large amounts of finance; reductions in inventories and receivables, and increases in payables, provide extra finance for the business.

Definition and Importance of Working Capital

A large part of a company's capital is usually tied up in assets such as buildings and machinery for a period of years. But companies also need some capital to finance short-term assets such as inventories and receivables, and there is a need for some cash for day-to-day operations. The amount of long-term capital available after financing fixed assets is known as 'working capital', which may be defined as:

> Long-term funds − non-current assets = working capital

From the balance sheet in Illustration 11.10 we can see that working capital was:

> Year 1   85,000 + 110,000 − 140,000 = £55,000
> Year 2   88,000 + 135,000 − 138,000 = £85,000

The more usual definition of working capital is:

> Current assets − current liabilities = working capital

From the balance sheet below we can see that working capital is:

> Year 1   175,000 − 120,000 = £55,000
> Year 2   145,000 − 60,000 = £85,000

The two definitions appear to be different, but provided all items on the balance sheet are classified under the same five headings, the two approaches will produce the same figure.

Balance sheets of Solverham Company Ltd as at 31 December		
	Year 1	Year 2
	£000	£000
Non-current assets (at cost)	200	220
Provision for depreciation	(60)	(82)
Net book value	140	138
Current assets		
Inventories	95	70
Receivables	80	50
Cash	−	25
	175	145
Total assets	315	283
Current liabilities		
Payables	40	60
Overdraft	80	−
	120	60
Non-current liabilities		
12% Debentures	110	135
Equity		
Share capital	50	50
Retained earnings	35	38
	85	88
Total liabilities plus equity	315	283

ILLUSTRATION 11.10

Although most businesses finance their inventories and receivables partly from their long-term funds, current assets are also partly financed by payables and other current liabilities. In year 2 Solverham (Illustration 11.10) had inventories of £70,000; £60,000 of this was financed by current liabilities. In some companies, particularly retailers, stocks are wholly financed by short-term creditors.

How Much Working Capital Should a Business Have?

There is usually a relationship between a company's turnover, and the amount of working capital they have. In Chapter 4, ratios 14, 15 and 16 express inventories, receivables and payables in relation to the amount of (cost of) sales. As turnover increases we can expect working capital to increase in proportion. If turnover goes up by 25 per cent, it does not mean that the amount of cash coming into the business immediately goes up by 25 per cent: there is likely to be an increase in inventories and receivables (partly financed by an increase in creditors).

But companies should not simply watch working capital drift upwards: there is a need for proper planning and control. There is, however, no ideal level for working capital. It is a question of balancing (a) *solvency* against (b) *profitability*.

A company that is very safe in terms of solvency will have lots more current assets than current liabilities. There will always be more than enough current assets, either in the form of cash or receivables (and even inventories) that will soon become cash, to meet short-term liabilities as they fall due. This short-term financial strength can be expressed in the form of *current ratios* and *liquidity ratios*. In Illustration 11.11, the first of the four companies (Alice Ltd) has most working capital, the strongest current ratio (3 : 1), and the strongest liquidity ratio (2 : 1). The fourth company (Dora Ltd) has the least working capital: a negative amount! Dora also has a very low current ratio (0.17 : 1) and a very low liquidity ratio (0.1 : 1).

	Alice Ltd £000		Bertha Ltd £000		Colin Ltd £000		Dora Ltd £000	
Non-current assets		150		150		150		150
Current assets								
Inventories	100		50		100		4	
Receivables	150		80		150		2	
Bank/cash	50		10		—		4	
	300		140		250		10	
Current liabilities								
Payables	100		80		200		60	
Overdraft	—		—		50		—	
	100		80		250		60	
Working capital		200		60		—		(50)
Net assets = capital employed		350		210		150		100
Profit		35		35		35		35
Return on capital employed		10%		16.7%		23.3%		35%

ILLUSTRATION 11.11

A company that is concerned more with profitability than with appearing to be solvent will concentrate on keeping down the amount of working capital. In order to maximize ROCE, companies need not only to maximize profits or returns, but also to minimize capital employed in relation to profits. Other things being equal, companies that manage with the least working capital are likely to be the ones that are most profitable.

Each of the four companies in Illustration 11.11 has the same amount of fixed assets, and the same amount of profit. The only differences between the companies are the amounts of working capital. As working capital decreases, so the ROCE increases. The company with the lowest amount of working capital (Dora Ltd has £50,000 *negative* working capital) has the highest ROCE.

In terms of solvency or liquidity, however, Dora looks very weak. There are payables of £60,000, but current assets amount to only £10,000. Few businesses would have such a pattern of working capital (perhaps a florist's shop; inventories would be low because fresh flowers do not keep for long). Retailers tend to sell mostly on a cash basis, and so a low receivables figure is to be expected. Retailers buy mostly on credit and so a significant creditors figure is normal.

Although there is no 'normal' level of working capital, we can see that higher levels of working capital are associated with higher levels of solvency; and lowering levels of working capital can increase profitability.

Overtrading

Having too little working capital is associated with 'overtrading'. This occurs when a company is trying to do too much business with too little long-term capital. If a company is generating lots of cash, and manages its working capital carefully, they may survive and prosper even if they appear to be overtrading. But having insufficient liquid resources (or access to them) to meet liabilities as they fall due is fatal for businesses.

The problem can start with a major outflow of cash, perhaps to buy additional fixed assets or another business; to repay a loan; or paying too much out as dividends. It is sometimes the result of success: rapid expansion can lead to a rapid outflow of cash (inventories, receivables and non-current assets: all increase) before the cash comes in from customers. High levels of inflation make the problem worse: the amounts of cash required to replace assets increase in line with inflation.

Overtrading can also be the result of failure. A company that makes substantial losses is likely to find that cash is haemorrhaging out of the business. A mild case of overtrading is easily treated with various tactics to bring in cash more quickly. Debtors can be pressed to pay more quickly; inventories can be reduced by control of new purchases and by extra efforts to clear stocks; and payments to creditors may be delayed.

A cash shortage, and the effects of reducing inventories and receivables, and increasing creditors, soon show up in reducing a company's current ratio. A trend of falling current ratios is a matter for concern.

In a serious case of overtrading the symptoms get worse, and attempts to deal with it can lead to further deterioration. The overdraft limit can often be increased, but if an increased limit is breached, the bank soon loses patience with a business that seems unable to manage its cash. If a company reduces its inventories too much, they will soon find that they are losing business because they are unable to supply what their customers want. Customers will go elsewhere, if they are pushed too hard to pay their bills too quickly. Creditors will usually put up with a little delay, but most will not tolerate repeated or increased delays. If a company cannot pay its bills without excessive delay, they soon find that they are unable to obtain supplies on credit. If they are to continue in business, they have to find cash to buy supplies, which makes the original problem worse.

Many of us have been in shops where the signs of overtrading are obvious. There is very little on the shelves because suppliers are no longer willing to sell to them on credit. Each day the shopkeeper hopes to bring in a few hundred pounds from customers so that they can go to their local cash and carry to replace what they have sold; they cannot buy very much because they have to use some of the cash to pay off some of the amounts due to whichever creditors are pressing hardest.

Often it is a wages bill that precipitates the crisis, especially at the stage when the bank is no longer willing to honour cheques because the business has (again!) exceeded its overdraft limit. At this stage desperate measures are needed. When difficulties first arise, surplus assets are sold off to raise cash. Towards the end, they even have to sell essential assets, and sell off stocks at ridiculously low prices, just to bring in some cash to survive another day. At this stage the business has little chance of survival.

It is not difficult to spot the early symptoms of overtrading, and good financial planning and management can avoid a crisis. The usual problem is trying to do too much with too little money, especially where there is too little long-term finance. Solutions include raising more long-term capital, and careful management of working capital and profitability, with a particular emphasis on cash budgeting so that crises can be identified and averted before they become critical to survival.

Managing Receivables

Financial managers may prefer to minimize the amounts tied up in receivables (debtors). This minimizes the requirements for external funding. If debtors are reduced, cash is brought into the business more quickly; the amount of capital employed is reduced; and profitability is increased.

Some businesses sell on a cash-only basis: there are no debtors. Some (such as mail order companies) require customers to pay in advance: their debtors can be negative. Others (particularly service providers) require part or full payment in advance; this reduces the amount tied up in receivables.

Offering credit facilities to customers may be an important part of marketing strategy, and it is usually essential when supplying governments and other major organizations. But it has its costs: bad debts, administration of customers' accounts, credit control (chasing customers to pay on time) and the cost of capital (money tied up in receivables may be used more effectively elsewhere). If a company is partly financed by an overdraft that costs 10 per cent per annum, and the level of their debtors is £100,000, then the cost of financing those debtors is £10,000 per annum. It is worth calculating whether the costs of offering credit facilities are justified by the contribution earned by the additional business generated.

If a business decides that it will sell on credit, the following three steps should be taken to encourage customers to pay on time, and to minimize losses through bad debts.

Accepting Credit Customers

It would be foolish to sell on credit to every Tom, Dick and Harry; there are always a few dodgy customers who will not pay up. There are various ways of deciding who is likely to be creditworthy.

1 *Personal judgement and the impression someone gives* These are still important, and no amount of investigation or calculation can eliminate the need for personal judgement. Even the most reputable companies and individuals (and even countries' governments) get into financial difficulties and are unable to pay their bills. But we should not rely on a smart suit and a flashy car being the guarantee of financial strength; they can be financed by excessive borrowing. A visit to a customer's premises can be revealing: many businesses with impressive Internet sites and publicity are operated from a back room above a shop, or a teenager's bedroom.

2 *Bankers' references* Although they may say very little that is useful, with current money laundering regulations, the mere fact that someone has a bank account is some indication that they exist, and have an address (or they did when they opened the account).

3 *Business annual reports and accounts* These can be checked before accepting a credit customer, and show what liabilities a business already had, and indicate their financial strength and ability to pay liabilities as they fall due. It is also worth calculating their creditors' ratio: how long they seem to take to pay existing creditors. It may be easier to rely on a credit rating agency to do the assessment.

4 *Ask other creditors how reliable a company is in paying its bills* This can be done formally, by taking up trade references. It may be more revealing if done informally, through business contacts. Often it becomes widely known when a particular company becomes a slow payer.

5 *Credit rating agencies* Agencies such as Experian, Moodies, and Standard and Poor provide information on the creditworthiness of individuals and firms. Information can be provided immediately by telephone or the Internet.

How Much Credit to Allow

The amount of credit allowed to customers should be limited in four ways.

1 *Time* It is important to be clear about how long customers are allowed to pay, perhaps within 30 days. It is wise to have a contract with the agreed terms for payment, with penalties for delay.

2 *Amount of money* There should be a credit limit for each customer, based on their size and creditworthiness. It could be millions of pounds for a government body, but perhaps only £100 for students!

3 *Maximum for an individual debtor* Many businesses rely too heavily on one or two major customers. If one such customer does not pay up, the business may go bankrupt. It is important for a business to know that there is not an individual debtor owing an amount large enough to bring the business down if they do not pay.

4 *Maximum total receivables figure* It may be prudent to estimate the maximum total receivables figure that the business can afford to finance. Profitable expansion usually

looks attractive, but if it involves additional working capital that the business cannot afford, it could be very risky.

Collecting the Money

The first step in collecting the money from debtors is to send out the paperwork promptly and correctly, and for it to be clear when payment is due. Small businesses are often lax about this: proprietors are often more keen on their product or service than they are on paperwork. Larger businesses usually have fairly tight – sometimes aggressive – credit control systems.

When payments come in, it is necessary to check carefully the amounts received; some customers are good at disputing invoices, delaying payments and taking discounts to which they are not entitled.

Offering cash discounts for prompt payment can be an effective way of encouraging customers to pay within, say, 14 days. But the cost of offering such discounts needs to be carefully calculated. A 10 per cent discount may encourage customers to pay up, say, one month early. But a 10 per cent discount for one month is very expensive – equivalent to 120 per cent per annum! Even a discount of 4 per cent may prove too expensive, as shown in Illustration 11.12. More modest discounts of, say, 1 per cent, may not be enough incentive for early payment. It might be more cost-effective to employ a competent credit controller to chase debtors to pay up promptly. Another approach is to charge interest on late payments.

It is important to have a credit control system that carefully monitors the payment record of customers, and what has been done about late payers. It is usual to produce an 'age analysis' of debtors, showing little detail where the sale took place only a month or two previously. But where amounts have been outstanding for more than 2 or 3 months the amounts and dates should be carefully detailed for each customer, together with what action had been taken, and what promises and payments have been received.

When payments do not come in on time the next step is a prompt and polite reminder. Problems arise when customers have still not paid a few weeks after the due date. There are three main approaches to get customers to pay up:

1 *Phoning them, following up promises to pay and visiting them* Sales staff are not usually keen on the sordid business of asking their customers for money. But sales to customers who do not pay are useless.

Last year the Vinelia Building Company's turnover was £12m. All sales were made on credit. Their debtors figure was £3m at the balance sheet date and that figure was typical of the figure throughout the year.

The company usually has a large overdraft and their cost of capital is 15 per cent per annum. The sales director recommends offering customers a 4 per cent discount for prompt payment and estimates that this would halve the debtors figure.

The costs and benefits of this proposal would be as follows:

Annual cost of discount: 4% × £12m	£480,000
Reduction in debtors: £1.5 million	
Annual interest savings on reduction: 15% × £1.5m	£225,000

The cost of offering the discount is more than the saving in interest.

ILLUSTRATION 11.12

The Vinelia Building Company (as in Illustration 11.12) is considering employing a credit controller, and instituting more effective procedures for collecting money from debtors. The annual cost of doing this is expected to be £40,000. If the average period taken by debtors to pay their bills is reduced from 3 months to 2½ months, would this expense be justified?

Reduction in debtors: half of 1 month's sales =	£500,000
Annual saving in interest £500,000 × 15% =	£75,000

Additional expenditure of £40,000 a year is justified if it has the effect of reducing the average level of debtors by £500,000, and reducing interest costs by £75,000 a year.

ILLUSTRATION 11.13

2 *Withdrawing supplies to customers* Sometimes it may be best to negotiate a compromise: supplies will continue if the customer pays for them on delivery, *and* begins to pay off some of the amounts due for previous supplies. Continuing to supply customers who do not pay can be fatal to a business.

3 *Threatening legal action* The threat should be enough to frighten most customers into paying promptly. Legal action can be very expensive, but threats are cheap: a routine letter (that appears to come) from solicitors may be cost effective.

The effects of improving credit control can be estimated, as shown in Illustration 11.13.

The Costs and Benefits of Different Approaches

The costs of having debtors include:

1 Cost of capital

2 Administration

3 Bad debts

4 Discount allowed

Companies need to evaluate the costs and benefits involved in different strategies. Sometimes they may want to increase sales by offering more attractive payment terms. If we know the contribution/sales ratio of a company,[5] we can estimate the additional profits that will be brought in by an increase in sales. We can also estimate the amount by which receivables will be increased by offering more attractive credit terms. If we also know the company's cost of capital, we can estimate the annual cost of an increase in debtors. We can then calculate if it appears to be worth while to offer a more generous credit terms to customers, as shown in Illustration 11.14.

Factoring and Discounting of Debtors

A business can outsource or subcontract almost any activity, including the management of debtors. With factoring, most of the money tied up in debtors (typically 75–80 per cent) can be turned into cash immediately. The factoring company provides the money, and charges

---

[5] Contribution as a percentage of sales, as illustrated on pages 351–2.

The Tightar Company specializes in surfacing driveways and minor roads. They have a strict credit control policy because they are short of funds, and depend on an overdraft that has an interest rate of 18% per annum.

They do not undertake work for public institutions or building contractors because such customers are slow to pay, taking on average 10 weeks.

The company's annual turnover is £520,000, and their average debtors figure at any one time is £30,000.

The direct costs of surfacing a driveway amounts to 40% of the selling price.

Would it be worth extending their average credit period to 10 weeks if they could double turnover?

Direct costs as a proportion of turnover	40%	
Contribution as a proportion of turnover	60%	
Proposed additional sales	£520,000	
Additional contribution (60%)		£312,000
Existing debtors figure		£30,000
New debtors figure	$\frac{10 \text{ weeks}}{52 \text{ weeks}} \times £1,040,000 =$	£200,000
Increase in debtors		170,000
Annual cost of increase in debtors	18% × £170,000 =	£30,600

It is worth while to pay interest on the necessary additional borrowings because the cost of the interest is substantially lower than the additional contribution generated.

ILLUSTRATION 11.14

interest for so doing; it also takes over the administration of the client's sales accounting, invoicing and credit control, for which they also charge a fee, typically of between 0.75 per cent and 2 per cent of turnover. These costs may be more than offset by savings in the business's own administration, and advantages in getting the money in more quickly so that it can be used for other, more profitable purposes. Factoring is likely to be particularly appropriate in small, rapidly growing businesses, where the business has relatively little expertise in credit control and the factor is likely to be more efficient and effective, with economies of scale in carrying out their specialist activity. Using a factor can mean that cash from debtors becomes readily available as the business expands, otherwise the need to finance working capital can be a significant constraint on growth: increased sales usually require increases in stocks and debtors that are only partly financed by creditors. Factoring can be a way of financing growth.

Factoring can be done confidentially so that customers do not know that a company's receivables are being collected by a third party. A business should be careful to calculate the costs and benefits of using a factor: it may seem to be more expensive, but if it is more effective in the long run, it may prove to be more economical. It usually has to be a long-term arrangement: once a business becomes reliant on getting the cash in quickly by using a factor, it is difficult to go back and establish a replacement source of finance, and to set up a credit control function again. Another disadvantage of factoring is that, sometimes, the factor may be unwilling to take on particular types of customer where they anticipate problems.

Invoice discounting is usually a short-term way of using debtors to make cash available quickly. In effect the debtors are 'sold' to a financial institution who provides around 75 per cent of the amount immediately. The client (not the financial institution) continues with the administration of debtors and continues to bear any risks of bad debts. This usually applies only to selected debtors, and can be a useful source of short-term finance.

Managing Inventories

Inventories of raw materials, work in progress and finished goods can be reduced by careful budgeting and planning, and the use of techniques such as the economic order quantity.

It is always handy to have lots of stuff in stock just in case it might be needed. But holding stocks is a very expensive business. There are all the costs involved in providing storage space, including rent, rates, lighting, heating, insurance, security and administration. But the most substantial costs of holding stocks are:

1 *The cost of capital*   A company's cost of capital might typically be between 10 per cent and 15 per cent per annum. This means that, just in terms of the cost of capital, it costs between £10,000 and £15,000 a year to have average stocks of £100,000.

2 *Obsolescence*   Clothes go out of fashion; publications go out of date; and technological items are soon superseded. Stocks of computers, software or mobile phones that are only a year or two old are worth very little. Inventories of goods for sale, and even raw materials and components, rapidly become out of date.

3 *Physical deterioration*   Inventories physically deteriorate – or even disappear – in various ways. Some things are eaten by rats and other creatures; some things evaporate, go mouldy or become unusable in a variety of ways.

Holding stocks is expensive typically costing perhaps 25 per cent per annum. A company that on average holds stocks of £100,000 is likely to incur costs of about £25,000 a year. In order to maximize profitability, there is pressure to reduce stock levels. Various approaches are used to achieve this.

Where stocks of finished goods appear to be excessive, there has presumably been a mismatch between the sales budget and the production budget – too much has been produced. This can be tackled by using appropriate control information more quickly, and considering special offers to clear existing inventories.

It is also worth concentrating only on the most valuable items in stock. Sometimes as much as 90 per cent of the value of stocks may be in only 10 per cent of the items. It may not be worth bothering too much about lots of small items of little value.

Economic Order Quantity (EOQ)

Various quantitative techniques are available for effective management of inventories. If the aim is to keep inventories at as low a level as practicable, there is a need to order small quantities at frequent intervals. But every time an order is placed, there are significant administrative costs: placing the order, checking what has been received, and checking and paying invoices. The administrative costs of ordering suggest that it would be better to order larger quantities less frequently. It is possible to balance these two factors, as shown in Illustration 11.15.

The Chemvee Company uses 10,000 special purpose disks each year, and pays 50p each for them. The administration cost associated with each order is £200, and stockholding costs are estimated at 25% per annum. Calculate the EOQ.

$$EOQ = \sqrt{\frac{2 \times \text{annual demand} \times \text{ordering cost}}{\text{Price per unit} \times \text{stockholding cost}}}$$

$$= \sqrt{(2 \times 10{,}000 \times 200) \div (50p \times 0.25)}$$
$$= \sqrt{4{,}000{,}000 \div 0.125} = 5{,}657$$

The EOQ is 5,657 units.

If the company orders 5,657 units at a time they will have to order (10,000 ÷ 5,657 = 1.77) just less than twice a year: about once in 29 weeks. The average annual ordering cost will be 1.77 × £200 = £354 per annum.

When they receive each new order, they will have 5,657 units in stock, which will be gradually whittled down to zero units. On average they will have half of 5,657 units in stock (2,828½ each costing 50p) amounting to £1,414. Annual stockholding costs amount to 25 per cent of the amount of stock (0.25 × £1,414 =) £354.

We can see that the EOQ is the quantity at which the annual stockholding cost is equal to the annual ordering cost. If the company ordered more often, the annual cost of ordering would increase. If they ordered larger amounts, the annual stockholding cost would increase.

A formula such as this is useful in drawing attention to two of the key variables in determining stock levels, and providing rough guidelines. In practice, it might be difficult to determine ordering and stockholding costs with the accuracy inherent in the use of the formula. Even annual demand may not be so predictable. A more serious weakness of the EOQ formula is that it ignores quantity discounts. It is often possible to negotiate price reductions in return for more substantial order quantities.

ILLUSTRATION 11.15

Just in Time

Supermarkets have fresh bread delivered every day, just in time to meet customers' demand. Similarly, manufacturers can have components delivered just in time to meet production schedules; this minimizes the amounts of inventories held. It depends on managing good quality relationships with suppliers. Traditional managers may be tempted to keep large inventories 'just in case' they are needed. But the pressures of financial management lead to the use of a variety of approaches to minimize inventory levels.

Managing Cash

Planning and control of cash (and bank) is an essential part of financing a business. New and rapidly expanding businesses are often short of cash; unplanned overdrafts can incur very high rates of interest. In serious cases the bank may withdraw support and the business is then unable to meet its liabilities. In some businesses, excessive amounts of cash can be a problem and lead to underperformance. The business may earn interest on its deposits at modest rates (currently 4 per cent or 5 per cent per annum), but shareholders expect their funds to be used more profitably. Sometimes companies have large hoards of cash that they keep to be ready to buy another business; sometimes companies have surplus funds and they do not seem to know what to do with them; and sometimes these surplus funds are returned to shareholders as extra dividends, or the company buys up its own shares on the market and cancels them.

Careful planning and control of cash should ensure that sufficient long-term funds are available to finance all long-term assets; that additional funds are retained or raised to meet planned high levels of investment whether in fixed assets or acquiring other businesses; and that working capital is properly planned and financed, partly from current liabilities. Overdrafts are an appropriate source of finance to meet temporary or seasonal requirements. Cash budgeting is an essential tool of financial management, and businesses should plan their financing requirements over a 3–5-year period. Cash budgeting is dealt with in Chapter 7, and the main approaches to raising finance are outlined in this chapter. Liquidity problems become apparent in interpreting financial statements, as shown in Chapter 4, and cash flow statements can be used to review a company's performance, as shown in Chapter 7.

Where a company has liquidity problems, the ideal solution may be to raise more equity finance (by issuing shares); but a number of approaches suggested below may minimize the problem in the short term.

Liquidity problems can be minimized by good housekeeping. Prompt banking of all receipts will minimize cash shortages and interest charges. Centralized banking should ensure that any cash shortages in one part of the business are offset by surpluses elsewhere. Payments should not be made ahead of schedule and sending a cheque rather than using a bank transfer helps to retain funds within the business for a few more days. But customers should be encouraged to pay by the fastest means. Creditors should be paid at the time of the month when the business normally has most money in the bank, not at the same time as they pay wages and salaries. It is also important to maintain good relationships with bankers, letting them see budgets, and keeping within agreed limits; the role of bankers can be vital when times are tough. Careful planning and monitoring can avoid liquidity problems.

Where there are more serious liquidity problems the business may need to take emergency measures that could include a desperate trip to the bank. Banks are always willing to help if they are sure that the customer will repay (and has assets as security), but can make high charges in situations that look risky, and may refuse to help if they have no confidence in the management of the business. Delaying payments to creditors may be necessary. Debtors can be encouraged to pay more quickly. Selling off stocks at low prices will bring in cash, at the expense of profits. Capital expenditure can be postponed or cancelled. Surplus assets can be sold off: many businesses have some assets that are underutilized. Sometimes large companies, in times of crisis, suddenly appear to discover that they have expensive head office buildings in the centre of London, or country houses, or sports grounds (or even executive jets) that they do not really need. Smaller businesses can consider transferring their main administrative office to the spare bedroom at home! And businesses can free up cash by selling off company cars and using taxis or bicycles instead, especially when the only realistic alternative is bankruptcy. It may be possible or necessary to defer the payment of taxes; this can usually be negotiated with the Inland Revenue, although, of course, interest will be payable. The payment of dividends can also be delayed, or reduced, or cancelled, although it looks better if this is planned in advance.

Some short-term crisis measures can do more harm than good, especially if there is an underlying problem, such as overtrading. But tackling a problem promptly and harshly is better than undue optimism, a key cause of business failure.

Managing Payables

To some extent inventories and receivables are financed by creditors, and such trade credit is an attractive source of finance. It is cost-free, and the amount of payables tends to increase in line with increases in sales, inventories and receivables. When a company has short-term liquidity problems, the easiest thing to do is to delay paying creditors. This does not cause much of a problem if it is only for a week or two, especially if, after a short-term blip, the company goes back to paying their creditors on time. But there is a danger that a company may be unable to resume normal payment periods, and that further delays will occur if they become too heavily dependent on creditors as a source of short-term funding.

Excessive delay in paying creditors is not cost-free. Creditors soon lose patience with slow payers and are likely to cut off supplies, take legal action, or add interest to the amount due. If supplies are cut off because of slow (or non-) payment, it may be difficult to get supplies on credit elsewhere, especially if a company gets a reputation as a poor payer.

There is much to be said for cultivating good relationships with suppliers, keeping to the terms of the contract, and concentrating on the quality of the relationship, including payment. A company that delays making payments is in a weak position when it comes to negotiating improvements in the quality of goods or service received from suppliers.

In some businesses, such as retailers, the amount of payables is greater than the total of current assets; in this case short-term creditors are, in effect, financing some of the company's long-term assets. But a 'normal' working capital cycle would show that inventories represent a number of days' sales; receivables represent a number of days' sales; and this is only partly offset by the number of days' sales represented by payables.

11.6 Other Sources of Finance

Companies are assumed to need funds to finance the purchase of fixed assets and inventories, and to pay expenses until the profits come rolling in, in the form of cash. But there are various ways of avoiding, or minimizing, the need to raise finance.

1 Non-current assets can be leased instead of buying them. Obviously this applies to premises, but most machinery, equipment and vehicles can be leased if necessary. It is sometimes possible to arrange for an initial rent-free period to minimize initial funding requirements. But most lessors will not rent out equipment to any Tom, Dick or Harry: the lessee usually needs to produce evidence that they are creditworthy.

2 Sale and leaseback: a business can raise finance by selling assets that it owns and wants to continue using, through a finance company (e.g. bank or insurance company), and then leasing the asset back from that company. This is often done with premises, and many chains of retail shops no longer own the freehold of their premises: they made a sale and leaseback arrangement. This can make sense both for the finance company and for the retailer. The finance company gets a guaranteed return in rental income at the going rate (say 5 per cent to 7 per cent per annum); the retailer continues to use the premises and raises additional funds at a reasonable cost. The transaction will look good if the premises are sold for more than their book value: the profit contributes to an increase in EPS. This may be further boosted if the funds raised are used to increase profits, or to reduce the number of shares.

A cautious proprietor may prefer to retain the freehold of business premises; it can be used to provide security for a loan where additional finance is needed.

3 Businesses often find that they have more fixed assets than they need, especially when they find themselves in financial difficulties. Warehouses can be 'rationalized': the company may find that it can manage with two instead of six, and raise substantial sums by selling off uneconomic premises.

4 Outsourcing or subcontracting some activities (e.g. computing, accounting, catering, manufacturing, cleaning, transport – indeed, almost anything) may free up surplus assets that can be sold to raise funds. It can also be used to minimize the finance required for expansion.

5 Careful management of working capital can effectively reduce the financing needs of a business; reductions in working capital can produce additional cash.

6 Increasing profits also generates additional funds. This can be done both by reducing costs (e.g. eliminating a layer of management, or transferring production to Morocco or China), or by increasing sales (the volume of sales, and/or selling prices).

7 Reducing dividends, or even not paying dividends for a year or two is another way of making more funds available.

8 Careful cash budgeting can also make more funds available when needed by delaying major payments at times when there is a particular shortage of cash. Sometimes the easiest way to deal with a cash shortage is to delay capital expenditure programmes.

Businesses rely mostly on funds contributed by their owners (sole proprietors, partners or shareholders); on borrowing money; and on generating profits that are ploughed back into the business. But there are more creative ways of financing businesses.

Summary

The published financial statements of companies show how they have been financed, and indicate the balance between safety and solvency on the one hand, and risk and profitability on the other. The safest way of financing a company is to issue more shares, but this can be an expensive business, and shareholders expect a high return. Borrowing is in many ways easier and cheaper, but excessive gearing can lead to excessive risk that can adversely affect share prices, and increase the cost of borrowing. Retained profits are also an attractive source of funds, and companies need to have dividend policies that strike a balance between keeping shareholders happy, and retaining profits to finance expansion, where such reinvestment is justified. High gearing can enhance profitability, particularly during a period of low interest rates, but it also increases risk. Similar issues arise with the management of working capital. Minimizing levels of inventories and receivables can minimize the need for external finance, and enhance ROCE. But lowering levels of working capital make companies look less solvent. There are various more creative ways of financing a business, and there are no 'correct' solutions. Policies on gearing, dividends and working capital change as circumstances change, and a combination of several different approaches to financing a company is usually appropriate.

Review of key points

- The three main sources of funds for companies are share capital, borrowing and retained profits.
- There is no requirement to pay dividends to ordinary shareholders; they bear most of the risk of the business, and, if the business does well, will get substantial rewards.
- Borrowing can 'gear up' the return to the owners of the business, but excessive gearing is risky.
- Profits may be paid out to shareholders as dividends, or reinvested in the business as they are earned.
- Dividend policy strikes a balance between retaining funds within the business that are needed, and maintaining a payment record to satisfy shareholders.
- Working capital is usually measured as current assets minus current liabilities.
- Insufficient working capital is likely to be associated with liquidity problems; excessive working capital restricts profitability.
- Debtors should be managed to minimize bad debts and to encourage debtors to pay up quickly.
- The cost effectiveness of different ways of managing debtors should be assessed.
- Carrying excessive stocks is expensive for companies.
- Careful planning and control of cash is essential.
- Creditors should be paid in accordance with agreed terms; some companies prefer the short-term financial advantage of delaying payment to their creditors.
- Calculations and estimates can be made of the costs and benefits of different policies for managing each element of working capital.
- Much of business activity can be financed without using share capital, borrowing or retained profits.
- Published financials statements indicate the way in which a business has been financed, its dividend and gearing policies, and the effectiveness of its working capital management.

Self-testing questions

1 What are the three main sources of finance for businesses?

2 What are the main differences between preference shares and ordinary shares?

3 Explain the advantages and disadvantages of a company increasing its gearing.

4 You are given the following information about two companies.

Self-testing questions (continued)

Summarized balance sheets as at 31 December

| | TimeBall Company | | DownsPier Company | |
	Year 6	Year 7	Year 6	Year 7
	£000	£000	£000	£000
Total assets *minus* current liabilities	300	342.2	300	284.1
Current liabilities				
9% Debentures	100	140	100	50
	200	202.2	200	234.1
Share capital	100	100	100	115
Share premium	–	–	–	15
Retained profits	100	102.2	100	104.1
	200	202.2	200	234.1

Summarized income statements for year ended 31 December

Sales	100	110	100	95
Gross profit	40	44	40	41
Operating profit	20	21.6	20	17.5
Interest	9	12.6	9	4.5
Pre-tax profit	11	9	11	13
Taxation	3.3	2.7	3.3	3.9
Profit after tax	7.7	6.3	7.7	9.1
Dividends	4	4.1	4	5
Retained profit	3.7	2.2	3.7	4.1

a You are required to calculate for each company for each year:
  i Capital gearing ratio
  ii Interest cover
  iii Dividend cover
  iv Proportion of profits paid out as dividends

b Explain what each shows.

c Comment on the financial performance and position of the two companies making use of appropriate ratios.

5 Why might a company want high levels of working capital?

6 Can a company operate with zero or negative levels of working capital?

7 How would you detect overtrading, and why does it matter?

8 What steps can be taken to speed up the collection of receivables? Why might a company deliberately allow an increase in the time taken for debtors to pay?

9 What factors are taken into consideration in the conventional model for calculating economic order quantities?

10 How can a company avoid having liquidity crises?

11 The Congle Company uses 40,000 wongles a year. Each wongle costs £1.25 to buy; stockholding costs are estimated to be 32 per cent per annum of the cost of the stocks held; each order costs £20 to place. What ordering quantity will minimize costs? How many orders will be placed each year? How often will goods be delivered, and what is the average stock level? What is the annual stockholding cost?

12 Fleshwick Traders has a large overdraft on which interest of 17 per cent per annum is being charged. The directors are considering offering cash discounts to customers to encourage prompt payment. Annual sales, all on credit, amount to £365,000, and the debtors figure at present is £90,000. The sales director considers that a discount of 2.5 per cent for settlement in 10 days would be taken up by about one-third of their customers. The finance director thinks that a larger discount would be required to achieve this result. Assuming that the sales level remained constant:

a Would it be worth offering the discount if the sales director is right?

b What is the largest discount the company could offer without a reduction in profits?

c Assume that each £1 of sales contributes 20p to fixed costs and profits. If the company decided to offer a 5 per cent cash discount for payment in 10 days, and it is taken up by one-third of their customers, how large an increase in sales would be required to maintain profits?

13 Stokeypokey Wholesalers Limited are proposing to set up a branch in Northern Ireland. Experience elsewhere suggests that sales will start off at £100,000 a month in January, and then increase by £100,000 a month until reaching £400,000 in April. Then sales will increase by £80,000 a month until they reach £640,000 in July. In August sales are expected to reach £700,000 a month and remain at that level until the end of the year. Customers are expected to pay 2 months after the sales are made.

The cost of purchases is 80 per cent of the sales figure, and they are paid for in the month following the purchase. In January purchases will amount to £240,000; then, each month they purchase the amount of goods required for the following month.

Rent of £100,000 per quarter is payable at the beginning of January, and then in March, June, September and December. Other expenses, payable in the month that they are incurred, are expected to amount to £10,000 per month for the first 4 months; they will increase to £15,000 a month in May, and then to £16,000 a month in August–December.

The only capital expenditure is for purchase of fittings with £50,000 payable in January and £50,000 in September. Depreciation is at 10 per cent per annum with a full year's depreciation being charged in the first year.

The Northern Ireland branch starts business with an interest-free loan of £1 million from Stokeypokey Wholesalers, which is put into a separate bank account.

Self-testing questions (continued)

i Prepare a summarized income statement for the first year of business.

ii Prepare a balance sheet as at the end of the first year.

iii Prepare a cash budget showing receipts and payments for each month for the year.

iv Comment on the results highlighting key learning points.

Assessment questions

1 Why might a company issue convertible preference shares rather than debentures?

2 The capital structure of two companies is as follows:

	Loborough plc	Hiborough plc
	£m	£m
Equity	180	50
11% Debentures	20	150
	200	200

The EBIT of both companies was as follows:

Year 1	£19m
Year 2	£22.8m
Year 3	£15.2m

The rate of corporation tax on profits is 25 per cent.

a Calculate the net profit after tax earned for ordinary shareholders for each year and for each company.

b Comment on the effect that gearing has had on the results.

3 The directors of the Palazine Company are seeking funding of £50m to finance an expansion programme. The summarized financial statements for the most recent year are set out below.

Income statement for the year ended 31 December year 6

		£000
Sales		120,000
Cost of sales		90,000
Gross profit		30,000
Distribution costs	8,000	
Administration expenses	12,000	(20,000)
Operating profit		10,000
Debenture interest		(5,000)
Net profit before taxation		5,000
Taxation		(3,000)
Net profit after taxation		2,000
Dividends		(1,000)
Retained profit for year		1,000

Assessment questions (continued)

Balance sheet as at 31 December year 6

		£000
Non-current assets		
Land and buildings (market value £55m)		45,000
Plant and machinery		18,000
Investments at cost (market value £30m)		45,000
		108,000
Current assets		
Inventories	8,000	
Receivables	5,000	
Cash	1,000	14,000
Total assets		122,000
Current liabilities		
Payables	23,000	
Proposed dividend[6]	1,000	24,000
Non-current liabilities		
10% Debentures (secured)		50,000
Equity		
Share capital	30,000	
Retained earnings	18,000	48,000
		122,000

The following suggestions have been made for raising the additional finance. You are required to explain the effects of each of the suggestions and to comment on their practicability.

The company could:

i   Issue more debentures

ii   Make a sale and leaseback arrangement on their premises

iii   Sell their investments (although some directors object to this as it would involve a loss of £15m)

iv   Reduce inventories by one-half

v   Halve the period that debtors are allowed to pay (all sales are on credit)

vi   Extend the period for paying creditors by 50 per cent

vii   Cancel the proposed dividend

viii   Use the reserves

ix   Issue more ordinary shares

x   Obtain a bank overdraft

4 The EPS and the dividend per share of Uppen Down plc for the last few years are shown below (in pence):

---

[6] It is now more usual that a dividend proposed in year 6 is not treated as a liability until year 7.

Assessment questions *(continued)*

Year	1	2	3	4	5	6	7
EPS	20	25	18	30	10	13	24
Dividend	10	10.4	10.8	11.2	11.7	12.2	12.7
Share price	300	400	200	270	250	270	300

a You are required to calculate the dividend cover for each year; the proportion of profits that was distributed as dividends; and the dividend yield based on the share price at the year end given above.

b Comment on the company's dividend policy.

c Since the end of year 7 the dividend yield, as shown in the *Financial Times*, has increased to 10 per cent. What is this likely to indicate?

5 How can a company operate with minimum levels of working capital?

6 Working capital should be managed to maximize profitability. Explain and comment.

7 What steps can be taken to minimize bad debts?

8 What are the main limitations of the EOQ model?

9 The Scottish Cake Company has annual sales of £1,200,000. Annual fixed costs are £150,000 and last year's profit was £50,000. At the year end the receivables figure was £100,000.

   The company has been offered a contract for supplying cakes to the Swaysco Supermarket Group in England. Sales would be £300,000 in a year, and Swaysco would require 3 months' credit. The Scottish Cake Company's cost of capital is estimated at 15 per cent per annum. Is the proposed expansion worth while if all customers are given 3 months' credit? Is the proposed expansion worth while if only Swaysco is given 3 months' credit?

10 The summarized balance sheet of the Warmel Trading Company as at 31 December last year was as follows:

	£	£
Fixed assets		3,000,000
Current assets		
Inventories	500,000	
Trade receivables	600,000	
Cash	10,000	1,110,000
Total assets		4,110,000
Current liabilities		
Trade payables		110,000
Equity		4,000,000
		4,110,000

Last year sales amounted to £3,600,000 and net profit before tax was £600,000. The company's target ROCE is 15 per cent. It is estimated that variable costs amount to 50 per cent of sales, and that fixed costs amount to £1,200,000 per annum.

Assessment questions (continued)

The purchasing manager is concerned about the very small amount of cash available and that the company may be unable to meet its current liabilities as they fall due.

The financial accountant says that the level of receivables is too high, and proposes to appoint a credit controller at an annual cost of £25,000. He reckons that by doing this the amount of debtors could be halved.

The sales manager believes that many customers are put off by the strict credit control policies, and would like to allow 3 months' credit to customers. If this policy was adopted he reckons that sales would increase by at least 10 per cent. The finance director estimates that such a policy would result in debtors taking, on average, 4 months to pay, that stocks and creditors would each increase by 10 per cent, and that bad debts would increase by £18,000 per annum.

Required:

a Evaluate the comments made by:

  i The purchasing manager

  ii The financial accountant

  iii The sales manager and finance director.

b What would be your recommendation and why?

11 The following information has been extracted from the most recent annual report and accounts of Greyhound Leather Manufacturers Ltd:

Income statement

	Year 1	Year 2
	£000	£000
Sales	20,000	22,000
Cost of sales	16,000	17,800
Gross profit	4,000	4,200
Operating profit	2,000	2,050
Net profit after tax	1,500	1,300

Balance sheet

	Year 1	Year 2
Non-current assets	6,200	12,680
Inventories		
Raw materials	1,600	2,000
Work in progress	400	420
Finished goods	2,000	2,500
Receivables	5,000	3,200
Bank	2,000	–
Total assets	17,200	20,800
Current liabilities		
Receivables	2,200	2,800
Overdraft	–	2,000
Equity	15,000	16,000
Total equity plus liabilities	17,200	20,800

Assessment questions (continued)

a The finance director is pleased with the management of working capital, but the chairman is more concerned about profitability. Making use of appropriate calculations you are required to analyse the financial management of the company and comment on the two points of view expressed.

b What is meant by the working capital cycle? Illustrate your answer with appropriate calculations for Greyhound Leather Manufacturers Ltd.

c What steps can a company take to improve stock turnover?

d The company uses one million hides of leather a year that they buy for £16 each. Stockholding costs are estimated to be 25 per cent per annum of the cost of the items in stock. Administration costs for placing and receiving an order are estimated to be £50. How many hides should the company order at a time (i.e. calculate the EOQ)?

e Illustrate the financial effects of implementing the EOQ in practice and suggest its limitations.

12 The directors of Woebun Standard Components plc have been very successful in persuading their customers to pay, on average, in one month. However, they believe that this policy is restricting sales and that sales would increase by 15 per cent if the average collection period for receivables was allowed to increase from one month to two months.

The selling price of the component is £40 per unit and variable costs per unit are £30. Annual sales revenue is £6 million. A sales increase of 15 per cent would lead to an increase in stocks of £400,000 and an increase in trade creditors of £100,000. Woebun expects a ROCE of 27 per cent per annum.

a On purely financial grounds, should the company allow its customers to enjoy the extended credit period of 2 months?

b Assess the practicability and financial viability of restricting the 2 months' credit to new customers only.

c What are the main causes and symptoms of *overtrading*? To what extent and in what ways can effective management of debtors avoid the problems of overtrading?

13 The Bonjarron Decorating Company uses 14,400 large size cans of white gloss paint in a year. They use different suppliers and, on average, pay £20 per can. They have limited storage space and reckon that the annual stockholding costs amount to 20 per cent of the cost of the stocks held. Administration costs amount to £50 per order placed.

a Calculate the EOQ.

b For what reasons might the company use (i) a much higher, or (ii) a much lower ordering quantity?

Group activities and discussion questions

1 What is the minimum amount of funding with which it is possible to start a business? Could a business be started with zero funds? What sort of business could each member of the group start, with little or no funding? Prepare a (very brief) business plan. Would it be necessary to raise substantial funding to develop the business so that it becomes large scale? How would you define 'large scale' (big enough to provide you with a suitable lifestyle; big enough for a stock market listing)?

2 Prepare a list of companies that are not currently paying dividends. (Look for shares with a zero yield in the *Financial Times*' listing.) Why are these companies not paying dividends? Each member of the group could research a number of companies. Can the companies be classified into groups, each with similar reasons for not paying dividends (e.g. developing new products/services; recent losses)?

3 Why are some companies high-geared and others low-geared? Each member of the group should examine the balance sheets of a number of companies, probably in different sectors. It may be easier to do this using the companies' websites. The group should agree the way in which gearing should be measured (e.g., is short-term borrowing to be included with long-term borrowing?). Are utility companies more highly geared than retailers? Are breweries more highly geared than oil companies? Can you identify what factors seem to be associated with high gearing and with low gearing?

4 Many small businesses may be seen as 'overtrading'. Accountants are too conservative about such things. To be successful, a rapidly expanding small business needs to sail close to the wind. Discuss these views.

5 Large businesses should not have working capital problems. It is easy for them to borrow large sums on a long-term basis. The problem for large businesses is not working capital; it is excessive gearing. Discuss.

6 Discuss the effects on just in time of increasing proportions of manufacturing (for the UK) taking placed in eastern Europe, Africa and Asia.

7 Can working capital, like manufacturing, be 'outsourced'? Could a company operate with zero or negative capital employed, make some profits, and, therefore, have a ROCE of infinity?

8 Large companies can bully small customers to pay up promptly, while they need not bother paying their own bills on time. Small companies have to pay up promptly if they are to continue to receive supplies, but they cannot force large customers to pay them promptly if they are to continue to make sales. Discuss these views.

9 How does cash budgeting for a business differ from the way in which you do your own personal cash budgeting. Should it differ? (Other than the amounts of money being very different!)

Financial accounting in context

Money talks

By Hugh Thompson

Accountancy Age, 23 February 2006

Discuss and comment on the following extracts from the press. To what extent do you think that governments should assist growing companies?

Source: Reproduced with permission by *Accountancy Age*.

RAISING FINANCE for growth is a subject that brings out a fairly predictable set of moans from finance directors and their advisers. The banks give you the run around, the government-backed schemes require too much bureaucracy and management time and the venture capitalists always ask far too much, too soon and give too little. Actually at a certain point, one begins to wonder how any growth is financed at all.

So it was nice to bump into Craig Brown, finance director of Kryson Resources, an AIM-listed company that is prospecting for gold in central Asia. 'We are in a bull market for mining and raw materials and so we haven't had any problems in raising money.'

But it isn't only mining companies that have benefited from easier finance. As the economy evolves and expands into areas such as the environment and the wilder areas of technology, so specialist funds have been created to cater for these sectors.

'Not only are there new funds but the banks generally have become more innovative and creative in their risk assessment,' explains Darren Jordan, a partner with Blick Rothenberg. 'Many are now treating commercial leases as assets. They are generally more sophisticated in their risk assessment, but they are well aware of the state of the economy and in recent weeks we have seen more caution creeping in. In terms of real innovation, I know of one company that raised money by borrowing from its employees.'

Jordan, like many, is quite scathing of the various government schemes that he feels, despite being much trumpeted, are simply not worth the hassle. 'There is always less than you think available and they demand so much in management time.'

Many companies realise that bank debt, however flexible, does not have the advantages of private equity or going to AIM when it comes to financing growth. Many are now looking to strategic partnering where large players take minority stakes in up and coming companies in their sectors. But for some, the price of having someone else on the board trying to call the shots is too high.

John May is an accountant who has helped many companies raise finance for growth. His advice is simple. 'It's often just a question of knocking on doors. Eventually you will find a lender who, because of the state of their book, and because they are more imaginative or they understand what you are talking about, will lend.

'Each lender is in a slightly different position. What is mezzanine or equity finance to some is a straight loan to others. Occasionally you do get originality. I had a bank recently that split a £5m offer into straight loan and revolving credit. It is important that companies work out what they want the money for and over what term.'

Unlike others, May praises the government guarantee loan schemes, although he does admit that, under present rules, there is pressure for banks to push companies down the factoring route.

Over the past few years, there has been something of a rush to finance growth by listing on AIM. Andy Wallfold is transactions manager of Marwyn Capital, which in the last year has put six management teams into shells for the purpose of acquiring and growing other companies.

'Many of these management teams have found that the private equity route is a bit restricting,' he says. 'Venture capitalists typically make one investment and want to make that pay quickly, while those pension funds and the like who invest in AIM companies are in it for a longer term.'

But many smaller companies will be looking for seed finance or even business angel backing before they look to AIM as a funding mechanism. One company that does both is the Catalyst Investment Group, which last year did 30 deals in the £50,000 to £1m bracket. Four times a year it also hosts an Entrepreneurs Lunch Club where would-be backers are entertained by three companies. This route raises about £2.5m a year.

Renwick Haddow, a director of the Catalyst Group, claims to be offered around 20 deals a week, 'and the main problem is always the same', he says. 'Companies feel if they are worth £6m, then they haven't done a day's business. I am really looking for a simple business that investors can understand and a strong management team.'

But while those providing finance for growth can point to a whole raft of venture capital, venture capital trusts, private equity and government guaranteed loans, others are not sure there is any new dawn in this area.

Mike Smart is the group managing director of the Gowi Group, which is involved in online recruitment and content management. In six years, the company has grown to a £6m turnover and 100 staff.

'I am still disappointed with the financial community,' he complains. 'The banks don't want to know about these government guarantees, private equity is not interested in the smaller player and the trusts don't really like technology companies like ours. We have raised money from friends, family and fools.'

Government grants

By Nigel Wilcock

Accountancy Age, 23 February 2006

R&D – Support for companies is now widely available through the R&D tax credit, which can be considered state aid by the European Union. There is a national DTI grant for R&D and a European grant regime called Framework 6, available to companies involved with pan European collaborative projects.

EMPLOYMENT & TRAINING – Funds are aimed at training providers and organised by the Learning and Skills Council. Grants are available through the regional development agencies.

ENVIRONMENTAL GRANTS – The EU makes provisions for national governments to provide funding under environmental schemes.

CAPITAL INVESTMENT in assisted area – Companies seeking funding must explain why the grant will allow the project to progress in the UK. The government will not pay more than a set percentage of the eligible expenditure.

REAL ESTATE DEVELOPMENT – Where there is gap between the end value of a development project and its cost, grant aid can meet the difference, albeit within set limits. These grants are used for regionally important development projects rather than small building schemes.

References and further reading

Berger, D. and J. Carlisle (2002) *The Motley Fool UK Investment Guide*. Boxtree.

Brealey, R., S. Myers and F. Allen (2005) *Corporate Finance*. McGraw-Hill.

Brett, M. (2003) *How to Read the Financial Pages*. Random House Business Books.

Financial Times (daily newspaper)

Investors Chronicle (weekly magazine)

Lumby, S. and C. Jones (2003) *Corporate Finance: Theory and Practice*. Thomson Learning.

McKenzie, W. (2003) *Financial Times Guide to Using and Interpreting Company Accounts*. FT Prentice Hall.

Modigliani, F. and M. Miller (1958) 'The cost of capital, corporation finance and the theory of investment'. *American Economic Review*, June, pp. 261–97.

Rees, B. (forthcoming) *Financial Analysis* (3rd edition). FT Prentice Hall.

www.ft.com

www.londonstockexchange.com

Investment Appraisal

❖ LEARNING OBJECTIVES

After studying this chapter you should be able to:

❖ Understand the difference between using cash flow and profit in making investment appraisals

❖ Calculate and interpret the return on investment (ROI), or return on capital employed of a project and appreciate its uses and limitations

❖ Calculate and interpret the payback period of a project, and appreciate its uses and limitations

❖ Understand the principles of discounting and calculate a project's net present value (NPV) and internal rate of return (IRR)

❖ Evaluate the strengths and weaknesses of discounted cash flow (DCF) approaches to investment appraisal

❖ Understand which cash flows are relevant and should be included in a DCF calculation, and which are not

❖ Appreciate the importance of cost of capital in investment appraisal, and evaluate the relevance of cost of capital calculations

❖ Understand that there is always uncertainty and risk in investment appraisal and appreciate various ways of dealing with this

12.1 Introduction

Financial accounting is concerned with reporting to shareholders on the success of management in achieving what shareholders want. It may be assumed that the objective is to maximize shareholders' wealth. To achieve this they should use proper investment appraisal techniques to ensure that shareholders' funds are used only to finance activities that will produce an adequate return. They must strike a balance between high-risk projects that seem to promise a high return, and safer projects producing a lower return. They should also be aware of a company's cost of capital. A company with a cost of capital of 10 per cent per annum will find that projects yielding 12 per cent per annum are attractive, and can increase the value of the company. Those with a higher cost of capital (e.g. 15 per cent) will find that fewer projects are attractive.

12.2 Investment

Individuals and companies invest money in the short term with the idea of getting back more, in the longer term, than the initial cost of the investment. This is a straightforward enough idea, but there are a number of issues that have to be addressed if we are to 'appraise' our investments properly.

1 How much do you need to get back to justify the amount invested?

2 How quickly does the money need to come back? If you can invest £100 today, and get back £300 after 50 years, the return might look brilliant, but the timing is terrible!

3 Risk. How sure are you that we will get back the amount suggested? There are various ways of allowing for risk and uncertainty in investment appraisal, but there is still a need for judgement, and to recognize that some uncertainty is inevitable in most businesses and projects.

Before considering the various approaches that are used in investment appraisal, it is necessary to be clear whether the returns that we expect an investment to make will be measured as:

a profit; or

b cash flow.

Profit and Cash Flow

Profits are measured in accordance with all the usual rules that apply to income statements. Profit, by definition, should always mean after depreciation has been charged as an expense. But as depreciation is not 'paid' (no cash goes out of the business), the annual *cash flows* from a project are usually much higher than the annual *profits*. This is clearly shown in Elizabeth's project in Illustration 12.1.

The first of our four methods of investment appraisal, return on investment, uses profit. The other three methods use cash flow.

Elizabeth was made redundant recently, and was given a severance payment of £55,000, which she uses to buy a special-purpose delivery vehicle. She employs a driver. Each year she receives money from customers for delivering goods; each year she pays all her expenses in cash (wages, petrol, repairs, insurance etc.); and each year she pockets what is left: this amounts to £15,500 a year, which she reckons is a pretty good return on her initial capital of £55,000.

Unfortunately, Elizabeth forgot to allow for depreciation. After 5 years the vehicle is worn out, and she manages to sell it for £5,000. She should have allowed £10,000 a year for depreciation.

In terms of cash flow, Elizabeth made £15,500 a year. In terms of profit she made only £5,500 a year.

In this simple business we can see that:

Profit	+	depreciation	=	cash flow
£5,500	+	£10,000	=	£15,500

ILLUSTRATION 12.1

12.3 Methods of Investment Appraisal

a Return on Investment (ROI)

The ROI, or accounting rate of return (ARR), is based on the return on capital employed (ROCE).[1] It uses accounting profits which are calculated after charging depreciation. It can be expressed as follows:

$$\frac{\text{Average annual profits}}{\text{Amount initially invested}} \times \frac{100}{1}$$

Elizabeth's return may be calculated as follows:

$$\frac{5,500}{55,000} \times \frac{100}{1} = 10\%$$

Using ROI is an appealing approach to investment appraisal in a number of ways. It is in many ways consistent with conventional financial accounting. If the performance of a company as a whole is judged on the basis of profitability, using ROCE, then it makes sense to judge the performance of each part of the business using a ROCE. If a company wants to achieve a ROCE of, say, 15 per cent per annum, they can be sure of achieving this if every part of the business, and every project achieves this return.

But calculating the return on the *initial* amount invested is likely to understate the returns that a company subsequently achieves. If a project has no scrap value, that is, the capital employed at the end of its life is zero, then the average capital employed is exactly half of the initial capital employed. The return on average capital employed will be double the ROCE.

With Elizabeth's project, the initial amount invested is £55,000. After 1 year's depreciation the amount of the investment will be reduced to £45,000. After 2 years it will be £35,000. After 3 years it will be £25,000. After 4 years it will be £15,000. At the end of 5

---

[1] ROCE is usually applied to the business as a whole, but it can be applied to parts of the business or individual projects.

years it will be down to £5,000. We can say that the *average* amount invested in the project is the amount halfway through its life, that is, after 2.5 years. The average amount invested is £30,000, calculated as follows:

$$\text{Average capital employed} = \frac{\text{Initial capital employed} + \text{Value at end}}{2}$$

$$£30,000 = \frac{£55,000 + £5,000}{2}$$

$$\text{Return on average capital employed} = \frac{5,500}{30,000} \times \frac{100}{1} = 18.3\%$$

Elizabeth
Return on initial capital employed   10%
Return on average capital employed   18.3%

It may be better to use the *average* amount invested, rather than the *initial* amount invested. This is less prudent: using the average amount invested shows a higher return. Elizabeth should not reject what might be a perfectly good project on the basis that it achieves a return on initial investment of 'only' 10 per cent.

The Trudo machine will cost £50,000, and will have a 4-year life with zero scrap value at the end of 5 years. It will generate cash flows as follows:

Year 1	10,000
Year 2	16,000
Year 3	20,000
Year 4	20,000
Total	66,000

To calculate average annual profit, it is necessary to calculate average annual depreciation charges.

There is no need to know what method or rate of depreciation will be used. The total amount to be written off, whatever method is used, is £50,000. The total cash flows are £66,000. The total profits must, therefore, be £16,000. Averaged over 4 years, the profits are £4,000 a year.

We could work out average annual profits as follows:

Average annual cash flows	£66,000 ÷ 4 =	£16,500
Average annual depreciation	£50,000 ÷ 4 =	£12,500
		£4,000

The return on initial amount of capital employed is:

$$\frac{£4,000}{£50,000} \times \frac{100}{1} = 8\%$$

The return on the average capital employed is:

$$\frac{£4,000}{£25,000} \times \frac{100}{1} = 16\%$$

ILLUSTRATION 12.2

A further illustration of the calculation of return on investment is provided in Illustration 12.2.

It is difficult to relate the ROI of a project to the company's cost of capital. It would be appealing to say that if a company's cost of capital is, say, 12 per cent, any project with a ROI of greater than 12 per cent should be accepted because it would increase the company's average return on capital employed, and so increase the value of the company. There are several important reasons why such a neat rule of thumb could lead to poor decisions.

1 There are different ways of calculating ROI, and care is needed to ensure that like is compared with like.

2 ROI ignores the timing of future cash flows and profits. It simply averages profits over the life of the project. It assumes that making £10,000 profit next year is the same as making £10,000 profit after 3 years. But shareholders want to see results within a relatively short period of time. The problem is shown in Illustration 12.3 with two projects: one generates cash flows and profits more quickly; the other generates more profit and cash flow, but over a longer period.

In Illustration 12.3 the Jaggie project makes only £40 profit, but the Lardie project makes £45 profit. The ROI is, therefore, higher for the Lardie project than it is for the Jaggie project. But the Jaggie project makes the money much more quickly, and might be a better project.

3 Use of ROI is also criticized because it depends on all of the usual assumptions in financial accounting. The usefulness of ROI is limited by variations in accounting poli-

Year	Jaggie Project Cash flow	Depreciation	Profit	Lardie Project Cash flow	Depreciation	Profit
0	(100)			(100)		
1	45	20	25	10	20	(10)
2	40	20	20	20	20	–
3	35	20	15	30	20	10
4	10	20	(10)	40	20	20
5	10	20	(10)	45	20	25
Total	140	100	40	145	100	45

	Jaggie	Lardie
Average annual profits	40 ÷ 5 = 8	45 ÷ 5 = 9
Average capital employed	50	50
Return on average investment	16%	18%

In deciding between Jaggie and Lardie we need a method of investment appraisal which takes into account not just the amounts of cash flows or profits that a project generates, but also the timing of them. It is better to get our money back sooner rather than later.

In both of these projects there are years when no profit is being made. But as long as a project is generating positive net cash flows it is usually worth continuing with.

ILLUSTRATION 12.3

cies, the use of 'creative accounting', and any questionable assumptions in measuring profits or capital employed.

ROI, or return on capital employed, is the only method of investment appraisal that uses profit figures as opposed to cash flow figures. The 'return' means profit, and in calculating profit, depreciation has to be deducted.

Other methods of investment appraisal are based on cash flows, not profit. Depreciation is not deducted from cash flows when calculating payback period, or discounted cash flow (see Illustration 12.3).

b Payback Period

The easiest way to deal with the timing of future returns is to ask the simple question: how quickly do we get our money back? A project that gives you your money back in 3 years is likely to be better than one that takes 5 years.

A quick look at Jaggie and Lardie shows that both require an initial investment of £100, but Jaggie pays it back much more quickly. After only 2 years Jaggie has already produced cash flows of £95, and will have paid back the full £100 a couple of months into the third year. But Lardie is much slower: it has not repaid the full £100 until the end of the fourth year.

As a method of investment appraisal payback period has a number of clear advantages:

1 It is easy to calculate, easy to understand and easy to present.

2 It is based on cash flow, not profit, and so is seen as being more objective with less dependence on questionable accounting assumptions.

3 It emphasizes the need for projects to repay quickly, which is important, especially if we take into account the cost of the funds invested in a project.

4 Projects with shorter payback periods are likely to be less risky than projects that take longer to pay back the initial investment. In forecasting the results of a project, we can be much more certain about costs and revenues in the first few years than we can be about what might happen 5 or 10 years into the future.

If we combine ROI with payback period we might make reasonable investment decisions. ROI takes into account all the profits that a project makes throughout its life; it ignores timing. Payback period considers only the length of time it takes for cash flows to amount to the amount of the original investment; it ignores cash flows after the payback period.

Rudi pays £100,000 for a 3-year lease on an office building that will generate cash inflows of £50,000 a year for 3 years, and then have no residual value.

Duri pays £100,000 for the freehold of some shop premises that will bring him cash inflows of £12,500 a year for many years into the future.

Rudi's payback period is 2 years.

Duri's payback period is 8 years.

ILLUSTRATION 12.4

Using only the payback period as a method of investment appraisal could lead to really silly decisions, as Illustration 12.4 shows.

If the two investments were compared solely on the basis of payback period, Rudi's is clearly the better investment. But in this case it is worth waiting longer to get a lot more money back. Duri's project is the better one (unless the cost of capital is very high).

The disadvantages of using the payback period are:

1 It ignores cash flows after the initial amount has been paid back.

2 It does not consider the timing of cash flows in a systematic way.

Looking at the payback period may be a convenient way of screening out projects that take far too long to pay back, but it does not indicate whether or not a project is worth while. A project must produce enough total cash flows, as well as doing so within a reasonable period. It is important to consider the *timing* of cash flows more precisely; this is best done using discounted cash flow.

c Discounted Cash Flow (DCF): Net Present Value (NPV)

It is obviously better to receive £100 today than to receive £100 in one year's time, even if we ignore risk and inflation. One hundred pounds received today can be invested, and after a year it might be worth £104, or more, depending on how successful the investment is. If we have to wait for the money, we lose the opportunity of using it to generate a return, even if the return is only 4 per cent interest. But shareholders expect a higher return than they could get from putting their money in a bank, and might expect the company to 'make', say 10 per cent per annum for them. Companies should have better investment opportunities than individuals.

If we have the choice of receiving £100 today, or £120 in a year's time, the decision is a little more difficult; but it is always worth waiting to receive money, *if* we are going to receive extra money to compensate for the delay. Indeed, that is the whole nature of investment: we pay out money in the short term in order to receive more back in the future. If a company's cost of capital is 10 per cent, it is better worth waiting a year to receive £120 than having only £100 today. Where a company's cost of capital is 10 per cent per annum, then the cost of waiting to receive money is 10 per cent per annum, and DCF should be used to calculate if it is worth waiting for the expected returns.

If we know the cost of a project, and the future cash flows it will generate, then it is a matter of arithmetic to determine whether or not an investment is worth while. If the company's cost of capital is 10 per cent, we apply a 10 per cent discount rate to future cash flows. If we have to wait 1 year to receive £100, that is the equivalent of receiving £90.91 today. This is because, if we received £90.91 today, we could invest it at 10 per cent for a year, and then it would give us exactly £100 in a year's time. If we have to wait 2 years for it, then the 'present value' is £82.64. If we have to wait 3 years for it, then the NPV is £75.13. If we have to wait 4 years for it, then the NPV is £68.30 and so on.

It is easy to check this. If we had £68.30 today, and it earned 10 per cent a year interest, at the end of 4 years it would amount to £68.30 × 1.1 × 1.1 × 1.1 × 1.1, which amounts to £100.[2]

---

[2] There are usually slight rounding differences with DCF.

If a company's cost of capital is 10 per cent per annum, we assume that they have investment opportunities that would enable £100 today to become £110 after one year. If this is the case, we can make the following statements:

1 Receiving £100 today is equivalent to receiving £110 after one year.

2 Waiting 1 year to receive £110 is equivalent to receiving £100 today.

3 Waiting 1 year to receive £100 is equivalent to receiving £90.91 today. This is because if we have £90.91 today, and we invest it at 10 per cent, we will make £9.09 interest in 1 year, which will give us (£90.91 + £9.09 =) £100 after 1 year.

4 Waiting 2 years to receive £100 is equivalent to receiving £82.64 today. This is because if we have £82.64 today, and we invest it at 10 per cent, we will make £8.26 interest in the first year, giving us (£82.64 + £8.26 =) about £90.90,[3] which, after another year at 10 per cent will give us £100.

5 We can look at any future cash flows and discount them in this way.

This is all very important in investment appraisal. The nature of investment is that we pay out money now, and expect to get returns in the future. To start with we need to work out what those future returns are likely to be, and to assess the timing of them. Then we need to 'discount' the future cash flows to take into account the cost of having to wait for them. We will continue to assume that the cost is 10 per cent per annum, but equivalent calculations can be made for any 'discount rate'.

We have already established that receiving £100 after

| 1 year | is equivalent to receiving | £90.91 today |
| 2 years | is equivalent to receiving | £82.64 today |

We can continue as follows:

| 3 years | £75.13 |
| 4 years | £68.30 and so on |

Present value table

	5%	10%	15%	20%	25%	30%
1	0.952	0.909	0.870	0.833	0.800	0.769
2	0.907	0.826	0.756	0.694	0.640	0.592
3	0.864	0.751	0.658	0.579	0.512	0.455
4	0.823	0.683	0.572	0.482	0.410	0.350
5	0.784	0.621	0.497	0.402	0.328	0.269
6	0.746	0.564	0.432	0.335	0.262	0.207
7	0.711	0.513	0.376	0.279	0.210	0.159
8	0.677	0.467	0.327	0.233	0.168	0.123
9	0.645	0.424	0.284	0.194	0.134	0.094
10	0.614	0.386	0.247	0.162	0.107	0.073

ILLUSTRATION 12.5

[3] There are usually slight rounding differences with DCF.

Year	Jaggie Project Cash flow	Discount factor	Net present value	Lardie Project Cash flow	Discount factor	Net present value
0	(100)			(100)		
1	45	0.9091	40.91	10	0.9091	9.09
2	40	0.8264	33.06	20	0.8264	16.53
3	35	0.7513	26.30	30	0.7513	22.54
4	10	0.6830	6.83	40	0.6830	27.32
5	10	0.6209	6.21	45	0.6209	27.94
Total	140		113.31	145		103.42

ILLUSTRATION 12.6

The easiest way of finding these 'discount factors' is to look them up in a present value table, as shown in Illustration 12.5.

We can then apply these discount factors to the cash flows of a particular project to find the 'present value' of the future cash flows, assuming a cost of capital of 10 per cent. This is applied to Jaggie and Lardie as shown in Illustration 12.6.

The cash flows in this illustration are from Illustration 12.6 in respect of Jaggie.

Year 1   Divide the cash flow by 1 + the discount rate. Divide the cash flow by 1.1 for a 10 per cent discount rate

$$\text{Cash flow } \frac{45}{1.1} = \text{£}40.91$$

Year 2   Divide the cash flow by 1.1 × 1.1 to allow for 2 years (i.e. 1.1 squared)

$$\text{Cash flow } \frac{40}{1.1 \times 1.1} = \text{£}33.06$$

$$\text{or } \frac{40}{(1.1)^2}$$

Year 3   Divide the cash flow by 1.1 × 1.1 × 1.1 to allow for 3 years (i.e. 1.1 cubed, or 1.1^3)

$$\text{Cash flow } \frac{35}{(1.1) \times (1.1) \times (1.1)} = \text{£}26.30$$

Year 4   Divide the cash flow by 1.1 × 1.1 × 1.1 × 1.1 to allow for 4 years (i.e. 1.1^4)

$$\text{Cash flow } \frac{10}{(1.1) \times (1.1) \times (1.1) \times (1.1)} = \text{£}6.83$$

Year 5   Divide the cash flow by 1.1 multiplied by itself 5 times to allow for five years (i.e. 1.1^5)

$$\frac{10}{(1.1)^5} = \text{£}6.21$$

ILLUSTRATION 12.7

After reducing all future cash flows using a 10 per cent discount factor, we can see that the total NPV for each of the projects is as follows:

Jaggie   £113.31 − £100 =   £13.31
Lardie   £103.42 − £100 =   £3.42

Although Lardie brings in more money than Jaggie, it is not worth waiting for. Jaggie earns enough to cover the cost of capital, and an extra £13.31. Lardie also covers its cost of capital, and has a positive NPV. But Jaggie has a greater NPV, and so is the better investment.

Discount rates can be applied in this way to most projects. Once the discount rate, or cost of capital has been decided, the best project is the one that produces the highest NPV.

If discount tables are not available, it is possible to work out the figures for Jaggie as shown in Illustration 12.7.

For those who are not particularly good at mathematics it is easier to use discount tables. But if you want to do it without tables, here are the three easy steps:

1 Decide on the discount rate, and add it to 1 as follows:

   5%   becomes   1.05
   10%   becomes   1.1
   15%   becomes   1.15

2 Multiply the figure given in (1) by itself once for year 1; twice for year 2; three times for year 3; four times for year 4 and so on.

3 Divide the cash flow for each year by the figure given in (2) above to 'discount' it to give the 'present value'.

When we have identified all the future cash flows, and then allowed for the delay in receiving them by 'discounting' them, we know the NPV of the future cash inflows. This can be compared with the amount of the initial outflow to see if the project has earned us the 10 per cent that we specified as the cost of capital. Investment decisions should be based on choosing those projects that give the maximum cash flows, after applying the appropriate discount rate. This is called the NPV.

d Discounted Cash Flow: Internal Rate of Return

With the NPV approach to investment appraisal, we need to select a discount rate; then the NPV of the project is calculated. With Jaggie the NPV was £13.31. With Lardie the NPV was £3.42. The answer will always be a sum of money[4] (it could happen to be zero).

If we do not know what discount rate to use, we could put the question the other way around: what discount rate would make future cash flows exactly equal to the amount of the initial investment? In other words, at what discount rate does the project break even, or give a zero NPV?

With the internal rate of return (IRR), we do not assume a discount rate. Instead we try to find a discount rate at which the NPV of the project is zero. The answer will always be a percentage. A quick glance at Jaggie and Lardie suggests that the IRR of Jaggie is well above

---

[4] The sum of money could be positive, negative, or zero.

Year	Jaggie Project Cash flow	Discount factor 20%	Net present value	Lardie Project Cash flow	Discount factor 15%	Net present value
0	(100)			(100)		
1	45	0.8333	37.50	10	0.8696	8.70
2	40	0.6944	27.78	20	0.7561	15.12
3	35	0.5787	20.25	30	0.6575	19.72
4	10	0.4823	4.82	40	0.5718	22.87
5	10	0.4019	4.02	45	0.4972	22.37
Total	140		94.37	145		88.78

ILLUSTRATION 12.8

10 per cent. As Lardie has a much smaller NPV, its IRR is likely to be not much above 10 per cent. In the calculations in Illustration 12.8, 20 per cent is chosen as a guess for Jaggie, and 15 per cent for Lardie.

When the cash flows of Jaggie and Lardie are discounted using higher discount rates, we can see that the totals amount to less than the £100 originally invested. Comparing these results with those shown using a 10 per cent discount rate we can say that:

Jaggie earns more than 10 per cent: it has a positive NPV of £13.31 when discounted at 10 per cent

Jaggie earns less than 20 per cent: it has a negative NPV of (£100 − £94.37 =) £5.63 when discounted at 20 per cent

Jaggie's IRR is between 10 per cent and 20 per cent; but it is closer to 20 per cent

Lardie earns more than 10 per cent: it has a positive NPV of £3.42 when discounted at 10 per cent

Lardie earns less than 15 per cent: it has a negative NPV of (£100 − £88.78 =) £11.22 when discounted at 15 per cent

Lardie's IRR is between 10 per cent and 15 per cent, but it is closer to 10 per cent

A better estimate of IRR can be made using interpolation.

We know that Jaggie's IRR is between 10 per cent and 20 per cent. It is 10 per cent plus a part of 10 per cent.

$$IRR = 10\% + \frac{13.31}{(13.31 + 5.63)} \times 10\%$$

$$= 10\% + 0.7 \times 10\%$$

$$= 17\%$$

We know that Lardie's IRR is between 10 per cent and 15 per cent. It is 10 per cent plus a part of 5 per cent.

$$IRR = 10\% + \frac{3.42}{(3.42 + 11.12)} \times 5\%$$

$$= 10\% + 0.24 \times 5\%$$

$$= 11.2\%$$

We can now compare the two investments, Jaggie and Lardie, using different approaches to investment appraisal.

	Jaggie	Lardie
Return on average investment	16%	18%
Payback period	2.14 years	4 years
NPV at 10%	£13.31	£3.42
Internal rate of return	17%	11.2%

Jaggie is clearly the better project. Lardie showed a better return on investment because it produces slightly more profits. But because Jaggie produces cash flows more quickly, it shows a shorter payback period, and it is better using DCF.

Advantages of using internal rate of return are:

1 It deals properly with the timing of all cash flows.

2 Seeing an answer as a percentage appears to be easy to understand and can be compared with a company's cost of capital.

3 It is difficult to know what a company's cost of capital is, and what discount rate should be used to calculate NPV. Using IRR sidesteps this. A company could simply rank all projects according to the IRR that each achieves; it would select the projects with the highest IRRs, and reject those with the lowest. Assuming that the company has only limited funds for investment, those funds would be allocated to the projects that have the highest IRR.

The main disadvantages of using internal rate of return are:

1 It involves more calculations than other methods.

2 It is technically flawed and can lead to incorrect decisions. This is particularly true where there are irregular patterns of cash flows (perhaps with inflows coming before outflows), and high discount rates.

A variety of different techniques for investment appraisal may be used. Sometimes the use of one technique rather than another can lead to a different, and perhaps a poor, investment decision. The best approach is to use DCF to calculate the NPV. In order to do this it is necessary to know what discount rate to use, or the 'cost of capital'.

Which Cash Flows to Include

It is easy to get lost in the technicalities and complications of DCF, and overlook the fact that the calculations can be no better than the basic data on which they are based. Estimates have to be made of the cost of the project, of the timing and amount of future cash inflows and outflows that it will generate, and the cost of capital. There is always an element of risk and uncertainty.

The appraisal should take into account all cash flows that would result from the project being undertaken, and exclude all cash flows that would arise whether or not the project is undertaken. There are a number of problem areas, including those shown below. It is important not only to have the best estimates of the amounts of the cash flows, but also to be clear about the timing of them.

1 *Working capital* Where a project involves expansion, there is usually a requirement for additional working capital (financing stocks and debtors) at the beginning, which is treated as a cash outflow. It is usually assumed that at the end of the project's life the additional working capital will no longer be required,[5] and so becomes a cash inflow.

2 *Installation* Where a new piece of equipment is being bought, the cash outflow for it should include any payments for installation and setting it up.

3 *Scrap values* If a new machine is being bought, there is often a cash inflow from the sale of the old machine. If this scrapping is a direct result of buying the new machine, then the cash inflow from the scrap value should be included in the appraisal. When the new machine comes to the end of its life we usually assume that there will be a cash inflow from selling it.

4 *Taxation* The amount of corporation tax to be paid should be included in the appraisal. This can be rather complicated[6] and there are two aspects to it.
   a If the project makes additional profits (which is usually the intention), additional corporation tax is payable.
   b The Inland Revenue allows profits to be reduced for tax purposes by substantial 'writing-down allowances' for depreciation[7] (usually more generous than the amounts that the company charges in their financial accounts).

Illustration 12.9 shows two methods of dealing with these amounts. Method 1 shows a single tax payment each year, with writing down allowances deducted from each year's profits. Method 2 deals with the writing down allowances separately from the tax on additional annual profits by calculating the amount for each year, discounting them, then deducting them from the initial cost of the asset. Method 2 is useful in 'sensitivity analysis' where the effects of differing assumptions are calculated.

5 *Relevant costs* Some costs will be incurred, and the payments made, whether or not the project is undertaken. A project may be charged its share of fixed overheads (e.g. the costs of providing a factory and its administration), but as those costs will be incurred whether or not the project is undertaken, the cash flows for fixed overheads are usually excluded.

6 *Sunk costs* There are often significant payments for market research and feasibility studies that are undertaken before a decision is made on whether or not to go ahead. As those costs have already been incurred or paid (they are 'sunk'), they are

---

[5] Inventories are sold; debtors pay up; there is an inflow of cash.

[6] Sometimes profit is made in one year, and the tax is paid in the following year. The actual timing of payments has to be taken into account in DCF computations.

[7] And 'balancing allowances': any 'loss' when the asset is sold at the end of its life. If it is sold at a 'profit', tax is payable on the excess of the sale proceeds over the amount to which it is written down for tax purposes.

irrelevant in deciding whether or not to go ahead, and should not be included in the appraisal.

7 *Opportunity costs* The cost of using an asset for a particular project is often the 'opportunity cost' and the best alternative use (see Illustration 12.10).

DCF and Taxation

A company is proposing to invest in a new machine that will cost £100,000. It will generate additional profits of £19,000 a year for 5 years. At the end of year 5 it is expected to have a scrap value of £10,000.

Corporation tax is 30 per cent of taxable profits; writing down allowance is 25 per cent per annum.

1 Calculate annual cash flows (before considering taxation).

Annual profits will be £19,000
Depreciation will be £90,000 ÷ 5 = £18,000 per annum
Cash flows (before considering taxation) will be £18,000 + 19,000 = £37,000 a year for the first four years, with an additional £10,000 in year 5.

2 Writing down allowance (WDA) is the amount calculated on the diminishing balance basis as follows:

Cost of asset	£100,000
Year 1 WDA 25%	25,000
	75,000
Year 2 WDA 25%	18,750
	56,250
Year 3 WDA 25%	14,062
	42,188
Year 4 WDA 25%	10,547
	31,641
Year 5 WDA 25%	7,910
	23,731
Proceeds of scrap	10,000
Balancing allowance	13,731

3 ***Method 1*** Calculate amount of tax payable based on profits after deducting writing down allowances. The DCF is then done on a single, all-embracing cash flow figure (see over).

ILLUSTRATION 12.9

Year	0	1	2	3	4	5
Profit before deducting depreciation		37,000	37,000	37,000	37,000	37,000
Writing down allowance		25,000	18,750	14,062	10,547	7,910
Balancing allowance						13,731
Taxable profit		12,000	18,250	22,938	26,453	15,359
Cash flows						
Tax payable (30%)		(3,600)	(5,475)	(6,881)	(7,936)	(4,608)
(Initial cost) annual CFs	(100,000)	33,400	31,525	30,119	29,064	32,392
						10,000
						42,392
10% discount factor	1.0	0.909	0.826	0.751	0.683	0.621
DCF	(100,000)	30,361	26,040	22,619	19,851	26,325
NPV						125,196
						(100,000)
						25,196

4 **Method 2** Two separate discounting calculations: (i) the cost of the asset together with the value of the taxation allowances, and the final scrap value; (ii) other cash flows, including profits, and the taxation on them.

Present value of writing down allowances

Year	0	1	2	3	4	5	Total
Writing down allowance		25,000	18,750	14,062	10,547	7,910	
Balancing allowance						13,731	
30% of WDA/ BA		7,500	5,625	4,218	3,164	6,492	
10% discount factor	1.0	0.909	0.826	0.751	0.683	0.621	
NPV		6,817	4,646	3,168	2,161	4,032	20,824

Cost of machine		£100,000
NPV of writing down allowances and balancing allowance		(£ 20,824)
Net cost of machine (after deducting taxation allowances)		£ 79,176
Deduct NPV of final scrap value £10,000 × 0.621		£ 6,210
NPV of net cost of machine		£ 72,966
Annual pre-depreciation profits	£37,000	
Deduct tax at 30%	£11,100	
Annual cash flows after tax	£25,900	
Annuity 10% for 5 years	× 3.791 =	£ 98,187
NPV		£ 25,221

The two different methods produce the same positive NPV of £25,200. There are slight rounding differences. The second method facilitates 'sensitivity analysis': the results of lower sales or higher costs can be calculated without changing the cost of the fixed asset.

ILLUSTRATION 12.9 continued

A company owns a machine that they originally bought for £100,000, and on which depreciation of £80,000 has been charged. They could sell it for scrap for £10,000; alternatively they could hire it out to another manufacturer, and the NPV of the rentals receivable for doing this would be £15,000.
   The net book value of £20,000 is irrelevant. The opportunity cost of using for another purpose is £15,000.

ILLUSTRATION 12.10

12.4 Cost of Capital

The preferred method of investment appraisal is 12.3(c) DCF – NPV, using a 'given' discount rate, perhaps 10 per cent. The best projects are those that show the highest NPV when discounted at 10 per cent. (In Illustration 12.6, Jaggie is better than Lardie.)

The choice of 10 per cent might almost be arbitrary and there is something to be said for having a clear policy: any project giving a positive NPV when discounted at 10 per cent is acceptable. This would work well if unlimited funds are available at a cost of no more than 10 per cent per annum. It is important to establish what the company's cost of capital is, to be used as a 'hurdle' rate, and there are various ways of approaching this.

1 *Opportunity cost* If there are plenty of projects available that show a positive NPV when discounted at 14 per cent, and only limited funds are available, then the hurdle rate should be 14 per cent, not 10 per cent. There is no point in tying up limited funds on projects that achieve only, say 11 per cent, if there is the opportunity to invest in projects that achieve 14 per cent or more. In Illustration 12.6 the company should not invest in a Lardie if they would then not have sufficient funds to invest in a Jaggie.

It is important that a company has a sensible hurdle discount rate for investment appraisal. If it is set too low, perhaps at 7 per cent, then the company is likely to invest in projects that barely earn their keep; that disappoint the owners of the business; and that result in the value of the business falling. If it is set too high, perhaps at 22 per cent, then the company is likely to reject projects that more than earn their keep. If projects that earn a good return are rejected, then the business loses opportunities to increase its value.

2 *Weighted average cost of capital* Companies are usually financed partly by borrowing, and partly by shareholders' funds. At first sight it is not difficult to establish the cost of borrowing: the interest rate on borrowings is usually specified. The cost of shareholders' funds is more difficult. As there is no requirement for companies to pay dividends on ordinary shares, we might be tempted to think that shareholders' funds have no real cost. They are 'free', and provided the company makes *some* profit, that is OK. But directors who do not meet shareholders' expectations in terms of profit will probably soon find themselves out of a job. Low profits lead to low share prices; low share prices invite takeover bids; and when another company acquires a company that is seen to be failing, they will soon get rid of the previous managers.

The cost of ordinary shareholders' funds depends on market expectations. The company should aim to invest in ways that increase the value of the company, not in ways that reduce it. Attempts to identify a company's cost of capital are attempts to identify the discount rate that projects must achieve in order to at least maintain the value of the company.

A company might be half-financed by borrowing, which costs 8 per cent per annum, and half-financed by shareholders' funds, which costs 14 per cent per annum. In this case the company's average cost of capital is 11 per cent. Another company might be 25 per cent financed by borrowing, which costs 8 per cent per annum, and 75 per cent financed by shareholders' funds, which costs 14 per cent per annum. In this case the company's weighted average cost of capital is 12.5 per cent.

$$25\% \times 8\% \quad = \quad 2\%$$
$$75\% \times 14\% \quad = \quad \underline{10.5\%}$$
$$\underline{12.5\%}$$

In calculating the weighting of the different types of capital (e.g. shareholders' funds 75 per cent; loan capital 25 per cent), it may be better to use the *market* value of shareholders' funds, and the *market* value of borrowings rather than the amounts shown on the balance sheet.

a *Cost of borrowing* A company might have issued £1 million of 10 per cent debentures, but that does not necessarily mean that the cost of those debentures is 10 per cent per annum. If the market value of debentures falls below the balance sheet value, the amount of interest payable remains the same, but the *effective* rate (interest payable as a percentage of market value) will be higher. Similarly, if the market value of debentures increases, the effective interest rate declines. A number of other factors have to be taken into consideration:

i Interest is an allowable expense for corporation tax purposes. If the company's effective rate of corporation tax is 25 per cent, then the effective cost of 10 per cent interest to the company is only 7.5 per cent.

ii Most debentures are redeemable at some future date, perhaps 5 or 10 years into the future. They may be redeemable at par (which is book value or face value); they may be redeemable at a discount (e.g. £100 debentures redeemable at £95), or they may be redeemable at a premium (e.g. £100 debentures redeemable at £110). The calculation of the cost of debentures can look like doing a DCF calculation to arrive at the internal rate of return as shown in Illustration 12.11.

b *Cost of equity (cost of ordinary shareholders' funds)* Establishing the cost of equity is more difficult: there is no requirement to pay dividends, and it might be tempting to think that there is no cost attached to shareholders' funds. Shareholders have money invested in the business, and if they are lucky they will receive dividends, and the value of their shareholdings will increase. If they are unlucky there will be no dividends, and the value of their shareholdings will decline.

In a small company, perhaps where all the equity is owned by one or two directors, they can do what they like. If they choose to regard shareholders' funds as having zero cost, and to invest in duff projects, that is their own business.

If a listed company decided that shareholders' funds are cost free, they might not produce enough profits or dividends; the market value of the shares would decline, and the directors will soon find their position threatened.

In order to determine the cost of a company's equity, we need to know what rate of return is needed to maintain, or increase, the value of the company. This really depends on shareholders' expectations. If they are expecting a return of 10 per cent, and the company generates 15 per cent, then the value of the company should increase. If they are expecting 15 per cent, and the company generates only 10 per cent, then we can expect the value of the company to decrease.

It is not clear how investors' expectations can be quantified. Even if we could find out what it is that determines future share prices, by the time we have found

The market value today of Air UK's 6% debentures is £80 for £100 par value. The debentures are redeemable at £105 4 years from today. The company is profitable and their effective rate of taxation is 30 per cent.

The cost of interest each year is 70 per cent of £6, which is £4.20. At first sight the cost of the loan capital looks like 70 per cent of £6 per annum, which is 4.2 per cent. But the effective cost is increased by the premium that is payable on redemption, and by the fact that the current market value of the debentures is well below the £100 par value.

The cash flows associated with it are shown in the second column below. As the cost of the debentures is likely to be more than 6 per cent, as a first guess we try discounting the cash flows at 10 per cent.

Year	Cash flow	Discount factor 10%	Net present value	Discount factor 15%	Net present value
0	(80)	1.0	(80)	1.0	(80)
1	4.2	0.9091	3.81	0.8696	3.65
2	4.2	0.8264	3.47	0.7561	3.18
3	4.2	0.7513	3.15	0.6575	2.76
4	109.2	0.6830	<u>74.59</u>	0.5718	<u>62.44</u>
			85.02		72.03

When discounted at 10 per cent, the future cash flows associated with the debenture are more than the price of the debenture now. The cost of the debentures to the company (in relation to the current market value) is, therefore, more than 10 per cent per annum.

When discounted at 15 per cent, the future cash flows associated with the debenture are less than the price of the debenture now. The cost of the debentures to the company (in relation to the current market value) is, therefore, less than 15 per cent per annum.

Interpolation suggests a cost of 10% + $\dfrac{5.02}{(5.02 + 7.97)} \times 5 =$ **11.9%**

If the company has nothing better to do with its money it should consider buying up the debentures on the stock market. But if the company's opportunity cost of capital is 12 per cent or more, it should be able to find a more profitable use of funds.

ILLUSTRATION 12.11

out, the picture would have changed; any model that predicts share prices, based on historic data, needs to be constantly updated to maintain credibility.[8] Sometimes companies seem to promise a lot, and their share price goes up and up. But if they then disappoint, the share price will collapse. It seems sensible to manage expectations: to plan and promise only what can be delivered with reasonable certainty.

In assessing shareholders' expectations, as in so many areas of accounting, we need to consider whether they should be expressed in terms of profit or cash flow. Return on capital employed and price/earnings (P/E) ratio are two indications of shareholders' expectations that are based on profits. The dividend growth model is based on dividends. The capital asset pricing model (CAPM) can also be used to assess a company's cost of capital. Companies should not undertake projects that are

---

[8] There is more chance of maintaining credibility than of revealing truth!

likely to lower the company's returns and share price. When they cannot find sufficiently profitable opportunities for investing available funds, they should return those funds to shareholders as dividends, or use them to buy up the company's shares. There are plenty of examples of companies that have invested surplus funds unwisely, and so have reduced the value of the company.

3 *Return on capital employed*   If a company has a return on capital employed of, say, 15 per cent, shareholders may expect this rate to continue in the future. If the company fails to achieve this, the share price is likely to fall. This does not, however, mean that the company's cost of capital for DCF purposes is 15 per cent. ROCE provides only a rough indication of shareholders' expectations, and there is no clear relationship between a company's return on capital employed and their cost of capital to be used for DCF.

4 *Price/earnings ratio (P/E)*   A company's P/E ratio is also an indication of investors' expectations about the future profits of a company. Where substantial growth is expected, the share price is likely to be high in relation to the current level of profits, and so the P/E ratio is high. Where growth in earnings is expected to be low, then the company's share price is likely to be low in relation to the current level of profits, and so the P/E ratio is relatively low. There is, however, no easy way to convert the P/E ratio into a cost of capital figure.

5 *Dividend growth model*   A company's share price in relation to the last known level of dividends is also a good indicator of shareholders' expectations. If a company has a low dividend yield, this means that the share price is high in relation to the last known level of dividends; shareholders' expectations are high, and future dividends are expected to grow at a relatively high rate. The growth rate in dividends over recent years can be calculated, and incorporated into a 'model', or formula, that indicates the cost of a company's equity capital, as shown in Illustration 12.12.

The cost of shareholders' funds is assumed to be the dividend yield on the shares (dividend expressed as a percentage of share price), adjusted for an assumed rate of growth.

Last year's dividend per share: 20p
Current share price: £5
Assumed rate of dividend growth: 15% per annum

1 Calculate next year's dividend: 20p + 15% = 23p
2 Express next year's dividend as a percentage of current share price: $\dfrac{23}{500} \times \dfrac{100}{1} = 4.6\%$
3 Add assumed rate of growth: 15% + 4.6% = 19.6%

Cost of equity capital is assumed to be 19.6%.

ILLUSTRATION 12.12

6 *Capital asset pricing model* (CAPM)   The CAPM assumes that the cost of capital is based on:

a 'risk-free' interest rate; to this is added

b an extra return to allow for the risk of investing in shares generally; this second element is adjusted to allow for

c the specific risk of a given company.

It is easy to find the 'risk-free' interest rate: it is the interest yield on government bonds, currently about 4 per cent.

The second element is more difficult to estimate, but we might say that in recent decades investors in ordinary shares have had returns of about, say, 8 per cent over and above the rate on government bonds.

The specific risk of a given company is measured as a 'beta', which might be average (1.0), or above average (say 1.2), or below average (say 0.8).

The cost of capital of a company with high risk might be:

$$4\% + (8\% \times 1.2) = 4\% + 9.6\% = 13.6\%$$

The cost of capital of a company with low risk might be:

$$4\% + (8\% \times 0.8) = 4\% + 6.4\% = 10.4\%$$

Calculations are complex, but the answers produced seem to be reasonable: typically the cost of equity may be between 10 per cent and 15 per cent per annum.

Evaluation of Different Approaches to Cost of Capital

It is difficult to establish the cost of ordinary shareholders' funds with any certainty, and without making some assumptions. Average returns on ordinary shares for the twentieth century can be calculated, and shareholders might expect this level of returns to continue. But in the first three years of the twenty-first century they were disappointed: returns on ordinary shares were negative, and share prices fell. In the following three years there was a return of growth. Although we do not know how long this will continue, it is reasonable to assume that there is little change in long-term expectations.

Estimates of the cost of borrowing are likely to be more accurate; and the cost of borrowing is likely to be lower than the cost of ordinary shareholders' funds because it is seen as being lower risk, and because interest is an allowable expense for corporation tax purposes.

Given that the cost of borrowing is likely to be lower than the cost of equity, it is worth calculating a weighted average cost of capital figure. This approach assumes that the more a company relies on borrowing, the lower its cost of capital is likely to be. But if a company relies too much on borrowing, the amount of risk increases, and this is likely to increase the cost of capital.

In practice many companies do not bother with the more sophisticated approaches to determining a 'correct' cost of capital figure. It is acceptable to choose a reasonable rate, and stick to it. For low-risk projects 10 per cent is acceptable. For higher-risk projects it could be increased up to about 15 per cent.

12.5 Uncertainty and Risk

All investment is based on assumptions about the future and there is usually some uncertainty about our forecasts, and a degree of risk. There are some 'risk-free' investments, such as lending money to the government by buying 'gilts'. But managers are more likely to be involved in evaluating projects where there is some uncertainty and risk in estimating:

1 The initial cost of the project: with major projects the initial capital expenditure often turns out to be much higher than was originally planned.

2 The cash inflows that the project will generate: forecasts may prove to be much too high, or much too low.

3 The cash outflows, including costs, that will be involved.

4 The timing: a project may take longer to be completed and to generate cash flows than was anticipated. And it is difficult to be sure how long a project will last. It is easy to 'assume' a 5-year life, but difficult to know how long it will really continue.

There are various ways of dealing with risk and uncertainty, all of which involve some subjectivity, but which help to give credibility to forecasts and appraisals.

One approach is to use a higher discount rate for projects that are seen as involving more risk than others. This is appealing but it is difficult to know how much extra risk there is, and by how much the discount rate should be increased.

A second approach, where there are several possible outcomes, is to apply probability theory to arrive at an 'expected value'. For example, if there is a 20 per cent chance that a cash flow will be £10,000, a 45 per cent chance that it will be £20,000 and a 35 per cent chance that it will be £30,000, the 'expected' cash flow can be calculated as follows:

$$20\% \times £10,000 = £\ 2,000$$

$$45\% \times £20,000 = £\ 9,000$$

$$35\% \times £30,000 = \underline{£10,500}$$

Expected cash flow £21,500

The actual cash flow for a particular project is unlikely to be the 'expected' figure calculated in this way. But if probabilities can be applied in this way to a number of different projects, on average the actual results are likely to be in line with what is expected. The problem is, of course, knowing what the probability is for any particular outcome.

A third approach is to recognize that a range of different outcomes is possible, and to produce one appraisal based on rather pessimistic assumptions, one based on rather optimistic assumptions and one 'realistic' appraisal between these two extremes. This may be attractive in terms of saying (a) this is the worst that is likely to happen; this is the downside risk; (b) this is the best that is likely to happen; and (c) this is what is most likely to happen. If (a) looks pretty dreadful, then a pretty good (b) might be needed to make the risk look worth while. This may give a useful 'feel' for a project, and provide a basis for considering other likely outcomes. It may not be too difficult to get agreement on a range of likely outcomes, which can help to get decisions made, but it is very subjective. There is no way of determining how dreadful the pessimistic assumptions should be, or how brilliant the optimistic assumptions should be.

A fourth approach is to use 'sensitivity analysis' to consider a wider range of different possible outcomes. The appraisal can be done again and again, using different assumptions, to see how sensitive it is to particular changes. It may be uncertain whether a project will last for 5 years, or 10 years, or somewhere in between. Sensitivity analysis might show that it is brilliant if it lasts for 10 years, but it is still viable if it lasts for only 5 years. It may be uncertain whether the initial project cost will be £1 million, or £2 million, or somewhere in between. Sensitivity analysis might show that it is a brilliant project if it costs only £1 million; a waste of money if it costs £2 million; and that, provided it does not cost more than £1.6 million, it is viable. Wherever there is uncertainty, the proposal can be recalculated to see how sensitive it is to a change in assumptions. This approach does not remove subjectivity, but it enables the financial effects of particular uncertainties to be quantified and provides a basis for judgement and decision-making.

Summary

In theory managers use investment appraisal techniques to ensure that a company's funds are used in ways that maximize shareholders' wealth. In practice managers may have their own agendas, favouring particular projects, seeking to impress their superiors, enhancing their reputation, increasing their personal remuneration packages and getting promotion by claiming credit for all that goes well, and blaming others for all that goes badly. It is easy to gain approval for a pet project by producing forecasts and appraisals that meet the company's criteria and show it as being viable. It is important that companies have 'post-investment appraisal' procedures in place that check if actual results are in line with the figures that were included in the appraisal, which the company approved. Successful managers will have done some, or all, of the following:

1 Made sure that actual results are in line with the original appraisals

2 Been promoted and transferred so that they are no longer around to take the blame

3 Kept a careful record of all the forecasts that made up the appraisal, and made sure that someone else is responsible for each element that made up the total appraisal. If the project does not come up to expectations, it is Bill's fault because the sales forecasts were wrong; or Jane's fault because she underestimated the original cost; or Jo's fault because production costs were way out of line.

Successful investment projects are the key to the financial success of a company, and to maximizing shareholder value. Management cannot avoid the results of their investment activities being assessed by the outside world through their published financial statements. For individual managers, taking credit for successful investment projects is important in success. All managers need to understand investment appraisals if they are to be the ones who take the credit, and not the ones who end up taking the blame. Good managers ensure that decisions are taken on the basis of information that is as honest as possible, with risks and uncertainties specified and taken into account. Good decisions are taken by responsible groups of managers who understand the limitations of the data, and the techniques used for appraising the data.

Review of key points

- The ROI of a project is calculated using profits, not cash flow, and is comparable with the return on capital employed for the company as a whole.
- The payback period is calculated using cash flows, not profits, and tells us how quickly a project is likely to pay for itself.
- DCF properly allows for the timing of cash flows.
- The NPV method of DCF is the preferred method of investment appraisal.
- It is necessary to know the company's cost of capital to use NPV.
- DCF calculations can be no better than the underlying data that are based on estimates, and there is always some risk and uncertainty.

Self-testing questions

1 How is ROI calculated?

2 The most recent annual report and accounts of the Row Sea Company shows that they made profit after tax of £1 million last year, and the balance sheet shows total shareholders' funds of £10 million. They are considering buying a ship that will cost £2 million and that will generate operating profits (after charging depreciation) of £180,000 a year.

   Would the investment increase the company's return on capital employed?

3 The PBP company has £1 million to invest, and are considering the following two projects:

   Project A will generate annual net cash flows of £200,000 for 8 years;

   Project B will generate cash flows of £400,000 in year 1, £350,000 in year 2, £300,000 in year 3, £100,000 in year 4, £50,000 in year 5, and then about £5,000 a year for another few years.

   On the basis of this information, and without considering DCF, which of the two projects is better?

4 What are the main advantages and disadvantages of using the following methods of investment appraisal:

   a ROI

   b Payback period

5 Is there a case for investing in the following project?

   A new machine costs £200,000 and will have a 5-year life with no residual value at the end. It is expected to generate profits of £35,000 a year for 5 years.

   What is the highest cost of capital at which the project would be acceptable?

Self-testing questions (continued)

6 The Peel Company is considering two alternative investment opportunities; a Kippering Project and a Queenies Project. Each would involve an initial outlay of £50,000 and is expected to have a 5-year life with no scrap value at the end. The additional cash flows (before deducting depreciation) that each project is expected to generate are as follows:

Year	Kippering	Queenies
	£	£
1	25,000	5,000
2	20,000	15,000
3	15,000	25,000
4	10,000	25,000
5	5,000	20,000

You are required to calculate the following for each project, and suggest how a decision should be made between the two projects:

a Average annual profits

b Return on initial capital employed

c Return on average capital employed

d Payback period

e NPV using 10 per cent discount factor

f NPV using 25 per cent discount factor

g An approximate internal rate of return

7 The Maroc Production Company is considering manufacturing and selling an economy video camera for use by small retailers for security purposes. A firm of management consultants has carried out a feasibility study for them at a cost of £25,000, which has not yet been paid. There would be two requirements for machinery:

a Some existing machinery could be modified at a cost of £100,000 to undertake the first stage of production.

b For the second stage of production, the company already has suitable machinery that is not in use; it has a book value of £80,000; it would be difficult to dismantle and dispose of, and its net realizable value at present is zero.

If the project goes ahead, maintenance costs of the machinery would be £10,000 per annum; there would be additional working capital requirements of £50,000 at the beginning of the project, which would be recovered at the end of 4 years; initial marketing costs, to be paid for as soon as soon as the project is approved, would be £60,000, and annual marketing costs would be £20,000 per annum for the full 4 years.

Self-testing questions (continued)

The costs and selling price per unit are expected to be:

	£	£
Selling price		60
Materials	11	
Direct labour	6	
Variable overheads	13	
General fixed overheads	12	
Interest	2	
		44
Profit		16

The management consultants have suggested that the product would have a 4-year life before being superseded by better cameras, and that the pattern of sales would be:

	Sales in units
Year 1	3,000
Year 2	7,000
Year 3	4,000
Year 4	1,000

The company's cost of capital is assumed to be 20 per cent per annum.

Making careful use of the above information, calculate the NPV of the project. Ignore taxation. Make and state appropriate assumptions where necessary.

Assessment questions

1 How is the payback period calculated? Why is it widely used although it can suggest wrong decisions?

2 The Leongwei Company decided that there would be no additional purchases of fixed assets unless they had been subject to investment appraisal and showed a positive NPV when discounted at 10 per cent. The policy was implemented 5 years ago, but the company's return on capital employed is still only 7 per cent per annum.

Explain the apparent inconsistency.

3 A project with an initial cost of £200,000 is expected to make profits of £44,000 per annum for 5 years, at the end of which it will have a scrap value of £20,000. Calculate:

a Average annual depreciation charge

b Average annual cash flows

c Payback period

Assessment questions (continued)

    d Total profits made during the five years

    e Return on initial investment

    f Return on average investment

    g NPV assuming a cost of capital of 20 per cent

    h Internal rate of return

4 Respirer Limited is a small company that specializes in the manufacture of electronic devices for surveillance purposes. Recently, they have been involved in producing devices to detect drugs, and the presence of live animals or humans, in import and export consignments. They have designed and produced a prototype of a device that they are calling the 'Kensington' and that can be worn by lorry drivers.

    A report from a large firm of management consultants suggests that in order to produce the device, the company will need to set up a new production line at a cost of £600,000, and that an old assembly shop could be used. The assembly shop originally cost £500,000 and depreciation on it of £350,000 has been charged, but it has not been used for a number of years. The company was planning to sell it for £120,000, but the consultants' report recommends that it is used to produce the new device; modifications to the workshop for this purpose will cost £80,000.

    The expected costs and selling price per unit of the Kensington are as follows:

	£	£
Selling price		110
Materials	18	
Labour	12	
Variable overheads	15	
General fixed overheads	8	
Interest	4	57
Profit		53

Anticipated sales in units are 5,000 in year 1; 10,000 in year 2; 16,000 in year 3; 12,000 in year 4 and 7,000 in year 5.

    Additional working capital requirements will be £250,000, which will be recovered at the end of the project. An initial advertising campaign costing £400,000 will be required at the beginning of the project; continuing marketing costs will be £130,000 per annum.

    It cost £80,000 to produce the prototype and those costs have been paid; the consultants' report cost £120,000, but those costs have not yet been paid.

    The company's cost of capital is 15 per cent.

    Making careful use of the above information, calculate the NPV of the project. Ignore taxation. Make and state appropriate assumptions where necessary.

5 The Bitchwood Company is considering two alternative investment proposals, details of which are as follows:

Assessment questions (continued)

		Proposal 1	Proposal 2
		£	£
Initial investment		100,000	120,000
Cash inflow	Year 1	35,000	30,000
	Year 2	30,000	30,000
	Year 3	30,000	35,000
	Year 4	25,000	50,000
	Year 5	15,000	40,000

Assume that the amount of the initial investment will be depreciated on a straight line basis over 5 years, and that there will be no residual value.

a Calculate for each proposal

  i Payback period

  ii Average annual profits

  iii Return on initial investment

  iv NPV using discounted cash flow and assuming a cost of capital of 10 per cent

  v Internal rate of return

b Which of the two projects would you recommend, and why?

Group activities and discussion questions

1 'The acceptability of an investment proposal depends on the company's cost of capital; a project that is acceptable to one company may not be acceptable to another.'

  'Accurate assessments of cost of capital are not possible; choosing a figure of between 10 per cent and 15 per cent is a reasonable approximation.'

  Explain, contrast and attempt to reconcile these statements.

2 With many well-publicized projects, it seems that proper investment appraisal techniques were not applied, were not possible or appropriate, or were ignored. Discuss this statement with reference to projects such as:

  a The Millennium Dome

  b Fees paid by telecommunications companies for third generation licences

  c The building for the Scottish Parliament in Edinburgh

3 To what extent is the proper use of investment appraisal techniques likely to stop the development of projects that are for the benefit of society?

4 Post-investment appraisal is essential to ensure that a company's investment appraisal techniques have been properly applied, but it is likely to reveal some uncomfortable facts. Discuss.

5 Sophisticated investment appraisal techniques are no substitute for sound judgement (or good luck). Discuss.

Group activities and discussion questions (continued)

6 Effective managers usually succeed in getting approval for the projects that they want. A knowledge of the company's investment appraisal procedures enables them to produce figures that ensure that projects will be approved. The existence of sound investment appraisal procedures does not to ensure that projected results are actually delivered. Discuss.

Financial accounting in context

Rail firm given two hours to sign £1bn deal

By Dominic O'Connell

Sunday Times, 6 August 2006

Discuss and comment on the following extract from the press, and what it reveals about the difficulties of implementing investment appraisal procedures in practice.

Source: Reproduced with permission by the *Sunday Times*.

THE SAGA OF GNER, the troubled train operator, took a fresh twist last night when it emerged that transport officials dramatically withdrew an offer of financial protection just hours before the company signed a £1.3 billion franchise agreement.

Rail sources said that GNER, owned by Sea Containers, was given a two-hour ultimatum either to sign the deal or see it snatched away and re-tendered.

GNER signed. But the deal has since gone sour and triggered a potential financial crisis at the company. GNER's problems have added to uncertainty over the future of Sea Containers, the Bermuda-registered transport group founded by tycoon James Sherwood, which is in the middle of a financial restructuring.

The drama unfolded in March last year when, after months of talks, GNER clinched a deal to continue running services between London and Scotland for 10 years. GNER agreed to pay £1.3 billion to the government over the franchise period.

Crucially, the franchise gave Sea Containers indemnity against the emergence of a rival operator, Grand Central Railways, a start-up rail firm that had lodged an application to start services on the line.

The safety net was revealed during a recent High Court case brought by GNER. Adrian Caltieri, planning and development manager, said the Strategic Rail Authority (SRA) had "immediately" offered protection when the question of Grand Central was raised.

"This protection was withdrawn by the SRA on 18 March 2005, just before GNER entered into the franchise agreement," he said.

Sources said transport officials withdrew the offer at a meeting in London, and gave GNER only two hours to sign up or see the franchise taken away. GNER accepted, and Grand Central was later given permission to start services. GNER challenged that decision in court, but lost.

Last night the Department for Transport would not comment on the detail of the negotiations, but said: "The franchise agreement is now in the public domain, and represents the final negotiated form of the agreement."

But GNER backed the claims of rail sources. It had included a competition "caveat" in its bid, which was withdrawn at the last minute, it said. "Obviously, being faced with such an ultimatum at the eleventh hour was a surprise, given the value that had previously been offered," a spokesman said.

"And the threat that the franchise would have to be re-tendered, if we did not sign there and then, put us in an impossible position.

"What is worse is that the verbal assurances that the SRA gave us at the time, that open access would not adversely affect GNER, have now been shown in the High Court to have been no use whatsoever."

References and further reading

Arnold, G. (2005) *Corporate Financial Management*. FT Prentice Hall.

Brealey, R.A., S.C. Myers and A.J. Marcus (2003) *Fundamentals of Corporate Finance* (4th edition). McGraw-Hill.

Dayananda, D., R. Irons, S. Harrison, J. Herbohn and P. Rowland (2002) *Capital Budgeting: Financial Appraisal of Investment Projects*. Cambridge University Press.

Drury, C. (2004) *Management and Cost Accounting*. Thomson Learning.

Lumby, S. and C. Jones (2003) *Corporate Finance: Theory and Practice* (7th edition). Thomson Learning.

CHAPTER 13

Planning, Decision-Making and Control

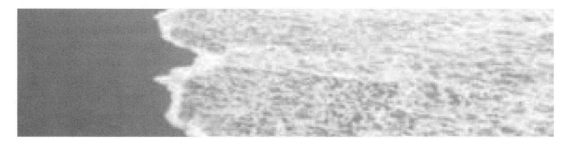

❖ LEARNING OBJECTIVES

After studying this chapter you should be able to:

❖ Explain the differences between financial accounting and management accounting

❖ Explain the functions and terminology of costing systems

❖ Produce and evaluate straightforward costing statements

❖ Understand and evaluate the differences between absorption costing and marginal costing

❖ Appreciate the assumptions on which costing information is based

❖ Explain the roles and functions of budgetary control systems and appraise their effectiveness

13.1 Introduction

Many businesses use financial accounting as a basis for planning future activities, making decisions between different courses of action, and for controlling their financial position and performance. They do not wait until the end of the year to see how things have turned out, after the balance sheet and income statement have been produced. Instead, they plan ahead. They decide what they want next year's financial results to look like. They set themselves a target,[1] perhaps to increase the return on share-holders' funds to 16 per cent, or to increase earnings per share to 13p. These objectives may be set out in the form of a planned or budgeted set of final accounts for next year, perhaps with a budgeted income statement, balance sheet and cash flow statement for each month. Then, as the year progresses, each month's actual results can be compared with what was planned. In this way some sort of financial control is established, and where the results that are actually achieved are not good enough, the need for corrective action becomes clear. This comparison and control takes place monthly, or more often.

Although financial accounting can provide a basis for planning, decision-making and control, a distinct area of accounting, called 'management[2] accounting' has developed. It includes costing systems and budgetary control systems, but the term may be used more widely to include all areas of financial management.

13.2 Management Accounting and Costing

Financial accounting has been developed within a framework of company law, mainly to provide information for shareholders and creditors rather than to provide information for the managers of a business. Managers can have whatever information they want as a basis for planning and controlling the business and making decisions. They do not need to rely on financial accounting, and systems of management accounting have been developed that differ from financial accounting in a number of ways, as shown in Table 13.1. Management accounting has developed from costing systems.

Costing systems were developed for two main reasons:

1 To establish the costs of producing different products.[3] This is needed to give some indication of what price should be charged for each product. It may also help to indicate which products are the most profitable, and which should be discontinued. But the approach traditionally used in financial accounting, *absorption costing*, can lead to misleading results, as shown below in Illustrations 13.1 and 13.3. It is better to use *marginal costing* in making such decisions

---

[1] They may have several targets, such as increasing market share, reducing short-term borrowings, and increasing profitability

[2] Or even 'managerial accounting', which may sound more impressive.

[3] Products or services, or orders, or contracts.

Financial accounting	Management accounting
Companies are required by law to produce financial accounting information	No formal requirements
The ways of producing and presenting the information are determined by company law and international accounting standards	No formal requirements. Statements are prepared in different formats for different purposes
Information is mainly a record of what has already happened	Information is a basis for decisions about the future and includes forecasts, plans and budgets
Emphasis on precise accuracy (balance sheets must balance) although this leads to delays in producing information	Emphasis on relevance and immediacy; approximations are acceptable
Information is intended mainly for users outside the organization, especially shareholders and creditors	Information is intended for directors and managers within the organization
Information is public	Information may be private
Published information is for the company as a whole (with some additional information for main segments)	More emphasis on detailed analysis
Annual reporting is a requirement (but monthly reporting is normal)	Emphasis on frequent production of control information

TABLE 13.1 Comparison of financial accounting and management accounting

2 To establish the cost of closing inventories.[4] This is needed for calculating profit. Gross profit is the difference between the revenue earned from sales, and the cost of the goods that have been sold. The cost of goods that have not been sold ('closing stocks'[5]) are carried forward to be shown as an expense in the following period; they are not charged as an expense until they are sold. Costs that have been incurred, therefore, have to be allocated between (a) cost of sales, which is treated as an expense on the income statement; and (b) closing inventory, which is carried forward on the balance sheet as a current asset.

Costing systems have also been developed to assist with other functions including:

3 Planning future activities, which includes detailed planning of costs

4 Controlling costs: if a business is to be profitable, it is important that costs do not spiral out of control, or beyond planned levels

5 Deciding between different courses of action. A costing system should produce information as a basis for such decisions, such as when a business considers investing in new machinery and needs to know how costs will change if one machine is used rather than another, or when considering reducing the price of a product with a view to selling more of it. Each decision requires costing information developed in a particular way[6] for the purpose of that decision.

---

[4] Or stocks.

[5] Or 'inventory'.

[6] It requires *relevant* costing information.

Costs of Producing Different Products

Illustration 13.1 shows an important problem in management accounting, and will be used to illustrate how conventional financial accounting information can be seriously misleading, if it is used to justify decisions that are foolish and damaging to the business.

At first sight the information looks credible and powerful. The story seems to be that the company is making only £13,000 a year profit. Tables and chairs are both profitable – they make £25,000 a year between them. But desks produce a loss of £12,000 a year. The obvious (but wrong!) conclusion is that the company should stop producing desks, and then their profit would increase from £13,000 to £25,000 a year.

A furniture manufacturing company produced three products last year, details of which are as follows:				
	Total **£000**	**Tables** **£000**	**Desks** **£000**	**Chairs** **£000**
Sales	757	254	276	227
Costs	744	240	288	216
Profit/(loss)	13	14	(12)	11

ILLUSTRATION 13.1

More detailed information about the costs is required before a sensible decision can be made. More detailed analysis is provided in Illustrations 13.3 and 13.4 below. The company will probably not be £12,000 better off if they stop making desks. They may even be worse off. Many of the costs of manufacturing furniture, such as providing the factory and all its machinery and the wages of supervisory staff, will remain much the same whether they produce desks or not. The share of those continuing costs that have been borne by desks will have to be charged to tables and chairs, if they stop making desks; then the other products might appear as loss makers.

Many different organizations face problems such as this. A university might find that their physics department is uneconomic: the total of all costs charged to the physics department is less than the revenues earned by that department. If the university then closes one department, many of the costs previously charged to it will continue at much the same level: all the central administration costs will continue; the university's computing system will probably continue as before (or be upgraded!); most of the costs of providing premises will continue at the same level (other departments or administrators will probably move into the premises previously occupied by physics). There will be savings on physics department staff costs, and on equipment, books and periodicals. But it is likely that the loss of revenues will be greater than any reduction in costs. Central administration charges then have to be reallocated to other departments, and perhaps another department will then appear to be uneconomic.

In most cases the use of conventional financial accounting (or 'absorption costing'[7]) information for decisions such as these is not appropriate. 'Marginal costing' usually provides a better basis for decision-making.

---

[7] Where total costs are charged to particular products, including 'fixed' overheads.

Cost of Closing Inventory

The Ragged Doll Company produced 10,000 dolls last year. They sold 8,000 of them for £20 each, bringing total revenues of £16,000.
  Total costs incurred by the company were £16,500.

ILLUSTRATION 13.2

In Illustration 13.2 the total costs incurred during the year (£16,500) were greater than the total revenues earned (£16,000), and it is tempting to conclude that they made a loss of £500. However, we must remember that the income statement shows that profit is calculated in two stages.

1 Gross profit is the difference between sales and the cost of goods sold.

2 The final profit figure is calculated after deducting all operating expenses, such as distribution costs and administrative expenses.

In order to calculate profit, we need to know how much of the £16,500 costs were costs of production (part of which is carried forward to the next year as 'closing stock'[8]), and how much was for operating costs[9] (which are all written off in the period in which they are incurred).

If we assume that £10,000 was for production costs, the remaining £6,500 was for operating costs. As only 80 per cent[10] of the dolls were sold, then only 80 per cent of the production costs are an expense of the current year; 20 per cent are carried forward to the next period. The income statement would appear as follows:

Sales revenue	£16,000
Production costs	£10,000
Deduct Closing stocks	£ 2,000
Cost of goods sold	£ 8,000
Gross profit	£ 8,000
Operating costs	£ 6,500
Profit	£ 1,500

An apparent 'loss' of £500 is, in accordance with normal accounting principles, a profit of £1,500. Establishing the figure for closing inventories is an essential part of profit measurement. If the figure is overstated, then profit is overstated. If the figure is too 'prudent', then profits are understated.

In a retailing organization it is relatively straightforward to calculate the cost[11] of closing inventories. In a manufacturing organization it is necessary to be clear which are production costs (a proportion of which is included in closing inventories), and which are operating

---

[8] Or inventory. The closing stock of one period becomes the opening stock of the next.

[9] Such as selling and distribution costs, and administrative expenses.

[10] 8,000 of the 10,000 produced.

[11] The net realizable value of inventories is, however, harder to establish, and closing stock should be shown at the lower of cost and net realizable value.

costs (which are treated as expenses when they are incurred). In order to arrive at a closing stock figure (which is necessary to calculate cost of sales, and to calculate profit), we need to *classify costs*.

Classification of costs

Costs may be classified in many different ways, but one of the most important distinctions is between *production costs* and *operating expenses.*

1 Production (or manufacturing, or factory) costs. At the end of the year some of these costs become part of cost of sales[12] on the income statement; and part is carried forward as closing inventory (to become the opening inventory, part of cost of sales, for the next period).

2 Operating expenses (or costs, or overheads) are all treated as expenses during the period in which they are incurred. They include selling and distribution costs, and administrative expenses. They do not include production overheads.

Absorption Costing

Absorption costing is intended to ensure that each product[13] bears its fair share of costs, and it has to be used in financial accounting to establish the amount for closing stock that should be carried forward to the following period. But absorption costing does not usually provide a good basis for making decisions; costing information that is more *relevant* is required. In Illustration 13.1 the company may consider giving up the production of desks because the costing information, on the face of it, shows them as making a loss. But it is worth investigating what costs have been charged to desks. A more detailed analysis, using absorption costing, is provided in Illustration 13.3. In examining these figures it is worth asking how fair and accurate the charges are to each product, and how relevant the resulting figures are.

	Total £000	Tables £000	Desks £000	Chairs £000
Sales	757	254	276	227
Direct materials	300	100	120	80
Direct labour	160	50	60	50
Prime cost	460	150	180	130
Production overheads	160	50	60	50
Production cost	620	200	240	180
Distribution and administrative overheads	124	40	48	36
Total costs	744	240	288	216
Profit	13	14	(12)	11

ILLUSTRATION 13.3 Absorption costing

[12] Or cost of goods sold.

[13] Or customer, or batch, or service.

Direct materials

This includes all the materials and components that become part of the finished product. Most organizations have a paperwork system that charges direct materials to particular jobs or customers. A builder should know how much is spent on bricks, cement, wood and fittings to construct a particular house. When a car is repaired the garage makes a point of producing a bill for the customer that details all the components and materials that have been used on that particular job.

Direct Labour

This includes the cost of people working directly on the product. There is usually a paperwork system that records how much time each employee spends on a particular job.[14] A builder should record what work each bricklayer, plasterer, joiner and so on is doing; that a particular job uses a bricklayer for 30 hours; a plumber for 20 hours; and so on. And the hourly rate of pay for each category of employee is easy to establish. Mechanics working in a garage have to record how much time is spent on each job, and the hours are clearly shown on the bill that is presented to the customer.

Prime Cost

Prime cost is simply the sum of direct material and direct labour costs.[15]

Production[16] Overheads

These are all the production costs (excluding direct materials and direct labour) that are counted as being part of the cost of the goods sold. They do not include general administrative, selling and distribution overheads. In a factory, production overheads would include rent, rates, lighting, heating and maintenance of the premises; the depreciation and maintenance of machinery; the costs of indirect labour in the factory, such as supervisors, storekeepers, maintenance staff and forklift truck drivers. The total cost of production overheads is easy to establish, but it is difficult to decide how much should be charged to each different product, and what basis would be 'fair'. In Illustration 13.3 production overheads have been charged to each product in proportion to direct labour costs. In this straightforward example the total labour costs happen to equal the total of production overheads, and so we can say that the overheads are charged to individual products using an overhead recovery rate of 100 per cent on direct labour.

There are many different ways of charging production overheads to different jobs, all of which are rather crude attempts at being fair. In modern, highly automated production

---

[14] Even with accountants, solicitors and architects who may not like to think of themselves as 'direct labour'. But where they work in professional practice, their time is directly charged to particular clients or jobs; it is the secretaries and receptionists who are the overheads. In a factory, however, the cost of accountants is part of administrative expenses.

[15] Prime cost sometimes also includes some 'direct expenses'. Most costs of equipment are included in production overheads; sometimes a special-purpose piece of equipment might be required for a particular job; the cost of hiring that equipment is then a 'direct expense' of that job. It is not included in general production overheads (which are spread out across the cost of all jobs).

[16] Sometimes called manufacturing, or factory, or workshop overheads.

processes, production overhead costs may be many times greater than labour costs. If overheads are charged out to different jobs on the basis of labour costs, the 'overhead recovery rate' could be much more than 100 per cent on direct labour; perhaps 500 per cent, or 1,000 per cent. Where labour costs are small in relation to production overheads a huge dollop of overheads, added to prime cost, can seem rather arbitrary and hard to justify.

Distribution and Administrative Overheads

It is also very difficult to arrive at any 'fair' basis for charging selling and distribution overheads to different products. In Illustration 13.3 they have been allocated on the basis of the total production cost of each product.[17] This may be an effective way of ensuring that each product bears a share of these overheads, but it is rather arbitrary, and may not be a sensible basis for making decisions (such as what the selling price for each product should be, or whether to discontinue a product).

Distribution and administrative overheads are all written off (treated as an expense) in the period in which they are incurred. A proportion of these costs is *not* included in closing stock (unlike production overheads, which have to be apportioned between cost of sales, and closing stock).

The above information is based on *absorption costing*, which is the traditional financial accounting approach to deal with costing information. For decision-making purposes *marginal costing* is likely to be more useful. Absorption costing information seems to suggest that the company should stop making desks, as if all the costs charged to desks would suddenly cease. A more useful analysis of costs would show which are:

1 Fixed costs, which would continue at much the same level, whether or not desks are produced. Such costs would include the rent, rates, lighting and heating of the factory, most of the costs of supervisory staff, and most machinery and maintenance costs

2 Variable costs, which vary directly in line with the volume of production. If the company stopped making desks, they would save all the costs of direct materials and direct labour. There would also be some reduction in production overheads – less power would be used, maintenance costs would probably be lower (if the machinery is used less), and there might be a reduction in 'indirect labour' costs (supervisors and others in the factory who are not direct labour).

When using costing information to make decisions, it is useful to be able to separate fixed costs from variable costs. Ways of doing this are outlined in the section on marginal costing below. The figures from Illustration 13.3 are presented in a marginal costing format in Illustration 13.4. Here it is assumed that production overheads are half-fixed, and half-variable, and that distribution and administrative overheads are mainly fixed (£78,000 fixed; £46,000 variable).

---

[17] Total production costs are £620,000. Distribution and administrative overheads are £124,000, which is 20 per cent of total production costs. The 20 per cent rate is then applied to the production cost of each product: for tables 20 per cent of £200,000 is £40,000.

	Total £000	Tables £000	Desks £000	Chairs £000
Sales	757	254	276	227
Variable costs				
Direct materials	300	100	120	80
Direct labour	160	50	60	50
Production overheads	80	25	30	25
Production costs	540	175	210	155
Distribution and administrative overheads[18]	46	15	18	13
Total variable costs	586	190	228	168
Contribution	171	64	48	59
Fixed costs				
Production overheads	80			
Distribution and administrative overheads	78			
Total fixed costs	158			
Profit	13			

ILLUSTRATION 13.4 Marginal costing

The following points emerge from the marginal costing presentation:

1 Each of the three products makes a 'contribution' towards fixed costs. Those costs will be incurred whether or not desks are made.

2 Desks make a contribution of £48,000. It might be 'fairer' if desks made a larger contribution. But if the company stops making desks, they will be £48,000 worse off;[19] and their (modest) overall profit would become a loss.

3 Using marginal costing, variable costs are charged to each product; but fixed costs are dealt with only in total (not charged to individual products).

4 *Contribution* may be defined as sales minus variable costs, and it is worth calculating it for each product.

5 *Contribution* is also equal to fixed costs plus profit; but fixed cost and profit are not shown for each product.

6 The above may be summarized as sales minus variable costs equals contribution, which equals fixed costs plus profit. This may be expressed as:

---

[18] Distribution and administrative overheads have been allocated to each product in proportion to total variable production costs. £46,000 is 8.52 per cent of £540,000; that percentage has been applied to the total variable production cost for each item; 8.52 per cent of 175,000 is £14,900, rounded to £15,000; 8.52 per cent of £210,000 is £17,900; 8.52 per cent of £155,000 is £13,200. Businesses are free to allocate overheads on whatever basis seems most appropriate to them.

[19] Unless they replace desks with a more profitable product, or increase the selling price of desks.

$$S - V = C = F + P$$

or

$$S - V = F + P = C$$

Absorption costing and marginal costing systems each provide information that is useful for different purposes.

13.3 Absorption Costing

Absorption costing is based on the idea that each product[20] 'absorbs' all the costs of production; both fixed costs and variable costs. Distribution and administrative overheads are not 'absorbed' by products, although they may be charged out in some way to make each bear its fair share of total costs.

In Illustrations 13.1 and 13.3, production overheads were charged out to different products on the basis of direct labour costs. Other bases may be used.

In Illustration 13.1, the same overhead recovery rate was used throughout the factory. In practice it is likely that some parts of the factory are more labour-intensive than others; some parts involve more expensive machinery, and so have higher production overheads in relation to labour costs. A factory is divided into a number of cost centres, such as a machining department, an assembly department and a finishing department; each of these can have a different overhead recovery rate, or even a different method of recovering overheads. A highly mechanized department is likely to have higher production overheads than one which is labour-intensive with relatively little machinery. This is shown in Illustration 13.5.

Cost Centres

The production overhead cost of each cost centre is established by *allocation* and *apportionment* of particular production overheads. Some costs may be specifically recorded for each cost centre, and so they can be allocated specifically and accurately to each cost centre. Supervisory staff may belong to a particular cost centre; electricity meters may record the power consumption of each cost centre; and the costs of maintaining machinery may be recorded for each machine and cost centre. Other costs are *apportioned* to cost centres on some arithmetic basis. Rent, rates, insurance, factory maintenance and heating and lighting may be apportioned to each cost centre on the basis of the number of square metres it occupies. The cost of supervisors and other staff costs may be apportioned to each cost centre in relation to the number of direct labour employees in each cost centre. Once the production overheads for each cost centre have been established, they are *absorbed* by (charged to) individual products.

---

[20] Or job, or batch, or order, or client.

The Dream-Kit Manufacturing Company is divided into three cost centres, details of which are as follows:

Budget for next year	Total/ average	Machining department	Assembly department	Finishing department
Production overheads	£1,140,000	£500,000	£400,000	£240,000
Direct labour cost	£460,000	£100,000	£200,000	£160,000
Percentage direct labour cost overhead recovery rate	248%	500%	200%	150%

ILLUSTRATION 13.5

In the Dream-Kit Manufacturing Company, it would be possible to take the *total* production overheads for the year and express them as a percentage of *total* labour costs, and arrive at an *average* overhead recovery rate of 248 per cent of labour cost, as shown in Illustration 13.5.

Production overheads, at 248 per cent of labour cost, would amount to about £377, using the average overhead recovery rate for the factory as a whole. It might be more accurate to use a different overhead recovery rate for each cost centre.

The machining department has very high production overheads in relation to direct labour costs, and the appropriate direct labour overhead recovery rate in that department would be 500 per cent. The finishing department has relatively low production overheads in relation to direct labour costs, and the appropriate direct labour overhead recovery rate in that department would be only 150 per cent. If the factory makes a number of different products, some of which require a lot of machining, and others which require more finishing than machining, it would not be fair to charge both with the same overhead recovery rate.

The table in Illustration 13.5 shows that each department could use a different percentage of direct labour cost as a way of charging production overheads to different products. A product that incurs high labour costs in the machining department would be charged much more for production overheads than one that incurred high labour costs in the finishing department.

It is clear that different departments have different levels of production overheads, partly because some have more machinery that is expensive to operate than others. It is perhaps reasonable to say that different products should be charged with overheads in relation to the time that they spend in each department.

The Dream-Kit Manufacturing Company wants to calculate the cost of manufacturing a new product, the Fantasy-Box. Each unit will incorporate components costing £10 and will incur direct labour costs as follows:

Direct labour	Machining	5 hours @ £20 =	£100
	Assembly	2 hours @ £10 =	£ 20
	Finishing	2 hours @ £16 =	£ 32
			£152

ILLUSTRATION 13.6

Using a different overhead recovery rate for each cost centre would show production costs of the company's new product, the Fantasy-Box (see Illustration 13.6), as follows:

Production overheads	Machining	500% of £100 =	£500
	Assembly	200% of £ 20 =	£ 40
	Finishing	150% of £ 32 =	£ 48
			£588

We now have two different versions of production cost:

	One cost centre	Three cost centres
Direct materials	£ 10	£ 10
Direct labour	£152	£152
Production overheads	£377	£588

The second method, using a different overhead rate for each cost centre, should be more realistic. It demonstrates that using more detailed analysis can produce very different overhead figures for a given product. The overheads to be charged to the Fantasy-Box have gone up from £377 to £588 because of changes made in the costing system. This could result in the product being seen as unviable.

In the above illustration, production overheads were charged to individual products on the basis of their labour *cost*. An alternative approach would be to do the calculation on the basis of labour *hours*.[21]

Many organizations charge customers using a combined labour overhead recovery rate. If a lawyer charges £200 an hour, that amount is calculated to cover overheads, not just the hourly rate the solicitor is paid. When a garage charges £50 per hour for repairing a car, the rate is not the amount paid to the mechanic; it is the mechanic's wage, plus an hourly rate to cover overheads.[22]

There are other ways of charging the production overheads of individual cost centres to particular products. Instead of using labour cost it is possible to use labour hours. In Illustration 13.6 the people working in the machining department are paid £20 per hour, perhaps because they are more skilled. In the assembly department they are paid only £10

---

[21] Using direct labour hours

Budget for next year	**Total/ average**	**Machining department**	**Assembly department**	**Finishing department**
Production overheads	£1,140,000	£500,000	£400,000	£240,000
Direct labour cost	£460,000	£100,000	£200,000	£160,000
Hourly pay rate		£20	£10	£16
Direct labour hours	35,000 hrs	5,000 hrs	20,000 hrs	10,000 hrs
Direct labour hour overhead recovery rate		£100	£20	£24

If production overheads are charged on the basis of the hours worked in each department, the amounts will be:

Production overheads
Machining	5 hours @ £100 =	£500
Assembly	2 hours @ £20 =	£ 40
Finishing	2 hours @ £24 =	£ 48
		£588

[22] And profit!

per hour, perhaps because they are less skilled. If we assume that a particular product incurs overhead costs in relation to the amount of *time* it spends in a particular department (which is different from the amount of labour cost in that department), we can use a direct labour hour overhead recovery rate. Two different approaches to dealing with overheads will produce two different cost figures, as the illustration shows.

Management should attempt to use the method of recovering overheads that most fairly or accurately reflects the costs incurred by each product in each cost centre, but there is no certain 'right' answer. And there are many variations and areas for subjectivity. Even within a given cost centre, the rate at which a product incurs overhead costs can vary, and an organization can be divided into any number of cost centres. Production overheads may be charged in different ways in different cost centres. Some may use a percentage on direct labour cost; some may use direct labour hours. Where there is particularly expensive machinery, a 'machine hour rate' may be used. The resulting cost figure, which somehow acquires credibility with management, can be a hotchpotch of several different approaches, each with a subjective or even arbitrary element.

A more sophisticated (or complex[23]) approach would be to use several different approaches at the same time, even within a given cost centre. Organizations may attempt to define different activities that are deemed to determine the amount of overheads that should be charged to a particular product. Some products may be charged more for overheads (regardless of labour cost or labour hours) because they require a particularly large number of components, or because machinery has to be reset several times during the production process, or because they require additional inspections. All these activities can be described as 'cost drivers', and an average cost per component issued, or per machine resetting, or per inspection can be calculated. Production overheads are then charged to individual products on the basis of these cost drivers, based on the different activities that incur production overheads. This approach is called 'activity-based costing', which is a more complex system of charging out costs, intended to be more accurate.

Evaluation of Absorption Costing

Absorption costing is the required method for valuing closing stocks. It is also useful in ensuring that all costs are 'recovered': that means charging every cost to a job or customer. If a business allocates only some of its costs to jobs, they could end up showing that all their jobs make some sort of contribution to overheads, but overall they make a loss.

The process of charging out all costs inevitably involves approximations and arbitrary elements. The basis for charging is usually established at the beginning of the year, based on budgeted figures. As the year goes by, actual figures are likely to be different from budgeted figures, and the amount of overheads charged to jobs during the year is likely to be different from the amount of overheads actually incurred. At the end of the year there are usually 'under-recovered' or 'over-recovered' overheads.

Developments such as activity-based costing are intended to make overhead charges more accurate. In Illustration 13.7 central overhead costs are allocated to three different

---

[23] Or perhaps (deliberately?) impenetrable.

cost centres on a single, simple basis (as a percentage of sales revenue), which ignores the factors that really 'drive' costs. Activity-based costing attempts to identify the 'drivers' for each cost, so that, for example, delivery costs are allocated to the different depots on the basis of miles covered (rather than being lumped in with other costs and allocated on the basis of sales revenue).

The Brigstow Autoparts Company operates from a main warehouse in Brigstow and imports spare parts for specialist sports cars, and sells them via three distribution depots; one in England, one in Wales, and one in Scotland. The company's budget for the coming year is summarized as follows:

	England £000	Wales £000	Scotland £000
Sales	10,000	8,000	6,000
Cost of sales	5,600	4,600	3,800
Gross profit	4,400	3,400	2,200
Local operating costs	2,720	2,660	1,620
Operating profit	1,680	740	580

Brigstow: Central costs

	£000
Warehouse	
Depreciation	200
Storage	160
Operating and despatch	240
Delivery	600
Head office	
Salaries	400
Advertising	160
Establishment	240
	2,000

Central costs are allocated to the three distribution depots as a percentage of the sales revenue of each depot, as follows:

	£000
Total sales	24,000
Total central costs	2,000
Central costs as a percentage of sales	8.33% (one twelfth)

	England	Wales	Scotland
Central costs	833	667	500
Operating profit	1,680	740	580
Net profit (loss)	847	73	80
Total £1,000,000			

Following the popularity of activity-based costing, management have decided their usual approach to allocating central overheads to the different distribution depots is too crude and simplistic, and that each category of central costs should be allocated in accordance with cost drivers (what it is that really incurs the costs at each depot). These have been defined as follows:

ILLUSTRATION 13.7

Depreciation: in proportion to the amount of space occupied
Storage: in proportion to the amount of space occupied
Operations and despatch: in proportion to the number of despatches
Delivery: in proportion to the number of delivery miles
Salaries: 10% of their time is spent on warehouse issues; the remainder is divided equally among the three depots
Advertising: to be allocated in proportion to sales
Establishment: to be allocated on the same basis as salaries.

The necessary information for the three depots is as follows:

	England	Wales	Scotland
Number of despatches	550	450	520
Total delivery distances (000 miles)	70	50	90
Storage space occupied (%)	40	30	30

The illustration continues as Self-testing question 4 on page 367.

ILLUSTRATION 13.7 continued

However, whatever methods of allocating overheads are used, and however complex they are, there is inevitably an arbitrary element, and, in making any particular decision, it is best to ensure that only the most appropriate or relevant specific costing information is used for that particular purpose. It is not possible to develop a costing system that produces costs that are accurate for all purposes.

13.4 Marginal Costing and Break-Even Analysis

The use of marginal costing was shown in Illustration 13.4. It is based on the idea of separating fixed costs from variable costs. Fixed costs stay much the same whether the volume of production is increased or decreased; the rent paid for a factory, or the cost of lighting and heating in it, are likely to stay the same whether production is increased by 20 per cent or reduced by 20 per cent. Variable costs vary directly in line with the volume of production; the cost of direct materials and direct labour will increase by 20 per cent if the volume of production increases by 20 per cent.

Many costs are, however, semi-fixed, or semi-variable. If the volume of production is increased by 20 per cent, there will be additional wear and tear on machinery, and the cost of power and maintenance are likely to increase, but not by as much as 20 per cent. It is not usually possible simply to categorize some costs as fixed and others as variable. It is easier to study their behaviour: identifying the amount by which costs increase when the volume of production increases.

Marginal costing is valuable for decision-making, but it is based on a number of simplifying assumptions and, like all accounting information, should be interpreted with care, bearing in mind its limitations. A straightforward example is provided in Illustration 13.8.

The Eat41 production company produced 1,000 frozen meals in September, and 1,100 in October. Total production costs were £2,500 in September and £2,600 in October.

Absorption costing would simply add up the costs, and divide them by the number of units produced, as follows:

	September	October
Production costs	£2,500	£2,600
Units produced	1,000	1,100
Cost per unit	£2.50	£2.36

ILLUSTRATION 13.8

Clearly, there are economies of scale: as the volume of production increases, the cost per unit falls. But marginal costing would make this more specific by separating variable costs from fixed costs. When the units produced increased by 100, production costs increased by £100, indicating that variable costs are £1 per unit. Fixed costs can be calculated by deducting variable costs from total costs and are, by definition, the same for each month.

Managers might want simple answers to simple questions such as 'How much does it cost to produce a meal?' Part of the answer should be 'It depends how many meals we produce'.[24] Marginal costing will tell us that the variable cost of producing a meal is £1, but that does not tell us anything about how much should be charged to cover overhead costs. Absorption costing tells us a cost per unit, but the cost keeps changing as the level of output changes and overheads are spread across different numbers of units produced. The answer to how much something costs to produce also depends on how overheads are dealt with.[25]

	September	October
Units produced	1,000	1,100
Variable costs[26]	£1,000	£1,100
Production costs	£2,500	£2,600
Fixed production costs	£1,500	£1,500

Similar calculations can be made, comparing the results of two months, even where we do not know the number of units produced.[27] If we look at the *difference* between the costs of one month and the costs of another, we know that amount is the variable costs (because fixed costs do not vary). We can use the sales figure to indicate the change in volume from one month to the next, as shown in Illustration 13.9, and calculate variable costs as a percentage of sales.

---

[24] Given our existing facilities and fixed production costs. These could, of course, be changed.

[25] It also depends on the purpose for which the costing information is required.

[26] Variable costs are £1 per unit.

[27] Or where the items produced are so different from each other that the idea of 'units' is irrelevant.

The sales and profit figures of the Building Repair Company were as follows:

	November	**December**
Sales	£250,000	£300,000
Profit	£40,000	£70,000

ILLUSTRATION 13.9

At first sight it seems that there is too little data in Illustration 13.9 to derive any significant information. But we can calculate total costs simply by deducting profit from sales. Then we can see by how much total costs have increased.

	November	**December**	**Increase**
Sales	£250,000	£300,000	£50,000
Profit	£ 40,000	£ 70,000	
Total costs	£210,000	£230,000	£20,000

When sales increase by £50,000, costs increase by £20,000. As fixed costs do not increase, all of the increase must be in variable costs. We can now see that variable costs represent 40 per cent of sales,[28] and we can use this to calculate the variable costs for each month. This can be deducted from total costs to show the amount of fixed costs per month, which should be the same for each month.

	November	**December**	**Increase**
Sales	£250,000	£300,000	£50,000
Profit	£ 40,000	£ 70,000	
Total costs	£210,000	£230,000	£20,000
Variable costs[29]	£100,000	£120,000	
Fixed costs	£110,000	£110,000	

When we know that variable costs are 40 per cent of sales, we can say that contribution (fixed costs plus profit) is 60 per cent of sales.

Break-Even Point

It may be useful to know at what point a business or product will 'break even', the level at which they make neither profit nor loss.

In Illustration 13.8, we know that the variable cost per meal is £1. If we assume that the selling price per meal is £3, then each meal makes a contribution of £2 towards fixed costs. We know that fixed costs amount to £1,500 per month. We, therefore, need to sell 750[30] meals per month in order to break even.

---

[28] £20,000 is 40 per cent of £50,000.

[29] Forty per cent of sales.

[30] 750 meals × £2 per unit contribution = £1,500, which is just enough to cover fixed costs and break even.

$$\text{Break-even point (in units)} = \frac{\text{Fixed costs}}{\text{Contribution per unit}}$$

We can also calculate the break-even point even where figures for units are not available or appropriate. In Illustration 13.9 we know that 60 per cent of sales is contribution (and 40 per cent is variable cost). We know that fixed costs are £110,000 per month; this is divided by the 60 per cent contribution/sales ratio[31] to calculate the break-even point.

$$\text{Break-even point (in £ sales)} = \frac{\text{Fixed costs}}{\text{Contribution/sales ratio}}$$

$$\text{Break-even point of the Building Repair Company} = \frac{£110,000}{0.6}$$

$$= £183,333$$

This can be 'proved' as follows.

	£
Sales	183.333
Variable costs (40% of sales)	73,333
Contribution	110,000
Fixed costs	110,000
Profit	0

During November their sales level was £250,000; this could fall by quite a lot (£66,666[32]) before they would risk making losses. Any further fall in sales, beyond the margin of safety of £66,666, would result in losses. In December sales increased to £300,000, and so the 'margin of safety' also increased (by £50,000) to £116,666.

January is often a very quiet month in the building trade and, even if a business is profitable for most of the year, the sales level could easily fall below the break-even point in January. If the Building Repair Company is concerned that January might be a loss-making month, they could consider boosting turnover in order to cover fixed costs by taking on work at lower prices for that month. At present most jobs are making a contribution of 60 per cent of the selling price towards fixed costs that will be incurred whether or not that work is done. If they lower quoted prices for January, they could still be making a contribution towards fixed costs and profit. It is necessary to separate fixed costs from variable costs in order to calculate the extent to which price reductions are appropriate.

In deciding between different courses of action, it is important to remember that some costs are fixed, regardless of the decisions being considered. Other costs are variable; they will change in relation to any decision to expand or reduce production. The most *relevant* costs should be considered, that is those that will be changed if a particular decision is taken.

---

[31] The contribution/sales ratio may be expressed as a percentage (60 per cent) or as a decimal (0.6). It is sometimes known as the profit/volume ratio, perhaps because once the volume of sales is above the break-even point, all of the contribution is profit.

[32] £250,000 − £66,667 = £183,333.

13.5 Evaluation of Absorption Costing and Marginal Costing

Absorption costing (or full costing) is the traditional financial accounting approach. It is the required method for valuing closing stocks and so for profit measurement in financial accounting. It is intended to ensure that all products, jobs and orders bear their fair share of overheads, and discourages the idea of cutting prices to obtain additional business.

In recent years production processes have become more automated and computer-controlled; this has resulted in much higher production overheads, and lower direct labour costs. This means that production overheads, as a percentage of direct labour costs, can be extremely high. As a result of this, a minor change in direct labour costs can have an exaggerated effect (when overheads are added) in the calculation of total production cost. Approaches in dealing with production overheads have become more sophisticated, usually aided by using spreadsheets, with more cost centres, each with different overhead absorption rates, and even with different methods of charging out overheads. With activity-based costing several different methods of charging out overheads within each cost centre are used. The emerging picture is steadily becoming more fair and accurate (and complex and impenetrable), but there is inevitably an arbitrary element, based on averages and approximations.

Absorption costing produces information that can easily lead to 'wrong' decisions. A product may be shown as unprofitable, and a business may consider dropping it. But marginal costing might show that the product is making a 'contribution' and that it is worth continuing with.[33] Calculations of cost per unit are misleading if the impact of fixed costs[34] is not taken into consideration: as production volumes increase, so the average cost per unit declines. It is often more useful to base decisions on the variable cost per unit rather than on the total absorption cost per unit.

Marginal costing, in distinguishing between fixed and variable costs, usually[35] provides a better basis for planning, decision-making and control. In planning for expansion, it is essential to recognize that some costs will increase in line with increases in output; others remain fixed. In decision-making, it is essential to use the costs that are most *relevant* for a particular decision: those costs that will change as a result of the decision, which are usually the variable costs. Fixed costs are often irrelevant in relation to particular decisions because they will continue at much the same level unless very radical decisions are made to change the way in which the business operates. Managers who are expected to 'control' their costs are likely to have more control over variable costs than they are over arbitrary allocations of fixed overheads.

Marginal costing has other advantages. It avoids much of the arbitrariness involved in allocating overheads. It demonstrates that costs vary with the level of output. It increases flexibility in quoting prices at below full cost level. Businesses might, for example, move into new markets with prices that are below full cost, but which still make a contribution to

---

[33] But it is always worth exploring more profitable products, or products that make a larger contribution.

[34] And economies of scale.

[35] Usually, but not always. In some areas of planning, decision-making and control fixed costs, and perhaps full absorption costs, are the most relevant information.

fixed costs and profits. Cost behaviour can be clearly demonstrated, in relation to changes in output levels, using break-even charts or profit/volume graphs. In deciding between different products, or in changing selling prices, the use of contribution per unit (rather than profit per unit) provides a better basis. It also has behavioural advantages: managers are more likely to be motivated to control costs over which they can have a direct effect; managers are not likely to be motivated to control central costs that seem to be allocated to their division on an arbitrary basis.

There is, however, an important danger with marginal costing. The idea that any product or customer is valuable, as long as some contribution is earned, can lead to there being too many sales at prices that cover little more than variable costs; the result would be that there is not enough contribution to cover fixed costs, and the business would operate at a loss.

Marginal costing is based on simplifying assumptions, such as the following:

1 Fixed costs can be clearly separated from variable costs. This is usually done by monitoring the actual behaviour of costs over a number of periods, and using simple arithmetic, or more complex formulae, to show what the relationship between sales or output has been with the amount of costs. It is then assumed that this relationship will continue in the future. This is usually a good approximation that deals with modest increases or reductions in output levels. But if a massive increase in production is proposed, fixed costs will probably not be fixed. And if significant production facilities are to be closed down and sold, and if staff are made redundant, then even 'fixed' costs disappear.

2 Fixed costs always remain at the same level. Most businesses can increase their sales by modest amounts without a significant increase in fixed costs. A restaurant, for example, could open for longer hours, and try to attract more customers at quiet times. But a point would be reached when they can accommodate no more customers without expanding their capacity, and taking on additional premises. Fixed costs would then take a step upwards. The same is true with many businesses. An airline can sell more seats, and increase the occupancy of its aircraft to 100 per cent; but if they then want more passengers, they have to have another aircraft.

3 Variable costs remain at the same level per unit. In practice bulk buying, and the effect of the learning curve,[36] can lead to lower direct material and labour costs. On the other hand, there may be increases in the cost of materials and components more generally.

4 Changes in costs are linear: if shown on a graph, increases in total and variable costs would be a straight line as output increases. This is an oversimplification: curves and steps are more likely in practice.

Absorption costing and marginal costing have important roles to play, but each has its limitations. In financial accounting, absorption costing tends to predominate. In management accounting, marginal costing tends to predominate. In planning, decision-making and control, the most relevant information should be used, taking both absorption costing and marginal costing into account.

---

[36] People get better and faster at doing a job as they do more of it.

13.6 Budgetary Planning and Control

Most businesses have some sort of financial plan or budget that is set and approved before the beginning of the year. Sometimes it is simply based on the previous year's income statement and balance sheet. The idea of 'control' is that each month[37] the results that are actually achieved are compared with the original plan or budget to see if the business is on course. Where actual results are different from what was planned, some corrective action is required.

In addition to a budgeted income statement and balance sheet, it is usually important to produce a cash budget; often this is required by the business's bankers. Cash budgets are dealt with in Chapter 7 (p. 177).

A full and formal system of budgetary control involves the production of a set of detailed budgets to include all the business's activities. There are budgets for sales, production, inventories, material purchases, direct labour costs, production overheads, distribution and selling costs, administration, capital expenditure and cash, all culminating in a budgeted income statement, balance sheet and cash flow statement. Managers in each area of the business are involved in setting the budgets.

A budget may be defined as a *plan*, quantified in monetary terms, prepared and *approved* prior to a defined period of time, showing details of income to be generated, and expenditure to be incurred, and capital to be employed, to attain a given *objective*. There may be several objectives, such as achieving a given return on capital employed or earnings per share (EPS), and perhaps improving the liquidity position, or reducing borrowings. It is not supposed to be a set of estimates, prepared by the finance department, to give an idea of what is likely to happen during the coming year. It is supposed to express the intentions of top management, detailed as a financial plan, with a commitment from all managers to achieve the results expected.

Budgetary control may be defined as the use of budgets that *relate the responsibilities of managers* to the requirements of a policy, and the continuous comparison of actual results with budgeted results to identify and implement specific actions to achieve the results intended, or to provide a basis for revising planned results. Objectives will not achieve themselves. The idea is that managers are responsible for achieving defined objectives, and actual results are monitored and compared with the established plan or budget.

A system of budgetary control has a number of functions. It ensures that the *objectives* of an organization are defined and quantified. It identifies *limiting factors* (e.g. an expected cash shortage) in advance so that they can be eliminated. Where particular expenses are included in an approved budget, it serves to *authorize* that expenditure. It means that the *responsibilities* of particular managers are defined, and authority for achieving plans is *delegated* to them. *Management by exception* is facilitated: senior management do not need to pay attention to every detail of results if they are in line with budget; they concentrate their efforts on exceptions where budgeted results are not being achieved. This is intended to ensure *control* of the business. It may improve the *motivation* of managers if they know exactly what they are expected to achieve, and some sort of *targets* are defined. This can serve as a basis for *performance evaluation*, and managers may be given financial incen-

---

[37] Or more frequently.

tives to achieve the performance specified in the budget. The planning process, with widespread management involvement, should also improve *communication* and *co-ordination* within the organization.

In practice budgetary control may not be as successful as intended. Realistic financial plans are needed to ensure that sufficient cash and other resources are available. But if the budget is also intended to motivate staff, it may be based on overambitious targets that do not provide a suitable basis for planning resources. Sometimes it is seen as an annual round of resource allocation, leading to competition between managers to increase the amounts that they are authorized to spend. Those managers who are most confident in dealing with finance may be the winners, perhaps at the expense of the organization as a whole. Budgets tend to be *incremental*:[38] each year's budget is based on the previous year's, with a bit added for inflation, and a bit more for growth. Almost all managers want to see their budgets growing; but then they have a real incentive to spend all the money allocated to them, perhaps finding important conferences to go to in sunny climates just before the end of the financial year;[39] they do not want to be caught out underspending, fearing that next year's budget will be reduced.

In the game of budgetary control, it is usually intended that managers should be involved in setting their own budgets. Then the accountants put all the individual budgets together in a master budget: the budgeted income statement, balance sheet and the cash budget. It may be that all the budgets fit neatly together revealing no cash shortages, and achieving all the intended targets, such as increasing return on capital employed, and EPS. Similarly, pigs might fly. It is more likely that once the first draft of the master budget is prepared, the finance director or senior management will insist on revisions: expenditure to be cut back, sales to be increased, capital expenditure to be reduced and deferred. All the careful planning put in by individual managers is overturned. But experienced managers know that this will happen, and so they put some 'slack' into the first version of the budget because experience tells them that the final version will be tougher. And the finance director knows that they know, and that they have included slack, so tougher cutbacks are demanded. But very experienced managers know this, and have included even more slack than the finance director would expect. But very experienced finance directors know this . . . and so all is set for another round of the game of budgetary control.

One approach to make budgetary control more effective, and to avoid the tendency for expenditure to drift upwards every year ('incremental drift'), is to use *zero base budgeting*. This means that, instead of taking the previous year's figures as a basis for planning future expenditure, the basis is taken as zero. The starting point is that each activity will spend nothing in the coming year, unless it can be justified. This may be valuable in some areas: perhaps there is no need for company cars if it is cheaper to use taxis; perhaps there is no need for a mail room if most communication is done by email. But it is usually too much hassle, expense and bureaucracy to review every activity every year, and incremental budgeting still predominates.

---

[38] It would be possible to have a zero base budgeting scheme, where increases in budgets are not assumed. Indeed, each manager would have to justify all expenditure from scratch each year.

[39] Or repainting the inside of cupboards. Many building and maintenance firms, and stationery suppliers, suddenly find that business bucks up in February and March, just before the financial year end in the public sector.

If budgets are seen as the official expressions of the plans and intentions of top management, they are likely to be taken seriously, and provide an effective means of controlling the business. They are likely to be less effective if they are seen as being a paperwork exercise produced by the finance department; a pointless extra burden for management; a sterile figure-producing exercise that provides information that managers do not understand, is irrelevant to their needs, and arrives in too much detail, and too late for them to act upon. If they are to be successful, management accountants must produce financial information that is relevant and effective in planning, decision-making and control in the business.

Summary

Financial accounting information can be used for planning, decision-making and control in an organization. But costing systems and budgetary control have been developed, along with management accounting more generally, to provide information more relevant to the needs of management. Absorption costing emerged from financial accounting so that the costs of different products can be calculated, and to establish the cost of closing inventories for the purpose of profit measurement. Marginal costing systems are usually seen as being more relevant for planning, decision-making and control. But each approach has its limitations, and, as with all accounting information, care is needed to manage an organization on the basis of the most appropriate information. The use of budgetary control systems for planning purposes is part of a control mechanism, and provides a basis for financial planning.

Review of key points

- Financial accounting is mainly concerned with providing information to shareholders, creditors and other users who are outside the business. Management accounting provides information for managers within a business and is less formalized.

- Costing and budgetary control are key elements of management accounting.

- Costs can be classified in different ways: an important distinction is between production costs (which are included in closing inventories), and other operating expenses (which are not).

- In calculating the costs of different products, an *absorption costing* system charges all production costs in calculating the profit made by each product.

- *Marginal costing* distinguishes between fixed and variable costs, and calculates the *contribution* made by each product.

- Marginal costing and break-even analysis provide useful information for planning, decision-making and control, but are based on a number of simplifying assumptions.

- Budgetary control can play an important role in planning and controlling a business, and provide useful information for decision-making.

Self-testing questions

1 The Golden Beach Holiday Centre operates three departments, details of which for last year are as follows:

	Total £000	Accommodation £000	Restaurant £000	Shop £000
Sales revenue	1,330	600	230	500
Direct materials	460	10	50	400
Direct labour	450	300	100	50
Overheads	320	200	60	60
Profit/(loss)	100	90	20	(10)

Overheads include general management and administration, plus the cost of providing premises, and are charged to the three departments on the basis of square metres occupied by each. It is estimated that £100,000 of the overheads vary in line with sales revenue; £220,000 is regarded as fixed. Management are considering closing down the shop as it is making a loss.

Restate the above information in marginal costing format, and make appropriate recommendations.

2 The Medical Manufacturing Company has two production cost centres, details of which are as follows:

Budget for next year	Total	Assembly	Testing
Production overheads	£1,200,000	£200,000	£1,000,000
Direct labour cost	£400,000	£200,000	£200,000
Direct labour hours	28,000 hours	20,000 hours	8,000 hours

You are required to calculate:

a The production overhead recovery rate as a percentage of direct labour cost:

   i   On average

   ii Separately for each cost centre

b The production overhead recovery rate on the basis of direct labour hours:

   i   On average

   ii Separately for each cost centre

c The average hourly wage rate for each cost centre

d The production cost of a new lie-detecting machine that requires components costing £150 and 3 hours of direct labour in the assembly department, and 5 hours of direct labour in the testing department

Self-testing questions (continued)

3 The results of the Queen's Pier Engineering Company for the last two months are summarized as follows:

	March	**April**
Sales	£120,000	£140,000
Profit	£ 40,000	£ 49,000

On the basis of this information you are required to estimate:

a Variable costs as a percentage of sales

b Contribution as a percentage of sales

c Fixed costs per month

d The monthly sales revenue at which the company would break even

4 Calculate the profit of each of the three distribution depots in Illustration 13.7 using activity-based costing.

Assessment questions

1 The Gollanic Manufacturing Company produces three types of gollane,[40] details of which for last year are as follows:

	Total	**Basic**	**Super**	**Commercial**
	£000	£000	£000	£000
Sales revenue	3,100	1,600	900	600
Manufacturing costs				
Direct materials	850	450	150	250
Direct labour	1,000	600	300	100
Production overheads	900	540	270	90
Total production costs	2,750	1,590	720	440
Distribution and administration overheads	310			

Production overheads are charged to individual products as 90 per cent of direct labour costs. Distribution and administrative overheads have traditionally been charged to products in proportion to sales revenue.

It is estimated that £600,000 of production overheads are fixed, and £300,000 varies in proportion to labour costs. Distribution and administrative overheads are regarded as being fixed for the foreseeable future.

The company is considering ceasing production of the basic model.

You are required to:

---

[40] A fictitious product.

Assessment questions (continued)

a Calculate the profit or loss made by each product using absorption costing, and charging the distribution and administrative expenses as suggested.

b Restate the above information in marginal costing format, and make appropriate recommendations.

2 The Garden Ornament Manufacturing Company has two cost centres. Budgeted figures for year 7 are as follows:

	Total	Moulding	Finishing
Direct labour cost	£300,000	£200,000	£100,000
Direct labour hours		10,000	10,000
Production overheads	£600,000	£420,000	£180,000

a Calculate the overhead recovery rate for each cost centre, assuming:

i A percentage on direct labour cost is used

ii A direct labour hour rate is used

b The company is negotiating an order to produce a batch of models of a recent prime minister. The costs of producing the batch are estimated as follows:

Direct materials	£1,200
Direct labour hours – moulding	120 hrs
Direct labour hours – finishing	60 hrs
Direct labour cost – moulding	£2,400
Direct labour cost – finishing	£600

Calculate the production cost of this batch assuming:

i A percentage on direct labour cost is used

ii A direct labour hour rate is used

3 The results of the Williston Company for the last two months are summarized as follows:

	May	June
Sales	£300,000	£350,000
Profit	£ 10,000	£ 50,000

On the basis of this information you are required to estimate:

a Variable costs as a percentage of sales

b Contribution as a percentage of sales

c Fixed costs per month

d The monthly sales revenue at which the company would break even

Group activities and discussion questions

1 It would be safer for managers to rely on financial accounting information (that is produced in accordance with official regulations, and is audited), rather than relying on management accounting information. Discuss.

2 In most businesses it is not possible to establish accurately the cost of producing a particular product or service. Discuss.

3 Would you expect management accountants to be popular or unpopular with other managers? Why?

4 In the long run all costs are variable; in the short run they are all fixed. Explain and comment.

5 Budgetary control (like many other management techniques?) has huge potential, but tends to become a pointless bureaucratic exercise in practice. Discuss.

Financial accounting in context

For richer, for poorer?
By Malcolm Howard FCMA

Letter to the editor, *Financial Management*, June 2006

Discuss and comment on the following extract from the press and what it suggests about the general applicability of break-even analysis.

Source: Reproduced with permission by *Financial Management*.

I READ WITH interest Victor Sheahan's amusing piece about how to calculate the optimum number of guests to invite to his wedding (Study notes, May). He calculated that €7,500 would cover fixed costs such as the dress, cake, flowers, priest, photographer and rings, while €55 per head would cover the variable cost of catering, stationery and postage. One the basis that typical wedding presents were valued in the €75 to €125 per person, he assumed that in his case the most generous relative would give a present valued at €200. He also assumed that the marginal value of each present would decline as numbers increased, but that the lowest value for a present would be capped at €50. Using these figures he calculated that the optimum number of guests would be 193.

Unfortunately, the technique he used is flawed in two ways. First, it's reasonable to assume that close relatives will be more generous than friends, but it cannot necessarily follow that the 194th guest will offer a present worth 75 cents less than that provided by the 193rd guest. A more reasonable assumption would be that relatives would generate a positive contribution, while the value of friends' presents would be lower than their variable cost if you cannot put a value on the fun and atmosphere they provide.

So, in financial terms, relatives should be invited and friends left out in the cold. But, since we need some friends, where do we draw the line at accumulating losses? This is where the second flaw comes in. Although the catering part is a variable cost, the venue itself is a semi-fixed or step cost. The bigger the floor space used, the more it is going to cost you. So what the couple need to do is draw up two lists of guests: "must haves" and "nice to invites". Suppose there were 100 each of "must haves" and "nice to invites" and the venues available could cater for 80, 160 or 240 people. It would be the step that would determine the decision. In this case the venue holding 160 would be chosen.

The couple would then have to agree on the 40 "nice to invites" who would miss out – a good preparation for the decisions they'd have to share in future.

References and further reading

Black, G. (2005) *Introduction to Accounting and Finance.* FT Prentice Hall.

Davies, T. and B. Pain, (2001) *Business Accounting and Finance.* McGraw-Hill.

Drury, C. (2004) *Management and Cost Accounting.* Thomson Learning.

Horngren, C., S.M. Datar and G. Foster (2005) *Cost Accounting: A Managerial Emphasis.* Prentice Hall.

CHAPTER 14

Bookkeeping to Trial Balance

❖ LEARNING OBJECTIVES

After studying Section 14.1 you should be able to:

- ❖ Record straightforward transactions using double entry bookkeeping

- ❖ Prepare a trial balance summarizing those transactions

- ❖ Introduce closing stock and convert the trial balance into a set of final accounts

After studying Section 14.2 you should be able to:

- ❖ Produce ledger accounts in a good format

- ❖ Record a wide range of transactions using double-entry bookkeeping, including discounts and returns

- ❖ Use a cash book and separate petty cash from bank transactions

After studying Section 14.3 you should be able to:

- ❖ Understand how accounting systems operate

- ❖ Appreciate the role of day books, ledgers and control accounts

- ❖ Prepare a simple bank reconciliation statement

14.1 Introduction

Businesses use double-entry bookkeeping to record all transactions. For a very simple operation it might be possible to keep only a cash account that records all the money that the business receives, and all the money that it pays out. But most businesses operate using credit (buying goods and paying for them later; selling goods and receiving payment for them later); they own fixed assets that have to be depreciated, and many are financed by borrowing. It is, therefore, necessary to keep account not only of what has been received and paid, but also of how much the business owes to various people, and of how much customers owe to the business (debtors), and of other assets. Double-entry bookkeeping has developed to meet this need. It is also useful in producing a trial balance.

The rules for double-entry bookkeeping are straightforward: a few rules, consistently applied, are all that is needed. There are more detailed rules for anyone who wants to be a bookkeeper (introduced in Section 14.2). But the basic principles, outlined below, are not difficult.

Rule 1

A cash account shows all receipts of cash on the left-hand side, and all payments of cash on the right-hand side, as shown below.

Cash Account

Receipts			Payments		
Date	Description	Amount	Date	Description	Amount
2007		£	2007		£
1 Jan	Capital – Catherine Fox	100,000	4 Jan	Rent	2,000
3 Jan	Loan from HSBS	50,000	5 Jan	Vehicle	20,000
8 Jan	Sales	3,300	6 Jan	Purchases of books	4,000

From the above it can easily be inferred what has happened.

Catherine Fox started a business (as a bookseller) on 1 January 2007 with £100,000 of her own capital, which she paid into a business bank account. The money was 'received' into the business cash or bank account. She then borrowed £50,000 from HSBS. The next day she paid rent of £2,000; then paid £20,000 to buy a vehicle; then she paid £4,000 to buy some books. Two days later she sold some books for £3,300.

Anyone with no training in accountancy would soon devise a system of record-keeping such as the above. Recording receipts and payments is essential to keep track of the business's money.

A professional bookkeeper would separate 'petty cash' (notes and coins) from money in the bank; but this need not trouble us here.[1] It is all money, and will be called cash.

But the above is too simple, and it is not double-entry bookkeeping.

---

[1] It is explained in Section 14.2.

Rule 2

Every transaction must be recorded twice: on the left-hand side of one account, and the right-hand side of another account.

The next steps should follow naturally. Payments must be on the right-hand side of the cash account; payments are usually to pay for assets, or expenses, or purchases of goods for resale. Separate accounts are needed for each of these, and the amounts will be recorded on the left-hand side of the asset, expense and purchases accounts.

Receipts must be on the left-hand side of the cash account. They may be from the original capital provided, or from borrowings, but are mainly from sales. Separate accounts are needed for each of these, and the amounts will be recorded on the right-hand side of the capital, loan and sales accounts.

These are illustrated below.

Capital Account

Date 2007	Description	Amount £	Date 2007	Description	Amount £
			1 Jan	Cash	100,000

HSBS Loan Account

Date 2007	Description	Amount £	Date 2007	Description	Amount £
			3 Jan	Cash	50,000

Sales Account

Date 2007	Description	Amount £	Date 2007	Description	Amount £
			8 Jan	Cash	3,300

Rent Account

Date 2007	Description	Amount £	Date	Description	Amount £
4 Jan	Cash	2,000			

Vehicle (Fixed Asset) Account

Date 2007	Description	Amount £	Date	Description	Amount £
5 Jan	Cash	20,000			

Purchases Account

Date 2007	Description	Amount £	Date	Description	Amount £
6 Jan	Cash	4,000			

There should be no difficulty in deciding what description to put for a transaction: it is simply the name of the account where the other half of the double entry is to be found. Payments for purchases are shown on the right-hand side of the cash account, and labelled as purchases; the transaction also appears on the left-hand side of the purchases account, labelled as cash.

But many, or most business transactions, are not conducted on a cash basis. Purchases are typically made on credit, and the payment is made a month or so later. Sales to other businesses are normally made on credit, and the money is received a month or so later.

Purchases and sales that take place on a credit basis must not be shown on the cash account when the transaction first takes place. Entries in the cash account will be made when the cash is received or paid. But there is a need to record the sales and purchases as soon as they are made – not least because there is a need to keep track of how much is owed to suppliers, and how much is owed to the business by customers.

Rules 3 and 4 seem to follow naturally from what we have already seen.

Rule 3

The purchases account records all purchases that have been made, whether they are on a cash basis, or are on credit.

Rule 4

The sales account records all sales that have been made, whether they are on a cash basis, or on credit.

Catherine Fox specializes in buying remaindered books on credit from UK publishers and selling them, on credit, to overseas colleges. Her purchases account and sales account for January are shown below.

Purchases Account

Date	Description	Amount	Date	Description	Amount
2007		£			£
6 Jan	Cash	4,000			
18 Jan	Pinwin Publishers	8,000			
22 Jan	Grohill Publishers	7,000			

Sales Account

Date	Description	Amount	Date	Description	Amount
2007		£	2007		£
			8 Jan	Cash	3,300
			10 Jan	College A	5,500
			27 Jan	College B	8,500

It is clear what has happened: she has bought books on credit from Pinwin Publishers and from Grohill Publishers, and she has sold books on credit to College A and to College B. No cash has changed hands in respect of these transactions (yet) and so the cash account is not affected. But she does need to keep track of her creditors and debtors. She must also follow Rule 2, and complete the double entry, as shown below.

Purchases made on credit are shown on the left-hand side of the purchases account, and on the right-hand side of the creditors account.

Pinwin Publishers (Creditors) Account

Date	Description	Amount	Date	Description	Amount
2007		£	2007		£
			18 Jan	Purchases	8,000

Grohill Publishers (Creditors) Account

Date	Description	Amount	Date	Description	Amount
2007		£	2007		£
			22 Jan	Purchases	7,000

Sales made on credit are shown on the right-hand side of the sales account, and on the left-hand side of the debtors account.

College A (Debtors) Account

Date	Description	Amount	Date	Description	Amount
2007		£			£
10 Jan	Sales College A	5,500			

College B (Debtors) Account

Date	Description	Amount	Date	Description	Amount
2007		£			£
27 Jan	Sales College B	8,500			

Catherine Fox will, in due course, pay some of what she owes to her suppliers, and these payments (like all payments) must be recorded on the cash account, as shown below:

Cash Account

Date	Description	Amount	Date	Description	Amount
2007		£	2007		£
1 Jan	Capital – Catherine Fox	100,000	4 Jan	Rent	2,000
3 Jan	Loan from HSBS	50,000	5 Jan	Vehicle	20,000
8 Jan	Sales	3,300	6 Jan	Purchases of books	4,000
			24 Feb	Pinwin Publishers	6,000
			25 Feb	Grohill Publishers	6,500

She also needs to complete the double-entry bookkeeping by recording the transactions on the left-hand side of her suppliers' accounts, as shown below.

Pinwin Publishers (Creditors) Account

Date	Description	Amount	Date	Description	Amount
2007		£	2007		£
25 Feb	Cash	6,000	18 Jan	Purchases	8,000

Grohill Publishers (Creditors) Account

Date	Description	Amount	Date	Description	Amount
2007		£	2007		£
25 Feb	Cash	6,500	22 Jan	Purchases	7,000

The balance on Pinwin's account now shows that Catherine Fox owes them £2,000. The balance on Grohill's account now shows that Catherine Fox owes them £500.

The money owed to Catherine Fox by her credit customers should, in due course, be received. These receipts, like all receipts, must be recorded on the left-hand side of the cash account, as shown overleaf.

Cash Account

Date	Description	Amount	Date	Description	Amount
2007		£	2007		£
1 Jan	Capital – Catherine Fox	100,000	4 Jan	Rent	2,000
3 Jan	Loan from HSBS	50,000	5 Jan	Vehicle	20,000
8 Jan	Sales	3,300	6 Jan	Purchases of books	4,000
26 Feb	College A	3,000	24 Feb	Pinwin Publishers	6,000
28 Feb	College B	8,500	25 Feb	Grohill Publishers	6,500

Again, it is necessary to complete the double entry by recording the amount that has been received on the right-hand side of the debtors accounts, as shown below.

College A (Debtors) Account

Date	Description	Amount	Date	Description	Amount
2007		£	2007		£
10 Jan	Sales	5,500	26 Feb	Cash	3,000

College B (Debtors) Account

Date	Description	Amount	Date	Description	Amount
2007		£	2007		£
27 Jan	Sales	8,500	28 Feb	Cash	8,500

The balance on the College A account shows that they still owe £2,500. College B has paid in full and so there is no balance remaining on their account.

The above example shows most types of transaction. There may be dozens of different types of expense (rent, rates, insurance, postage, stationery, telephone, wages, salaries and so on), but in principle they are all the same. They are shown on the left-hand side of an expense account, such as electricity, and on the right-hand side of the cash account when it is paid.

It is not difficult to understand the words left and right. But the words 'debit' and 'credit' often seem to cause problems. But they are just more professional-sounding words for the same simple idea.

Rule 5

Recording a transaction on the left-hand side of an account is called debiting it. Recording a transaction on the right-hand side of an account is called crediting it. If an account has more debited to it than credited to it, it is said to have a debit balance. If an account has more credited to it than debited to it, it has a credit balance.

Enough transactions have been illustrated above to be able to make the following generalizations:

- A sales account has a credit balance
- A purchases account has a debit balance
- An expenses account has a debit balance
- An asset account has a debit balance
- A creditors account has a credit balance (unless we have paid our suppliers too much by mistake!)

- A debtors account has a debit balance (unless our customers have paid us too much by mistake!)
- A cash or bank account has a debit balance, provided more has been received than paid out. If more has been paid out than received it will have a credit balance; that is an overdraft.

If every transaction is recorded twice, on the debit side of one account, and on the credit side of another account, the totals of all the debits must equal the totals of all the credits. This can be checked and summarized in the form of a trial balance, as shown below;

Trial balance of Catherine Fox as at 28 February 2007

	Debit	Credit
Capital		100,000
Loan		50,000
Vehicle	20,000	
Cash (£164,800 − £38,500)	126,300	
Pinwin (Creditor)		2,000
Grohill (Creditor)		500
College A (Debtor)	2,500	
Rent	2,000	
Purchases	19,000	
Sales		17,300
	169,800	169,800

It is called a 'trial' balance because we are trying to see if it balances, or if there are errors and omissions. If it does not balance, there is definitely something wrong. If it does balance, there could still be some errors: items completely missing, or 'compensating errors', such as where a debit item and a credit item for the same amount have been omitted.

The trial balance is also useful in summarizing all transactions. Even if there have been hundreds of sales, we just have one figure for the total. A cash account may have hundreds of debits and credits, but on the trial balance we just show the one figure. In the above trial balance there are two creditors; a normal business might have hundreds, but the trial balance would show just one figure for the total amount of creditors (or payables).

The trial balance provides most of the information that is needed to produce a balance sheet and an income statement, but some additional information is usually needed. Each 'adjustment' to the trial balance must involve a debit and a credit, otherwise it would not balance.

In the case of Catherine Fox, the figure for closing stock (the amount of unsold books at the end of the period) must be added to the trial balance. It will appear on the balance sheet as a current asset, and it will be deducted from purchases to arrive at the cost of goods sold on the profit and loss account. If her closing stock is £6,000, her profit and loss account and balance sheet can be prepared as follows:

Income statement of Catherine Fox for the two months ended 28 February 2007

	£	£
Sales		17,300
Cost of goods sold		
Opening stock	0	
Purchases	19,000	
	19,000	
Less Closing stock	6,000	
		13,000
Gross profit		4,300
Expenses – rent		2,000
Net profit		2,300

Balance sheet as at 28 February 2007

	£	£
Assets		
Fixed assets – van		20,000
Current assets		
Inventories	6,000	
Receivables	2,500	
Cash	126,300	134,800
		154,800
Equity and liabilities		
Equity		
Capital		100,000
Profit for year		2,300
		102,300
Non-current liabilities		
Loan from HSBS		
Current liabilities		50,000
Payables		2,500
		154,800

When looking at a balance sheet and income statement like this for the first time, it is a good idea to check where each item has come from. It is important to note that the profit figure calculated at the end of the income statement account is added to the capital figure on the balance sheet.[2]

Practice questions are provided in Self-testing questions (Carlos; Killip) at the end of this chapter (see pp. 391–2), with answers at the end of the book (see pp. 479–81). Additional practice questions (A Florist; Moorey) are also provided at the end of the chapter (see pp. 393–4). These questions require production of double-entry accounts, a trial balance, and a balance sheet and income statement. Questions in Chapter 15 begin with the trial balance and do not require double-entry bookkeeping.

---

[2] In a company's income statement, any amount for dividends that shareholders receive is deducted to arrive at a 'retained' profit for the year. These items are shown on a separate 'statement of changes in equity' which links the income statement with the balance sheet.

14.2 Bookkeeping in Practice

Section 14.1 provides enough information about bookkeeping to understand how a system works, to be able to record straightforward transactions, and to understand how a trial balance is produced. In practice bookkeeping systems are more sophisticated and this section explains how bookkeeping operates in practice.

Balancing Accounts

In Section 14.1 there were very few transactions and it is easy to see what the balance on an account is. For example, in the account of a creditor, Grohill Publishers, there was a debit item of £6,500 and a credit item of £7,000. As the credit item is greater than the debit item, we say that there is a credit balance on the account.

Where there are more transactions on the account (e.g. Catherine Fox's cash account), we have to add up all the debit items, which made a total of £164,800; then add up all the credit items, which made a total of (£38,500); then deduct the credit items from the debit items to arrive at the balance on the account, which is (£164,800 − £38,500 =) £126,300; this is a debit balance because the total of debits is greater than the total of credits.

Calculating the balance on an account is done at the end of a period, typically monthly, and the balance is recorded twice on the account (as a debit, and as a credit, keeping to the rules of double entry), and shown as a balance carried down (c/d), and then as a balance brought down (b/d) as shown in two of Catherine Fox's accounts below.

Grohill Publishers (Creditors) Account

Date	Description	Amount	Date	Description	Amount
25 Feb	Cash	6,500	18 Jan	Purchases	7,000
28 Feb	Balance c/d	500			
		7,000			7,000
			1 Mar	Bal b/d	500

Cash Account

Date	Description	Amount	Date	Description	Amount
1 Jan	Capital	100,000	4 Jan	Rent	2,000
3 Jan	Loan from HSBS	50,000	5 Jan	Vehicle	20,000
8 Jan	Sales	3,300	6 Jan	Purchases of books	4,000
26 Feb	College A	3,000	24 Feb	Pinwin Publishers	6,000
28 Feb	College B	8,500	25 Feb	Grohill Publishers	6,500
			28 Feb	Balance c/d	126,300
		164,800			164,800
1 Mar	Balance b/d	126,300			

Remaining balances on accounts, including creditors, debtors, cash and other assets and liabilities, are summarized in the form of a balance sheet that is, in effect, a statement of remaining balances. Accounts that deal with expenses and revenues are dealt with differently: the balances are transferred to the profit and loss account, which is part of the double-entry bookkeeping system. The profit and loss account is summarized and presented in the form of an income statement.

Cash and Bank

Accountants often use the word 'cash' to include both petty cash (coins and notes) and money that it is in the bank. But in practice it is necessary to record the two separately. Some businesses (e.g. retailers) accumulate large amounts of cash that they pay into the bank on a regular basis. Other businesses are operated mainly through bank accounts, but it is usually necessary to keep a cash float to pay modest routine expenses (e.g. window cleaning, newspapers, coffee).

It is often convenient to combine petty cash and bank into a single cash book, using separate columns, as shown in Illustration 14.1.

Date	Folio	Description	Cash	Bank	Date	Folio	Description	Cash	Bank
2 Jan		Balance	100	23,000	4 Jan	Abc123	Office expenses	8	
3 Jan	Xyz123	Sales	800		6 Jan	Lmn123	A Supplier		8,000
5 Jan	Xyz124	Sales	950		7 Jan	Lmn199	B Wholesaler		11,000
8 Jan	Xyz125	Sales	700		8 Jan	Abc199	Refreshments	52	
9 Jan		Contra		2,390	9 Jan		Contra	2,390	
							Bal c/d	100	6,390
			2,550	25,390				2,550	25,390
10 Jan		Bal b/d	100	6,390					

ILLUSTRATION 14.1

In this illustration the business is probably a retailer. Large amounts of cash are received each day. At the end of the week most of the cash is paid into the bank as a 'contra' entry. A float of £100 of petty cash is retained for small expenses, and perhaps to provide change. Suppliers are paid by cheque; all cheque payments are recorded in the bank column on the credit side.

In a large firm it is useful to have a folio column that gives a reference number to show where else in the accounting system the item is recorded. This can help with reconciliations and finding errors. For simplicity folio columns have been excluded elsewhere in this book.

Discount Allowed and Discount Received

Businesses often allow a cash discount of perhaps 2.5 per cent or 5 per cent for prompt settlement of accounts.

Discount allowed is an expense, and reduces the amount owed by debtors, and is accounted for as follows:

> Debit discount allowed account
> Credit the debtor's personal account

The total on the discount allowed account is treated as an expense on the profit and loss account.

Discount received reduces the amount owed to creditors, and is treated as income to be added to gross profit, and is accounted for as follows:

> Debit the creditor's personal account
> Credit discount received

The amounts shown for sales and purchases are not affected by discounts allowed and received. The full amount (before deducting any cash discounts) is shown for sales and purchases. Discounts allowed and received are dealt with in the profit and loss account, after calculating gross profit, and are included in the profit for the year shown on the income statement.

Discount allowed and received should not be confused with 'trade discounts'. Suppliers often charge higher prices to the general public than they do to wholesalers and other businesses. These trade discounts are not entered into the accounting system. The transactions are recorded at the price actually charged.

A 'Three-Column' Cash Book

When recording the amounts paid to creditors (or received from debtors), it is convenient to record the amounts of discount received (or discount allowed) at the same time using discount columns in the cash book for this purpose. The 'three columns' of the cash book are cash, bank and discount. In practice such a cash book would have more columns, as shown in Illustration 14.2 (where the folio column has been omitted).

Date	Description	Discount allowed	Cash	Bank	Date	Description	Discount received	Cash	Bank
1 Jan	Balance b/d		250	120,000					
1 Jan	Katherina	140		2,860	1 Jan	Office expenses		60	
2 Jan	Bianca	200		4,400	2 Jan	Cleaning		120	
2 Jan	Sales		10		3 Jan	Petruchio	20		1,980
3 Jan					3 Jan	Grumio	30		2,770
4 Jan					4 Jan	Hortensio	15		885

ILLUSTRATION 14.2 Shrew Enterprises' cash book

In Shrew Enterprises most sales are on credit. When Katherina send a cheque for £2,860 the cash account is debited with £2,860; discount allowed will be debited with £140; and the total amount credited to Katherina's account is £3,000.

Shrew Enterprises pay a few expenses out of petty cash. They started with £250 in cash, but within a few days they have paid out £180. They will soon need to top up their petty cash by taking money out of the bank. This will be recorded as a contra entry by debiting the cash column, and crediting the bank column.

They also have creditors to pay. When they pay £1,980 to Petruchio it is shown as a credit in the bank column, and the £20 discount received is shown in the discount column. The total amount debited to Petruchio's account will be £2,000.

The cash book may be seen as being both a day book (see Section 14.3) and part of the double-entry system. At the end of a period the totals of the discount allowed (and discount received) columns are debited (or credited) to the profit and loss account.

Returns Inwards and Returns Outwards

Customers often return goods that they have received to the supplier for a variety of reasons. Where the original sale was made on credit, the returns are accounted for as follows.

Returns inwards (or sales returns) are goods that a business has sold, but then they are returned by the customer.

> Debit returns inwards account
> Credit the debtor's personal account

The total on the returns inwards account is deducted from the total sales figure shown on the income statement.

Returns outwards (or purchases returns) are goods that a business has bought, but then returns to the supplier. They are recorded as follows.

> Debit creditor's personal account
> Credit returns outwards

The total on the returns outwards account is deducted from the total purchased figure shown on the income statement.

The recording of discounts and returns is shown in Illustration 14.3.

Extracts from the ledger accounts of G. Maye

Sales Account

| | 1 Mar | Bal | 56,000 |

Purchases Account

| 1 Mar | Bal | 20,000 | |

S. Oldrick (Debtor)

| 1 Mar | Bal | 23,000 |

Cass Hawin (Creditor)

| | 1 Mar | Bal | 11,000 |

Returns Inwards

| 1 Mar | Bal | 5,000 |

Returns Outwards

| | 1 Mar | Bal | 3,000 |

During March the following transactions took place:

3 Mar	Sales on credit to S. Oldrick	£14,000
6 Mar	Purchases on credit from Cass Hawin	£7,000
12 Mar	Purchases on credit from Cass Hawin	£4,000
16 Mar	Returned goods to Cass Hawin	£2,500
19 Mar	Sales on credit to S. Oldrick	£21,000
21 Mar	S. Oldrick returned goods	£4,600
26 Mar	Sales on credit to S. Oldrick	£18,000

ILLUSTRATION 14.3

28 Mar   Paid the balance on Cass Hawin's account after taking 4% discount
30 Mar   Received a cheque from S. Oldrick for £50,730 who had taken discount of £2,670

Solution

Purchases Account

1 Mar	Bal	20,000	
6 Mar	C. Hawin	7,000	
12 Mar	C. Hawin	4,000	

Sales Account

			1 Mar	Bal	56,000
			3 Mar	S. Oldrick	14,000
			19 Mar	S. Oldrick	21,000
			26 Mar	S. Oldrick	18,000

S. Oldrick (Debtor)

1 Mar	Bal	23,000	21 Mar	Returns inwards	4,600
3 Mar	Sales	14,000	30 Mar	Discount allowed	2,670
19 Mar	Sales	21,000	30 Mar	Cash	50,730
26 Mar	Sales	18,000	31 Mar	Bal c/d	18,000
		76,000			76,000
1 Apr	Bal b/d	18,000			

Cass Hawin (Creditor)

16 Mar	Returns outwards	2,500	1 Mar	Balance	11,000
28 Mar	Discount received[3]	780	6 Mar	Purchases	7,000
28 Mar	Cash	18,720	12 Mar	Purchases	4,000
		22,000			22,000

Returns Inwards

1 Mar	Bal b/d	5,000	
21 Mar	S. Oldrick	4,600	

Returns Outwards

			1 Mar	Bal b/d	3,000
			12 Mar	C. Hawin	2,500

Discount Allowed

30 Mar	S. Oldrick	2,670

Discount Received

			28 Mar	C. Hawin	780

ILLUSTRATION 14.3 continued

Returns inwards and returns outwards affect the amount of gross profit. The figures to be included in the income statement from Illustration 14.3 are as follows:

	£
Sales	109,000
Deduct Returns	(9,600)
	99,400
Purchases	31,000
Deduct Returns	(5,500)
	25,500

Discounts received and allowed do not affect gross profit. Discount received is added to gross profit. Discount allowed is a normal expense shown after calculating gross profit.

---

[3] Four per cent of (£11,000 + £7,000 + £4,000 − £2,500 =) £19,500 = £780.

Accruals and Prepayments

The normal rules for double-entry bookkeeping apply to accruals and prepayments. For the purpose of preparing final accounts from a trial balance, particularly in an examination, the adjustments can be made directly on to the balance sheet and profit and loss account or income statement. But in practice full double entry is required, as shown below.

Accrual

A company pays its electricity bill quarterly as follows:

3 April	£800
5 July	£600
4 October	£700

The company's year end is 31 December and the fourth electricity bill has not been received, recorded or paid by that date. It has to be accrued. It may be estimated, or the actual bill, for example £750, may be used for the accrual. It is likely to be received early in January before the financial statements have been finalized. The three payments will have been recorded early in the year. (Debit electricity;[4] Credit cash.) At the end of the year it is necessary to add £750 to the amount of the expense for electricity; it is also necessary to show £750 as a short-term creditor (an accrual) on the balance sheet. The bookkeeping is done as follows:

Electricity Account

Date	Description	Amount	Date	Description	Amount
3 April	Cash	800			
5 July	Cash	600			
4 Oct	Cash	700			
31 Dec	Accrual c/d	750	31 Dec	Profit and loss a/c	2,850
		2,850			2,850
			1 Jan	Accrual b/d	750

This may seem a complicated way of proceeding, but it achieves three things:

1 The full amount of the electricity charge for the year (£2,850) is shown on the profit and loss account[5] (debit profit and loss account; credit electricity account) although all of it has not yet been paid as at 31 December.

2 The balance brought down at 1 January (a credit balance) is the balance that will be shown on the balance sheet as an accrual, part of short-term creditors.

3 When the final bill for the year, £750, is actually paid, early in the following year, the bookkeeping will be: debit electricity; credit cash. The electricity account already

---

[4] Alternatively, the account might be called 'lighting and heating'.

[5] The term 'profit and loss account' is still used for recording transactions; the summary of it for final presentation is usually called an 'income statement'.

shows a credit balance brought down of £750; this will offset the payment that is in respect of the previous year so that the new year, in effect, starts with a zero balance.

Carriage Inwards and Carriage Outwards

The cost of transporting goods, whether inwards or outwards, is an expense and is included on the trial balance as a debit. Often there is no cost for carriage inwards because the seller pays delivery costs. Where the buyer pays the delivery costs (or carriage inwards), the expense is added to the cost of purchases and so affects the gross profit figure.

The cost of carriage outwards does not affect the gross profit. It is a normal expense and is included in the income statement, often as part of 'distribution costs'.

Sales of Fixed Assets

Companies usually have a number of categories of non-current (or fixed) assets (e.g. land and buildings; plant and machinery; fixtures and fittings; vehicles). They should maintain two types of accounts for each category.

1 *Fixed assets at cost (or valuation)* This shows all fixed assets that the company owns, usually at the original cost price; the account has a debit balance. Sometimes a fixed asset is revalued, then the amount on the fixed asset is changed. If it is an increase in value, the fixed asset account is debited, and the increase is credited to capital reserves, which is shown as part of equity on the balance sheet.

2 *Provision for depreciation* This shows the cumulative (or aggregate) depreciation that has been built up over a number of years; the account has a credit balance. Each year the depreciation charge is debited to the profit and loss account (to be included in expenses on the income statement), and credited to the provision for depreciation account. The credit balance on the provision for depreciation account increases each year until some fixed assets are sold.

On the balance sheet the amount shown for fixed assets is the net book value. The cumulative depreciation figure is deducted from the cost (or revalued amount) to give the net book value.

When a fixed asset is sold it is necessary to remove it from both of the above accounts: the original cost must be taken from the fixed asset at cost account; and the amount of depreciation that has been charged for it must be taken from the provision for depreciation account. Both amounts are transferred to a 'disposal of fixed asset account', or a 'sale of fixed asset account', as shown in Illustration 14.4.

As can be seen in that illustration, the machine that is disposed of has to be removed from the machinery at cost account and transferred to the disposal of fixed asset account. This is done by crediting the machinery at cost account, and debiting the disposal of fixed asset account.

The Salov Company bought a machine some years ago for £85,000; cumulative depreciation in respect of the machine amounts to £55,000. The machine was sold last week for £5,500. The company's fixed asset account, and their provision for depreciation account had balances brought forward as shown below immediately before the disposal.

Machinery at cost account

Balance brought forward	£85,000		

Provision for Depreciation on Machinery Account

		Balance brought forward	£55,000

The accumulated depreciation in respect of the machine that is sold has to be removed from the provision for depreciation on machinery account, and transferred to the disposal of fixed asset account. This is done by debiting the provision for depreciation on machinery account, and crediting the disposal of fixed asset account.

The effect of these two transactions is shown below.

Machinery at Cost Account

Balance brought forward	£85,000	Disposal of fixed asset	£20,000

Provision for Depreciation on Machinery Account

Disposal of fixed asset account	£16,000	Balance brought forward	£55,000

Disposal of Fixed Asset Account

Fixed asset at cost	£20,000	Provision for depreciation on machinery	£16,000

After these two transfers, the balance on the disposal of fixed asset account is a debit of £4,000. This is the net book value of the machine. As the machine was sold for £5,500, a profit on sale of £1,500 was made. This profit is credited to the profit and loss account, and debited to the disposal of fixed asset account. The cash received is debited to the cash account, and credited to the disposal of fixed asset account. The effect of these two transactions is shown below.

Disposal of Fixed Asset Account

Fixed asset at cost	£20,000	Provision for depreciation on machinery	£16,000
Profit and loss account	£1,500	Cash	£ 5,500
	£21,500		£21,500

The effects of a sale of fixed assets is included in Self-testing question 6 (Ellie's Limited) in Chapter 15.

ILLUSTRATION 14.4

14.3 Bookkeeping Systems

Bookkeeping systems are designed, or have evolved over the years, so that they achieve a number of objectives:

1 All transactions are recorded, using double entry.

2 They facilitate the production of trial balances and balance sheet and income statements.

3 Transactions can be traced and verified by the organization's own staff, and by external auditors.

4 Errors can be identified, traced and corrected.

5 Several different people can work on different parts of the system at the same time; there are separate books and ledgers for different parts of a system, whether it is hand-written or computerized.

6 One part of the system, or set of records, is used to check on another part of the system.

7 It is unlikely that one person, working alone, can commit fraud. It is more difficult to prevent or detect fraud where there is collusion between a number of different individuals.

Ledgers, Day Books and Journals

All transactions end up being included in double-entry accounts in a 'ledger'. This is usually done on a computer using an accounting package. In a small business, with very few transactions, everything may be recorded in a single 'general ledger'. In a large organization there are likely to be several day books[6] and ledgers in which each individual transaction is recorded.

Where there are hundreds or thousands of items of sales, each item is usually recorded in a sales day book (or sales journal) and the total amount for a week or a month's sales is shown in the ledger. Similarly, there is likely to be a purchases day book (or purchases journal). There might also be a purchases returns (or returns outwards) journal and a sales returns (or returns inwards) journal.

The main day books are:

1 Sales day book

2 Sales returns day book

3 Purchases day book

4 Purchases returns day book

5 General journal

6 Cash book(s)

A general journal may be used to record one-off or special transactions such as adjustments to the trial balance at the end of the period, or corrections of errors.

---

[6] Or 'journals', or 'books of prime entry'.

There may be several cash books (petty cash, bank) or a combined one. They may be analysed to show the amounts for different sorts of transaction (e.g. expenses, payments to creditors, receipts from debtors). The cash book is regarded as being both a day book (showing each individual transaction) and a ledger in its own right.

It is essential to keep a separate personal account for each individual creditor and each individual debtor to be clear what transactions have taken place, and the net amount owed to or by each individual. Where a business has a large number of different suppliers and credit customers, their personal accounts are kept in two different ledgers:

1 The sales or debtors ledger

2 The purchases, or creditors, or bought ledger

3 The remaining accounts may be included in a general or impersonal ledger. Sometimes a nominal ledger is maintained that includes all accounts for revenues and expenses, which are transferred to the profit and loss account (presented as an income statement). Some accounts may be included in a private ledger to which most accounts staff would not have access.

Control Accounts

Where a business has many debtors, it is likely that some errors are made in individual personal accounts, and it is important that the bookkeeping system checks for such errors so that they can be corrected.

It is possible to arrive at the total figure for debtors at the end of a period without examining the individual debtors accounts. The figure can be arrived at by starting with the total amount of debtors at the beginning of the period, then adding all credit sales made during the period (minus any sales returns); from that is deducted any discount allowed to debtors, and any amounts of money received from them. The remaining balance should be equal to the total on the individual personal accounts.

It is useful to have this total on the debtors control account that can be used in the trial balance and to prepare the final accounts, even before errors on individual personal accounts have been corrected.

The position is similar with a creditors control account, but the opposite way around. For example, the amount owed to creditors is a credit balance (whereas the amount owed by debtors is a debit balance); payments are made to creditors (whereas money is received from debtors); discount may be received from creditors (whereas discounts are allowed to debtors); and returns are made outwards to creditors (whereas they are received inwards from debtors).

Bank Reconciliations

The cash book, or the bank column of a cash book, shows the amount of money that the business has in its bank account. When a statement is received from the bank, the amount on that statement will almost certainly differ from the balance in the cash book, for several reasons.[7] The following adjustments apply where the business has money in the bank.[8]

1 The business writes cheques and records them in their cash book as payments. But the bank does not know about these 'unpresented' cheques for several days. The amount for unpresented cheques should be deducted from the amount shown on the bank statement in order to reconcile with the cash book.

2 The bank statement is often prepared before recording deposits made by the business on the day of the statement. Any such deposits should be added to the amount shown on the bank statement.

3 Where a business has investments, it is likely that the bank will receive and record dividends or interest on behalf of the business before they are recorded in the business's cash book. In this case, the bank's figures are likely to be correct and it is necessary to update the cash book.

4 A business often does not know what bank charges have been made until the statement has been received. The amounts shown on the bank statement for bank charges must then be entered in the cash book as payments.

The above adjustments are shown in Illustration 14.5.

Grenaugh Ltd's cash book showed a debit balance of £13,000 on 31 December year 9.

The bank sent them a statement, showing the same date, but that there was £16,400 in the bank.[9] Further investigation revealed the following:

1 Unpresented cheques amounted to £5,000
2 On 31 December Grenaugh Ltd had deposited £2,000 cash into the bank, but this was not shown on the bank statement
3 The bank statement showed dividends received of £500 that had not yet been recorded in the cash book
4 The bank charges for December amounted to £100

Balance according to cash book	£13,000
Add Dividends received	500
Deduct Bank charges	(100)
Updated cash book balance	£13,400
Balance according to bank statement	£16,400
Deduct Unpresented cheques	(5,000)
Add Cash deposited on 31 December	2,000
Updated bank statement balance	£13,400

ILLUSTRATION 14.5

---

[7] Part of the difference is because, from the business's point of view, money in the bank is an asset. But from the bank's point of view, they owe money to the business, and so in the bank's books the amount is a liability. The bank statement will show a credit balance where the business's cash book shows a debit balance. (If there is an overdraft, it is the other way around.)

[8] Where there is an overdraft the adjustments are the other way around. For example, unpresented cheques are added to the overdraft shown by the bank statement, not deducted.

[9] A credit balance of £16,400 in the bank's books.

Summary

It is essential that all transactions are recorded accurately, and that bookkeeping systems are designed to ensure that every item can be traced and verified, and that most errors are shown up. Every transaction is recorded twice; once as a debit and once as a credit. The total of all credits must be equal to the total of all debits. Bookkeeping systems are necessary to keep track of all assets and liabilities, and to ensure that there is an accurate record of all amounts owed to and by the business. They are also necessary to provide the basic information for producing balance sheets and income statements. The first section of the chapter provided an outline of bookkeeping sufficient for most users of financial statements. More detail was provided in the second and third sections.

Review of key points

- Every transaction is recorded twice, on the left-hand side (debit) of one account, and on the right hand side (credit) of another.
- All receipts of cash are recorded on the debit side of the cash account; all payments are recorded on the credit side.
- Not all transactions are shown in the cash account. In many businesses most sales and purchases take place on credit.
- The trial balance provides a summary of all transactions, and is the basis for producing a balance sheet and income statement.
- Bookkeeping systems in practice include more detail than is shown in most textbook examples.
- The term 'cash' is often used loosely to include both bank transactions and petty cash transactions; the two must be recorded separately in practice.
- Bookkeeping systems include mechanisms such as reconciliation statements and control accounts as a check on accuracy.

Self-testing questions

1 Complete the double entry for each of the following transactions:

  a Sales made for cash are credited to the sales account and debited to the

    _____

  b Sales made on credit to Smith are debited to the Smith account, and credited to the _____

  c Purchases made for cash are credited to the cash account, and debited to the

    _____

  d Purchases made on credit from Anirroc Company are debited to the purchases account, and credited to the _____

  e Smith, a debtor, pays us part of what he owes; the amount is credited to the Smith account and debited to the _____

  f The provision for bad debts is increased by £30. This amount is debited to the income statement (perhaps via a profit and loss account) as an expense, and credited to the _____

2 Which of the following accounts normally have a credit balance (as shown on a trial balance): sales, purchases, debtors, creditors, fixed assets, share capital, share premium?

3 Which of the following accounts normally have a debit balance (as shown on a trial balance): expenses, fixed assets, receivables, cash at bank?

4 Which of the following statements is true?

  a Accounts for assets and expenses have credit balances.

  b Accounts for liabilities, share capital, retained earnings and overdrafts have credit balances.

5 Record the following transactions of Carlos using double-entry bookkeeping; summarize them in the form of a trial balance, and prepare an income statement for the three-month period, and a balance sheet as at the end of the period.

1 July	Carlos started a business dealing in second-hand cars and opened a business bank account with £40,000
3 July	Carlos borrows £15,000 from the Spano Bank
5 July	Pays £5,000 to rent premises
8 July	Buys furniture and equipment for £11,000
13 July	Buys cars on credit from Motosales Ltd for £50,000
19 July	Pays general expenses of £2,500
27 July	Sells one car for £4,000 cash
3 Aug	Sells cars on credit to Minki Cabs for £18,000
10 Aug	Buys one car for £3,300 cash
16 Aug	Buys cars on credit from Motosales Ltd for £22,000

30 Aug   Pays £40,000 to Motosales Ltd

6 Sept   Pays general expenses £3,300

14 Sept   Receives £15,000 from Minki Cabs

21 Sept   Sells cars for £24,000 cash

The stock of unsold cars remaining at the end of September was £38,100 at cost. Ignore depreciation.

6 Record the following transactions of Killip using double-entry bookkeeping; summarize them in the form of a trial balance, and prepare an income statement for the one-month period and a balance sheet at the end of that period.

1 Aug   Started business as a management consultant with £5,000 capital, which was paid into the bank

2 Aug   Paid £4,100 for a computer, printer, scanner and photocopier

4 Aug   Paid £500 rent for office for one month

6 Aug   Arranged advertising in the *Journal of Man* at a cost of £250, to be paid for a month later

7 Aug   Bought stationery on credit from Dubya Smith at a cost of £120

11 Aug   Received £650 for work done for two small clients

15 Aug   Paid travelling expenses of £135

20 Aug   Completed work for OneAlpha Ltd and invoiced them for £2,200

23 Aug   Paid £700 to a subcontractor

29 Aug   Paid £80 to Dubya Smith

31 Aug   Receives £550 from OneAlpha Ltd

Depreciation should be ignored.

7 Cass Hawin's bookkeeper had not balanced the cash book on 31 March year 7. They received a bank statement, dated 31 March year 7, which showed an overdraft of £2,000. Further investigation revealed the following:

i   Unpresented cheques amounted to £1,500

ii   On 31 March Cass Hawin had deposited £3,600 cash into the bank, but this was not shown on the bank statement

iii The bank statement showed interest received of £200, which had not yet been recorded in the cash book

iv   The bank charges for December amounted to £150

Required:

a Show the necessary adjustments to the bank statement; and

b Show what the cash book balance should be *before* making any necessary adjustments.

Assessment questions

For the purpose of questions 1–3 there is no need to separate 'petty cash' from 'bank' transactions. They can be combined in a single 'cash account'.

1 Complete the double entry for each of the following transactions:

a The owner of a business pays additional capital to the company; the cash account is debited and it is credited to the _____

b A business repays a loan; the cash account is credited and it is debited to the _____

c The provision for bad debts is reduced by £50; the provision for bad debts account is debited and it is credited to the _____

d Drawings paid are credited to the cash account and debited to the _____

e A loss arising on the sale of a fixed asset is debited to the income statement and credited to the _____

f Closing inventory is shown as a debit item on the balance sheet and is credited to the _____

g A supplier allows a cash discount of £24; this is credited to the income statement and debited to the _____

h Costs of delivering goods to customers of £123 are incurred with Rodo Transport Ltd. This amount is credited to the Rodo Transport Ltd Account and debited to the _____

i A customer returns goods as being unsatisfactory; the amount is debited to the sales returns (or returns inwards) account, which is eventually deducted from sales on the income statement. It is credited to the _____

j The cost of buying a new fixed asset (a car costing £20,000) has inadvertently been debited to the account for travelling expenses. To correct this error the travelling expenses account is credited and it is debited to the _____

k How would the answer to (j) differ if the car had been bought on credit from BWM Garages Ltd?

2 Record the following transactions of A Florist using double-entry bookkeeping; summarize them in the form of a trial balance, and prepare an income statement for the month of January, and a balance sheet as at the end of the period.

1 Jan	Started business with £10,000 capital, paid into the bank
2 Jan	Bought second-hand van; paid £4,000 by cheque
3 Jan	Bought flowers on credit from Miss Daisy, £700
4 Jan	Sold flowers for cash, £120
5 Jan	Bought flowers, paying by cheque, £456
6 Jan	Paid one month's rent, £408
7 Jan	Sold flowers on credit to the University of Eastminster, £999

[handwritten: Dr. Bank Cr. Capital.]

Assessment questions (continued)

14 Jan   Sold flowers in Berwick Street Market for cash, £236

20 Jan   Paid Miss Daisy £400

28 Jan   Received a cheque from University of Eastminster for £899

At the end of January the closing stock of flowers amounted to £210, at net realizable value. Depreciation should be ignored.

3 Record the following transactions of Moorey using double-entry bookkeeping; summarize them in the form of a trial balance, and prepare an income statement for the one-month period and a balance sheet at the end of that period.

1 Apr   Started business selling electronic equipment with £800,000 capital which was paid into the bank

1 Apr   Paid £560,000 for a retail shop

2 Apr   Bought shop fittings on credit from Quirky Fitters for £101,000

3 Apr   Paid £460 for advertising

4 Apr   Purchased electronic goods from a car boot sale, paying cash, £800

5 Apr   Received £150 for first sales

7 Apr   Purchased goods on credit from Sinofacturers for £34,000

8 Apr   Sold goods on credit to Eccentainers amounting to £18,000

15 Apr   Cash sales, £230

24 Apr   Paid General Expenses, £333

28 Apr   Paid £51,000 to Quirky Fitters and £25,000 to Sinofacturers

31 Apr   Received £12,500 from Eccentainers

At the end of the month stocks of goods remaining were £22,600.

Depreciation should be ignored.

4 Banner Ltd's cash book showed a debit balance of £8,000 on 30 June year 4. The bank sent them a statement, showing the same date, but that there was £11,800 in the bank.[10] Further investigation revealed the following:

i   Unpresented cheques amounted to £6,000

ii   On 30 June Banner Ltd had deposited £3,000 cash into the bank, but this was not shown on the bank statement

iii   The bank statement showed dividends received of £1,000 that had not yet been recorded in the cash book

iv   The bank charges for December amounted to £200

Prepare a bank reconciliation statement showing the updated cash book and bank statement balances.

---

[10] A credit balance of £11,000 in the bank's books.

Group activities and discussion questions

1 a Accountants cannot do their job effectively if they do not have a detailed understanding of the business's bookkeeping systems.

b Bookkeeping is done by technicians and computers; it is not a matter for managers and accountants.

Discuss these two statements. With which do you most agree, and why?

2 The power of accountants and accountancy lies mainly in their control of the official financial recording system. Discuss.

3 A French balloonist landed in a field somewhere in the south of England. He hailed a passer-by and said 'Can you tell me where I am, please?' The passer-by said 'You are in a wicker basket in a field.' The Frenchman said 'You are an accountant, aren't you?' The Englishman said 'Yes. How do you know?' The Frenchman said 'Because your information is totally accurate and totally useless.' Explain and comment.

Financial accounting in context

Iris launches against Line50

By Kevin Reed

Accountancy Age, 27 July 2006

Discuss and comment on the following extract from the press. Do you think that software can eliminate the need for accountants to be able to do bookkeeping?

Source: Reproduced with permission by *Accountancy Age*.

A NEW PRODUCT to launch against Sage's ubiquitous Line50 accounting software has been revealed by rival technology company Iris.

Known as Iris Accounts Office, the product aims to eat into Sage's dominance of the small business software market. Both companies have spent years trying to secure the lucrative software market for accounting practices and their clients.

While Iris has a bigger market share among accounting practitioners than Sage, Line50 has proved the most popular accounting software for small businesses.

Iris director Rob Steele said feedback from practices representing 2,500 clients viewed the products as 'relevant': 'That's just from the first month of practice workshops. We're extremely confident it will be viewed well,' he said.

Practitioners' clients remain in charge of their own data, and can 'synchronise' their information with that held by the practice when required, such as towards year end.

Steele said this 'drip-feed' of information between the two parties was implemented because many small businesses were not yet ready to have their business information hosted on the internet, preferring to keep control of data onsite.

References and further reading

Black, G. (2005) *Introduction to Accounting and Finance*. FT Prentice Hall.

Davies, T. and B. Pain (2001) *Business Accounting and Finance*. McGraw-Hill.

Weetman, P. (2006) *Financial and Management Accounting: An Introduction*. FT Prentice Hall.

Wood, F. and A. Sangster (2005) *Business Accounting* vol. 1 (10th edition). FT Prentice Hall.

CHAPTER 15

Trial Balance to Final Accounts

❖ LEARNING OBJECTIVES

After studying this chapter you should be able to:

- ❖ Understand how a trial balance summarizes all transactions that have been recorded

- ❖ Classify items on a trial balance as being income, expenses, assets, liabilities or equity

- ❖ Produce balance sheets and profit and loss accounts (or income statements) from trial balances for sole traders, companies and partnerships

- ❖ Incorporate a wide range of adjustments into final accounts

- ❖ Deal with a variety of different profit-sharing arrangements in partnerships

15.1 Introduction

This chapter deals with the conversion of a trial balance to a set of final accounts, incorporating a range of different adjustments. A trial balance summarizes all the transactions that have been recorded by an organization and provides the main information for producing a set of 'final accounts', that is a balance sheet and an income statement. Additional information and 'adjustments' are required to complete the process.

A balance sheet shows assets, liabilities and equity. The way in which these are presented has been changed several times in recent history; most recently following the widespread adoption of International Accounting Standards (IASs). When dealing with trial balances it may be easiest to think of a balance sheet as follows.

Debit	**Credit**
Assets	Liabilities
	Equity

An income statement (or profit and loss account) shows revenues (or income) and expenses, the difference being profit. The format for presenting these statements has varied over the years, but when dealing with trial balances it may be seen as follows.

Debit	**Credit**
Expenses	Income or Revenues

If the above two simplified tables are combined, they begin to look a bit like a trial balance.

Debit	**Credit**
Assets	Liabilities
	Equity
Expenses	Revenue (or Income)

The above table should help to avoid mistakes in dealing with items on a trial balance. Almost all debit items are either assets to be shown on the balance sheet, or expenses to be shown on the income statement. Almost all credit items on a trial balance are either revenues (or income) to be shown on the income statement, or liabilities to be shown on the balance sheet.

A long trial balance can be daunting but becomes more user-friendly if each item is labelled as being one of the above.

15.2 Sole Traders

The way in which a simplified trial balance can be converted into a balance sheet and income statement is shown in Illustration 15.1.

A simplified trial balance might appear as follows:

Trial balance of Sim Pull as at 31 December year 8

	Debit	Credit
	£	£
Land and buildings	200,000	
Creditors		10,000
Capital as at 1 January year 8		150,000
General expenses	80,000	
Sales revenue		120,000
	280,000	280,000

This would be easily converted into (not very well presented) final accounts, as follows.

Balance sheet of Sim Pull as at 31 December year 8

	£		£
Land and buildings	200,000	Creditors	10,000
		Capital	150,000

Income statement of Sim Pull for year ended 31 December year 8

	£		£
General expenses	80,000	Sales revenue	120,000

The above final accounts do not balance because a profit of £40,000 has been made, and this has to be shown on both the income statement and the balance sheet, where it can be added to capital (if it is not a company), or shown as a separate item, as follows.

Balance sheet of Sim Pull as at 31 December year 8

	£		£
Land and buildings	200,000	Creditors	10,000
		Capital	150,000
		Profit	40,000
	200,000		200,000

Income statement of Sim Pull for year ended 31 December year 8

	£		£
General expenses	80,000	Sales revenue	120,000
Profit	40,000		
	120,000		120,000

Most trial balances look much more complex than Sim Pull's above because:
a   there are more items; and
b   there are adjustments to be made.

ILLUSTRATION 15.1

Additional Items

The items that most frequently appear on trial balances are shown below, categorized under the main headings to indicate where they appear in final accounts.

Assets

Assets are usually classified as long term ('fixed assets') or short term ('current assets').

Non-current assets (or fixed assets)

Premises, land, buildings
Furniture, fixtures, fittings
Plant, machinery
Vehicles, ships, aeroplanes
Goodwill

Current assets

Inventories (or stocks)
Receivables (or debtors)
Prepayments or payments in advance
Cash and bank

Liabilities

Long term

Debentures, loans, mortgages

Short term

Payables (or creditors)
Accruals
Overdraft
Taxation; proposed dividends (in company accounts)

Equity

Capital (called 'share capital' in a company)
Retained profits
Profit and loss account
Drawings (not in company accounts): these are a debit item, to be deducted from capital

Revenue (or *Income*)

Sales or turnover
Dividends, interest, rent, commissions received or receivable
Discount received

Expenses

There are probably hundreds of different expenses, sometimes grouped together under general headings such as distribution costs or administrative expenses. Examples of expenses include: wages, salaries, rent, rates, insurance, postage, telephone, stationery, travelling expenses, carriage inwards, carriage outwards, lighting and heating.

Provisions are like negative assets. A provision for depreciation is shown as a deduction from non-current (fixed) assets on the balance sheet. A provision for bad debts is shown as a deduction from receivables (or debtors) on the balance sheet.

How to Tackle a Trial Balance Question

There are many different ways of tackling a trial balance question, perhaps using an extended trial balance. The following stages often prove to be the fastest way of scoring marks in an examination:

1 Make sure that you have the format of a balance sheet and income statement memorized. Set the format out, using a whole page for each statement and writing on alternate lines, leaving space for adjustments. You should then be clear where most items from the trial balance should appear, and there should be space for any additions or alterations.

2 Copy each item from the trial balance on to the balance sheet or income statement in the appropriate place.

  At this stage do not bother with adding up (the totals may have to be changed later, and there are not usually many marks in an examination for adding up), and do not try to do the adjustments until every item has been copied from the trial balance to the appropriate place. If you try to do adjustments before completing the copying-out of trial balance items, you may get confused or omit items, such as the second part of an adjustment.

3 Do each adjustment in turn, making sure that each item is dealt with *twice*; usually this is once on the income statement, and once on the balance sheet.

4 Add up to produce sub-totals under each heading, and profit figures, and to balance. There is no point in attempting to calculate profit until all the adjustments have been done.

Stages 2, 3 and 4 are demonstrated in Illustration 15.4 (Jimmy's Junk, p. 405).

The 'extended trial balance'[1] approach is more time consuming, but it is also more systematic and thorough. Items are dealt with using several columns: debits and credits from the trial balance; adjustments; and columns to show the amounts for the balance sheet and income statement

Adjustments

1 Closing Inventory (Stock)

Most businesses are likely to have unsold stocks (or inventories) at the end of the period. A closing inventory is usually introduced as an extra item after completing the trial balance. It has to appear twice in the final accounts as a:

■ Debit on the balance sheet, shown as a current asset

■ Credit on the profit and loss account, deducted from purchases in calculating cost of sales (or cost of goods sold); this can be shown directly on the income statement to avoid bothering with double-entry bookkeeping in an examination

The bookkeeping for dealing with these is shown in Chapter 14, Section 14.2, but there is no need to do the detailed bookkeeping in order to produce correct final accounts from a trial balance in an examination.

Illustration 15.2 shows how to deal with the adjustment for closing inventory.

---

[1] Illustrated in the website of this book.

Trial balance of Rikki Bloderick as at 30 June year 2

	Debit £	Creidt £
Bank	56,000	
Capital		27,000
Lighting and heating	6,000	
Payables (debtors)	5,000	
Purchases	118,000	
Receivables (creditors)		13,000
Rent and rates	26,000	
Sales revenue		220,000
Inventories at 1 July year 1	12,000	
Wages and salaries	37,000	
	260,000	260,000

Adjustments

1 Closing inventory as at 30 June year 2 amounted to £15,000

Prepare the income statement for the year ended 30 June year 2 and the balance sheet as at that date.

Solution

The first part of the income statement will compare the sales revenue figure for the year with the cost of goods sold to arrive at the gross profit.

The trial balance includes stocks available for sale at the beginning of the year (£12,000) and purchases made during the year (£118,000). The amount of goods available for sale was, therefore (£118,000 + £12,000 =) £130,000, but not all those goods were sold during the year. We are told that the closing inventory of goods unsold at the end of the year amounted to £15,000. The cost of the goods that were sold during the year was, therefore (£130,000 − £15,000 =) £115,000.

Income statement of Rikki Bloderick for the year ended 30 June year 2

	£	£
Sales revenue		220,000
Opening inventory	12,000	
Purchases	118,000	
	130,000	
Deduct Closing inventory	15,000	
Cost of goods sold		115,000
Gross profit		105,000
Lighting and heating	6,000	
Rent and rates	26,000	
Wages and salaries	37,000	69,000
Net profit		36,000

Balance sheet as at 30 June year 2

Current assets		
Inventory	15,000	
Receivables	5,000	
Bank	56,000	76,000
Current liabilities		
Payables		13,000
Equity		
Capital as at 1 July year 1		27,000
Add Profit for year		36,000
		76,000

ILLUSTRATION 15.2

2 Depreciation

Most businesses have some fixed assets that should be depreciated each year. A trial balance usually includes a number of fixed assets that are shown at cost (debit items). It is best to leave this figure unchanged and to deal with 'provision for depreciation' as a separate item. A balance sheet usually shows the original cost of the asset, and the provision for depreciation, and then the net book value, as follows.

Extract from balance sheet as at 31 December year 6

Plant and machinery at cost	£50,000
Deduct Provision for depreciation	£15,000
Net book value	£35,000

Trial balances include a provision for depreciation (a credit item), which is usually the figure left from the previous year. In the above illustration it could be that the £15,000 provision for depreciation figure on the trial balance was £10,000 (as at 31 December year 5); to that £5,000 is added (and charged as an expense, a debit, on the profit and loss account) to give a new provision for depreciation as at 31 December 2006.

The bookkeeping for dealing with depreciation is shown in Chapter 14, Section 14.2; the idea of depreciation is explained in Chapter 2. Illustration 15.3 shows how to deal with the adjustment to the trial balance.

Extract from trial balance as at 31 December year 6

	Debit £	Credit £
Plant and machinery at cost	50,000	
Vehicles at cost	80,000	
Provision for depreciation on plant and machinery as at 31 December year 5		10,000
Provision for depreciation on vehicles as at 31 December year 5		35,000

Adjustments

1 Provision for depreciation is to be made on plant and machinery at 10 per cent per annum on cost (straight line basis).
2 Provision for depreciation is to be made on vehicles at 25 per cent per annum on a diminishing balance (or reducing balance) basis.

The calculations could be shown as a 'working' on the face of the balance sheet, or a note, as follows:

Item	At cost	Provision for depreciation		Net book value
Plant and machinery		As at 31 Dec year 5	10,000	
		Charge for year	5,000	
	50,000	As at 31 Dec year 6	15,000	35,000
Vehicles		As at 31 Dec year 5	35,000	
		Charge for year	11,250	
	80,000	As at 31 Dec year 6	46,250	33,750

The net book value of the vehicles at the beginning of the year was (£80,000 − £35,000 =) £45,000. The depreciation charge for the year is 25 per cent of that balance (25 per cent × £45,000 =) £11,250.

ILLUSTRATION 15.3

You should now be in a position to tackle Self-testing questions 1–4 (Noddy; Mona Ramsey; Sally Glen; Mary Rushen), which are to be found at the end of this chapter (see pp. 417–18). Answers are supplied at the end of the book.

3 Drawings

Most sole traders withdraw money from their businesses from time to time, especially if it is profitable. If drawings have already been recorded, the amount has been taken from the bank, and the amount withdrawn is shown as a debit item on the trial balance; that amount is then shown as a deduction from capital plus profit on the balance sheet.

If drawings are shown as an adjustment, because they have not yet been recorded, the amount should be taken from the bank, and shown as a deduction from capital plus profit on the balance sheet.

4 Accruals

There are usually some expenses (e.g. electricity) that have not yet been recorded or paid at the end of the year. The amount of the required adjustment is:

- Shown as a debit on the income statement, increasing the amount of the expense that has already been recorded
- Shown as a credit on the balance sheet, as a current liability

5 Prepayments

There are usually some expenses (e.g. rent) that have been paid in advance at the end of the year, so part of the expense that has already been recorded (and included on the trial balance) is in respect of the following year. The amount of the prepayment is:

- Shown as a debit on the balance sheet, as a current asset 'prepayments', alongside receivables
- Shown as a credit on the income statement reducing the amount of the expense that has already been recorded

6 Provision for Bad Debts

Where a provision for bad debts already exists, it is usually necessary to change the amount at the end of the year.

When there is an *increase* in a provision for bad debts, the *amount of the increase* is included as an expense (a debit) on the income statement. The increase is added to (credited to) the existing provision for bad debts. This credit balance is shown as a deduction from receivables on the balance sheet.

When there is a *reduction* in a provision for bad debts, *the amount of the reduction* is credited to the income statement (as if it is additional income, or perhaps as a negative expense). The reduction is deducted from the provision for bad debts that is shown as a deduction from receivables on the balance sheet.

A provision for bad debts is general, perhaps taken as 5 per cent of debtors.

7 Bad Debts Written Off

Bad debts written off are specific, where it is known that the debtor will not be paying. It is easier to keep the writing-off of specific bad debts separate from any provision for bad debts. The amount to be written off is:

- Shown as a debit (an expense) on the income statement
- Treated as a credit on the balance sheet by reducing the amount shown for receivables

These adjustments are illustrated in Illustration 15.4 (Jimmy's Junk).

Trial balance of Jimmy's Junk business as at 31 December year 9

	Debit £	Credit £
Bank	18,010	
Capital as at 31 December year 8		90,950
Fixtures and fittings at cost	1,200	
General expenses	14,000	
Insurance	5,000	
Interest paid	7,000	
Inventory at 31 December year 8 (opening stock)	3,000	
Lighting and heating	12,000	
Loan from Bank of Ruristan		100,000
Payables (creditors)		32,000
Provision for bad debts		1,880
Provision for depreciation on delivery van as at 31 December year 8		9,760
Provision for depreciation on fixtures and fittings as at 31 December year 8		720
Provision for depreciation on premises as at 31 December year 8		24,000
Purchases	47,000	
Receivables (debtors)	41,100	
Sales revenue		225,000
Shop premises at cost	300,000	
Delivery van at cost	20,000	
Wages	16,000	
	484,310	484,310

Adjustments

1 Closing inventory as at 31 December year 9 amounted to £4,000.
2 Depreciation is to be provided on shop premises on a straight line basis at 2 per cent per annum.
3 Depreciation is to be provided on fixtures and fittings on a straight line basis at 10 per cent per annum.
4 Depreciation is to be provided on the delivery van at 20 per cent per annum on a diminishing balance basis.
5 The electricity bill for the 3 months ending on 28 February year 10 amounts to £2,700, and has not yet been recorded in the accounts.
6 The amount shown for insurance includes £1,200 for the 3-month period 1 November year 9 to 31 January year 10.
7 A specific debt of £1,100 is to be written off as irrecoverable.

ILLUSTRATION 15.4

8 The provision for bad debts is to be adjusted to be 5 per cent of debtors.
9 On 31 December Jimmy took drawings from the business of £18,000, which have not yet been recorded.

Prepare the income statement for the year ended 31 December year 8 and the balance sheet as at that date.

Solution in three stages
The following solution is designed to show three stages of producing final accounts from a trial balance. In stage 1 the figures that are taken from the trial balance are shown in normal type. Stage 2 adjustments are shown in **bold**. The results of the final stage, adding up, are shown in *italics*.

Income Statement of Jimmy's Junk for the year ended 31 December year 9

	£	£	£
Sales revenue			225,000
Opening inventory		3,000	
Purchases		<u>47,000</u>	
		50,000	
Deduct Closing stock		**4,000**	
Cost of goods sold			<u>*46,000*</u>
Gross profit			*179,000*
General expenses		14,000	
Wages		16,000	
Interest		7,000	
Insurance	5,000		
	− 400	*4,600*	
Light and heat	12,000		
	+ 900	*12,900*	
Bad debt written off		**1,100**	
Increase in provision for bad debts		**120**	
Depreciation: premises		**6,000**	
Depreciation: fixtures and fittings		**120**	
Depreciation: vehicle		**2,048**[2]	
			<u>*63,888*</u>
Net profit			*115,112*

Balance sheet of Jimmy's Junk as at 31 December year 9

Non-current assets	Cost	Provision for depreciation	Net book value
Shop premises	300,000	24,000	
		+ 6,000	
		30,000	*270,000*
Fixtures and fittings	1,200	720	
		+ 120	
		840	*360*
Delivery van	20,000	9,760	
		+ 2,048	
		11,808	<u>*8,192*</u>
			278,552

ILLUSTRATION 15.4 continued

---

[2] Van at cost £20,000, minus provision for depreciation as at 31 December year 8, £9,760, gives a net book value of £10,240 at the beginning of the year. The depreciation charge is 20 per cent of £10,240 = £2,048.

Current assets				
Inventory			4,000	
Receivables		41,100		
Bad debt written-off		1,100		
		40,000		
Provision for				
bad debts	1,880			
Increase	120	2,000	*38,000*	
Prepayment			**400**	
Bank	18,010			
Drawings	18,000		10	
			42,410	*42,410*
TOTAL ASSETS				320,962
Equity				
Capital as at			90,950	
31 December year 8				
Add Profit for year			*115,112*	
			206,062	
Deduct Drawings			18,000	*188,062*
Current liabilities				
Accrual		900		
Payables		32,000		*32,900*
Non-current liabilities				
Loan from Bank				
of Ruristan				100,000
				320,962

ILLUSTRATION 15.4 continued

Additional Adjustments

There may be other adjustments when trial balances are produced in practice, for example to correct errors. When a trial balance is first produced it is only a 'trial': the accountant is trying to see if it will balance. If not, a 'suspense account' is sometimes put in to make up the difference; errors are then traced, and each correction is debited to the correct account, and credited to the suspense account (or credited to the correct account, and debited to the suspense account) until the trial balance balances.

Normal bookkeeping principles apply to all adjustments to the trial balance, and these are shown in Chapter 14.

15.3 Companies

In most ways the final accounts of companies are much the same as for sole traders. The main differences are as follows:

1 There are prescribed formats for company final accounts, as explained in Chapters 1 and 2. There is more freedom for sole traders to present financial statements in their own way.

2 The owners of companies receive payments as *dividends*; the equivalent payments to sole traders are called *drawings.*

3 In companies *share capital* is shown in an account that is kept separate from retained earnings and dividends. In sole traders profits are usually added to the figure for capital, and drawings are deducted from capital.

4 In companies there is a heading for *shareholders' funds* which can include a number of items such as: *ordinary share capital, preference share capital, share premium, retained profits, general reserves and revenue reserves and capital reserves.* In sole traders a single capital account usually includes all that the owners have invested in the business, capital and profits.

5 Companies are liable to pay *corporation tax*, and a profit before tax figure is shown, and also a profit after tax figure. At the end of the year it is usually necessary to estimate the amount of corporation tax payable, and this is included as a debit in the income statement, usually as the final deduction before showing profit for the year. It is included as a credit, as a current liability on the balance sheet (in the way that an accrual is treated). Sole traders are liable to pay income tax as individual people; there is no taxation on the profits of the business itself.

6 A trial balance often shows that an *interim dividend* has already been paid (a debit item). In addition, companies usually propose a *final dividend*, which is dealt with as an adjustment to the trial balance. In addition, companies usually propose a *final dividend*, which used to be dealt with as an adjustment to the trial balance. Final dividends are not now recognized until approved at the annual general meeting, after the financial statements have been produced. They are shown the following year on the 'Statement of changes in equity'.

7 Legislation requires that many expenses are disclosed in company accounts; these are often shown as notes to the accounts. The specified formats for income statement accounts require relatively little disclosure. Examples of expenses that must be disclosed, although they are included within more general headings on the income statement, are directors' fees, auditors' fees and expenses. The profit and loss accounts[3] of sole traders usually disclose expenses in some detail, according to the preferences of the individual concerned.

8 Most companies have to pay some *interest* (finance expense), whether on long-term loans such as *debentures* or on overdrafts. It can be useful to show profit before charging interest ('operating profit') and profit after charging interest ('profit before taxation').

A simplified company trial balance question for Scarlett Ltd is shown in Illustration 15.5.

---

[3] The term 'profit and loss account' is still used, particularly for working statements, part of the double-entry system of accounting. The 'income statement' is the final statement, in good form, suitable for showing to people outside the business.

The trial balance of Scarlett Ltd as at 31 December year 4

	Debit £	Credit £
Administrative expenses	24,000	
Cash	48,500	
Distribution costs	57,000	
Interim dividend paid	4,500	
Inventories (stocks) at 31 December year 3	14,000	
Payables (creditors)		53,000
Property and plant at cost	660,500	
Provision for depreciation on property and plant as at 31 December year 3		135,000
Purchases	730,500	
Retained earnings as at 31 December year 3		69.000
Receivables (debtors)	68,000	
Sales		900,000
Share capital, ordinary £1 shares		450,000
	1,607,000	1,607,000

Adjustments
1 Inventories (stocks) as at 31 December year 4 amounted to £18,000.
2 The depreciation charge on plant and equipment for the year ended 31 December year 4 is to be £48,000.
3 A final dividend of 2p per share is proposed.
4 Corporation tax of £15,000 is to be provided.

Income statement of Scarlett Ltd for the year ended 31 December year 4

	£	£
Revenue (from sales)		900,000
Cost of sales		
Opening stock	14,000	
Purchases	730,500	
	744,500	
Deduct Closing stock	18,000	726,500
Gross profit		173,500
Distribution costs	57,000	
Administrative expenses	24,000	
Depreciation	48,000	129,000
Profit before tax		44,500
Corporation tax		15,000
Profit after tax		29,500

Statement of changes in equity for the year ended 31 December year 4

Balance as at 31 December year 3 (450,000 + 69,000)	519,000
Profit for the period	29,500
Dividends[4]	(13,500)
Balance as at 31 December year 4	535,000

ILLUSTRATION 15.5

---

[4] £4,500 plus (2p per 450,000 shares) £9,000.

Balance sheet as at 31 December year 4

	£	£
Assets		
Non-current assets		
Property and plant at cost	660,500	
Deduct Provision for depreciation		
(135,000 + 48,000)		183,000
		477,500
Current assets		
Inventories	18,000	
Trade receivables	68,000	
Cash	48,500	
		134,500
Total assets		612,000
Equity and liabilities		
Equity		
Ordinary share capital		450,000
Retained earnings		
(69,000 + 29,500 − 4,500 − 9,000)		85,000
		535,000
Current liabilities		
Payables (creditors)	53,000	
Proposed dividend	9,000	
Corporation tax	15,000	
		77,000
		612,000

ILLUSTRATION 15.5 continued

Additional Adjustments

There may be other adjustments with company financial statements, for example the issue or redemption of shares and debentures. Care is needed to ensure that dividends are properly dealt with, and there may be additional accruals for interest payable. Sometimes it may be necessary to write down the value of assets. Closing inventories, for example, should be shown at the lower of cost and net realizable value. Any reduction in the amount shown for assets is shown as a credit to the balance sheet item (reducing the amount of the asset), and as a debit on the income statement (reducing profit). As always, normal bookkeeping principles apply to all adjustments. You should now be able to tackle Self-testing question 6 (Ellie's Ltd) at the end of this chapter. A solution is provided at the end of the book.

15.4 Partnerships

In most ways the final accounts of partnerships are much the same as for sole traders. The main differences arise because there is a need (a) to divide the profit between the partners; and (b) to keep separate accounts for each of the partners, for capital, drawings and current transactions.

A partnership's profit and loss account is prepared in the same way as for a sole trader until the net profit is arrived at. After that there is an 'appropriation account' on which the amount of profit due to each partner is calculated.

A partnership's balance sheet is prepared in the same way as for a sole trader, except that (a) there is a separate capital account for each partner; and (b) in addition to the capital accounts there is a 'current account' for each partner to keep track of the amounts of profits credited to each, and the amount of drawings taken.

In the simplified Illustration 15.6, it is assumed that there are no accruals, prepayments, and the only adjustments are for depreciation and closing stock.

Trial balance of Orry, Mona and Michael as at 31 December year 7

	Debit £	Credit £
Cash	95,200	
Expenses	44,400	
Premises	280,000	
Provision for depreciation on premises at 31 December year 6		33,600
Purchases	240,000	
Sales		400,000
Stocks at 31 December year 6	25,000	
Capital accounts at 1 January year 7		
Orry		160,000
Mona		100,000
Michael		30,000
Current accounts at 1 January Year 7		
Orry		30,000
Mona	40,000	
Michael	29,000	
	753,600	753,600

Adjustments

1 Stock at 31 December year 7 amounted to £35,000.

2 The provision for depreciation on premises is to be increased by £5,600.

Income statement of Orry, Mona and Michael for the year ended 31 December year 7

	£	£
Sales revenue		400,000
Opening stock	25,000	
Purchases	240,000	
	265,000	
Deduct Closing stock	35,000	
Cost of sales		230,000
Gross profit		170,000
Expenses	44,400	
Depreciation	5,600	50,000
Net profit		120,000

ILLUSTRATION 15.6 (Part 1)

Explanations

The profit is calculated in the same way as with a sole trader. In most cases there would be more assets and expenses, more adjustments, and additional items such as debtors and creditors.

In a sole trader the net profit is simply added to the capital account on the balance sheet, which should then balance.

In a partnership it is necessary to know how the profit is to be divided between the partners. If there is £120,000 profit to be divided equally between three partners, it would be possible simply to credit £40,000 to each of the partner's capital accounts, and that would be the end of the matter. The balance sheet (1) of Orry, Mona and Michael would balance if the £120,000 profit was added to the capital or current accounts.

More detail is usually required because:

1 The partners do not necessarily share the profits equally. In this example Orry has much more money invested in the business (£160,000 + £30,000 = £190,000) than Michael who seems to draw almost as much money out of the business as he has invested in it. But perhaps it is Michael who does most of the work, and deserves a regular salary. Orry may be more or less retired ('a sleeping partner'), but as he has a substantial sum invested in the business (and perhaps he set it up in the first place), he deserves some extra return. It might be agreed that Michael should have a 'salary' from the profits of £40,000 a year; that Orry should have half of the remaining profits; and that Mona and Michael should have one-quarter each. Balance sheet (2), opposite, shows the effect of appropriating the profits in this way.

2 There are usually separate accounts for partners':

   a Capital, with the amounts remaining much the same from year to year, unless there is a major change

   b Current accounts, which change regularly each year as appropriations of profit are credited to them, and drawings debited to them

   c Drawings, which may be shown in a separate account, and debited to the current accounts at the end of the year

ILLUSTRATION 15.6 continued

Balance sheet (1) of Orry, Mona and Michael as at 31 December year 7 (before appropriation of profits)

Non-current assets

Premises			280,000		
Deduct Provision for depreciation (33,600 + 5,600)			39,200		
				240,800	

Current assets

Inventories			35,000		
Cash			95,200		
				130,200	
				371,000	

Capital accounts

Orry	Mona	Michael			
160,000	100,000	30,000	290,000		

Current accounts

Orry	Mona	Michael			
30,000	(40,000)	(29,000)	(39,000)		
			251,000		

ILLUSTRATION 15.6 (Part 2)

Balance sheet (2) of Orry, Mona and Michael as at 31 December year (after appropriation of profits)

Non-current assets

Premises			280,000	
Deduct Provision for depreciation (33,600 + 5,600)			39,200	
				240,800

Current assets

Inventories			35,000	
Cash			95,200	
				130,200
				371,000

Capital accounts

Orry	Mona	Michael		
160,000	100,000	30,000	290,000	

Current accounts

	Orry	Mona	Michael		
	30,000	(40,000)	(29,000)		
Salary			40,000		
Profit	40,000	20,000	20,000		
	70,000	(20,000)	31,000	81,000	
					371,000

ILLUSTRATION 15.6 (Part 2) continued

Other Issues in Partnership Accounts

Partners can agree among themselves to share the work and benefits of the partnership business in any way they like, and this is best done with a formal written agreement. In the absence of any agreement to the contrary, the provisions of the 1890 Partnership Act apply, the key parts of which are that partners share profits and losses equally; they share equally in the management of the business; there are no partners' salaries, interest on capital or drawings; if a partner loans money to the business, interest will be allowed at 5 per cent per annum; and no new partner can be admitted unless all agree. The partnership is dissolved if one partner resigns, dies or becomes bankrupt or insane.

A New Partner Joins

When new partners are admitted, it is fair that they should contribute something towards the goodwill that has already been generated by the existing partners. The current value of goodwill is not usually shown on partnership balance sheets, but it needs to be agreed for the purpose of admitting a new partner; this may be dealt with as shown in Illustration 15.7.

> Rue and Blue are in partnership sharing profits equally; they do not include goodwill on their balance sheet. They agree to admit Ayre who will have one-fifth of profits. The new profit-sharing ratios will be 2 : 2 : 1. It is agreed that (a) goodwill amounting to £100,000 should be introduced on the balance sheet; (b) Ayre should pay £80,000 into the partnership; and (c) that the goodwill should then be written off.
>
> **a** Debit goodwill £100,000
>   Credit the capital accounts of Rue £50,000; Blue £50,000
> **b** Debit cash £80,000
>   Credit Ayre's capital £80,000
> **c** Debit the capital accounts of Rue £40,000; Blue £40,000; Ayre £20,000
>   Credit goodwill £100,000
>
> The effect of this is that Ayre has paid £80,000 into the partnership, but is left with a credit of only £60,000 because he has paid £20,000 for his share of goodwill.
>   It would be quicker simply to debit Ayre's capital with £20,000, and credit £10,000 each to Rue and Blue.
> Another alternative would be to continue to show the goodwill on the balance sheet, and to amortize it each year.
>
> **ILLUSTRATION 15.7**

Change in Profit-Sharing Ratios

When existing partners agree to change their profit-sharing ratios, similar procedures take place. Goodwill is valued and credited to the partners in their old profit-sharing ratios. It may then be written off in their new profit sharing ratios.

A Partner Leaves; Dissolution

When a partner retires or leaves, the partnership has to be dissolved, even if it is immediately replaced by a similar partnership with many of the same individuals. It is important that the leaving partner(s) are credited with their full share of the value of the business. In principle the assets and liabilities are sold off (or transferred to other individuals), and cash is then paid to the leaving partners equal to the balances remaining on their capital and current accounts. In practice it is necessary to establish the amount of goodwill and credit to the partners' capital accounts. All assets and liabilities are transferred to a realization account. The assets and liabilities are then disposed of (or transferred to a new business at agreed amounts). The amounts realized are likely to be different from their book values, and so a profit or loss arises on realization. This profit or loss (which is the balance remaining on the realization account) is then transferred to the partners' capital accounts in their profit sharing ratios. The balance remaining on the leaving partners' capital account is then the amount that is due to be paid to them. This may be paid immediately in cash, or other terms (e.g. loans; instalments; taking over particular assets) may be agreed.

A general example of partnership accounts is provided in Illustration 15.8, with additional questions at the end of the chapter (see pp. 421 and 423–4).

Before preparing the appropriation account, the profit and loss account of Knobby and Bee-Gears showed a net profit of £150,000, and their summarized balance sheet as at 31 December year 2 was as follows:

	£	£
Net assets		700,000
Profit for year (before appropriation)		150,000
Capital accounts		
Knobby	500,000	
Bee-Gears	100,000	600,000
Current accounts		
Knobby	50,000	
Bee-Gears	(40,000)	10,000
Drawings accounts		
Knobby	(10,000)	
Bee-Gears	(50,000)	(60,000)
		700,000

ILLUSTRATION 15.8

The partnership agreement provides for charging interest on drawings at the rate of 10 per cent of the balances on the drawings accounts at the end of the year; interest on capital is to be 5 per cent per annum; Bee-Gears is to receive a salary of £30,000 a year; Knobby is to be credited with two-thirds of remaining profits and Bee-Gears with one-third.

Appropriation account of Knobby and Bee-Gears for the year ended 31 December year 2

	£	£
Net profit		150,000
Interest on drawings		
Knobby	1,000	
Bee-Gears	5,000	6,000
		156,000
Salary – Bee-Gears	30,000	
Interest on capital		
Knobby	25,000	
Bee-Gears	5,000	60,000
		96,000
Share of profit		
Knobby	64,000	
Bee-Gears	32,000	96,000

Summarized balance sheet of Knobby and Bee-Gears as at 31 December year 2

	Knobby	Bee-Gears	
Net assets			700.000
Capital accounts	Knobby	Bee-Gears	
	500,000 Cr	100,000 Cr	
			600,000 Cr
Current accounts	Knobby	Bee-Gears	
	50,000 Cr	(40,000) Dr	
Interest on drawings	(1,000) Dr	(5,000) Dr	
	49,000 Cr	(45,000) Dr	
Salary	–	30,000 Cr	
Interest on capital	25,000 Cr	5,000 Cr	
Share of profit	64,000 Cr	32,000 Cr	
	138,000 Cr	22,000 Cr	
Drawings	(10,000) (Dr)	(50,000) (Dr)	
	128,000 (Cr)	(28,000) (Dr)	100,000
			700,000

Explanations

The profit and loss account and balance sheet have already been prepared in the usual way, taking into account depreciation, accruals and other adjustments. The net profit to be allocated between the partners is £150,000, which is a credit balance remaining on the profit and loss account. For each appropriation of profit (salary, interest on capital, share of profit), the bookkeeping is to debit the profit and loss appropriation account, and to credit the current account of each partner.

The idea of charging interest on drawings is rather different. The charge (the debit) is made to the partners' current accounts; the credit is to the profit and loss account, which has the effect of increasing the amount to be divided between the partners.

At the end of the year 2 the partners' drawings accounts can be netted off against their current accounts. The drawings accounts for year 3 will then show only the drawings made in year 3. Knobby may think that Bee-Gears ought to be charged more interest because he still has a debit balance on his current account in year 3, even before making any drawings.

The partners' capital accounts usually remain unchanged from year to year, unless it is agreed that additional capital is introduced (or withdrawn).

Summary

The basic recording of financial transactions, using double-entry bookkeeping, is the same with sole traders, companies and partnerships, and most of the adjustments to trial balances are much the same. Unincorporated businesses (sole traders and partnerships) are free to present their balance sheets and 'profit and loss accounts' in traditional ways, often including expenses in some detail. The term 'income statement' is used for a final, published version of a profit and loss account.

With sole traders it is acceptable for profits to be added to capital, and for drawings to be deducted from capital. In partnerships there are usually separate accounts for each partner's capital, current transactions and drawings.

In company accounts share capital must be clearly separated from other reserves and retained earnings. Company financial statements are governed by Companies Acts and accounting standards; and the formats shown in IAS 1 for balance sheets and income statements are generally being adopted.

Review of key points

■ The trial balance is a summary of all transactions that have been recorded in the double-entry bookkeeping system, and is the basis for preparing balance sheets and income statements.

■ Adjustments and additional information are required to produce a balance sheet and income statement. Each of these has to be dealt with twice: once as a debit, and once as a credit.

■ Adjustments for closing stock, depreciation, accruals, prepayments, provisions for bad debts and bad debts written off are the same in all types of organization.

■ Drawings are deducted from capital in sole traders' accounts. In partnerships, drawings are shown separately from capital, and separately for each partner.

■ A company's income statement concludes by showing profit for the period. Dividends are shown on a separate statement 'changes in equity for the period'.

■ Balance sheets and income statements for all types of organization are increasingly following the formats illustrated in IAS 1.

Self-testing questions

1 The trial balance of Noddy's Business as at 31 December year 6 is as follows:

	Debit	Credit
	£	£
Shop premises	400,000	
Capital as at 1 December year 6		370,000
General expenses	120,000	
Payables (creditors)		20,000
Sales		130,000
	520,000	520,000

Prepare an income statement for the year ended 31 December year 6, and a balance sheet as at that date.

2 The trial balance of Mona Ramsey as at 30 September year 3 was as follows.

	£	£
Bank	24,321	
Capital		27,000
General expenses	8,000	
Inventory at 1 October year 2	20,000	
Payables (creditors)		13,000
Purchases	188,000	
Receivables (debtors)	11,000	
Rent, rates and insurance	17,000	
Sales revenue		267,321
Wages	39,000	
	307,321	307,321

Self-testing questions (continued)

Adjustments

i Closing Inventory as at 30 September year 3 amounted to £15,000.

Prepare an income statement for the year ended 30 September year 3, and a balance sheet as at that date.

3 The trial balance of Sally Glen's business as at 31 December year 8 is as follows:

	£	£
Bank	23,000	
Capital as at 31 December year 7		370,000
General expenses	8,000	
Inventories at 31 December year 7	18,000	
Provision for depreciation on premises as at 31 December year 7		21,000
Provision for depreciation on delivery van as at 31 December year 7		14,000
Payables (creditors)		20,000
Purchases	242,000	
Receivables (debtors)	60,000	
Rent, rates and insurance	23,000	
Sales revenue		365,000
Shop premises at cost	350,000	
Delivery van at cost	32,000	
Wages	34,000	
	790,000	790,000

Adjustments

i Closing inventory as at 31 December year 8 amounted to £19,000.

ii Depreciation is to be provided on shop premises on a straight line basis at 2 per cent per annum.

iii Depreciation is to be provided on the delivery van at 25 per cent per annum on a diminishing balance basis.

Prepare an income statement for the year ended 31 December year 8, and a balance sheet as at that date.

4 The trial balance of Mary Rushen's business as at 30 June year 5 was as follows.

	£	£
Capital as at 30 June year 4		238,200
Cash and bank	7,400	
Fixtures and fittings at cost	44,000	
Freehold buildings at cost	400,000	
General expenses	13,000	
Inventories at 30 June year 4	12,000	
Payables (creditors)		18,000
Provision for depreciation on freehold buildings as at 30 June year 4		80,000

Self-testing questions (continued)

Provision for depreciation on fixtures and fittings as at 30 June year 4		30,800
Purchases	155,000	
Receivables (debtors)	8,000	
Repairs and maintenance	10,600	
Sales revenue		320,000
Wages	37,000	
	687,000	687,000

Adjustments

i   Closing inventory as at 30 June year 5 amounted to £7,000.

ii Depreciation is to be provided on freehold buildings on a straight line basis at 2.5 per cent per annum.

iii Depreciation is to be provided on the fixtures and fittings on a straight line basis at 10 per cent per annum.

Prepare an income statement for the year ended 30 June year 5, and a balance sheet as at that date.

5 The trial balance of Brad Head as at 31 December year 3 was as follows.

	£	£
Bank	6,400	
Capital as at 31 December year 2		35,000
Fixtures and fittings at cost	22,000	
General expenses	9,000	
Interest paid	3,500	
Inventories at 31 December year 2	28,000	
Lighting and heating	19,000	
Loan from SHC Bank		50,000
Payables (creditors)		31,000
Plant and machinery at cost	220,000	
Provision for bad debts		1,800
Provision for depreciation on vehicles as at 31 December year 2		15,000
Provision for depreciation on fixtures and fittings at 31 December year 2		13,200
Provision for depreciation on plant and machinery as at 31 December year 2		24,000
Purchases	255,000	
Receivables (debtors)	98,100	
Rent, rates, and insurance	65,000	
Sales revenue		660,000
Vehicles at cost	60,000	
Wages	44,000	
	830,000	830,000

Self-testing questions (continued)

Adjustments

i   Closing inventory as at 31 December year 3 amounted to £13,000.

ii   Depreciation is to be provided on plant and machinery on a straight line basis at 10 per cent per annum.

iii   Depreciation is to be provided on fixtures and fittings on a straight line basis at 10 per cent per annum.

iv   Depreciation is to be provided on the delivery van at 20 per cent per annum on a diminishing balance basis.

v   An electricity bill for the 3 months ending on 31 January year 4 amounts to £3,000 and has not yet been recorded in the accounts.

vi   Rent for the 3 months ending on 28 February year 4, amounting to £6,600, was paid at the beginning of December year 3.

vii   A specific debt of £2,100 is to be written off as irrecoverable.

viii   The provision for bad debts is to be adjusted to be 2.5 per cent of debtors.

ix   On 31 December year 3 Brad Head took drawings from the business of £6,000, which have not yet been recorded.

Prepare a profit and loss account for the year ended 31 December year 3, and a balance sheet as at that date.

6   The trial balance of Ellie's Ltd as at 31 December year 1 was as follows.

	Dr £	Cr £
Inventories at 1 January year 1	19,500	
Trade receivables	61,000	
Trade payables		13,400
Share capital: 100 £1 shares		100
Share premium		11,600
Retained profits at 1 January year 1		17,100
Printing and stationery	2,400	
Provision for bad debts		600
Wages and salaries	12,300	
Purchases	167,000	
Sales revenue		248,300
Cash at bank	450	
Rent	1,500	
Electricity	1,100	
Fixtures and fittings at cost	12,000	
Fixtures and fittings: provision for depreciation at 31 December year 0		2,000
Van at cost	8,400	
Van: provision for depreciation at 31 December year 0		4,200
Van: disposal proceeds		4,750
Car at cost	20,000	

Car: provision for depreciation at		
31 December year 0		5,000
General expenses	1,400	
	307,050	307,050

Additional information

i   Inventories as at 31 December year 1 was £21,000.

ii   Rent prepaid as at 31 December year 1 was £400.

iii   Accrued electricity as at 31 December year 1 was £200.

iv   A debtor of £500 is to be written off.

v   The provision for bad debts is to be increased to £650.

vi   Depreciation is to be provided for the year as follows: fixtures and fittings; 25 per cent per annum on a reducing balance basis and vehicles; 25 per cent per annum on a straight line basis.

vii   The company's accounting policy is to charge no depreciation in the year that a fixed asset is sold.

viii   Corporation tax of £15,000 is to be provided.

ix   The directors propose a dividend of £20 per share.

Prepare an income statement for the year ended 31 December year 1 and a balance sheet as at that date.

7   The trial balance of Bulgham, Dhoon and Barony as at 31 December year 9 is as follows.

	£	£
Cash	47,000	
Furniture at cost	90,000	
General expenses	45,000	
Inventories as at 31 December year 8	37,000	
Provision for depreciation on		
furniture as at 31 December year 8		27,000
Purchases	320,000	
Rent	28,000	
Sales revenue		490,000
Capital accounts as at 1 January year 9		
Bulgham		40,000
Dhoon		30,000
Barony		20,000
Current accounts at 1 January year 9		
Bulgham		10,000
Dhoon	22,000	
Barony	28,000	
	617,000	617,000

Self-testing questions (continued)

Adjustments

i Inventory as at 31 December year 9 amounted to £31,000.

ii Furniture is to be depreciated on a straight line basis at 10% per annum.

iii Rent of £6,000 was paid on 30 November year 9 for the 3-month period ending on 28 February year 10.

iv Profits are to be appropriated as follows:

- 5 per cent interest on capital to each partner
- Salaries of £18,250 each to Dhoon and Barony
- The remaining profits are to be divided equally among the 3 partners

There were no drawings during the year.

Prepare an income statement for the year ended 31 December year 9, and a balance sheet as at that date.

Assessment questions

1 The trial balance of E. Zee's Business as at 31 December year 7 was as follows.

	Debit £	Credit £
Workshop	170,000	
Payables (creditors)		15,000
Capital as at 1 December year 7		145,000
General expenses	50,000	
Sales revenue		60,000
	220,000	220,000

Prepare an income statement for the year ended 31 December year 7, and a balance sheet as at that date.

2 The trial balance of Isabella Stanley as at 31 March year 9 was as follows:

	£	£
Administration expenses	43,000	
Bank	61,000	
Capital		30,000
Inventory at 1 April year 8	18,000	
Payables		33,000
Purchases	234,000	
Receivables	17,000	
Sales revenue		370,000
Selling expenses	26,000	
Distribution costs	34,000	
	433,000	433,000

Assessment questions (continued)

Adjustments

i Closing inventory as at 31 March year 9 amounted to £22,000

Prepare an income statement for the year ended 31 March year 9, and a balance sheet as at that date.

3 The trial balance of Michael Orry's business as at 31 March year 2 is as follows.

	£	£
Administrative expenses	43,000	
Capital as at 31 March year 1		250,000
Cash and bank	170,000	
Drawings	36,900	
Distribution costs	11,000	
Inventories at 31 March year 1	18,000	
Payables		18,000
Plant and machinery at cost	180,000	
Provision for depreciation on plant and machinery as at 31 March year 1		108,000
Provision for depreciation on vehicles as at 31 March year 1		21,000
Purchases	120,000	
Receivables	16,000	
Repairs and maintenance	27,900	
Rent and rates	36,200	
Sales		390,000
Vehicles at cost	48,000	
Wages	80,000	
	787,000	787,000

Adjustments

i Closing inventory as at 31 March year 2 amounted to £21,000.

ii Depreciation is to be provided on plant and machinery on a straight line basis at 10 per cent per annum.

iii Depreciation is to be provided on vehicles on a reducing balance basis at 25 per cent per annum.

Prepare an income statement for the year ended 31 March year 2, and a balance sheet as at that date.

4 Andreas, Jude and Sandy are in business together sharing profits in the proportion 3 : 2 : 1. Their partnership agreement provides for interest on their fixed capital balances of 8 per cent per annum, and that Sandy should receive a salary of £13,400 per annum.

Their trial balance as at 30 June year 3 was as follows.

Bank	42,800	
Business expenses	38,150	
Capital accounts at 30 June year 2		
Andreas		120,000
Jude		150,000
Sandy		100,000
Creditors (payables)		8,000
Current accounts at 30 June year 2		
Andreas		15,000
Jude		13,000
Sandy	4,600	
Debtors (receivables)	11,150	
Drawings accounts at 30 June year 3		
Andreas	51,000	
Jude	72,000	
Sandy	38,400	
Plant and equipment at cost	290,000	
Goodwill	100,000	
Inventories as at 30 June year 2	12,000	
Provision for eepreciation		
as at 30 June year 2		50,000
Purchases	78,900	
Sales		283,000
	739,000	739,000

Adjustments

i   Fixed assets are to be depreciated at the rate of 20 per cent per annum on a reducing balance basis.

ii   Closing inventory amounted to £18,900.

iii   Business expenses of £2,735 have been incurred but not yet recorded.

iv   A provision for bad debts amounting to 10 per cent of debtors is to be created.

Prepare a profit and loss appropriation account, and an income statement for the year ending 30 June year 3, and a balance sheet as at that date.

5 The trial balance of Faraway Retailers Limited as at 31 December year 1 is shown below.

	Dr	Cr
	£000	£000
Inventories as at 1 January year 1	545	
Trade receivables	705	
Trade payables		600
Share capital: £1 shares		1,500
Share premium		750
8% Debentures		1,200
Retained profits at 1 January year 1		190
Printing and stationery	750	

Assessment questions (continued)

Provision for bad debts		40
Wages and salaries	890	
Distribution costs	100	
Bad debt written off	20	
Purchases	3,350	
Sales		7,900
Cash at bank	51	
Rent and rates	320	
Electricity	55	
Debenture interest	48	
Land and buildings at cost	3,000	
Land and buildings provision for depreciation as at 31 December year 0		90
Fixtures and fittings at cost	1,500	
Fixtures and fittings provision for depreciation as at 31 December year 0		600
Plant and machinery at cost	2,800	
Plant and machinery provision for depreciation at 31 December year 0		1,264
	14,134	14,134

Additional information

i The stocktake on 31 December year 1 revealed the following:

	Cost £000	Net realizable value £000
Home furnishing	500	1,000
Clothing	440	410

ii Rent and rates includes a rent payment of £144,000 for the period 1 April year 1 to 31 March year 2.

iii Electricity for the 3 months ended 31 January year 2 of £18,000 was paid in February year 2.

iv A debtor of £5,000 is to be written off.

v The provision for bad debts is to be adjusted to be 5 per cent of debtors.

vi Depreciation is to be provided for the year as follows: land and buildings 2 per cent per annum, straight line; fixtures and fittings 20 per cent per annum, straight line; plant and machinery 25 per cent per annum, reducing balance.

vii A full year's debenture interest is payable.

viii Corporation tax of £615,000 is to be provided.

ix The directors propose a dividend of 40p per share.

Prepare an income statement for the year ended 31 December year 1, and a balance sheet as at that date.

Group activities and discussion questions

1 Would you rather be in business as a sole trader, in a partnership, or in a company? Why?

2 What are the various ways of sharing profits between partners, and why are they used?

3 Is there, or should there be, a standard format for the financial statements of unincorporated businesses? Why or why not?

4 Why is there a need for 'adjustments' to a trial balance at the year end?

5 Bookkeeping records transactions; trial balances, balance sheets and income statements summarize and present the results of those transactions. It is unrealistic to expect such summaries to be 'useful', except in a very narrow sense. Discuss. How useful would you like financial statements to be? How realistic is it to expect financial statements to meet the needs of various users of accounts, given the way in which they are derived?

Financial accounting in context

The simple life
By The Rt Hon John Redwood MP

Accountancy Age, 19 January 2006

Discuss and comment on the following extract from the press. In what ways could formal accountancy requirements be reduced?

Source: Reproduced with permission by *Accountancy Age*.

SMALL COMPANIES have to tell the authorities twice what their turnover and profits have been in the previous year – HM Revenue & Customs needs to know so it can take its cut, while Companies House needs to know to add the information to a public record.

My idea to make life a little easier for the harassed company accountant and secretary is to say 'one return is enough'. The company would still have to supply the figures HMRC needs to agree the tax assessment. The HMRC computer would then be programmed to send on all the figures that were needed for publication through Companies House from the company's own return to HMRC.

The task could be made easier for both HMRC and the companies concerned by the publication of an online standard format of reporting turnover, profit and other relevant figures.

It is difficult to see why people should object. Under the scheme, no more information would be made public and no more information would be shown to HMRC than at present. A company would avoid being responsible for the Companies House compliance annually.

Of course, the company itself would still have to notify Companies House of changes in share structure or directors in the normal way as these occurred. The HMRC form could contain a reminder that all relevant changes of share structure and personnel still have to be notified as they arise.

Nor should the government object. It is true it would have to set up the original system to send the relevant information on, but with modern computing it would be neither difficult nor expensive. A long time ago, Companies House set up a shuttle document with my encouragement, to remind companies annually of what they had filed about their structure and could send back a nil change return easily as a result. This addition would take care of the ever changing figures for activity and profit.

Stuff and nonsense

A reply by Mark Saunders

WITH THIS announcement, it seems the Conservative Party is attempting to make proposals that support the notion of reducing the administrative burden on SMEs.

While this should be encouraged, they are sadly misguided if they think that a single declaration of company results will satisfy all needs. Killing two birds with one stone is never that simple.

One of the most fundamental reasons why this will not work in practice is that the filing requirements for smaller companies at Companies House are much less than the requirements of HM Revenue & Customs.

While full accounts are submitted to HMRC for all companies, small companies are only required to submit abbreviated accounts to Companies House.

The most notable of these differences is that small companies (that meet two of the following criteria: an annual turnover of £5.6m or less, a balance sheet total of £2.8m or less and the average number of employees 50 or fewer) only submit an abbreviated balance sheet and notes without any profit and loss information at all.

The only way that a single declaration would work is if HMRC reduced the amount of information that it requires from all companies, or if small companies were required to make more information publicly available through Companies House, thus defeating the object of the exercise. Both options seem unlikely, with the latter simply being commercially unacceptable.

While this proposal is impractical, it does raise important points. It is a sad fact that UK companies are already required to place more information than many other European countries on public file, while small companies in the US do not need to file any information publicly at all.

Perhaps the Conservatives would gain more favour with small businesses by looking at these facts rather than making proposals that make a complex system even more so.

References and further reading

Black, G. (2005) *Introduction to Accounting and Finance*. FT Prentice Hall.

Davies, T. and B. Pain (2001) *Business Accounting and Finance*. McGraw-Hill.

Weetman, P. (2006) *Financial and Management Accounting: An Introduction*. FT Prentice Hall.

Wood, F. and A. Sangster (2005) *Business Accounting* vol. 1, (10th edition). FT Prentice Hall.

CHAPTER 16

Cash Flow Statements and Incomplete Records

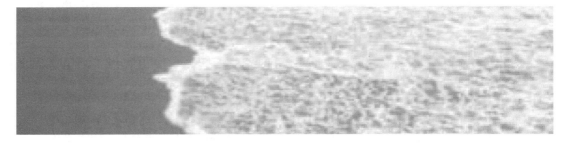

Chapter Contents

❖ LEARNING OBJECTIVES

After studying this chapter you should be able to:

❖ Explain the differences between cash flow and profit

❖ Compare opening and closing balance sheets to explain how the amount of cash has changed during the year

❖ Produce cash flow statements in a format suitable for publication

❖ Produce a balance sheet and profit and loss account from incomplete records

16.1 Cash Flow Statements

A company's balance sheet shows how much cash (bank) they have. Comparing this year's balance sheet with last year's shows whether they have more or less cash now than a year ago, or whether their overdraft has increased. It is worth comparing the profit that the company has made with what has happened to their cash balances.

The Stuaper company (Illustration 16.1) made a profit during year 2, but they ended up with less cash at the end of the year than they had at the beginning. This is not unusual. If we compare the balance sheets at the end of years 1 and 2, we can see what has happened to a lot of their cash. Where assets have increased (items 1,2 and 3 below), we can assume that cash has flowed out of the business to pay for them. Where liabilities have been reduced (items 4 and 5), we can assume that cash has flowed out of the business to (re)pay them. In total, £140,000 has flowed out of the business to buy more assets or to pay liabilities.

Cash balances have decreased from £160,000 to £40,000: an outflow of £120,000.

But these outflows of cash have been partly offset by the fact that the company has made a profit. The balance sheet shows that retained earnings have increased from £150,000 to £170,000: the company must have made (at least) £20,000[1] profit.

		£000
1	Non-current assets have increased, so it seems that they have bought more fixed assets during the year	50
2	Inventories have increased, so it seems that more money is tied up in inventories	20
3	Receivables have increased, so it seems that more money is tied up in receivables	20
4	Current liabilities have gone down, so it seems that more money has been paid out	10
5	Borrowings have gone down, so it seems that cash has been paid out to repay them	40
6	Total outflows of cash	140
7	Reduction in cash balance	120
8	Increase in retained earnings	20

One way of preparing a cash flow statement is simply to compare each item on this year's balance sheet with last year's. Every increase in assets, or reduction in liabilities,[2] is an outflow of cash. Every decrease in assets, or increase in liabilities,[3] is an inflow of cash. Arithmetically this will reconcile this year's cash balance with last year's. But this is not satisfactory for a number of reasons.

1 A reconciliation is not an explanation, and it is better to present a cash flow statement in accordance with International Accounting Standards (IASs) to make comparisons easier.

2 One simple figure for an increase (or decrease) in fixed assets is not satisfactory because (at least) two things have usually happened.

---

[1] Some profits have been paid out as dividends. The balance sheet shows only the *retained* earnings.

[2] Or equity.

[3] Or equity.

Simplified balance sheet of Stuaper Company as at 31 December

	Year 1 £000	£000	Year 2 £000	£000
Non-current assets		200		250
Current assets				
Inventories	60		80	
Receivables	40		60	
Cash	160	260	40	180
		460		430
Current liabilities				
Trade payables		40		30
Non-current liabilities				
Borrowings		70		30
Equity				
Share capital	200		200	
Retained earnings	150	350	170	370
		460		430

Simplified income statement of Stuaper Company for the year ended 31 December

	Year 2 £000
Sales revenue	660
Cost of sales	(440)
Gross profit	220
Operating expenses	(120)
Operating profit	100
Finance expenses	(7)
Profit before tax	93
Corporation tax	(30)
Profit after tax	63

ILLUSTRATION 16.1

a additional fixed assets have been bought (and some may have been revalued or disposed of); and

b fixed assets have been depreciated.

Careful examination of the notes to the accounts might show that the depreciation charge for the year was £25,000, and £75,000 was spent on buying additional fixed assets. The net figure of £50,000 does not tell us what we want to know.

3 The £20,000 increase in retained earnings is not a very useful figure. It is more useful to know how much the *operating profit* was (before deducting finance costs, taxation and dividends) as a first step to finding out how much cash was generated from operations. If we find that the company paid dividends of £43,000 during the year, the total profit after tax would be £63,000, leaving additional retained earnings of £20,000.

IAS 7 requires that cash flows should be classified under three headings.

1 Operating activities
2 Investing activities
3 Financing activities

Although international standards are not totally prescriptive about what should be included under each of the headings, Illustration 16.2 complies with generally accepted practice.

Summarized balance sheet of Kione Halby as at 31 December

	Year 1 £000	£000	Year 2 £000	£000
Non-current assets				
Machinery at net book value	20		15	
Vehicles at cost	—	20	45	60
Current assets				
Inventories	30		50	
Receivables	30		35	
Cash	10	70	—	85
Total assets		90		145
Current liabilities				
Trade payables		20	18	
Overdraft			4	22
Non-current liabilities				
Debentures				50
Equity				
Share capital	40		40	
Retained earnings	30	70	33	73
		90		145

Summarized income statement of Kione Halby for the year ended 31 December year 2

	£000
Sales revenue	200
Cost of sales	(170)
Gross profit	30
Profit on sale of fixed asset	1
Depreciation of machinery	(5)
Other operating expenses	(11)
Profit for the year	15

Additional information
i   During the year machinery, which had a net book value of £3,000, was sold for £4,000.
ii   The motor vehicles were bought on the last day of year 2, and no depreciation will be charged on them until year 3
iii Dividends paid were £12,000.

Ignore interest and taxation.

ILLUSTRATION 16.2

Cash flow statement of Kione Halby for the year ended 31 December year 2

	£000	£000
Cash generated from operating activities		
Operating profit	15	
Depreciation	5	
Other items		
Profit on sale of machinery	(1)	
		19
Increase in working capital		
Increase in inventories	(20)	
Increase in receivables	(5)	
Decrease in payables	(2)	(27)
Interest paid	–	
Taxation paid	–	–
		(8)
Cash used in investing activities		
Purchase of machinery	(3)	
Purchase of vehicles	(45)	
Disposal of fixed assets	4	(44)
Cash used in financing activities		
Debentures issued	50	
Dividends paid	(12)	38
		14
Decrease in cash during year		
Opening balance	10	
Closing balance	(4)	14

The net book value of machinery at the beginning of the year was £20,000; machinery with a net book value of £3,000 was sold, and depreciation of £5,000 was charged; these would reduce the balance to £12,000. The balance at the end of the year was £15,000 indicating that additional machinery of £3,000 had been purchased.

In the above statement the convention has been adopted that outflows of cash are shown in brackets.

ILLUSTRATION 16.2 continued

Cash generated from/used in operating activities

The above presentation shows cash generated from operating activities in three stages:

1 *Profit plus depreciation and similar items* This is almost always an inflow of cash. Even when a business makes a loss, this is often more than offset by the depreciation charge for the year. The figure for Kione Halby is an inflow of £19,000.

2 *Changes in working capital* This is typically an outflow of cash when a business is expanding. But careful management, reducing inventories and payables, and delaying paying creditors, can produce an inflow of cash. Kione Halby had an outflow of £27,000.

3 *Interest and taxation* These are usually outflows of cash. However, sometimes a company receives more interest than it pays out; and negative tax charges do exist (for example after losses, and/or substantial writing-down allowances for new fixed assets). Illustration16.2 is simplified, and Kione Halby made no payments for interest or taxation. Overall, in a successful business, there should be a cash inflow from operating activities. But with Kione Halby there was an overall outflow of cash of £8,000 from operating activities because of the substantial increase in working capital.

Cash Generated from/used in Investing Activities

The main items here are purchase of non-current assets such as fixed assets, or other businesses, which are outflows of cash. There are usually some inflows as well resulting from sales of fixed assets or parts of the business. Kione Halby paid £48,000 for additional fixed assets, which was slightly offset by receipts of £4,000 for selling old fixed assets. The net cash outflow was £44,000.

Cash Generated from/used in Financing Activities

Inflows and outflows are about equally likely under this heading. Dividends paid are usually shown as an outflow of cash under this heading, together with the repayment or redemption of debentures and shares. Inflows result from additional borrowings, or from raising more share capital. Kione Halby obviously needed a lot more cash (to finance the increases in working capital and the additional fixed assets), and they raised £50,000 by issuing debentures. This was offset by paying dividends of £12,000, leaving a net cash inflow from financing activities of £38,000.

The total of the three categories of cash flows added together show a net outflow of £14,000 as follows.

	£
Cash used in operating activities	(8,000)
Cash used in investing activities	(44,000)
Cash generated from financing activities	38,000
Net cash outflow	(14,000)

The total of the cash flows in each of these categories must be equal to the difference between the cash that the business had at the beginning of the year, and the amount at the end of the year. Kione Halby started the year with £10,000 in the bank; they ended the year with an overdraft of £4,000; this means that £14,000 had flowed out of the business. The cash flow statement shows the main items that made up that outflow.

16.2 How to Prepare a Cash Flow Statement

In order to prepare a cash flow statement, it is important to have a clear format in mind, such as the one shown in Illustration 16.2. Then it is helpful to list each of the items that have to be found from the balance sheet, income statement or notes to the accounts, as shown in Illustration 16.3. It is a good idea to leave a line or two between each item as there are likely to be additional figures or 'adjustments'[4] to be slotted in.

Cash generated from operating activities

1 Operating profit
2 Depreciation
3 Other items

Increase in working capital

4   Increase in inventories
5   Increase in receivables
6   Decrease in payables
7 Interest paid
8 Taxation paid

Cash used in investing activities

9 Purchase of fixed assets
10 Disposal of fixed assets

Cash used in financing activities

11 Repayment of loan
12 Dividends paid
13 Other items

Decrease in cash during year

ILLUSTRATION 16.3

There is almost no limit to how complicated financial statements can be, and a competent and experienced accountant would be needed to produce a decent cash flow statement for any large listed company. The following provides a guide to how the main figures can be found in reasonably straightforward situations. The items are numbered in Illustration 16.3 for convenience; this numbering has no official statues. The format illustrated complies with international standards, but some variations are also acceptable.

1 Operating profit should be easy to find on an income statement, even if it is not separately labelled as such. It is the amount of gross profit left after deducting all operating expenses, and before any finance income, finance expenses or taxation.

   It may be useful to see what cash flows have been generated before deducting interest and taxation, but these obviously have to be paid. They are usually shown as separate items (7 and 8 in Illustration 16.3).

2 Depreciation is regarded as being a cash inflow because operating profit is calculating after charging depreciation for the year, as if depreciation was an outflow of cash, but it is not an outflow; it is charged as an expense, and so has to be added back to profit as if it is a cash inflow.

---

[4] It sounds better if you are 'making an adjustment' rather than just correcting a mistake!

Depreciation is not usually shown as a separate item on the face of an income state-ment; it is tucked away in the notes, usually the note that applies to fixed assets on the balance sheet. There is a schedule that shows the balance at the beginning of the year[5] for fixed assets; the balance at the end of the year, and the explanation of the differ-ences: additional fixed assets acquired during the year, and disposals of fixed assets during the year. There is a similar schedule for depreciation showing the total cumula-tive depreciation at the beginning of the year, the depreciation charge for the year (the figure that goes on the cash flow statement), the amount of depreciation for fixed assets disposed of, and the total cumulative depreciation remaining at the end of the year.

3 There are often other items which, like depreciation, have been charged as expenses, but there has been no outflow of cash. These have to be added back to profit. They include amortization; write-offs for impairment of goodwill and other assets; and increases in provisions.

Some of these items can be the other way around: profits have been boosted by items that produce no cash flows, and which, therefore, have to be deducted from operating profit. A reduction in a provision is an example of this.

There is also a problem with any profit or loss arising from the sale of fixed assets. If a fixed asset is sold during the year for more than its net book value, the profit arising is correctly treated as part of profit in preparing the income statement. The total amount of cash received on disposal of a fixed asset is shown under item 10 of Ilustration 16.3, and this includes the amount of profit as part of the cash inflow. As the profit on dis-posal cannot be included twice on a cash flow statement (as part of profit; and as part of the proceeds of disposal), it has to be taken out of the profit figure; this is done by deducting it from profit, as if it is a cash outflow.

If a fixed asset is sold for less than its net book value, the loss is correctly charged against profit when the income statement is prepared (even if it is not separately ident-ified). But as there is no cash outflow for that loss, the amount has to be added back to profit in preparing the cash flow statement. The proceeds of disposal are shown under item 10 in the cash flow statement.

4 The increase in inventories is easily calculated, comparing this year's balance sheet with last year's. If the difference between the two inventories figures is an increase, the amount is shown on the cash flow statement as an outflow of cash. If inventories have decreased, the cash flow statement shows this as an inflow of cash.

5 The increase in receivables is easily calculated, comparing this year's balance sheet with last year's. If the difference between the two receivables figures is an increase, the amount is shown on the cash flow statement as an outflow of cash. If receivables have decreased, the cash flow statement shows this as an inflow of cash.

6 The increase in payables is easily calculated, comparing this year's balance sheet with last year's. If the difference between the two payables figures is an increase, the amount is shown on the cash flow statement as an inflow of cash. If payables have decreased, the cash flow statement shows this as an outflow of cash.

---

[5] The fixed assets are shown at cost (or revalued amount).

7 It is easy to find the interest charge for the year on the income statement: it is labelled as 'finance costs'. In some cases there is also 'finance income' (interest receivable), and it is acceptable to show a single net figure for interest on a cash flow statement.

The amount shown on the cash flow statement should be the amount actually paid (or received) during the year, which is sometimes different from the amount shown on the income statement. The income statement should show the amount *due* during the year; the cash flow statement should show the amount actually paid. Sometimes an amount due for the year ended on 31 December is not actually paid until January of the following year.

8 It is easy to find the taxation charge for the year on the income statement. Sometimes this might not be the same as the amount actually paid during the year, which is required for the cash flow statement. The amount actually paid can be calculated if sufficient information is available, as shown in Illustration 16.4.

	At 31 December year 5	At 31 December year 6
Balance sheet extract from current liabilities		
Corporation tax	£50,000	£60,000

The income statement showed a tax charge of £58,000 for the year ended 31 December year 6.

To calculate the amount actually paid during year 6, we can assume that the whole of the £50,000 shown as a current liability at the end of year 5 was payable during year 6.

During year 6 an additional £58,000 became payable, making a total of £108,000 due to be paid. By the end of year 6 only £60,000 was still due to be paid. We can, therefore, assume that the difference, £48,000, was actually paid, and this is the figure to be shown on the cash flow statement.

ILLUSTRATION 16.4

9 The amount paid for additional fixed assets can be found in the (balance sheet) notes to the accounts, as explained in 2 above (additional fixed assets acquired during the year). There may be several different items included under the general heading of non-current assets.

Any increase in the amount of non-current assets that is due to a revaluation involves no cash flows and is not included on a cash flow statement.

10 The amount included on a cash flow statement for disposals of fixed assets must be the actual amount of cash received, not the book value. The book value of assets disposed of is easily established. As explained in 2 above, the balance sheet notes to the accounts in respect of fixed assets shows both the cost[6] of the assets disposed of, and the depreciation relating to them; the difference between the two is the net book value. The sale proceeds are the book value, plus any profit arising, or minus any loss arising. Profits or losses on disposals of fixed assets are included in the income statement, but it may be necessary to hunt around in the notes to find the amounts.

---

[6] Or revalued amount.

11 If any loans have been repaid, the amounts can be established by comparing this year's balance sheet with last year's. There may be increases or reductions in non-current borrowings, or both. Details are provided in the notes to the financial statements.

12 Dividends paid are usually included as a cash outflow under the financing activities heading. The figure can be hard to find, especially since changes to financial statements in 2006. Dividends are no longer shown on the income statement, and the basis on which they are shown has changed. Dividends that have been *proposed* are not now recognized in financial statements until they have been declared or paid. It is often necessary to hunt around in the notes to find the amounts of dividend declared, and the amounts paid. There is usually a note of the amount declared, normally in pence per share (which needs to be multiplied by the number of shares to arrive at the total amount). Care is needed to ensure that the cash flow statement includes the amounts actually paid; this usually means the final dividend for the previous year, plus the interim dividend for the current year; it excludes the final dividend for the current year. In published financial statements the easiest way to find the amount of dividends paid during the previous year is to look at the cash flow statement, rather than trying to calculate the figure yourself. In the questions at the end of this chapter, the required figure is provided.

13 Other items include the cash inflows arising from issue of any shares during the year, including the amount of premium. The company may also have bought its own shares and cancelled them, which involves an outflow of cash. The overall picture is easily seen by comparing two years' balance sheets, and more detail (such as the number of shares issued or redeemed) is provided in the notes to the accounts.

16.3 Incomplete Records

Many small businesses do not bother to record fully all transactions using double-entry bookkeeping. Sometimes they hand over a pile of papers and their bank statements to an accountant who is expected to construct a full set of accounts from these 'incomplete records'. It is usually straightforward to produce a summary of receipts and payments for the year, based on the business's bank statements. The accountant will not really know whether or not all receipts really did go into the bank; reliance has to be placed on what the proprietor of the business remembers or says. The proprietor will probably remember any payments made for the business in cash, especially those that will reduce their tax liability. They may find it harder to remember any cash receipts that would increase it.

In the two examples in Illustration 16.5, a summary of the bank statement is provided, but this is insufficient information to be able to calculate profits.

Additional information also enables us to produce balance sheets. The balance sheet at the beginning of the year is fairly straightforward, as shown in Illustration 16.5, Answer part 2 (p. 440). After the profit for the year has been calculated we can produce the balance sheet at the end of the year. Depreciation has to be deducted from fixed assets, and the profit for the year has to be added to the balance shown for capital at the beginning of the year.

The summarized bank accounts are available for Ahmed and Leong. Ahmed started the year with £20,000 in the bank. By the end of the year this had increased to £30,000; an increase of £10,000. Leong started the year with £15,000 in the bank; by the end of the year the bank balance had increased to £41,000, a much more substantial increase of £26,000. At first sight it seems that Leong is doing better than Ahmed because Leong has generated more cash.

In this instance, most of the big differences between cash flow and profit do not apply. Neither business has acquired fixed assets; there has been no borrowing or repayment of loans; and there has been no additional capital introduced, or withdrawn. The differences between cash flow and profit are due to the application of the accruals concept – the normal way of measuring profit.

Summarized bank statements

	Ahmed		Leong	
	£	£	£	£
Opening balance: cash at bank		20,000		15,000
Receipts from debtors	67,000		142,000	
Receipts from cash sales, banked	30,000		10,000	
	97,000		152,000	
Payments to trade creditors	77,000		91,000	
Payments for expenses	10,000		35,000	
	87,000		126,000	
Increase in cash balance during year		10,000		26,000
Closing balance: cash at bank		30,000		41,000

The cash figures alone do not give sufficient information about the performance of a business; they do not enable us to measure profit. Neither of the two businesses kept proper sets of double-entry accounts, but they are able to produce a record of stocks, debtors and creditors at the beginning and end of the year as follows:

	Ahmed		Leong	
	1 January	31 December	1 January	31 December
	£	£	£	£
Stocks	10,000	14,000	16,000	12,000
Debtors	8,000	11,000	9,000	7,000
Creditors	9,000	6,000	8,000	11,000

Additional information

Ahmed began the year with fixed assets of £30,000 on which depreciation of £5,000 is to be charged. Leong began the year with fixed assets of £50,000 on which depreciation of £10,000 is to be charged.

As is clear from the summarized bank account, there have been no purchases or sales of fixed assets, and neither of the owners has taken money out of the business as drawings. The owners state that all receipts from sales have been banked, and that there were no receipts or payments that did not go through the bank account.

There is now sufficient information to prepare the profit and loss accounts of the businesses.

The sales figure must include the money received from cash sales, and money receivable from debtors.

ILLUSTRATION 16.5

Answer (Part 1): Ahmed
Summarized income statement of Ahmed for the year

	£	£	£
Cash sales	30,000		
Receipts from debtors	67,000		
Deduct opening debtors	(8,000)		
Add Closing debtors	11,000		
Sales			100,000
Opening stock		10,000	
Payments to creditors	77,000		
Deduct opening creditors	(9,000)		
Add Closing creditors	6,000		
Purchases		74,000	
		84,000	
Deduct Closing stock		(14,000)	
Cost of goods sold			70,000
Gross profit			30,000
Expenses	10,000		
Depreciation	5,000		(15,000)
Net profit			15,000

In determining the correct sales figure for the year, the figures on the bank statement are inadequate. The figure for cash sales (receipts of money from sales paid directly into the bank) is probably acceptable as it is. But some of the amount shown for receipts from debtors is for sales that took place in the previous year. At the beginning of the year, Ahmed was owed £8,000 by debtors. During the year he received £67,000 from debtors, but £8,000 of this was for the previous year. The figure of £59,000 is still not the correct figure for sales for this year. At the end of this year debtors owed Ahmed £11,000; this is for sales that have been made this year, but the money will not be received until next year. The correct figure for sales to debtors is, therefore, £67,000 − £8,000 + £11,000 = £70,000. Cash sales are added to credit sales to give the total sales figure for the year (£70,000 + £30,000 = £100,000).

It is a similar story in determining the correct purchases figure for the year. In this instance it seems that there are no purchases that have been paid for in cash. The total figure of cash paid to creditors includes payments for purchases that were made last year. At the beginning of this year Ahmed owed £9,000 to creditors. During the year he paid £77,000 to creditors, but £9,000 of this was for the previous year. But £68,000 is not the correct figure for purchases for this year. At the end of this year Ahmed owes £6,000 to creditors. The correct figure for purchases from creditors is, therefore, £77,000 − £9,000 + £6,000 = £74,000.

To arrive at gross profit we do not simply deduct purchases from sales; a stock adjustment is required, and a summary of the bank statement does not provide the information required. Gross profit is the difference between sales, and the cost of goods sold. When we have arrived at the purchases figure, we need to add opening stocks to it, and deduct closing stocks from it to arrive at the cost of goods sold.

Net profit is arrived at after deducting all expenses. Most expenses are shown on the bank statement as payments; sometimes these have to be adjusted to allow for accruals and prepayments. In some businesses there may be additional expenses that have been paid out of cash received from sales.[7] Depreciation has to be shown as an expense in calculating profit, but it is not a payment, and so does not appear on the bank statement. Fixed assets and depreciation are part of the additional information that is essential to calculate profit from information from incomplete records.

ILLUSTRATION 16.5 continued

---

[7] If any expenses have been paid directly from the money received for cash sales, the amount must be included as part of sales, and also be included as an expense in the income statement.

When all this information is taken into account we can see how a 'receipts and payments' basis is converted into an accruals basis for profit. Ahmed's profit figure can be reconciled with his increase in cash as follows.

Ahmed	£	£
Net profit		15,000
Add Depreciation		5,000
		20,000
Deduct		
Increase in inventories	(4,000)	
Increase in receivables	(3,000)	
Decrease in payables	(3,000)	(10,000)
Increase in cash		10,000
Opening balance	20,000	
Closing balance	30,000	

This reconciliation is, of course, like a simplified cash flow statement.

Answer (Part 2)
Balance sheet at beginning of year

	Ahmed		Leong	
	£	£	£	£
Fixed assets		30,000		50,000
Inventories (stocks)		10,000		16,000
Receivables (debtors)		8,000		9,000
Cash		20,000		15,000
		68,000		90,000
Payables (creditors)		9,000		8,000
Capital		59,000		82,000
		68,000		90,000

Balance sheet at end of year

	Ahmed		Leong	
Fixed assets		25,000		40,000[8]
Inventories (stocks)		14,000		12,000
Receivables (debtors)		11,000		7,000
Cash		30,000		41,000
		80,000		100,000
Payables (creditors)		6,000		11,000
Capital	59,000		82,000	
Profit for year	15,000	74,000	7,000	89,000
		80,000		100,000

ILLUSTRATION 16.5 continued

Companies are required by law to keep proper accounting records, but many small, unincorporated businesses do not bother. They manage by keeping a careful eye on their bank account and controlling their receipts and payments. But it is also important to be able to measure profit, and to appreciate how it differs from a 'receipts and payments' basis of accounting.

---

[8] The amounts for fixed assets and for capital are shown for the first time here.

Summary

Both profits and cash flows are important to businesses, and comparing this year's balance sheet with the previous year's indicates what has happened to each during the year. Profits accumulate as 'retained earnings', which are part of equity (except to the extent that they have been paid out as dividends or drawings). The amount of cash at the year end is shown under current assets; this can be compared with the previous year's; and comparisons can be made with each item on the balance sheet to see which changes during the year have generated additional cash, and which have used it up. The income statement provides better information about profits, and the cash flow statement provides better information about cash flows in a (nearly) standardized format. A cash flow statement is not the same as a list of receipts and payments, or a summarized bank statement.

Cash flows are at least as important as profits in running a business, and it is important to monitor both. Some small businesses rely on 'incomplete records', with relatively little information other than bank statements (often accompanied by shoe boxes full of invoices). But most need to know how much profit they have made, and accountants often have to produce income statements and balance sheets from incomplete records.

Review of key points

- The differences between this year's balance sheet and last year's provide a crude indication of the main cash flows during the year.
- Cash flow statements should be produced in a standardized format with separate flows identified for operating activities, investing activities, and financing activities.
- Published financial statements include the detailed information required to produce a cash flow statement; they also include a cash flow statement.
- Many small businesses do not keep records of all transactions and rely on summaries of receipts and payments.
- Incomplete records can, with some additional information, be converted into income statements and balance sheets.

Self-testing questions

1 You are required to produce a cash flow statement for Daubyhaven Ltd for the year ended 31 December year 2.

Summarized balance sheet of Daubyhaven Ltd as at 31 December

	Year 1		Year 2	
	£000	£000	£000	£000
Non-current assets				
Machinery at cost	120		130	
Provision for depreciation	(60)	60	(68)	62

Self-testing questions (continued)

Current assets				
Inventories	30		50	
Receivables	30		35	
Cash	10	70	–	85
Total assets		130		147
Current liabilities				
Trade payables		20	18	
Overdraft			12	30
Non-current liabilities				
Debentures		30		20
Equity				
Share capital	50		60	
Retained earnings	30	80	37	97
		130		147

During the year ended 31 December year 2:

i A machine that originally cost £15,000, and on which £12,000 depreciation had been charged, was sold for £4,500.

ii Operating profit, including the profit on the sale of the machine, was £35,000.

iii Interest of £2,000 was paid, taxation of £8,000, and dividends of £18,000.

2 You are required to prepare a cash flow statement for Fistard Neash plc for the year ended 31 December year 6.

Summarized balance sheet of Fistard Neash plc as at 31 December

	Year 5		Year 6	
	£m	£m	£m	£m
Non-current assets				
Intangible assets		100		90
Property, plant and equipment	120		140	
Provision for depreciation	(50)	70	(66)	74
Current assets				
Inventories	40		65	
Receivables	60		55	
Cash	10	110	8	128
Total assets		280		292
Current liabilities				
Trade payables		45		40
Non-current liabilities				
Debentures		55		6
Equity				
Share capital	150		170	
Share premium	–		40	
Retained earnings	30	180	36	246
		280		292

Self-testing questions (continued)

Income statement of Fistard Neash plc for year ended 31 December year 6

	£mill
Sales revenue	440
Cost of sales	(330)
Gross profit	110
Profit on sale of Scottish factory	7
Distribution costs	(47)
Administrative expenses	(40)
Impairment of goodwill	(10)
Operating profit	20
Finance costs	(2)
Profit before taxation	18
Corporation tax	(4)
Profit for the year	14

During the year ending 31 December year 6:

i The Scottish factory had originally cost £24 million, and depreciation of £8 million had been charged on it. It was sold for £23 million.

ii Dividends paid were £8 million.

iii Interest of £2 million and taxation of £4 million were paid.

3 Produce statements showing the profit made by Leong in Illustration 16.5, and a reconciliation of profit and cash flow. The statements should be in the same format as those shown for Ahmed on pages 439 and 440.

4 From the following incomplete records supplied by Jack Kit, a clothes retailer, you are required to produce an income statement for the year ended 31 December year 3, and a balance sheet as at that date. In addition, as an arithmetic check on your work, you should produce a balance sheet as at the beginning of year 3 and a cash flow statement for the year.

Summarized bank statement of Jack Kit for year 3

	£	£
Balance at bank on 1 January year 3		20,000
Add Receipts		
Receipts from debtors	120,000	
Cash from sales paid in	60,000	
Loan from Mortgage Co	170,000	
	350,000	
Deduct Payments		
Payments to creditors for clothes purchased	125,000	
Wages	25,000	
General expenses	20,000	
Purchase of premises	187,000	
	357,000	
		(7,000)
Balance at bank on 31 December year 3		13,000

Self-testing questions (continued)

Additional information

	At 1 January year 3	At 31 December year 3
Debtors	10,000	12,000
Creditors	15,000	17,000
Stocks	14,000	16,000
Fixtures and fittings	18,000	
Premises	–	187,000

It was agreed that £1,800 depreciation should be provided on fixtures and fittings. No depreciation would be provided on the premises as they were acquired immediately before the year end.

Assessment questions

1 You are required to produce a cash flow statement for Ballamauda Ltd for the year ended 31 December year 2.

	Year 1		Year 2	
	£000	£000	£000	£000
Non-current assets				
Machinery at cost	80		70	
Provision for depreciation	(40)	40	(44)	26
Current assets				
Inventories	50		35	
Receivables	38		28	
Cash	–	88	90	153
Total assets		128		179
Current liabilities				
Trade payables	30		39	
Overdraft	16	46	–	39
Non-current liabilities				
Debentures		–		40
Equity				
Share capital	40		40	
Retained earnings	42	82	60	100
		128		179

During the year ending 31 December year 2:

i A machine that had originally cost £10,000, and on which £6,000 depreciation had been charged, was sold for £3,400.

ii Operating profit, after deducting the loss on the sale of the machine, was £32,800.

iii Interest of £2,400 was paid, taxation of £6,400, and dividends of £6,000.

Assessment questions (continued)

2 You are required to produce a cash flow statement for Soldricton plc for the year ended 31 December year 4.

Summarized balance sheets of Soldricton plc as at 31 December

	Year 3		Year 4	
Non-current assets	£m	£m	£m	£m
Intangible assets		50		55
Property, plant and equipment	90		104	
Provision for depreciation	(30)	60	(44)	60
Current assets				
Inventories	30		36	
Receivables	44		48	
Cash	=	74	8	92
Total assets		184		207
Current liabilities				
Trade payables	28		20	
Overdraft	13	41	–	20
Non-current liabilities				
Debentures		–		38
Equity				
Share capital	90		90	
Retained earnings	53	143	59	149
		184		207

Income statement of Soldricton plc for year ended 31 December year 4

	£m
Sales revenue	216
Cost of sales	(144)
Gross profit	72
Loss on sale of machinery	(4)
Distribution costs	(24)
Administrative expenses	(20)
Impairment of goodwill	(6)
Operating profit	18
Finance costs	(3)
Profit before taxation	15
Corporation tax	(4)
Profit for the year	11

During the year ended 31 December year 4:

i The company sold machinery that had cost £12 million, and on which £5 million depreciation had been charged, for £3 million.

ii The company bought a number of manufacturing businesses in South Asia for £37 million, of which £26 million was for property, plant and equipment, and £11 million for goodwill.

Assessment questions (continued)

iii Dividends paid were £5 million.

iv Interest of £3 million and taxation of £4 million were paid.

3 You are given the following summarized balance sheets and income statements for the Solverham Company for the past two years.

Balance sheet of Solverham Company as at 31 December

	Year 1 £000	£000	Year 2 £000	£000
Fixed assets at cost		200		220
Provision for depreciation		(60)		(82)
Net book value		140		138
Current assets				
Inventories	95		70	
Receivables	80		50	
Cash	—	175	25	145
		315		283
Current liabilities				
Payables	40		60	
Overdraft	80	120	—	60
Non-current liabilities				
12% Debentures		110		135
Equity				
Share capital	50		50	
Retained earnings	35	85	38	88
		315		283

Income statement for the year ended 31 December

	Year 1	Year 2
Sales	520	500
Cost of sales	376	375
Gross profit	144	125
Administration expenses	35	36
Depreciation	20	22
Distribution costs	22	24
Operating profit	67	43
Interest paid	14	17
Net profit before tax	53	26
Taxation paid	16	8
Net profit after tax	37	18

Dividends paid in year 1 were £10,000, and in year 2 were £15,000.

Required:

a Prepare a cash flow statement for the year ended 31 December year 2.

b Explain how cash flow differs from profit.

Assessment questions (continued)

c The company's managing director is pleased that the company has money in the bank having paid off a significant overdraft. He is particularly pleased that he ignored his chief accountant who said that the company could not afford to buy more fixed assets or to increase the dividend. Critically assess the chief accountant's advice.

4 Malcolm, the son of the founder of Solverham plc, is aware that the managing director of the company believes that the company is strong, and is doing well, but the chief accountant says that the company's position is rapidly deteriorating. You are required to produce a report on the company's financial position and performance, based on the information given for question 2. Your answer should include calculations of the ratios shown below for each year, and comments on them.

a Current ratio

b Liquidity ratio

c Capital gearing ratio

d Interest times cover

e Return on shareholders' funds

f Return on total long-term capital employed

g Operating profit as a percentage of sales

h Asset turnover

i Gross profit ratio

j Distribution costs as a percentage of sales

k Administrative expenses as a percentage of sales

l Sales/fixed assets

m Sales/current assets

n Stock turnover ratio

o Debtors ratio

p Creditors ratio

5 Mr Downund has been running a signwriting business for many years, and it continues to provide him with a high standard of living. The volume of business has declined in recent years, and he no longer employs any staff. But he maintains a healthy and increasing bank balance, and is happy with his business. Then he employs an accountant, and provides her with the following information:

Summarized bank account of Mr Downund for year 13

Receipts	£	Payments	£
Opening balance	30,000	Trade creditors	40,000
Receipts from debtors	65,000	Materials	32,000
Cash sales	8,000	General expenses	18,000
Sale of surplus equipment	12,000	Personal drawings	29,000
Sale of premises	50,000	Balance carried down	46,000
	165,000		165,000

Assessment questions (continued)

At the beginning of the year stocks of materials amounted to £8,000; by the end of the year this had reduced to £2,000. At the beginning of the year debtors amounted to £22,000; by the end of the year this had reduced to £7,000. At the beginning of the year creditors amounted to £16,000; by the end of the year this had increased to £24,000, but Mr Downund had taken to buying materials in a local cash and carry warehouse rather than using his traditional supplier. He was also doing a number of smaller jobs for cash, and estimated that he had received about £8,000 for such work that he had not paid into the bank but had spent on his own living expenses.

The amount shown for general expenses included £5,000 paid for rent as Mr Downund has sold his premises because they were underutilized. A year ago he had total fixed assets of £75,000, including £40,000, which was the original cost of the premises; he sold half of his equipment. His accountant said that equipment should be depreciated at 10 per cent per annum on a straight line basis.

Mr Downund was happy with his lot, but his accountant made him unhappy. What did she do?

You are required to show the balance sheets at the beginning and end of the year, and the profit and loss account for the year, in as much detail as the above information permits.

Group activities and discussion questions

1 A small business is more likely to prosper and to control its operations effectively by monitoring cash flows than by listening to its accountant. Discuss.

2 In what ways is a cash flow statement likely to be useful?

3 Why should small businesses produce accruals-based accounts (as opposed to relying on controlling cash and banking)?

4 The published accounts of companies have steadily become more complicated, with additional statements, notes and disclosures, as required by accounting standards. Conventional financial accounting is a waste of time and effort for small businesses. Discuss.

References and further reading

Black, G. (2005) *Introduction to Accounting and Finance*. FT Prentice Hall.

Davies, T. and B. Pain (2001) *Business Accounting and Finance*. McGraw-Hill.

Weetman, P. (2006) *Financial and Management Accounting: An Introduction*. FT Prentice Hall.

Wood, F. and A. Sangster (2005) *Business Accounting* vol. 1 (10th edition). FT Prentice Hall.

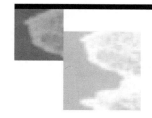

Answers to Self-testing Questions

1 A balance sheet shows assets, liabilities and share capital. Expenses, sales and profit for the year are shown on the income statement.

2 Non-current assets (fixed assets) are intended to be retained and used by the business for more than a year.

Current assets are cash and things that are intended for conversion into cash within a year.

3 Land and buildings; plant and machinery; furniture, fixtures and fittings; vehicles, ships and aircraft.

Furniture owned by a furniture shop and intended for sale is a current asset. Vehicles owned by a garage and intended for sale are a current asset.

4 Assets minus liabilities equals equity.

5 Individual assets may be worth more or less than the balance sheet value.

A successful business as a whole (including unrecorded goodwill) should be worth more than the balance sheet shows because of the profits that it now produces, and expectations for the future.

6 a Current ratio = current assets : current liabilities

$$45,000 : 22,000 = 2.05 : 1$$

b Liquidity ratio = current assets excluding inventories : current liabilities

$$21,000 : 22,000 = 0.95 : 1$$

c

	Existing		Revised	
	£	£	£	£
Non-current assets		50,000		50,000
Current assets				
Inventories (at cost)	24,000		20,000	
Trade receivables	12,000		12,000	
Cash	9,000	45,000	17,000	49,000
Total assets		95,000		99,000
Current liabilities				
Trade payables		22,000		22,000
Equity				
Share capital	50,000		50,000	
Retained earnings	23,000	73,000	27,000	77,000
		95,000		99,000

d Current ratio = 49,000 : 22,000 = 2.2 : 1

Liquidity ratio = 29,000 : 22,000 = 1.3 : 1

As the business now has £4,000 less inventory, and £8,000 more cash, both the current ratio and the liquidity ratio have improved, or become stronger.

7 a £83,000, being the increase in shareholders' funds

b £83,000 + £10,000 − £20,000 − £30,000 = £43,000

8

	Domer Castle	Warmer Castle
Current ratio	34 : 17 = 2 : 1	34 : 17 = 2 : 1
Liquidity ratio	26 : 17 = 1.5 : 1	15 : 17 = 0.88 : 1
$\dfrac{\text{Debentures}}{\text{Debentures + Equity}}$	100 ÷ 331 = 30.2%	200 ÷ 331 = 60.4%
EBIT ÷ interest payable	31,000 ÷ 10,000 = 3.1 times	32,000 ÷ 20,000 = 1.6 times

Warmer appears to be weaker. The two companies have the same current ratio, but a large part of Warmer's current assets is stocks and so they have a much lower liquidity ratio. Warmer also has much higher capital gearing and their interest cover is low.

9 a i   Non-current assets   −£80,000

Cash   +£100,000

Retained earnings   +£20,000

ii   Inventories   −£30,000

Receivables   +£80,000

Retained earnings   +£50,000

iii   Cash   −£40,000

Payables   −£40,000

b

	Existing		Revised	
Non-current assets		158,000		78,000
Current assets				
Inventories (at cost)	110,000		80,000	
Trade receivables	120,000		200,000	
Cash	20,000	250,000	80,000	360,000
Total assets		408,000		438,000
Current liabilities				
Trade payables		120,000		80,000
Equity				
Share capital	250,000		250,000	
Retained earnings	38,000	288,000	108,000	358,000
		408,000		438,000

Chapter 2

1 The balance sheet is *as at* a particular date. An income statement is for a particular *period*, such as for a year.

A balance sheet shows assets, liabilities and equity (which includes all retained profits). An income statement shows revenues, expenses and the current year's profit.

2 An expense is the cost incurred in earning the revenues of a particular period. Some assets become expenses. Assets such as unsold inventories and non-current (fixed) assets may be seen as stores of value that have not yet been used up in generating revenues. Fixed assets become recognized as expenses as they are depreciated. Inventories become expenses when they are sold. Receivables become expenses if they are written off as bad debts.

3 Closing inventories are shown at the lower of cost and net realizable value. The valuation of closing stock has a direct effect on profits. If closing stock is overstated by £1 million, then profits are overstated by £1 million.

If closing inventories were shown at selling price, the company would be taking credit for profits before sales are made; it is not a good idea to claim profits that have not yet been earned.

4 Depreciation is charged to write off the cost of the fixed asset over a number of years, depending on its economic life. If an asset is shown at a revalued amount rather than at cost, then the revalued amount is written off in the same way.

5 Capital expenditure adds to fixed assets that are then written off (depreciated; an expense) over a number of years. Examples would include a retail shop buying a new delivery vehicle, having an extension to the shop built, and buying new tills. Revenue expenditure is written off during the period in which it is incurred. Examples include lighting, heating and cleaning. (Some revenue expenditure is included in closing inventories that are carried forward and written off in the period in which they are sold.)

6 Profit after tax for the year, £12,000. This is because:

a it is the amount that has been earned for them after charging all expenses and taxation; and

b it is the basis for dividend decisions; dividends are the amounts actually paid to shareholders.

7 Kingsdun Company

	Delivery van £	Boring machine £
Cost	25,000	25,000
Year 1 depreciation	6,250	2,500
Net book value at end of year 1	18,750	22,500
Year 2 depreciation	4,688	2,500
Net book value at end of year 2	14,062	20,000
Year 3 depreciation	3,516	2,500
Net book value at end of year 3	10,546	17,500
Year 4 depreciation	2,636	2,500
Net book value at end of year 4	7,910	15,000

8 Dargate Retailing Company

Product	Cost price £	Mark-up %	Selling price £	Gross profit %
Fargs	100	25	125	20
Gargs	100	10	110	9.09
Hargs	50	100	100	50
Jargs	40	100	80	50
Kargs	80	50	120	33⅓
Largs	50	20	60	16⅔
Margs	30.77	30	40	23.1
Nargs	45	11.11	50	10
Pargs	75	33⅓	100	25

9 Banterbury Company Ltd

	Year 3 £000	%	Year 4 £000	%
Turnover	100	100	120	100
Cost of sales	60	60	73	60.83
Gross profit	40	40	47	39.17
Distribution costs	(12)	12	(14)	11.67
Administration expenses	(9)	9	(12)	10
Operating profit	19	19	21	17.5
Interest payable	(3)	3	(3)	2.5
Profit before taxation	16	16	18	15
Tax on profit for year	(4)	4	(3)	2.5
Profit after tax for the year	12	12	15	12.5

Turnover has increased by 20 per cent, but most costs have increased by a larger percentage than sales. Expressing all items as a percentage of sales, we can see that cost of sales has increased slightly, and so gross profit has gone down. There has been an increase in operating costs as a percentage of sales, and so operating profit as a percentage of sales has gone down. There has been no change in interest costs, and the company is fortunate that the amount of tax payable has gone down: the effect of these two is that there has been an increase in profit after tax as a proportion of sales.

The small improvement in profit as a percentage of sales is mainly due to the lower tax charge. Cost of sales and operating costs have both increased by a bigger proportion than sales. These results suggest that management have not been very successful in getting more profits out of the increase in sales.

Shareholders' funds are £109,000, and the profit after tax earned for them is £15,000, a return on shareholders' capital employed of 13.8 per cent, which is satisfactory.

Chapter 3

1 The main users are investors and creditors. These include existing shareholders and those who are considering investing in the company. Creditors include trade creditors and short- and long-term lenders.

They want to know about the company's financial position, including its solvency and ability to survive; its financial performance, including its profitability; and its cash flows.

There may be many other potential users with wide information needs, but most of financial accounting concentrates on those specified above.

2 Creditors are interested in a company's ability to repay them. They are interested in assets as security, the total amount of debt, interest cover and cash flows.

Shareholders are more interested in prospects for future dividends and increases in the market price of their shares. They are particularly interested in profitability and growth.

3 The main framework is laid down by the Companies Act 1985. Additional requirements are specified by 'accounting standards'. Statements of Standard Accounting Practice (SSAPs) have been superseded by Financial Reporting Standards (FRSs). For major companies, International Financial Reporting Standards (IFRSs) have been predominant since 2005, and these are increasingly followed by most businesses. Differences between UK and International Financial Reporting Standards have largely been eliminated, and the International Accounting Standards Board (IASB) is now working on minimizing differences between their standards and those of the American Financial Accounting Standards Board (FASB). Directors are free to disclose any additional information that they wish, provided they also adhere to the official standards.

4 There is a lot of criticism of auditors partly because financial scandals receive a lot of publicity. Most such scandals are not the fault of the auditors; it is often the auditors who first draw attention to a problem. When something has gone wrong it seems to be easy to blame the auditors, and even to sue them and hope to get financial compensation. Some criticism of arrangements for auditing is justified, particularly in relation to auditors' questionable independence. There is also the problem that rules for defining and valuing assets are not totally clear-cut, and if directors choose to adopt their own methods, it is difficult for auditors to prevent them.

5 The main influences on the development of accounting in the UK have been companies and directors and the need for accountability; accountants, auditors, the professional accountancy bodies and standards setters; and governments and company law. In addition, stock markets and the requirements of bankers and creditors have been influential. In recent years the role of theory has been increasingly emphasized.

Chapter 4

1 a Current assets : current liabilities (e.g. 1.8 : 1)

  b Current assets minus stocks : current liabilities (e.g. 0.9 : 1)

  c Capital requiring a fixed return (e.g. debentures) as a percentage of total long-term capital (equity plus debentures). This is often expressed as $\dfrac{D}{D+E}$ e.g. 35% It may also be expressed as $\dfrac{D}{E}$

  It is usually calculated using balance sheet values. It may be calculated using market values. Preference shares and all borrowings may be included with D.

  d Earnings before interest and taxation ÷ interest payable (e.g. 5 times)

2 It might take a long time to convert stocks into cash; they are not a very 'liquid' asset.

3 Net profit for the year, after taxation, as a percentage of equity (including all reserves and retained earnings) as shown on the balance sheet.

4 The 'return' is earnings before interest and taxation. If debentures are included as part of capital employed, the interest payable on them should be included as part of the return on capital employed (ROCE). It is important that the numerator and the denominator are consistent: where borrowings are included in the denominator, the interest on those borrowings should be included in the numerator. Return on ordinary share-holders' capital employed is usually measured after charging taxation for the year. If borrowings are included in capital employed, and earnings before interest and taxes (EBIT) is used as the numerator, it is taken before charging taxation; this is a matter of convenience, not a matter of principle.

5 An increase in the gross profit ratio does not tell us anything for sure about sales. They may have increased; selling prices may have increased. But an increase in the gross profit ratio may be entirely attributable to a reduction in cost of sales as a percentage of sales, which could be due to more effective buying, or reductions in purchase prices.

6 The company's financial position looks reasonably strong with some improvement in year 2. The current ratio is lower, but the liquidity ratio has increased. The gearing looks rather high, but has reduced; the company has reduced its long-term bor-rowing slightly; shareholders' funds have increased slightly; and interest cover has increased.

  The company's current assets look rather high, and this can have an effect on prof-itability. They have generated substantial amounts of cash, and the cash balance is now excessive and should be used profitably. It may be the company's intention to further reduce its long-term borrowing.

  The company has managed to increase its profitability slightly: both measures of ROCE have improved. But they appear to be struggling with sales and costs. Sales have increased slightly (5 per cent), but the gross profit margin has gone down a little. Operating costs have been kept under control (a slight decrease); and because of reduced borrowings, there has been a significant reduction in interest payable. After taxation, there has been an improvement in net profit as a percentage of sales.

Overall utilization of capital employed has hardly changed, but there have been improvements in the management of stocks and debtors. Stock turnover looks very slow, but has been improved substantially. The length of time that debtors take to pay has also been reduced substantially.

More detailed analysis of each item of expense as a percentage of sales could be undertaken; more detailed analysis of each item of assets and liabilities in relation to sales could be made. But the analysis shown below brings out the main points outlined above. The overall impression might be of reasonably successful financial management struggling to improve financial performance in difficult market conditions.

Solvency	Year 1	Year 2
Current ratio	1,868 : 434	2,100 : 600
	4.3 : 1	3.5 : 1
Liquidity ratio	688 : 434	1,100 : 600
	1.6 : 1	1.8 : 1
Gearing ratio	1,000 ÷ 2,434	900 ÷ 2,400
	41%	37.5%
Interest cover	295 ÷ 100	305 ÷ 90
	2.95 times	3.39 times

Profitability		
Return on ordinary shareholders' capital employed	135 ÷ 1,434	150 ÷ 1,500
	9.4%	10%
EBIT as a percentage of long-term capital employed	295 ÷ 2,434	305 ÷ 2,400
	12.1%	12.7%
Gross profit ratio	375 ÷ 3,600	384 ÷ 3,780
	10.42%	10.16%
Operating profit/sales	295 ÷ 3,600	305 ÷ 3,780
	8.19%	8.07%
Net profit after tax sales	135 ÷ 3,600	150 ÷ 3,780
	3.75%	3.97%
Sales net assets	3,600 ÷ 1,434	3,780 ÷ 1,500
	2.51 times	2.52 times
Stock turnover (days)	$\frac{1,200}{3,225} \times 365$	$\frac{1,000}{3,396} \times 365$
	136 days	107 days
Debtors ratio (days)	$\frac{600}{3,600} \times 365$	$\frac{500}{3,780} \times 365$
	61 days	48 days

Chapter 5

1 Profit is measured as a guide to dividend decisions; to indicate how successful or otherwise the management of the company is; as a basis for taxation; to guide investors in making decisions to buy, sell or hold shares; to guide creditors; to indicate the economic efficiency of the company and so to contribute to the efficient allocation of resources in the economy. It is also used for many different purposes, for example in relation to wage claims and price controls. It does not really indicate how much cash a company has generated.

2 The balance sheet can show the amount of profit made during a year by comparing the net asset value (or equity) on the balance sheet at the beginning of the year with the equivalent figure on the balance sheet at the end of the year. If the amount has increased the difference is profit, but two adjustments have to be made. Any dividends paid must be added to the amount of the increase; any additional share capital subscribed must be deducted.

This approach differs from using income statements because it is based on asset valuation (rather than measurement of income and expenses) but it is expected to produce the same answer.

3 Turnover and profit figures are shown separately for continuing operations and discontinued operations.

Exceptional items are separately disclosed, including profits or losses on the sale or termination of an operation; costs of a fundamental reorganization or restructuring; profits or losses on the disposal of fixed assets.

Segmental reports show sales, operating profit and assets for each segment in which the business operates.

Information is also available on the performance of investments; the performance of subsidiaries, associates and joint ventures, and simple investments can be monitored.

4 The calculation of profit requires a cost of sales figure that uses a closing stock figure; closing stock is shown at the lower of cost and net realizable value. Net realizable value requires prediction of how much the stock would sell for.

Profit calculation also requires figures for depreciation; this necessitates estimates of the future life of a fixed asset, and its residual value.

5 Current purchasing power (CPP) uses a general price index. Current cost accounting (CCA) deals with specific price changes.

CPP is based on maintaining capital in general purchasing power. CCA is based on maintaining the operating capability of the business.

6 a Mary's opening balance sheet

| Inventory 100 @ £10 | £1,000 |
| Capital | £1,000 |

b Income statement for year

Sales 1,000 @ £15		£15,000
Cost of goods sold		
Opening inventory 100 @ £10	1,000	
Purchases 1,000	11,000	
	12,000	
Closing inventory 100 @ £12	1,200	10,800
Gross profit		£4,200

c Balance sheet at end of year

Inventory 100 @ £12	£1,200
Cash (£15,000 − £11,000)	£4,000
	£5,200
Capital	£1,000
Profit	£4,200
	£5,200

d The business has only £4,000 cash available to give to charity. Profits of £4,200 have been made, but part of these were required to finance the additional cost of replacing stocks. If all the profit was given to charity, the business would have either to borrow money, or to reduce its operating capability (i.e. hold less stock).

e If 'last in first out' (LIFO) had been used, the most recently purchased items (at £12 each) would have been sold. Closing inventory would have been £200 less; cost of goods sold would have been £200 more; profit would have been £200 less. These are simplifying assumptions, but the profit for the year would have equalled the cash available to be paid out to charity. But the closing stock figure on the balance sheet would have been unrealistic, and the business would not have been able to finance the existing level of stocks. LIFO is an inadequate solution to the problem.

7 a Jackie's opening balance sheet

Vehicle	£30,000
Capital	£30,000

b Income statement for typical year

Sales		£40,000
Expenses	£20,000	
Depreciation	£3,000	£23,000
Profit		£17,000

c Jackie will take £17,000 out of the business each year. The business generates £20,000 cash a year. But profit is after charging depreciation of £3,000 a year. Each year £3,000 cash is retained in the business.

d Balance sheet at end of 9 years

Vehicle at cost	£30,000
Less Provision for depreciation	27,000
	3,000
Cash	27,000
	30,000
Capital	30,000

e Jackie has maintained capital in terms of money: there is still £30,000 in the business at the end of 9 years. The depreciation charge means that the annual £20,000 generated as cash was not taken out of the business. Only the £17,000 profit was taken out.

But, after 9 years, the cost of replacing the vehicle has probably increased substantially; perhaps it has doubled. The business would then be able to buy only half a taxi. In terms of operating capability, the capital of the business has been halved over the 9-year period because no allowance has been made for the increase in prices of the fixed assets.

Chapter 6

1 The three ratios may be calculated on a 'per share' basis, or for the company as a whole. The results should be the same.

   a The price/earnings (P/E) ratio indicates whether the share price is expensive or cheap in relation to the most recent profits. It is calculated by dividing the share price by the earnings per share (EPS). A high P/E ratio (e.g. 30+) suggests that investors are optimistic about future increases in earnings. A low P/E ratio (e.g. 10 or less) suggests that investors are not very optimistic about future growth.

   b The dividend yield indicates whether the share price is expensive or cheap in relation to the most recent dividends. It is calculated by dividing the most recent year's dividend per share by the share price. A high dividend yield (e.g. 5 per cent or more) suggests that shares are cheap in relation to the most recent dividend. A very high dividend yield (e.g. 8 per cent or more) suggests that there are serious concerns about the company: perhaps the share price has collapsed, and/or the level of dividends is not expected to be maintained at last year's level. A low dividend yield (e.g. 2 per cent or less) suggests that investors are optimistic about future growth.

   c The dividend times cover relates the most recent year's dividends to the amount of profits earned in that period. It helps to indicate how 'safe' the dividends are. It is calculated by dividing the amount of earnings by the amount of dividends. A high cover (e.g. 2.5 or more) suggests that dividends are relatively safe. A low cover (e.g. 1.2, or even less than 1) suggests that the company would have difficulty maintaining the dividend, especially if there was a fall in earnings.

2 The market value of a successful company is likely to be higher than its balance sheet value. This is partly because balance sheet values may be understated. It is mainly because the market value of a business is largely influenced by its profitability, and expectations that it will be at least maintained, and will probably increase. The value of a successful business as a whole, as a going concern, with internally generated goodwill that is unrecorded, is normally higher than the value of a collection of dead assets.

   Sometimes the market value of a company falls below the net asset value, especially when the company is doing badly. In these circumstances the company may unwittingly attract an asset-stripping takeover bid. Another company may be attracted to buy up the assets of the company at a low price, and then split up the various parts of the company and sell them at a profit.

   In some companies (e.g. property companies) assets may be fully valued, and prospects for growth in earnings are limited; the market value may then be lower than the net asset value.

3 The dividend yield refers to the last known dividend. The next dividend may be lower, or it may be zero. High dividend yields are associated with low share prices, and question marks about how likely the dividend is to be maintained.

4 The figures are shown in full below.

	Alemouth plc	**Beermouth plc**
Share capital (20p shares)	£1,600,000	£ 2,000,000
Reserves	£3,200,000	£18,000,000
	£4,800,000	£20,000.000
Net profit after tax for year	£3,520,000	£1,200,000
Dividends for year	£3,200,000	£800,000
Number of shares	8,000,000	10,000,000
Market price of shares	£4.40	£1.80
Market capitalization	£35,200,000	£18,000,000
EPS	£0.44	£0.12
Dividend per share	£0.40	£0.08
P/E ratio	10	15
Dividend times cover	1.1 times	1.5 times
Dividend yield	9.09%	4.44%
Net assets per share	£0.60	£2.00

5 The dividend yield of Alemouth plc is very high, which is associated with a low share price (the P/E ratio is only 10), a low dividend cover (1.1 times) and pessimism about future prospects.

6 The market capitalization of Beermouth is only £18 million although their net asset value is £20m. In most companies the market value is higher than the net asset value. There could something seriously wrong with Beermouth's balance sheet: perhaps the assets are over-valued, or there is a significant unrecorded liability; perhaps the company is about to be sued for something. It is more likely that the market value of the company is very low because the company is expected to be making losses. The company's ROCE (£1,200,000/£20,000,000) was only 6 per cent last year. If the company makes losses of more than £2 million in the current year, the net asset value would soon fall below the current market capitalization (which might then rise or fall, depending on investors' expectations).

Chapter 7

1 The accruals concept means that profit is not based on cash flows; it is not the difference between cash received during a period, and cash paid out during that period. The accruals basis of accounting means that profit is the difference between revenues earned during a period, and the costs incurred in earning those revenues. Revenues (sales and other income) are recognized when they are earned, not when the cash is received. Similarly, expenses are not recognized when payments are made; instead, they are 'matched' against the revenues earned during the period.

The accruals concept is important in financial accounting because profits are different from cash flows; a business can be profitable and expanding, but be short of cash. A business can generate cash (e.g. by selling off assets), but be running at a loss.

If business accounts were based entirely on 'receipts and payments', there would be no balance sheet, and no measurement of profit. The accruals concept is essential for the preparation of balance sheets and income statements.

2 A very successful business will have serious cash shortages if their profits are poured into additional assets. This may be healthy expansion of inventories and receivables in line with sales, and investment in additional fixed assets, and buying shares in other companies. It may be unhealthy if poor control results in too many assets being bought, excessive inventory levels, and fixed assets that are not profitably utilized.

The situation could also arise if substantial loans are repaid, and if the company pays out more as dividends than it earns as profits.

3 If a company's depreciation charge is greater than its losses, it can still produce a positive cash flow. If a business is declining, additional cash could come in from reducing asset levels (inventories are sold off, debtors pay up, and excess fixed assets are sold). But this could not continue indefinitely. Eventually fixed assets will be fully depreciated and/or sold off, leaving little more than a cash shell.

4 Free cash flow is the amount of cash flow that a company has generated during a period when it is free to spend as it wishes. It is based on cash flow from operations after deducting non-discretionary payments such as interest and taxation (and including any dividends received). The company is free to spend as much of this free cash flow as it wishes on additional investments in fixed assets, paying dividends and repaying loans. The figure should be reduced to allow for the fact that there is usually some *essential* replacement of fixed assets.

a £7,000 minus essential asset replacement = approx. zero

b £4,100 minus, say £3,100 = £1,000; £5,500 minus, say, £2,200 = £3,300

5 It is true that Deek Lining plc produced positive cash flows in year 4, but this was mainly as a result of reducing assets. Reducing stocks and debtors produced £500,000, and sales of fixed assets produced £1,100,000. The increase in the amount owed to creditors produced another £100,000.

It is also true that additional fixed assets were bought, but this amounted to only £150,000, while the proceeds of selling fixed assets were £1,100,000. Borrowings were substantially reduced, as the chairman stated, and, as a result, there was a reduction in the amount of interest paid.

The most serious feature of year 4 was the substantial loss (£1.2m), compared with a profit of £3.4m in year 3. This demonstrates clearly the difference between cash flow and profit: although they made a loss in year 4, they produced a positive cash flow.

Year 3 generally looked more healthy, with a substantial profit, although they ended the year with less cash than they had at the beginning. It may be that they overexpanded in year 3 (with too much cash going into additional assets) and that some rationalization and careful housekeeping (including control of working capital) was required in year 4.

The increase in dividend is not justified by earnings: the company made a loss in year 4.

Although the chairman's statements are correct, it is difficult to justify the overall view that the company had a successful year in year 4. They made a substantial loss, and seemed to be selling off assets in order to raise additional cash.

6 Rachel

Rachel: budgets for year 3

b Cash budget

	Jan £	Feb £	Mar £	Apr £	May £	Jun £	Jul £	Aug £	Sep £	Oct £	Nov £	Dec £	Total £
Receipts													
From debtors	2,500	2,500	5,000	5,000	10,000	10,000	10,000	10,000	6,000	6,000	10,000	10,000	87,000
Payments													
Operating expenses	1,000	1,000	2,000	2,000	2,000	2,000	1,200	1,200	2,000	2,000	2,000	500	18,900
Fixed overheads	1,000	1,000	1,000	1,000	1,000	1,000	1,000	1,000	1,000	1,000	1,000	1,000	12,000
	2,000	2,000	3,000	3,000	3,000	3,000	2,200	2,200	3,000	3,000	3,000	1,500	30,900
Net receipts	500	500	2,000	2,000	7,000	7,000	7,800	7,800	3,000	3,000	7,000	8,500	56,100
Opening balance	1,000	1,500	2,000	4,000	6,000	13,000	20,000	27,800	35,600	38,600	41,600	48,600	1,000
Closing balance	1,500	2,000	4,000	6,000	13,000	20,000	27,800	35,600	38,600	41,600	48,600	57,100	57,100

a Budgeted income statement

	Jan £	Feb £	Mar £	Apr £	May £	Jun £	Jul £	Aug £	Sep £	Oct £	Nov £	Dec £	Total £
Sales	5,000	5,000	10,000	10,000	10,000	10,000	6,000	6,000	10,000	10,000	10,000	2,500	94,500
Expenses													
Operating expenses	1,000	1,000	2,000	2,000	2,000	2,000	1,200	1,200	2,000	2,000	2,000	500	18,900
Fixed overheads	3,000	3,000	3,000	3,000	3,000	3,000	3,000	3,000	3,000	3,000	3,000	3,000	36,000
	4,000	4,000	5,000	5,000	5,000	5,000	4,200	4,200	5,000	5,000	5,000	3,500	54,900
Profit	1,000	1,000	5,000	5,000	5,000	5,000	1,800	1,800	5,000	5,000	5,000	(1,000)	39,600

d Drawings should not exceed profit of £39,600

c

	£
Profit	39,600
Depreciation	24,000
	63,600
Increase in debtors (£12,500 − £5,000)	7,500
Increase in cash	56,100

Chapter 8

1 Depreciation, valuation of inventories, the distinction between capital expenditure and revenue expenditure, provisions for bad debts, other provisions, impairment of goodwill.

2 Low depreciation figures; profits/losses on sales of fixed assets; other exceptional items; provisions; asset (re)valuations; capitalizing items in the grey area between capital and revenue expenditure; showing alternative EPS figures.

3 There is no agreed definition of creative accounting. At the moderate end of the spectrum of creative accounting practices, some exercise of judgement is perfectly legal. At the other extreme, deception is illegal.

4 Accounting standards could reduce or eliminate choices of accounting policy, and require additional disclosures. More effective systems for monitoring and enforcement could also be developed.

5 There may be a conflict of interest between the auditors' wish to earn additional fees from consultancy and their need to remain independent from directors. In practice it is the directors who determine the appointment and remuneration of auditors, although this is subject to approval by the shareholders. Many of the problems are criticisms of the arrangements for auditing rather than of the auditors themselves.

6 The Platto Company

	Draft income statement for year ended 31 December year 8 £000	Budgeted income statement for year ended 31 December year 9 £000	Answer (i) Revised income statement for year ended 31 December year 8 £000	Answer (ii) Actual income statement for year ended 31 December year 9 £000
Sales revenue	800	790	800	758
Opening inventory	80	90	80	50
Purchases	650	636	650	636
	730	726	730	686
Closing inventory	(90)	(88)	(50)	(88)
Cost of sales	640	638	680	598
Gross profit	160	152	120	160
Profit on sale of asset				25
				185
Impairment			(55)	
Depreciation	(40)	(38)	(40)	(26)
Operating expenses	(90)	(92)	(90)	(92)
Profit	30	22	(65)	67

iii When the Uppit Company took over the Platto Company, it looked as if Platto's profits were steadily declining (from £30,000 in year 8 to £22,000 in year 9). Uppit produced a rapid improvement: they showed that Platto was not making a profit at all – they made a loss of £65,000 in year 8. By year 9, Uppit had turned this around: a profit of £67,000 was produced. But this was all done by 'creative accounting': there was no real improvement in the company's performance. Two extra charges were made against profits in year 8 (writing down inventories, impairment of fixed assets); this led to extra profits in year 9 (a lower opening stock figure; a profit on sale of fixed assets). Both of the additional charges in year 8 proved to be too high: the inventories sold for more than their supposed net realizable value; and the assets in Chipping Sodbury sold for more than their supposed fair value. There was no real improvement in performance (and they no longer have Chipping Sodbury!).

Chapter 9

1 Wm Morrison Supermarkets plc: ratios for 2005

Ratio	2006			2005		
1 Current ratio		820.7 : 1,806.6	0.45 : 1		1,324 : 1,712.4	0.77 : 1
2 Liquidity ratio		421.2 : 1,806.6	0.23 : 1		900.2 : 1,712.4	0.53 : 1
3 Capital gearing ratio	296.6 / 1,022.7 / 1,319.3			274.7 / 1,016.7 / 1,291.4		
	3,648.6 / 1,319.3 / 4,967.9	1,319.3 / 4,967.9	26.6%	4,005.9 / 1,291.4 / 5,297.3	1,291.4 / 5,297.3	24.4%
4 Interest times cover		$(262.9) \div (73.2)$	Not covered		$256.2 \div (86.5)$	2.96 times
5 Return on shareholders' funds		$(250.3) \times 100$ / 3,648.6	Negative		105×100 / 4,005.9	2.62%
6 Return on total long-term capital employed		$(262.9) \times 100$ / 4,967.9	Negative	5,297.3 / (78.4) / 5,218.9	256.2×100 / 5,218.9	4.91%
7 Operating profit as a % of sales		$(262.9) \times 100$ / 12,114.8	Loss		256.2×100 / 12,103.7	2.1%
8 Asset turnover	6,623.4 / 820.7 / (1,806.6) / 5,637.5	12,114.8 / 5,637.5	2.15 times	6,375.7 / 1,324.8 / (1,712.4) / 5,988.1	$12,103.7 \times 100$ / 5,988.1	2.02 times
9 Gross profit ratio		$2,977.8 \times 100$ / 12,114.8	24.6%		$3,011.7 \times 100$ / 12,103.7	24.9%
10 Staff costs as a % of sales		$1,716.9 \times 100$ / 12,114.8	14.2%		$1,568.3 \times 100$ / 12,103.7	13%
11 Other operating costs as a % of sales	256.9 / 124.2 / 9.2 / 1,133.5 / 1,523.8	$1,523.8 \times 100$ / 12,114.8	12.6%	259.2 / 40.0 / 0.4 / 887.6 / 1,187.2	$1,187.2 \times 100$ / 12,103.7	9.8%
12 Sales/fixed assets		$12,114.8 \div 6,623.4$	1.83 times		$12,103.7 \div 6,375.7$	1.90 times
13 Sales/current assets		$12,114.8 \div 820.7$	14.76 times		$12,103.7 \div 1,324.8$	9.14 times
14 Stock turnover ratio		399.4×365 / 9,155.5	15.9 days		424.6×365 / 9,110.3	17.0 days
15 Debtors ratio		157.4×365 / 12,114.8	4.7 days		224.2×365 / 12,103.7	6.8 days
16 Creditors ratio		$1,471.2 \times 365$ / 9,155.5	58.7 days		$1,437.2 \times 365$ / 9,110.3	57.6 days
17 Price/earnings ratio		$199 \div (9.46)$	Negative		$177 \div 4.14$	43
18 Dividend yield		0.037×100 / 1.99	1.9%		0.037×100 / 1.77	2.1%
19 Dividend cover		Loss	Negative		$4.14 \div 3.7$	1.1 times
20 Net assets per share		$3,648.6 \div 2,673m$	£1.36		$4,005.9 \div 2,658m$	£1.51

2 Current ratio; liquidity ratio; capital gearing; interest cover. Profits, quality of assets, and cash flows are also important. Z scores take into account various combinations of similar information including working capital, total gross assets, retained earnings, earnings before interest and tax, market value of equity and book value of debt.

3 Turnover, operating profit, net assets, for each class of business and for each geographic sector.

4 Tate and Lyle

	Food Americas	Food Europe	Sucralose	Sugars Americas	Sugars Europe	Total
Year to 31 March 2006						
Operating profit/net operating assets	20.5%	(50.7%)	37.2%	22.4%	13.8%	4.1%
Operating profit/sales	12.2%	(30.2%)	45.1%	10.3%	4.2%	2.0%
Sales/net operating assets	1.67 times	1.68 times	0.83 times	2.18 times	3.24 times	2.01 times
Year to 31 March 2005						
Operating profit/net operating assets	8.3%	7.1%	63.6%	45%	23.6%	15.3%
Operating profit/sales	3.9%	5.3%	36.5%	15.2%	5.9%	6.9%
Sales/net operating assets	2.11 times	1.35 times	1.74 times	2.96 times	4.02 times	2.23 times

In 2006 profitability declined substantially with the overall ROCE falling from 15.3 per cent to 4.1 per cent. The main problem was Food Europe where a modest return became a substantial loss. The return on capital employed for Food Americas increased substantially, but it declined in all other products. Sucralose continued to be very profitable, but its return on capital employed declined from 63.6 per cent to 37.2 per cent, mainly because of the substantial increase in operating assets devoted to that product: the company has been investing in it.

The decrease in return on capital employed was due both to a decrease in the operating profit/sales margin, and to reduced utilization of assets. The operating profit/sales margin decreased with all products (except for Sucralose; a remarkable success story), suggesting that the company had difficulty in charging sufficiently high prices, perhaps because of a competitive market. Utilization of assets declined with all products except Food Europe, where there was a substantial reduction in the amount of assets devoted to the product.

5 The key ratios for Gobbiediggan International plc are calculated as follows:

Segment	UK		Africa		South America	
	Year 1	Year 2	Year 1	Year 2	Year 1	Year 2
Operating profit ÷	80 ÷ 900	78 ÷ 760	40 ÷ 200	44 ÷ 175	20 ÷ 40	21 ÷ 60
Operating assets	8.9%	10.26%	20%	25.1%	50%	35%
Operating profit ÷	80 ÷ 800	78 ÷ 860	40 ÷ 300	44 ÷ 270	20 ÷ 100	21 ÷ 180
Sales	10%	9.1%	13.3%	16.3%	20%	11.7%
Sales ÷	800 ÷	860 ÷	300 ÷	270 ÷	100 ÷	180 ÷
Operating assets	900	760	200	175	40	60
	0.89	1.13	1.5	1.54	2.5	3.0

It is true that profits in the UK are declining, in spite of a modest increase in sales. However, the UK produces the bulk of the company's profits; the amount of capital employed has declined, and the profitability of the UK (in terms of ROCE) has increased. The UK may be a mature market, with limited long-term prospects, but for the foreseeable future it is still very important and profitable to the company.

It is true that sales are declining in the Africa market, but profits are increasing; profitability (in terms of ROCE) is higher than the UK and is increasing. The decline in sales may be a one-off blip, and the company should investigate its causes, and try to increase sales before abandoning the market.

It is true that the South America market has had an additional investment of £20,000, but this sum is small compared with the substantial increase in sales, and the high level of profitability. The ROCE declined, but this may be because it will take a little while for the additional investment to generate substantial additional profits.

The ratios may suggest that the company has a reasonable balance of different markets. It may also suggest priorities for developing each of the markets.

Chapter 10

1 The ASB's *Statement of Principles* defines assets as 'rights or other access to future economic benefits controlled by an entity as a result of past transactions or events'. Their definition of liabilities is 'obligations of an entity to transfer economic benefits as a result of past transactions or events'.

2 The purposes of asset measurement and reporting of assets are:

a To complete the double-entry system, and check on its accuracy, and to produce a list of balances to be transferred to a new ledger.

b To account for what has happened to the funds subscribed by shareholders by showing the assets in which they are invested.

c To give creditors information indicating the creditworthiness of the firm, showing that it has assets worth more than the amount that the firm owes.

d To provide up-to-date asset values so that the company does not have 'secret reserves', and to avoid unwelcome takeover bids based on hidden asset values.

e To provide up-to-date asset values as a basis for increased borrowing.

f As a basis for measuring profit, with profit measurement based on the increase in equity.

3 Methods of asset valuation include:

i   Historic cost (HC)

ii   HC less depreciation

iii   Net realizable value

iv   Economic value or net present value (NPV)

v   Replacement cost

vi   Face value

vii   Face value less a provision

viii Market price

ix   Directors' estimate of market value

x   Valuer's report

xi Insurance values

xii HC adjusted for inflation

xiii Various combinations

4 HC accounting requires fixed assets to be depreciated so that a proper charge is made against profits for the asset being 'used up'.

Inventories should be shown at the lower of cost and net realizable value; if they were always shown at cost, profits would be overstated if the assets could be sold only at a price significantly lower than cost.

Various other provisions, such as provisions for bad debts, are also created.

5 a Fixed assets: intangible.

Examples: deferred development expenditure; concessions, patents licences, trademarks; goodwill; payments on account

b Fixed assets: tangible examples: land and buildings; plant and machinery; fixtures and fittings; tools and equipment

c Fixed assets: financial examples include investments in shares, debentures and government securities

d Current assets: examples include inventories of raw materials and consumables; work in progress; finished goods and goods for resale

e Debtors and prepayments

f Investments (which may be held as fixed assets or as current assets)

g Cash and bank

6 a Current liabilities: examples include bank overdrafts; payments received on account; trade receivables; bills of exchange payable; other creditors including taxation and social security; accruals and deferred income.

b Non-current liabilities: examples include debentures and loans

c Provisions for liabilities and charges: examples include pensions and similar obligations; taxation including deferred taxation.

7 The main 'liabilities' that do not seem like other liabilities are provisions. Provisions for depreciation and for bad debts do not seem to be like obligations to transfer economic benefits. They are more an estimate of what has happened, and an appropriate charge against profits.

A provision for deferred taxation may not result in any payment in the foreseeable future. Provisions for pensions may seem to have been inappropriate if made at a time when the value of the pension fund's investments is very low; subsequent increases in the value of investments may mean that the provision is no longer required.

Sometimes provisions are created, and partly reversed at a later date.

8 Any additional share capital is an increase in equity, but is not revenue. Revaluations of assets, and restatements of amounts invested overseas in foreign currencies, can increase equity, but would not usually be regarded as revenues. Other credits to the income statement, such as reductions in provisions, would increase equity, but it is more debatable whether or not they should be regarded as revenues.

9 The payment of dividends, and reductions in share capital (e.g. the company buying back its own shares on the stock market) are decreases in equity, but are not expenses. Equity is also reduced when assets and investments are revalued downwards, and when provisions are created or increased; these may be more debatable, but prudence would suggest that they should be regarded as expenses.

10 a The small effects are with expenses like rates that are paid in advance, and it is necessary for the income statement to include only those expenses that relate to the period of the profit and loss account. There are also usually some 'accruals' at the end of the year: expenses that belong to the period that has just ended, but which have yet to be recorded.

    b A much bigger effect is with fixed assets. These are not regarded as an expense when they are purchased; the cost is charged to the income statement over a number of years as depreciation.

    c Another large effect is with closing inventories. The expense for the period is the cost of the goods that were sold. The cost of goods that were bought, or manufactured, but not sold, is carried forward and charged as an expense in the next period.

11 Cost of sales; distribution costs; administrative expenses; finance expense (interest).

12 Exceptional items are no longer formally defined, but separate disclosure is still expected. Financial Reporting Standard (FRS) 3 defined them as 'material items that derive from events or transactions that fall within the ordinary activities of the reporting entity and which individually or, if of a similar type, in aggregate, need to be disclosed by virtue of their size or incidence if the financial statements are to give a true and fair view'. The main non-operating exceptional items are profits or losses on the sale or termination of an operation; costs of a fundamental reorganization or restructuring; and profits or losses on the disposal of fixed assets.

    Exceptional items are separately disclosed; all are taken into account in calculating the basic earnings per share figure.

13 They could claim that the life of the fixed asset is so long that depreciation or amortization would be immaterial; that the asset is maintained; and that an annual impairment review takes place to ensure that this is the case. There is now no requirement for systematic amortization of goodwill; instead, an annual impairment review has to take place, and it is possible that this will find that no write-down is required.

Chapter 11

1 i Owners' capital, which is share capital in the case of a company

   ii Borrowing, which may be short (e.g. overdraft) or long term (e.g. debentures)

  iii Retained profits

In addition, expansion can be funded in a variety of ways such as factoring debtors, sale and leaseback of premises.

2 Preference shareholders receive a fixed rate of dividend. No dividend can be paid to ordinary shareholders unless the preference dividend has been paid. There is no fixed rate of dividend for ordinary shareholders: they may receive very substantial dividends, or none at all.

Preference shares are usually *cumulative*, which means that if their dividend is not paid for one or more years, all arrears of preference dividends must be paid before any ordinary dividends are paid.

3 The main advantages of gearing (or borrowing) are that, if the company is successful, it can 'gear up' the return to ordinary shareholders. If a company can borrow money at, say, 7 per cent, and invest it to earn, say, 10 per cent, the whole of the extra profits belongs to the ordinary shareholders. The more the company borrows, the more profit it will make. Such borrowing also has the advantage that it enables companies to finance expansion relatively quickly, and at a relatively modest cost. Interest is an allowable expense for corporation tax purposes. If the alternative to borrowing is to issue ordinary shares, the issue costs of shares are likely to be higher, and shareholders are likely to expect a higher return in due course.

The main disadvantage of gearing is the risk of borrowing too much, and the company getting into difficulty. If a company has excessive borrowing, suppliers and lenders may be reluctant to do business with them. As long as a company has to pay only, say, 7 per cent for its borrowing, and is able to earn, say, 10 per cent, they should be all right. But if interest rates rise very much, or (more likely) if earnings are significantly reduced – or the company has no earnings – in particular years, they are likely to get into serious financial difficulties. Substantial borrowing is usually secured on some of the company's assets, and if the company is unable to meet the repayments, the lenders may require the assets to be sold, and the company could be forced into liquidation.

High gearing exaggerates the effects of changes in earnings before interest and taxation on earnings for ordinary shareholders. When EBIT is good, it is very, very good for the ordinary shareholders. But when EBIT is bad, it can be horrid for the ordinary shareholders – there may be no dividends, and the share price may collapse. High gearing is associated with high risk.

4 a

	TimeBall Co		DownsPier Co	
	Year 6	Year 7	Year 6	Year 7
Debentures	100	140	100	50
Debentures + equity	300	342.2	300	284.1
i Capital gearing ratio	33⅓%	40.9%	33⅓%	17.6%
Operating profit ÷ interest	20	21.6	20	17.5
	9	12.6	9	4.5
ii Interest cover	2.2 times	1.7 times	2.2 times	3.9 times
Profit after tax	7.7	6.3	7.7	9.1
Dividend	4	4.1	4	5
iii Dividend cover	1.9 times	1.5 times	1.9 times	1.8 times
iv Proportion of profit paid as dividend	52%	65%	52%	55%

b i   The capital gearing ratio shows the proportion of net assets financed by borrowing.

The TimeBall Company increased its fixed assets plus current assets less current liabilities; a small part of this was financed by retained profits; it was mainly financed by additional borrowing. It became a higher risk company.

The DownsPier Company reduced its fixed assets plus current assets less current liabilities; this was needed, plus an issue of additional shares, and a small amount of profit retained during the year, to provide enough to pay off half of the borrowing. The company's risk was reduced.

ii   The interest times cover shows how much the company is earning in relation to the amount of interest payable. In year 6 the interest cover of both companies was very low (2.2 times), which means that nearly half of their EBIT was committed to interest payments. A serious dip in EBIT could make it very difficult for the company to pay the necessary interest.

In year 7 the TimeBall Company's interest cover was lower, meaning that the situation became more risky. The DownsPier Company's interest cover increased significantly (though it is still on the low side), and risk was reduced.

iii   The dividend cover shows how much profit after tax was available to pay the dividend that the company chose to pay. The TimeBall Company's profit after tax was lower in year 7 than in year 6, and there was a very small increase in dividend, both of which reduced the cover.

The DownsPier Company's profit after tax increased significantly (by 18 per cent), but the increase in dividend was more substantial (25 per cent) and so the dividend cover was reduced.

iv   The proportion of profits paid out as dividend is the same information as in (iii) above, but expressed the other way around (the reciprocal expressed as a percentage).

c

	TimeBall Co		DownsPier Co	
	Year 6	Year 7	Year 6	Year 7
Return on shareholders' capital employed				
Profit after tax	7.7	6.3	7.7	9.1
Shareholders' capital employed	200	202.2	200	234.1
ROSCE	3.85%	3.1%	3.85%	3.9%
Return on total long-term capital employed				
Operating profit	20	21.6	20	17.5
Debentures + equity	300	342.2	300	284.1
Return	6.7%	6.3%	6.7%	6.2%

In year 7 the TimeBall Company increased their operating profit, but because of extra debenture interest, their profitability was reduced.

In year 7 the DownsPier Company managed a small increase in the return on ordinary shareholders' capital employed; although their operating profit was lower than in the previous year, their debenture interest was halved. The ordinary shareholders had put more money into the company, and they earned just enough to make it worth while.

Gross profit/sales %	40%	40%	40%	43%
Operating profit/sales %	20%	19.6%	20%	18.4%

The TimeBall Company maintained the same gross profit ratio from year 6 to year 7, but their operating profit as a percentage of sales declined; this must have been due to operating expenses increasing more than sales.

The DownsPier Company's gross profit ratio increased from year 6 to year 7; perhaps they concentrated on their most profitable lines, and the total amount of sales declined. Their operating profit as a percentage of sales declined, although the gross profit had increased. This was because operating expenses had increased, both as a percentage of sales, and in total.

The TimeBall Company expanded sales and borrowing in year 6, and their financial position was weaker, as shown by the gearing ratio and interest times cover. But the expansion was not (yet?) worth while, and profitability declined. They managed a small increase in dividends, but this was not justified by profits.

The DownsPier Company seems a little safer. Sales declined, and borrowing was reduced, and the gross profit ratio increased, and the amount of net profit increased. The return on ordinary shareholders' capital increased very slightly, and there was a substantial increase in dividend, more than was justified by the increase in profits.

5 High levels of working capital make life easier for managers. Sales can be made to anyone without worrying about collecting the money in. Having large amounts of stock is convenient to satisfy all demands. Having substantial sums of money in the bank is also very convenient; there is no need to plan it properly, and there is always money available. High levels of working capital also lead to high current ratios that make the company look financially stronger in terms of their ability to pay their creditors as they fall due.

6 Debtors can be reduced to little or nothing (or even negative) if customers are required to pay in advance. Some businesses have no stocks, or ensure that deliveries are 'just in time'. If there is a significant creditors figure, then working capital can be negative. This is not unusual with retailers.

7 At first, it arises with attempts to expand with insufficient long-term capital. There might be significant increases in fixed assets, stocks and debtors; but then the business finds that it is unable to finance these. Creditors increase; current and liquidity ratios fall; and the company runs out of money. It may then have to operate on a cash-only basis, and start to sell off assets.

8 Prompt paperwork, with invoices and reminders; follow-up letters and telephone calls; personal visits. Threatening to cut off supplies, and/or legal action. Implementing threats. Offering cash discounts for early payment. Charging interest on late payment.

A company might deliberately increase the length of time that customers are allowed to pay if this is likely to lead to increases in sales, and to generate additional profits greater than the cost of financing the additional debtors.

9 Stockholding costs; and the costs of ordering (which may include placing the order,

monitoring receipt, and payment of invoice). It also considers the volume of usage during the year, and the price per unit.

10 By careful planning and monitoring of cash receipts and payments; ensuring that there are sufficient funds to meet all planned requirements; and not authorizing unplanned payments.

11 Congle

Applying the economic order quantity (EOQ) formula the ordering quantity will be the square root of:

$$\frac{2 \times 40,000 \times £20}{1.25 \times 0.32} = \sqrt{\frac{1,600,000}{0.4}} = \sqrt{4,000,000} = 2,000$$

The number of orders each year will be 40,000 ÷ 2,000 = 20.

The annual ordering cost = £20 × 20 times per annum = £400.

Goods will be delivered (365 ÷ 20 =) every 18 days.

The average stock level will be half of the amount delivered, i.e.

$$\frac{1}{2} \times 2,000 \times £1.25 = £1,250$$

The annual stockholding cost is £1,250 × 32% = £400.

12 Fleshwick traders

Annual cost of debtors now: £90,000 × 17% = £15,300.

Annual sales are £365,000, i.e. £1,000 per day.

Existing debtors figure is £90,000, i.e. 90 days.

Expected reduction in debtors applies to one-third of debtors, i.e. £30,000.

Reduction is from 90 days to 10 days, i.e. a reduction of eight-ninths.

Eight-ninths of £30,000 is £26,667.

Annual interest saved is 17% of £26,667 = £4,533.

Annual cost of discount on one-third of annual sales is £121,667 × 2.5% = £3,042.

a It is worth offering the discount because the amount of interest saved is greater than the cost of the discount offered.

b The annual interest saved is £4,533; discount costing up to £4,533 could be offered without reducing profits. £4,533 as a percentage of eight-ninths (one-third of annual sales) £121,667 is 3.726%.

c Five per cent discount to one-third of existing customers would cost £6,085.

The annual interest saved would be £4,533.

The additional cost would be £6,085.

The additional contribution required would be £1,552.

Additional annual sales to achieve this contribution (contribution is one-fifth of sales) is 5 × £1,552 = £7,760.

This is near enough for most purposes, but for the mathematically inclined it is rather simplistic. A more accurate calculation would be as follows:

Let I = the increase in sales required to finance the discount.

The cost of the discount is ⅓ (365,000 + I) × 0.05, less the interest saving, which is 17% of eight-ninths of one-third of (365,000 + I). This will be equal to the amount of the additional contribution required, which is 20% of the additional sales. We can say, therefore, that:

$$[\frac{1}{3} (365,000 + I) \times 0.05] -$$

$$[0.17 \times \frac{8}{9} \times \frac{1}{3} \times \frac{90}{365} (365,000 + I)] = 0.2 \times I$$

The amount of the additional contribution required (solving the above equation) is £7,913.

13 Stokeypokey

i   Income statement

	£000	£000
Sales		6,180
Cost of sales		4,944
Gross profit		1,236
Rent	400	
Other expenses	165	
Depreciation	10	575
Net profit		661

ii   Balance sheet as at end of year

	£000	£000		£000
Fixed assets at cost		100	Capital/Loan	1,000
Less Provision for depreciation		10	Creditors	560
		90	Profit	661
Current assets				
Inventories	560			
Receivables	1,400			
Prepayment	100			
Cash	71	2,131		
		2,221		2,221

iii

	Jan £000	Feb £000	Mar £000	Apr £000	May £000	Jun £000	Jul £000	Aug £000	Sep £000	Oct £000	Nov £000	Dec £000
Receipts from debtors	–	–	100	200	300	400	480	560	640	700	700	700
Payments for purchases		240	240	320	384	448	512	560	560	560	560	560
Rent	100		100			100			100			100
Fittings	50									50		
Expenses	10	10	10	10	15	15	15	16	16	16	16	16
Opening balance	1,000	840	590	340	210	111	(52)	(99)	(115)	(201)	(77)	47
Net receipts	(160)	(250)	(250)	(130)	(99)	(163)	(47)	(16)	(86)	124	124	24
Closing balance	840	590	340	210	111	(52)	(99)	(115)	(201)	(77)	47	71

Workings	Jan	Feb	Mar	Apr	May	Jun	Jul	Aug	Sep	Oct	Nov	Dec
Sales	100	200	300	400	480	560	640	700	700	700	700	700
Purchases	240	240	320	384	448	512	560	560	560	560	560	560

iv The business looks highly profitable. Stokeypokey plans to put £1 million into the Northern Ireland branch, and expects to earn £661,000 profit: a return on capital of just over 66 per cent per annum.

The gross profit ratio is expected to be 20 per cent. The net profit/sales ratio is expected to be 10.7 per cent. The main reason for the high return on capital employed is that capital employed is fairly low, partly because the premises are rented.

Although profits look very good, it will take a little longer to generate cash flows to match. Rapid expansion in sales means that cash receipts from debtors tend to lag behind payments. A rapidly expanding and profitable business is often 'cash hungry' in the early stages. In this venture the branch pays out more cash than it receives in each of the first 9 months, and the initial £1 million will not be sufficient to avoid an overdraft by September.

By careful planning it might be possible to avoid an overdraft. Perhaps they could arrange to delay some payments in September, such as for the additional fittings, or make an extra effort to get debtors to pay more quickly in August.

Depreciation is an expense in calculating profit, but it is not a cash payment.

Chapter 12

1 ROI takes the average annual profits during the life of a project and expresses them as a percentage of the capital employed in the project. It is sometimes based on the initial capital employed, and sometimes on the average capital employed over the life of the project.

2 The company's return on capital employed is 10 per cent (£1 million as a percentage of £10 million).

The ROI of the proposed project is 9 per cent (£180,000 as a percentage of £2 million). But these figures are not strictly comparable: the £1 million is after tax, and the £180,000 is operating profit (before tax).

If the company had surplus funds, the new ship would increase the company's return on capital employed because there would be no increase in capital employed, and profits would increase. If the £2 million needed was in the bank, the increase in profits would depend on the amount of interest receivable that was lost as a result of buying the ship.

If the company had to raise additional equity, the total return on equity would be lowered because (a) the 9 per cent return is lower than the existing 10 per cent return, and (b) the additional £180,000 is operating profit: it would be less after tax.

If the ship was financed by borrowing, the company's return on equity would increase, assuming that the cost of borrowing was less than 9 per cent per annum.

3 Cash flows

Year	Project A	Project B
	£000	£000
0	(1,000)	(1,000)
1	200	400
2	200	350
3	200	300
4	200	100
5	200	50
6	200	5
7	200	5
8	200	5
Total	1,600	1,215

The payback period of Project A is 5 years. The payback period of Project B is just less than 3 years.

Project A produces substantially more cash flows than Project B. If the time value of money is not considered, Project A is much better.

If discounted cash flow (DCF) was used whether or not it is worth waiting for the extra money would depend on the discount rate used.

4 a ROI is based on profits and so is compatible with financial accounts. The answer is expressed as a percentage that appears to be easy to understand. It is relatively easily calculated and understood.

However, the approach ignores the timing of the cash flows. A project may have a good ROI but not be worth while if the delay in receiving it is too long.

b Payback period is easy to understand and easy to calculate. It uses cash flows rather than profits, and the emphasis is on getting back the money quickly.

But payback period ignores cash flows received after the end of the payback period. Use of payback period could lead to a project being accepted that makes very little money, but pays back quickly, and a very profitable project could be rejected because it takes a little longer to pay back.

5 The project will generate £35,000 profits a year for 5 years, giving total profits of £175,000. This looks poor.

But, profits are measured after charging depreciation, which amounts to £40,000 a year. Annual cash flows are, therefore, £75,000 a year.

Using a discount rate of 10 per cent, the project gives a net present value of about £84,300 as follows:

Year 1	$0.909 \times 75,000 =$	68,175
Year 2	$0.826 \times 75,000 =$	61,950
Year 3	$0.751 \times 75,000 =$	56,325
Year 4	$0.683 \times 75,000 =$	51,225
Year 5	$0.621 \times 75,000 =$	46,575
	$3.790 \times 75,000 =$	284,300

After deducting the initial cost of the investment (£284,300 − £200,000) the net present value (NPV) of the project is £84,300, which makes it acceptable if the company's cost of capital is 10 per cent.

The project would still be just about acceptable with a cost of capital of 25 per cent (£75,000 × 2.689 = £201,675) because the net present values of the future cash flows would still be slightly above the initial cost.

6

		Kippering	Queenies	
a	Average annual profits	£	£	
	Total cash flows	75,000	90,000	
	Total depreciation	50,000	50,000	
	Total profits	25,000	40,000	
	Average annual profits	5,000	8,000	
b	Return on initial capital employed	10%	16%	
c	Return on average capital employed	20%	32%	
d	Payback period	2½ years	3.2 years	
			£000	£000
e	NPV using 10%	1 0.9091	25 22,727	5 4,545
		2 0.8264	20 16,528	15 12,396
		3 0.7513	15 11,269	25 18,782
		4 0.6830	10 6,830	25 17,075
		5 0.6209	5 3,105	20 12,418
			60,459	65,216
			(50,000)	(50,000)
	NPV		10,459	15,216
f	NPV using 25%	1 0.800	25 20,000	5 4,000
		2 0.640	20 12,800	15 9,600
		3 0.512	15 7,680	25 12,800
		4 0.410	10 4,100	25 10,250
		5 0.328	5 1,640	20 6,560
			46,220	43,210
			(50,000)	(50,000)
	NPV		(3,780)	(6,790)
g	Approximate internal rate of return		10,459	15,216
	10% plus a proportion of 15%		(10,459 + 3,780)	(15,216 + 6,790)
			0.735 × 15	0.691 × 15
			11.02	10.36
		+10	21.02%	20.36%

7 If it is decided to go ahead with the proposal, the additional cash outflows at the beginning of the project would be:

Modifications to existing machinery	£100,000
Additional working capital	£ 50,000
Initial marketing costs	£ 60,000
	£210,000

The book value of the other machine is irrelevant; it has no alternative use or disposal value, and so there is no 'opportunity cost'.

The cost of the consultants' report has already been incurred whether the project goes ahead or not, and so is irrelevant.

The cash flows generated by each unit of sales are:

Selling price		£60
Variable costs		
Materials	11	
Labour	6	
Variable overheads	13	£30
		£30

The costs of general fixed overheads and interest will be incurred whether or not the project goes ahead, and so they are not relevant.

	Year 0	Year 1	Year 2	Year 3	Year 4
Sales (units)	–	3,000	7,000	4,000	1,000
'Contribution' at £30 per unit		90,000	210,000	120,000	30,000
Machinery	(100,000)				
Working capital	(50,000)				50,000
Marketing	(60,000)	(20,000)	(20,000)	(20,000)	(20,000)
Maintenance		(10,000)	(10,000)	(10,000)	(10,000)
Net cash flow	(210,000)	60,000	180,000	90,000	50,000
20% discount factor	1.0	0.833	0.694	0.579	0.482
Present value	(210,000)	50,000	124,920	52,110	24,100

The NPV of the project discounted at 20 per cent is (£251,130 − £210,000 =) £41,130

Chapter 13

1 Golden Beach Holiday Centre

	Total £000	Accommodation £000	Restaurant £000	Shop £000
Sales revenue	1,330	600	230	500
Variable costs				
DM	460	10	50	400
DL	450	300	100	50
VO*	100	45	17	38
Total variable costs	1,010	355	167	488
Contribution	320	245	63	12
Fixed costs	220			
Profit	100			

*Variable overheads of £100,000 are (100/1,330) about 7.5 per cent of sales revenue.

The shop makes a contribution of £12,000 to fixed costs that would be incurred whether or not the shop continues. Consideration could be given to alternative, more profitable use of the premises occupied by the shop; outsourcing the operation of the shop and charging a rent of more than £12,000 a year; and the need for a shop to operate within the complex (are there other acceptable shops nearby?).

2 Medical Manufacturing Company

Budget for next year	Total	Assembly	Testing
Production overheads	£1,200,000	£200,000	£1,000,000
Direct labour cost	£400,000	£200,000	£200,000
Production overheads as a % of direct labour	300%	100%	500%
Direct labour hours	28,000	20,000 hrs	8,000 hrs
Hourly pay rate	£14.29	£10	£25
Production overheads per direct labour hour	£42.86	£10	£25

a i 300%; **ii** 100%; 500%

b i £42.86; **ii** £10; £25

c £14.29 per hour; £10; £25

d

Direct materials	£150
Direct labour	
Assembly 3 hrs	£ 30
Testing 5 hrs	£125
Production overheads	
Assembly	£ 30
Testing	£100
	£435

3 Queen's Pier Engineering Company

	March	April	Change
Sales	£120,000	£140,000	£20,000
Profit	£ 40,000	£ 49,000	
Total costs	£ 80,000	£ 91,000	£11,000
Variable costs	£ 66,000	£ 77,000	
Fixed costs	£ 14,000	£ 14,000	

a Variable costs are 55 per cent of sales (£11,000 / £20,000).

b Contribution is, therefore, 45 per cent of sales.

c Total costs = sales minus profit. Fixed costs are total costs minus variable costs. Fixed costs are £14,000 per month.

d Break-even point = fixed costs ÷ contribution/sales ratio. £14,000 ÷ 0.45 = £31,111

4 Brigstow Autoparts Company

		England £000	Wales £000	Scotland £000
Sales		10,000	8,000	6,000
Cost of sales		5,600	4,600	3,800
Gross profit		4,400	3,400	2,200
Local operating costs		2,720	2,660	1,620
Operating profit		1,680	740	580
Central costs				
Depreciation (40 : 30 : 30)		80	60	60
Storage (40 : 30 : 30)		64	48	48
Operating and despatch (550 : 450 : 520)		86.8	71.1	82.1
Delivery (70 : 50 : 90)		200	142.9	257.1
	Warehouse			
Salaries (10 : 30 : 30 : 30)	40	120	120	120
Advertising (5,000 : 4,000 : 3,000)		66.7	53.3	40
Establishment (10 : 30 : 30 : 30)	24	72	72	72
Reallocation (550 : 450 : 520)	64	23.2	18.9	21.9
		712.7	586.2	701.1
Net profit		967.3	153.8	(121.1)
Total £1,000,000				

Chapter 14

1 a Sales made for cash are credited to the sales account and debited to the *cash account.*

b Sales made on credit to Smith are debited the Smith Account, and credited to the *sales account.*

c Purchases made for cash are credited to the cash account, and debited to the *purchases account.*

d Purchases made on credit from Anirroc Company are debited to the purchases account and credited to the *Anirroc Company (Anirroc is a creditor).*

e Smith, a debtor, pays us part of what he owes; the amount is credited to the Smith account and debited to the *cash account.*

f The provision for bad debts is increased by £30. This amount is debited to the income statement as an expense, and credited to the *provision for bad debts account.*

2 Sales, creditors, share capital, share premium

3 All of them.

4 Statement (b) is true.

5

Carlos Cash Account

Date	Description	Amount £	Date	Description	Amount £
July 1	Capital	40,000	July 5	Expenses (rent)	5,000
July 3	Spano Bank	15,000	July 8	Furniture and equipment	11,000
July 27	Sales	4,000	July 19	Expenses	2,500
Sept 14	Minki Cabs	15,000	Aug 10	Purchases	3,300
Sept 21	Sales	24,000	Aug 30	Motosales	40,000
			Sept 6	General expenses	3,300

Carlos Capital Account

Date	Description	Amount £	Date	Description	Amount £
			July 1	Cash	40,000

Spano Bank (Loan) Account

Date	Description	Amount £	Date	Description	Amount £
			July 3	Cash	15,000

General Expenses Account

Date	Description	Amount £	Date	Description	Amount £
July 5	Cash (rent)	5,000			
July 19	Cash	2,500			
Sept 6	Cash	3,300			

Furniture and Equipment Account

Date 2004	Description	Amount £	Date	Description	Amount £
July 8	Cash	11,000			

Purchases Account

Date 2004	Description	Amount £	Date	Description	Amount £
July 13	Motosales Ltd	50,000			
Aug 10	Cash	3,300			
Aug 16	Motosales	22,000			

Motosales Ltd (Creditor) Account

Date	Description	Amount £	Date 2004	Description	Amount £
Aug 30	Cash	40,000	July 13	Purchases	50,000
			Aug 16	Purchases	22,000

Sales Account

Date	Description	Amount £	Date 2004	Description	Amount £
			July 27	Cash	4,000
			Aug 3	Minki Cabs	18,000
			Sept 21	Cash	24,000

Minki Cabs (Debtors) Account

Date 2004	Description	Amount £	Date 2004	Description	Amount £
Aug 3	Sales	18,000	Sept 14	Cash	15,000

Trial balance as at 30 September

	Debit £	Credit £
Capital		40,000
Spano Bank loan		15,000
Cash	32,900	
General expenses	10,800	
Furniture and equipment	11,000	
Purchases	75,300	
Creditor (Motosales)		32,000
Sales		46,000
Debtors (Minki Cabs)	3,000	
	133,000	133,000

Income statement of Carlos for the three months ending 30 September

	£	£
Sales		46,000
Cost of sales		
Opening stock	0	
Purchases	75,300	
Deduct Closing stock	38,100	
Cost of goods sold		37,200
Gross profit		8,800
General expenses		10,800
Loss		2,000

Balance sheet of Carlos as at 30 September

	£	£
Fixed assets		
Furniture and equipment		11,000
Current assets		
Stocks	38,100	
Debtors	3,000	
Cash	32,900	
		74,000
		85,000
Capital	40,000	
Loss	(2,000)	
		38,000
Loan		15,000
Payables (creditors)		32,000
		85,000

6 Killip's ledger accounts

Cash Account

Date	Description	Amount £	Date	Description	Amount £
1 Aug	Capital	5,000	2 Aug	Office equipment	4,100
11 Aug	Sales	650	4 Aug	Office expenses (rent)	500
31 Aug	OneAlpha Ltd	550	15 Aug	Travelling expenses	135
			23 Aug	Salaries and subcontracting	700
			29 Aug	Dubya Smith	80

Capital Account

Date	Description	Amount £	Date	Description	Amount £
			1 Aug	Cash	5,000

Office Equipment Account

Date	Description	Amount £	Date	Description	Amount £
2 Aug	Cash	4,100			

Office Expenses Account

Date	Description	Amount £	Date	Description	Amount £
4 Aug	Cash (rent)	500			
7 Aug	Dubya Smith (stationery)	120			

Advertising Account

Date	Description	Amount £	Date	Description	Amount £
6 Aug	Journal of Man	250			

Journal of Man (Creditor) Account

Date	Description	Amount £	Date	Description	Amount £
			6 Aug	Advertising	250

Dubya Smith (Creditor) Account

Date	Description	Amount £	Date	Description	Amount £
29 Aug	Cash	80	7 Aug	Office expenses	120

Sales Account

Date	Description	Amount £	Date	Description	Amount £
			11 Aug	Cash	650
			20 Aug	OneAlphaLtd	2,200

Travelling Expenses Account

Date	Description	Amount £	Date	Description	Amount £
15 Aug	Cash	135			

OneAlpha Ltd (Debtor) Account

Date	Description	Amount £	Date	Description	Amount £
20 Aug	Sales	2,200	31 Aug	Cash	550

Salaries and Subcontracting Account

Date	Description	Amount £	Date	Description	Amount £
23 Aug	Cash	700			

Trial balance as at 31 August

	Debit	Credit	Calculation of balances
Cash	685		6,200 − 5,515
Capital		5,000	
Office equipment	4,100		
Office expenses	620		500 + 120
Advertising	250		
Journal of Man		250	
Dubya Smith		40	120 − 80
Sales		2,850	650 + 2,200
Travelling expenses	135		
OneAlpha Ltd	1,650		2,200 − 550
Salaries and subcontracting	700		
	8,140	8,140	

Income statement for month ending 31 August

Sales		2,850
Office expenses	620	
Advertising	250	
Travelling expenses	135	
Sales and subcontracting	700	1,705
Profit		1,145

Balance sheet as at 31 August

Fixed assets		
Office equipment		4,100
Current assets		
Debtors	1,650	
Cash	685	2,335
Total assets		6,435
Current liabilities		
Journal of Man	250	
Dubya Smith	40	290
Equity		6,145
Capital	5,000	
Profit	1,145	
		6,145
		6,435

7

Cass Hawin: bank reconciliation		
Balance according to cash book	£ **	
Add Interest received	200	
Deduct Bank charges	(150)	
Updated cash book balance	£100	
Balance according to bank statement	£(2,000)	
Unpresented cheques	(1,500)	increasing the overdraft
Add Cash deposited on 31 March	3,600	reducing the overdraft
Updated bank statement balance	£100	

**The balance in the cash book would be £50 (debit) before recording the interest received (debit) and the bank charges (credit).

Chapter 15

1 Noddy

Income statement of Noddy's Business for year ended 31 December year 6

	£
Sales	130,000
General expenses	(120,000)
Profit	10,000

Balance sheet as at 31 December year 6

		£
Shop premises		400,000
Total assets		400,000
Creditors		20,000
Capital	370,000	
Profit	10,000	
Equity		380,000
Total liabilities and equity		400,000

2 Mona Ramsey

Income statement of Mona Ramsey for the year ended 30 September year 3

	£	£
Sales revenue		267,321
Opening stock	20,000	
Purchases	188,000	
	208,000	
Deduct		
Closing stock	15,000	
Cost of goods sold		193,000
Gross profit		74,321
General expenses	8,000	
Rent, rates, insurance	17,000	
Wages	39,000	64,000
Net profit		10,321

Balance sheet as at 30 September year 3

		£
Current assets		
Inventory	15,000	
Receivables	11,000	
Bank	24,321	50,321
Total assets		50,321
Current liabilities		
Payables		13,000
Equity		
Capital at 1 October year 2	27,000	
Profit for year	10,321	37,321
		50,321

3 Sally Glen

Income statement of Sally Glen for the year ended 31 December year 8

	£	£
Sales revenue		365,000
Opening inventory	18,000	
Purchases	242,000	
	260,000	
Deduct Closing inventory	19,000	
Cost of goods sold		241,000
Gross profit		124,000
General expenses	8,000	
Rent, rates, insurance	23,000	
Wages	34,000	
Depreciation: premises	7,000	
Depreciation: vehicle	4,500[1]	
		76,500
Net profit		47,500

[1] Van at cost £32,000, minus provision for depreciation at 31 December year 7, £14,000, gives a net book value of £18,000 at the beginning of the year. The depreciation charge is 25 per cent of £18,000 = £4,500.

Balance sheet of Sally Glen as at 31 December year 8

Fixed assets	Cost	Prov for depn	Net book value
Shop premises	350,000	21,000	
		+ 7,000	
		28,000	322,000
Delivery van	32,000	14,000	
		+ 4,500	
		18,500	13,500
			335,500
Current assets			
Inventory	19,000		
Receivables	60,000		
Bank	23,000		102,000
Total assets			437,500
Current liabilities			
Payables			20,000
Equity			
Capital as at 31 December year 7		370,000	
Add Profit for year		47,500	
			417,500
Total liabilities and equity			437,500

4 Mary Rushen

Income statement of Mary Rushen for the year ended 30 June year 5

		£
Sales		320,000
Opening inventory	12,000	
Purchases	155,000	
	167,000	
Deduct Closing inventory	7,000	
Cost of goods sold		160,000
Gross profit		160,000
General expenses	13,000	
Repairs and maintenance	10,600	
Wages	37,000	
Depreciation: freehold buildings	10,000	
Depreciation: fixtures and fittings	4,400	
		75,000
Net profit		85,000

Balance sheet of Mary Rushen as at 30 June year 5

Fixed assets	Cost	Prov for depn	Net book value
Freehold buildings	400,000	80,000	
		+ 10,000	
		90,000	310,000
Fixtures and fittings	44,000	30,800	
		+ 4,400	
		35,200	8,800
			318,800
Current assets			
Inventory	7,000		
Receivables	8,000		
Cash and bank	7,400		22,400
Total assets			341,200
Current liabilities			
Payables			18,000
Equity			
Capital as at 30 June year 4	238,200		
Add Profit for year	85,000		323,200
			341,200

5 Brad Head

Income statement of Brad Head for year ended 31 December year 3

Sales revenue		660,000
Opening inventory	28,000	
Purchases	255,000	
	283,000	
Closing inventory	13,000	
Cost of sales		270,000
Gross profit		390,000
General expenses		9,000
Light and heating		
19,000+2,000		21,000
Rent, rates, insurance		
65,000−4,400		60,600
Wages		44,000
Depreciation:		
fixtures and fittings		2,200
Depreciation: MV		9,000
Depreciation:		
plant and machinery		22,000
Increase in provision for		
bad debts		600
Bad debt written off		2,100
Total expenses		170,500
Operating profit		219,500
Interest paid		3,500
Profit for the year		216,000

Balance sheet as at 31 December year 3

Non-current assets	Cost	Depn	NBV
Fixtures and fittings	22,000	13,200	
		2,200	6,600
Plant and machinery	220,000	24,000	
		22,000	174,000
Vehicles	60,000	15,000	
		9,000	36,000
			216,600
Current assets			
Inventories			13,000
Receivables (98,100−2,100)	96,000		
Provision for bad			
debts (1,800+600	(2,400)		93,600
Prepayment			4,400
Cash (6,400−6,000)			400
Total assets			328,000
Current liabilities			
Payables			
Equity			
Capital at 31 Dec year 2	35,000		
Profit for year	216,000		
Drawings	(6,000)		245,000
Current liabilities			
Payables	31,000		
Accruals	2,000		33,000
Non-current liabilities			
Bank loan			50,000
			328,000

6 Ellie's Limited

Income statement of Ellie's Limited as at 31 December year 1

	£	£
Sales		248,300
Cost of goods sold		
Opening inventory	19,500	
Purchases	167,000	
	186,500	
Less Closing inventory	21,000	165,500
Gross profit		82,800
Printing and stationery	2,400	
Wages	12,300	
Bad debt written off	500	
Increase in provision for bad debts (650 − 600)	50	
Rent (1,500 − 400)	1,100	
Electricity (1,100 + 200)	1,300	
Depreciation on furniture and fittings		
(25% × 10,000)	2,500	
Depreciation on cars		
(25% × 20,000)	5,000	
Profit on disposal of van		
(8,400 − 4,200 − 4,750)	(550)	
General expenses	1,400	26,000
Operating profit		56,800
Corporation tax		15,000
Profit after tax		41,800
Proposed dividend (100 × £20)		2,000
Retained profit for year		39,800

Balance sheet of Ellie's as at 31 December year 1

Fixed assets	Cost	Accum depn	Net book value
	£	£	£
Fixtures and fittings	12,000	4,500	7,500
Vehicles	20,000	10,000	10,000
			17,500
Current assets			
Inventories		21,000	
Receivables (61,000 − 500)	60,500		
Less Provision for bad debts	(650)	59,850	
Prepaid rent		400	
Cash		450	
		81,700	
Current liabilities			
Payables	13,400		
Accruals	200		
Taxation	15,000		
Dividend	2,000		
		30,600	51,100
			68,600
Equity			
Share capital			100
Share premium			11,600
Retained profits as at 31 December year 0		17,100	
For year to 31 December year 1		39,800	56,900
			68,600

Note

Dividends payable are now not normally recognized until after they have been approved by shareholders. It may be assumed that the above financial statements were finalized after the annual general meeting.

7 Bulgham, Dhoon and Barony

Income statement of Bulgham, Dhoon and Barony for the year ended 31 December year 9

	£	£
Sales revenue		490,000
Opening inventory	37,000	
Purchases	320,000	
	357,000	
Deduct Closing stock	31,000	
Cost of sales		326,000
Gross profit		164,000
General expenses	45,000	
Rent (28,000 − 4,000)	24,000	
Depreciation	9,000	78,000
Net profit		86,000

Profit and loss appropriation account

Interest on capital		
Bulgham	2,000	
Dhoon	1,500	
Barony	1,000	4,500
Salaries		
Dhoon	18,250	
Barony	18,250	36,500
Profit share		
Bulgham	15,000	
Dhoon	15,000	
Barony	15,000	45,000
		86,000

Balance sheet as at 31 December year 9

Non-current assets

Furniture at cost		90,000
Deduct Provision for depreciation (27,000 + 9,000)		36,000
		54,000

Current assets

Inventories		31,000	
Prepayment		4,000	
Cash		47,000	
			82,000
			136,000

Capital accounts:	Bulgham	Dhoon	Barony	
	40,000	30,000	20,000	90,000

Current accounts:	Bulgham	Dhoon	Barony	
	10,000	22,000 Dr	28,000 Dr	
Interest	2,000	1,500	1,000	
Salaries	–	18,250	18,250	
Share of profit	15,000	15,000	15,000	
	27,000	12,750	6,250	46,000
				136,000

Chapter 16

1 Daubyhaven Ltd

Cash flow statement of Daubyhaven Ltd for year ended 31 December year 2

Cash generated from operating activities

1	Operating profit	35,000	
2	Depreciation*	20,000	
3	Other items: profit on sale of machine	(1,500)	
			53,500
	Increase in working capital		
4	Increase in inventories	(20,000)	
5	Increase in receivables	(5,000)	
6	Decrease in payables	(2,000)	
			(27,000)
7	Interest paid	(2,000)	
8	Taxation paid	(8,000)	
			(10,000)
			16,500
	Cash used in investing activities		
9	Purchase of fixed assets**	(15,000)	
10	Disposal of fixed assets	4,500	
			(10,500)
	Cash used in financing activities		
11	Repayment of loan	(10,000)	
12	Dividends paid	(18,000)	
			(28,000)
			(22,000)
	Decrease in cash during year		
	Opening balance	10,000	
	Closing balance	(12,000)	

Notes

*At the beginning of the year the provision for depreciation was £60,000. During the year it was reduced by £12,000 in respect of a machine that was sold to £48,000. It ended the year as £68,000 which means that it must have increased by £20,000, being the year's depreciation charge.

**At the beginning of the year machinery at cost was £130,000. During the year it was reduced by £15,000 in respect of a machine that was sold to £115,000. It ended the year as £130,000, which means that it must have increased by £15,000, being the additional purchases of machinery.

2 Fistard Neash plc

Cash flow statement of Fistard Neash plc for year ended 31 December year 6

			£m
Cash generated from operating activities			
1	Operating profit	20	
2	Depreciation*	24	
3	Impairment of goodwill	10	
	Profit on sale of Scottish factory	(7)	47
	Increase in working capital		
4	Increase in inventories	(25)	
5	Decrease in receivables	5	
6	Decrease in payables	(5)	(25)
7	Interest paid	(2)	
8	Taxation paid	(4)	(6)
			16
Cash used in investing activities			
9	Purchase of fixed assets**	(44)	
10	Disposal of fixed assets	23	
			(21)
Cash used in financing activities			
11	Redemption of debentures	(49)	
	Issue of shares ***	60	
12	Dividends paid	(8)	3
			(2)
Decrease in cash during year			
	Opening balance	10	
	Closing balance	8	

Notes

*At the beginning of the year the provision for depreciation was £50m. During the year it was reduced by £8m in respect of the Scottish factory that was sold to £42m. It ended the year as £66m, which means that it must have increased by £24m, being the year's depreciation charge.

**At the beginning of the year plant, property and equipment at cost was £120m. During the year it was reduced by £24m in respect of the Scottish factory that was sold to £96m. It ended the year as £140m, which means that it must have increased by £44m, being the additional purchases of property, plant and equipment.

***Share capital increased by £20m, and share premium increased by £40m. This indicates that shares with a nominal value of £20m were issued for £60m.

3 Ahmed and Leong

	Ahmed	Leong
	£	£
Net profit	15,000	7,000
Add Depreciation	5,000	10,000
	20,000	17,000
(Increase)/decrease in inventories	(4,000)	4,000
(Increase)/decrease in debtors	(3,000)	2,000
(Decrease)/increase in creditors	(3,000)	3,000
Increase in cash	10,000	26,000
Opening balance	20,000	15,000
Closing balance	30,000	41,000

4 Jack Kit

Income statement of Jack Kit for year ended 31 December year 3

	£	£	£
Sales			
Receipts from debtors	120,000		
Less: from previous year	(10,000)		
Plus: this year's debtors	12,000		
Cash sales	60,000		182,000
Cost of sales			
Opening stock		14,000	
Payments to creditors	125,000		
Less: from previous year	(15,000)		
Plus: this year's creditors	17,000		
Purchases		127,000	
		141,000	
Deduct Closing stock		16,000	125,000
Gross profit			57,000
Wages	25,000		
Expenses	20,000		
Depreciation	1,800		46,800
Net profit			10,200

Balance sheet of Jack Kit as at 31 December year 3

Fixtures and fittings	
(18,000 − 1,800)	16,200
Premises	187,000
Inventories (stocks)	16,000
Receivables (debtors)	12,000
Cash	13,000
Total assets	244,200
Payables (creditors)	17,000
Loan	170,000
Capital	47,000
Retained earnings	10,200
	244,200

Balance sheet of Jack Kit at beginning of year 3

Fixtures and fittings	18,000
Inventories (stocks)	14,000
Receivables (debtors)	10,000
Cash	20,000
Total assets	62,000
Creditors	15,000
Capital	47,000
	62,000

Jack Kit made a profit of £10,200 during the year, but his cash balance fell from £20,000 to £13,000. The business did much better than the cash figures suggest. Indeed, he managed to pay a deposit of £17,000, and buy new premises.

Cash flow statement of Jack Kit as at 31 December year 3

		£
Cash generated from operations		
Operating profit		10,200
Depreciation		<u>1,800</u>
		12,000
Increase in inventories	(2,000)	
Increase in receivables	(2,000)	
Increase in payables	<u>2,000</u>	<u>(2,000)</u>
Cash flow from operations		10,000
Cash used in investing activities		
Purchase of premises		(187,000)
Cash generated from financing activities		
Loan		<u>170,000</u>
Decrease in cash		<u>(7,000)</u>
Opening cash balance	20,000	
Closing cash balance	13,000	

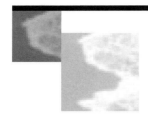

Answers to Activities

4.1 Druisdale plc

Ratio	Year 5		Year 6		Comment
Current ratio	120 : 60	2 : 1	120 : 80	1.5 : 1	Looks weaker because of increased current liabilities
Liquidity ratio	60 : 60	1 : 1	60 : 80	0.75 : 1	Looks weaker because of increased current liabilities
Gearing ratio	60/240	25%	40/240	16.7%	Lower, less risky, because of reduced borrowings
Interest cover	60/5	12 times	69/4	17¼ times	Higher, less risky, because of reduced borrowings, reduced interest and increased operating profit

4.2 Druisdale plc

Ratio	Year 5		Year 6		Comment
5 Return on shareholders' capital employed	40/180	22.2%	50/200	25%	Profitability for shareholders has increased because profits have increased more than the increase in shareholders' capital employed
6 Return on total long-term capital employed	60/240	25%	69/240	28.75%	Overall profitability in the use of assets has increased
7 Operating profit as a percentage of sales	60/300	20%	69/350	19.7%	Profit as a percentage has declined, indicating an increase in costs as a percentage of sales
8 Asset turnover	300/240	1.25 times	350/240	1.46 times	Overall increase in profitability is due to improved utilisation of assets (sales have increased; assets have not)

Relationship between ratios 6, 7 and 8
Year 5   25 ÷ 20 = 1.25
Year 6   28.75 ÷ 19.7 = 1.46

4.3 Druisdale plc

Ratio	Year 5		Year 6		Comment
9 Gross profit ratio	100/300	33⅓%	120/350	34.3%	The margin between buying prices has improved by increasing selling prices and/or reducing the cost of purchase
10 Distribution costs as a % of sales	15/300	5%	20/350	5.7%	Distribution costs have increased by a bigger proportion than sales
11 Administrative expenses as a % of sales	25/300	8⅓%	31/350	8.9%	Administrative expenses have increased by a bigger proportion than sales

4.4 Druisdale plc

Ratio	Year 5		Year 6		Comment
12 Sales/fixed assets	300/180	1.67 times	350/200	1.75 times	Sales have increased by a bigger proportion than fixed assets, thus improving the utilization of fixed assets
13 Sales/current assets	300/120	2.5 times	350/120	2.92 times	Sales have increased, current assets have not, thus improving the utilization of current assets
14 Stock turnover ratio	$60 \div 200 \times 365$	109.5 days	$60 \div 230 \times 365$	95.2 days	Stock levels have remained constant while turnover has increased
15 Debtors ratio	$40 \div 300 \times 365$	48.7 days	$50 \div 350 \times 365$	52 days	Debtors have increased by a bigger proportion than sales, indicating that it is taking a few days longer to get money in from debtors
16 Creditors ratio	$60 \div 200 \times 365$	109.5 days	$80 \div 230 \times 365$	127 days	Creditors have increased by a bigger proportion than cost of sales, and it is taking even longer than an already long period to pay them

Comments on profitability

Overall profitability (measured as return on capital employed, ratios 5 and 6) increased from year 5 to year 6. This was not due to an improvement in the profitability of sales, which declined (ratio 7). It was due to improved utilization of assets (asset turnover, ratio 8, increased).

The problems with the profitability of sales were due to an increase in distribution costs and administrative expenses; the gross profit ratio increased, suggesting that there was not a problem with the cost of sales or selling prices.

The improved utilization of assets applied to both fixed assets and current assets. Stock turnover increased, although this was offset by a slowing down in the collection of debtors. The period taken to pay creditors is excessive, and increased; but this increasing reliance on funding by debtors contributed to the increase in profitability.

4.5   Druisdale plc

Ratio	Year 5		Year 6		Comment
17 Price/earnings ratio	£5.60 ÷ 40p	14	£7.50 ÷ 50p	15	Share price has increased by an even bigger proportion than earnings per share (EPS); suggests optimism
18 Dividend yield	25p ÷ £5.60 × 100	4.5%	30p ÷ £7.50 × 100	4%	Dividend has increased by a significant proportion, but the share price has increased by an even bigger proportion so that dividend is a smaller proportion of the share price
19 Dividend cover	40/25	1.60 times	50/30	1.67 times	Dividends have increased almost in line with profits, but there is a slight increase in cover
20 Net assets per share	£180/100	£1.80	£200/100	£2.00	Net assets per share have increased as profits have been retained; but the market price is much higher than the underlying asset value

4.6   Garwick Ltd

Ratio	Year 7	Year 8
1 Current ratio	2.47 : 1	1.5 : 1
2 Liquidity ratio	1.88 : 1	0.85:1
3 Capital gearing ratio	53.3%	42.9%
4 Interest times cover	4.75 times	7.67 times
5 Return on shareholders' funds	31.4%	37.5%
6 Return on total long-term capital employed	25.3%	32.9%
7 Operating profit as a % of sales	18.8%	21%
8 Asset turnover	1.35 times	1.57 times
9 Gross profit ratio	30.7%	32.7%
10 Distribution costs as a % of sales	6.9%	6.4%
11 Administrative expenses as a % of sales	5%	5.5%
12 Sales/fixed assets	2.02 times	1.83 times
13 Sales/current assets	2.4 times	3.67 times
14 Stock turnover ratio	52.1days	64.1 days
15 Debtors' ratio	50.6 days	53.1 days
16 Creditors' ratio	88.6 days	98.6 days
17 Price/earnings ratio (P/E)	17	19
18 Dividend yield	4.3%	3.5%
19 Dividend cover	1.4 times	1.5 times
20 Net assets per share	£0.35	£0.40

Comments

In year 7 the current and liquidity ratios were strong, but they had declined to worrying levels in year 8.

In year 7 the gearing ratio was high, and the interest times cover was low, indicating heavy reliance on long-term borrowing. The level of gearing was lower (safer), and the interest cover was stronger in year 8.

The company had reduced its reliance on long-term borrowing mainly by reducing the amount of cash held.

The level of overall profitability was high, and increased in year 8 (ratios 5 and 6) . The increase was due both to an increase in the profitability of sales (ratio 7) and in the utilization of assets (ratio 8).

The increase in the profitability of sales was due both to an increase in the gross profit ratio, and to a decrease in distribution costs as a percentage of sales; this was offset by an increase in administrative expenses as a percentage of sales.

The improvement in the utilization of assets was due entirely to an increase in the turnover of current assets; the utilization of fixed assets declined (because the amount of fixed assets increased by a bigger proportion (20 per cent[1]) than the increase in sales (just less than 10 per cent[2]).

The improvement in the utilization of current assets was due partly to the reduction in the amount of cash, and partly to the increase in stock turnover; these were offset by the deterioration in the debtors ratio. The amount of net assets was also reduced (and so capital employed was reduced[3]) by the increase in creditors.

Overall, there was a good improvement in profitability, but some concern about solvency and excessive liabilities remains.

The share price increased substantially, and the increase in the P/E ratio indicates investors' optimism about the company. The amount of dividend paid by the company increased substantially (by 25 per cent), but the share price increased by a greater proportion, and so the dividend yield declined; a reduction in dividend yield may be seen as an indicator of the market's confidence in the company. There may be questions about the sustainability of dividends (cover was only 1.4 times in year 7), but this improved a little in year 8.

The market value of the company is much higher than the balance sheet value of it (the share price is much higher than the net assets per share).

---

[1] From £50,000 to £60,000.

[2] From £101,000 to £110,000.

[3] And so return on capital employed was increased.

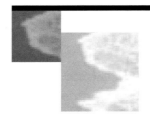

Glossary

The word 'company' is used in this glossary although most of the definitions apply to other businesses and entities.

A

Absorption costing A traditional costing method in which individual products bear their share of both fixed and variable production costs.

Accounting standards These have been issued as *SSAPs*, *FRSs* (UK and Ireland); *IASs*, and *IFRSs* (international). US standards are issued by the US Financial Accounting Standards Board (FASB).

Accrual An accrual is an expense that has been incurred but not yet recorded at the year end; the trial balance has to be adjusted to incorporate accruals. Accruals are only a small part of the accruals concept.

Accruals concept On an income statement revenue is recorded in the period when it is earned and not when the cash is received; expenses are recorded in the period in which they are incurred and not when they are paid; expenses are matched against revenues. This is distinct from the cash (or receipts and payments) basis of accounting.

Acid test *See **liquidity ratio**.*

Assets Simply: something of value that a company owns. More fully: a resource controlled by the enterprise as a result of past events and from which future economic benefits are expected to flow to the enterprise; this definition emphasizes control not ownership.

Associate An associate company is not a subsidiary company but it is one over which an investing company has significant influence, usually by owning between 20 per cent and 50 per cent of its shares.

Auditing The annual process whereby all but small companies are subject to qualified accountants checking their financial statements, ensuring that they have been prepared in accordance with the Companies Acts and relevant accounting standards, and that they show a true and fair view.

B

Balance sheet A statement of *assets*, *liabilities* and *equity* as at a given date, typically at the end of a year, or a month.

Bonus issue An issue of shares to existing shareholders where no money changes hands. Reserves or retained earnings are re-designated as share capital.

C

Capital expenditure Expenditure incurred in buying, creating or adding to tangible fixed assets.

Cash A current asset; it includes petty cash and bank. It can be negative, usually shown as an overdraft, a *current liability*.

Cash flow The term has no precise meaning but is sometimes used as if it means profit plus depreciation. All companies produce cash flow statements that show separately cash flows from operating activities, investing activities and financing activities.

Cash flow statement One of the principal statements in a published set of accounts, it shows cash flows generated by/used in operating activities, investing activities and financing activities.

Concepts The idea of four fundamental accounting concepts (prudence, consistency, accruals and going concern) has been superseded by emphasis on relevance and reliability.

Consistency Consistent accounting treatment is given to similar items within a given year and from year to year.

Consolidated financial statements Financial statements of a group of companies that includes 100 per cent of the assets, liabilities, revenues and expenditure of all subsidiary companies, even if they are only, say, 60 per cent owned. The amounts in respect of *minority interests* are separately shown on the financial statements.

Cost of sales In a retailing organization this is opening inventory plus purchases minus closing inventory. In a manufacturing organization it is opening inventories plus costs of production, minus closing inventories. Also known as cost of goods sold. It is deducted from sales revenue to arrive at *gross profit*.

Costs Costs may be classified as *fixed costs* and *variable costs*; or as *production costs* (which include *production overheads*) and other *overheads*, which include distribution costs (selling and distribution overheads), and administration overheads. Production costs may be classified as *direct materials*, *direct labour* and *production overheads*. *Prime costs* comprise direct materials and direct labour (and *direct expenses*, if any). *See also opportunity cost*.

Creditors *See payables*.

Creditors: amounts falling due after more than one year These are now called *non-current liabilities*.

Creditors: amounts falling due within one year These are now called *current liabilities*.

Creditors' ratio The relationship between trade payables (creditors) and purchases (or cost of sales) usually expressed as a number of days.

Current assets *Assets* such as *inventories*, *receivables* and *cash*, which are held short term (less than one year); or are turned into cash within a year.

Current cost accounting (CCA) A system of accounting that adjusts for changing values following SSAP 16.

Current liabilities Amounts due to be paid within a year.

Current purchasing power accounting (CPP) A system of accounting that adjusts for inflation following (P)SSAP 7.

Current ratio The ratio of *current assets* to *current liabilities* that indicates a company's ability to meet its current liabilities as they fall due. A ratio of 3.2 : 1 is fairly high, or safe; a ratio of 0.6 : 1 is low, suggesting that the company does not have enough current assets to meet its current liabilities. Also known as the *working capital ratio*.

D

Debtors' ratio The relationship between debtors and sales, usually expressed as a number of days.

Depreciation Simply: the systematic writing down of the amount of a fixed asset. More fully: the measure of the economic benefits of fixed assets that have been consumed during the period.

Direct expenses (Much less frequently encountered than direct labour and direct materials.) Costs of the type that would normally be treated as part of *production overheads*, but instead are treated as part of *prime cost* because they are directly attributable to a particular job, product or service. For example, a car repair business would normally treat machinery costs as being part of production overheads; but if a special-purpose machine has to be hired to repair a specialist car, the cost of hiring that machine would be treated as part of the cost of repairing that car, and not included in general production overheads.

Direct labour The costs of remunerating employees who work directly on a product or service to be sold; these labour costs are separately identified and charged to particular products or services (as opposed to being treated as part of *production overheads*). Part of *prime cost* which, when *production overheads* are added, make up total *production cost*.

Direct materials The cost of direct materials and components that are separately identifiable and enter into and become constituent elements of a product or service to be sold. Part of *prime cost* which, when *production overheads* are added, make up total *production cost*.

Discounted cash flow (DCF). A method of investment appraisal using net present value (NPV) and/or internal rate of return (IRR).

Dividends Amounts paid out to shareholders, usually twice a year (interim dividend, final dividend). Usually out of profits. Sometimes companies pay more dividends than they have earned as profits.

Dividend cover Net profit after tax (or profit available to pay dividends) divided by dividends payable for the year.

Dividend yield The most recent annual dividend per share as a percentage of share price.

E

Equity The total of shareholders' funds including ordinary share capital, share *premium*, and all reserves and retained earnings.

Exceptional items The term now has no precise definition but there is usually separate disclosure of unusual or non-recurring items, such as write-downs of inventories, impairment of property, plant and equipment, restructuring, profits or losses on disposal of investments or tangible fixed assets. All these affect earnings per share.

Expectations gap The difference between what many seem to expect of auditors and what they actually do.

Extraordinary items These have in effect been abolished.

F

Finance cost Interest payable.

Finance income Interest receivable.

Financial Reporting Standards (FRSs) These were issued by the Accounting Standards Board, but have now been superseded by *IASs*.

Fixed assets Now normally known as *non-current assets*.

Fixed costs Costs (such as rent for the premises, or most salaries) that tend to remain at the same level when there are changes in the volume of production or sales. In *marginal costing* fixed costs are separated from *variable costs*. (Some costs are semi-variable.)

G

Gearing The relationship between long-term funding that requires a fixed return (such as debentures), and equity. The first of these is often represented as D; and the second as E. It may be calculated showing D as a percentage of D plus E; or, more simply, showing D as a percentage of E. Also known as capital gearing or *leverage*.

Going concern The assumption that the business will continue in operational existence for the foreseeable future.

Goodwill The amount paid to acquire a business over and above the fair value of its net assets. It is an intangible asset and subject to annual impairment reviews.

Gross profit Sales revenue minus *cost of sales*.

Gross profit ratio Gross profit as a percentage of sales.

Group accounts See *consolidated financial statements*.

I

Impairment Goodwill is not now systematically amortized; it is subject to an annual impairment review.

Income statement A statement of sales revenue, costs and net profit for a period (e.g. one year). Used to be known as a profit and loss account.

Incomplete records Some small businesses do not keep proper double-entry accounting records and accountants need to construct balance sheets and income statements from incomplete records that usually comprise bank statements and a variety of documents such as invoices.

Interest cover Operating profit (or profit available to pay interest) divided by interest payable.

Interest times cover Profit available for paying interest (usually operating profit) divided by the amount of interest payable (finance costs).

International Accounting Standards (IASs) These are now being superseded by *IFRSs*.

International Financial Reporting Standards (IFRSs) These are issued by the International Accounting Standards Board.

Inventories Raw materials, components, work in progress, finished goods, and goods held for resale. Formerly known as *stocks*.

J

Joint venture A business jointly owned by several other business, none of whom has a controlling interest.

L

Leverage *See **gearing**.*

Liabilities Simply: something that a company owes. More fully: a present obligation of the enterprise arising from past events, the settlement of which is expected to result in an outflow from the enterprise embodying economic benefits.

Liquidity ratio The ratio of current assets excluding inventories to ***current liabilities*** that indicates a company's immediate ability to meet its current liabilities as they fall due. A ratio of 1.8 : 1 is fairly high, or safe; a ratio of 0.4 : 1 is low, suggesting that the company does not have enough liquid assets to meet its current liabilities. Liquid assets include cash and receivables, but exclude inventories. Also known as the ***quick assets ratio*** or ***acid test***.

M

Marginal costing A costing system in which individual products are charged with variable but not fixed production overheads; useful in decision-making and break-even analysis.

Mark-up Percentage added to cost price to arrive at selling price. This is *not* the same as gross profit ratio.

Minority interest Where an investing company partly (e.g. 60 per cent) owns a subsidiary company, 100 per cent of the subsidiary company's figures are included in the group financial statements; the figures for the 40 per cent owned by outside shareholders are separately identified as minority interest.

N

Nominal value *See **par value**.*

Non-current assets Formerly known as ***fixed assets***. Assets that are held for long-term use (more than one year) including tangible assets such as property, plant and equipment; intangible assets, such as ***goodwill***, patents and trademarks: and financial assets that are investments such as shares and debentures.

O

Operating costs These are the main difference between gross profit and profit before tax. Two are normally disclosed, distribution costs and administrative expenses.

Opportunity cost The value of a benefit sacrificed in favour of an alternative course of action. If a business owns premises that are currently unoccupied, the cost of using them for a particular purpose should not be regarded as zero; the 'opportunity cost' of using them for that purpose is the amount that they could have earned from the best alternative use (e.g. renting them out).

Overheads All costs other than ***direct materials***, ***direct labour*** (and ***direct expenses***, if any). There are ***production overheads***, distribution costs (which comprise selling and distribution overheads) and administration overheads.

Overtrading Attempting to do too much business with too little long-term capital, which often leads to difficulty in paying liabilities as they fall due.

P

Partnership A business owned and controlled by a number of people in partnership. It is not incorporated and so not subject to Companies Act requirements.

Par value Each share has a theoretical, or par, or nominal value that is of little importance.

Payables Amounts that a business owes and is required to pay, for example, trade payables (creditors).

Preference shares Shares with a predetermined rate of dividend, now usually classified as being either equity or liabilities.

Premium Shares are normally issued at a premium above their nominal or par value. For example, a

20 pence share might be issued for 30 pence, which means the premium is 10 pence. On a balance sheet, share premium is very much like share capital.

Price earnings ratio (P/E ratio) This is share price divided by earnings per share.

Prime cost of production The total of *direct materials*, *direct labour* (and *direct expenses*, if any). It excludes production and other overheads.

Production cost Includes *prime cost* and *production overheads*.

Production overheads The costs of providing a production or manufacturing facility that are not directly attributable to individual products or services. It includes rent and rates for the factory premises, depreciation and repairs for machinery, and wages and salaries for people in the factory who are not part of *direct labour*. These costs are allocated and apportioned to individual products in an *absorption costing* system.

Profit and loss account Now usually known as an income statement. The term 'profit and loss account' may still be used as part of the double-entry bookkeeping system, and in the process of producing the final statement that is called an *income statement*.

Provision A liability of uncertain timing or amount.

Prudence Prudence was regarded as a fundamental accounting concept. It stated that a prudent approach should be taken to recognition of assets and revenues, but that all known liabilities and expenses should be provided for.

Q

Quick assets ratio See *liquidity ratio*.

R

Receivables Money due to be received from customers who may be referred to as trade debtors. Part of current assets.

Return on shareholders' funds (ROSF) or return on equity (ROE) Net profit after tax as a percentage of equity.

Return on total long-term capital employed Operating profit as a percentage of long-term funding (equity plus long-term borrowings).

Revenue expenditure Costs incurred in earning revenues during the period; it excludes *capital expenditure*.

Rights issue An issue of shares to existing shareholders at a price below the current market price.

S

Segmental reporting Diversified companies report separate figures for sales, operating profit, and net assets for each of their business and geographic segments.

Share premium See *premium*.

Sole trader A business owned and controlled by one person. It is unincorporated and so not subject to Companies Act requirements.

Statements of Standard Accounting Practice (SSAPs) These were issued by the Accounting Standards Committee, but have now been superseded by *FRSs*.

Stewardship Directors are assumed to be stewards of shareholders' funds and so directors are accountable to shareholders.

Stocks See *inventories*.

Stock turnover ratio The relationship between inventories (stocks) and cost of sales (or purchases) usually expressed as a number of days.

Subsidiary company A company controlled by another company, which usually owns more than 50 per cent of its shares.

V

Variable costs These costs (e.g. *direct material* costs) tend to vary in proportion to the level of production or sales. In *marginal costing*, variable costs are separated from *fixed costs*. Some costs may be regarded as semi-variable, or semi-fixed.

W

Working capital The excess of *current assets* over *current liabilities*. It can be negative.
Working capital ratio *See current ratio.*

Z

Z score A combination of ratios that can predict financial distress.

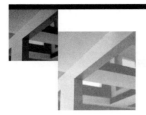

Index